HEAVEN IN THE AMERICAN IMAGINATION

Heaven in the American Imagination

Gary Scott Smith

OXFORD UNIVERSITY PRESS

OXFORD
UNIVERSITY PRESS

Oxford University Press, Inc., publishes works that further
Oxford University's objective of excellence
in research, scholarship, and education.

Oxford   New York
Auckland   Cape Town   Dar es Salaam   Hong Kong   Karachi
Kuala Lumpur   Madrid   Melbourne   Mexico City   Nairobi
New Delhi   Shanghai   Taipei   Toronto

With offices in
Argentina   Austria   Brazil   Chile   Czech Republic   France   Greece
Guatemala   Hungary   Italy   Japan   Poland   Portugal   Singapore
South Korea   Switzerland   Thailand   Turkey   Ukraine   Vietnam

Copyright © 2011 by Oxford University Press, Inc.

Published by Oxford University Press, Inc.
198 Madison Avenue, New York, New York 10016

www.oup.com

Oxford is a registered trademark of Oxford University Press.

Library of Congress Cataloging-in-Publication Data
Smith, Gary Scott, 1950–
Heaven in the American imagination / Gary Scott Smith.
   p.   cm.
ISBN 978-0-19-973895-3
1. Heaven.—Christianity.   2. Heaven.   3. Future life—Christianity.
4. Future life.   5. United States—Religion.   I. Title.
BT846.3.S65 2011
236'.240973—dc22   2010037448

9 8 7 6 5 4 3 2 1

Printed in the United States of America
on acid-free paper

To my mother, Arlene Smith, who has embodied the life of heaven on earth.

A minister concluded his sermon by asking
parishioners to stand up if they wanted to go to
heaven. Everyone except one man rose. "Brother,"
asked the incredulous pastor, "don't you want to go
to paradise when you die?" The holdout declared,
"When I die? Sure! I thought you were getting up a
group to go right now."

Heaven goes by favor; if it went by merit, you
would stay out and your dog would go in.
—MARK TWAIN

Preface

During a children's sermon at an evangelical
church, the director of children's ministries asked,
"What do you have to do to go to heaven?" She,
like most of the congregation, expected one of the
children to answer, "Accept Jesus as your savior."
Instead, a little boy responded, "Be dead."

WHAT IS MORE alluring, intriguing, controversial, and confusing than heaven? Is
heaven a reality or a fantasy? Is it God's home or a human invention? Is it an inspiration for earthly action or an escape from earthly problems? Is it a helpful source of
comfort and consolation or a harmful opiate that dulls people's sensitivities to their
actual condition? Is it a place of continuous worship or a perpetual playground? Is it
a realm of eternal rest or of vigorous activity? Is it a site of static perfection or of
everlasting progress? Is it an exhilarating, enchanting paradise or a boring, dull
place?

Americans have described heaven's wonders as luscious, stunning, spellbinding,
exhilarating, and captivating. We regularly use the adjective *heavenly* in literature to
describe life's most joyful experiences.[1] To the faithful, majestic mountains, cas-
cading waterfalls, breathtaking canyons, magnificent cathedrals, pealing organs,
angelic choirs, and sensational symphonies all pale in comparison to the dazzling
beauty and splendor that awaits them in heaven. If God could create such a spectacular earth and endow human beings with such marvelous gifts, the heavenly home,
which He has prepared for them to live in forever, must be even more fantastic.

Throughout our history, a large percentage of Americans have believed that
heaven exists and have expressed a desire to go there, although most have not been
in a hurry to arrive. Americans' depictions of heaven have been significantly shaped
by their understanding of biblical teaching (heaven is mentioned about 550 times in

the Bible), but they have also been powerfully affected by their cultural settings and personal needs.[2] Their differing interpretations of scripture, coupled with dissimilar cultural trends and people's diverse life experiences, have contributed to competing portraits of paradise. Moreover, Americans have proposed conflicting views of how people gain entry to heaven. While many Christians have claimed that people get to heaven only by accepting Jesus Christ as their savior, others have contended that heaven is a reward for righteous conduct.

This survey focuses on key aspects of authors' views of heaven and salvation and does not present their positions fully or discuss their nuances. Moreover, many Americans' understanding of heaven changed over time and involved inconsistencies. Synthetic historical works rarely have the space to analyze such matters in detail. However, I have tried to represent the views of various authors faithfully and as fully as space limitations allow.

Although this book is titled *Heaven in the American Imagination*, I do cite some non-American authors, primarily British and Canadian, whose works were published in the United States and helped shape American perceptions of heaven. Moreover, I focus considerably more on Protestant than on Catholic, Jewish, and sectarian authors and on evangelical more than on theologically liberal writers because their views of heaven were more widely embraced. While Americans have espoused numerous religious perspectives, Protestant evangelicals have been the largest and most influential group throughout our history. As late as 1850, Catholics constituted only about 10 percent of the American population, and theological liberalism arose as a significant challenge to biblical orthodoxy only in the 1880s. Since 1970, evangelical denominations and congregations have grown substantially while most mainline Protestant communions have declined. Today, 40 percent of Americans claim to be born again or to accept Jesus as their personal savior.[3] I also pay relatively little attention to Swedenborgianism, Spiritualism, or Native American, Buddhist, Hindu, or Muslim views of heaven because these groups have relatively few adherents in the United States and have not had nearly as great an impact upon American conceptions of heaven as have Christian portraits.[4]

The vast amount of material on heaven, coupled with space limitations, also led me to focus on books and printed sermons and to pay much less attention to articles, diaries, and letters. Arguably, these former works had the greatest influence on American beliefs about what heaven will be like and how people can get there. Only the chapter on slavery and the Civil War utilizes many letters and diaries. I supplement the views of these books and sermons by discussing hymns and, more recently, songs, jokes, movies, television shows, and survey data. Lisa Miller argues convincingly, based on her six years of interviews with dozens of Americans, that many portraits of heaven today rely much less on church creeds, sermons, and the writings of scholars than they do on movies, television, novels, "residual messages from parents, grandparents, and Sunday school lessons—and especially on their own individual experiences of transcendence."[5] However, this is much less true for Americans before 1930 (and even 1960), when mass media played little or no role and church teachings were more respected and understood. Nevertheless, this book is primarily about how educated, religiously committed Americans imagined heaven.

Americans have disagreed about the nature of heaven because the sources of information about it are limited, shrouded in mystery, and amenable to different interpretations. Heaven is also baffling because it entails both a future existence after time ends and the world is either destroyed or recreated and a present realm that exists somewhere in time and space where God, the angels, and saints dwell. Reflecting this perplexity, in their depictions of heaven, Americans have often not clearly distinguished between the life of its residents before and after the last judgment and general resurrection. Therefore, differentiating between the intermediate and postresurrection states is often difficult, but, whenever possible and appropriate, distinctions are noted.

For the sake of readability, I have usually modernized spelling and punctuation and removed italics and some capitalization in quoted materials. The pattern for quotations is that unless there are quotations within a single sentence that refer to different pages, first quotation, second quotation, and so forth refer to material quoted in sequential sentences.

Acknowledgments

AT TIMES I thought I would never finish this book. That I did is a testimony to the grace of God and a tribute to the scholars upon whose work I built and the many colleagues and students who assisted me.

I wish to thank my Grove City College colleagues Gillis Harp and Paul Kemeny for reading draft chapters of my book. Two other colleagues, Beverly Carter and Collin Messer, furnished helpful suggestions. Historians David Kling of the University of Miami and Richard Pointer of Westmont College also provided astute critiques of chapters. I am also grateful to Grove City College graduates Leah Ayers Stapleton, Timothy Witt, Miranda Bailey, Heather Shaw, and Sean Varner, who did independent studies on various topics related to my book, and to graduates Elizabeth Miller, Kim Stains, Caroline Harp, and Andrew Welton, who helped with research. Special thanks go to my student assistant Emily Steer, who devoted countless hours to helping with this book. Grove City College librarians Conni Shaw and Joyce Kebert greatly aided my work by procuring hundreds of books and articles for me through interlibrary loan.

I especially want to thank Theo Calderara, senior editor at Oxford University Press. His suggestions were immensely helpful in conceptualizing, organizing, and focusing my book. Moreover, he carefully read the entire manuscript and made many invaluable suggestions about how to reshape it to make it more readable and engaging. I am also grateful to Oxford University Press editorial assistant Charlotte

Steinhardt, to production editor Tamzen Benfield, who oversaw the book's production process, and to Mary Anne Shahidi for her meticulous copyediting of my manuscript.

As she does with almost everything I write, from books to articles to op-eds, my wife Jane provided research assistance, wise counsel, and excellent stylistic suggestions. Her love, encouragement, and support were essential to my writing of this book.

Contents

Introduction 1

1. *The Puritans: Celebrating the Glory of Heaven* 10

2. *Jonathan Edwards and the First Great Awakening:
   Heaven Is a World of Love* 29

3. *The Early National Era and the Second Great Awakening* 47

4. *Heaven as Home: The Victorians and Heaven, 1830–1870* 70

5. *Slavery, the Civil War, and Heaven* 87

6. *Heaven in the Gilded Age: Dwight L. Moody and the Princes of the Pulpit* 109

7. *Heaven in the Progressive Years: Personal Growth, Service, and Reform* 134

8. *Shifting Conceptions of Heaven from the Roaring Twenties to the Fabulous
   Fifties* 158

9. *New Currents and Old Streams, 1960–2000* 177

10. *Heaven in a Postmodern, Anxiety-Ridden, Entertainment-Oriented, Therapeutic,
    Happiness-Based Culture* 204

Conclusion 227

NOTES 239
INDEX 317

HEAVEN IN THE AMERICAN IMAGINATION

Heaven itself cannot be described, but the human concept of heaven can be.
—JEFFREY BURTON RUSSELL, *A History of Heaven*

Soon you will read in the newspaper that I am dead. Don't believe it for a moment. I will be more alive than ever before.
—DWIGHT L. MOODY, QUOTED IN J. C. POLLOCK, *Moody*

INTRODUCTION

DOES HEAVEN EXIST? If so, what is it like? And how can one get in? Human beings have pondered and debated these questions for millennia. The ancient Babylonians, Egyptians, Greeks, and Romans all depicted a future existence where heroes rested, pharaohs resided, or the righteous picnicked in Elysian Fields. Australian Aborigines, as well as early Polynesians, Peruvians, Mexicans, and Native Americans, all had concepts of an afterlife.

Many other Americans have also been deeply interested in life after death. From the works of Puritan Increase Mather, to the sermons of theologian Jonathan Edwards, to the writings of nineteenth-century revivalist Dwight L. Moody, to the books and sermons of evangelist Billy Graham, and the novels of Mitch Albom and Alice Sebold, many have offered visions of heaven or explained how to get there. Evangelicals have led the way, but mainline Protestants, Catholics, Jews, Mormons, Spiritualists, New Agers, Muslims, and numerous others have also described heaven and its entrance requirements.

Studying ideas about heaven is a daunting task. It involves examining works of art, music, sociology, psychology, folklore, liturgies, sermons, poetry, fiction, memoirs, diaries, letters, devotional books, and systematic theologies. Artists, musicians, social scientists, philosophers, theologians, pastors, evangelists, and novelists have portrayed the nature of heaven or speculated about the prerequisites for admission. Thousands of books, articles, and essays on heaven have been published, countless sermons have been preached about the subject, and songs about heaven have been popular. Jokes, works of art, and kitsch about heaven have proliferated in recent decades. The Puritans, proponents of the First Great Awakening of the 1730s and 1740s, and antebellum Americans displayed great interest in the afterlife. The carnage of the Civil War intensified focus on heaven, and the novels of Elizabeth Stuart Phelps, most notably *The Gates Ajar* (1868), sold hundreds of thousands of copies. Between 1870 and 1900, dozens of additional books, mostly written by evangelical Protestants, provided vistas of heaven. Fueled in part by world events, especially those in Israel, and conjecture about the end-times, a new surge of literature about heaven filled the shelves of bookstores between 1970 and 2000. Meanwhile, numerous accounts of near-death experiences (NDEs) also focused attention on the afterlife.[1]

Recently, interest in heaven has become even greater. Polls consistently find that high percentages of Americans believe in heaven and expect to spend eternity there. Polls show that between 80 and 90 percent of Americans believe in heaven. A Gallup poll reported that 77 percent of Americans rated their chances of getting to heaven as "good" or "excellent."[2] Sebold's *The Lovely Bones* (2002), the tale of a murdered four-teen-year-old girl who watches events on earth while exploring heaven, and Albom's *The Five People You Meet in Heaven* (2003), a story about an octogenarian amusement park worker's life review while in heaven, have more than five million copies in print and have been made into movies. Anthony DeStefano's *A Travel Guide to Heaven* (2003), a highly speculative tour of the wonders and joys of paradise, made several appearances at the top of Amazon.com's best-seller list. These imaginative portraits of the afterlife both reflect and fuel Americans' interest in heaven.[3] In another best seller, *90 Minutes in Heaven,* Texas pastor Don Piper describes the marvels of heaven he experienced during his alleged sojourn there. Descriptions of NDEs are widely appealing because they can be used to support diverse worldviews and provide powerful testimony for life after death.[4] Numerous pop, rock, country, and religious songs focus on heaven. Perhaps the best known of these songs is Los Lonely Boys' "Heaven," which has been widely played on both pop and country stations:

In this crazy world, how far is heaven…
Cause I know there's a better place
Than this place I'm living.[5]

While Americans' visions of heaven are often rooted in religious traditions, they have been closely connected to what was happening on earth. As Alan Segal argues, Americans tend to imagine an afterlife containing what they judge to be the "best, most lasting, virtuous, and meaningful" aspects of this life and "eliminating those things" they consider "the most difficult, frustrating, evil, and inessential." Depictions of the afterlife, he adds, "are mirrors of our cultural and social needs" that can be promoted and manipulated. The types of heaven people hope for, historian Paul Carter contends, provide an "unconscious commentary on what they cherish or regret in this world."[6] The general political, economic, and social climate has helped shape various conceptions of heaven as reflected in literature, sermons, art, and music. When peace and prosperity prevail, Americans have typically either ignored the afterlife or emphasized its kinder, gentler aspects. In times of depression and war, Americans have tended to view heaven as a place where people can escape earth's problems and sin.

People's desires and personal life experiences significantly influence their understanding of heaven. "We build heaven out of our joys," suffering, grief, and experiences, asserted America's leading pulpiteer Henry Ward Beecher in 1872, "taking the best and noblest things, and arranging them" to fit "the imagination." Views of heaven, Unitarian pastor John Haynes Holmes contended in 1915, invariably assume "the form of that particular kind of life" each group considers ideal. "Descriptions of heaven," insisted Catholic John Shea in 1972, "reveal the soul of the culture."[7]

Perhaps this is because the Bible, the sacred scripture of the vast majority of Americans, says little about what heaven is like. Christ used parables and similes to describe heaven's glories, Increase Mather maintained, because mortals could not comprehend its riches. The Bible's description of heaven, James Campbell declared in 1924, portrayed "in human language things for which there are no earthly equivalents." "When the Bible describes...the new earth," wrote Bill Arnold, "it consistently uses metaphorical language" because even the inspired authors could see the next life only "through a glass darkly."[8]

At various times, Americans have pictured heaven as an unparalleled paradise, an unending banquet, a celestial city, a refuge of the redeemed, a glorious kingdom, a magnificent home, a haven from the world's ills, a posh vacation resort, a perpetual playground, and a therapeutic center. America's preeminent theologian Jonathan Edwards called the saints' eternal residence "a garden of pleasures...fitted in all respects" to be "an abode of heavenly love."[9] Those who referred to heaven as the New Jerusalem emphasized its "security, safety and stability," varied occupations, cultural enrichment, educational opportunities, and sense of community.[10] The image of a heavenly home connotes reunion with family, tranquility, love, intimacy, and comfort.[11] Following Karl Marx, some Americans have complained that longing for an imaginary heaven gives the poor and oppressed false hope that their privation and exploitation will be redressed above and prevents them from working to remedy injustice on earth. Others have countered that their vision of heaven enables individuals to cope with earthly disappointment, suffering, and sorrow. DeStefano's *Travel Guide* portrays heaven as "Disney World, Hawaii, Paris, Rome, and New York all rolled up into one," "the ultimate playground, created purely for our enjoyment." For Albom and Sebold, by contrast, in heaven one listens to her inner child, repairs her self-esteem, and finally reaches closure.[12] These contemporary pictures of heaven reflect Americans' preoccupation with personal fulfillment, entertainment, and pleasure.

THE PRINCIPAL FEATURES OF HEAVENLY LIFE

Throughout American history, theologians and pastors have generally depicted heaven as a physical place of dazzling beauty, unending delight, and greatly expanded knowledge. Evangelists R. A. Torrey and Billy Sunday both asserted that heaven "is a place," not "merely a state or condition." Jesus, argued Hal Lindsey, author of several 1970s best sellers on the end-times, "is already preparing an incredibly beautiful room for each one in His Father's house."[13]

Various authors have depicted heaven as the antithesis of earth—as safe, orderly, clean, beautiful, fragrant, a realm of "abundant food, splendid clothes, delightful music, and running water—all luxuries denied to so many on earth." In the "celestial Paradise," Ebenezer Pemberton averred in 1770, the saints enjoyed "unfading Honours" and "incorruptible Treasures." People's reason, intellectual curiosity, imagination, aesthetic instincts, and emotions, argued Princeton Seminary professor A. A. Hodge, would all be stronger in heaven.[14]

Many Americans, especially in recent years, have insisted that heaven will be incredibly stimulating and enjoyable. God created heaven for His children, asserted Timothy Dwight, and "adorned and enriched it with everything" essential "to their happiness and glory." God will spend eternity, Anne Sandberg contended, making His children "happy and fulfilled." Heaven, proclaimed Foursquare pastor Daniel Brown, will be "beyond our wildest expectations."[15]

American Christians have also accentuated the saints' phenomenal knowledge. The redeemed, explained Increase Mather, "have a perfect Understanding of the holy Scriptures" and "a far greater...knowledge of the Works of Creation." In heaven, averred Presbyterian James M. MacDonald, all mysteries are explained; "every hard doctrine" is understood. "The difference between the knowledge of [Isaac] Newton and the most illiterate peasant," proclaimed the *Encyclopedia of the Presbyterian Church* (1884), "will be far exceeded by the difference between the knowledge of the Christian on earth and in heaven."[16]

Most American Christians have also insisted that individuals will retain personal identity after death. "No valid objections can be deduced," Augustus C. Thompson asserted in 1854, to show that personal identity will not be preserved in heaven.

"What satisfaction would there be in talking to Isaiah or Paul," Walter Rauschenbusch declared in 1917, if people did not "remember what books they wrote?" Speaking for most Christians, Jay D. Robison maintained that while the Bible does not explicitly teach personal identity in heaven, the scriptures constantly assume it, and the concept of a last judgment in which individuals are held accountable for their earthly deeds implies it.[17]

Not only will people retain their identity in heaven, but they will also recognize their family and friends there. The concept of mutual recognition, Presbyterian J. M. Killen insisted in 1857, was "deeply imbedded in our moral constitution." Having one's friends in heaven, J. Aspinwall Hodge averred, would not "detract from worshipping Christ" as some claimed; full fellowship with the Lord was "only possible in communion with His people." Almost everyone agrees, John Gilmore alleged in 1989, that the redeemed will "recognize each other in heaven."[18]

Americans have also looked forward to spending time in heaven with the heroes of the Bible and church history. Edwards insisted that the saints would converse with the patriarchs "and saints of the Old and New Testaments." Billy Sunday looked forward to talking with heaven's superstars—Abraham, Noah, Moses, Joseph, Samuel, Isaiah, Daniel, John, Peter, Paul, Luther, Calvin, Spurgeon, and Moody.[19]

Although a few acknowledged that Jesus said nothing explicitly about the occupations of the saints, many others confidently explained the work they would do. The redeemed, wrote Edwards, "are employed in praising and serving God." Episcopalian Phillips Brooks asserted in 1897 that heaven would entail "active, tireless, earnest work." Heaven, author Randy Alcorn maintained in 2004, will feature "bustling activity" and events "involving music, the arts, education, religion, entertainment and athletics."[20]

While describing heaven's topography, activities, and attractions, numerous ministers and authors from the Puritans to the present have exhorted Christians to adopt a heavenly perspective while on earth. God commanded Christians, asserted Timothy Dwight, "to set their affections on things above."[21] Concentrating on heaven, many maintained, gives believers a transcendent perspective and an incomparable identity, satisfies their hearts' deepest longing, empowers them to serve God energetically in this world, helps them cope with suffering and failure, and prepares them to serve God after death.[22]

GETTING TO HEAVEN

Americans have debated not only what heaven will be like, but also how people get there. Most Christians have argued that individuals gain admission only by accepting

Jesus Christ as their savior and Lord. Christ, Congregationalist pastor James Pierpont claimed in 1712, is "the only suitable" foundation on which individuals could build to attain "eternal blessedness." "I would as soon as think of climbing to the moon on a rope of sand," evangelist George Whitefield asserted in 1770, as trying to "get to heaven by works!" "Jesus Christ," Moody maintained, "is the 'open sesame' to heaven. Anyone who tries to climb up some other way is a thief." People can never fulfill God's requirement for entrance to heaven, Billy Graham asserted, because His "standard is nothing less than perfection." Individuals, therefore, must accept Jesus Christ as their savior, the one who lived a perfect life and died on the cross to reconcile them to God.[23]

Others have insisted instead that their good works will get them to heaven. They have reasoned that if their good deeds outweigh their bad ones on God's eternal scale, God will reward them with eternal life. Or they have concluded that God is like a college math professor who grades on the curve; as long as their conduct places them in the top half, they will be admitted into heaven. "The most prevalent and popular assumption about heaven," John Gilmore insisted in 1989, is that it "is earned by the ethical and upright." In recent Gallup polls, about 70 percent of Americans have agreed that "people who have led good lives are eternally rewarded" in heaven. A 2008 Pew poll reported that only 30 percent of Americans thought that people's beliefs were the primary grounds for their admission to heaven. Throughout American history, evangelists have complained that many have thought that their "civil, honest, decent lives" entitled them to go to heaven.[24]

Unitarians, Universalists, liberal Protestants, Catholics, and Jews have been the most likely to contend that good deeds play a crucial role in people's admission to paradise. Rejecting Jesus' deity, Unitarians and Universalists have generally avowed that "salvation is by character" and insisted that "religion is a matter of deeds, not creeds."[25] Most liberal Protestants have accepted the deity of Christ but repudiated the doctrine that He died on the cross to reconcile sinners to God. They have minimized humanity's sinfulness and claimed that people gain salvation by emulating Christ's sacrificial example, developing virtuous character, and acting compassionately. Liberals have stressed the similarities between the good life on earth and the life to come, concentrated on improving people's personalities, and argued that moral growth will continue in heaven.[26] Beginning with Progressive Orthodoxy at Andover Seminary in Boston in the 1880s, many evangelical liberals have rejected the long-standing Protestant argument that everyone's eternal destiny is determined by whether they accept Christ as their savior while on earth. They have contended instead that many will have the chance to respond to the gospel in an intermediate state after death and that the concept of future probation is more just and humane than the traditional Christian position that many of those who never heard the gospel are damned.

Guided by the teaching of the Council of Trent (1545–1563), most American Catholic leaders have asserted that salvation involves "faith cooperating with good works." They have also argued that in justification, God infuses grace into the hearts of believers, changing their spiritual and moral nature.[27] Many Protestants have countered that in the act of justification, God imputes the righteousness of Christ to those who trust Him as their savior. Over the years, Catholic and Protestant theologians and clergy have debated the nature of salvation and the role works play in it. In 1983, American Catholics and Lutherans issued a joint statement on justification, declaring that "our entire hope of … salvation rests on Jesus Christ and on the gospel." Nevertheless, Catholics and Protestants still often disagree about how people get to heaven, especially about whether most believers must be purified in purgatory before God will admit them to heaven.[28]

Jews reject the Christian concept that Jesus is the messiah who reconciles individuals to God by His atoning death on the cross. Instead, they emphasize developing a close relationship with God, obeying His laws, and helping others. For Jews, salvation is not "a miraculous treasure" given to humans "by divine grace, but rather a task imposed by God" to live righteously and love other people. God does not provide atonement for human sins; the proper response to sin is to turn to God, forsake evil, and obey His commandments. Focusing on obtaining compensation or avoiding punishments in the afterlife is selfish, Jews argue, and diminishes the virtue and value of individuals' earthly acts.[29] Since its creation in Pittsburgh in 1885, advocates of Reform Judaism have competed for adherents with the Orthodox and Conservative branches. While traditionalists contend that a messiah will someday come to redeem the Jewish people, Reform Jews exhort people to work to bring to earth an era of world peace, righteousness, and prosperity.[30]

CONCLUSION

As the ensuing pages will show, American portraits of paradise have differed substantially. Although most Americans have claimed to derive their images of heaven solely from the Bible, they also display their dreams, hopes, and visions of the good life. As a result, their depictions of celestial life shed substantial light on what Americans have most treasured and feared in various eras. Although Christians and Jews have based their depictions of heaven on the Bible, these depictions have varied greatly from the Puritans to the present. American Christians have largely agreed that heaven is a spectacular, delightful place whose residents are aware of their own identities and histories, enjoy fellowship with friends and family, enthusiastically worship God, do meaningful work, and experience fantastic joy. However, deeply influenced by their own life experiences and their different political, social, economic, and cultural circumstances, they have sharply disagreed about what heavenly life will be like.

The Puritans depicted a God-centered heaven where the redeemed constantly worshipped the Trinity in a beautiful, blissful environment and where all the perplexities of life were explained.[31] While Jonathan Edwards agreed that heavenly life revolved around glorifying God, he also accentuated the communion of the redeemed. During the Victorian age (roughly 1840 to 1900) perceptions of heaven shifted in both Europe and America from a God-centered heaven that focused on worshipping and serving the Trinity, to a more human-centered heaven revolving around family and fellowship. Deeply affected by the nation's increased emphasis on individualism and voluntarism, during the mid-nineteenth century heaven was depicted principally as a heavenly home where relationships with earthly family members were extremely important. During the antebellum years, Southern slaves combined African and biblical ideas to produce a distinctive portrait of the afterlife that emphasized God's punishment of cruel owners and rewarding of faithful slaves and provided hope and comfort. The tragedy and suffering of the Civil War evoked tremendous interest in heaven.

During the late nineteenth and early twentieth centuries, many depictions of heaven emphasized service, education, and personal growth as these concepts, promoted by the Social Gospel movement and Progressivism, became dominant in American society. By 1900, these themes had replaced rest and worship as the principal occupations of heaven's residents and realizing earthly dreams became as important as glorifying God. After 1930, the increasing growth of theological liberalism, the fundamentalist counteroffensive, and the rise of neo-Orthodoxy produced disagreements among Protestants over the reality and nature of heaven. Fundamentalists largely ignored heaven, while most liberal seminary professors and some pastors rejected belief in heaven and hell as actual places and saw them instead as states of mind.[32] The "death of God" theologians of the 1960s and 1970s abandoned the concept of heaven, while many African-American and feminist theologians, advocates of the theology of hope, and liberation theologians echoed the arguments of the Social Gospelers that Christians must work primarily to establish a just society on earth rather than help individuals get to heaven. Recently, evangelicals, Mormons, and New Agers—groups who espouse very different perspectives—have most discussed the afterlife.

Much more than Protestants, Catholics have retained the theocentric conception of heaven, portrayed a mystical, reflective, abstract heaven, and stressed the beatific vision of God. Numerous Catholics have criticized Protestants for stressing the fellowship of the saints and neglecting this intuitive, spiritual communion with and delight in God.[33]

American Jews have generally paid less attention to and speculated less about the afterlife than Christians. While Orthodox Judaism retains the traditional rabbinic belief in the resurrection and heaven, Reform Jews have rejected the concept of a bodily resurrection and eternal rewards. They tend to view heaven as a spiritual state rather than a specific place and to conceive of immortality as living on through one's children or accomplishments. Since God is just, other Jews counter, an afterlife is necessary to redress the injustices of earth.[34]

While disagreeing significantly about the nature of the afterlife, for the past four centuries, Americans have also vigorously debated on what grounds individuals get into heaven. These disagreements shed light on what has most troubled, perplexed, and inspired various groups of Americans during different eras. Their conceptions of paradise reveal what they most highly cherished and desired. Examining how Americans envisioned heaven provides a better understanding of their earthly aims, struggles, and joys.

The happiness of heaven is beyond all imagination.

—INCREASE MATHER, *Meditations upon the Glory of the Heavenly World*

Heaven is a most glorious, ravishing and excellent place.

—JAMES HILLHOUSE, *A Sermon Concerning the Life*

There is not a sermon which is heard, but that it sets us nearer to heaven or hell.

—JOHN PRESTON, *A Patterne of Wholesome Words*

1

THE PURITANS

Celebrating the Glory of Heaven

THE PURITANS EMERGED in the 1560s and sought to purge the Church of England of elements that they believed owed too much to Roman Catholicism. They attempted to ground the church's doctrines, organization, and worship on the principles taught by John Calvin and implemented in large part in Geneva, Switzerland. The Puritans strove to reform the church, produce godly pastors, promote spiritual revival, and live out a comprehensive biblical worldview. Although they were a minority movement everywhere, except in parts of New England, and were often persecuted in England, the Puritans had a significant religious, intellectual, political, and economic impact in the years from 1570 to 1725. The Puritans "have frequently been described as rationalists, capitalists, political revolutionaries, and members of a new and upwardly mobile middle class," but first and foremost Puritanism was a religious movement that emphasized corporate worship, biblical study, prayer, theological reflection, and the spiritual life. The Puritans stressed the authority of the Bible, promoted literacy, and preached the necessity of personal regeneration. They accentuated the doctrine of creation, God's providential activity in the world, and the concept of "calling"—both a general calling to serve God in all areas of life and a particular calling to serve God through specific vocations.[1]

Smearing of Puritans is as old as Puritanism itself, and negative stereotypes still abound. As theologian J. I. Packer explains, "pillorying the Puritans...has long been a popular pastime on both sides of the Atlantic."[2] They have often been denounced as cranky, petty, vain hypocrites who attempted to control the behavior of others and tried to prevent anyone from having fun. These "religious fanatics" were allegedly overly scrupulous, legalistic, and concerned about minutia. They have also been accused of being workaholics who never relaxed or engaged in recreation. As with most stereotypes, these contain a kernel of truth.

In recent decades, many scholars have portrayed the Puritans more positively. Led by American historians Perry Miller and Edmund Morgan, scholars have argued that the Puritans were generally conscientious and cultured citizens who worked vigorously to establish a Christian commonwealth in both England and America. Their quest to build a Christian society while battling the New England weather and wilderness (and, sadly, often Native Americans) helped produce in the Puritans strong character and led them to see themselves as God's "soldier-pilgrims." As they worked to establish their New Jerusalem in Massachusetts and Connecticut, they asserted that both God and Satan claimed ownership of the world and that no neutral ground existed in the war between them.[3]

The Puritans had substantial shortcomings, as their own sermons often bewailed. They frequently failed to live up to their own moral standards, pretentiously assumed that they were the new Israel, interpreted God's providence in self-serving ways, tended to be self-righteous, treated outsiders harshly, banished dissenters, mistreated Indians, and created an overly stringent legal system based on Old Testament laws.[4] Nevertheless, few groups in history can match their theological understanding, knowledge of the scriptures, emphasis on spiritual experience, and practice of self-examination. They established schools and a college (Harvard) and strove to develop godly families and base church practices on biblical principles. Convinced that the Bible was relevant to every facet of life, the Puritans tried to use it to guide all aspects of daily living.

Before settling in the colonies, many American Puritan leaders were educated and ministered in Europe, especially England. They continued to interact with clergy across the Atlantic and read many of the books their English counterparts wrote. In New England, Puritanism was "more prone to intolerance and heavy-handedness, to complacency, to legalism, [and] to inner decay" than it was in England. Their belief that they were God's new Israel gave them great confidence that their theological positions were biblically correct and that their social arrangements were scripturally mandated, limiting their willingness to discuss these matters or compromise with Christians who espoused other perspectives. The constant jeremiads of Puritan preachers decrying sin, sloth, and spiritual apathy testify to the great concern about these problems in colonial New England. The Half-Way Covenant of 1662, which permitted baptized individuals who had not joined the church to have their children baptized, was adopted because many second-generation New Englanders could not meet the strict qualifications for church membership.[5] Alarmed by this wide-spread spiritual lethargy, many Puritans preached sermons urging laypeople to con-template the joys of heaven and the terrors of hell.

Many scholars emphasize that the Puritan conception of heaven was theocentric, focusing on the glory and majesty of God and Christ, and the power and splendor of the Father and the Son does loom large in their understanding of heaven. According to this conception, heaven exists primarily for God and celestial life revolves around glorifying, worshipping, and serving Him.[6] However, more than most historians and theologians have noted, the Puritans also underscored the fellowship of the saints and the rewards the redeemed received in heaven. The Puritans repeatedly asserted that only those who responded to God's call and received Jesus Christ as their savior and Lord would be admitted to heaven. Good works, although required of Christians, did not help people get in. Puritan pastors urged their parishioners to set their sights on heaven not only to prepare for the life to come but to help inspire them to live a faithful, zealous Christian life on earth. They continually argued that good deeds and righteous conduct were essential elements of believers' pilgrimage to heaven and were richly rewarded in paradise to help motivate Christians to labor arduously to accomplish their errand in the wilderness. As the Puritans carried out their earthly vocations, buried many children at a tender age, and constantly studied the scripture, heaven was often on their minds.

THE SPLENDOR OF HEAVEN

Puritan pastors performed many roles—they were preachers, teachers, shepherds, physicians of souls, counselors, and disciplinarians—and no one did so better than Increase Mather (1639–1723), president of Harvard College, pastor of North Church in Boston, and author of numerous treatises on theology, eschatology, and biblical exposition, as well as many volumes of published sermons. Highly respected on both sides of the Atlantic, he wrote more extensively about the nature of heavenly life and the necessity of preparing properly for eternity than any other American Puritan. His son, Cotton, who served at North Church with him, also discussed the afterlife and salvation in many of his more than 450 books and pamphlets. Both Mathers had a tremendous influence on colonial American political, social, and religious thought.[7]

For the Mathers and other Puritan divines, "the Happiness of Heaven" was "beyond all Imagination." Heaven, Increase insisted, infinitely surpassed the earth "in all that is desirable." Its residents, James Hillhouse rhapsodized, experienced "majesty and glory" that the eye had never before beheld, a "Triumphant Song of

Victory over the Devil and the World" that the ear had never heard, and "Joy, Pleasure, and Satisfaction" that "the Heart [had] never Conceived."[8]

The garden that the Second Adam had prepared for humanity, Cotton Mather proclaimed, was much more "a place of Beauty, of Pleasure, of Tranquility" than the one Adam tilled in Eden. Even if a minister spent his whole life studying "the Glory of Heaven," Increase reasoned, he would not be able to explain "a millionth part" of its "blessedness." Believers should not be disappointed with what they owned in this world, he argued, "because they are going to an Infinitely Better & more Desirable World." Nothing that believers experienced on earth compared with "the bliss awaiting the redeemed in heaven." "Were the Sun ten thousand times brighter than it is," Mather exulted, its glory would still only be a small fraction of heaven's.[9]

Puritan ministers frequently contrasted the wonder and glory of heaven with the suffering, pain, and persecution Christians endured on earth. Because happiness depended on holiness and they would be completely holy in heaven, Increase Mather argued, the redeemed were assured that they would always be happy there, which would "more than compensate for all their Afflictions in this world." If people never died, Hillhouse argued, the "Saints would have the worst Lot of any in the World"; but "all men must die," which would end the misery of the redeemed and bring them complete happiness in heaven. As Michael Wigglesworth put it in his widely read *The Day of Doom* (1662):

> Eternal Life will recompense thy pains,
> If found at last, with everlasting gains....
> Nor shalt thou grieve for loss of sinful pleasures,
> Exchanged for heavenly joys and lasting treasures.[10]

Christians might lose their houses and lands, William Gearing, announced, but they would someday "possess a great kingdom." Believers might be imprisoned, banished, or experience great sorrow, but this suffering paled compared to "the rivers of pleasure...at God's right hand." Christians might even be killed, but the rewards of paradise were a hundredfold greater than those of earthly life. Hillhouse argued that earthly privation and problems often stimulated people to pursue heaven. "Is your Estate wasting, your Family dwindling away & your Trade decaying? Had not you lost these, it may be you had lost your Soul forever."[11]

At the heart of the Puritan view of heaven was its residents' relationship with God. In the beatific vision, the saints experienced "the full fruition and the sweet embraces of the thrice Blessed Trinity." By beholding, adoring, and serving "the Great, the Glorious, and the Immense GOD of all Perfection," Hillhouse claimed, the saints will gain inconceivable pleasure. Glorified souls, he exclaimed, will derive "inexpressible Joy and Comfort" from fully comprehending God's compassion and goodness. For Edward Pearse, love, joy, admiration, and holiness characterized heavenly life. The saints will reside forever "in our Father's house," relish their fellowship with the Father, Son, and Holy Spirit, and rejoice "with the glorious Host of Saints and Angels." Experiencing the "soul-ravishing and transforming Sights" of God and Christ will perpetually delight and satisfy their souls.[12]

The first thing God created, Increase Mather proclaimed, was a heaven for His people to dwell eternally with him. The saints bask in the beatific vision. They needed nothing else, Mather claimed, to make them happy (although he and other Puritans also emphasized the joy that heavenly rewards and their mutual fellowship gave the saints). Although the heavenly residents cannot see God or completely comprehend Him, they continually feel His presence. "Loud Acclamations of Joy," heralded Nathaniel Henchman, pastor of the First (Congregationalist) Church of Lynn, Massachusetts, rang throughout heaven whenever a saint ascended to glory. Wigglesworth proclaimed,

> O glorious Place! where face to face
> Jehovah may be seen....
> For God above in arms of love
> doth dearly them embrace....[13]

Puritan devotional exercises sought to prepare believers for heavenly worship by helping them anticipate the unfettered adoration of God they would experience there. Poets and pastors celebrated paradise's glorious worship of the Trinity. Poet Edward Taylor asserted that his praise would be perfect only in heaven when "Angels shall set the tune."[14]

Christ taught His disciples to pray "Thy Will be done on Earth as it is in Heaven," Increase Mather declared, which implied that glorified saints conform completely to the will of God. In heaven the commandment to love God with all one's heart, soul, and mind is totally fulfilled. "A Blessed Harmony," Hillhouse concluded, exists in heaven between the will of the saints "and the Divine Pleasure." Because heavenly residents are "so fully like God," Gearing reasoned, they "love Him perfectly." Their wills and affections are transformed so that they want only what God wills.[15]

While accentuating the saints' adoration of God the Father, Puritans also emphasized Christ's radiance and splendor and the incredible joy of communing with Him in heaven. Christ, Increase Mather declared, "shines in the highest Heaven with a greater glory, than the Sun does in the visible heavens." The intensity of Christ's glorified body, Gearing asserted, obscures "the brightness of [the] sun, moon, and stars as the brightness of the sun" overwhelms "the light of a fire." Jesus, Mather maintained, "is an Inestimable and Inexhaustible Treasure." Being with Him for even one day, he effused, was better than enjoying all the earth's comforts for a thousand years.[16]

While laboring energetically to establish a city on a hill in Massachusetts, the Puritans frequently described Christians as pilgrims who were journeying to their true home in heaven. "The world is not only a strange Land," wrote Edward Pearse, "but a waste howling Wilderness" where people lived "among wild Beasts" and battled "Lusts within, and Devils without." In the "Warfare" of earthly life, Christians endured wounds, bruises, and bloodshed. Their experience was similar to the wounded and half-dead traveler on the road from Jerusalem to Jericho, but after they died the saints sat on "a Throne of Triumph." "The Servants of God," Mather proclaimed, "are Strangers and Sojourners on the Earth." Christians were "going home…to their Fathers [*sic*] House," and, therefore, their hearts, treasures, and desires should "center there." Believers who had little in this world should not be discontented. Christians were only tenants on earth, but they will inherit all heaven's riches.[17] Although "this world is not our home," Mather asserted, Christ's followers "should be content to live longer in this world if the Lord" willed so that they could "Serve & Glorify" Him. Paul was willing to postpone "the Joys of Heaven for eleven years" in order to do Christ's work on the earth. Many Puritan pastors urged Christians to view their civil callings primarily as a way of glorifying God rather than as a means of sustaining their families.[18]

The difficulty of carving a civilization out of the wilderness, the long hours many worked, frequent battles with Indians, their sometimes contentious relationship with England, the primitive state of medicine, and numerous other trials all contributed to Puritans often depicting heaven as a place without any troubles or afflictions. Gearing argued that the saints will be free from "all the temptations and rage of Satan," the fear of death, the persecution of the wicked, all weakness in serving God, and their many earthly obligations. Believers' "wondrous Consolations" in paradise, Cotton Mather rejoiced, would compensate for the "various Evils" they endured on earth. In heaven, Increase Mather averred, Christians will no longer have to battle against the guile and power of sin. They will never "be guilty of any Actual Sin, in Word, Thought or Deed." Pearse promised that the saints would shift "from an unavoidable necessity of Sinning, to an absolute impossibility of Sinning."[19]

The Puritans highly valued education as a tool for studying, understanding, and applying the Bible to everyday life and promoting "religious and social cohesion." Thus, during their first two decades in Massachusetts, they founded Harvard College and passed laws requiring towns to establish schools to teach youth their foundational religious truths and social standards.[20] Reflecting this interest in education, the saints possessed phenomenal knowledge in the Puritan conception of heaven.

The saints, Increase Mather argued, conform completely to God's will and have perfect knowledge. Mather expected to learn more in one day in heaven than he could "by a Thousand Years [of] hard Study in this World." The faculties of the saints will be so "enlarged, and their capacities so perfected," Hillhouse alleged, that they could understand the presently incomprehensible "great Mysteries of Redeeming Grace." Their ability to see "far into the dazzling Perfections of Almighty GOD, and Heavenly things" would make the saints incredibly happy.[21]

In addition to worshipping and communing with God, Puritans asserted, residents of heaven delighted in their fellowship with each other. The saints, Increase Mather reasoned, must know one another; "otherwise there would be little comfort in their communion." Hillhouse maintained that residents of heaven will enjoy a "Great, Glorious, Excellent and incomparable Society." Because they agree in God and among themselves, Gearing declared, the saints "see the image of God shining clearly and gloriously in each other." While fellowshipping with earthly friends and relatives and developing new friendships, heavenly residents, Puritans asserted, would also converse with the patriarchs, prophets, and apostles.[22]

For the Puritans, man's chief end on earth was to "enjoy God and glorify Him forever." Devout Puritans attended church services twice each Sabbath, gathered for midweek meetings in their homes or churches, had regular family and personal devotions, and faithfully studied the Bible to understand and apply its teachings. Thus the principal activity that they envisioned occurring in heaven—worship—was an extension of their earthly passion. The saints, Hillhouse asserted, will enjoy "a Blessed Rest" from all their "Toilsome Duties" and will spend eternity singing songs of admiration, astonishment, and joy to Jesus. Heavenly residents, exclaimed Pearse, will spend an "Eternal Sabbath...employed in the highest Acts of Worship and Adoration." They will forever sing "Praises, Doxologies, and Halleluja's to God and the Lamb." To combat spiritual lethargy and inspire them to honor Christ more fully on earth, Increase Mather wished that Christians, like Stephen before his death, could see "the Heavens Opened, and JESUS Sitting at the Right hand of God, and Thousands of Millions of Saints & Angels Worshipping before him."[23]

The Puritans rejected the doctrine of soul sleep, the belief that souls have no awareness between death and their resurrection on Judgment Day, and taught instead that at death people went directly to heaven. At the moment of death, asserted Mather, the soul immediately goes into God's presence. After a person died, Nathaniel Henchman stated, his body lay in "the silent grave," "resting in hope," while his soul was "instantly Convoyed (by Guardian Angels) into Abraham's Bosom"; "not a moment intervenes between his being absent from the Body and present with the LORD."[24]

Although people's heavenly bodies had new qualities, Puritans insisted, they remained "Materially and Substantially" what they were before death. The Mathers, Jonathan Mitchel, and many other Puritan divines agreed that people's bodies would be reunited with their souls on the Day of Judgment. Historian Robert Middlekauff has argued that the resurrection body the Puritans envisioned in the millennial state "was not really a body at all." It did not require food or sleep; it felt no pain and experienced no disease; "it had no senses; it was incorruptible; and it was completely under the control of the spirit." Although the glory of the saints' bodies were not equal to Christ's, Increase Mather maintained, the composition of their bodies was similar to His. The bodies of the saints "are not Perfected until the Resurrection," he argued, "but their Souls are Perfected as soon as they leave their Bodies, and go to the Heavenly World." Many scriptures intimated, Mather added, that the separated "Souls of Believers are immediately Happy" after "the Death of their Bodies." The saints' previously "vile Bodies," Hillhouse contended, would be refashioned and made similar to "the glorious Body of Christ." Their spiritual bodies will not hunger, thirst, or grow weary. Every imperfection will be removed; people's ignorance, spiritual dullness, lukewarm affections, and tendency to make poor decisions will all be eradicated. Unless the saints were made perfect, Hillhouse reasoned, they could not have "Satisfaction, Comfort, or Joy" in heaven. Based on his understanding of Paul's teachings, Mather concluded that the resurrected body is incorruptible, gloriously adorned, phenomenally powerful (much stronger than Samson), and spiritual (it had no need of food or drink).[25]

HEAVENLY REWARDS

The Puritans insisted that salvation was by grace alone through faith alone, argued that God prompted and empowered the redeemed to do good works, and emphasized that people's primary motive for wanting to go to heaven should be to worship and serve God in a totally unencumbered way. Nevertheless, based on their understanding of scripture and to motivate earthly saints to live righteously, construct a Christian commonwealth, and endure suffering, they frequently stressed that believers would receive great rewards in heaven. Cotton Mather expected God to praise the saints "before the entire universe" for their faithful service. They would reign with Christ and help "separate the just from the damned." Heaven's residents, Nathaniel Henchman contended, would enjoy "Everlasting Happiness" in the "Mansions of Glory" God prepared for them. Hillhouse urged Christians to live in "constant expectation" of receiving "a Crown of Glory."[26]

While God required righteous conduct primarily to promote His glory, He would richly recompense it in heaven. Increase Mather argued that Christians' good works, especially their "charity to the Lord's poor," would "follow them to the Heavenly World." Those who "have done far greater Service for God, and have been more Active Instruments in Glorifying his Name than Others," he claimed, would receive "a more abundant Reward." Celestial rewards, Mather declared, were commensurate with both the quality and quantity of people's good deeds. Those who "have been Instruments of Converting many Sinners" and those who have suffered the most for Christ would have the most honor in heaven. This promise of greater heavenly recompense for greater earthly service, he avowed, should inspire Christians to diligently serve God. Heaven's abundant rewards would more than offset Christians' earthly privation and suffering. The estate of "the richest man in the world," Increase Mather maintained, was vastly inferior "to what the meanest saint has in another World." Therefore, believers who had had "Little of this World's Good[s]" should be content and focus on their future heavenly bounty and bliss. Moreover, meditating on heaven, Mather and Hillhouse promised, would help Christians endure earthly trials and cope with affliction.[27]

For these and other reasons, Puritans exhorted Christians to concentrate on heaven. Do believers value heavenly things more than earthly things?, Increase Mather asked. "Do we think much of heaven every day?" "If our Hearts and Treasure are in Heaven," he averred, "our Thoughts will be much there." Mather also exhorted his coreligionists to "do on Earth, what is done in Heaven" in order to honor Christ and advance God's kingdom. Christians' earthly worship, Cotton Mather argued, should be "a Conversation with Heaven." The redeemed should emulate what the saints were doing in the intermediate state, converse with them, and share their joys.[28]

THE WAY TO HEAVEN

In an age with few creature comforts, little medical knowledge, and no painkillers or anesthesia, and grueling work, pain and suffering were a common occurrence and death was an ever-present reality. Although disease was not as prevalent in New England as in other places in the world and its residents lived longer than their contemporaries in other colonial regions or in Europe, most parents lost a child before he or she reached adulthood, and some endured much greater loss. Judge Samuel Sewall and Cotton Mather each had fourteen children. Only two of Sewall's children outlived him, while only Samuel Mather survived Cotton. Samuel Danforth, a pastor at Roxbury, Massachusetts, lost eight of his twelve children before they reached age eight. Therefore, from an early age, children were repeatedly warned that their existence was precarious. Sermons, parents, teachers, and the books they later read all stressed that sudden death was likely and exhorted them to prepare for it.[29]

Puritan pastors encouraged their parishioners to get ready for death, not to fear death if they were properly prepared, and not to mourn excessively when Christian family members and friends died because they were with God in paradise. Eulogizing a recently deceased Christian, Henchmen declared that "the prospect of his approaching" death did not frighten him, "but rather filled him with…holy Joy" because he was "desirous to depart."[30] Two things made Christians "Long for Heaven," Mather maintained: "a Well-grounded Assurance" that they were going there and frequent thoughts of the blessedness they would enjoy.[31] He counseled Christians "not to grieve inordinately" when godly friends and close relatives died. Remembering their great gain "should moderate our Sorrow."[32]

People could gain entry into heaven, Puritans insisted, only by accepting Christ's substitutionary death on the cross as paying for their sins. Salvation, Henchman argued, depended entirely "upon the Sovereign free Grace of GOD through Christ." "No other Righteousness" than Christ's, Increase Mather asserted, could justify individuals in God's sight. In atoning for their offenses by dying on Calvary's cross, Christ provided a way to reconcile sinners to God. Jesus could accomplish this reconciliation, Mather reasoned, only if He were both God and man. Christ's blood was "infinitely Meritorious"; it alone brought "real Remission" for sins.[33] By conforming perfectly to God's law, Mather maintained, Jesus earned the "title to Eternal Life in Heaven." God transferred this title to those who trusted in Christ as savior and Lord by imputing His righteousness to them. To be admitted to heaven, individuals needed "a better Righteousness than the Scribes and Pharisees had," an alien righteousness that only Christ could supply. To receive God's favor, Mather alleged, individuals must confess that they were rebels and denounce their sin. "A Repenting Sinner," declared Cotton Mather, renounced all hope of being justified by his own deeds, and clung to the "Righteousness of the Lord Jesus Christ, as his only Hope." To be fit for the heavenly world, Mather added, individuals must be regenerated by the Holy Spirit, which transformed their minds. The doors to heaven, he warned, would be shut against all those who did not have "a Sincere, and Thorough Conversion." People must put on the robe of Christ's righteousness, Edward Pearse declared, to cover all their sin and make them fit for heaven.[34]

Believing in Christian doctrine, Puritans argued, was not sufficient to "bring a Soul to Heaven." Many in hell, Increase Mather contended, had done that. Like other Calvinists, Puritans believed in the antimony of God's absolute sovereignty and unconditional election and human free agency and the necessity of individuals responding to God's effectual call to salvation. Although true faith was God's gift, it always prompted "Evangelical Repentance." To enter heaven, Mather maintained, individuals must experience "a New and Heavenly Birth." In regeneration they received a new heart and a renewed mind so that they loved what God loved.[35]

Although the Puritans viewed salvation as God's gift, they considered it the goal of life's journey "rather than an achieved state." Therefore, it must be "prepared for, stage by stage, anticipated, hoped for, [and] worked toward."[36] American Puritans argued, as did their English counterpart John Bunyan in *Pilgrim's Progress* (1678), that Christians "must Fight and Run" for heaven "because the Devil, the Law, Sin, Death and Hell" all strove to derail those who were traveling toward heaven. A "lazy and cowardly professor," James Hillhouse asserted, could not expect to "win Heaven." Instead, Christians must run the "spiritual Race with Patience, looking to Jesus." As Christ focused on the "Joy that was set before him," so must his earthly followers. Those who did not diligently battle until the Day of Judgment, he warned, would not be saved. At that point "the Gates of Heaven [will] be bolted" and people's "fighting and racing" could not help them. "Many who...made their way" to heaven's gates would knock and plead but would be denied entrance. "You must not think to go to heaven on a feather bed," declared Thomas Hooker; "if you will be Christ's disciples, you must take up his cross; and it will make you sweat."[37]

Both Hooker, one of the founders of Connecticut, and Thomas Shepard, pastor of First Church in Cambridge, Massachusetts, two of the leading first-generation Puritan ministers, urged New Englanders to "seek Christ with all their power." Shepard argued that "a complex and extended process of repentance must precede" individuals' conversion. Hooker listed eighteen rules people needed to follow to prepare properly for salvation, which focused on truly understanding the horrors of sin so that their hearts were "pierced and broken."[38] Puritan preachers also delineated the stages through which an individual must pass in the conversion process. While conversion was a pivotal experience in people's pilgrimage to heaven, they stressed, it was not an isolated event but part of a lifelong process. "Gradual growth in...sanctification" and developing a deeper relationship with Christ was also essential to spending eternity with God.[39]

Puritan primers, almanacs, popular verses, manuals, and sermons all used similar language to exhort individuals to prepare for death. Patrick Ker's *The Map of Man's Misery* (1685) is representative of the many devotional manuals written to aid people in this process. Ker proclaimed: "Then lead a Holy Life, Fast, Read, and Pray...That thou may'st sing back from Mount Zion high, Death Where is thy Sting? Grave where's thy Victory?" Shepard argued that believers' weekly preparation for the Sabbath was "a miniature version" of their "lifelong preparation for glory and eternal rest." Each Sabbath was a stage on the road to heaven, "a resting place on the journey," which helped the faithful obtain eternal "rest with Christ in Heaven." Neglecting to get ready for and observe the Sabbath, therefore, was a serious sin because it both violated God's laws and robbed Christians of potential heavenly benefits.[40]

An individual's painstaking self-examination to achieve assurance of his justification could last several days or even many months and often involved extensive conversation with his pastor. Many pastors urged their parishioners to seek "renewed conversions" in order to experience the stages of redemption more deeply. "True Believers," Increase Mather insisted, underwent "Further degrees of Mortification and Sanctification."[41]

Although "the quest for salvation was at the core of everything the devout Puritan thought and did," God's inscrutable will made complete confidence in one's own or anyone else's salvation impossible. Paradoxically, Puritans strove to obtain assurance of their election while asserting that salvation was "both predetermined and undetectable." However, their belief that certain "marks" indicated God's election led them to seek to identify these signs in themselves and other church members. Because these signs had to be interpreted and could be feigned, they were not conclusive evidence of sainthood.[42] Nevertheless, external behavior was a generally reliable indicator of people's inner condition. While ministers stressed that Christ's atonement was limited and warned that "few shal be saved," they often preached and wrote about God's mercy, love, and "offer of free grace."[43]

To test their salvation, James Pierpont counseled people to ask, "Does the Beauty, the Suitableness, the Sufficiency, of my Saviour mightily affect me? Do I cheerfully commit myself into His Precious and Saving Hands? Do I joyfully trust in Him for all the Blessings of Goodness?" A true work of grace, he explained, made people hunger for "the Enjoyments and Employments of the Heavenly World" and strive to follow Christ's commandments. Shepard argued that continual upright conduct supplied compelling evidence of election. Those who fulfilled the conditions of God's covenant and sought "Christ with a cleansed heart" were "entitled to assurance of salvation." If an individual "customarily, voluntarily, deliberately" pursued a "righteous course," he argued, it could be safely concluded that Christ had regenerated him and freed him from bondage to sin. For Cotton Mather, the marks of salvation included loving God with all one's heart, adoring the Savior, doing "the Things that please God," regretting all one's sins, and loving one's neighbor as oneself.[44]

Puritan clergy reminded their parishioners that they might die at any moment. Many tombstones contained the words "Behold and think of death." The prospect of God's judgment, ministers argued, should prompt people to repent continually and live righteously. Thousands of sermons sounded a "now or never" theme. They stressed that people were rarely converted after age thirty and used the sudden death of individuals to drive home the point that anyone could perish in an instant. After two young men drowned when they fell through the ice in a pond, Increase Mather warned the students at Harvard that no one knew "the Time of his Death" and that God might shoot more arrows "that shall suddenly strike some of you ere long." However, pastors also urged Christians who led godly lives not to "fear the King of Terrors."[45]

Sermons and books supplied examples of people who died well and of others who died in despair. Thomas Shepard's first wife provided a positive model of how to spend one's last earthly moments by repeatedly professing her belief that after death she would be reunited with her compassionate savior in heaven.[46] On the other hand, chapbooks, broadsides, and published sermons provided numerous tales of anguish. For example, Leonard Hoar, the third president of Harvard, "told awful stories of the dying process—of people trembling" in desolation "as Satan flung his final arrows at the dying."[47]

Thus Puritan pastors sent people a mixed message. Death entailed judgment, so people must prepare to meet God by constantly obeying His laws and monitoring their spiritual condition. At the same time, ministers sought to assure the pious that God would receive them into His kingdom. Those who trusted in Christ, lived righteously, and had a clear conscience would pass peacefully from earth to heaven. Many clergy emphasized that because God alone knew the spiritual state of individuals on their deathbed, neither the dying nor their loved ones should worry excessively. Moreover, in their wills, Puritans typically expressed confidence in God's abundant mercy and Christ's atoning death on their behalf. Wills often declared people's commitment to Christ, rarely referred to uncertainty about their eternal state, and never conveyed despair about death.[48]

Although God saved people at conversion, Puritans insisted, individuals would not enjoy full salvation until they were "perfectly united with Christ" in heaven. To them, death was simultaneously a source of anxiety and hope, which impelled and enticed them to pursue greater piety. Those whose faith prompted them "to prepare and provide for another life," John Cotton argued, were true saints. Like athletes or soldiers, Puritans trained for a future engagement—life in heaven—through their devotional exercises on earth. Their confession of sin, meditation, and strict self-examination were "rehearsals for the Last Judgment." In *Preparatory Meditations upon the Day of Judgment*, Cotton Mather compared getting ready for eternity to a theatrical rehearsal. Their daily devotions prepared the saints for their everlasting union with Christ in glory. Shepard "began to long to die and think of being" with God, while poet Anne Bradstreet claimed that she heard God calling her home. Cotton Mather claimed that, in his later years, his father Increase had many heavenly visions. Jonathan Mitchel meditated daily so that "Heaven is here begun upon earth: shall I be thinking on and talking with Christ" throughout eternity "and not discourse with him one quarter of an hour in a day now?"[49] For Puritans, their future perfect union with Christ would be the culmination of "a lifetime of spiritual preparation." Conversion placed pilgrims on the road to heaven, while their private devotions and public worship equipped and empowered them to get to their heavenly destination. Numerous works such as John Corbet's *Self-Imployment in Secret* aimed to prepare Puritans for death and eternity. The journey to heaven, Puritans proclaimed, was strewn with difficulties. In many ways, taking the road that led to hell was much easier, and people's innate depravity inclined them to prefer that path. The road to heaven was "Up Hill all the Way," Mather declared; getting to heaven required "Swimming against the Stream." Because many enemies tried to block their progress, pilgrims "must fight every step" of the way.[50]

For Puritans, the path to heaven was indeed narrow and demanding. Their leaders warned that even many members of the visible church would not be saved. Increase Mather lamented that many were "deceived with False Hopes" until it was "too late for them to mend their Error."[51] People could "excel in morality," faithfully perform their religious duties, express love for "the Worship and Ordinances of God," know the scriptures thoroughly, be good citizens, helpful neighbors, and honest in all their dealings, and fear the terrors of hell and still not be not be permitted to enter God's eternal kingdom. Some would suffer greatly because of their religious convictions, losing their property, liberty, and lives—and still miss heaven. The doors of heaven would be shut even to "many gifted Preachers of the Gospel" who had fruitful ministries, Mather warned, because they had not been regenerated.[52]

Their preoccupation with worldly amusements and material things, James Pierpont predicted, would prevent countless people who "had very Promising Hopes of an Everlasting Happiness" from reaching heaven. Eternity, he argued, would be especially horrible for these individuals. The higher the hope people had for heaven "in this Life, the more horrendous" would "their despair be when these Hopes are not realized." Moreover, Pierpont claimed, God's wrath is proportional to people's "foolish & vain Hopes of going to Heaven." Such views often made even a devout saint's last days on earth uncomfortable, if not frightening. As James Fitch put it, contemplating death often made a person's "flesh tremble." "Some poor Souls," Edward Pearse declared, enter "Heaven through a throng of doubts and unbelief, difficulties and despondencies, through many fears and temptations." They were, as the apostle Paul put it, "scarcely saved," while others went to paradise "triumphantly, with a Crown upon their Heads." The witness of the Holy Spirit made some confident that they would forever "possess the fullness…of God and Christ." They entered into eternal life "without any Rebukes from God" or their own consciences, "without any stumbling through doubting or unbelief." Those "who have all things set right" with God, Pearse proclaimed, "die both happily and comfortably." To ensure that they did not deceive themselves and were ready for heaven, Mather counseled New Englanders to continually examine themselves, pray earnestly, regularly do good works, and "walk closely with God."[53]

Most Puritans believed they were living in the latter days when God was using catastrophes to end history and complete His kingdom. They saw clues in astrology, weather patterns, and the course of earthly events that the world was progressing toward its appointed end.[54] Increase Mather insisted that God used calamities and heavenly signs to chastise His people and compel them to contemplate their eternal state. Comets could serve as "presages of miserable Dearths and Scarcity," and the "Devastations and Desolations" of wars might foreshadow Christ's Second Coming. Mather was especially intrigued by the comet of 1680, the largest one he had ever seen.[55] Such signs were "tokens of God's anger" intended to "awaken men out of their Lethargyes." He exhorted people who saw blazing stars to repent and pray that God did not send a "destroying Angel" to earth. Similarly, Mather declared that a 1706 earthquake was a divine warning to people to repent to avoid the horrors of hell. However, Mather judged the sins of the Puritans, especially their pride, profaneness, and worldliness, to be "surer and blacker signs of judgment than any signs in heaven."[56] Mather and other Puritan pastors also proclaimed that the "Great Day of our Lord[']s Second coming" was close at hand to inspire New Englanders to live righteously.[57]

Many today associate the Puritans with the use of hellfire and brimstone to promote conversion, and this link is well-founded. Because the path to heaven was filled with obstacles, Puritans reasoned, avoiding hell was difficult. "Many who think they have escaped," warned Solomon Stoddard, the pastor of the Congregationalist Church in Northampton, Massachusetts from 1672 to 1729, "will not." Sharing much of the medieval tradition's doctrine and rhetoric about hell, Puritan ministers seeking to win souls stressed its horrors. Speaking for most of them, Samuel Danforth declared that "bold and presumptuous sinners" could be saved only if they came to fear the "Vengeance of God." "O Sinners," Hillhouse asked, "can you think of Dwelling Eternally with the Devil, and your old Companions in Sin?" "Can you think of taking up your Everlasting Habitation in unquenchable Fire?" In a sermon, strikingly similar in parts to Jonathan Edwards's "Sinners in the Hands of an Angry God," Increase Mather warned, "O Christless Sinner...thy soul is hanging over the mouth of hell by the rotten thread of a frail life: if that break, the devouring Gulf will swallow thee up for ever" in the unquenchable "Ocean of Fire." The scriptures, he added, warned people to flee "the exceeding Greatness and severity" of "hell's torments."[58]

In addition to prompting people to turn to God, Stoddard contended, "the fear of hell" helped deter sin. The "fear of the displeasure of parents, the justice of rulers," and "divine vengeance in this world" all helped restrain sin, "but the fear of hell" was "much more powerful." During the last twenty years, he complained in 1713, behavior had grown worse and worse. Many seemed "to be incorrigible and obstinate in their pride, luxury, and profaneness" because they were "not afraid of hell." People feared poverty and sickness, but they did not fear hell. Public ridicule, desire to avoid shame, and "a sense of [God's] mercies and deliverances" would not make most people repent and reform; only comprehending "the terrible anger of God" toward sin and the fear of going to hell could accomplish that.[59]

The fantastic promises of heaven and the horrific perils of hell, Puritans argued, should prompt Christians to work diligently to convert others. Christians must recognize that most people were not properly prepared for eternity. The desire to "save Precious...Souls from Eternal Death," Increase Mather contended, should inspire Christians to do their utmost to proclaim the gospel. Evangelism was crucial, Puritan divines contended, because individuals' spiritual condition at death irrevocably determined their destiny. "The Soul[']s Eternal State," asserted Pearse, "is absolutely fixed and unchangeably determined." Nothing could be done to help people after they died. "There is no repenting...no turning to God in the Grave," he warned.[60]

CONCLUSION

More than most other American Christians, the Puritans lived with one eye on eternity. Well versed in scripture, frequently reminded of the perilousness of life in sermons, books, and poems, eager to reap the rewards of heaven, and desirous of being reunited with loved ones, many of them thought frequently about the nature of heaven and how to get there. Few Puritans saw illness, death, or "natural" disasters as accidental. They believed that God sent these things to prompt people to assess their relationship with Him. Speaking for a host of Puritan preachers, Pearse proclaimed, "To be ready to live with God for ever in Heaven when we...die, is the great Work we have to do...in our present Pilgrimage." For Puritans, experiencing conversion, worshipping on the Sabbath, participating in the Lord's Supper, and engaging in private devotions were all "preparatory stages on the way to the final goal, the eternal life of glory."[61] These activities made them ready to enjoy their relationship with God and Christ in heaven.

Puritans believed that God was the author and finisher of human redemption and that good works neither justified individuals nor proved their Christian conviction; God saved souls and motivated people to do good deeds not to "puff up human pride, but to enhance his glory." For Puritans, these works were also a means of thanking God for His gift of salvation, building a godly earthly society, and helping bring the millennial kingdom.[62] Puritan doctrine involved a tension between the belief in God's election of individuals and His promise that they would persevere in the faith to the end of their earthly lives and the conviction that the pilgrimage to paradise was extremely difficult and people must labor diligently to attain heavenly bliss. As Peter Thuesen explains, the Puritans believed paradoxically that God's covenant of grace was "both conditional and absolute": God's choice of particular individuals was sovereign and inscrutable, but they must respond in faith to God's gracious offer and live righteously. Thuesen argues perceptively that the Puritans strove to balance "a healthy anxiety" about people's spiritual state (to help promote godly behavior and the construction of their city on a hill) with assurance of salvation. Therefore, Puritan piety dialectically combined "self-abasement with meditation on heavenly joys"—a spiritual discipline that aimed to produce "ecstatic agony." Like the pain superstar athletes endure that enables them to excel, the constructive pain of ecstatic agony aided Puritan warriors in their battle against the flesh, the Devil, and social evils and helped them to someday gain their heavenly reward. While emphasis on virtuous behavior and the obstacles in the heavenly path was stronger in times of theological challenges to the Puritan mission, perceived declension, and civil strife, Puritans from John Winthrop to the Mathers consistently stressed that those who wanted to spend eternity with God must obey His laws and develop sanctified hearts on earth.[63]

As stated, the Puritans displayed greater interest in both the end-times and heaven during theological and social crises, especially during the Pequot War in the 1630s, the debate over the standards for church membership and communion that produced the Halfway Covenant of 1662, King Philip's War in the 1670s, King William's War (1688–1697), and the witchcraft trials of the 1690s. Nevertheless, while each generation confronted different challenges and had distinct emphases, there was a "continuity and unity" to Puritan preaching and theology largely because of their central focus on the salvation of souls. Although the message and meaning of occasional sermons (primarily fast and election ones) often reflected New England's changing political and social conditions, Harry Stout argues, the two sermons most laypeople heard on Sundays and the one many listened to midweek were remarkably consistent in the years between 1630 and 1730, and typically stressed otherworldly themes.[64] Similarly educated at Harvard, Oxford, and Cambridge, the clergy almost all shared the same worldview. By the 1690s, some ministers had espoused heterodox doctrines, including a few who gained positions at Harvard, prompting Congregationalists to found Yale College in 1701, but the large majority of them remained orthodox Calvinists.[65]

For the Puritans, religion "was embedded in the fabric of everyday life," coloring how they thought about parenting, community, work, recreation, and life beyond the grave. As David Hall has shown, numerous Puritans incorporated folk religion and elements of magic into their belief system, including "wonder stories, holy curses, and witch-hunting," and some were much more religiously devout than others, but several factors indicate that most Puritans shared their ministers' beliefs about heaven and salvation. First, as Stout points out, the average Puritan church-goer listened to about 7,000 sermons in his lifetime, totaling about 15,000 hours. Before the 1760s, laypeople heard few if any competing messages, making the sermon "the only regular voice of authority." Moreover, the Puritans were a highly literate group who had easy access to the Bible in English and to inexpensive books about the Bible, theology, and Christian living written for laypeople.[66] The first generation who settled the Boston area primarily included godly individuals who embraced the Puritan theology and lifestyle and were committed both to building a righteous community and passing on their spiritual heritage to their children. Although many in subsequent generations rejected their parents' faith (sometimes only for a while), family devotions, religious instruction in school, regular church attendance, colonial laws, social expectations, and friendships with religiously committed individuals combined to keep most Puritans in the fold. Finally, countless diaries and letters testify that many ordinary Puritans held the same understanding of salvation and heaven as did pastors and professors.[67]

The Puritans were more introspective about their spiritual state, more sensitive to their own sinfulness, and held themselves to more rigorous moral standards than American Christians of any other era. They frequently exhorted one another to receive Christ as their savior and work out their salvation with fear and trembling so that they could spend eternity with God and loved ones and enjoy the glories of heaven. Continual stress on God's unconditional election and the numerous impediments on the road to heaven made many Puritans insecure and anxious about their own salvation. Subsequent generations of American Christians have held themselves to less stringent standards and consequently have experienced less apprehension about their eternal destiny. While some later Christians rhapsodized as much about the wonders of heaven, no other group of believers stressed the horrors of hell or the difficulties pilgrims encountered in the journey to the celestial city as much as the Puritans did. The harshness and challenges of their lives, their study of scripture, their rich devotional life, their substantial theological reflection, the books they read, and the sermons they heard led many Puritans to stress the necessity of a new birth experience, ponder the joys of heaven, warn people to avoid the terrors of hell, and encourage each other to live righteously to assure that they were admitted to God's hallowed home.

The Puritan conception of heaven resembled the community they sought to achieve on earth: a stable, secure, well-ordered, tightly knit commonwealth where residents had the same values, commitments, and goals. Both the earthly city on a hill they strove to create and the heavenly Jerusalem they envisioned prized hierarchy, strict adherence to biblical norms, subordination of individual interests to the common good, strong social discipline, and a loving community of like-minded saints who espoused a shared ideology. More than most groups in American history, the Puritans sought to systematically exclude all deviant and contentious individuals in order to maintain social harmony and religious purity.[68] In many ways their conception of heaven was a replica of the godly society they strove to build on earth.

JONATHAN EDWARDS

AND THE FIRST GREAT

AWAKENING

Heaven Is a World of Love

My heaven is to please God, and glorify him, and give all to him, and to be wholly devoted to his glory.
—DAVID BRAINERD, diary entry in Jonathan Edwards, *The Life of David Brainerd*

The heaven I desired was a heaven of holiness; to be with God, and to spend my eternity in divine love, and holy communion with Christ. My mind was very much taken up with contemplations on heaven, and the enjoyments there; and living there in perfect holiness, humility and love.... Heaven appeared exceedingly delightful, as a world of love; and that all happiness consisted in living in pure, humble, heavenly, divine love.
—JONATHAN EDWARDS, *Heaven Is a World of Love*

How can you better employ your strength, use your means, and spend your days, than in traveling the road that leads to the everlasting enjoyment of God; to his glorious presence; to the new Jerusalem; to the heavenly mount Zion; where all your desires will be filled, and no danger of ever losing your happiness?
—JONATHAN EDWARDS, "The Christian Pilgrims"

IN THE POPULAR mind, Jonathan Edwards is much more associated with his sermon "Sinners in the Hands of an Angry God" than with another of his sermons, "Heaven Is a World of Love." Many anthologies of American literature include the former, while few, if any, contain the latter. Most educated Americans have heard of Edwards's sermon on hell; it is among the best known sermons in American history. Only scholars in American religious history and some Reformed pastors know of his sermon on heaven. Nevertheless, Edwards's homily on heaven is much more typical of his preaching. He delivered numerous sermons that focused on heaven and only a few that primarily dealt with hell.[1] Although many Americans continue to picture Edwards as a stern, harsh, gloomy Puritan who relished preaching hellfire and brimstone diatribes, he was a compassionate pastor who strove to help his flock live by biblical truths and properly prepare for heaven. To Edwards, heaven was a marvelous place where the redeemed would bask in the love and savor the glory of God the Father and Christ the Son.

Widely considered America's greatest theologian, Jonathan Edwards was also a gifted preacher, teacher, and expositor of the Bible. Following his graduation from Yale in 1721, graduate study in theology in New Haven, work as a Congregationalist pastor at a church in New York City, and service at his alma mater as a tutor, Edwards became the pastoral assistant to his grandfather Solomon Stoddard at Northampton, Massachusetts, in 1726. After Stoddard's death in 1729, Edwards became the church's sole minister, a position he held until he was forced out in 1751 as a result of a theological dispute. For the next six years Edwards served as a missionary to Native Americans in nearby Stockbridge, Massachusetts, before accepting the presidency of the College of New Jersey (later Princeton). He died several months later from a smallpox vaccination. Edwards played a leading role in the First Great Awakening, a series of colony-wide religious revivals in the 1730s and 1740s, serving as one of its principal evangelists and organizers as well as its chief scribe and defender.[2]

English Calvinist George Whitefield was as important to the awakening as Edwards. The itinerant evangelist spoke to hundreds of large and small groups from Georgia to Nova Scotia in churches, colleges, and open air forums. Unlike Edwards, Whitefield is largely forgotten today. However, he was the most famous religious figure of the eighteenth century, and before being surpassed in prominence by Benjamin Franklin in the 1750s, the best known man in America. Referred to by newspapers as the "marvel of the age," Whitefield's shrewd use of marketing, powerful oratory, and captivating messages attracted huge crowds and won thousands to Christ on both sides of the Atlantic. Over his lifetime, he preached more than 18,000 sermons to an estimated ten million listeners.[3] A leading Boston pastor called Whitefield "one of the most extraordinary characters of the present age" whose "zealous, incessant and successful labors, in Europe and America, are without a parallel." Other keys leaders of the awakening were Presbyterian pastor and revivalist Gilbert Tennent, Presbyterian evangelist and educator Samuel Davies, and Dutch Reformed minister Theodore Frelinghuysen who labored in the Raritan Valley of New Jersey.[4]

Although some scholars dispute whether a "great awakening" actually occurred, most contend that it deeply affected American life and religion. It brought thousands to Christ, poured vitality into many congregations, and strengthened the denominations that most emphasized evangelism, the new birth experience, and vital Christian piety—Baptists, Presbyterians, and Congregationalists. The awakening also provoked significant controversy over theology and worship practices and contributed to schism, most notably among Presbyterians with their Old Side/ New Side division of 1741 to 1758. It inspired the founding of colleges—Princeton by the Presbyterians, Brown by the Baptists, Rutgers by the Dutch Reformed, and Dartmouth by the Congregations—and helped prepare the way for the American Revolution by giving colonists a shared sense of religious identity, greater familiarity with each other, and stronger bonds.[5] In their efforts to win converts and to moti-vate Christians to witness and live righteously, the awakening's proponents empha-sized the allures and wonders of heaven and explained how to get there.

Other leaders of the awakening published dozens of pamphlets and sermons, but Edwards's voluminous writings on theology, biblical exposition, and eschatology, as well as several collections of sermons, have been much more influential, both in his own time and since his death.[6] Dozens of Edwards's sermons discuss celestial themes, and numerous ones are principally about heaven. As a young man, Edwards wrote that trying "to describe the excellence, the greatness or duration of the happiness of heaven by the most artful composition of words would" simply "darken and cloud it," but as a mature pastor he often tried.[7] More than almost any other American, Edwards asserted that love dominated and defined heaven—the love among the three members of the Trinity, the love between God the Father, Christ the Son, and the Holy Spirit and individual saints, and the saints' love of one another.

THE CHARACTERISTICS OF HEAVEN

Like the Puritans, Edwards and other revivalists conceived of heaven as theocentric, accentuating its magnificence and God's awesome presence. Scripture, Edwards declared, repeatedly referred to "the highest heaven" "as the house of God" "where God dwells with his family." Although God "is everywhere present," both testaments portrayed His "being in heaven, in a special and peculiar manner." Although "God built heaven chiefly for an habitation for Christ," Edwards argued, He "gloriously adapted" it "to be a blissful" abode "and an eternal possession" for the saints.[8]

In various sermons and treatises, Edwards portrayed heaven as a realm where the saints eternally praise God, delight in their intimate relationship with Christ, grow (especially in knowledge), and enjoy social harmony. Heaven, he explained, provides its residents with "inexpressible pleasure" that immensely exceeds all the "delights in this world." Edwards titled one of his sermons "Nothing upon Earth Can Represent the Glories of Heaven," but he employed such biblical similes as a crown, a kingdom, a treasure, and a city to describe it. These images, he asserted, indicated that God's celestial home is a place of brilliant light, fantastic happiness, and dazzling splendor.[9]

For Edwards, heaven revolved around the triune God, who displays incredible love for the saints and perfectly provides for their happiness. "Heaven is the palace…of the high and holy One, whose name is love." God the Father designed heaven to be the eternal "place of his glorious presence." The "eternal Three in One," the "infi-nite fountain of love," resides in heaven. The saints, Edwards declared, will have "per-fect union with God." They will see God clearly, fully conform to Him, and serve

Him perfectly. Basking in the beatific vision, the saints will "dwell with God the father," who they love with all their "hearts on earth; and with Jesus Christ," their "beloved Savior…and with the Holy Spirit," their "Sanctifier, and Guide, and Comforter." Christ is the "effulgence of God's glory," by which God's "glory shines forth in heaven." As "the Sun of righteousness," God illuminates "the heavenly Jerusalem."[10] The saints will see in God everything their hearts desire, everything "that tends to excite and inflame love," "everything that is lovely," and everything that evokes "their esteem and admiration." Like the angels, the saints will comprehend God's infinite glory, stupendous majesty, and perfect holiness and be completely sated by His love. Like Christ, the saints will rest "in the bosom of the Father" and feel "immense joy" in His love. Only intimacy with Him can truly satisfy their souls. At the same time, Edwards asserted, the Father will savor the excellent qualities, happiness, and loveliness of people He created in His own image. Making His creatures happy gives God as much pleasure as exercising His goodness or holiness.[11]

Heaven, Edwards rejoiced, will have none of the barriers that inhibited Christians from communing with God while they were on earth; "every separating wall" between God and man will be smashed and every impediment will be eradicated. In heaven, Edwards explained, the saints understand the previously "unfathomable depths" of God's wisdom and His "infinite" holiness. The "eternal, immortal, [and] invisible" King cannot be directly viewed, but God can be seen in and known through Christ. The saints, Edwards rhapsodized, will "eat and drink abundantly, and swim in the ocean of [God's] love, and be eternally swallowed up on the infinitely bright, and infinitely mild and sweet, beams of divine love." They will share in Christ's "ineffable delights" as He enjoys His Father. The central, unending event of heaven, Edwards maintained, "is the wedding feast of Christ and his bride, the church." At this feast, God entertains his saints with "amazing exercises of infinite and mysterious wisdom, showing the…infinite riches of his wisdom, and…[the] wonderful exercises of his power."[12]

God's love, Edwards asserted, is the basis for all heaven's "good principles" and "amiable and excellent actions." Heaven "is a garden of pleasures, a…paradise, fitted in all respects" to serve as the abode of divine love. God arranged everything in heaven to promote love and "mutual enjoyment." The saints will know, Edwards declared, that God has always loved them and will always love them, and they will passionately love God. The holiest saints will be the happiest and the closest to God. They will "penetrate further into the vast…distance" between themselves and God and will delight in "annihilating themselves" so that God will "be all."[13]

Edwards urged Christians not to crave "the world and its enjoyments," but rather to "desire heaven." Above all things, believers should yearn "to be with God" and

Jesus. Only this heavenly communion, he argued, could truly satisfy the soul. Several things contributed to the happiness of the inhabitants of heaven during the intermediate state: appreciating its arrangements, experiencing God's amazing love, and observing "God's mercy towards his church."[14]

Christ, Edwards argued, is "the King of heaven, and its most bright and precious jewel." Jesus "sits on the right hand of God, as the King" of angels and the entire universe. Christ's "glory and sweetness" furnishes heaven's "fullness, and glory, and happiness." As the "Alpha and Omega" and "the sum of all" things, He will "be exalted in glory." As the "sun of the new Jerusalem," Jesus supplies this world with vigor, beauty, fragrance, and joy. Because the "beloved Son of God" shed his blood on the cross and endured "extreme sufferings in obedience to his Father's will," God gave Christ even greater glory in heaven. Moreover, His crucifixion laid the foundation for renewing "all things both spiritual and external" and making them beautiful and splendid.[15]

At the end of time, Edwards contended, Christ will "appear in the most dreadful…manner to the wicked," but He will "appear as a Lamb to his saints" and treat them gently and lovingly. Although Christ is the glorious, exalted Lord, Edwards explained, He will not regard the saints as "subjects and servants"; instead in heaven He will "freely and intimately converse with them as friends and brethren." The inhabitants of heaven will see the splendor of Christ's "divine nature…the beauty of all his perfections," and His "great majesty, almighty power…infinite wisdom, holiness, and grace." They will also see His grandeur "as God-man and Mediator." The saints will understand much more fully than they did while they were on earth, how Christ's death demonstrated His "eternal and unmeasurable" love for them. Christ's "exaltation in heaven," Edwards asserted, will fill the saints with tremendous awe and adoration, but this will not separate them from their savior. Rather, it will heighten their joy as He grants them "intimate access" and "freely and fully" communicates Himself to them. The redeemed, Edwards declared, will be able to talk personally with Jesus and fully "enjoy his love, as his friends and spouse." On earth, the elect are "betrothed to Christ," while in heaven they are "married to him" and intimately converse with Him in "perfect mutual love." They will share His "infinite pleasure" in communing with His Father.[16]

While Edwards's portrait of heaven was based upon his interpretation of the Bible, it was shaped by his experiences as a pastor and revivalist. During the First Great Awakening, spiritual dreams, trances, and mystical experiences were common and caused considerable controversy. Most of them centered around believers' relationship with God and Jesus, and some of them included alleged visits to or visions of heaven. While some clergy, most notably Charles Chauncy, denounced these ecstatic encounters as inauthentic, misinterpreted, and harmful, Edwards generally defended them as genuine manifestations of the Holy Spirit, but he advised people to wait to see what fruit they produced.[17] Both Edwards and his wife Sarah had numerous rapturous experiences in which they felt immersed in the wonder and love of God and Jesus. In words that echo his descriptions of heaven, Edwards wrote about a memorable spiritual encounter in 1740: "The person of Christ appeared ineffably excellent, with an excellency great enough to swallow up all thought and conception."[18]

Edwards expected the saints to grow throughout eternity in holiness, love, understanding, and happiness. "There is eternal progress" and continual discovery in heaven. The "happiness of heaven," he added, "is progressive" and gloriously advances. Much of it involved beholding God manifesting Himself "in the work of redemption." The redeemed will continually "discover and enjoy" more of God's glory. As the saints understand God's perfection more fully, they will love Him more deeply and delight in Him more.[19]

For some, Edwards's focus on the happiness of heaven may seem ironic, given his work ethic (most days he spent twelve to thirteen hours studying and writing) and minimal interest in recreation and earthly pleasures (though he did like to walk and ride a horse). Scholars have described him as a "killjoy," as "not given to levity or the sorts of diversions that...appealed to his contemporaries." While Edwards walked to get exercise and enjoy nature, he also used his solitary walks to contemplate, pray, and commune with God and always took pen and ink along to record his thoughts.[20]

Given Edwards's passion for biblical study and theological reflection, it is not surprising that he especially emphasized that heaven's residents will "increase in their knowledge." The saints will understand the design and aims of all God's activity throughout time, which were currently "hidden, intricate, and inexplicable." While in the Puritan conception, the saints entirely focused on heavenly activities, Edwards claimed that during the intermediate state, heavenly residents closely observed the advancement of the church and God's kingdom on earth. Like the angels, they rejoiced when souls were converted on earth. Their happiness greatly increased, Edwards proclaimed, as they saw "the success of the gospel after Christ's ascension, its conquest of the Roman empire, and the Reformation"; and the saints "will exceedingly rejoice at the fall of antichrist and the conversion of the world to Christianity" in the end-times. Those in heaven, he insisted, had "infinitely greater advantages" over Christians on earth in fathoming "how Christ's kingdom" flourished; they could better understand God's marvelous acts and phenomenal accomplishments as well as Satan's opposition "and how he is baffled and overthrown." While life often appeared confusing to Christians on earth, the saints could "see the wise connection of events, and the beautiful order of all things...in the church in different ages." The redeemed, asserted Edwards, have a much better vantage point in heaven for viewing "the state of Christ's kingdom in this world" than they did while they were on earth, just as the man who is on top of a mountain can see much more than one who is in a forest or a valley. Mortals have "a very imperfect view of God's providence in the world"; they see only "a very small part of the scheme." Edwards argued that as the saints recognize the perfection of His work, they ascribe more glory to God. Observing what is happening on "earth does not disturb the[ir] tranquility" because the saints understand that "even the failings of the church militant work ultimately for God's glory and the church's own good."[21]

Heavenly residents, Edwards averred, will also better understand their own earthly experience. Although the saints will comprehend the foolishness and "vileness" of much of their earthly behavior and "the evil and folly of sin" "a thousand times" better, "they will not experience any...sorrow or grief for it" "because they will perfectly see" how God used it to promote His glory. Edwards expected the saints to clearly remember their lives on earth, especially the sins from which they had been saved, their experience of regeneration, God's mercies to them, their good works, and the circumstances of their death. The saints, Edwards, contended, would even recognize that humanity's fall brought great blessings. If people "had not fallen," their "glory and happiness" in heaven would have been greatly reduced. Without the fall, the saints "would never have had such...an intimate union" and communion "with the Father or Son." Christ would have remained "at an infinite distance from man" because He would have only possessed "the divine nature," and people would have remained "at an infinite distance from the Father" if they have not been brought close to Him by their union with "a divine person."[22]

For Edwards, the chief tasks of the saints were to worship and serve God, contemplate His creation and grandeur, rule with Christ over His kingdom, and help judge the world at the end of time. Scripture did not clearly reveal what particular tasks people do in heaven, he argued, but it did teach that they constantly praised and served God. Music is central to worship in heaven because it is "the best [and] most beautiful...way" people could express "a sweet concord of mind." Adoring and serving God and admiring his beauty and glory, Edwards insisted, would "fill up eternity." The saints, Theodore Frelinghuysen insisted similarly, will worship "the Lord day and night in His temple," exclaiming, "'Blessing, and honor and glory, and power, be unto him that sitteth upon the throne, and unto the Lamb forever and ever' (Rev. 5:13)." The saints, Edwards added, will eternally ponder the splendor of God, His magnificent design of creation, and "the wonders of God's providence."[23] Moreover, they will be "made kings and priests," "rule over the nations" and help Christ judge "the world at the last day." Before the final judgment, the saints will share Christ's "joy and glory" as His kingdom prospers on earth and the gospel advances. Edwards expected the inhabitants of heaven to have "different offices" as they did "in the church on earth." Unlike some other American Christians, Edwards did not portray rest as an important feature of heaven, but he did call heaven a blessed "haven of rest" for those who had "passed through the storms and tempests of this world."[24]

The saints, Edwards proclaimed, will delight in serving God because doing so "is just and right," produces wonderful benefits, and pleases God. Moreover, it promotes God's glory, helps conform them to God, and enables them to express their love for Him. The saints will recognize that the service they render to God "is but a small recompense" for His "great redemption." Heavenly inhabitants will acknowledge that God is worthy to be the "absolute sovereign of the world" because of His "infinite wisdom, justice, and holiness." God's accomplishment of His perfect purposes will bring the saints immense pleasure. Heaven, Edwards explained, will be a place "of action and employment" where the saints work more energetically than they did on earth. No longer plagued by the infirmity of their flesh and the corruption of their hearts, heaven's residents will work as "easily, freely and naturally as the sun shines." Reflecting on this should make Christians "ashamed of their...sluggishness in God's service," drowsiness in worship, and "coldness in prayer."[25]

In sharp contrast to the Puritans, Edwards argued that heaven was "built, and designed, [and] prepared for a great multitude." God's abundant mercy and Christ's meritorious sacrifice would provide salvation for "millions of millions." Anticipating the First Great Awakening's outreach to African Americans, Native Americans, and impoverished whites and its willingness to allow women to speak in the church, Edwards pictured God's celestial kingdom as having "sufficient and suitable accommodation[s]...for great and small, for high and low, rich and poor, wise and unwise, bond and free; persons of all nations, and all conditions, and circumstances." Samuel Davies and George Whitefield, who held many interdenominational evangelistic meetings, also stressed the worldwide scope and ecumenical character of heaven. When warriors "from every corner of the earth" passed "in review before their General in the fields of heaven, with their robes washed in his blood, with palms of victory in their hands and crowns of glory on their heads," Davies declared, "what a glorious army will they make!" "Father Abraham," Whitefield asked,

"Whom have you in Heaven? Any Episcopalians?"
"No!"
"Any Presbyterians?"
"No!"
"Any Independents or Seceders, New Sides or Old Sides, any Methodists?"
"No! No! No!"

"Whom have you there, then, Father Abraham?"

"We don't know those names here! All who have come are Christians—believers in Christ, men who have overcome by the blood of the Lamb and the word of his testimony...."

"Then... God help us all, to forget having names and become Christians in deed and in truth."[26]

THE NATURE OF THE SAINTS, HEAVENLY LIFE, AND THE ESCHATON

Both Edwards and Whitefield taught that the saints' principal attribute is that they will be like Jesus. The saints, Edwards repeatedly declared, will share Christ's nature and grandeur. Christ will give His people "the glory of his person"; their souls will be "like his soul, their bodies [will be] like... his glorious body"; they will share His riches and pleasures. When Jesus returned, "the bodies of all the living saints" will "be changed to be like Christ's glorious body." Whitefield agreed that the bodies of the saints were like "Christ's most glorious body." Their earthly bodies that suffered from "gout and gravel" and hindered their spiritual life would not inhibit them in the hereafter. Christians' bodies were "sown in corruption," but they will "be raised in incorruption." In heaven, the body and soul of the saints would be reunited. Therefore, no matter how weak or sick a Christian currently was, he would soon have a strong, vigorous body.[27]

"At death the believer not only gains a perfect and eternal deliverance from sin and temptation," Edwards explained, but is made totally holy, completing God's work of sanctification. Lacking all deformities or defects, the redeemed will "be perfectly pure and... lovely in heaven." Their "hearts are full of love." There is "no sin, no pride, no malice, [no] hating one another, no hurting one another... no death, no old age, [and] no winter" (spoken like a true New Englander). In heaven, people's "capacities will be exceedingly enlarged," all their desires will be fulfilled, and their happiness will never end. Moreover, in direct contrast to earth, the saints progressively "become more and more youthful... vigorous, active... and beautiful."[28]

Like the earlier Puritans and unlike later American Christians, Edwards said relatively little about either the ability of the saints to recognize each other in heaven or their fellowship there. Although he placed more emphasis on the saints' fellowship with God the Father, Christ the Son, and the Holy Spirit, Edwards did not agree with Thomas Aquinas and John Calvin that the saints' relationship with one another was either nonexistent or inconsequential. "The special affection" Christians had for particular individuals on earth would continue in heaven. Nothing would hinder heaven's inhabitants from thoroughly enjoying each other's love. Relations in heaven, Edwards asserted, will be "very near and dear," and no one will ever feel slighted or that her "love is not fully and fondly returned." Residents of heaven will also enjoy fellowship with the patriarchs, Old and New Testament saints, and angels. They will all dwell together harmoniously and happily in "the heavenly Jerusalem."[29]

Despite such statements, Edwards wrote little about heavenly fellowship, which may be explained in part by his personality. Although he grew up in an affectionate family (and as the only boy among eleven children, he was often doted over) and had a loving marriage, Edwards had few close friends and spent little time socializing. "Deeply spiritual, intensely hardworking, intellectual, introspective, and somewhat withdrawn," Edwards cherished his time alone to study and reflect. His chief disciple and first biographer, Samuel Hopkins, asserted that many found the theologian to be "stiff and unsociable" until they got to know him. "Not a man of many words," and rather "reserved with strangers," Edwards rarely visited his parishioners at their homes and had trouble "making small talk." "His brittle, unsociable personality contributed" to his dismissal by his Northampton congregation.[30]

The much more gregarious Whitefield stressed personal recognition and the communion of the saints more than Edwards. He inferred from the fact that Peter identified Moses and Elijah at Christ's transfiguration and that the rich man recognized Lazarus "sitting in Abraham's bosom" "that departed saints do … know each other in heaven … by intuition and immediate revelation." The "blessed prospect" "of seeing the Lamb sitting upon the throne" surrounded by "Abraham, Isaac, and Jacob" and "all the redeemed company" should inspire Christians to strongly "desire to go to heaven." Whitefield hoped that their conviction that they would someday be reunited with their parents, spouses, and children who had been "follower[s] of Jesus" would prevent Christians "from sorrowing as persons without hope" and wanting their loved ones to return to "this evil world."[31]

As did the Puritans, Edwards taught that believers go directly to heaven at death. After "the souls of true saints … leave their bodies at death," he declared, they dwelled "in the immediate, full, and constant view" of Christ. This was a foretaste of what they would experience after "the consummation … when all things" were "in their fixed and eternal state." After His "perfect and complete victory" over all His enemies at the Day of Judgment, Christ, Edwards attested, would return to heaven even more triumphantly than He had after His resurrection and ascension. Thereafter, heaven will be made "much more glorious" while hell will "be made more terrible."[32]

Disagreeing with Increase Mather, Edwards argued that the saints would spend eternity in heaven, not on a renovated and refurbished earth. God, Christ, and the saints would reside eternally in heaven, "not [in] this lower world, purified and refined." Scripture taught, he asserted, that heaven is "God's fixed abode." Because the New Testament repeatedly referred to heaven "as the place of God and Christ, and the angels" and "the proper country of the saints," Edwards expected the redeemed to remain there forever. At Christ's Second Coming, Christians who had endured "hatred, reproach, and contempt" and had been unjustly "reviled and condemned" will be removed from earth and "fully vindicated" in heaven. Then the world will "be turned into a great furnace" with "the fiercest and most raging heat" where "all the enemies of Christ and his church shall be tormented forever." "All the persecutors of the church of God" will "burn in [this] everlasting fire"; they will "suffer torments far beyond" what they had inflicted on the saints.[33]

HEAVEN'S "GLORIOUS REWARDS"

Edwards wrote little about the fellowship of the saints, but he discussed extensively their spectacular rewards. Although people's earthly deeds played no role in their salvation, Edwards argued, they did earn them heavenly rewards. Those who were the most obedient, holy, and fruitful would reap the richest heavenly recompense. Although the saints would not obtain their ultimate rewards until after the final judgment, they received "glorious rewards" immediately after death. Several factors, he argued, indicated that the saints had different "degrees of glory in heaven." First, God's word encouraged people to pursue greater rewards. Second, Jesus described heaven as having "many mansions," implying that it had "seats of various dignity and different degrees...of honor and happiness."[34] Third, this concept was consistent with the angels' disparate degrees of glory and disciples' different privileges. Fourth, scripture directly taught that heavenly rewards "will be in proportion to men's works" on earth. For example, I Corinthians 3:12–15 declared that each person's deeds will be evaluated and those of some Christians (their "wood, hay, and stubble") will count for nothing. Fifth, God could properly compensate those who did good works only by giving them additional happiness. Finally, Edwards argued, God promised to reward the saints "to encourage them" to be diligent "in his work and service." Faithful Christians, added Whitefield, will receive "a crown, a kingdom, an eternal and exceeding weight of glory."[35]

Edwards maintained that Christians' "future degrees of glory" depended on their level of holiness, the amount of their "self-denial and sufferings" for God, and the quality of their work to advance God's kingdom and aid others. As long as Christians did "so righteously," Edwards avowed, they should eagerly seek "the highest degrees of glory possible" and earnestly strive to obtain "heavenly treasures." "The least addition to heavenly glory," he declared, "will be more worth than all the high things of this world put together." Moreover, those who have the most glory in heaven will be able to praise God most fully and effusively because they will know Him the best and enjoy Him the most. Therefore, ignoring "any of the blessings God has offered to stir us up to our duty" was sinful. "Self-love, when directed and regulated by the will and word of God," he added, "is a good principle."[36]

The saints' different levels of rewards, Edwards alleged, did not diminish the happiness of or evoke envy among those who had less glory. Heaven's incredible blessings ensured that all the saints were happy, he avowed, but God sovereignly determined their capacity for happiness. "Every vessel may be full," Edwards explained, but "some may hold more than others." It did not diminish the happiness of saints to see others who had more glory because perfect love prevailed in heaven, permitting no pride or jealousy. Heaven's hierarchy of glory does not diminish anyone's joy because all the saints are enthralled by God's love and want the complete happiness of everyone else. For Edwards, the superior rewards in heaven were having a more magnificent resurrection body, higher levels of holiness, and a greater ability to know, worship, and enjoy God.[37]

In addition to promising them future rewards, Edwards argued, God gave Christians previews of heaven to aid them in their earthly pilgrimage and to stimulate them to do good works. On earth, Christians experienced samples of "heavenly pleasures and delights," such as godly conduct and joy to help them anticipate heaven. For Edwards, the Lord's Supper was "a foretaste of the ineffably sublime heavenly communion." The glimpses of heaven Christians enjoyed on earth, "such as the peace and rest that Christ gives," created a "longing for their fulfillment."[38]

Edwards urged Christians to remember that their true "hearts and treasure are in heaven." He exhorted believers to "think often of all that is in heaven, of the friends who are there, and the praises and worship there, and of all that will make up the blessedness of that world of love. Let your conversation be in heaven (Phil. 3:20)." He hoped that reflecting on the blessings of heaven would motivate Christians to "earnestly to seek after it."[39]

THE TRUE CHRISTIAN'S LIFE IS A JOURNEY TOWARD HEAVEN

Like Martin Luther and their Puritan forefathers, Edwards and other leaders of the First Great Awakening argued that God would admit into heaven only those individuals who had been justified by faith. Scripture taught, he wrote, that Christ paid for heaven for believers. "We cannot purchase it for ourselves." People could not be "saved by their own righteousness." Christ merited heaven by His complete obedience and sacrificial death for human sin upon the cross. Because He did not need this merit (He was perfect and had no sin to atone for), God applied it to those who accepted Christ as their savior and Lord. To go to heaven, Edwards argued, individuals "must first be made fit" by being clothed with Christ's righteousness. Individuals must be "born again"; they must undergo a "blessed renovation" of their "hearts by the Holy Spirit" that implanted "divine love in them." No matter how "moral and strict, sober and religious" individuals were, he warned, they would go to hell unless they were born again. Jesus Christ is "the way, and the truth, and the life," Edwards proclaimed, the only door to heaven.[40]

As Calvinists, Edwards, Whitefield, Frelinghuysen, Stoddard, Davies, and most other leaders of the First Great Awakening believed that God predestined individuals for salvation. Although people could not repent and be saved unless God prompted them to do so through the Holy Spirit, God normally worked through means (especially preaching) to save sinners. Since no one knew who the elect were, preachers exhorted everyone to forsake their sin and accept Jesus as their personal savior. They insisted that God's sovereign grace alone effected redemption and that people's works played no role in salvation. Their opponents, known as Arminians, denounced Calvinist soteriology as biblically unsupported, unjust, and a barrier to moral effort.[41]

"The doctrine of our regeneration, or new birth in Christ Jesus," Whitefield proclaimed, is "clearly taught in sacred writ, the very hinge on which the salvation of each of us turns, and a point" with "which all sincere Christians, of every denomination, agree." Tragically, however, few of those "who call[ed] themselves Christians" "experimentally understood" this crucial concept. Many believed that Christ was the sole "Mediator between God and men" and the only way of salvation. They did not recognize, however, that they "must be regenerated … born again … renewed … in the inmost faculties of their minds" before they could "truly call Christ" Lord or "share in the merits of his precious blood." Whitefield argued that God would forever banish those without a "wedding garment" from heaven. To be admitted, sinners must come to Christ, who is the way, "the resurrection and the life" and be converted by the Holy Spirit.[42]

Edwards, Whitefield, and other revivalists protested, as had the Puritans, that many hoped to get to heaven by their own efforts, especially by participating in religious observances such as worship and fasting. Many, Edwards complained, acted "devout at church," but led immoral lives; they wanted to gain admission to heaven without giving up their vices. "They seem to think," he wrote, "that a little religion" on the Sabbath and festival days "will atone for their sensuality and loose behavior on other days." Their "little religion" would not be enough to permit them to enter heaven. "If everyone who "hoped for heaven" got there, Edwards reasoned, heaven would be "full of murderers, adulterers…drunkards, thieves, robbers, and licentious debauchers." Those who imagined that all that was required to gain entrance to heaven was to attend church and adhere "to the outward forms of religion"—praying, "reading the word of God, and taking the sacraments," Whitefield declared, were sadly mistaken. Many wrongly concluded, Theodore Frelinghuysen argued, that their civil righteousness—obeying the law without injuring or wronging anyone, giving everyone his due, and acting justly—provided a passport to heaven. "Some hope to obtain Heaven" without relying on Christ's holiness, complained Samuel Finley, a Presbyterian pastor and president of the College of New Jersey. No one would "be pardoned without an Heart-purifying Faith" or accepted by God "without the imputed Righteousness of Christ."[43]

Edwards observed that almost everyone tried "to be religious sometime" before they died because no one intended to go to hell. Being religious, however, was not enough. People must choose either "this world" with its sinful delights, which led to "eternal misery," or deny themselves and obey God's commandments, which led to "heaven and eternal glory." Many foolishly tried to have both, Edwards declared; they wanted to go to heaven and to enjoy this world; they wanted both salvation "and the pleasure and profits of sin." If they could attain heaven without living righteously and serving God, he contended, many "would be glad to have" it, but individuals must choose either "heaven and holiness, or the world and hell." Despite their fallen nature, people could determine whether it is better to live "a life of self-denial, and enjoy eternal happiness" or pursue "a worldly, carnal, wicked life," revel in "sinful enjoyments," and "burn in hell forever." God would consign those who tried to have it both ways, Edwards alleged, to "the lake that burns with fire and brimstone forever." While some followed "the straight and narrow way to life" in Zion "and laboriously travel[ed] up the hill against the inclination and tendency of the flesh," others ran swiftly toward "the bottomless pit" of hell.[44]

Whitefield argued similarly that many wavered "between Christ and the world," vainly trying "to reconcile God and Mammon, light and darkness, Christ and Belial." The world, more than the word of God, directed both their principles and practices. They based their decisions, he claimed, either on conventional morality or what best suited their "own corrupt inclinations" rather than on "what scripture requires." Criticizing the growing materialism in colonial America, Whitefield protested that their desire for earthly pleasures and "inordinate love of money" led many people to be "almost Christians." The incredible blessings of eternal life, Whitefield reasoned, were well worth temporarily renouncing "a few transitory riches." Christ "shed his precious blood" to purchase people's total lives, he added, but sadly many tried to "only give him half" of themselves. Whitefield urged his hearers to present "God their whole hearts, and no longer halt between two opinions": if the world and pleasure were God, "let us serve that; but if the Lord…be God, let us…serve him alone."[45] He warned indecisive individuals that God might "cut you off before you have another invitation" to receive Christ as their savior. Respond to Jesus "while he knocks at the door of your souls" so you never hear Him say, "depart, ye cursed, into everlasting fire, prepared for the devil and his angels." Just "as the company of the blessed increases the happiness of heaven," Whitefield claimed, "the company of the damned will increase their torments" in hell.[46]

In addition, Whitefield accused many church members of being Pharisees who "trusted in their own righteousness" because they led "civil, honest, decent lives." "Harlots, murderers, and thieves," he alleged, would "enter the kingdom of God" before them. No one's good works could justify her; "only the blood of Jesus Christ" could cleanse individuals "from the filth and pollution" of their sins and reconcile them to God. Although their works did not contribute to their salvation, God required people to do good deeds after He redeemed them. Only those who were converted, empowered, and sanctified by the Holy Spirit, Whitefield declared, could do truly good works.[47]

Like the Puritans, Edwards and Whitefield contended that while redemption was by grace, people must work out their salvation with fear and trembling. Edwards urged his hearers and readers to employ all their strength and means to travel "the road that leads to the everlasting enjoyment of God." Getting to the heavenly Mount Zion, he argued, required denying oneself, obeying God's commands, and acting compassionately. Many who hoped to go to heaven, Edwards averred, would not do so because they lacked holiness, which was an "absolutely necessary" prerequisite. Holiness, he maintained, involved conforming one's "heart and life to God," emulating Jesus, and following God's laws. Edwards counseled Christians to strive to attain a "high seat in God's house…above by seeking eminent holiness." Those on "the way to the world of love" must also "live a life of love." "Because the essence of heavenly life is a loving union with God, those who do not love God will not be able to enjoy heaven." Companionship was very desirable whenever people traveled, Edwards stated, but it was especially beneficial as they journeyed to paradise.[48]

Edwards also urged people to reject the "world and its enjoyments" and continuously think about and "desire heaven." Christians should be willing to exchange loving families, children who had promising futures, delightful social relationships, a good name, the respect of others, and comfortable accommodations to attain heaven. Believers must take up their crosses daily, follow Christ, deny all their "sinful inclinations and interests," and travel heavenward.[49]

Like Edwards, Whitefield stressed that believers must become more spiritually minded, obey Christ, and act righteously to prepare for heaven. Because heavenly happiness is spiritual, Whitefield asserted, people would not be suited to take part in God's wonderful inheritance unless their "carnal minds" were made spiritual. Until their depraved natures were totally renovated, people could not relish heaven's pleasures. "Nothing short of a thorough…conversion" would make sinners ready "for the kingdom of heaven."[50] True Christians, he argued "are willing to follow the Lamb" wherever "he leads them. They hear, know, and obey his voice. Their affections are set on things above…their citizenship is in heaven.… [T]hey habitually…walk with…God." Because Christ lived in the redeemed, their hearts were pure and their conduct was upright. Only those whose demeanor and actions caused them to be "persecuted for righteousness sake," he maintained, could expect to inherit the kingdom of heaven.[51]

While acknowledging that "the way to heaven" involved many difficulties, Edwards did not focus on them nearly as much as his Puritan predecessors. Nor did he emphasize, as did the Puritans and others, that "the righteous" were "scarcely saved." However, he did urge those who focused on "the worthless, fading things of this world" instead of on pursuing a place in heaven to "consider three things": that earthly life was very brief; that those who had no mansion in heaven when they died would reside forever in hell because "no middle place" existed; and churchgoers who died unconverted would "have the worst place in hell."[52]

While accentuating the traits that should characterize Christians on their pilgrimage to Zion, Edwards assured believers that their "inheritance in heaven is fixed, certain, and incorruptible." This conviction, he argued, should moderate Christians' mourning when their loved ones died. Rather, Christians should rejoice when those who spent their lives journeying toward heaven reached the destination they so intensely desired and fervently sought.[53]

Although Edwards spoke eloquently and passionately about the pleasures and privileges of heaven, he also painted one of the world's most horrific portraits of hell in his "Sinners in the Hands of an Angry God." God held those who refused to repent "over the Pit of Hell." They "deserved the fiery Pit" and were "already sentenced to it" because "justice demands that sinners be punished."[54] Despite such statements, Stephen Holmes pointed out, compared with his Puritan predecessors, Edwards was reluctant to provide "graphic descriptions of hell." While using language that alarmed and shocked his listeners, he usually did not stress "the pains of hell itself," but their immediacy, inescapability, and perpetuity. The saints, Edwards asserted, will "take great notice of" "the misery of the damned in hell." Seeing "the wrath of God executed on ungodly men" will not cause them grief, uneasiness, or dissatisfaction; "on the contrary…it will excite them to joyful praises."[55] The saints will extol God when they see the damned, Edwards argued, because they love only the things God loves, and He abhors those in hell; they will recognize that God's punishment of sinners demonstrates His majesty, justice, and power; and they will understand the horrors from which they have been spared and therefore will appreciate God's grace and love even more. Therefore, viewing sinners' agony intensified the elect's love and "fullness of the joy." For Edwards, hell, like all other aspects of God's work in creation and redemption, was a means of increasing His glory.[56]

Although numerous ministers and evangelists proclaimed the perils of hell during the First Great Awakening, Whitefield complained that many people did not believe hell existed. The promise of eternal happiness agreed so fully with human "inclinations and wishes" "that all who call themselves Christians" willingly subscribed to it. However, the doctrine that an "eternity of misery awaits the wicked in a future state" and an "infinite disproportion [exists] between an endless duration of pain, and [a] short life spent in pleasure" is "so shocking," he asserted, that many rejected it.[57] Whitefield probably exaggerated the extent of disbelief in hell, but by the middle of the eighteenth century, it was no longer the source of terror it had been for the Puritans.

CONCLUSION

While promoting revival, revitalizing congregations, and safeguarding biblical orthodoxy, the leaders of the First Great Awakening placed significant emphasis on heaven. Edwards's vision of heaven is one of the most detailed and winsome in Christian history. In numerous sermons and sections of theological tomes, he described heaven's contours, characteristics, and spectacular blessings. In his portrait, God the Creator and Jesus the Redeemer dominate the celestial realm. Basking in their relationship with the Father and the Son and enjoying fellowship with one another, the saints praise and serve God, grow in holiness and knowledge, observe the progress of the church on earth (until the end of time), and experience indescribable happiness in a world of amazing, astonishing love. Edwards also highlighted the fantastic rewards the saints would enjoy as a result of their earthly holiness, suffering for God's kingdom, and good works. His depiction of heaven has significantly affected the way countless American Christians, especially Reformed ones, have viewed heaven.

Edwards, Whitefield, and other leaders of the First Great Awakening, like the Puritans, insisted that individuals must be born again to enter heaven. As did the Puritans, they described the difficulties on the journey to heaven and warned that those who trusted in their moral behavior or civic righteousness would not get there.

However, they did not see the obstacles on the path to paradise as quite so imposing or those who would reach the final destination as so few as did their New England predecessors. Although Arminians refuted their understanding of election, and many others thought (or hoped) that good conduct would provide a passport to paradise, the challenge to orthodox conceptions of salvation was not nearly as intense or extensive as it became during the early national and antebellum years as growing numbers of deists, free thinkers, Transcendentalists, Unitarians, and Universalists offered alternative perspectives.

Heaven consists in perfect holiness, in beholding, worshiping and admiring the glories and perfections of the Deity, in an uninterrupted enjoyment of the love of God.

—JAMES B. SMITH, ed., *The Posthumous Works of the Reverend and Pious James M'Gready, Late Minister of the Gospel, in Henderson, Kentucky*

A wonder working god, who violates his own laws, and acts inconsistently with the principles which he himself has established, is no God at all.

—KERRY S. WALTERS, *Elihu Palmer's 'Principles of Nature' Text and Commentary*

3

THE EARLY NATIONAL ERA

AND THE SECOND GREAT

AWAKENING

IN AMERICAN HISTORY, religious decline has often followed revival, and it did during the decades immediately after the First Great Awakening. Several factors contributed to the waning of revival fires. Although many saw God's providential hand in their seemingly miraculous victory over Britain, the Revolutionary War was hard on religion. Many ministers left their parishes to serve as chaplains in the Continental Army; hundreds of churches were destroyed, damaged, or diverted to other uses; and few funds were available to pay pastors, repair churches, publish religious literature, or finance evangelistic efforts. Moreover, the war divided Americans into patriots and loyalists, many of whom were preoccupied by the battle for independence, and Christian pacifist groups (Anabaptists and Quakers) that tried valiantly to remain neutral. Despite the frequent claim that there are no atheists in foxholes, war has rarely been a time of religious revival, and the Revolutionary War was no exception. Although many Americans praised God for their new constitution, George Washington's willingness to serve as the nation's first president, and the fledgling republic's success in maintaining its independence, Americans generally focused more on their new economic opportunities than spiritual matters, on earthly gain more than heavenly reward. Land was readily available, trade expanded, and transportation and communication improved as many roads, canals, and railroads were constructed. Farmers and artisans began to produce for a market economy, and a new group of businessmen invested in factories, banks, and ships. Meanwhile, increasing attacks on Christian orthodoxy, the greater "complexity of economic relationships," and the impact of population growth, migration, and the market battered the foundations of traditional community life.[1]

A lively debate rages today over the faith of America's founders. Some claim that almost all the founders were deists rather than orthodox Christians. Others counter that most of the nation's founders were devout Christians. The truth lies somewhere in between. Many of the most prominent founders—Washington, Thomas Jefferson, Benjamin Franklin, John Adams, and James Wilson—are best described as theistic rationalists, a worldview that combines facets of natural religion, Christianity, and rationalism, with rationalism being the most important element. While most deists denied that God was directly involved in the world, that Christ was divine, and that the Bible was God's infallible revelation, theistic rationalists maintained that God played an active role in human affairs, saw the Bible as divinely inspired, and considered prayer to be valuable. For them, religion's primary role was promoting morality, which they considered indispensable to the success of a republic.[2]

Other founders, however, most notably John Jay, Samuel Adams, Benjamin Rush, Elias Boudinot, John Witherspoon, Roger Sherman, Patrick Henry, and Charles Carroll were orthodox Christians. Although the founders disagreed about whether salvation depended on character, conduct, and virtue or personal trust in Christ's death on the cross to atone for sin, almost all of them believed in life after death, generally along traditional Christian lines.[3]

During the late eighteenth and early nineteenth centuries, numerous "religious salespeople" offered Americans "a variety of methods of salvation, passageways to heaven…and blueprints for constructing the New Jerusalem." Some Americans accepted the basic principles of Enlightenment deism and rejected the Christian contention that Jesus was the divine redeemer. For them, a person's disposition in the afterlife depended on his earthly conduct rather than on his acceptance of Jesus' sacrificial death on his behalf. Others espoused religious skepticism, atheism, or universalism. Revolutionary War hero Ethan Allen and deist author and publicist Elihu Palmer led the assault on Christian orthodoxy. John Murray, a chaplain during the war and a Boston pastor, and Hosea Ballou, often called the father of American Universalism, argued that all people would be saved.[4] Therefore, while orthodox Christians living in the revolutionary and early national periods sounded many of the same themes about heaven as their predecessors, they had to defend the conventional view in the face of much greater skepticism and unbelief, deist attacks, and the outright denial of immortality. Moreover, they had to uphold the orthodox view of salvation against claims that upright conduct and good works were the passport to paradise and the doctrine that everyone eventually went to heaven regardless of their behavior.

As the nineteenth century began, revival erupted on both the Western frontier and in the East. Led by James McGready, Timothy Dwight, Lyman Beecher, Asahel Nettleton, and Charles Finney, the Second Great Awakening (1800–1840) lasted longer than the First and had a much greater impact on American society than its predecessor. Although its proponents failed to abolish slavery or stop the removal of Native Americans from their ancestral lands, their efforts stamped Christian values deeply onto American life in the middle decades of the nineteenth century. They created a Benevolent Empire consisting of two dozen voluntary organizations that planted churches, opened colleges, established Sunday schools, published Christian books and evangelistic tracts, and alleviated numerous ills in American society.[5] In their books, articles, and sermons designed to convert sinners and strengthen the faith of believers, prominent revivalists and ordinary pastors painted vivid pictures of heavenly life, especially stressing the saints' relationship with God, celestial worship, and progress in knowledge, love, and power. Much more than did subsequent generations, they warned their readers and listeners of the suffering that awaited them in hell if they refused to repent of their sins and accept Jesus as their savior.

A THEOCENTRIC HEAVEN

The leaders of the Second Great Awakening described heaven in substantial detail. Like their Puritan and First Great Awakening predecessors, they depicted a theocentric heaven characterized by worshipping and communing with God. They accentuated the importance heaven had for everyday life and the saints' perpetual development and celestial rewards. By comparison, they focused much less on heavenly recognition and fellowship.

Numerous pastors and evangelists agreed with James McGready, a Presbyterian minister who played a pivotal role in the camp meeting revivals in Logan County, Kentucky, in 1800, that the "glory and blessedness" of the saints "is unspeakable, incomprehensible, and indescribable."[6] If Enoch, the apostle John, or Paul came to earth, McGready reasoned, they would declare that language could not "express the ten thousandth part of the boundless glories...of the heavenly state." All Christians could say was that heaven involved an "exceeding and eternal weight of glory" that people had neither seen nor conceived. Paul's declaration that "God is able to do exceeding abundantly above all we are able to ask or even to think" will be strikingly fulfilled in heaven, declared Charles Finney, a theologian, president of Oberlin College, social reformer, and the nation's most influential evangelist during the antebellum years. Presbyterian John Witherspoon agreed. Witherspoon served as the president of the College of New Jersey (later Princeton) from 1768 to 1794 and taught theology to an incredibly distinguished group of graduates that included 114 pastors, 33 U.S. congressmen, 20 U.S. senators, 13 state governors, 3 U.S. Supreme Court justices, 1 vice president, and 1 president. The richest, most gorgeous attire, "the most sumptuous and delicate fare" the world offered, he argued, paled compared with the "rivers of pleasures...at God's right hand."[7]

Despite such disclaimers, many did attempt to describe the wonders of paradise, especially the saints' relationship with the Trinity. Heaven consists of "perfect holiness," McGready declared, "in beholding, worshiping and admiring the glories and perfections" of the Father, Son, and Holy Spirit, as the redeemed enjoyed the marvelous love of and an uninterrupted communion with the triune God. The mere taste of God's love, McGready maintained, made "the dying bed a couch of...holy delight" and brought bliss to the martyr "blazing at the stake" or "being torn in pieces upon the rack." Like his Puritan forebears, Ezra Stiles, a Congregationalist minister, theologian, and author, who served as president of Yale from 1778 to 1795, asserted that the saints would behold God intuitively, be assimilated into Him, experience "his love and protection," understand "the grand plan of the universe," and perpetually grow in moral perfection. Going well beyond the Puritans (and sounding like later Mormons), Stiles effused that "bathed in the beatific vision of the Deity, the soul blossoms in God;...it is transfused with the divinity itself." The saints would lose their self identity and "be swallowed up" in God's ineffable glory.[8]

As the finished product of "divine workmanship," heaven, declared Timothy Dwight, a Congregationalist pastor and president of Yale from 1795 to 1817, displayed "the beauty and greatness of the Infinite Mind" in its "most exquisite forms." God's goal, he proclaimed, is to adorn "this world of glory...with unrivalled beauty," stock it with His "richest blessings," fill it with the "proper inhabitants," and "reign over it." Heaven's incomparable joy and wonderful pleasures would inspire the saints to admire, love, and praise God. The glorious character of the "forgiving, redeeming, and sanctifying God," "his wonderful works of creation," and His astonishing providence would enrapture the saints. The splendor of His residence, "the saints' reverence for his perfections," "their devotion to his service," their rewards, and the amazing nature of His government all displayed God's awesomeness. Edward Payson, who served a Congregationalist Church in Portland, Maine, claimed that contemplating God's "goodness, holiness, justice, mercy...and sovereignty," His "infinite power, unerring wisdom, [and] omnipresence," and all His "natural and moral perfections" would completely satisfy the saints. The redeemed would be encircled by God's everlasting power, faithfulness, and love and assured that nothing could separate them from His love. The saints will love God perfectly "with all their heart, and soul, and mind, and strength," Payson proclaimed. "Their whole desire" will be "to glorify and exalt him." Echoing Jonathan Edwards, he exulted that the saints would "be entirely...swallowed up in God"; "completely absorbed in the contemplation of his ineffable, infinite...glories," they will be totally unconscious of time. Innumerable ages may pass before they even "think of asking how long they have been in heaven." The saints, Witherspoon insisted, will never be able to exhaust the fullness and richness of God's nature. God's glory is so astounding, argued James Dana, a Connecticut Congregationalist pastor, that it may need to be gradually revealed in heaven in order not to overwhelm newcomers.[9]

Revivalists and ministers also emphasized the saints' communion with Christ. Being with Christ and beholding his glory, McGready asserted, is the centerpiece of heaven. "Clothed in the righteousness of Jesus," he explained, "we shall walk...the golden streets of the New Jerusalem." The saints will sit enthralled at the feet of Jesus, declared Levi Hart, a pastor in Preston, Connecticut, listening to His words and savoring His love. Heavenly inhabitants, avowed Payson, will "explore the heights and depths" of the Redeemer's love, continually "see new wonders, glories and beauties," and respond with songs of praise.[10]

Numerous depictions of heaven during the Second Great Awakening emphasized the saints' close relationship with members of the Trinity. Payson, for example, pictured God sitting on His throne and Jesus, "the friend, the brother, the Redeemer," residing at His right hand. Surrounding them was an innumerable throng of saints and angels who were enveloped in a "boundless flood of light and glory" and praised the Trinity with one voice. "Their superior brightness" distinguished the patriarchs, prophets, apostles, and martyrs from other members of this heavenly host. Because they know God intimately and immediately, Payson concluded, the saints no longer needed any means of grace, the Sabbath, symbols of Christ's crucified body, or human teachers. Nor do they need the Bible because they have arrived at the destination to which it points and "intuitively understand all its doctrines."[11]

John Witherspoon insisted that the saints would engage in acts of adoration, gratitude, trust, and submission. In heaven, as on earth, the "first duty and chief end of man" would be to give God the glory He deserved. Therefore, saints would contemplate "the glorious excellence of the divine nature," and their adoration of God would be perfect and blissful. Their trust in God and surrender to Him would be "infinitely more complete" and pleasurable in heaven than it was on earth. They would quickly and joyfully accept God's will and "consecrate themselves to his service." The entire plan of God's providence, which people discerned only "a small detached part" of on earth, would "be opened to their view."[12]

Pastors and evangelists described many other features of heaven. Unlike earth, Edward Payson declared, celestial life had "no buying and selling, no planting or building, no places devoted to business or amusement." Moreover, the saints no longer had "bodies to provide for, families to care for," or social duties to perform. The redeemed, he rejoiced, would lose all their earthly imperfections and devote themselves to thought, reflection, and meditation. Heaven's inhabitants, Witherspoon declared, would enjoy perfect happiness, which was unattainable on earth with its many evils and its afflictions, which were necessary "to purge away the dross of sin." The saints would be "forever freed from the dangerous and deadly consequences of sin," separated from the wicked, and released "from the rage, malice and subtle temptations" of the Devil, McGready maintained. Completely unified in their affections and pursuits, heaven's residents, Hart heralded, would love, serve, and enjoy God and zealously promote His kingdom. Ebenezer Pemberton, a Presbyterian who pastored congregations in New York and Boston, stressed that peace, order, and harmony would prevail in paradise. If people could experience such exquisite gratification on earth despite their fallen nature, Witherspoon argued, they will have even more ravishing delights in heaven when their senses "are refined and purified" and liberated from their current insatiable cravings. Heaven's residents, Dwight maintained, will experience no sorrow, pain, confusion, "ungratified desire, disappointment, discontent, reproaches of conscience," or fear of God's wrath. No more will people's "strength be wasted by weariness, their health impaired by languor and pain, or their comfort and peace destroyed by enemies and dangers." Moreover, the saints will suffer no more pain because of family friction, friends who are alienated from God, or the devastation of the world. They will no longer have to battle lust, "struggle with temptations," or "endure the stings of scorn" or malice "or the iron hand of oppression."[13] The saints will have no "private, separate interests," Dwight insisted; everyone will share the same views and promote the common good. Witherspoon argued that the saints would realize the extent of their guilt, the price Christ paid for their redemption, the horrors of hell they had escaped, and the glory they possessed. Their sense of "unworthiness as sinners" would make God's "unmerited grace and mercy" much more valuable and enliven the saints' worship. The redeemed, Dwight added, would continually rejoice that Christ secured their admittance to heaven by His "great sacrifice" on the cross.[14]

While near-death experiences did not attract widespread popular attention until the 1970s, during the antebellum years several revivalists and pastors discussed these experiences and visions of heaven or hell they or others had to help confirm biblical portraits. Both Lyman Beecher and Edward Payson claimed to view heaven on their deathbeds. Beecher had "a glorious vision of heaven," which included seeing "the King of Glory himself." Shortly before his death, Payson awoke from a dream, exclaiming, "I am going...to the heavenly Jerusalem, to an innumerable company of angels, to the...church of the first born, and to God the Judge of all." Soon thereafter he wrote to his sister that "the celestial city" was fully in view. "Its glories beam upon me, its breezes fan me, its odors are wafted to me, its sounds strike upon my ears, and its spirit is breathed into my heart."[15]

Charles Finney insisted that there was no good reason to doubt these experiences. The Bible taught that angels conveyed Christians to heaven, so it was reasonable to assume that the redeemed actually saw what they professed to see in their dying hours. Throughout history many dying believers had claimed to hear music from heaven and to see angels surrounding them. Physician David Nelson reported that he had heard many sinners describe "awful shapes and hear dreadful sounds" on their deathbeds and beg that horrific creatures be removed. Finney also discussed the alleged near-death experience of William Tennent, a leader in the First Great Awakening. While apparently dead, Tennent went to heaven, where, like the apostle Paul, he saw "unspeakable things."[16]

HEAVENLY RECOGNITION, FELLOWSHIP, FOCUS, PROGRESS, AND REWARDS

Neither heavenly recognition nor fellowship of the saints was a major theme during the years from 1770 to 1840, especially among leaders of the Second Great Awakening. Christians during this period placed more emphasis on contemplating the joys of heaven, progress in paradise, and celestial rewards. A few did accentuate the marvelous communion heaven's inhabitants would experience. God created people to enjoy relationships, John Witherspoon explained, and corporate worship especially pleased Him. Fellowship among "the innumerable company of the redeemed above" gathered from around the globe would be much richer than that on earth. Christians could spend time with Enoch, Elijah, Isaiah, other prophets, the apostles, martyrs, church fathers, and the Reformers, Ezra Stiles promised, while also communing with departed friends, relatives, and acquaintances. Ministers and laypeople who had "walked together for years in harmony, love and sweet fellowship" on earth, he added, would have even more delightful fellowship in heaven. Both Asahel Nettleton, a pastor, theologian, and evangelist who led thousands to Christ during the Second Great Awakening, and Timothy Dwight insisted that friendships will be stronger in heaven. The saints' moral purity and perfect love, Nettleton maintained, would enable them to develop deeper relationships. Dwight described heavenly camaraderie as devoted, total, and unending. The redeemed will be reunited with companions who understand their worth, possess the same character, delight in the same activities, and pursue the same ends. Everyone will love his neighbor as himself, he added, fulfilling Christ's second great commandment. Spouses will not be married in heaven, but their partnership will be even richer.[17]

Although Christianity was largely confined to Europe and the Americas in the years before 1840 and the modern missions movement was in its infancy, several influential Christians, like their First Awakening peers, pictured heaven as populated by a multiracial, geographically diverse throng. Its residents would consist of people who spoke every language and belonged to every ethnic group and nation on the earth, McGready asserted. God will gather His elect from all parts of the world, Witherspoon asserted, to create a "great and general assembly of the church of the first born." All other distinctions and designations will be abolished, and the saints will commune as "one pure and unmixed society" who all share a new name—the redeemed. Heaven "had three gates on every side," declared Edward Payson, to show that the way is open "from all parts of the world." Its inhabitants will come from the East, the West, the North, and the South.[18]

During the late eighteenth and early nineteenth centuries, numerous pastors and evangelists urged Christians to focus on heaven. Witherspoon exhorted Christians to recognize that they were pilgrims and strangers on earth, renounce the world, reflect upon the wonders of heaven, and prepare to receive their eternal inheritance. This could best be done by worshipping regularly and passionately because worship would be central to heavenly life and the happiness of its residents. He complained that many seemed too busy or proud to worship while the worship of others was "cold and formal"—they performed the rituals of worship but did not understand their underlying meaning and power. Levi Hart counseled believers to moderate their grief when Christian friends and relatives died because they would someday enjoy a heavenly reunion.[19] A lively hope of heaven, Witherspoon avowed, could help Christians cope with worldly anxieties, sickness, and the "reproach of the ungodly." As had the apostles, Dwight asserted, ministers should accentuate the prospects, joys, and glories of heaven. He encouraged Christians to meditate on heaven's sublime, alluring, and delightful features; by participating in the earthly church, they had already figuratively entered the New Jerusalem. McGready contended that as Christians "wrestle[d] with principalities and powers," dealt with taxing trials, and fought their "way to heaven inch by inch," God was shaping and polishing them to be stones in "the heavenly building." Payson exhorted Christians to add gems to the crowns they would cast before Christ in heaven by praying more often and fervently, doing greater good works, and growing "in grace and knowledge." Anticipating their jobs in heaven would help Christians to someday perform them, give them a more godly spirit, and enable them to triumph over the flesh, the Devil, and the world. By breaking "the charm of the world," overcoming the power of sin, and giving people a deeper desire to know God, revivals, Finney claimed, provided a "foretaste of heaven." Dana exhorted believers to seek the better country, concentrate on Christ's promises, and finish their course. By reviewing their lives in light of the splendor and perfection of God and heaven, Payson argued, people could best determine the number, magnitude, and heinousness of their sins. They should ask themselves how "impious, profane...language" sounded in heaven and how not keeping the Sabbath holy was viewed there.[20]

As their new nation advanced in size, productivity, trade, and technology, many Christians accentuated the progress the saints would make in knowledge, wisdom, love, and power and their important roles in heaven. Paralleling their society's increasing emphasis on personal autonomy, on familial bonds "as essentially voluntary, private," and promoting personal growth, and on the individual as "the conceptual building block of society," many revivalists and pastors asserted that the saints would experience endless advancement.[21] Eulogizing one of his parishioners, Lyman Beecher, a Congregationalist revivalist, pastor, and seminary president, declared that "in heaven his knowledge is growing, his mind is expanding, and his holiness and joy will increase forever." Ezra Stiles and Timothy Dwight, successive presidents of Yale, maintained, as Dwight put it, that the saints continually attained "higher perfection" in "knowledge, power, and love" as they better understood the works of God. On earth, Christians were like children "standing on the bank of a mighty river" who could not see its source or destination and therefore did not comprehend its beauty, usefulness, or progress. In heaven, by contrast, Christ would explain all God's plans and accomplishments and unravel all mysteries. The saints would understand God's providential direction of the church, the purpose of their own difficulties and temptations, and the earthly displays of God's mercy. Heaven's residents, James Dana proclaimed, constantly came "nearer to the fountain of intellectual light, and life, and joy." McGready asserted that the saints' capacities would expand forever and their understanding of God's goodness, justice, and mercy would continuously increase. Heavenly inhabitants, he claimed, would comprehend "how all things worked together for their good—how all their losses, afflictions, woes and sorrows" served to accomplish divine purposes. The saints' knowledge would multiply so dramatically, Finney predicted, that they would eventually know exponentially more than everyone in the world did collectively.[22] Although the worship of God was paramount in heaven, Dwight maintained, the Bible taught that the saints will also be assigned jobs based on their talents to accomplish the purposes of heaven. God used people's "faculties, attributes, and employments" to make the heavenly system work effectively. Everyone will conclude that their roles are perfectly suited to them, and no one will be jealous of the offices and tasks allotted to others.[23]

Ezra Stiles devoted great attention to the subject of heavenly rewards. In his funeral sermons, he stressed that the Bible used both metaphors such as "eating of the tree of life," resting in Abraham's bosom, serving as "pillars in the temple of God," and "shining as stars in the kingdom of the Father" as well as literal descriptions such as the crown of life and the crown of glory that would never fade. The saints would be assigned "greater, higher, and more glorious" tasks than they had on earth. They would also be made princes and priests and exalted above the archangels. The Redeemer promised, Stiles added, that those who had "been faithful over a few things" would be placed in charge of many things. Ruling with Jesus over the universe was a phenomenal honor "for worms of the dust." Every good work individuals did on earth, Stiles insisted, would increase their heavenly reward. Every soul they helped save would enhance their eternal happiness and enable them to shine with "a more distinguished luster through eternal ages."[24]

As commercial life increasingly provided metaphors for moral experience and models for life such as investments, returns, and profits, both James Dana and Edward Payson urged Christians to pursue heavenly rewards. Dana argued that people's celestial recompenses differed greatly depending on their God-given talents, opportunities, and faithfulness. As a result of their different attainments, the saints would receive different mansions; moreover, they would have "various kinds and degrees of glory" based on their earthly "knowledge, purity and love." However, he concluded, everyone would "be fully satisfied" with their own mansions and "rejoice in those prepared for others." The bliss of all heavenly inhabitants would be complete, regardless of their temperament or character. The more Christians "do for God in this world," Payson proclaimed, "the brighter will" their "celestial crown be." Since the saints will cast their crowns at the Redeemer's feet, they should want them to shine as brightly as possible. "Can you be content," he asked, if your crown is "the least glorious" one laid before Christ? "Every good work," "acceptable prayer," and "sincere attempt to grow in grace and knowledge," he promised, will add more gems to it.[25]

SALVATION: GOD'S GIFT OR A HUMAN ACHIEVEMENT?

Like the Puritans and the leaders of the First Great Awakening, the principal promoters of the Second Great Awakening argued that to be fit for heaven, individuals must be regenerated by the power of the Holy Spirit and born again. However, only a few of them, most notably Timothy Dwight and Asahel Nettleton, defended the Calvinist view of salvation espoused by the Puritans, Edwards, Whitefield, and the Tennents, which emphasized God's election of individuals and the role of His irresistible grace in redemption. Many other key figures in the Second Great Awakening, led by Charles Finney, instead adopted an Arminian perspective that placed much greater stress on man's role in responding to God's offer of salvation. Meanwhile, significant number of skeptics, deists, theistic rationalists, Unitarians, and Universalists contended either that salvation depended on individual's character and virtue—rather than on their trust in Christ's substitutionary atonement (that Christ satisfied God's wrath against sinners by dying on the cross for them)—or that everyone would ultimately be saved.[26] Therefore, proponents of the Second Great Awakening had to deal with much stronger challenges to the orthodox understanding of salvation than their predecessors had.[27] Belief that salvation was a reward for virtuous behavior received strong support from the emphasis both the new commercial society and the public schools placed on individual character and conduct.[28]

Deists, Unitarians, and Universalists all maintained that Jesus was not God, but was "more than a man." "He existed before the world" was created and "came from heaven to save our race." Jesus was "a teacher and witness to the truth" who continues to act "for our benefit" and "is our intercessor with the Father." Speaking for most Universalists, Hosea Ballou asserted that although Christ was a man, he was God's representative. Much more than a moral example, he was "Lord" and the "Captain of our salvation" who displayed God's love. Ethan Allen repudiated the doctrines of the incarnation and the virgin birth as archaic, but like Jefferson, he admired Jesus as a wise moral philosopher. Elihu Palmer, by contrast, chastised deists for believing that Jesus had a commendable character; the facts of the New Testament undermined this assessment.[29]

Rejecting the concept of Christ's substitutionary atonement, deists, theistic rationalists, and Unitarians generally contended that people best served God by loving and helping others and deserved heaven principally because of their exemplary ethical behavior. For them, dogmas and creeds were unimportant and sometimes detrimental. Unitarians' leading spokesperson, William Ellery Channing, denounced the doctrine that Jesus purchased people's "forgiveness and future happiness" by His death on the cross and instead stressed Christ's character and mission as an example, teacher, and messenger of God. Self-inspection, piety, moral conduct, and fulfilling one's duties were central to Christianity. The pastor of Boston's Federal Street Church sought to help individuals develop their spiritual potential, engage in "upright and useful action," and exhibit "modest, unassuming" goodness. Christians should surrender their wills to God, abandon their worldly interests, fulfill their obligations, and make sacrifices for others.[30]

Deists Palmer and Allen also rejected the traditional Christian conception of salvation. Both of them exalted reason and repudiated the central features of Christianity: the veracity and value of the Bible, miracles, the traditional doctrines of God, sin, and salvation, and the biblical system of morality. While many others shared their views, few were willing to publicly and directly denounce the core dogmas of Christianity. Most deists and skeptics during the revolutionary and early national periods had a background much more similar to Palmer than Allen: they "were either cosmopolitan, elite intellectuals or freethinking artisans in major seaports, not frontier farmers." Building on French and British Enlightenment philosophers, most notably Rousseau, Voltaire, Hume, and Bolingbroke, Palmer and Allen argued that reason is superior to revelation in understanding God and the nature of the universe. They deprecated the clergy and creeds as superstitious, antiquated, faulty sources of knowledge and instead stressed the importance of independent thinking and experience in determining truth and personal convictions.[31] Christian theology, Palmer protested, in his *Principles of Nature* (1802), offered a defective perspective of the universe, insulted the Creator, and either distorted or contradicted "scientific deductions." The Bible's "extravagant accounts" contradicted the testimony of people's senses and "the instructive guide" of human experience. Tenets that accorded with reason, experience, and conscience, Allen asserted in *Reason the Only Oracle of Man* (1784), were God's true revelation.[32]

Palmer denounced the dogma that Jesus died to atone for human sins and that moral virtue had "no saving efficacy" as "perverted" and "destructive." The Christian doctrine of salvation, he added, ruined man's "confidence in his own energies," debased his faculties, vitiated his social affections, and crippled his "most useful qualities." Palmer denounced life after death as another folly of Christianity, which did not "serve the cause of virtue, or lead to the practice of genuine morality." Allen repudiated the idea that people "are born into the world in a state of enmity to God and moral good" and "are under his wrath and curse." The clergy's claim that individuals must be born again and possess a special kind of faith to enter heaven, he alleged, gave them great power. Because the exact nature of the afterlife could not be verified on earth, pastors and priests had been able to control perceptions of heaven and coerce people into accepting their schemes of salvation. Allen called on Americans to "break the fetters" with which the clergy had bound them, exalt reason, and recognize that God dealt with individuals on the basis of their behavior, not their beliefs. Allen agreed with Universalists that in a rational universe ruled by a benevolent deity, everyone would attain heaven. If God denied salvation to those who had no knowledge of the Bible because of the times or places in which they lived, he protested, He was guilty of malicious favoritism.[33]

Allen expected the clergy to wage war on him "in the name of the Lord," and they did. They denounced him as "an awful Infidel" and "a profane and ignorant Deist."[34] Timothy Dwight led the assault, preaching 200 sermons condemning natural religion and deism, and each year delivering a series of them to students at Yale.[35] Dwight castigated Allen for repeating "every rotten, worn-out dogma of the English deistical writers." By attacking "truth, virtue, providence, and the Creator," Allen displayed the "deformity, the venom, and the ill nature of the toad." Dwight deprecated *Reason the Only Oracle of Man* as flimsy and unconvincing, but he provided no specific criticisms of Allen's magnum opus. Most other reviewers of Allen's book also ignored its arguments, "moving directly to insults."[36]

Some of the nation's most prominent founders as well as less known pastors agreed with Unitarian, Universalist, and deist spokespersons that entrance to heaven was determined by works, not faith. For Jefferson, Washington, Franklin, and Adams, virtuous behavior, not correct belief, was the key to spending eternity with God. Jefferson, who affirmed much of biblical morality but could not accept several pivotal Christian doctrines, put it bluntly: if he were to found a new denomination, its fundamental principle would be "that we are saved by our good works which are within our power, and not by our faith which is not within our power." Those who consistently lived by "the moral precepts" all religions taught, Jefferson wrote in 1813, "will never be questioned, at the gates of heaven, as to the dogmas in which they differ." Heaven, he declared, contained no Quakers, Baptists, Presbyterians, Episcopalians, or Catholics. On entering paradise, people left "those badges of schism behind" and were united by their commitment to essential moral truths. Washington did not express his views of salvation as forthrightly as Jefferson, but he concurred that behavior, more than belief, made individuals acceptable to God. No person, "who is profligate in his morals," Washington maintained, "can possibly be a true Christian." Although Franklin substantially qualified his position in private, publicly he trumpeted the message that living virtuously was the way to heaven. "The Soul of Man is immortal," Franklin declared, "and will be treated with Justice in another Life respecting its Conduct in this." Adams argued similarly that "virtue will be rewarded and vice punished in a future state."[37]

Other founders and early presidents, by contrast, asserted that people were admitted to heaven because of their trust in Jesus as their savior, rather than their character and conduct. Elias Boudinot, a lawyer, statesman, and dedicated Presbyterian layman, declared that people must repent and believe the gospel; salvation could be attained only through Christ. "Whoever believed on him" would be saved, while all who refused to believe would be damned. "My faith, my trust, my hope of salvation," wrote John Jay, an Episcopalian who served as president of the Continent Congress, the nation's first chief justice of the Supreme Court, the governor of New York, and the president of American Bible Society, is in Christ, "and in him only." "My only hope of salvation is in the infinite, transcendent love of God manifested to the world by the death of His Son upon the cross," proclaimed Philadelphia physician Benjamin Rush. Upon the Bible, testified Andrew Jackson, "I rest my hope for eternal salvation, through the merits and blood of our blessed Lord and Saviour, Jesus Christ."[38]

Although they disagreed about the role individuals played in their own salvation, the leaders of the Second Great Awakening echoed the conviction of these statesmen and their Puritan and evangelical predecessors that salvation was God's gift, not man's achievement. While they concurred with religious liberals that character and conduct were important, they saw them as the fruit, not the basis, of salvation. Speaking for them, Timothy Dwight declared, "Christ alone is" the "hope for forgiveness, acceptance, and eternal life"; "salvation is a reward not of works, but of the grace of God." Only those who trusted in Christ's righteousness would be accepted into heaven, he asserted, but sadly many instead were relying on their own righteousness: their faithful attendance of religious services, fulfilling of their moral duties, religious character, and knowledge of scripture. All the revivalists stressed that individuals must be born again to gain admittance to heaven. In Asahel Nettleton's words, repentance and redemption was "the only gate" by which people could enter heaven. Those who strove to attain heaven by living morally, Nettleton contended, would be denied entrance not "because they did not do more, but because they trusted in what they did." Very few people are saved in old age, Dwight averred, so the longer the impenitent lived, the more sin they committed and the greater their condemnation and misery would be throughout eternity.[39]

No one could be saved, John Witherspoon and James McGready argued, without experiencing the new birth, which Christ strongly stressed. In the new birth, McGready explained, God transformed people's hearts, implanted "a new principle of spiritual life" in their souls, and gave them a "heavenly inheritance." Their wills, memories, consciences, and affections became "subservient to the designs of God," and they received new eyes, tongues, minds, and hearts. The world's statesmen and philosophers, he lamented, had no desire to be "made new creatures in Christ Jesus." No matter how upright people's "conduct and conversation" were, if they were not "born from on high," "the wrath of God like a mighty deluge" would sweep them into "the lowest hell." All the "prayers, tears, resolutions, vows and good works" of the unsaved, McGready alleged, "were so abominable in the sight of God, that it would be just for him to send" them to hell. It was as impossible for the unregenerate "to satisfy divine justice" and receive God's favor as it was for them to stop the course of the sun. Regeneration, McGready avowed, "is absolutely necessary" to make individuals "pleasing in the sight of God." Those who were not born again were totally "unfit for heaven" because God demanded that people be clothed in Christ's righteousness. "The flaming sword of divine vengeance" guarded the gate of paradise and prohibited "unholy sinners" from entering. A dead carcass "in the last stage of putrefaction" was not nearly as "abominable" to human sensibilities, he declared, as is "the unregenerate soul, in the sight of a God of immaculate purity."[40]

"If you are not washed in the blood, and sanctified by the Spirit of Christ," Edward Payson announced, "heaven will never open to you its gates." Those who relied upon their upright conduct or pretended "to trust in the righteousness of Christ, without imitating his example and obeying his commands," Payson proclaimed, remained in their sins. And people had no chance to repent after they died. Anyone pronounced a sinner "at the judgment day," he asserted, would be "treated as a sinner forever." Payson urged sinners to tell God "that you do not deserve his assistance; that you are justly condemned already, and merit nothing but eternal condemnation." Those who accepted Christ's "obedience, suffering and death" as paying for their iniquity would "be saved from the guilt and power of sin," adopted into God's family, and receive through Christ everything "necessary to prepare and qualify them" to enjoy their "heavenly inheritance." When people arrived in heaven, Payson asserted, they would proclaim, "My salvation was wholly of the Lord. Jesus is the author, the finisher, and rewarder of my faith."[41]

While asserting that redemption was ultimately God's work, Finney assigned individuals a major role in the process of salvation. He argued that the Bible ascribed conversion to four agents: the Holy Spirit, the truth, the preacher, and the sinner himself. Although the Spirit converted "sinners by the power of persuasion," the unredeemed must not "wait for some mysterious influence, like an electric shock, to change their hearts." In response to God's prompting, they must change their hearts themselves, as the Bible commanded. Finney chastised those who, trying to magnify God's glory and grace, considered the sinner "a helpless, unfortunate creature" who could not "do what God requires of him"—repent and gain a new heart. Instead, the sinner was "a guilty, voluntary rebel" who had both the ability to alter his heart and many reasons to do so. Therefore, rather than "waiting and praying for God to change" their hearts, sinners "should at once summon" their powers and shift "the governing preference" of their minds. Doing so involved confessing one's sins, accepting "Christ really and fully" as one's savior, denying oneself totally, ceasing all immoral practices, and preferring God's glory to one's own happiness. Finney repeatedly asserted that this position neither diminished God's majesty nor contradicted scripture's declaration that a new heart was "the gift and work of God" because the Holy Spirit helped transform people's hearts.[42]

Finney exhorted the unsaved not to delay repentance because they thought that the time would be more favorable later. Many who had assumed this, he warned, were presently suffering in hell. He urged sinners not to wait for deeper belief, stronger feelings, or God to change their hearts for them. While taking these steps, the unredeemed must rely totally on Christ's atonement for their salvation and "forever relinquish the idea" that they had "done any good" that would commend them to God.[43] To motivate the unredeemed to repent immediately, Finney related a story Jonathan Edwards had told. An intemperate neighbor of Edwards "dreamed that he died and went to hell." He was granted permission to return to earth for a year, but if he did not reform, he would go back to hell. Edwards told his neighbor that the dream was a solemn warning from God to forsake his sins. For a while, the man stopped drinking and attended church, but well before the year ended, he resumed his old pattern. Intoxicated one night, he fell headlong down a stairway, broke his neck, and died. Consulting his journal, Edwards discovered that this happened exactly one year after the man had his dream. Unless people accepted Christ as their savior and stopped sinning, Finney warned, a similar fate might befall them.[44]

Finney was one of the nineteenth century's most influential leaders and its most important evangelist. He made the Methodist "anxious bench"—requiring those who wanted to be converted to come to the front of the meeting place at the end of the service—a staple of subsequent American revivalism.[45] Many Second Great Awakening evangelists, especially Congregationalists and New School Presbyterians, accepted Finney's "new measures," including "protracted meetings"—nightly services for several weeks in one locale—because they produced so many converts. Lyman Beecher and some others rejected these techniques, arguing that they inhibited rather than aided efforts to save the lost. Numerous Reformed Christians, most notably Asahel Nettleton and German Reformed minister John W. Nevin, denounced these measures as theologically erroneous and offensive to God.[46] In *The Anxious Bench* (1844), Nevin, while endorsing revivals, protested that urging people to come forward at the end of a service to publicly accept Christ overemphasized human action in salvation and promoted false conversions based on emotion rather than reason and will. William McLoughlin explains the core controversy: "While Calvinists contended that conversion was two-thirds passive (people repent but God gives them faith to believe and regenerates them)," Arminians such as Finney "saw conversion as two-thirds active—people repent and have faith, and then God regenerates them."[47]

While they disagreed about the process of salvation, proponents of the Second Great Awakening joined forces to combat the growing advocacy and acceptance of universalism. Although Universalists' argument that everyone would be saved "exposed and challenged the Protestant drift" away from the traditional Calvinist position of salvation, revivalists understandably spent more energy attacking the Universalist doctrine than battling each other over the relative importance of God's sovereignty and human action in redemption.[48] *The Mystery Hid from Ages, or the Salvation of All Men* (1784) by Charles Chauncy, the pastor of the First (Congregationalist) Church in Boston for 60 years, generated a debate that produced more than 75 books and articles in the late eighteenth and early nineteenth centuries.[49] In the ensuing years, John Murray, Elhanan Winchester, and other Universalists established thriving congregations and traveled widely to promote their theology. The creation of a Universalist denomination in 1834 (which by the 1840s included more than 300 ministers and about 700 congregations) and Universalists' aggressive evangelistic efforts on the frontier (Methodist revivalist Peter Cartwright complained that everywhere he went, Universalists had already spread their heretic views) evoked hundreds of books, pamphlets, and sermons by evangelicals.[50]

Leading Universalist Hosea Ballou served thirty-five years as the pastor of the Second Universalist Society in Boston. He founded the *Universalist Magazine* in 1819 and often moderated the annual Universalist General Convention. Strongly influenced by Allen and Chauncy, Ballou published *A Treatise on the Atonement* (1805), in which he asserted that as a result of Christ's redeeming love, God would reconcile all people to Himself regardless of what they believed or did on earth. Christ died on the cross not to satisfy God's wrath but to win individuals to Himself by displaying His love for them. In *An Examination of the Doctrine of Future Retribution* (1834), Ballou argued that God would not punish anyone in the after-life.[51] The central premise of Universalism—that all would be saved—coincided both with popular understandings of compassion and sympathy and the antebellum American commitment to broad political participation and social equality, contrib-uting to its growing acceptance in the first half of the nineteenth century. Deeply influenced by Jeffersonian democracy, Universalists rejected both the Calvinist con-cept of an elect and the notion of an American aristocracy. Reason dictated that a benevolent God would save everyone; the idea that God would choose to redeem only some was both antiegalitarian and offensive. Universalists contended that few ministers taught the concept of election and that most Americans viewed hell as "a prison for a few incorrigibles" and rejected infant damnation as "a relic of a crueler age."[52]

Finney debated Universalists on several occasions, and Dwight and Nettleton censured Universalist tenets in their preaching and prose. Dwight protested that many embraced universalism because it enabled them to feel safe "while continuing in a state of impenitence and unbelief." Some Universalists, he charged, soon became atheists, while others became deists who denied God's word and true character. Still others rejected the need for Christ's atonement and regeneration, concluding that they had nothing for which to be forgiven. They reasoned that they were acceptable to God because of their abundant good works, upright behavior, and zealous performance of religious duties. The scripture, Dwight warned, contained no hint that God loved sinners; instead it sounded "terrible alarms" to awaken "every impen-itent transgressor."[53]

Nettleton rebutted the Universalist argument that because people received all the punishment they deserved in this life, everyone would go to heaven after they died by pointing to the judgment scene of Matthew 25, where the sheep and goats were separated, and to God's destruction of the wicked in Noah's day and of those living in Sodom. He also accused Universalists of using the Greek word for "everlasting" inconsistently. When applying the word to the future state of the righteous, they interpreted it to mean an endless duration; but when they applied it to the future punishment of the wicked, they argued that it referred to a limited period.[54]

In a sermon in Rutland, Vermont, in 1805, Lemuel Haynes, an African-American Calvinist, rebutted Ballou's position. Universal salvation was not a "new fangled scheme"; it had been proclaimed throughout history beginning with the devil who strove to convince Adam and Eve that they would not die if they disobeyed God. If future punishment did not exist or was only temporary, he reasoned, Satan would not work so diligently to try to convince people there was no hell.[55]

Universalists were divided over whether some people would be temporarily punished after death. Some of them insisted that Christ's atonement covered all human sin and that people's sense of duty was sufficient to ensure that they usually followed the moral law. Therefore, after death, everyone would go directly to heaven. Other Universalists countered that many individuals needed to be purified to make them fit to spend eternity with God. Moreover, they agreed with orthodox Christians and Unitarians that the threat of punishment was necessary to motivate many people to obey God's commandments consistently.[56] Despite this disagreement, Universalists echoed the increasing emphasis early nineteenth-century Americans placed on individual freedom and personal responsibility as they strove to construct their "republic of virtue" and build a commercial empire.[57] Usually ignoring the difference between these two groups, evangelicals protested that Universalism promoted social chaos by removing all sanctions against sin. Dwight, for example, claimed that Universalism fostered "love of sinning" and provided "safety for the sinner." Expressing this widespread concern, Haynes closed his sermon with a poem mocking the concept of universal salvation:

> But all his children reach fair Eden's shore,
> Not e'er to see their father Satan more.
> The tottering drunkards shall to glory reel,
> And common strumpets endless pleasure feel.
> Blest are the haughty, who despise the poor,
> For they're entitled to the heavenly store.
> Blest all who laugh and scoff at truth divine,
> For bold revilers endless comfort find.
> Blest are the clam'rous and contentious crew,
> To them eternal rest and peace are due.
> Blest all who hunger, and who thirst to find
> A chance to plunder and to cheat mankind:

Such die in peace—for God to them has giv'n,
To be unjust on earth, and to go to heaven....
Go riot, drink, and ev'ry ill pursue,
For joys eternal are reserv'd for you.
Fear not to sin, till death shall close your eyes;
Live as you please, yours is th' immortal prize.[58]

Reformed theologians asserted that Christ's atonement on the cross accomplished the salvation of the elect, while Universalists claimed that it guaranteed the salvation of all people. Repudiating both positions, Finney contended that Christ simply made salvation possible for all who trusted Him as their savior. He espoused the "governmental" theory of the atonement, which viewed Jesus' death as demonstrating God's willingness to forgive sins rather than actually compensating for sins. Therefore, he reasoned, Christ's atonement did not pay the debt of all sinners in the way that Universalists maintained; instead, it conveyed God's compassion for humanity, satisfied the demands of His law, and made possible the salvation of all who repented and were regenerated.[59] The Universalist idea that people could "be saved without doing anything" was "preposterous." The Bible, by contrast, taught that "the salvation of the righteous is difficult, and that of the sinner, impossible." Universalists, he alleged, expected everyone "to become religious at some time—perhaps after death—perhaps after being purified from their sins by purgatorial fires" because they realized that everyone must become holy in order to "see God and enjoy His presence."[60]

Evangelicals attacked Universalism not only for depreciating the importance of character, holiness, and good works and misconstruing the nature of Christ's atonement but also for ignoring God's justice. Belief that everyone would ultimately be saved, "no matter how monstrous their sins or great their infidelity," they complained, contradicted the biblical teaching that God was just.[61]

While arguing that salvation was by grace through faith, Second Great Awakening revivalists also stressed that Christians were required to live righteously and do good works in response to God's gracious gift of redemption. James McGready insisted that the new birth implanted "a vital principle of holiness" within the redeemed, and he and others urged Christians to cultivate godliness. To prepare for "a glorious immortality," Ezra Stiles asserted, believers must strive for moral purity. Payson urged Christians to run with "vigor and alacrity the race set" before them. People must "become holy in heart and life," Finney argued, because without holiness they could neither be admitted to nor enjoy heaven.[62]

Although disagreeing about the process of salvation, Finney and Nettleton pointed to similar indicators that people were truly saved. The redeemed, Finney claimed, had a deep faith in Christ, a strong love of God, "a habitual disposition to obey" His commandments, and "an abiding preference" for "God's glory over every-thing else." Those who genuinely desired "to dwell with Christ," Nettleton averred, adored God and faithfully served Him on earth.[63]

THE HORRORS OF HELL

More than any group of American Christians other than the Puritans, the revivalists of the Second Great Awakening defended the traditional view of hell and used its terrors to promote conversion. In sharp contrast to Unitarians and Romantics, who accentuated human goodness and potential, and Universalists, who asserted that all would go to heaven, Dwight, McGready, and Finney warned that the impenitent would go to hell, a place of horrible suffering. They repudiated the common argu-ments that either no punishment occurred after death or that it would only be pro-visional, that the concept of hell clashed with universalistic scripture passages, that it was unfair to inflict everlasting punishment on people for temporal acts, that end-less punishment could not be reconciled with God's benevolence and served no purpose, and that the punishment of the wicked was inconsistent with the happiness of God and the residents of heaven. Many revivalists insisted that the Bible often referred to the chastisement of the wicked as everlasting.[64]

In *Principles of Nature*, Elihu Palmer argued that because people are "finite and imperfect" agents, they could not perform any infinite acts. Therefore, the doctrine that they "deserve[d] an infinite punishment" was "unjust and unreasonable." It clashed with both "the nature of human actions" and the "principle of distributive justice." Moreover, it inflicted the same severe penalty—endless punishment—on "the smallest offender" and the "most abandoned criminal." People should "love and practice virtue," Palmer proclaimed, not to avoid going to hell, but to promote the common good and increase their own earthly happiness.[65]

Although people were finite beings, Dwight countered, their obligation to God was infinite. Violating such an obligation was "plainly an infinite evil," and, there-fore, finite beings could commit a crime that was "infinitely heinous" and deserved eternal punishment. People could not comprehend God's designs, Dwight added, and thus could not understand either how hell was compatible with God's goodness or the purposes it served. "It is impossible," he reasoned, "for us to determine how great, how numerous, or how useful the consequences" of "the punishment of the impenitent" were. Finney agreed that although the damnation of sinners was tragic, God had good reasons for it.[66]

Those who claimed they could not be happy in heaven if they knew that others were in hell, Finney protested, thought that they were more benevolent or wise than

God. Rather, the saints' confidence that God's moral government prevailed would make them happy. They would have no more reason to be unhappy than the virtuous did when criminals were punished on earth. The saints would even accept their spouses, children, or parents being in hell because they would recognize that God always did what was right. A sinner's own pious mother, Finney averred, "would not open heaven's gate" to admit him if she had that power because she knew he "would disturb the bliss of heaven." "God's provision of hell for impenitent sinners," McGready alleged, was "an act of boundless goodness and love." It helped deter sin, affirmed the divine government, and promoted "the general good of the universe." Wise legislators fined and imprisoned "notorious offenders" not because of anger or delight in their misery but to ensure "the order, peace and welfare of society." Similarly, to enhance His glory and honor and to further "the happiness and general good of his creatures," God severely punished those who refused to repent.[67]

Moreover, revivalists contended, the unredeemed would not enjoy heaven if God admitted them. Even "the most moral sinner," Finney asserted, was much closer to being "a devil than a Christian." After their thorough "training in selfishness and sin," the unregenerate were fit only for the company of Satan and his angels. If forced to directly behold God's glory and holiness, such individuals would immediately "dive into the darkest cavern of hell" to escape His awesomeness. To avoid spending eternity with others so opposite in nature and performing repulsive tasks, McGready argued, the unregenerate would leap over "the high battlements of heaven" into "the burning furnace of hell." How could people who were unable to tolerate a prayer meeting for one hour, Finney asked, enjoy worshipping and serving God forever? Being in heaven "would be worse" for sinners "than being in hell." Unless sinners were regenerated, Nettleton asserted, they would detest "the holy employments and enjoyments of the heavenly state." They would protest that it had no pleasant activities or companions and beg to return to earth. The unredeemed considered the Sabbath to be boring and worship services to be burdensome. What pleasure could the unsaved gain, McGready inquired, from beholding the glory of a Being they abhorred? An Islamic paradise—"a heaven of carnal pleasures, and fleshly gratifications—would suit" their tastes much better than the biblical heaven.[68]

Many accentuated the dreadfulness of hell. Abolitionist Theodore Wright, who founded a black Presbyterian congregation in New York City, declared that both the "glories of heaven" and the ceaseless horrors of hell compelled Christians to faithfully serve their "Lord and Master." God "provided an atonement through Jesus Christ," Finney proclaimed, because "it is an awful thing to go to hell!" Jesus declared that in hell "myriads of desperate wretches" would rage "against God and all the good." Because of their refusal to repent, many would go to this abode of "endless suffering." It did not matter if hell involved literal fire or something else that fire represented, Finney argued; either way "the sinner's future woe is very terrible." Hell's residents, Finney insisted, would have no chance to turn to God, and the concept of annihilation "utterly lacked all foundation either in Scripture or reason." Christ taught in the parable of Lazarus and the rich man that "the state of both the righteous and the wicked is...fixed forever." How terrible it will be, Dwight declared, to be "forever guilty, despised, and abhorred" and to live perpetually with a "debased character" in a world of mourning, lamentation, and woe.[69]

Dwight urged his auditors to escape "from the wrath to come," Finney accentuated "the agonies of the second death," and Nettleton warned that the behavior of those currently in hell had been no worse than that of sinners presently on earth, but McGready and Payson employed the threat of hellfire even more.[70] McGready proclaimed, "Every moment" without "Christ, you are suspended over eternal burnings...by the hand of a sin avenging God, who is angry with you" and may at any time allow "you to fall irrecoverably into the flames." Multitudes, he warned, were presently suffering "the flames of God's vengeance" in hell because they had "stifled the voice of conscience" and "put off the work of salvation," intending "to become pious [shortly] before death." The image of fire conveyed "all the miseries, pains and tortures that an infinite God can inflict." "At this very moment," he warned in another sermon, "thousands are...beginning to feel the pangs and tortures, which will never end!" The misery of the damned would be multiplied by "the dreadful and racking accusations" of their consciences and their hideous company—"black horrible devils" and "the ungodly wretches of the human race." As awful as these tortures and torments were, McGready declared, being eternally separated from God, Christ, and heaven was even worse. Payson agreed that those who refused to accept Christ as their savior would plunge into "wretchedness and despair" and "devouring flames." Their own passions, desires, and consciences would continually prey upon hell's inhabitants, a condition as awful as God regarding them "with severe displeasure."[71]

Others made even more audacious claims. After Ethan Allen's death in 1789, Ezra Stiles consigned the arch infidel to hell. Stiles wrote in his diary that "the profane and impious Deist" was lifting "up his eyes, being in Torments." Congregationalist theologian Samuel Hopkins insisted that people must overcome their self-love by "disinterested benevolence" and totally submitting to God's will—which included the willingness to be damned to advance God's glory.[72] He argued further that the saints would find the sight of hell "most entertaining." The perpetual punishment of the wicked would make the redeemed much more aware of their happiness. It also would constantly remind them of the "infinite evil of sin" and enable them to clearly see and celebrate "the goodness of God and his astonishing mercy in their redemption," as well as the "power, dignity, worthiness, love and grace" of Christ their redeemer. "However great an evil" the "endless misery" of millions might seem, it was just and "essential to the…highest glory and happiness of God's eternal kingdom."[73]

CONCLUSION

From 1770 to 1840, numerous pastors, theologians, revivalists, founders, and politicians displayed great interest in the contours of heaven and the conditions for admittance. During these decades, Americans won their independence from Britain, established a new nation, doubled its size, framed a venerable constitution, celebrated republicanism and individualism, advanced significantly in agriculture, commerce, industry, and technology, and experienced another widespread revival. From the Revolution to the Civil War, a synthesis of republican principles and Christian values strongly influenced American colleges, courts, pulpits, and social mores. Most Americans assumed that Christian virtue was essential to the success of republican institutions and that these institutions supplied the freedom necessary for Christianity to thrive.[74]

During the revolutionary, early national, and antebellum periods, numerous deists, free thinkers, and Unitarians attacked conventional Christian understandings of God, the Bible, the means of salvation, and the nature of heaven. Meanwhile, Universalists repudiated the orthodox view that individuals had to accept Jesus as their savior and Lord to gain entry to heaven, arguing instead that everyone would eventually be admitted regardless of whether they repented of their sins or led a godly life on earth. As a result, Christians were forced to defend the traditional doctrines of redemption. The revivalists of the Second Great Awakening took the lead in responding to these assaults and in depicting the splendors of heaven. In their portrait, the majesty and glory of God loomed large as the saints reveled in His awesomeness, their intimate communion with the Trinity, and the wonders of the New Jerusalem. Influenced by their society's increasing emphasis on the individual and growing economic opportunities, many leading Christians stressed the saints' progress in knowledge, love, and power and heavenly rewards. More than any group other than the Puritans, revivalists upheld the traditional view of hell, argued that divine justice required it, explained the purposes it served, and emphasized its horrors to stimulate sinners to accept Jesus as their savior.

Heaven is a home, in which there is assembled
already a great and glorious and happy family.
—WILLIAM BRANKS, *Heaven Our Home*

"My Father's House! How sweet a designation of
locality as well as personal affection!"
—GEORGE CHEEVER, *The Power of the
World to Come*

A warm faith in this doctrine [of heavenly
recognition] has a tendency to elevate, strengthen,
and purify all our earthly affections.
—HENRY HARBAUGH, *The Heavenly Recognition*

Heaven will be no heaven to me if I do not
meet my wife there.
—ANDREW JACKSON

HEAVEN AS HOME

The Victorians and Heaven,

1830–1870

IN THE MIDDLE decades of the nineteenth century, Americans' vision of heaven changed dramatically, from one centered on God to one focused on humans. Some authors continued to stress the worship and contemplation of God in heaven and used the hope of heaven to promote conversion. However, the subjects of heavenly recognition, the fellowship of the saints with loved ones and the heroes of the Bible and church history, and infant salvation received much more emphasis than in earlier (and later) periods. From 1830 to 1870 the picture of heaven as a celestial home, largely modeled on the most cherished features of the Victorian home, became widely accepted. Americans accentuated the phenomenal beauty and the "dazzling and luminous appeal" of heaven and the fantastic life the saints would enjoy there. In the heaven they imagined, the redeemed lived harmoniously with one another and loved ones clasped hands again.[1]

In the mid-nineteenth century, both fictional and allegedly factual accounts "of deathbed scenes and celestial communications" became very popular. This "consolation literature" included mourners' manuals, guidebooks for prayer, poems, hymns, fictional works, and biographies that sought principally to comfort the bereaved. The authors of these death manuals, Ann Douglas argued, were not primarily concerned "with the kind of life a believer must pursue on earth to attain heaven." Instead, they asserted that the celestial kingdom was accessible "to earthly intelligence" and stressed "the similarities between the two worlds which made communication possible." Moreover, many of them depicted "heaven as a continuation and a glorification of the domestic sphere."[2]

Articles in magazines and journals, sermons, poems, tracts, novels, and hymns all portrayed heaven as a home beyond the skies. Ministers as different as Unitarian William Ellery Channing and Congregationalist Austin Phelps insisted that in heaven, homes would be restored, families reconstituted, and friends reunited. Especially popular was Englishman William Branks's *Heaven Our Home* (1864), which sold very well on both sides of the Atlantic, going through sixty printings in Britain alone. Rather than portraying eternal life as principally a beatific vision of God or an everlasting rest, he described it as "a home with a great and happy and loving family in it." In the 1840s and 1850s, Henry Harbaugh, a Lutheran who taught at Mercersburg (German Reformed) Seminary in southern central Pennsylvania, published three widely read books on heaven. He also argued that heaven is "our father's home, with ... familiar homelike scenes." Dozens of authors urged Americans to approach their "heavenly inheritance like children long absent going home."[3]

These consolatory works, penned primarily by devout women and theologically moderate ministers, promised the bereaved that they could know about the heavenly lives of deceased loved ones in minute detail and strove to make heaven comprehensible and accessible to people on earth. The most popular, influential, and controversial of these works was Elizabeth Stuart Phelps's *The Gates Ajar* (1868). Written to help those who were grieving the loss of sons, husbands, or brothers who died in the Civil War, it depicts a blissful, domestically-oriented heaven where war veterans chat with Abraham Lincoln and young girls play the piano. One of its heroines instructs her young daughter to confide in her dead father and to expect God to someday satisfy all her desires in heaven. In her later novels, *Beyond the Gates* (1883) and *Between the Gates* (1887), Phelps describes heaven's "eating habits, occupations, lifestyles, [and] methods of child care and courtship." Such accounts of heaven, Charles Jackson asserts, helped transform the previously awesome celestial world "into a state much like that of life in middle-class America." Some protested that these portraits of paradise transferred "the baggage of this world" to life after death.[4]

Phelps had an impressive pedigree and an excellent education. She was the granddaughter of Moses Stuart and daughter of Austin Phelps, who both taught at Andover Seminary, the nation's first and arguably most influential seminary in the nineteenth century. Moreover, she was tutored in religion by another of its leading professors, Edward A. Park. In these books, she portrayed heaven as "an idealized New England projected into the skies." Like proponents of the New Theology, which arose at Andover in the 1880s, Phelps expected "the same laws of natural growth and progress" that operated on earth to function in heaven.[5] Written as a series of diary entries, *The Gates Ajar* is set in the closing months of the Civil War.

Mary Cabot, a twenty-four-year-old resident of Homer, Massachusetts, mourns her brother Royal, who has died in the war. Aided by her Aunt Winifred, Mary eventually overcomes her doubts about God and her fears about various features of the afterlife.

Mary rejects the austere and dull heaven of Deacon Quirk and the local Calvinist minister, the aptly named Dr. Bland. In their theocentric heaven, "the glory of God is the primary consideration," as disembodied souls contemplate "the infinite mind of an impersonal sovereign." Quirk suggests that Roy is so immersed "in worshipping before the great White Throne" that he is paying no attention to this miserable earthly sphere, which pales compared to heaven's "exceeding weight of glory." In one of his sermons, Bland declares, "I expect to be so overwhelmed by the glory of the presence of God, that it may be thousands of years before I shall think of my wife." Bland also insists that earthly family members and friends have "no special affections" in heaven. Such assertions cause Mary to lament that in this "dreadful Heaven" Roy did not think of her or remember how she loved him. Singing and worshipping were all-consuming. "God wants it all. . . . I am nothing any more to Roy." Mary complains that Bland's conception of God and description of heavenly life make her cringe. "I do not doubt that we shall glorify God primarily and happily," she declares, "but can we not do it in some other way than by harping and praying?"[6]

Winifred offers Mary a very different portrait of heaven. God, she promises, "will never separate . . . us from each other." She claims that heaven's residents talk, play, joke, attend concerts, read novels, marry, and raise children. Winifred maintains that individuals do the same things in heaven that they do on earth—"comforting, teaching, helping, [and] saving people." Moreover, she contends, "our absent dead are very present with us." Winifred assures Mary that Roy remembers and loves her and knows what she is doing and feeling and therefore can help her.[7]

Phelps's novel exalts the Victorians' glorification of the home and strong desire for stability and decorum. Sounding a theme that resonated with most mid-nineteenth century Americans, Winifred declares that heaven is "a happy home" because this is the best thing humans can imagine. In heaven people enjoy books, art, and music, and family and friends are even dearer to them than they are on earth. The infinitely ingenious God designed heaven with endless variety and unlimited charms to delight the saints. Winifred quotes a little Swedish girl who, gazing at the stars, exclaimed, "O father, if the wrong side of heaven is so beautiful, what must the right side be like?"[8]

Mary eventually rejects the "conventional" conception of heaven as a place "where the glory of God" crowded out "all individuality and all human joy," where a "great blank ocean" swallowed up "all the little brooks" of human bliss. Repudiating the view that God is "an abstract Grandeur" who must be pleased out of fear, Mary comes to see Him as a "dear and real" "living Presence." Regaining her faith, Mary rejoices that she will someday be reunited with her brother in a heaven that shares many similarities with her New England village and its surrounding streams, meadows, and forests. *The Gates Ajar* teaches that God admits all well-intentioned individuals into heaven and that the existence of hell does not disturb the happiness of the saints because its few residents are despicably evil.[9]

By combining elements of "sacred allegory, sentimental romance, Platonic dialogue," the sermons of progressive ministers, and the confessional diary with realistic features of key aspects of contemporary New England life, Phelps hoped to reassure Americans who, goaded by Darwinian evolution and an increasingly aggressive assault on orthodox Christianity, were questioning immortality. Her fable, Helen Sootin Smith explained, "expressed philosophically" what its many "readers felt or hoped." Moving beyond the typical abstractions and generalities about heaven, Phelps provided "concrete images" that delighted some readers while irritating others.[10] *Gates Ajar* is a mirror that reflects the "deepening disquiet" of many Americans about "the traditional images of heaven," which to them seemed to be "cold, impersonal, and unattractive." Although its prose sounds sentimental, stilted, and maudlin to contemporary ears, it expressed the fears, hopes, and dreams of many Victorians on both sides of the Atlantic. Undoubtedly speaking for many of them, Phelps' father, Austin, confessed that his "conception of heaven as a place... not unlike this world," a primary part of the appeal of *Gates Ajar*, gave him the strength to live on earth.[11]

Much of the religious press, by contrast, denounced Phelps's novel as irreverent, immoral, and injurious. Some editors and ministers claimed that her conception of the life to come had unleashed an "evil spirit" that assaulted "accepted theology" and threatened to destroy the world. An Episcopal seminary professor denounced her attempt to furnish paradise "with toys and playthings for children," pianos, sports, and games as a "wretched and degrading travesty of the heavenly state." Phelps's assumption that in heaven "natural fools, artists and artisans, acrobats and bird fanciers" would continue "their idiotic conduct" rather than develop their religious affections was ludicrous. Mark Twain castigated her conception of the afterlife as "a mean little ten-cent heaven about the size of Rhode Island." Equally critical is historian Jackson Lears, who argues that by reducing heaven "to domestic proportions," Phelps and like-minded moralists "denied death," "trivialized life," and "unwittingly reinforced the cultural dominance of their own class, the educated bourgeoisie."[12]

THE NATURE OF HEAVEN

Unlike Phelps, some other leading writers of the period frankly confessed that their knowledge of heaven was limited and promised to stick to what the scriptures taught about the afterlife. The Bible, Harbaugh declared, primarily used "figures, images, and symbols" to portray heaven. Many accounts of paradise, he complained, contained either "too much wild and unwarrantable speculation" or "too much vague spiritualistic use of the figurative language of the Bible," both of which misled people. He sought "to steer between these two extremes. When I speculate—if the carrying out of Bible truths to their legitimate consequences by the assistance of scripture allusions and established rational and analogical laws of interpretation, can be called speculation—it shall be tame, and tempered with…modesty and reverence." Almost everything we know about heaven from Christ's teachings, Harbaugh declared, "is indirect and incidental." The Savior, he stressed, discussed people's earthly duties much more than their heavenly privileges. It is not necessary to have a complete picture of the palace before dining with the king, added James W. Kimball, a Yale graduate, businessman, and author; we know that the king's "house will be worthy of him." Although much of Revelation "is entirely beyond our comprehension," he asserted, even spiritual babes could understand other parts of it, especially that heaven's chief occupation is praise.[13]

Like Christians of earlier eras, some Victorians strongly emphasized the importance, magnificence, and wonder of the relationship heavenly inhabitants would enjoy with God and Jesus. "Every redeemed soul," exulted James MacDonald, who served Presbyterian congregations in New York City, Princeton, and Trenton during the mid-nineteenth century, "upon being admitted into heaven" will initially "be so completely absorbed in the contemplation" of God that they will pay little attention to anyone else. Edward Griffin, who pastored large congregations in Newark, New Jersey, and Boston, taught at Andover Seminary, and served as president of Williams College, declared that the saints enjoyed "a constant sense of God's favor, and uninterrupted communion with him." The absence of a temple in heaven, Kimball proclaimed, meant that the saints had direct access to God. He expected the saints' "friendship and fellowship with Christ" to be so fulfilling that they would never need human consolation.[14]

The saints' wills "perfectly accord with the will of God," John Kerr declared; they have "no separate desires and inclinations." Heaven's inhabitants recognize that everything God "does is wisest and best." The saints clearly see "the excellence of His laws and the equity of His government" and "cheerfully acquiesce in all His judgments." They will worship God perfectly with no irreverence, "wandering thought[s]…[or] worldly affections or desires," MacDonald claimed. Moreover, he argued, heavenly residents will admire and celebrate God's "infinite wisdom and goodness." They will understand how numerous events that perplexed them on earth, including sickness, premature death, and "the afflictions of the righteous," demonstrated God's "wisdom, justice, and mercy" and served His purposes. MacDonald maintained that the inhabitants of heaven obey cheerfully because they love God and recognize that He is the "rightful Lawgiver and Governor" whose injunctions are founded on "truth and mercy."[15]

Numerous authors emphasized Christ's radiance and rejoiced that the saints had an intimate relationship with Him. "Heaven without Christ," Rufus Clark, pastor of the influential Maverick (Congregationalist) Church in Boston, heralded, "would be like the firmament without a sun." Magnificent royal palaces and splendid heavenly cities will surround the Savior who is "the most intense delight of the church triumphant." "Christ will appear in his glory to all residents of heaven," Branks maintained, and "commune with them face to face throughout all eternity." In heaven, Kimball averred, the saints will be like Jesus and "love him...for what he is." Christ will graciously answer every question the redeemed ask, avowed George Wood, a U.S. Treasury Department official.[16]

Other aspects of the portrait of heaven pastors and professors painted during the years from 1830 to 1870 were also similar to their predecessors' conception of paradise. Some of them emphasized the growth Christians would experience in heaven, although not as much as others did in later periods. Christians living in the mid-nineteenth century underscored the beauty, majesty, holiness, and delights of heaven and the immense knowledge its residents possessed. They described the heavenly landscape as picturesque and extremely varied, as a place of "lush green fields, gently rolling hills, and quiet streams." Offering his readers a "travel guide" to an "exotic land," Harbaugh insisted that heaven's beauty would surpass that of Eden. James MacDonald cautioned Christians "not to conceive of heaven only as a sort of better earth," and many commentators, while focusing on the saints' rich relationships with family and friends, pictured a very otherworldly paradise. Heaven, Edward Griffin explained, is a realm of "resplendent and varied beauty." Paradise, Clark asserted, is characterized by light, the emblem of "loveliness, beauty, truth and happiness." It contained no sea because the sea is a symbol of "change, instability, and disappointment." The "mansions of the redeemed," John Kerr exclaimed, "are infinitely superior in splendor and glory" to the most sublime works of nature. Heaven, Wood declared, "fulfills all human desires."[17]

Griffin envisioned the saints wearing crowns and sitting around "Christ on his throne," playing "golden harps," singing, and enjoying "unspeakable ecstasies." They will express "perfect love and gratitude" toward God. Heaven's inhabitants will no longer sin or be buffeted by Satan. They will comprehend "the infinite evil of sin," "the transcendent wonders of redemption," "and the astonishing reach" of God's mercy. The saints will continuously learn about God's wisdom, goodness, power, justice, mercy, and truth.[18]

During an era when newspapers and magazines proliferated, numerous public libraries were established, many scholars gave lectures in the lyceum circuit, common schools were created, and Protestant denominations founded hundreds of colleges, many emphasized the unparalleled knowledge the saints would attain. "The feeblest infant" in heaven, Griffin alleged, "probably knows more of God than all the divines on earth." The perfect knowledge they possessed did not exclude progress, but it prevented error. The saints, Rufus Clark announced, had "discriminating reason" and "a keen, spiritual vision," and knew all truth. Like Jonathan Edwards, Griffin maintained that the saints will understand all "the mysteries of redemption," the "wonders of creation," the purposes of "the sufferings of the damned," God's "boundless" mercy, and "the whole history of God's administration in all worlds." The more people advanced in knowledge and holiness, the more they would love God and delight in Him. "Who can imagine," John Kerr asked, "the heights which may be ascended…the worlds which may be explored…and the degree of knowledge" which "the heirs of eternal life" will "ultimately attain?" As the saints' grew intellectually, their "benevolence, curiosity," and other "noble and generous affections" would also become stronger. William Ellery Channing agreed that heavenly residents will forever increase in "the likeness, and knowledge and enjoyment of the Infinite Father."[19]

Several facts, Harbaugh asserted, demonstrate that the saints are aware of life on earth: the rich man in hell knew what was happening on earth, Paul "expected to rejoice in heaven" as he viewed the ongoing results of his ministry, Hebrews 13:1 pictures the saints watching us "with intense interest," and the saints constantly communicated with angels who participated in earthly life. Scripture plainly taught, Harbaugh added, that the saints "affectionately remember" people on earth and "supplicate and intercede" for them.[20]

While discussing the saints' phenomenal knowledge, understanding, and perspective, the leading interpreters of heaven in the middle decades of the nineteenth century also described it as "a place of perfect rest" "from which pains and conflicts are forever excluded." The Book of Revelation portrays "a vision of peace and rest," declared Maine judge and abolitionist Woodbury Davis, where "the weaknesses, wants, trials, pains and sorrow of the present life" are all absent and "sacrifice, intercession and forgiveness" are not necessary.[21]

In *Future Life or Scenes in Another World* (1858), George Wood envisioned heaven's residents enjoying a rich cultural, social, and educational life. Handel, Haydn, Beethoven, and Mozart all continued to compose great music, while Dante and Beatrice asked newly arrived saints about the progress of the gospel on earth, the subject the redeemed cared about most. Heavenly inhabitants listened to one of Handel's new oratorios, heard a sermon by John Howe, a chaplain to Oliver Cromwell, and observed a dispute between allopathic and a homeopathic doctors over the merits of their medical practices. They attended a "great Convocation for the Advancement of Knowledge" "in a distant world" at which "all the great minds of the ages" were present. The saints also witnessed numerous biblical scenes including Abraham preparing to sacrifice Isaac, David slaying Goliath, and Jesus' birth in Bethlehem, baptism in the Jordan, temptations in the wilderness, and public ministry. In Wood's vision of heaven, whenever they wished, people could replay the life of the "glorious savior from his cradle to his ascension" as well as the events of their own lives. Meanwhile, the Apostle Paul traveled to "far-off worlds" to broadcast God's wisdom and love as displayed in His "redemption of the world."[22]

For Victorians, heaven was not as lively a place as it would be in the Progressive era, but some did see it as a place of "intense activity" where residents engaged in a wide variety of tasks. Augustus Thompson, who pastored a Congregationalist church near Boston, argued that in the Bible, the word *rest* signified freedom from both temptation and fatigue. The resurrection body could engage in strenuous labor without becoming weary. Delivered from "the hindrances of this world" and the "enfeebling effects of sin," the saints, like the angels, would serve God energetically. Although serving and praising God would be the saints' "noblest employment," Griffin contended, they would also "go on his errands to different worlds," study "the mysteries of his nature and the wonders of his works," and discuss these lofty "and exhaustless themes" with others. Archibald Alexander, a professor at Princeton Theological Seminary, maintained that God would send the saints "as messengers to distant worlds" to be either "instruments of justice or mercy."[23]

Like their counterparts in other eras, authors writing in this period entreated Christians to think frequently, deeply, and joyfully about heaven and underscored the benefits of doing so. Griffin challenged Christians to visit this "delightful land" daily in their thoughts "and to make excursions through its glorious regions." Walk down its "golden streets," he declared; "traverse its flowery fields, and examine its objects one by one." Believers should collect as much information as possible about the place where they planned to spend eternity and where many of their deceased friends had gone. Because it was "rarely a subject of conversation in Christian social circles," Branks lamented, "our views of heaven are dim and obscure. Heaven is out of sight, and too much out of mind." Did Christians think about their friends in heaven as much as ones who were in foreign countries? Habitually reflecting on the life and rewards of heaven, Branks asserted, comforted Christians and helped inspire them to serve God energetically on earth. Focusing on heaven, John Kerr added, enabled believers to cope with "the trials, disappointments, and calamities of life."[24]

"GOING HOME": HEAVENLY RECOGNITION, FRIENDS, AND FELLOWSHIP

All these themes were important during the middle decades of the nineteenth century, but the concept of heaven as a celestial home where the saints enjoyed rich fellowship with family members, friends, and heroes of the faith was especially prominent. While accentuating paradise's grandeur and magnificence, the most popular portrait incorporated many "features of a middle-class parlor" and highlighted the reunion of family and friends.[25] The Victorian domestic ideal dominated mid-nineteenth-century American culture. The novels of Harriet Beecher Stowe, Susan Warner, and Timothy Shay, poems in women's magazines, and the lithographs of Currier and Ives all celebrated it, and many ministers and pious female authors conflated domestic and religious values. As an industrial, market economy replaced subsistence farming, the focus of the family shifted from production to fulfilling psychological and emotional needs. Many women stopped performing agricultural and revenue-raising tasks and assumed the role of cultural and moral guardians. The Cult of True Womanhood that emerged in the 1820s limited the role of women to homemaking and nurturing children, stressed purity and piety, and elevated the home. As the nation's birthrate declined throughout the nineteenth century, parents, especially mothers, were able to give each child more attention. The bourgeoisie conceived of the home as "an oasis of tenderness and affection in a desert of ruthless competition." It was a sanctuary, "a haven in a heartless world," a refuge from the world's demands and problems where sympathy, affection, and virtue reigned. In the mid-nineteenth century, this idealized conception of the home became the dominant description of heaven, the place millions of Americans longed to go after death.[26] Good Christian homes provided "a glimpse of heaven," while heaven was "the perfect home."[27]

The phrase "my Father's House," asserted George Cheever, pastor of the Church of the Puritans in New York City, aptly described Christians' eternal destination and conveyed God's "personal affection" for them. For believers in Jesus, William Branks declared, death "is going home" to join "a great and glorious and happy family" over which God presided lovingly. Much more than the best homes on earth, Branks maintained, heaven "softens even the hardest heart, revives holy associations, and awakens a longing…to return to it." He counseled Christians to view heaven the same way a bride did as she anticipated her new home. Irish Presbyterian pastor J. M. Killen, whose books about heaven were very influential in the United States, rejoiced that the redeemed constituted "the family of God" because "the word family is one of the sweetest, holiest," most tender terms in human vocabulary. The saints' "warmest affections" are in heaven; it is "the longed-for dwelling-place" of their dearest friends. For Harbaugh, heaven was "our father's home, with…familiar homelike scenes," "not the cold ivory hall of a strange king." Like their future heavenly abode, Branks counseled, Christians' earthly homes should be places of love, union, peace, and harmony. Many hymns celebrated "celestial housekeeping" and portrayed family reunions. "Our Home with Jesus," for example, declared that "my heavenly home is bright and fair" and promised that Christians would someday "be gathered home."[28]

Authors of this era expected family members and friends to enjoy rich, robust, and rewarding fellowship in their heavenly home. Pastors and laypeople from Lutheran Henry Harbaugh to Unitarian James Freeman Clarke frequently declared their firm hope in a heavenly reunion of loved ones. Your friends who died in Jesus, J. Duncan promised, "are waiting to receive you." Christians' relationships with their family and friends will be "truer and more satisfying" in heaven than on earth, Boston pastor F. W. P. Greenwood asserted.[29] Christians would not be joyful in heaven, Kimball alleged, if they could not intimately converse with their earthly loved ones. Recognizing "the triumph of His grace" in earthly friends, MacDonald maintained, would enhance the saints' love and admiration for Christ. Griffin expected parents and their children and ministers and their parishioners to have especially endearing relationships. The perfect fellowship of heaven, he added, would surpass the most wonderful "communion with Christian friends on earth."[30]

While ministers often used "the threat of family division" to obtain conversions and encourage Christian piety and conduct, many women of all social classes also expressed their hope that their families would be reconstituted in heaven and urged their loved ones to live faithful Christian lives so they could be admitted. Sad because her sister was moving to Georgia, an upcountry farmer's wife urged her to "press on heavenword [*sic*]." Someday they would joyfully meet again on its happy shores "to part no more."[31] "Why should we not haste and fly to see our home [in heaven] and greet our parents?" asked Sarah Gould in *The Guardian Angels, or, Friends in Heaven* (1857). In Harriet Beecher Stowe's *Uncle Tom's Cabin* (1852), the dying little Eva derives comfort from her belief that she will soon be reunited with Uncle Tom and Mammy in paradise.[32]

Numerous authors promised that the saints would also enjoy "intimate friendship" with angels, the "patriarchs, prophets, apostles, [and] martyrs." The glorified, Griffin stated, would have "perfect friendship with angels." They would talk with Abraham, Isaac, Jacob, Moses, David, Daniel, Peter, and Paul and learn more about the wondrous events "recorded in the Bible." In heaven, Thompson declared, the saints would converse with "the venerable reformers, martyrs and Puritans" such as John Bunyan and Jonathan Edwards. Harbaugh rejoiced that Christians will "sit down at the celestial feast" with the patriarchs, prophets, church fathers, martyrs, and Reformers. Meeting in glory "the great and good of all ages, and all lands," especially Abraham, Isaac, Moses, David, Paul, John, Augustine, Aquinas, Luther, and Calvin and hearing about their "trials and triumphs" would produce "heavenly felicity." "The saints of every age" and nation, J. M. Killen argued, will fellowship above with the patriarchs and apostles, with "Christian fathers as well as Israel's and Judah's prophets—modern reformers as well as ancient seers…the most advanced believer and the weakest babe in Christ." Sarah Gould also expected to fellowship with the apostles and the "innumerable company of the martyrs" in God's eternal kingdom.[33]

Personal recognition was essential to this conception of heaven as an eternal home where intimate family relationships, close friendships, and warm fellowship prevailed. "No idea about heaven," Mark Schantz stated, was more important during the antebellum years. Therefore, many of the leading books on heaven in the mid-nineteenth century marshaled arguments to support this doctrine. The "recognition of friends in heaven follows necessarily from two facts," Branks argued, "that heaven is a home" and that all its residents constitute "one family." If family members did not recognize one another, heaven could "not be a home of love." Many, asserted Augustus C. Thompson, conceived of heaven "mainly as a rendezvous for friends" and thought that "future bliss" consisted almost entirely of renewing "domestic attachments." Every "enlightened" Christian, he alleged, longed to be reunited with friends in heaven.[34]

Mid-nineteenth century Christians argued first and foremost that heavenly recognition accorded with scripture. Rufus Clark admitted that few passages supplied "direct and unqualified proof" for this doctrine, but he insisted that the Bible provided enough evidence to convince "all true disciples of Jesus." Although neither the Old nor New Testament taught future recognition directly, Thompson declared, the scriptures contained nothing that conflicted with this belief. Human expectations, "the absence of adverse testimony," and incidental biblical teachings, he asserted, all assured Christian friends that they would "know one another in the future world." Harbaugh underscored the typical scriptural arguments: Christ taught the concept of heavenly recognition, most notably in His parable of the rich man and Lazarus; Jesus repeatedly described heaven as having the same social features as earth; Christ's transfiguration demonstrated the doctrine; "Paul's words of comfort to the Thessalonian Christians on the death of their friends" testified to it; and Revelation 5:9, which states that "the saints in heaven remember and speak" about people on earth, implied it. Because Moses and Elijah could be identified after death, some reasoned, other saints would also be recognizable.[35]

Between 1830 and 1870, pastors and professors also used many other arguments to defend heavenly recognition, including the widespread belief in the concept and the consolation it brought. All groups throughout all ages, Clark asserted, had believed that their friends in heaven awaited their "arrival at their blissful home." Branks claimed that "even those who did not enjoy the light of revelation" expected to recognize their friends in the afterlife. Would this belief be "so universal," Thompson asked, "if it were unreasonable or unscriptural?" God "would not have implanted either the belief or desire" of recognition in people's hearts if it were untrue, Killen asserted, nor would the Holy Spirit allow Christians to use a "delusion" to comfort one another when they mourned the loss of loved ones.[36]

Killen insisted further that the scriptures implied that people maintained their memories throughout eternity. Moreover, people could preserve their identity only if their memories continued, which meant that they would recognize individuals they knew on earth. The loss of personal memories, John Kerr alleged, would virtually eliminate individuality, which would "frustrate the purposes of [both] penal justice" and "redeeming love."[37]

Although Christ "loved all his people," Killen explained, He displayed "a peculiarly strong regard" for some, demonstrating that having "specific attachments" did not prevent exercising universal love. If Jesus had particular friends on earth, He undoubtedly had them in heaven, so others could as well. Harbaugh agreed that Christ endorsed having special friendships "by his own example." If divine beings showed greater affection for some individuals, Harbaugh concluded, it must also be permissible and even desirable for human beings.[38]

Several other considerations, Killen and Harbaugh claimed, justified belief in heavenly recognition. If the saints did not recognize each other, Killen reasoned, their ignorance in heaven in this respect would be greater than it was on earth, which contradicted the biblical promise that their knowledge would be "vastly enlarged" in the future state. Moreover, mutual recognition, he contended, was indispensable to the saints' love, knowledge, fellowship, and rewards and to fully appreciating God's providence. Strangers, Killen added, could not enjoy intimate relationships. The ability of friends and relatives to discuss their earthly circumstances and concerns in heaven, Harbaugh explained, would enhance their happiness.[39]

Mid-nineteenth century Christians also strove to refute numerous objections raised against the idea of heavenly recognition. That the scriptures did not "directly, clearly, and fully" reveal this doctrine, Harbaugh reasoned, showed it "was taken for granted" in the first century A.D. and did not need to be propounded "formally as a doctrine." Harbaugh repudiated the contention that recognition was impossible because individuals dramatically changed after death. People's bodies and spirits, he pointed out, could undergo great changes without destroying their marks of identity and peculiar characteristics. Just as individuals retained the same external features after they were converted, the "power, glory and immortality" they experienced in heaven would not change their outward appearance. The saints could also recognize each other by their inward spiritual qualities.[40]

Because heavenly residents were "entirely and eternally" occupied with the Savior, a few asserted, they had "no time or desire" to commune with their friends. Killen countered that "the Redeemer's love" for His Father was not "incompatible with his love" for His saints and, therefore, their love of Him would not reduce their love for one another. Harbaugh insisted that the Bible nowhere taught that the saints would do nothing but gaze at Christ. Although "the Lamb is the bright and glorious centre" of heaven, He is also "the Sun" that "animates all the social circles of the saints which surround Him." A related objection was "that all earthly relations" would "be swallowed up, superseded, or set aside" in heaven. While the saints' "affections will be vastly elevated, sanctified, [and] increased," Harbaugh countered, earthly friendships would not cease.[41]

Others protested that heavenly recognition would "introduce partiality into Heaven" or could not be reconciled with Jesus' declaration that the saints are not married. Friends could love each other more than they loved other saints without producing any ill effects, Harbaugh countered, because jealousy was impossible in heaven. Moreover, Christians usually did not envy the warm attachments other believers had to their friends and relatives on earth. Just because people were not married in heaven, asserted Harbaugh, did not mean that they did "not know each other." If Jesus intended to make that point, He could have said that earthly ties do not extend "beyond the grave."[42]

The most difficult argument defenders of mutual recognition combated was that realizing that some of their loved ones were not in heaven and seeing "the lost in hell" would bring the saints suffering and distress. If people did not recognize one another in the hereafter, Killen observed, the saints would not know whether any of their family or friends were saved, which would cause great anxiety and pain. Moreover, Christ's tenderness for people far surpassed that of even the most sensitive saints, and His knowledge that many were not in heaven did not interfere with His "perfect felicity." The "views, affections, and desires" of heaven's residents will conform so closely to God, Killen averred, that they will not be unhappy about the absence of certain friends and relatives. Harbaugh acknowledged that this objection, more than all others, caused some "to doubt the doctrine of recognition." He reasoned that God might erase the saints' memories of any earthly relationships that might cause them pain. On earth, he declared, the grief of those whose impenitent relatives died is "assuaged by a kind of 'hope against hope'" that they were perhaps saved and in heaven. "This sweet and consoling uncertainty," he added unconvincingly, might continue in the future life, in part because "heaven is spacious." Harbaugh also contended that the saints will "entirely and cheerfully" accede to God's decision to not admit certain individuals to heaven.[43]

Many stressed that belief in the doctrine of heavenly recognition had significant benefits. Harbaugh insisted it helped "elevate, strengthen, and purify" Christians' "earthly affections" and make their relationships "more holy and heavenly" because they regarded them as unending. Thompson contended that the concept inspired believers to be more heavenly minded, love their friends and relatives more deeply, and work more vigorously to convert them so that they could spend eternity together.[44] This conviction, Harbaugh proclaimed, could also motivate sinners to accept Christ as their savior so that they could reside forever with their loved ones. It also greatly consoled Christians who mourned the loss of their pious loved ones. Finally, Harbaugh declared, belief that many friends and loved ones awaited them in heaven comforted Christians as they faced their own death by giving them "an unquenchable desire to leave this foreign land and return home."[45]

Their conception of heaven as an eternal home led many to discuss the topic of infant salvation. Like some Christians before and almost all after them, Victorian Christians affirmed that all those who died as infants would be saved—indeed, they constituted a large percentage of heaven's population. Infants, who were precious and cherished on earth, Harbaugh reasoned, would also be one of heaven's major "treasures and attractions." Belief that deceased infants were immediately received into heaven and taught "the lessons of angelic wisdom and love" by "celestial guardians," Harbaugh announced, provided great consolation. In various works, especially manuals to help those mourning the death of young children, authors sought to comfort parents in an age when, they claimed (incorrectly), one half of all people died in infancy. "Assurance that little children" went to heaven when they died because of Christ's atonement for them, George Cheever asserted, "should greatly mitigate the grief of parents and friends." Like Harbaugh, he pictured infants and young children "growing up in heaven…in the image of Jesus" perhaps under "the guardianship and teaching" of angels. Because so many died as infants or children, heaven was "one vast ecstatic holy school of youthful happy spirits."[46] Moreover, he argued, infants were much safer in heaven "than they would be in…impious homes on earth." In addition, most of them had advantages over adults because they had led "lovely and pleasant" lives, "untarnished by actual sin," and "free from every unpleasant association." How could any sane person ever doubt "the final salvation of infants and little children?" asked William Holcombe, a Swedenborgian physician. When the Israelites rebelled in the wilderness, God spared all those under twenty years old and later allowed them to enter the Promised Land "because they were not considered morally responsible for participating in the sins of their fathers." Therefore, he concluded, God would not exclude anyone who died under the age of twenty from heaven.[47]

Some mid-nineteenth century parents "attempted to convince themselves that death benefited their children," Sean A. Scott contended, because it helped them cope with "the troubles and trials of life." An Indiana Quaker concluded that her two deceased infants had been mercifully removed before "one blot of sin…had stained their…purity." Others regarded the death of their young children as a "solemn admonition" to adults to draw "nearer to the Saviour" by concentrating on the treasures they enjoyed in heaven. Meanwhile, in articles in popular magazines such as *Godey's Lady's Book* and in novels, some authors, most notably Harriet Beecher Stowe, argued that "deceased infants became angels in heaven who helped rescue and purify the souls of family members on earth." Undoubtedly speaking for many, a resident of Flint, Michigan, resolved after her daughter died " 'to live in such a way' that she could" meet her "little angel in heaven" someday.[48]

Heavenly rewards were much less discussed in this period than heavenly recognition and fellowship. Some prodded Christians to seek celestial rewards and stressed that compensation differed in heaven, but few said anything about the nature of these rewards. "Your toils and self-denials," Edward Griffin promised the faithful, will "be recompensed a thousand fold" in paradise. To obtain the maximum "heavenly felicity," Kimball declared, Christians should pray, exercise faith, and minister to others as Jesus did. Although God accepted individuals into heaven based solely on Christ's atonement, He rewarded them based on their character and actions. Individuals' knowledge in heaven, Kimball maintained, would depend in large part on their earthly preparation; happiness in heaven would be contingent on the choices people made in this life. Those whose conduct is "narrow-minded, selfish, and inconsistent" and did little to serve Christ, he warned, would receive fewer heavenly blessings.[49] Those who followed Christ most faithfully on earth and spurned worldly pleasures, Kimball promised, will receive the highest honors of heaven.[50]

Christian authors in these years also gave little attention to either precisely where the saints would spend eternity or to the nature of the resurrection body. Griffin argued that after Christ's Second Coming and the final judgment, the saints would usually dwell in the highest heaven but would "occasionally visit and reside" on a renovated earth. Although the earth had been marred by sin, Jesus will restore it "in tenfold splendor," and it will shine with greater glory and beauty than before sin defaced it. The church fathers, Reformers, and most Protestant theologians and biblical expositors since the Reformation, Griffin claimed, espoused this position. The Bible revealed that the new heavens and new earth were part of Christ's "vast plan" to eliminate all instability, decay, and consequences of sin. Harbaugh, by contrast, contended that God was preparing heaven to be the saints' eternal home and would not renovate the earth. "The scriptures," he added, portrayed heaven as "God's peculiar dwelling place" where the saints, angels, and Christ constitute "one great happy society." "Can we believe that this insignificant earth" will be the site of this everlasting bliss? While many argued that the resurrection body would be recognizable, only a few attempted to explain its other features. MacDonald, for example, argued that the saints' glorified bodies would have four "peculiar properties": incorruptibility, glory, power, and spirituality.[51]

GETTING TO HEAVEN: TRUSTING IN THE RIGHTEOUSNESS OF CHRIST

Mid-nineteenth century Protestants agreed almost unanimously that in order to spend eternity with God, individuals must repent of their sins and accept Jesus Christ as their redeemer and master. They warned individuals not to trust in their own righteousness for salvation, insisted that their eternal destiny was fixed forever in this life, and urged believers to persevere in their faith. "The prevailing notion appears to be," James Kimball complained in 1857, "that even though men make [a] shipwreck of [their] life" and a few "trained swimmers" may have "some advantage in fording the Jordan of death," the rest will still get to heaven, as Paul and his companions got to shore at Melita, "some on boards, and some on broken pieces of the ship" and in heaven "God will then pour out his gifts on all, with lavish and indiscriminate munificence." This idea, Kimball maintained, "is at war with good sense, reason, and revelation."[52]

While proclaiming that salvation is by grace, Protestant leaders exhorted believers to strive to emulate Christ's earthly pattern, cultivate "virtues that can be perfected in heaven," and prepare their hearts, minds, and affections for spending eternity with God. Christ's life, precepts, and example, Kimball contended, indicate that heaven will be populated by "the kindly, the sympathetic, the pure in heart," and especially those who "lived for the happiness of others." Its residents will be "those who have chosen the service of Christ" over "all the pleasures, gaieties, and business of the world."[53]

It was important as well for Christians to demonstrate their faith by how they died. Throughout the nineteenth century, obituaries frequently included deathbed scenes. Lyman Beecher's first wife passionately described her anticipation of going to heaven to the family and friends who witnessed her last hours on earth. Numerous accounts featured dying believers' composure, faith in God, acceptance of death, and hope of heaven as they imparted wise counsel and encouragement to the loved ones surrounding them. Novels also underscored this point. For example, in her deathbed scene in Louisa May Alcott's *Little Women*, Beth displayed great assurance and joy about going to be with God. William B. Sprague, an influential Presbyterian pastor in Albany, New York, exhorted Christians to display "a triumphant and elevated faith" as they died to testify to "the all-sustaining power of the gospel."[54]

Meanwhile, a few, as the Puritans, Edwards, and the revivalists of the First and Second Great Awakening had done, used hellfire as an evangelistic technique. Griffin beseeched his hearers to flee from hell's "shame and everlasting contempt," from its "infinite torture and endless burnings," and from the "fury of devils." Remembering their lost "opportunities and privileges," he warned, increased the sorrow of hell's residents. In hell, people's selfishness, malice, and envy raged "without restraint." "Overwhelmed with guilt," "the damned" saw God as "their eternal enemy." Emphasizing that the Bible never even hinted that hell's fire is figurative, he charged people to feast on God's tender and boundless love to avoid making their eternal bed there.[55] However, compared with emphasis on hell during the Second Great Awakening, its infrequent mention in the middle decades of the nineteenth century is striking. Focus on making money, getting ahead, and the kinder, gentler aspects of heaven, including family reunions, coupled with debates over slavery, fears of disunion, and the calamity of the Civil War, combined to largely push hell from public discussion.

CONCLUSION

A plethora of monographs, articles, poems, sermons, novels, and manuals for mourners described the contours of heaven from 1830 to 1870. Christians continued to accentuate the beauty, splendor, holiness, and bliss of heaven, the phenomenal knowledge of its residents, and zealous worship of the Trinity. However, prompted by the Victorian quest to construct loving, decorous, stable homes on earth and the cult of domesticity, the principal portrait of heaven was as the ideal home where the perfect Father watched over His celestial children and robust relationships flourished among individuals who had loved each other on earth. Heavenly recognition, warm fellowship, and pleasurable interactions loomed large in the biblical analyses of William Branks, Henry Harbaugh, and other ministers and the imagined worlds of Elizabeth Stuart Phelps, Harriet Beecher Stowe, Susan Warner, Louisa May Alcott, and other novelists. More than their predecessors and successors, various mid-nineteenth century authors, prompted by their focus on heaven as the ultimate home, promised that all those dying in infancy would go there and grow in Christian virtues under the tutelage of the saints or angels. Like evangelicals in other periods, most Protestants living in the four decades surrounding 1850 exhorted Americans to trust in Christ's perfect obedience and atoning death in order to be reconciled with God and admitted to heaven.

In heaven "Dere's no sun to burn you...no hard trials...no whips a-crackin'...no stormy weather...no tribulation...no evil-doers....All is gladness in de Kingdom."
—THOMAS FENNER, *Religious Folk Songs of the Negro*

If dere ain't a heaven, what's colored folks got to look forward to? They can't git anywhere down here.
—ANNE BELL, in George Rawick, ed., *The American Slave*

It will be infinite gain to be translated to heaven.
—STONEWALL JACKSON on his deathbed

Although we may never meet here again, I will meet you in Heaven where partings are not known. Oh I would not exchange the peace & happiness that this "blessed hope" gives me, for the wealth of all the world.
—JAMES C. BATES, *A Texas Cavalry Officer's Civil War*

5

SLAVERY, THE CIVIL WAR,

AND HEAVEN

AMERICAN SLAVES, MORE than any other group, saw heaven through the prism of their earthly circumstances. As victims of oppression, dehumanization, and brutality, slaves rejected the portrait of heaven (and hell) painted by white Southerners and crafted their own. Masters and white ministers typically assigned blacks a subordinate place in heaven and warned them that their earthly obedience and work ethic would play a significant role in how and where they spent eternity. Slaves, by contrast, depicted a joyous, beautiful, bountiful heaven characterized by rest, feasting, and lively worship without any of the privations they had experienced on earth. While blacks generally accepted the evangelical Protestant position that admission to heaven depended on receiving Jesus as one's personal savior, they sometimes asserted that all those who had endured the hardships and horrors of slavery deserved to go heaven regardless of what they believed. Slaves expected heaven to supply the material comforts, relaxation, freedom, dignity, and opportunities denied to them on earth. Moreover, in heaven, either blacks and whites would be equal or blacks would be superior because of the affliction and misery they had suffered at the hands of whites. Many blacks insisted that because of the heinousness of their sin few, if any, slaveholders would be allowed to enter heaven.

Prior to the First Great Awakening, most slave owners opposed trying to convert slaves to Christianity for several reasons. They believed it might make them more dissatisfied, distracted, and defiant. It implied that slaves had souls and were spiritually equal to whites. It might encourage slaves to seek freedom. And there was widespread belief that it was immoral to own fellow Christians as slaves. However, by the mid-nineteenth century, growing numbers of Christians supported endeavors to evangelize slaves. Christian abolitionists stressed that their eternal destiny was at stake, and some argued that converted slaves would be more content, docile, and obedient. A combination of moral and prudential arguments, especially the contention that blacks did not have to be freed if they became fellow believers, eventually convinced most slaveholders to encourage (or at least permit) their slaves to accept Christianity. As a result of the efforts of the evangelists of the First Great Awakening, later missionaries, and some masters, after 1740, and especially after 1780, significant numbers of slaves adopted the religion of their oppressors.[1]

During the antebellum years, slaveholders fashioned a version of the gospel designed to produce better slaves. Although many masters genuinely cared about the spiritual welfare of their slaves, most of them were more eager to produce submissive, compliant, and productive slaves. Most masters recognized that "religion was a more subtle, more humane, and more effective means of control than the whip." To help motivate them to be obedient and compliant, masters and their minister allies described "the joys of heaven and the horrors of Milton's, if not the Bible's, hell."[2] Southern whites' selective form of Christianity emphasized that slaves could obtain rewards in the hereafter by their acquiescence, deference, and patience. White spokespersons, Norrece T. Jones, Jr., averred, "almost exclusively" employed texts that exhorted slaves to "pray, obey, and stay!" and constantly reminded them that their salvation depended upon their "faithfulness, honesty, and obedience." Such behavior, masters and white ministers promised, would please God, give slaves the greatest earthly happiness, and guarantee heavenly blessings. As Thomas Webber explained, most masters concluded "that blacks should be taught enough [about Christianity] to ensure their heavenly salvation" and to increase "the fruits of their labor on earth." Speaking for them, Episcopal rector Alexander Glennie declared that those who obediently followed Jesus Christ—and their masters—would "inherit everlasting life." Not surprisingly, the principal text white preachers used, according to Charles Colsock Jones, a Presbyterian evangelist, was the Apostle Paul's admonition, "servants, obey in all things your masters according to the flesh; not ... as menpleasers; but in singleness of heart, fearing God: And whatsoever ye do, do it heartily, as to the Lord, and not unto men." Jones and others developed catechisms to instruct slaves that accentuated "duty, humility, obedience and the afterworld."[3] By stressing the brevity of life, God's impending judgment of human deeds, and the prospects of eternal joy in heaven or perpetual suffering in hell, the Southern bourgeoisie strove to convince slaves to share their interests, submit to their demands, work more vigorously, and forgo efforts to escape.[4]

Numerous slaves testified that masters and white ministers frequently contrasted the splendors of heaven with the horrors of hell. Slaves whose lives were upright, they promised, would enjoy the astounding beauty and sumptuous material benefits of heaven—its golden streets, pearly gates, and ever flowing milk and honey.[5] Revivalists and pastors also used the threat of death and family separation and the promise of family reunions in heaven to induce conversions. All who accepted Jesus as their savior, Presbyterian evangelist Daniel Baker declared, could join the "Household of Faith" and would not have to suffer endless separation from their loved ones.[6] Few of them, however, stated or implied that blacks would be equal with whites in the afterlife because the concept of a multiracial heaven contradicted their contention that God sanctioned slavery. Instead, Southern whites usually depicted a segregated heaven where blacks would be second-class citizens. A South Carolina slave recalled hearing sermons portraying blacks' role in heaven as "working in God's kitchen."[7] Some members of the Southern power elite blatantly declared that blacks would still be inferior to whites in heaven. A white minister told slaves that "there will be a wall" with holes in it between them and their mistress and master that would permit blacks to see them as they walked by.[8] Whites also frequently stressed the torments of hell awaiting slaves "who cheated, lied, stole, ran away, plotted rebellion or engaged in other acts of sabotage." Former slave Henry Box Brown, for example, claimed that masters used religion "to keep the slaves in a docile and submissive frame of mind, by instilling into them the idea that if they do not obey their masters, they will infallibly go to hell." Ted Ownby pointed out that the heaven Confederate soldiers described in their letters rarely included slaves, possibly because they did not think anyone would work in the hereafter so slaves would not be needed. Moreover, by the end of the war, Southern whites, especially those who struggled to control their slaves while away fighting, saw blacks as "threats to the household rather than extended parts of it" and therefore did not picture them as part of the affectionate celestial family they envisioned.[9]

Assuming that slaves generally accepted their oppressors' version of Christianity, some scholars have concluded that religion functioned primarily as an opiate or an escape for slaves. In the early twentieth century, Southern historian U. B. Phillips maintained that slaves generally adopted the form of Christianity their masters and white pastors taught them, a view that "enjoyed a long life in American slave historiography." For example, Orlando Patterson asserted in 1982 that while "it would be simplistic to interpret the role of religion in the slave South solely" as a device the master class used to preserve its control, that was essentially how religion functioned. Masters promised their slaves pie in the sky in an effort to convince them to passively accept their exploitation and not to challenge white control or try to escape. Many other scholars, while acknowledging that whites emphasized heaven's rewards and hell's terrors to help make blacks docile and submissive, insist that blacks devised their own version of Christianity that better suited their needs as an oppressed group. As Lawrence Levine put it, "slaves simply refused" to accept "a religion defined and controlled by white intermediaries and interpreters."[10]

Largely rejecting whites' account of the gospel, blacks accentuated other aspects of the Christian message that enabled them to survive the dehumanization, heartache, and hardships of their bondage. While many of them looked forward to heavenly bliss and compensation and divine retribution for their suffering and adversity, the Bible's emphasis on liberation, justice, and equality also helped inspire, comfort, and give them hope on earth. Their life circumstances and the recognition that whites selectively employed scripture to exploit them prompted slaves to critically assess whites' teaching about salvation, morality, and the afterlife.[11] Resisting efforts to use Christianity to manipulate and control them, slaves devised their own interpretation of the gospel that enhanced their dignity, strength, and courage. Many slaves disavowed their masters' version of Christianity "as a compensatory and otherworldly religion" that encouraged them to accept their bondage as God's will, epitomized by the Negro spiritual that declared, "Take this world but give me Jesus."[12] While agreeing that voluminous evidence "illustrates the perennial preoccupation" of both slaves and free blacks "with the promise of everlasting life" during the antebellum years, Timothy Smith repudiated the claim that this hope made slaves content with their condition and stifled their efforts to change them. The Christianity they crafted helped them cope with the harshness of their everyday life, provided them the psychic space they needed to deal with debasement, and gave them hope of liberation, if not in this life, at least in the life to come.[13] "Narratives, tales, songs, sermons, aphorisms, prayers, and other slave sources" demonstrate that slaves rejected their masters' conception of a heaven where racism and subordination persisted and of a hell where disobedient, lazy slaves suffered for eternity. Convinced that this portrait of heaven could not be reconciled with a loving and just God who valued all human beings equally, they recast heaven and hell in light of "their own experiences, values, and traditions" as "an abused and exploited people."[14]

HEAVEN: THE NEGATION OF SLAVERY

Because slaves' focus on the hereafter was so strong and their conception of heaven was so vivid, some scholars have concluded that it led them to fixate on a peaceful, restful afterlife filled with material and spiritual delights and to ignore their earthly woes and grievances. "This interpretation," Lewis Baldwin claims, fails to recognize "the complex interrelationship between worldly and otherworldly concerns implicit in the spirituals, narratives, tales, and other slave sources." While many slaves greatly anticipated experiencing the "freedom, justice, and pleasure" denied to them in this world, some also strove to obtain independence, dignity, and greater fulfillment on earth. Sermons and songs taught them that God had liberated the Jews from Egyptian captivity and Daniel from the lion's den. As one spiritual asked,

> My Lord delivered Daniel,
> Why can't he deliver me?

The slaves' view of heaven as "the very negation of slavery," David Roediger asserts, forcefully indicted earthly injustices. Rather than offering compensatory hope, many spirituals that celebrated the glories of heaven also either openly or subtly condemned the maltreatment of blacks on earth.[15]

Slaves strongly identified with both Moses and Jesus, often merging them into a single this-worldly and otherworldly deliverer. While many blacks saw Jesus as their savior from sin, they also emphasized that, like them, Jesus had been mistreated. He understood their pain and deprivation, and He promised them ultimate freedom in heaven.[16] "God was a God of justice," they asserted, "the Lord of history, who intervened in human affairs to cast down the mighty and uplift the lowly. And a whole cloud of biblical witnesses supported their case: the children of Israel freed from Egyptian bondage, Shadrach, Meschach, and Abednego safe in the fiery furnace, and…the litany of prophets, apostles, and martyrs whose lineage they claimed as their own."[17] Slave preachers stressed that individuals must accept Jesus' atonement for their sin in order to obtain everlasting bliss and avoid unending hellfire, but they also urged their brothers and sisters to pray fervently and believe that God would "unshackle the chains which mortals had forged, linked, and anchored." One of them explained that he was forced to preach that if slaves obeyed their master, they would go to heaven. He knew that God had something better for them, but he could only tell about it slyly. "That I done lots. I tells 'em iffen they keeps prayin' the Lord will set 'em free." Slave songs about "Going over Jordan," "I Done Started for the Kingdom," and "Canaan's Happy Shore" often had a dual reference point: getting to heaven and attaining freedom. Both Frederick Douglass and Harriet Tubman testified that many slaves identified heaven with the North and Canada. Moreover, slaves rejected "a rigid separation of the sacred and the secular"; their songs such as "Didn't My Lord Deliver Daniel," "Joshua Fit de Battle ob Jericho," and "Go Down Moses" referred to deliverance in both this world and the next. Slave songs such as these, historian Eugene Genovese contended, often referred simultaneously to the afterlife, returning to Africa, going anywhere they could be free, and an undefined place where they could love one another without restraint or fear. Most slaves craved earthly freedom, but many of them, Thomas Webber argues, also longed for heaven because, given whites' commitment to preserving the peculiar institution, they could obtain freedom from physical, emotional, and sexual abuse and attain true fulfillment only in their celestial home.[18]

Slaves readily accepted the Christian idea of heaven in part because their West African heritage taught them both to believe that the spirits of the departed wandered through the world and to anticipate joyous reunions with their ancestors in the hereafter.[19] The belief that they would experience a blissful afterlife in Africa after they died, David Roediger contends, comforted many slaves. In his 1837 autobiography, fugitive slave Charles Ball insisted that all African-born slaves assumed that after death they would "return to their own country and rejoin their former companions." Even slaves who became devout Christians sometimes mixed African conceptions of the afterlife with biblical teaching. As did many Africans, numerous slaves claimed to have had "vision travels" in which they either went to heaven, where they saw God, and visited with deceased relatives, or to hell, where they felt intense heat. For example, one former slave told a WPA interviewer, "One time I...went rite up to heaven an' saw de angels playin' on golden strings stretched over all heaven. They wuz singin' 'Happy Home, Sweet Home, Where Never Comes de Night.'" Slave preacher John Jasper claimed in numerous sermons that he had had seen God's throne and conversed with "patriarchs, prophets, apostles, and martyrs."[20]

In many ways the slaves' conception of heaven was the opposite of their everyday life, stressing the absence of earthly ordeals, suffering, and toil. In the next world "Dere's no sun to burn you...no hard trials...no whips a-crackin'...no stormy weather...no tribulation...[and] no evil-doers....All is gladness in de Kingdom."[21] In heaven, the oppressed would "lay down dat heavy load." Slaves looked forward to living in "bright mansions above," to feasting with Jesus at His welcome table, singing and shouting, and never being forced to leave. No one would be hungry in this land of milk and honey. And there would be no sadness, sorrow, parting, quarreling, or backbiting. Slaves would be "Done wid driber's dribin'," "Done wid massa's scoldin.'" Another song proclaimed,

When I get to heaven, gwin be at ease.
Me and my God gonna do as we please,
Gonna chatter with the Father,
Argue with the Son.
Tell 'um 'bout the world I just come from.

In heaven it would always be Sunday, the one day of the week that most slaves did not have to work, when they could visit with each other, hold their own worship services, receive encouragement and consolation from slave preachers, commiserate, and feel a greater sense of worth.[22]

Slaves, like most whites in mid-nineteenth-century America, envisioned a celestial family reunion. Blacks rejoiced that heaven would have "no auction blocks, slave catchers, drivers, and traders to destroy family ties and relationships with friends." Their spirituals declared that departed loved ones were happy in heaven and expressed their confidence that they would someday rejoin them around God's throne. Their hope in heavenly reunion helped reduce the sorrow that relatives and friends felt when they were separated by sale. Before those who were sold left their plantations, slaves sang such lyrics as "When we all meet in Heaven, There is no parting there."[23]

God's justice was prominent in slaves' portrait of heaven. While unfairness and discrimination prevailed in this world, justice would triumph in the afterlife.[24] Many black sermons and songs celebrated God's "eternal order of justice and love" that "rebuked all unjust orders." Spirituals affirmed blacks' belief that God's righteousness would reign in the hereafter as individuals were rewarded or punished for their earthly deeds. Slaves conceived of heaven as a place of spiritual equality and just deserts. Speaking for most slaves, one man scoffed at the assumption of many whites that "when dey go to Heaven de colored folks would be dar to wait on 'em." A just God would not allow that. Occasionally a white minister had the courage to state that "God made no distinction between the souls of white masters and black slaves," which greatly pleased slaves.[25]

In the heaven slaves imagined, they would also experience the dignity and worth denied to them on earth. Their admission to heaven would validate their humanity. Although masters and many other whites defined them as uncivilized brutes or mere commodities, in God's eyes they were valuable, precious human beings for whom His Son died. They would spend eternity worshipping and serving God and Jesus in the glorious paradise God had constructed for them. Because of Christ's death and resurrection slaves could ultimately become what God created them to be—people of immense worth that no oppressor could take from them. In heaven no one would belittle them for their skin color or earthly servitude.[26] Their conviction that they would be equal with (and perhaps superior to) whites before God in heaven helped many blacks cope with the dehumanization and despair they suffered on earth and emboldened some of them to protest their mistreatment. Their religion, argues Paul Escott, enabled slaves to develop "a mental universe independent" of their masters'. It supplied "solace for their grief," a moral code that inspired their resistance, and "a spiritual vision that affirmed" their "humanity and dignity" as they dealt with "a suffocating burden of degradation." "Slavery's vast assault upon their humanity," Timothy Smith contends, compelled slaves "to discover in the religion of their white oppressors a faith whose depths few of the latter had ever suspected," empowering many of them "to reconcile suffering and hope, guilt and forgiveness, tyranny and spiritual freedom, self-hate and divine acceptance." Moreover, that faith gave some of them "the strength to throw off their bonds."[27]

Far from being a tranquilizer or a form of escape that led them to accept their plight passively, blacks' hope in heaven helped inspire many of them to live courageously on earth. Their passionate singing of such lines as "I've started to make heaven my home" and "marching up the heavenly road, I'm bound to fight till I die" testified to their belief that God's kingdom was breaking into the present order and advancing higher values and goals. Therefore, they could "git on board" the "gospel train" because nothing, not the cruelty of whites, the savagery of slavery, or even their own death, could prevent it from reaching its ultimate destination. Belief that God's kingdom was present in this world, James Cone has avowed, led many slaves to see themselves as God's agents who must reject, even revolt against, values and practices that thwarted the kingdom's progress. Their vision of heaven as "a place of eternal freedom and triumph" helped inspire Gabriel Prosser, Denmark Vesey, and Nat Turner to instigate slave insurrections and Frederick Douglass and Harriet Tubman to escape to the North, denounce slavery, and work with the Underground Railroad. Their hope in heaven emboldened many others to rebel, run away, or challenge injustice. As one spiritual asserted,

Before I'll be a slave,
I'll be buried in my grave
And go home to my Lord
And be free.[28]

White and black evangelicals perceived the process of salvation similarly during the antebellum years: God called sinners by name, showed them the glory of heaven and the torments of hell, and saved them through the shed blood of Jesus. However, blacks, especially slaves, experienced salvation differently from whites. Their conversion to Christianity typically enabled them to see themselves as valuable in God's eyes, "endure the harshness and uncertainties of their bondage," and gain the strength to do their daily work, cope with separation and sale, and remain sane. While many slaves believed that individuals must accept Christ as their savior to gain entrance to heaven, some concluded that "the whips and scorns of slavery" "were a sure ticket of admission to heaven when presented at the pearly gates."[29]

The West African belief that witches, thieves, and other wicked people were prohibited from paradise was similar to the Christian view. Accepting the biblical notion of judgment, most slaves thought the saved would go to heaven and sinners would be punished eternally in hell. While Second Great Awakening evangelists stressed the torments of hell that awaited the impenitent, most slaves rejected their owners' attempt to use hellfire and damnation to coerce them into obedience. Their spirituals and worship services rarely mentioned hell, and most "slaves had little interest in hell except as an eternal depository for slaveholders."[30] Some slaves referred to the South as hell. When they or their loved ones "were whipped, maimed, burned, lynched, or sold on the auction block," they experienced the horrors of hell.[31] As a slave poem explained:

> My body is weak and sickly
> But it done serve marse well
> I'se gonna land in heaven
> Already been through hell.[32]

Prior to 1800, many blacks envisioned a heaven where they dwelled harmoniously and equally with whites, but after that date this portrait was widely questioned and sometimes rejected. For example, Jupiter Hammon, a lifelong slave who lived on Long Island, declared in 1786, "Those of us who have had religious masters, and have been taught to read the Bible, and have been brought by their example and teaching to a sense of divine things, how happy shall we be to meet them in heaven, where we shall join them in praising God forever." In 1837, Charles Ball claimed, by contrast, that slaves did not picture a heaven where whites and blacks lived in "perfect equality and boundless affection." The few favored whites permitted to pass through the pearly gates would not enjoy "equal rank with those" God "raised from the depths of misery, in this world."[33]

"Slaves knew enough of the orthodox theology of the time," Frederick Douglass declared, "to consign all bad slaveholders to hell." Other slaves concluded that no masters would be permitted to enter heaven. Simply owning slaves, some argued, was sufficient to damn "even the most benevolent master's soul." Slave owners were culpable, Henry Garnet asserted, because they locked "heaven's door against Negroes" by making "it impossible for them to obey the Ten Commandments, to love God supremely, to love their neighbors as themselves, to keep the sabbath day holy, to search the Scriptures, or to bring up their children in respect for God's laws." In one slave tale, Mac informed his fellow slaves of their master's impending doom:

"there's only two places to go after you die…Heaven or Hell. And since Boss can't go to Heaven, there's no other place for him to go but to Hell."[34] Still other blacks believed that no one who supported slavery in any way would be allowed into heaven. They reasoned that because "slavery was a sin, those who practiced, sanctioned, or perpetuated it were sinners" and, therefore, were not fit to spend eternity with God. A few slaves even asserted that no white people would be admitted to paradise.[35]

Heaven could not truly be heaven for the ex-slave, Charles Ball argued, unless he was "avenged of his enemies." God would not permit those who tore husbands and wives apart, took children from their parents, profited from the coerced labor of others, raped teenage girls and slave wives, and whipped people for petty offenses to reside in heaven with oppressed blacks who had toiled so hard to get there. God would consign their oppressors to hell, where they would endure the same exploitation and mistreatment they had inflicted on slaves. Many blacks derived consolation by thinking about the delights they would enjoy in heaven and the torments their masters would suffer in hell. "A favorite or kind master or mistress" might occasionally "be admitted into heaven," Ball contended, as a favor to or through the intercession of a slave, rather "than as a matter of strict justice to the whites." Slaves were ready to receive eternal rest "on account of their present sufferings," but they were not willing to "admit the master and mistress to an equal participation in their enjoyments—this would only be partial justice and half way retribution."[36] When they saw whites riding in fancy carriages, slaves frequently commented to each other: "That is all the heaven you will ever get." Statements such as these strongly challenge Eugene Genovese's claim that most slaves had little interest in gaining revenge for the way they were treated and expected to be reconciled with whites in heaven.[37]

Many blacks believed that wicked slaves—those who were flagrantly profane, who betrayed, abused, cheated, murdered, or maltreated fellow slaves, or who cooperated with whites to preserve slavery—would join their masters and mistresses in hell. This conviction demonstrates "the tremendous importance which the slaves attached to the need for community among the oppressed."[38]

THE CIVIL WAR, DEATH, AND HEAVEN

The Civil War was arguably the most religious war in world history. Christian beliefs played a major role in inspiring both Yankees and Confederates to engage in the long, bloody, grueling fratricide. No other war in history included such extensive efforts to win combatants to Christ or produced so many converts. Moreover, their conviction that a glorious heavenly life awaited those who died in the conflict gave many the courage and perseverance to fight in a war with very high casualty rates. The war's massive death toll prompted an outpouring of talk about the afterlife.[39] Like other Americans of the time, those who fought in the Civil War and their family members who remained at home generally visualized heaven primarily as a place where those separated by death would be reconstituted as loving families. Their picture of paradise was a major source of comfort and consolation for those who lost loved ones in the war.[40]

Pastors, professors, journalists, combatants, and their wives and parents offered many religious explanations for the war and for the spiritual benefits it produced. Many on both sides zealously claimed that God supported them. Significantly outnumbered and outsupplied, and burdened with providing a moral defense of slavery, Southerners especially emphasized their Christian heritage and convictions. They insisted that their new nation was more godly than the North and used the Bible to justify slavery. Until the final days of the war, they fervently asserted that their cause was God's cause; they fought to defend their way of life against an unwarranted Northern invasion. Innumerable Southerners considered Christianity to be the primary basis of their personal and their nation's identity, and their faith played a crucial role in maintaining morale during the protracted conflict.[41]

Most Northerners also claimed to be Christians and insisted that they fought to achieve biblical principles of justice and freedom. Like Jefferson Davis, Abraham Lincoln called for several national days of prayer and fasting, and the words "In God We Trust" were first stamped on U.S. coins during the war. The war, some rejoiced, was prompting many Northerners to repudiate materialism, practice self-denial, and deepen their faith.[42] Numerous ministers argued that the conflict was rejuvenating and purifying America to enable it to fulfill its God-ordained mission of spreading religious and political liberty to the world. As Julia Ward Howe's 1864 "Battle Hymn of the Republic" asserted, many Northerners considered Union soldiers to be locked in an "eschatological conflict with the forces of evil." Leading Northern pastors, including Methodist Gilbert Haven, Unitarian Cyrus Bartol, and Congregationalist Horace Bushnell, compared the death of Union troops with Christ's act of sacrifice on the cross. Their martyrdom helped atone for America's sin of slavery, while the war motivated Americans to reform and cleanse their nation.[43]

Whether they wore blue or gray, slain soldiers were seen in their respective regions as agents of redemption who gave their lives for higher purposes: preserving the Union, ending slavery, and crushing a rebellion or achieving independence and defending their homeland, families, and treasured values. Northerners and Southerners alike saw soldiers' sacrifice as serving God and helping bring His kingdom on earth.[44] Many soldiers believed that strong faith and religious devoutness contributed significantly to victory in battle. Although God intended their respective side to win the war, many argued, their sin might prevent that from happening.[45] Many in both the North and South also assumed that committed Christian soldiers would fight more courageously and diligently and accept the hardships of war more willingly.[46]

The Civil War was the United States' most tragic and psychically devastating war. As Drew Gilpin Faust has pointed out, the number of soldiers who perished between 1861 and 1865 "is approximately equal to American fatalities in the Revolution, the War of 1812, the Mexican War, the Spanish American War, World War I, World War II, and the Korean War combined." Compared with the size of the nation's population, the rate of death during the Civil War was seven times that of World War II. Moreover, those who died in this internecine conflict defied widespread cultural beliefs "about who should die, when and where, and under what circumstances." The Civil War generation was much more accustomed to death than contemporary Americans are; the infant mortality rate was substantially higher, and such antebellum epidemics as the 1853 Yellow Fever outbreak in New Orleans rivaled the casualty rates of the war's major engagements. Nevertheless, the extent of the war's victims—623,026 deaths and 1,094,453 casualties—was unprecedented. Almost every family suffered loss, deeply affecting the way Americans perceived both their earthly lives and the hereafter. The war's carnage challenged the "fundamental assumptions about life's value and meaning" as well as the prevailing idea "of how life should end."[47]

In mid-nineteenth-century America, dying was considered an art and most people strove to achieve a "Good Death" by following the principles laid out in sermons, tracts, health books, poems, and stories. In the ideal scenario, an elderly person departed this world while at home surrounded by family and friends after uttering last words that testified to his faith in Christ and provided spiritual instruction for those present. It was widely assumed that how an individual died confirmed the way she had lived and predicted her eternal destiny. Consequently, a person's loved ones typically scrutinized and interpreted the dying individual's faith and worthiness for salvation as demonstrated during his last hours. The Civil War violated this model because thousands of young men died either instantly, unattended, or in a delirious state. They therefore could not reveal their last thoughts and provide closure for their loved ones or grounds for hope of their salvation. As a result, whenever they could, fellow soldiers, nurses, physicians, and chaplains strove to furnish "the dying man and his family with as many of the elements of the conventional Good Death as possible" and to help the dying and "their loved ones...believe they had died well." Deceased soldiers' closest companions often wrote letters to family members providing, if possible, a description of their comrades' last moments to assure kin that they had died in accordance with the conventional model. Such news supplied the grieving with "the ultimate solace"—the promise that a loved one had gone to heaven. Witnesses especially reported professions of faith by dying soldiers because this most reassured family members that God would admit them to heaven. These condolence letters served as models for obituaries, which often quoted the letters.[48] Funeral sermons and biographies of slain soldiers, published in both the North and South, reinforced the concept of the Good Death by detailing the righteous lives, Christian conviction, and holy deaths of their subjects. These sources reveal Americans' preoccupation with preserving "the transcendent symbolic and substantive importance of life's last moments" even in the midst of the carnage and chaos of the Civil War and the widespread desire to assure loved ones that the quality of their lives and manner of their deaths demonstrated that these soldiers deserved eternal life.[49]

Mark Schantz argues that antebellum Americans' view of death and the afterlife made it easier for soldiers "to kill and be killed" and for their loved ones to emotionally accept their deaths. Influenced primarily by evangelical Protestantism, Romanticism, and the culture of ancient Greece, most soldiers strove to meet "death with a spirit of calm resignation," aware that their society prized heroic action and confident that eternal rewards awaited them. Their views of the hereafter, concern about how they would be remembered, deathbed behavior, and the antebellum image of death combined to create a cultural climate that made the slaughter of the Civil War possible. Large numbers of Americans were able to "face death with resignation and even joy" because they possessed "a comforting and compelling vision of eternal life." For most of them, heaven was not an ethereal, vague region, but rather "a material place" where individuals "would be perfected and the relations of family and friendship restored."[50] Their confidence that they would spend eternity with God and loved ones in a magnificent abode without any trials or suffering enabled many soldiers to fight fearlessly and furiously, contributing to the war's astounding death tolls.

Nothing helped Americans deal with the tragedy and anguish of the Civil War, Schantz argues, more than their picture of "an eternal world of bliss and perfection." "They held no banner higher than the one that proclaimed that they would all live again, gloriously, in eternity." Diaries, letters, war songs and poems, and newspaper articles all testify that the promise of heaven supplied Americans whose lives were torn apart by the war with great hope, encouragement, and consolation. Interest in the afterlife was not confined to theologians, ministers, and philosophers, but was widespread among Americans.[51]

Numerous factors helped motivate and sustain Civil War combatants: their sense of duty; "loyalty to comrades, community, or cause"; "personal pride and courage"; "fear of the consequences of failure"; "ideals of manhood and honor," desire for vengeance, confidence in their leaders and fellow soldiers; and support from those at home. For many soldiers, Christian faith and the conviction that they would obtain eternal life reinforced these other incentives for fighting. Numerous ministers and military officers insisted that Christian soldiers were more courageous and conscientious because they did not fear death.[52] Many Americans assumed that the stronger a soldier's faith and godliness, the braver he would be on the battlefield and the more God would protect him. The demeanor of three Confederate military leaders—Robert E. Lee, Stonewall Jackson, and J. E. B. Stuart—who displayed amazing composure under fire, convinced many Southerners that God gave fortitude to those with great faith.[53] Their faith also helped many soldiers cope with the loss of scores of comrades and the continual threat of their own demise. Those who were struck down had God's guarantee of eternal life. Numerous soldiers testified in letters and diaries that their assurance of personal salvation strengthened their resolve to fight.[54]

Hundreds of letters and accounts of the war show how soldiers' belief in the afterlife inspired their courage on the battlefield. In *Christ in the Camp or Religion in the Confederate Army*, J. William Jones, who served as a chaplain in the Army of Northern Virginia, provides dozens of illustrations of fatally wounded soldiers who died peaceably because of the bliss and fellowship with friends they expected to experience in heaven. Numerous parents assured their sons that if they fell in battle, God would receive them, "cleansed in the blood of Jesus, into His kingdom."[55] Jones's account of the death of a member of the Thirteenth Virginia Infantry features the stock elements of the Good Death: the "youthful hero" was mortally injured during one of his regiment's "most splendid charges." Accepting "death with calm resignation," he told "the weeping loved ones" surrounding him, "I trust in Jesus and am not afraid to die." After dying triumphantly, he departed to "that brighter, better home above, where 'war's rude alarm' never disturb[s], and loved ones never part."[56] Countless dying Confederate and Union soldiers testified that they would spend eternity with God and their family and friends in a place that had no sorrow, desolation, or death.[57] Speaking for them, Major Augustus M. Gordon, after being wounded at Chancellorsville, averred, "I am not afraid to die, for I know I am going to be with Jesus." Thousands of Christian soldiers, a Southerner proclaimed, had "gladly yielded up their lives, cheered and sustained by the glorious hope of a better life in heaven." A member of the 47th Illinois regiment claimed that whenever he stood beside an open grave, he saw Jesus in His "resplendent beauty and glory" on the other side welcoming his fallen comrade home. A Union chaplain wrote that both the Catholics and Protestants in his regiment believed they would go to heaven if they died in combat.[58]

Perhaps no one illustrated the prevailing perception of death and the assurance of heavenly delights better than Stonewall Jackson. No account of any other

Confederate or Union soldier's death was more widely circulated. After being fatally injured at Chancellorsville in May 1863, Jackson declared that concentrating on "God and heavenly things" brought him "great comfort and peace." Informed that his recovery was very unlikely, he responded that "it will be infinite gain to be translated to heaven." As Jackson's funeral train traveled toward Lynchburg, Virginia, most mourners were assuaged by their conviction that the general was already enjoying his heavenly reward. Jones asserted that Jackson "had won the victory" and had gone "to wear the 'crown of rejoicing.'" Jackson had been promoted, a eulogist proclaimed, "from the high places of his earthly fame, to the infinitely higher places of heavenly glory."[59]

Ministers in both the North and South insisted that God sent the "thick and trying" afflictions of the war to make people dissatisfied with this world and to induce them to "seek that bright, saintly home" that lay "far beyond the...panics, convulsions and woes of this present life." God intended "every pain, disease, loss, cross, and bereavement...to loosen the bonds" that fastened people to earth and motivate them to "seek the things...above." Earthly ordeals would make heaven "more delightful." The New Jerusalem would be "a radiant, ever-blooming, all-satiating contrast" to the "sorrows, trials, and dying scenes of earth."[60] Large numbers of Confederate and Union soldiers expressed their longing for and expectation of going to heaven, and chaplains regularly reassured grieving family members that their slain sons were in heaven.[61] Chaplains and soldiers frequently informed parents that their sons had "died in hope of a blissful immortality."[62]

The heaven Americans envisioned during the Civil War clearly displays their most pressing concerns. Like others in the decades immediately before and after the conflict, they pictured heaven as a happy home of affectionate reunions.[63] As Drew Gilpin Faust argues, Victorian Americans, both Christians and Jews, expected their cherished home life and family ties to continue in heaven. Reid Mitchell contends that many Union soldiers imagined a heaven that was "very much like the idealized Victorian home" where friends and family could resume their relationships. Similarly, many Southerners, Ted Ownby maintains, saw heaven as "a happy place full of enjoyable human contacts." Tender, adoring families lived blissfully in a realm that had no "work, pain, disciplining patriarchs, or anything threatening or sinful." This view, Ownby points out, differed sharply from "everyday Southern home life and gender relations." While the Northern bourgeoisie exalted "domestic privacy, affection, motherly sentiment, and childish innocence," the typical antebellum Southern farm family revolved around hard work, paternalism, and discipline rather than warmth and affection. Power relations and concerns about honor, two very important aspects of Southern antebellum society, were absent in Confederate portraits of heaven. Ownby concludes that Confederate soldiers envisioned a heaven so similar to their

Yankee counterparts', and so at odds with the "everyday lives and ideals common in the antebellum South," to help reassure "themselves and their family members about the ultimate value of their relationships." This romanticized picture of the afterlife also helped Confederates deal with trying to practice "patriarchy in absentia." Their absence from home, their wives' greater assertiveness in their households, and their failure to win the war made maintaining their traditional male roles very difficult. Confederate soldiers imagined the hereafter as a compassionate and caring domicile, Ownby claims, to reduce the tensions involved in trying to simultaneously rule and love in their earthly households.[64]

Ministers, friends, spouses, and popular authors assured soldiers that they would live after death and comforted their loved ones by promising them that even if soldiers' whereabouts were unknown, they would not be lost forever. Belief that they would spend eternity with their kin was a major source of solace.[65] "My Dear Parents," a Confederate stationed in Corinth, Mississippi, wrote, if we "never meet on earth again...I hope that we will meet again in that world that is all pleasure, peace and joy." In many of his letters to his wife, Confederate William Nugent pictured their family residing happily in the "'Mansion not made with hands' beyond the surging billows of life's troubled sea."[66] Many wives exhorted their soldier husbands to become Christians so that they could spend eternity together. After his conversion in 1863, William Gale promised his wife that he would "lead a new life" so that they could be together "through all time." "The idea that when we go to our final rest you will go to everlasting life and bliss and I to everlasting damnation agonizes me," William Dorsey Pender wrote to his wife. Seeking to console his parents after his brother died, David Blair of Ohio wrote, "We have reason to hope that Morrow is now in a better mansion than a military hospital....I hope & pray," he added, "that we may meet [someday] where wars are not practiced and where there are pleasures evermore." Future president William McKinley hoped that his family and friends would be consoled by the "thought that if we never meet again upon earth, we will meet around God's throne in Heaven." After his father's death in 1863, Union chaplain Joseph Hopkins Twichell promised his mother that he was walking "golden streets," seeing Jesus "face to face."[67]

Augusta Jane Evans's 1864 novel, *Macaria; or, Altars of Sacrifice* accentuates the allure of heaven more than any other book written during the conflict. "Probably the single most popular piece of literature in the Confederacy," her novel, like Harriet Beecher Stowe's *Uncle Tom's Cabin* (1852), provides a "comforting prospect of heaven." Its heroine Irene exhorts her beloved Russell to live a righteous life so that if he is killed in combat, they will spend eternity together in heaven. He promises to so live that they will enjoy "reunion beyond the grave." As the book ends, Russell lies dying in a field hospital, but he has kept his vow to live as a faithful Christian. Irene declares that she can endure earthly loneliness, knowing that they will "soon meet in Heaven."[68]

Not surprisingly, the portrait of heaven Americans painted during the conflict stressed the absence of war's woes. Letters, diaries, sermons, and poems often described heaven as a place where death, suffering, and separation from loved ones did not exist.[69] In this "happy world" "sorrow & pain is not known."[70] A soldier from Indiana rejoiced that the afterlife involved no more trials, temptations, or dangers. Alfred Fielder of the 12th Tennessee Regiment Infantry declared that heaven entailed "no sickness, no pain, no death," and no separation of spouses. Thomas Hampton imagined heaven as a refuge "where wars & rumors of wars are no more." After months of living in tents, many dying soldiers looked forward to residing in "bright mansions" in "that beautiful city."[71] Many soldiers and their wives also pictured paradise as a place of perpetual rest from labor. Knowing that "dear friends are now enjoying the rest prepared for the righteous beyond the grave," J. Miles Pickens asserted, provided great consolation.[72]

Compared with earlier eras, Christians said little during the Civil War about worshipping the Trinity after death. Confederate Joshua Callaway anticipated "cast[ing] our crowns at the feet of Jesus and spend[ing] eternity in singing his praises." Recognition that they would soon "surround the throne of God in heaven," "clothed in the pure robe of Christ's righteousness," forever singing "songs of praise to the Lamb," wrote Captain Hugh A. White, should make Christians ecstatic.[73] Such statements about communing with God and Jesus in the hereafter, however, are relatively rare.

REVIVALS, REDEMPTION, AND DEATH IN A RIGHTEOUS CAUSE

While Americans speculated considerably about the nature of heaven during the Civil War, most of them were more concerned with getting there than with its specific features. Dozens of revivals occurred among Northern and Southern troops. The American Bible Society, the United States Christian Commission, the YMCA, and various denominations distributed millions of hymnbooks, New Testaments, scriptural selections, and evangelistic tracts. And thousands of chaplains, pastors, and soldiers asserted that individuals must accept Jesus Christ as their savior to gain admission to heaven. Most soldiers "believed that there was a heaven to gain and a hell to shun." They accepted the doctrine that "those who died in Christ" would have heavenly bliss as readily as they did the concept of divine providence.[74] These convictions prompted countless soldiers, when on the verge of battle, to solicit God's favor or to prepare to meet Him by reading the Bible intensely, praying fervently, and promising to forsake drinking, gambling, cursing, and whoring.[75] However, a significant number of officers, enlisted soldiers, civilians, and even some clergy suggested or explicitly stated that faithful service in the war would by itself ensure entry into paradise.

An estimated 150,000 Southern soldiers (about 10 percent of all who served) were converted during the war, mainly through revival services. Sermons, testimonies of converted soldiers, prayer meetings, Sunday schools, and the distribution of tracts all contributed to this result.[76] Northern regiments also experienced revivals, but Union troops (between 100,000 and 200,000 soldiers) who were converted constituted a smaller percentage of combatants. Three factors help account for this difference. First, many more Southern soldiers had an evangelical Protestant background that strongly emphasized conversion. Second, Southerners were under greater stress because the smaller number of available men and shortages of materiel forced them to serve longer tours of duty with fewer furloughs. Finally, Southern soldiers were younger on average (many were teenagers), which made them more receptive to conversion.[77] Revivals among Southern troops occurred most often after battles with high death tolls, especially losses, and a much higher percentage of common soldiers than officers professed faith in Christ. Many Confederate and Union officers, however, supported revival services, reasoning that Christian soldiers would obey orders more faithfully, exhibit greater discipline, and fight more effectively if they felt called by God to serve and had less fear of death. In addition, having more religiously devout soldiers, officers thought, would help ensure that the "God of Battles" continued to favor their respective sides. Both armies created Christian associations in their brigades and regiments that operated Bible classes, set up camp libraries to dispense religious literature, and helped soldiers face the fear of "dying abandoned and alone" that haunted many of them.[78] Adding in those who entered the army as Christians, a sizable percentage, perhaps half of the members of both armies, professed to be Christians. The revivals, Bible studies, and worship services helped many soldiers cope with the hardships and dangers of the war.[79] Strikingly, although most Southern civilians shared Confederate soldiers' perception that their armed conflict with Northerners was a holy war and also heard many evangelistic sermons, their rate of conversion was not nearly as great as that of military personnel, suggesting that the prospect of dying played a significant role.[80]

In their sermons and conversations with soldiers, chaplains stressed the fundamental tenets of Christianity and exhorted men to accept Christ as their savior, grow in their faith, and forsake the evils of camp life—drinking, gambling, swearing, and relations with prostitutes.[81] Although they stressed that becoming a Christian provided soldiers with worldly benefits—fellowship and community with other believers, "victory over temptation," and tranquility in the midst of the uncertainties of war—most chaplains, other ministers, and the religious newspapers that were disseminated widely among the troops focused primarily on providing "a simple, straightforward, evangelistic" message. Numerous sermons, diaries, and letters, Steven Woodworth maintains, "placed enormous emphasis on the need for a genuinely and profoundly felt religion of the heart." Many proclaimed that by suffering for guilty human beings, "the innocent Son of God" purchased salvation and a place in heaven for those who repented of their sins and trusted Him as their savior. Most sermons at revival meetings were "simple, direct" pleas for "personal conversion . . . through God's saving grace and the atonement of Christ."[82] Preachers often used such texts as "'Except ye repent ye shall all likewise perish,' 'What must I do to be saved?' and 'The wages of sin is death, but the gift of God is eternal life through Jesus Christ our Lord.'"[83] After their sermons, clergymen usually invited soldiers who wanted to declare their faith in Christ to come to the front to pray.[84] Those who trusted Christ as their savior, ministers promised, would go to heaven after they died. Funeral sermons for both soldiers and civilians frequently accentuated biblical passages that taught people must be washed in Christ's blood to gain admittance to His eternal kingdom.[85]

The most popular theme of evangelistic sermons, Kurt Berends explains, was that death could occur at any moment, a point many tracts and articles in religious newspapers reinforced. The war's staggering death toll made this topic a natural one. Sermons such as "Time Is Short" told the sad stories of sinners who failed to repent. Rejecting the Reformed conviction that God took the initiative in saving souls, many sermons, letters to soldiers, and conversion accounts urged people to choose God immediately.[86] Seeing their regiments shrink in size "from hundreds to handfuls" vividly reminded soldiers that their chance of surviving future gory battles was slim and motivated many of them to respond to the gospel message in order to avoid eternal damnation.[87] Sermons and tracts warned "death stares you in the face. The next battle may be your last." Everyone, declared a Southern newspaper, would ultimately serve either in God's victorious heavenly army or Satan's vast division that would be "defeated, accursed and punished forever." Other tracts exhorted soldiers to renounce their sins and embrace Jesus so they could live with God forever.[88] Numerous newspaper articles warned soldiers that they would spend eternity in hell if they did not repent.[89] Meanwhile, chaplains, Christian nurses, and devout soldiers tried to persuade mortally wounded combatants to repent of their sins and accept Christ as their savior.[90]

For many civilians and soldiers, admission to heaven depended exclusively on accepting God's gracious invitation and trusting in Christ's redeeming work. "If I am ever permitted to join the hosts of the redeemed in heaven," declared Alice Chapin, "it will be all of Grace." Only "a living faith" in Jesus, David Lough maintained, would enable people to reach "the blissful shores of a never ending eternity." In the words of one Confederate, "I put my trust in the merits of a crucified Redeemer, and depend on him alone for salvation."[91] Soldiers' favorite hymns, including "Rock of Ages," "There Is a Fountain Filled with Blood, Drawn from Emmanuel's Veins," and "Jesus, Lover of My Soul," also testified to their belief that Christ's death atoned for their sin.[92]

Explicitly or implicitly rejecting this position, numerous military personnel and civilian commentators promised soldiers that anyone who died in battle would be admitted to heaven. Some ministers and many Union soldiers argued that those who died "with a clear conscience" defending their nation's righteous cause would gain "entrance into the heavenly kingdom." Before his men charged a Confederate position at Spotsylvania Courthouse in May 1864, Emory Upton told them, "Some of us have got to die, but remember you are going to heaven." Numerous soldiers thought that they could earn God's favor by their meritorious actions or expected to find forgiveness during the final hours of life as had the thief crucified beside Christ.[93] For example, George Allen, who served with the Fourth Rhode Island Volunteers, insisted that the "noble and heroic sacrifice" of one of his fallen comrades had "gained for him a crown of glory in that better land beyond the skies." Charles B. Haydon, a Michigan attorney who fought in battles from Bull Run to Knoxville, claimed that God would reward any "soldier who does his best in his country's cause."[94] As previously noted, many soldiers considered the death of their comrades to be a form of martyrdom.[95] Writers of condolence letters often emphasized that their faithful performance of duties, patriotism, and courage showed that deceased soldiers deserved to go to heaven.[96]

Sean A. Scott concludes that Northern civilians were more likely than soldiers to claim that virtuous living was the basis for admission to heaven. Many letters, he notes, imply that "human endeavor, rather than the imputed righteousness of Christ" provided the grounds for people gaining residence in heaven. Numerous Northern civilians, Scott contends, believed that soldiers, by dying in combat, earned a "ticket to heaven and would receive special recognition there." Helen Sharp admonished her husband John, serving in the Second Iowa, to "live right so that if you do fall[,] you will fall Zionward." A Minnesota mother assured her son that if he died on the battlefield, he could exchange his soldier's "garb for a crown of glory at Christ[']s right hand."[97] Scott admits, however, that some of those who emphasized obeying God's commands and upright living, "if asked to clarify their opinion, might have disavowed the idea that moralism alone could provide access to heaven." Given the evangelical Protestant tenor of the era, many Americans considered righteous behavior to be a supplement to or evidence of salvation, rather than its source.[98]

Reflecting this perspective, many tracts, chaplain's sermons, and funeral sermons reminded soldiers and civilians that they were sinners who were unfit to stand before a holy God. Because death in battle was likely, carelessness about "eternal consequences" was "madness."[99] Directly repudiating the claim that those who died to accomplish a righteous end earned salvation, a Southern tract declared that soldiers could "storm cities, win battles," achieve the independence of their "beloved country, and gain imperishable renown," but without faith in Christ, they would not enter heaven. Unlike Muhammad, Jesus did not "promise eternal life" to those who fell defending their county.[100]

In the years after 1875, ministers and lay Christians would focus much less on hell than had the Puritans and First and Second Great Awakening revivalists. However, this trend was already evident during the Civil War. Some chaplains, pastors, and tracts such as the *Sufferings of the Lost* described in excruciating detail the agony the impenitent would endure in hell.[101] Soldiers, however, discussed the horrors of hell much less than the attractions of heaven. Most of them who mentioned hell did so obliquely and indirectly. Union sergeant Alexander Coe wrote that he had heard a minister who "preached the principle of hell fire and damnation in the true Methodist style," but such statements were rare.[102] Many officers and common soldiers even denounced sermons that threatened eternal damnation. A Wisconsin colonel ordered that no one preach the doctrine of hellfire to his regiment because "every one of my boys who fall fighting in this great battle of liberty is going to Heaven."[103] Echoing an argument that many slaves used, a member of the Army of Northern Virginia declared in 1864 that Confederates "had such a hell of a time in this country that the good Lord would not" damn them "in the next."[104] Northern civilians dealt with this "grisly topic with utmost delicacy." Most of them, especially staunch Unionists, consigned only traitors (Northern rebels) to hell.[105]

CONCLUSION

During the crucible of the Civil War, focus on heaven was extensive. The conflict's shocking death count and the fear of death it engendered prompted millions of Americans to think about the nature of heaven and the basis for getting there. However, other wars, including ones with equally furious fighting and gruesome consequences, have rarely triggered such vast soul-searching and reflection on the afterlife. Several factors played a prominent role in the tremendous interest in salvation and the hereafter during the Civil War years: the nation's evangelical Protestant ethos; the strenuous efforts of chaplains, pastors, denominations, and Christian organizations to minister to the spiritual needs of both soldiers and civilians; cultural currents that promoted a romantic, idealized, sentimental perspective of life; and nagging problems pertaining to authority relationships that were exacerbated by more than three million men being away from their homes and jobs. In this context, the thousands of sermons, tracts, articles in religious publications, and novels discussing the features of the afterlife and the proper passage to it evoked widespread reflection about heaven and the grounds for admission. The massive separation and loss the Civil War brought led heaven to be depicted primarily as a place of family reunion. The struggle of blacks to endure antebellum Southern slavery and of all Americans to cope with the war's carnage strongly shaped their portraits of heaven and understanding of its entrance requirements.

One of the greatest riches of heaven will be the
possession of those desires of the soul, which are so
often sought after down here, but are never
completely found—such as infinite knowledge,
perfect peace, and satisfying love.
—DWIGHT L. MOODY, *Heaven*

6

HEAVEN IN THE GILDED AGE

Dwight L. Moody and the

Princes of the Pulpit

There is a real heaven which is better than we can
imagine—which is larger, noble, brighter, more
blessed in every part.
—HENRY WARD BEECHER, *"The Heavenly State"*
and "Future Punishment"

The soul in heaven must sing not only for joy at
Christ's victory and at its own graduation from
struggle, but also for the continual delight of its
Savior's realized presence, its perfect communion with
Christ.... It sees Jesus entirely, and loves Him entirely,
and is perfectly satisfied to rest in His affection.
—PHILLIPS BROOKS, *The New Song in Heaven*

IN THE YEARS following the Civil War, Americans worked to rebuild their nation
and restore normality to their everyday lives. Industrialization significantly changed
the face and nature of American society as Andrew Carnegie, John D. Rockefeller,
Jay Gould, and their fellow entrepreneurs established empires in steel, oil, railroads,
and other enterprises. Americans strove to move beyond the tragedy and dislocation
of the war, adjust to an increasingly industrial and urban society, and absorb and
assimilate new waves of immigrants. This influx of immigrants, most of whom were
Catholics, Jews, or unchurched individuals from Eastern Europe, inspired an upsurge
of nativism and demands to restrict immigration and devise more stringent natural-
ization laws. New developments in geology and biology transformed the way most
educated Americans saw the earth's origins, while the new social sciences helped
reshape their understanding of human nature, government, and society. Larger numbers of students attended colleges and universities, and these institutions played a
more important role in American life. In the face of immense prejudice and
discrimination, African Americans labored diligently to supply their daily needs and
create a better life. Political corruption, most notoriously New York City's Tammany
Hall and the scandals of the Ulysses S. Grant administration, rocked the nation.
Never before, wrote Robert Wiebe, "had so many citizens held their government in

such low regard." Many Americans lamented that politicians governed to advance their own private interests rather than to promote the common good.[1]

Taking its name from Mark Twain and Dudley Warner's satirical 1873 novel, which lampooned the era's speculators, self-promoters, and business tycoons, the Gilded Age featured the frantic pursuit of fortune and ostentatious lifestyles, epitomized by George W. Vanderbilt's 295-room private home, Biltmore, in Asheville, North Carolina, and 50-room homes at Newport, Rhode Island, where some of the super rich spent their summers.[2] Excessive opulence, conspicuous consumption, and extravagant displays were common among the affluent. In the nation's largest cities, the rich attended the opera and theater and hosted lavish parties while the poor worked ten to fifteen hours a day for subsistence wages and resided in overcrowded, dirty, vermin-infested, dilapidated tenements. Cities teemed with filth, crime, and prostitution. Although the Gilded Age was characterized by substantial economic growth, a vastly enlarged industrial sector, and rising per capita income, numerous crises wracked the era. The speed, scale, and thoroughness of American industrialization from 1870 to 1895, as it rapidly surpassed England and Germany to become the world's leading industrial nation, was unprecedented. Worldwide depressions in both the 1870s and 1890s brought "chronic overproduction and dramatically falling prices" to all industrial nations as they coped with "constant market uncertainties" and stiff business competition at home and abroad. Credit tightened for farmers, while workers endured "wage cuts, extended layoffs and irregular employment." Many violent strikes and labor riots, most notably an 1877 railroad stoppage in numerous cities, the Haymarket Square bombing in Chicago in 1886, the 1893 strike at Carnegie's Homestead Works, and the walkout of 4,000 workers at the Pullman Place Car Company near Chicago in 1894, shocked and scared millions of Americans.[3] The Grange movement, the Knights of Labor, farmers' alliances, Edward Bellamy's Nationalist Clubs, Populists, and the American Federation of Labor all strove to remedy various social ills and improve the lives of their members.

Alan Trachtenberg has argued that during the Gilded Age the industrial capitalist system, aided by new forms of transportation and communication, expanded across the country, producing a "more tightly structured society with new hierarchies of control" and changing the conception of America. Corporations increasingly dominated American economic life, producing "subtle shifts in the meaning of prevalent ideas...regarding the identity of the individual, the relation between public and private realms, and the character of the nation." Massive economic and social change, numerous (often bloody) industrial strikes, political skirmishes, and continued discrimination against blacks and Native Americans affected the era's beliefs, institutions, social practices, and intellectual life. In *Our Country* (1885), Congregationalist home missionary Josiah Strong warned that "an almost impassable gulf" existed between industrial workers and their employers. His book, which sold more than half a million copies, sought to inspire Protestants to combat the perils of massive immigration, the growing numbers and political influence of the nation's Catholics, the debauchery of the cities, socialism, and the callousness of the affluent—all of which allegedly threatened the United States' mission to civilize its western region and Christianize the world.[4]

The nation's economic and social woes led many Americans to yearn for greater order, stability, and control. As millions moved from the countryside to the cities, the sense of community seemed to be breaking down. Massive waves of immigrants spoke dozens of languages, espoused a variety of ideologies, usually lived in separate neighborhoods and felt suspicious about each other, and competed with each other and native-born Americans for jobs. The urban, industrial, increasingly bureaucratic world confronted Americans with new values such as punctuality and efficiency. The long-accepted Protestant moral code was under assault by various forms of determinism that attributed people's actions to economic or social forces beyond their control, by the practice of compartmentalizing life and judging its components by different ethical standards, and by a "quantitative ethic" that measured value by the wealth of entrepreneurs, the size of companies or machines, or the seats in churches and the numbers of converts at crusades.[5] In William Dean Howells's *A Hazard of New Fortunes* (1890), Basil March deplores the "lawless, godless" world that lacked "intelligent, comprehensive purpose," expressing Americans' widespread fear that the breakdown of community and shifting moral values threatened traditional emphasis on the common good and sound character. Seeking to combat these trends, Henry Ward Beecher and others used the pulpit and print to assure anxious citizens that the creation of stronger character and the exercise of greater virtue and self-discipline could help preserve social order and harmony.[6] Meanwhile, others strove to restore order to their fragmenting world through crusades to curb drunkenness and the abuses to which it contributed, to reemphasize Protestant values in classrooms, and to promote patriotism through "the worship of the Constitution, the flag, and America's heroes." By the end of the Gilded Age, Jackson Lears contends, many on both sides of the Atlantic were dissatisfied with modern culture's "ethic of self-control and autonomous achievement," "cult of science and technical rationality," and "worship of material progress." Deeply distressed, many longed for authentic experiences and meaningful encounters with God.[7]

During this era, outstanding orators filled many of the nation's podiums and pulpits, and a plethora of books and sermons provided portraits of heaven. Through their preaching and publications, urban revivalists, led by Dwight L. Moody, and prominent pastors extolled the glories of the celestial realm and urged people to prepare properly for heaven.[8] Their sermons were published in newspapers across the nation, often on the front page. Henry Ward Beecher, who served Plymouth (Congregational) Church in Brooklyn, was the Gilded Age's most renowned minister. Only T. DeWitt Talmage, pastor of neighboring Central Presbyterian Church, rivaled his showmanship, and Beecher consistently preached to a larger audience than Boston's Phillips Brooks. Beecher, who also edited two influential journals, spoke to 3,000 congregants every Sunday, and his sermons were frequently published as books. Talmage was arguably the most popular preacher of the last quarter of the nineteenth century. More than 8,000 people attended his church's two Sunday services, and his sermons were published in 3,500 newspapers and in three leading journals, reaching an estimated 25 million people around the globe. From 1869 until 1891, Phillips Brooks addressed large crowds at Trinity Episcopal Church on Copley Square, "achieving an international reputation" few American ministers have equaled. After his death, Englishman James Bryce contended that no American since Abraham Lincoln had been "so warmly admired and so widely mourned" as Brooks.[9] Finally, these years were the heyday of a group of gifted Reformed theologians whose tomes discussed heaven, most notably Charles Hodge and A. A. Hodge of Princeton Theological Seminary, W. G. T. Shedd of Union Theological Seminary in New York, and James P. Boyce of Southern Baptist Theological Seminary in Louisville.

During the Gilded Age, theological liberalism became an important force in American Protestantism. Enlightenment philosophes, some founding fathers, Unitarians such as William Ellery Channing and Ralph Waldo Emerson, and Congregationalist Horace Bushnell all helped pave the way for the various forms of theological liberalism that gained many adherents in the 1870s and 1880s. Liberalism was a response to biblical criticism, the conclusions of the natural and social sciences (especially sociology and psychology), new views of history, and subjectivist and idealistic philosophy. Phenomenal advances in biology, geology, and paleontology challenged traditional theological positions and fostered belief that the scientific method was superior to revelation as a means of analyzing and explaining the world. As these intellectual forces buffeted society, many educated Americans concluded that revivalist Protestantism contradicted modern knowledge. This, coupled with the social and economic turmoil of the era, led many to seek theological alternatives.

Although liberals were a diverse group, they generally either modified or repudiated the orthodox dogmas of original sin and human depravity and espoused an optimistic view of human nature. Liberals believed that God worked to achieve His ends through "the entire evolutionary process—in nature, society, and the human conscience." Influenced by Herbert Spencer, who saw the universe as evolving inexorably to achieve higher ends, and "cosmic optimist" John Fiske, they labored to hasten the coming of God's kingdom in this world and bring "greater peace, prosperity, and human felicity" on earth. Liberals generally emphasized religious experience, ethics, and social progress.[10] The most important form of Protestant liberalism during the late nineteenth century was the "New Theology" developed by the faculty at Andover Seminary in the early 1880s. Some of the nation's most prominent pastors, theologians, and social reformers—Beecher, Brooks, Lyman Abbott, William Newton Clarke, Williams Adams Brown, Theodore Munger, George A. Gordon, Newman Smyth, and Washington Gladden—also championed this "Progressive Orthodoxy" or evangelical liberalism.

While theological liberals became more numerous and assertive during the Gilded Age, evangelical Protestants continued to sponsor countless evangelistic crusades, send thousands of missionaries overseas, and control many large churches, colleges, and seminaries. Although their portraits of paradise shared many similarities, liberals and conservatives diverged on important issues pertaining to the nature of heavenly life and the grounds for salvation. Even more than during the antebellum years, a serious and sustained assault battered the traditional conception of heaven. Meanwhile, many Americans either repudiated or downplayed the conventional notion of hell and religious leaders debated whether those who did not hear the gospel message on earth would have a chance to respond to it after death.

Although the motif of heaven as a celestial home remained popular during the Gilded Age, other themes became as important. Elizabeth Stuart Phelps's *Gates Ajar* enjoyed immense popularity in the three decades after its publication in 1868. By 1900, it had sold 80,000 copies in the United States and more than 100,000 in England. Entrepreneurs marketed a "gates ajar" "collar and tippet, cigar, funeral wreath, and patent medicine."[11] Moreover, two sequels, *Beyond the Gates* (1883) and *Between the Gates* (1887), also sold well.

At the same time, revivalists, "princes of the pulpit," and other pastors, professors, and authors continued to emphasize some aspects of the theocentric conception of heaven depicted by the Puritans and leaders of the First and Second Great Awakenings, especially the happiness, holiness, love, and knowledge the saints would enjoy in the hereafter. Gilded Age Christians also stressed heavenly recognition and fellowship and the importance of properly preparing for life in paradise, but they focused less on heavenly rewards than did many groups in earlier eras. Finally, some of them accentuated the activism, service, and progress of the heavenly realm, themes that became much more pronounced in the Progressive years.

During the Gilded Age, Jonathan Butler argues, revivalists' desire to produce conversions significantly shaped their conceptions of the next world. To motivate sinners to repent, revivalists depicted the afterlife as "more bright and benevolent" than did their First and Second Awakening predecessors. Earlier preachers, Talmage explained, had warned sinners of the wrath to come, while current ministers trumpeted "the joy to come!"[12] Revivalists often nostalgically pictured paradise as reflecting "the 'good old days' of antebellum American life." Their heaven "idealized and sentimentalized traditional middle-class values" and glorified the nation's rural past. Sentimentalism reigned supreme in fiction, the theater, the lecture circuit, and the pulpit of the Gilded Age. Troubled by how new social and industrial developments were affecting the family, Moody and other revivalists portrayed a celestial realm that embodied cherished Victorian values. They depicted mothers as "queen of heaven" and God as "a benign, exacting father" who invited his children to return home. Talmage called heaven a "great home circle," while Andover Seminary professor Austin Phelps labeled paradise "homelike." The saints will enjoy "the purest and most perfect social pleasures," declared F. J. Boudreaux, a Jesuit priest, in "our heavenly home."[13]

Meanwhile, the world's numerous wars, widespread crime, drunkenness, sexual immorality, and disease led Moody and other revivalists—most of whom were premillennialists who expected morality to grow continually worse until Jesus returned—to picture the earth as a wrecked ship. They strove to rescue individuals from this sinking vessel by supplying them with gospel life preservers. More than 100 of the approximately 1,200 songs in the Gilded Age's most widely used revivalist hymnbook, *Sacred Songs and Solos*, focus on heaven, and many of them sharply contrast the hardships of earth with the pleasures of paradise.[14]

Beecher, Brooks, and other theological progressives, like the Social Gospelers of the next generation, tended to view the world much more optimistically. Most of them were postmillennialists who assumed that the social and moral conditions on earth would gradually improve until Christ established His kingdom here. While revivalists and other premillennial theological conservatives saw decline and decay, they saw growth and improvement. As conservatives became increasingly pessimistic about the state of American culture, liberals celebrated its moral and social progress. Beecher "promised a generation scarred by the hellfire and damnation of the old orthodoxy" that they could attain happiness on earth as well as in heaven. Beecher reportedly asserted that he could not work with Moody because the evangelist "believes that the world is lost" and "is seeking to save from the wreck as many individuals as he can. I believe that this world is to be saved, and I am seeking to bring about the Kingdom of God on earth."[15]

THE NATURE OF HEAVEN: OLD THEMES AND NEW PORTRAITS

Gilded Age authors generally admitted that their knowledge of heaven was limited. The Bible, Presbyterian pastor Robert Patterson professed, focused on "how to get there" rather than furnishing a detailed description of paradise. Unitarian William

R. Alger asserted that the New Testament supplied only "a few fragmentary intimations" and scattered "incidental hints" of the future life. Undoubtedly exaggerating, Talmage claimed that people had asked him a thousand questions about heaven he could not answer. The New Testament, Beecher argued, did not even specify whether "heaven is a condition or a place." Not a single passage in the New Testament explicitly stated that friendships continued in heaven or explained what work the saints would do. "Intelligent commentators and preachers," he maintained, had long taught that pictures of heaven were not meant "to be taken literally," but rather were "designed to kindle hope, joy, and courage." As a result, the "prime truth" both Beecher and Brooks preached was the evanescence of earthly life and the "permanence of the future life."[16]

Moody, by contrast, alleged that the Bible contained considerable information about heaven, so depictions of the afterlife were not "mere speculation." "If God did not want [us] to think" and talk about heaven, He would not have divulged so much about it. Should not those who "are going to spend eternity in...a grand and glorious world where God reigns" "try to find out who is already there, and how to get there?"[17]

During the Gilded Age, pastors, professors, and other Christian authors placed less emphasis on the majesty and splendor of heaven and the relationship of the saints with the Trinity than did their predecessors. Jackson Lears argues that by accommodating itself to a secular mindset during the 1870s and 1880s, theological liberalism "lost much of its emotional power" and minimized "the intense spiritual ecstasy of communion with God." On the other hand, Richard Rabinowitz contends that a shift occurred in the middle decades of the nineteenth century from a more moralistic to a more devotional form of religious experience, which stressed that Christians could enjoy a "private realm of experience" unaffected by the demands of society and their growing feeling of inadequacy as life became more complex and specialized. As technical rationality, bureaucracy, and clock time increasingly governed external behavior, many Americans sought release and comfort in the personal, emotional realm. Many of those whose religious experience became more subjective and psychological "and less theological and abstract" found appealing the intimacy with God that some conservative Protestants, especially Reformed ones, Catholics, and a few theological progressives depicted as central to heaven. People were originally created to "live in the immediate presence" of their Maker, W. G. T. Shedd asserted, and in heaven they would do so. The "incomprehensible blessedness of heaven," declared theologian Charles Hodge, sprang from the beatific vision. The splendor and joy of the heavenly state were "inconceivable."[18]

Others also accentuated the redeemed's rich and robust fellowship with God. Daniel Goodwin, a theology professor at the Episcopal Divinity School in

Philadelphia, exulted in the "holy and happy worship" of heaven and the "personal communion" the saints would enjoy with God and Christ. "Life in heaven...without the presence of God," Moody reasoned, would be like earthly life "without health." The saints, Austin Phelps proclaimed, would gain "a new sense of the personality, the perfections, and the friendship of God." Like most other American Catholics, F. J. Boudreaux considered the beatific vision the centerpiece of heaven. It consisted, he explained, of three distinct but inseparable aspects: the sight, love, and enjoyment of God. "It would be easier to go near an immense fire and not feel the heat, than to see God in His very essence and yet not be set on fire with divine love," he declared. The redeemed will see God "clearly, intuitively, though not exhaustively," which will give them "a love far greater" than they "ever had, or could have, for anyone in this world." Their perpetual occupation, he alleged, is "to contemplate God's infinite beauty" and to love, praise, and thank Him for His past and future benefits.[19]

Others celebrated the communion they expected to have with Christ. When Moody arrived in heaven, he wanted to find the Savior "who bought me with his own blood." Talmage was eager to see the One who pardoned his sin and defeated his enemies. Southern Baptist theologian J. L. Dagg promised that the saints would fellowship with Jesus "who loved us, and gave himself for us." Boston pastor and missions advocate A. J. Gordon wrote in his 1893 hymn "The King in His Beauty":

I shall see Him, I shall be like Him,
By one glance of His face transformed;
And this body of sin and darkness
To the image of Christ conformed.[20]

Phillips Brooks also described heaven in very theocentric terms. Awed by God's presence, the saints, he insisted, would completely trust Him. They would also rejoice in Christ's triumph over evil and death and cast their crowns at His feet. Heaven's residents would sing for joy because their struggle with sin had ended and they had "perfect communion with Christ." They would see Jesus completely and love Him fully, which would totally sate the saints' mental, moral, and spiritual appetites.[21]

For Moody and others, heaven was primarily a place of praying, adoring God, and singing. Those who delighted in worshipping God on earth, Presbyterian pastor Samuel Spear promised, would find heavenly worship even more enthralling. "The predominant character" of heaven is praise, Patterson proclaimed, led by "magnificent choirs" and musicians playing "their harps to the glory of the Most High." On the other hand, the *Encyclopedia of the Presbyterian Church in the United States of*

America declared that "the common notion" of the saints as continually "standing up and singing is too childish to be entertained."[22]

Other Protestants and Catholics continued to stress the happiness, love, and holiness of heaven. Because "the glory of God" shines "in the face of Jesus Christ," Dagg announced, paradise is a "world of bliss." Love and holiness, author Lucy Larcom declared, are the centerpiece of heaven. "Only in Heaven," Boudreaux reasoned, can "all the conditions of love…be fulfilled," and, therefore, only there will love "produce pure and perfect happiness." The saints will love God "purely, unselfishly, [and] ardently."[23] In paradise, Shedd proclaimed, the continual "conflict between the flesh and the spirit" will cease, and the saints will see sin as "odious and abominable." Others added that heaven's inhabitants would enjoy "perfect purity." Boudreaux rejoiced that the passions of people's depraved nature will not be part of heaven.[24]

While some continued to portray heaven in largely theocentric terms, other depictions of the afterlife mirrored the social and economic developments of the Gilded Age. By 1880, Lears maintains, Americans "were far more able—and eager—than their ancestors to avoid both physical and emotional discomfort." Thanks to improvements in medicine and transportation and central heating and indoor plumbing, the upper classes and some members of the middle class enjoyed a much more pleasant life. As creature comforts increased, revivalists, princes of the pulpit, theologians, and other authors portrayed heaven as a realm of supreme material and emotional well-being without any heartache, privation, or social problems. When Christians died, Spear stated, they bade "permanent farewell to misery" and entered "a state of perfect and eternal happiness." The redeemed, Austin Phelps promised, would enjoy "the exhilaration of perfect health." Reflecting both the era's improved medical facilities and equipment and its social ills, Talmage depicted heaven as having no hospitals, dispensaries, medicines, ambulances, wheelchairs, crutches, or eyeglasses. He rejoiced that women would no longer have to work long hours stitching clothing to make money or fear being verbally or physically abused by their drunken husbands.[25]

As previously noted, the Gilded Age was a period of great anxiety. Its social ills and rapid changes produced bewilderment, irritation, disappointment, political ferment, class conflict, protest movements, and strikes. George M. Beard's *American Nervousness* (1884) examined the "causes of the breakdowns, distempers, [and] anxieties" afflicting the urban middle class, produced in part by the fear "of impending chaos…and rampant city mobs." Speaking for many critics, Henry George lamented in *Social Problems* (1883) that more specialized jobs and the increasing use of machines reduced workers' independence, rendered their skills less necessary, diminished their control over their lives, inhibited their intellectual development, and harmed their bodies. Millions of Americans felt "confused, angered, and frustrated" by the nation's "increasingly rigid stratification" system and the many obstacles that blocked upward mobility. These aggravations helped produce portraits of heaven in which various earthly evils were absent, greatly enhancing the saints' happiness and holiness. The New Jerusalem, Moody declared, has "no pain, sorrow, sickness, death, darkness, or tempter." Because Satan was excluded, J. Edmosson avowed, there was no temptation, evil, or possibility of suffering in heaven. Fanny Crosby's "Safe in the Arms of Jesus," which became very popular after it was sung at Ulysses S. Grant's funeral in 1885, sounded similar themes:

> Safe in the arms of Jesus, safe from corroding care,
> Safe from the world's temptations, sin cannot harm me there.
> Free from the blight of sorrow, free from my doubts and fears.[26]

Expressing the widespread concern about the pace and pressures of Gilded Age urban life with its "hustle and bustle of shipping, selling, and shopping," intense competition, timetables for commuters, and emphasis on speed, Phillips Brooks declared that he looked forward to never feeling hurried in heaven. Heaven, Boudreaux argued, would end "all labor, struggle, and fatigue."[27]

As high school and college attendance significantly increased, standards were established for many professions, graduate programs were created, doctorates were awarded, journals and books multiplied, and knowledge was more highly valued, many other Christians accentuated the phenomenal knowledge the redeemed possessed in heaven. "In the next world," Shedd asserted, "all doubts and perplexities" would vanish and residents would clearly perceive "divine things." Although people's knowledge in the future state would not be as extensive, exhaustive, or profound as "that of the Omniscient One," he added, they would have "direct, accurate, and unceasing" knowledge. As the saints perfectly conformed to God and studied His "character, works, and government," Dagg asserted, they continually made new discoveries. In paradise, Robert Patterson alleged, every person understood "more about the secrets of the earth...than all...the world's geologists," more about human history "than all its historians," and more about "science than all its natural philosophers." In paradise, Talmage proclaimed, all questions are answered and all riddles are solved. "Christ, the heavenly Teacher," claimed Ellen White, the founder of the Seventh Day Adventists, "will explain" to the saints "the truths" and their experiences "they could not in this life understand."[28]

Exhibiting his age's increased concern with sports, physical fitness, and "muscular Christianity," Talmage contended that the saints' magnificent, powerful resurrected bodies would enhance their bliss. After God raised the righteous from their graves, Talmage asserted, He would dramatically refashion them until the difference between a brawny gymnast and "the emaciated wretch" in a leprosy hospital was less radical than that between people's present bodies and their "gloriously resurrected" ones. Heaven's residents, Talmage trumpeted, will be "strong, supple, unconquerable, immortal athletes."[29]

Rejecting the typical Gilded Age conception of heaven, Unitarian pastor William Alger complained that throughout history, humans had conceived of heaven as "a definite, exclusive, material abode." They had depicted paradise as either an Elysian region on earth, an idyllic "isle beyond the setting sun," "the whole globe, renovated by fire and peopled with a risen and ransomed race," or a "halcyon spot in the sky" characterized by "inaccessible splendor" and "eternal blessings." Various groups had converted their "grandest and happiest conditions," "enhanced by the removal" of all limitations and evils, into their notion of heaven. Because God is "the Infinite Spirit," "except in his various incarnations," He could not be enthroned in any particular place and gazed upon by worshippers. Therefore, Alger urged Christians to reject "the vulgar idea of heaven as an exclusive spot in space." Instead, heaven should be regarded in three different ways: "as an individual experience," "a social state," and "a far-off universal event." "As a private experience," heaven is the harmonious intercourse individuals enjoyed with God on earth. "As a public society," it "is the blessed communion" of believers on earth. "As a final consummation," heaven would be the public declaration of God's will "in the total harmony of the universe," in which all individual wills acceded to His designs and purposes.[30]

"THE BUSIEST PLACE IN THE UNIVERSE"

Although they did not stress the themes of growth, progress, and service as much as Christians would in the Progressive years, some Gilded Age writers, echoing their era's emphasis on technology, the entrepreneurial spirit, problem solving, and industriousness and its faith in progress, insisted that heaven would be an active place. Also influenced by proponents of muscular Christianity, manly endeavor, and athletics who insisted that physically fit individuals could achieve more in all fields, they pictured the afterlife as involving, in the words of Phillips Brooks, "tireless, earnest work." The Book of Revelation's declaration that "there was silence in heaven for half an hour" led Talmage to conclude that it is "the busiest place in the universe." Heaven, he reasoned, must be a very eventful realm if "it could afford only thirty minutes of recess." The redeemed, he asserted, will be honored as victors over the trials of their age: "the temptations of the stock exchange," "professional allurements, domestic infelicities...physical distress, [and] depression." In another sermon, Talmage declared that "Broadway at noonday is quiet compared with the business of heaven." God would use the redeemed to accomplish "great projects."[31]

During the Gilded Age, the term *middle class* first entered the lexicon, and its members distinguished between having a career and doing a job. Occupations became much more diverse as many more Americans became managers, salesmen, insurance agents, wholesalers, accountants, engineers, and physicians. Advice manuals promised that the industrious, persevering, and thrifty would achieve success. The Gilded Age's energetic, dynamic society contributed to dozens of depictions of heaven as a lively place where the saints engaged in meaningful activity in varied employments. Patterson labeled portraits of paradise in which people did nothing except gaze at Jesus and sing as "very incomplete." Instead, he alleged, the saints actively served God by doing tasks for which their gifts and training equipped them. Heavenly residents, others added, would have "the most glorious [forms of] employment," while all the "mean and degrading toils" of earth (presumably the tedious, monotonous, back-breaking work in factories, mines, and fields) would be eliminated. Paradise, claimed Ellen White, "will provide endless opportunity for learning and growth." For the saints, Dagg declared, "inaction would be torture, rather than bliss." Talmage insisted that the employments of heaven would be as diverse as those of earth; astronomers, chemists, mathematicians, historians, explorers, musicians, artists, theologians, and even lawyers, physicians, and soldiers (but apparently no manual laborers) would continue their occupations. Congregationalist professor and pastor Asa Mahan expected the afterlife to include new evangelistic crusades. "The next great commission," he declared, would be to "preach the glad tidings to every creature" throughout the entire universe. Austin Phelps predicted that the saints would travel to "the most distant...stars" to serve God in various ways. Theologian A. A. Hodge wrote that in their "eternal home," the redeemed would utilize their reason, imagination, aesthetic instincts, and affections, as well as gratify all their tastes and develop all their capacities.[32]

Throughout the Gilded Age, most notably at spectacular expositions in Philadelphia in 1876 and Chicago in 1893, Americans celebrated the wonders of technology and exhibited enterprises and inventions they believed would help spread affluence and republican values. Politicians, businessmen, journalists, and clergy all enthusiastically endorsed the nation's material progress. Sermons and lectures expressed the widespread conviction that technological innovations and increased material comforts substantially benefited humanity. The centennial exposition in Philadelphia featured "power looms, lathes, sewing machines, presses, pumps...and locomotives." Even more impressively, it displayed the Remington typewriter, Thomas Edison's "multiplex" telegraph, Alexander Graham Bell's telephone, a huge steam engine, and a 7,000-pound electric pendulum clock. Meanwhile,

Americans rode in streetcars and elevators, ate processed foods, and wore machine-made clothing, and new machines and tools in factories and on farms altered traditional "forms, rhythms, and patterns of physical labor." Popular prints, such as John Gast's 1873 *American Progress*, testified to the nation's preoccupation with advancement and growth. It depicts animals and Indians fleeing as "civilizing" agents—hunters, prospectors, pony-express riders, and farmers—arrive.

Concerned that the industrial order inhibited the independence and mobility that had previously permitted all honest, assiduous Americans to better their lives, some promised that no barriers would hinder individual growth in heaven. Theological liberals and conservatives both emphasized that moral and intellectual progress occurred in heaven as the saints grew in happiness, understanding, character, and love. Beecher anticipated gradually growing into "a true son of God" while in heaven. On earth his insight into God was "like a little lake," but in heaven he would have "a full vision of the infinite…ocean of the divine nature." Others insisted that the saints' minds "will eternally progress" and that people's character slowly improved in heaven. The faculties of the redeemed, Charles Hodge averred, will be continually enlarged. Universalist pastor G. W. Quinby argued that because people entered heaven with radically different amounts of knowledge and spirituality, their levels of achievement and rate of advancement in knowledge and affection would vary greatly.[33]

Only a few Gilded Age authors specifically mentioned the concept of service in heaven, though it would become a watchword for the next generation. Service, Lucy Larcom argued, "is the law of the heavenly life." Christ, aided by the saints, continued to render loving service to those for whom He died. Those who were most faithful on earth, she reasoned, would be assigned more challenging tasks in the afterlife. Saints would have their "own special and peculiar ministries" just as they did on earth.[34]

Daniel Goodwin sharply disagreed with this portrait of heaven. In its discussion of the "employments of the heavenly state," he argued, scripture refers "scarcely at all to intellectual activity and expansion and enjoyment, to artistic development, to growth or gratification in scientific or philosophical knowledge or specula-tion…which some modern Christians" considered the "constituents of heavenly blessedness."[35]

HEAVENLY RECOGNITION, FELLOWSHIP, AND REWARDS

Although Gilded Age Christians did not accentuate heavenly recognition or fellowship as much as their antebellum predecessors, these themes remained very important to them. Many pastors and professors strongly defended the doctrine of heavenly recognition, arguing that it was highly reasonable, almost universally accepted, and clearly taught in scripture. The final judgment required that individuals have self-identity and awareness so that God could hold them accountable for their actions, and the interest those in heaven had in earthly affairs strongly implied the doctrine. The Bible asserted that people's memory continued in heaven, which meant that individuals must recognize others. The concept made sense because some features of people's moral temperament and character would distinguish them forever. In addition, the saints could complete certain tasks only if they recognized one another, such as thanking those who played a major role in their salvation and Christian growth. Finally, the deathbed reports many gave of seeing departed loved ones in heaven confirmed the doctrine. Both Methodist bishop Randolph Foster and Unitarian William Alger stressed that humanity's widespread "belief in reunion hereafter" testified to its truthfulness. Virtually all commentators, Alger asserted, conceived of the afterlife "as a social state in which" personal appearances "and memories are retained, fellow-countrymen are grouped together, and friends [are] united."[36]

The doctrine of recognition, avowed Episcopal rector George Zabriskie Gray, "runs through the Bible [and] is assumed in every part." The Apostle Paul, Gray claimed, repeatedly expressed his hope of communing with his converts in heaven. According to the Bible, Patterson averred, the saints retain their personalities and recognize one another. Many passages, Foster declared, indisputably taught that at the final "judgment a thorough memory of the entire life will remain," including one's "thoughts, words, feelings, and actions." People's "personality, intellect, emotion[s], will," and knowledge of all their earthly endeavors, he insisted, will continue in heaven. Four facts, Foster added, indicate that the saints have "a vivid recollection" of earthly "persons, things, and events": "the only way we can know ourselves is by our consciousness of past activities"; people could not "enjoy rewards or endure punishment for deeds" they did not remember; individuals could not fully appreciate heaven without reflecting on "the sins and suffering" from which Christ redeemed them; and heaven and hell only had "moral significance" "in relation to this life." Talmage assured the hundreds who wrote him about the subject that the doctrine of future recognition was not "a guess, a myth, [or] a whim," but rather "a granite foundation" upon which Christians could "build a glorious hope."[37]

Presbyterian pastor J. Aspinwall Hodge refuted several objections to the concept of future recognition, including that the union of the body and soul was so complete that the soul could do nothing without a body, that the Bible taught soul sleep, and that "parents could not be happy in heaven" if any of their children were not there. "The inability to recognize others," he declared, "would only increase people's . . . anguish, leaving them forever uncertain about the destiny of their loved ones and causing people to begin eternity as absolute strangers." Moreover, the doctrine of heavenly recognition was very comforting because it promised that Christians would spend eternity with many of their loved ones. Boudreaux reasoned that the saints would love everything that God loves and would not "love those whom He does not and cannot love." God is not unhappy because some people reject Him and are lost forever, and, therefore, the saints will not be either.[38]

Many authors accentuated the fellowship of the saints. The contention that awareness of their friends' presence would inhibit the saints' worship of Christ, J. Aspinwall Hodge argued, was wrong. Corporate worship, he maintained, was much more inspiring than "solitary awe." In fact, heavenly residents could fully commune with the Lord only as they fellowshipped with one another. Foster refuted the claim that "the saints will be so absorbed … in acts of worship, that they will have" neither "time nor inclination for … communion among themselves." God wanted the saints to minister together and grow "in greatness and power." Disagreeing with most Christians of all eras, Foster alleged that marital and family relations would not continue in heaven. The focus in heaven, he proclaimed, is on "the one great family of which God is the Father, and we [are] children." Husbands and wives and parents and children would simply share the common affection that united all the saints. Newman Smyth argued that social relationships were "absolutely indispensable" to people's full "growth and perfection" in heaven. One of heaven's great blessings, Charles Hodge asserted, would be to converse with its "high intelligences," especially the "patriarchs, prophets, apostles, martyrs." Boudreaux looked forward to communing with Peter, Paul, Saint Patrick, Francis of Assisi, Dominic, Ignatius of Loyola, and Teresa of Avila. Talmage wanted to talk with Adam, Joshua, Moses, George Whitefield, John Wesley, Charles Finney, and David Livingstone. He also anticipated getting to know those whose earthly contributions had been underappreciated, including doctors who died treating yellow fever and cholera, nurses who cared for the sick in hospitals for contagious diseases, and railroad engineers who sacrificed their lives to preserve the safety of passengers. While others wanted to study chemistry in heaven or "to meet Shakespeare, Milton, and Dante," Talmage confessed that he was much more interested in "the company of Jesus and my dear friends on earth." "It is not the jasper streets and golden gates that attract us to heaven," Moody declared, but the presence of spouses, children, friends, angels, and biblical heroes. In the afterlife, declared Lucy Larcom, we will need the friendship, guidance, and love of others to attain "spiritual heights." The fellowship of the saints, Boudreaux asserted, will be fantastic because they will love and be loved perfectly.[39]

Rejecting the widely espoused view that people's environment determined their behavior, many Christians defended the importance of human efforts and "the value of a properly trained and disciplined 'character'" and insisted that individuals were responsible for their deeds and moral choices. Some revivalists and pastors also asserted that people's character and actions would determine their rewards in the afterlife. "According to the Bible," Samuel Spear stated, "the reward[s] of the righteous" depended upon "their moral record" and character. Newman Smyth complained that many Protestants were ignoring the "Scriptural and rational truth" of differences in glory and blessing in the hereafter. Numerous parables of Christ taught that people's eternal rewards would differ, and Jesus urged believers to lay up treasures in heaven. Although everyone would be holy and happy in heaven, Patterson proclaimed, the saints' capacity for enjoyment would differ immensely, as would their closeness to God's throne and the degrees of splendor of their mansions. The saints, Boudreaux argued, would derive differing amounts of happiness from the beatific vision depending on the merit of their earthly lives. The saints, A. A. Hodge maintained, would have different ranks and offices based on their "natural capacities" and "fruitfulness on earth." In Henry Ward Beecher's novel *Norwood*, Pastor Buell insists that "there are infinite degrees of excellence and of happiness in heaven." Some enter paradise as kings "after a prosperous voyage," while others arrive with nothing after a shipwreck. Thus some are "well advanced," while others are paupers. Those who had a last-minute conversion experience enjoy less heavenly rewards than "those whose earthly life" involved "a long career of virtue and self-denial."[40]

SETTING OUR SIGHTS ON HEAVEN

Gilded Age Christians exhorted individuals to focus on heaven and emphasized the many benefits of doing so. Those who set their hearts "on things above," Moody maintained, experienced abundant life on earth. "The cardinal truth that the soul lives forever through Jesus Christ," Beecher announced, is "the most nourishing, the most hope-inspiring, [and] the most regenerating doctrine." A correct understanding of heaven, he affirmed, made people "bold, strong, enduring...teachable, and Christlike." Christ's followers, Brooks asserted, began "to live the everlasting life" on earth and experienced its "generous charity" and "abounding and inspiring peace." Meditating on paradise, he added, enabled Christians to push aside their "cares and troubles" and "bring the new song of heaven" to earth. Recognizing that "a great cloud of witnesses" carefully observed their lives on earth, Methodist Bishop Matthew Simpson declared, could help believers cope with trials, temptations, and sorrows. To ensure that humans did not yearn to stay permanently on earth, Talmage reasoned, God made them despise many of its circumstances and desire the splendors of heaven. Smyth urged Christians to allow the "grand, majestic power of the world to come" to direct their passions and pursuits in this life.[41]

Various pastors and evangelists also exhorted Christians to prepare properly for paradise. Echoing the themes of Horace Bushnell's *Christian Nurture* (1847), Beecher argued that the best way to groom children for heaven "is to surround them" with the finest "conditions of human society" to exert "a powerful... influence" on their moral development. Brooks challenged believers to cultivate a heavenly character to get ready for the life above. Moody compared being heaven-bound with rising in a helium-filled balloon. The more of the world's ballast people discarded, the higher they would ascend. "Everybody wants to enjoy heaven after they die," he complained, but many "don't want to be heavenly minded while they live." "The unregenerate man likes heaven better than hell," Moody added, "but he likes the world the best of all." Those who are the most "humble, faithful, [and] self-sacrificing" on earth, Lucy Larcom promised, would not have to learn a new language, form new habits, or make many new acquaintances in heaven. They would discover that "they had already been living in heaven" while on earth. To "be a saint in heaven," Ellen White reasoned, an individual "must first be a saint on earth" because death would not change "the traits of character" people cherished in this life. Studying "the Bible's vision of heaven," Patterson proclaimed, could inspire the faithful to live more Christ-like lives on earth and prepare more effectively for "the world of glory." Boudreaux argued that people's "earthly holiness" determined their "degree of happiness in heaven." Christians could "vastly increase" their future glory by helping the poor and teaching the truths of the gospel.[42]

UNLOCKING THE GATE OF HEAVEN

Speaking for theological conservatives, Moody, Talmage, and Shedd, an evangelist, pastor, and professor, respectively, and three of the leading Christian voices of the Gilded Age, asserted that individuals must accept Jesus Christ as their savior and master to enter heaven. Moody strove to ensure that all his sermons were "fit to convert sinners with." He summarized his message as the "Three R's"—"ruin by sin, Redemption by Christ, and regeneration by the Holy Ghost"—and labeled the new birth the most important biblical doctrine. Only those whom the Holy Spirit made new creations would go to heaven. Individuals "must believe on the Lord Jesus Christ and not merely about Him." Many, he protested, were trying "to earn salvation. This miserable word 'try' is keeping thousands out of heaven." Neither money nor good works, Talmage avowed, could "unlock the gate of heaven." Its gatekeepers would admit only those who know the password—Jesus—and are washed in His blood. Only the one "who trusts in Christ's...atonement" and receives a new heart,

Shedd argued, "will be able to look" at "the holy countenance of God" and "the dread record of his own sins, without either trembling or despair."[43]

The rhetoric of theological progressives like Beecher and Brooks sometimes sounded like that of evangelicals. "Give your heart to the Lord Jesus Christ," Beecher proclaimed. No person, he added, can become a Christian "by his own simple, unaided power." The Holy Spirit must work in individuals' hearts to make them Christians. Jesus was "God's appointed sacrifice for sin," people's "only hope," and the world's "only Savior." God dwells in men and women, Brooks declared, "by His Holy Spirit, in the great work of … personal regeneration." Those who received God into their hearts and lived "by Him and for Him" experienced a "wondrous moment of conversion," which baptism, confirmation, and other church rituals feebly tried to typify.[44] Despite such statements, both Beecher and Brooks paid little attention to the Pauline doctrine of justification by grace through faith alone. Almost completely ignoring the grounds upon which God reckoned sinners to be righteous, they and other evangelical liberals stressed that Christ's death was exemplary rather than pro- pitiatory. Rather than satisfying the "demands of God's justice," the cross challenged Christians to serve and suffer for others. By strongly emphasizing morality, progres- sives sometimes implied that people earned salvation through their virtuous con- duct rather than received it as God's free gift.[45] For example, Beecher declared that individuals' actions and character determined their destiny. Those who "have done good rise to honor and glory," while those who "have done evil sink to shame and woe." Gary Dorrien summarizes Beecher's core theology as: the example of "Jesus, the perfectly God-conscious redeemer," helps liberate human beings from their self- ish impulses and make them right with God. "To be saved is to experience the fulfillment of one's moral and spiritual personality" as "the indwelling spirit of Christ" triumphs over one's animal nature. For Beecher and other evangelical lib- erals, salvation was "the gift of God," but it was not "an unmerited gift. For, in the end, righteous character 'is the achievement of the personal will' and 'can be won, in the deepest sense, only by the soul for itself.' "[46]

Unitarian William Alger denounced the doctrine that faith in Christ's vicarious atonement was the only gateway to heaven as "narrow and repulsive." "The true method of salvation," Alger asserted, is to develop "a good character through divine grace and the discipline of life." Everything that brought people's will "into loving submission to the infinite Father" and molded their character in accordance with divine teachings furthered salvation. Whatever substituted virtues for vices led people "through some gate into paradise." Christ came to exhibit "the true type of being" and "the true style of motive and action" to help people reproduce it. "Salvation through Christ consists not in the technical belief that he shed his blood for our redemption," Alger argued, but in deriving from Him the willingness to shed our "own blood for the good of others."[47]

Although disagreeing over the role of faith and works in salvation, both theological conservatives and progressives exhorted believers to pursue holiness, strive to develop Christ-like character, and do good deeds. "Salvation is a gift," Moody declared, "but we have to work it out, just as if we had received a gold mine for a gift." The parable of Dives and Lazarus, Shedd maintained, taught that those who made the enjoyment of this life their chief end would suffer in the afterlife while those who suffered "in this life, for righteousness' sake" would "be happy in the next." Beecher reprimanded those who thought they had "a title to heaven" because they were "called, elected, sealed, and adopted," but whose conduct was "no better, more...spiritual...or holy" than that of nonbelievers. If a person "resolutely aims" for heaven, he will "reach it in the end, however much he may wander off his track." Some the world considered saint-like, he predicted, "will barely gain admittance" to heaven, while others whose lives were filled with "doubt and dread" "will have [an] angelic welcome." One of the characters in Beecher's novel *Norwood* denounced bereavement as "a great heretic" because it prompted most people to believe that their friends were saved, no matter what their belief or conduct.[48]

Several authors urged Christians to develop upright character and spiritual maturity to prepare for heaven. Individuals would carry the moral character they attained on earth into the future life, Spear stated, where it would be perfected. Shedd urged Christians to cultivate the spiritual disciplines because their "disposition and character" remained eternally unchanged. It is foolish "to think that we shall be at home in heaven," Lucy Larcom, asserted, "if we find its air too pure for our breathing here."[49]

The New Theology that arose in the 1870s and 1880s primarily at Andover Seminary preached a perspective on salvation similar to that of Unitarians like Alger. Its proponents taught a doctrine of future probation and implied that all people could ultimately be saved. They sought to modify traditional Christian beliefs to fit with the results of biblical criticism and new scientific theories, especially evolution, to make them more palatable to modern people. This school of thought viewed theology as an "evolutionary development that should adjust to the standards and needs of modern culture" rather than as "a fixed body of eternal truths."[50] While retaining traditional theological language, its advocates largely ignored God's transcendence and wrath and instead focused on His immanence and love. They rejected human depravity and considered religious experience much more important than correct doctrine. Like Unitarians, they stressed the example and teachings of Christ more than His atonement and exalted ethics and character. Winthrop Hudson argues that the New Theology revolved around "the doctrine of the Incarnation, interpreted in terms of divine immanence." Its advocates identified Christ with what they "conceived to be the finest cultural ideals, the noblest cultural institutions, and the best scientific and philosophical thinking." Accentuating God's benevolence and humanity's righteousness, they insisted that the world was inexorably moving toward redemption "quite independently of grace through Christ, except as he was present 'in the spirit of the world.' "[51]

By the 1880s, the eternal destiny of the unevangelized, brought to the fore by American missionaries' encounters with many new groups around the world, provoked heated debate in seminaries, missions boards, and denominational periodicals, especially in New England. During the next two decades, the doctrine of future probation produced substantial controversy, especially at Andover Seminary and among Congregationalists, whose General Council delegates sharply disagreed about the issue.[52] As Daniel Williams explains, during the 1880s three primary answers were given to the question "Is the gospel absolutely necessary to salvation?" Some contended that all who died without repenting, whether or not they had heard the gospel, would go to hell. Most theological conservatives maintained that reason, conscience, and the physical universe were sufficient to reveal God's existence, power, and holiness to those who never heard the gospel. Therefore, God justly condemned heathen who died without repenting of their sin, even if they never heard of Christ. Adopting a doctrine of "future probation," advocates of Progressive Orthodoxy countered that people need to hear the gospel message in order to repent and be saved, but those who never heard it on earth would be given an opportunity after death to learn about and respond to "God's love as revealed in Christ."[53]

The trustees of Andover Seminary refused to appoint Newman Smyth to a chair in theology in 1881 because he championed the doctrine of future probation. Passages pertaining "to the future life," Smyth claimed, constituted "a comparably small part" of the Word of God. Moreover, the biblical writers who received the "fullest revelations were the most conscious that they prophesied in part" and that people could not conceive all that God revealed. Smyth admitted that the passages where Paul discussed "the final completion of God's kingdom," including Jesus' descent into Hades to preach to the dead, "did not teach explicitly a second probation." However, Christ's mission to Hades completed His prophetic office, which required that salvation be universally proclaimed. The most reasonable deduction, Smyth asserted, was that Christ went to Hades to preach to disobedient unbelievers in prison. This passage and other verses that threw indirect light on the subject implied that those who had not heard the gospel would have an opportunity to do so after death.[54]

Smyth admitted that this doctrine might lead some who heard the gospel message to "cherish fallacious hopes" that they would have "a second probation after death." He stressed that the scriptures urged people to accept Christ as their savior before death and did not promise heaven to those who rejected Him on earth. However, failing to take these "hints and possibilities of Scripture" pertaining to a second probation into account, Smyth averred, made God appear to be unjust and led to "un-Scriptural dogmatism" about how God dealt with those who died without hearing the gospel. The scripture insinuated that God and Christ continued to work in Hades in the interval between death and the last judgment, which offered Christians "peace, comfort, and hope" about the destiny of those who had no contact with Christianity.[55]

The Reformers, Smyth contended, had correctly rejected the Catholic Church's "corrupt doctrine of purgatory," which was saturated with "the poison of meritorious works and penance." He held out hope, however, that, as the scriptures intimated and the church fathers had considered, the intermediate life might contain "processes of purification and perfecting" to prepare people to go to heaven after the final judgment. Rejecting universalism, he argued that eventually every person would either be "drawn by a sweet and resistless attraction" to God's throne of grace or repelled from God "by the evil magnetism of their own sinful desires."[56]

Many professors at Andover agreed that those who were not exposed to the gospel on earth would hear it in the hereafter. They denounced the selective provision of the gospel and "the damnation of countless millions" who never heard it as cruel and unjust. Advocates of the New Theology defended future probation as a much more humane alternative, insisted that almost everyone would be saved, said little about eternal punishment, and implied that moral improvement played a major role in salvation.[57]

Theological conservatives repudiated the doctrine of future probation. James Strong, a professor of theology at Drew Theological Seminary, a Methodist institution, and best known for his *Exhaustive Concordance of the Bible* (1890), denounced the concept as "the Roman Catholic fable of purgatory revamped for Protestant ears" and as "wholly unscriptural." The Bible contained no "supplemental plan or provision of atonement, mercy, or redemption." God gave the angels only one trial, declared Strong, so why would He give humans two? Moreover, future probation "would be utterly useless" for two reasons. First, moral character is so fixed by terrestrial life that a postmortem opportunity would not lead to "a change of mind or reformation of life." Second, he asked, would those who did not accept the gospel during this second probation be given even more opportunities? If they did not repent, would they then be punished or, as some argued, annihilated? Annihilation, he insisted, "is wholly unwarranted by Scripture," contrary to scientific principles, and unjust. Therefore, most people who rejected the biblical doctrine that the wicked would be punished forever believed that all would be saved. However, this general amnesty for sinners would make them "more hardened and audacious" in the afterlife. In addition, the "sacred delights" of heaven would not be attractive to the unregenerate because heaven's happiness depended upon holiness, which they lacked.

Theologian A. A. Hodge rejected the increasingly popular claim that people had another opportunity to repent between their death and the final resurrection for four reasons: the Bible did not teach it; it was based upon the "unchristian principle that God owes all men a favorable opportunity" to receive Christ; Christ and the apostles implied that people had only one chance to be saved; and "the law of habit" and "confirmed moral character" indicated that sinners will be "far more obdurate" after death than they are on earth and thus would not repent even if they had another opportunity.[58]

Some who repudiated the concept of future probation entertained the possibility that a significant number of non-Christians would be saved before their death. Samuel Spear asserted that Hebrews 2:3—"How shall we escape if we neglect so great a salvation?"—taught that people had no other recourse if they rejected the gospel on earth. It was not plain how God would treat those who died before they had the maturity "either to accept or reject the Gospel" or those who had no knowledge of the message of salvation. However, those who failed to respond to the gospel on earth would not have a second chance. Daniel Goodwin argued that the final judgment is eternal and irreversible. All individuals "had a fair, though, perhaps, not an equal opportunity on earth. Each will be judged according to the opportunity he has had." People will be condemned only because of their own sins, not because of their ignorance. If any person could stand "before God and truly say: 'I am conscious of no sin, I have ever lived up fully to my light and opportunities and abilities'" he "will not...be punished." His belief that the Judge of all the earth would treat everyone justly led Goodwin to conclude that many heathen would be saved as well as the billions who died in infancy. However, he repudiated the Universalists' claim that God willed the salvation of everyone. In citing various biblical passages to support this contention, they failed to consider the different connotations of the word *will*, which could mean desire, good pleasure, command, or purpose. The texts they quoted asserted that Christ atoned for everyone, that God's benevolence is universal, or that God is ready to redeem all who repent; they did not teach that God would save everyone.[59]

While many theological conservatives renounced this new concept of future probation, almost all Protestants rejected the long-standing Catholic doctrine that all Christians who did not achieve perfection on earth must be purified in purgatory to make them fit to enter heaven. Speaking for them, Charles Hodge argued that the two biblical passages Catholics typically employed to justify their belief in purgatory—Jesus' declaration that the sin against the Holy Spirit would never be forgiven and John's statement in Revelation 21:27 that nothing defiled or detestable could enter heaven—did not teach that people would be sent to a place of purification before being admitted to paradise. Although the custom of praying for the dead had developed in the early church, this "superstitious practice" had no scriptural support. The concept of purgatory contradicted the Bible's clear message that if an individual repented of his sins, believed Jesus is "the eternal Son of God," trusted "simply and entirely" in His atoning sacrifice on the cross, and endeavored to lead a holy life, he would "certainly be saved." Moreover, Hodge protested, the doctrine assumed that good deeds are meritorious and thus denied the biblical doctrine that people are saved by grace, not by works. Finally, he argued, Catholics based their dogma "of absolution and of the power of the keys over souls in purgatory" primarily on "the special gifts granted to the Apostles and to their successors." However, "the Apostles never claimed, never possessed, and never pretended to exercise, the power" Catholic priests assumed in remitting sins. Purgatory's central premise—that Christ's merits atoned only for original sin and therefore each person must pay for his own postbaptism sins either by penance or purgatory—A. A. Hodge protested, was unfounded. Similarly, Goodwin denounced purgatory as a "full-blown figment" of Catholic "superstition and priestcraft" that had no support in scripture, was not taught by the early church, was not included in any ecumenical creed, and contradicted salvation in Christ alone.[60]

CHANGING CONCEPTIONS OF HELL

Closely connected to this debate over future probation and purgatory was disagreement between liberals and freethinkers on one side and theological conservatives on the other about the concept and nature of hell. In an 1870 sermon, Beecher proclaimed (inaccurately) that nobody believed anymore in hell as "a place of literal fire and brimstone." He asserted that most Christians affirmed the idea of future punishment but taught that "it is remedial and educatory" and would eventually make individuals holy, a position sometimes labeled the Restorationist view. "I preach the love of God," he added, and "that all punitive elements are under the control of love."[61] Seven years later, Beecher denounced the concept of hell, prompting many other evangelical liberals to reconsider this doctrine. "If I thought God" sent people "to eternal punishment," he announced, "my soul would cry out: 'Let there be no God!' My instincts would say: 'Annihilate him!'"[62] In 1878, the editor of *Popular Science Monthly* alleged that most Americans considered the concept of hell obsolete. The advance of knowledge, new views of human nature, and growing emphasis on more humane sentiments, he asserted, had destroyed the hell of Jonathan Edwards. That same year, Octavius Brooks Frothingham, the founder of the Free Religious Association, also attacked the doctrine of hell, declaring that it was only a "shadow of its former self." Revivalists still spoke of it "with extreme reserve and reluctance," but they usually emphasized "the persuasions of love" instead of the torments of hell. They could not totally abandon the concept because it logically followed from their "dogmas of depravity and redemption" and was essential to their general scheme of salvation. Repudiating this doctrine, Frothingham claimed, would destroy the orthodox Christian theological system, but this must be done because neither "the language of scripture" nor the nature of God justified belief in the conventional Christian doctrine of hell.[63]

By the 1870s, Jonathan Butler argues, most revivalists no longer used "terror tactics." During the Gilded Age, evangelists stressed the blessedness of heaven much more than the awfulness of hell to prod sinners to repent. Although noting that some denominational presses and "colportage societies still published tracts warning sinners of the horror awaiting them at death," James Moorhead contends similarly that hell was less emphasized after the Civil War. Butler maintains that Moody "preferred saccharine sermons on heaven to harsh and vindictive" ones on hell. The evangelist feared that preaching traditional views of hell and eternal punishment would alienate many of his listeners and supporters. Moody never repudiated the traditional doctrine of hell, but he thought he could more effectively win converts by accentuating God's love and the wonders of heaven than by scaring people with images of hellfire and damnation.[64]

Other conservatives, however, continued to defend the conventional view of hell. "Nothing in the Scriptures," declared A. A. Hodge, "suggests that the suffering of the lost shall ever end." The Bible explicitly refuted the idea that sinners would eventually be restored "after an indefinite period of purifying discipline" either during the intermediate state or after the final judgment. Eternal punishment, he added, was not inconsistent with God's benevolence, which He exercised in conjunction with His wisdom, holiness, and justice. God, Shedd argued, did not wantonly or arbitrarily inflict eternal retribution on sinners. What caused torment in hell was primarily its residents' memory of their sin and perception of their wickedness. People would be miserable, Shedd declared, principally because they would see their sin as God did. Goodwin repudiated the increasingly accepted position that the punishment of hell was disciplinary and intended to reform offenders and therefore was temporary, not permanent. Goodwin rejected the Universalist argument that although biblical writers taught "the doctrine of eternal punishment," it was not revealed by God but borrowed from the heathen and the Pharisees.[65]

Talmage contended that the nation's leading denominations still affirmed that hell was as certain as heaven, and he refused to ignore or minimize the reality of hell. He noted that many people first denied that the fire of hell was literal, then they denied that hell was everlasting, and finally they rejected the concept of future punishment and permitted "all the thieves, pickpockets, and debauchees of the universe

[to] go to glory." This view, he protested, assured "the villains of the world" that they would someday "sit in the laps of patriarchs and apostles." However, he argued, eight New Testament passages directly stated that hell involved literal, eternal fire. Talmage also contrasted the glorious bodies of the redeemed with the wretched bodies of the wicked. The drunkard's blotches would cause him to be greatly disfigured, and the "lascivious and unclean wretch" would reek with the "filth that made him the horror of the city hospital." He exhorted people to choose the radiant, Christ-like body of heaven for eternity, not the worn out, infernal one of hell.[66]

Like Christians in other eras, some Gilded Agers stressed that non-Christians would not be happy in heaven even if God did admit them. For the unregenerate, Moody declared, heaven would be hell. Those who could not tolerate attending church services on earth would detest heaven's eternal worship. Those who had spent their lives rebelling against God, Ellen White asserted, would feel tortured by heaven's perfection, purity, peace, love, joy, and melodious music.[67]

CONCLUSION

Gilded Age Christians, whether they were evangelicals or theological liberals, painted a picture of heaven that shared many similarities with both earlier and later generations. They continued to stress the worship of God and Christ, heaven's homelike qualities, mutual recognition, and fellowship. More than Christians in most other periods, they emphasized the happiness, holiness, and love of heaven. As technological developments and unprecedented opportunities dramatically changed their lives, they accentuated, more than earlier generations, the concepts of vigorous and varied activities, progress, and personal growth, themes that became dominant in Progressive portraits of paradise. Differences in theological perspective led to disagreement over some features of heaven as well as debates over how individuals were saved and the existence, nature, duration, and purpose of hell. Christian positions on these matters diverged even more sharply in the thirty years that followed the Gilded Age.

Who could think…that…such an energetic
personality as our President [Theodore Roosevelt]
would be content with unending days without
definite and absorbing labors?
—LEVI GILBERT, *The Hereafter and Heaven*

[Heaven is] a wonderland of undiscovered
possibilities, full of things to be done and to be
learned and to be enjoyed.
—WILLIAM ADAMS BROWN, *The Christian Hope*

Our business is not to prepare for another life, but
to utilize this life…not to anticipate a kingdom of
heaven out there beyond the grave, but to bring in a
kingdom of heaven right here upon the earth.
—JOHN HAYNES HOLMES, *Is Death the End?*

Do you realize that every day spent in hard service
will make Heaven that much richer and every day
and hour frittered away will make heaven that
much poorer?
—R. A. TORREY, *Gospel for Today*

7

HEAVEN IN THE

PROGRESSIVE YEARS

Personal Growth, Service,

and Reform

FROM 1890 TO 1920, American life became more urban, industrialized, comfortable, and segregated. Cities grew in size, and factories multiplied. By 1904, corporations were producing three-quarters of all American goods. The middle class swelled. Unemployment, strikes, labor violence, child labor, poverty, and prostitution were prevalent. Jim Crow laws relegated blacks to separate neighborhoods, schools, and cars on trains and prevented most of them from voting. Most Native Americans were confined to reservations where destitution abounded, schools were inferior, and jobs were scarce. Chinese laborers were prohibited from immigrating to the United States, and both Chinese and Japanese Americans faced harsh discrimination.

The Social Gospel movement, which arose in the 1880s, tried to remedy the nation's numerous social and economic ills. Its advocates—ministers, college and seminary professors, social workers, novelists, journalists, photographers, and volunteer workers—strove to redesign social institutions, curb corporate power, improve factories, stop municipal corruption, and end social abuses. Led by Washington Gladden and Walter Rauschenbusch, many labored to help families escape poverty, new immigrants adjust to American life, and millions to gain better housing and medical care. Most proponents of the Social Gospel were theologically liberal Protestants, but some were conservative Protestants or Catholics. They created hundreds of "institutional churches" to provide a wide range of services to the residents of their neighborhoods. They exhorted capitalists to improve working conditions and wages and to share profits with workers, but they did little to aid blacks, Native Americans, Chinese Americans, or other victims of discrimination. As they fought to achieve these ends, many leaders of the movement argued that refashioning earth to mirror heaven was as important as preparing people to go to heaven.[1]

In the early twentieth century, this attempt to reconstruct society on the basis of Christian principles became closely connected with the Progressive movement. Many of its key leaders, including presidents Theodore Roosevelt and Woodrow Wilson, prominent politician William Jennings Bryan, Wisconsin governor and senator Robert LaFollette, and Toledo mayor Samuel "Golden Rule" Jones, were deeply influenced by social Christianity. The Progressive crusade sought to make American government more democratic, responsive to the people, and active in combating social ills. They worked to bring some of the attributes of heaven Social Gospelers accentuated to life on earth.

During these years, new theological currents, originating primarily in Germany, began to deeply affect American seminaries, colleges, and congregations and influenced what many educated Americans believed about the Bible, theology, and heaven. Supplied with a systematic foundation by Colgate Theological Seminary professor William Newton Clarke and Union Seminary professor William Adams Brown and popularized by editor and Brooklyn pastor Lyman Abbott and numerous other ministers and educators, liberal theology by 1900 had made deep inroads into most major Protestant denominations. Liberalism was a diverse, eclectic movement whose proponents strove to adapt "religious ideas to modern culture." They accentuated the immanence of God, the goodness of humanity, the moral theory of Christ's atonement, personal religious experience, emotions, and ethics.[2] In their view of heaven, service, personal growth, and progress became as important as worship, contemplation, and fellowship had been to earlier generations. While both theological liberals and conservatives underscored these themes in the years from 1890 to 1920, conservatives focused more on what they expected heaven to be like and what people must do to get there. Conservatives also placed greater stress on heavenly recognition, relationships, and rewards. During this thirty-year period, religious liberals and conservatives also developed differing views of death and hell. Many liberals questioned, and some repudiated, the traditional conception of hell. Although most conservatives affirmed the conventional view of hell as a place of eternal punishment, only a few of them used the threat of hellfire to goad sinners to repent.

As the nineteenth century ended, mainstream American views of heaven were changing. As we have seen, earlier Protestant portrayals had generally highlighted "release from earthly struggle, total abolition of sin, and unceasing adoration of God." They had typically viewed the principal activity of heaven as glorifying God rather than fulfilling earthly desires. By the 1890s, heaven began to assume a new appearance and revolve around different activities. The growth of cities, increased mass production, and technological advances helped substantially improve material life. Meanwhile, the average work week for those employed in manufacturing decreased from about 60 hours in 1890 to 47 in 1920. This, coupled with the invention of labor-saving devices for the home, gave many people more leisure time and creature comforts. Housing improved for many Americans, and new forms of recreation and entertainment became readily available. Deflation and mass production reduced the cost of many items, and urban department stores, most notably A. T. Stewart's in New York and John Wanamaker's in Philadelphia, fueled middle-class material desires and enabled millions to enjoy a surfeit of consumer goods, including better and more varied food and new conveniences ranging from Kodak cameras to Gillette safety razors.[3]

As the nation became more prosperous and powerful and more Americans enjoyed a higher standard of living, many concluded that the best features of this world were "writ large" in heaven and that achieving earthly dreams was as important there as worshipping God. Heaven, asserted New York Presbyterian pastor David Gregg, "is the holy life of earth glorified and perfectly arranged and grandly transfigured." He and others stressed the continuity of heavenly and earthly life; Christians would continue "their spiritual pilgrimage on the other side precisely where they had left off here."[4] As American society placed greater emphasis on individual achievement and personal fulfillment, Christians called for crusades to evangelize the world in a single generation, and novels celebrated adventure and success, many Protestants argued that self-development would be a major aspect of heavenly life. While Americans praised "the strenuous life" and muscular Christianity, numerous authors depicted heaven as a place of energetic and productive endeavor and service. As the number of middle-class Americans grew and work became less tedious and provided greater satisfaction, heaven was frequently depicted as a site of ceaseless activity where residents fully utilized their talents.[5]

The widely espoused conception of heaven as a realm where the redeemed "walk the golden streets, wear crowns," play harps, and sing hymns of praise, Methodist editor Levi Gilbert argued in 1907, had "largely lost its attractiveness." Most Christians had concluded that God had better things to do than forever sit on a throne listening to the saints express awe about His perfections. As Jesus declared, God continued to work, and He would assign Christians important tasks in heaven.

By studying "the secrets of God's world," the saints, Gilbert insisted, would be able to expand the powers of their minds and souls. An "energetic personality" such as President Theodore Roosevelt would require "definite and absorbing labors" to be happy in heaven. Gilbert and others rejoiced that Americans were increasingly picturing heaven "as a spiritual kingdom, whose foundation walls may be laid on earth."[6]

William Adams Brown also rejected the traditional depiction of heaven as a place of "untroubled bliss," "weary repetition," and "deadening routine" where there was "nothing to achieve" or anticipate. Thankfully, this view of heaven was being modified "in accordance with the spirit of the age" and the teachings of Jesus. In the new conception, productive labor replaced perpetual rest. Heaven, he asserted, is "a wonderland of undiscovered possibilities, full of things to be done and to be learned and to be enjoyed." Although the fullness of God's kingdom lay in the future, it had begun "here and now."[7]

Humorist Mark Twain also criticized the stereotypical late-nineteenth-century image of heaven as boring and uneventful and portrayed a more active, entertaining celestial realm. In one of his short stories, Captain Stormfield encounters an old man in heaven who tells him that "singing hymns and waving palm branches…is…as poor a way to put in valuable time" as anyone "could contrive." Those who tried "eternal rest" quickly discovered "how heavy time" hung "on their hands." Active individuals (presumably most Americans) "would go mad in six months" in a heaven with so little to do. In Twain's paradise, people chose their own occupations "and all the powers of heaven" helped them succeed if they did their "level best."[8]

In another essay, Twain lampooned other aspects of the traditional conception of heaven. It did not have "a single feature" that most Americans actually valued. It consisted principally of diversions that the typical Christian "cares next to nothing about…on earth, yet is quite sure he will like in heaven." The standard portrait of paradise entirely omitted the "ecstasy that stands first and foremost in the hearts of every individual"—sexual intercourse. On earth, people risked their reputations and even their lives to enjoy sex. Repudiating notions of Victorian sexuality, he claimed that "from youth to middle age all men and all women prize copulation above all other pleasures combined," but in heaven prayer replaces sex. Most depictions of paradise also featured an unending church service where the saints sang constantly and played musical instruments. On earth, however, few people liked to sing or played instruments, most people could not endure going to church for more than an hour and a quarter a week, and forty-nine out of fifty considered the Sabbath to be a "dreary bore." Moreover, the conventional view of heaven clashed sharply with another earthly reality. On earth, whites refused to associate with blacks and everyone hated the Jews, but in heaven, everyone supposedly mixed, prayed, and sang hosanna together—whites, blacks, and Jews, without distinction.[9]

"REFASHIONING THE PRESENT WORLD": HEAVEN AND THE SOCIAL GOSPEL

Social Gospelers often exhorted Christians to concentrate on improving conditions on earth rather than preparing for the glories of celestial life. Led by Congregationalist Washington Gladden, who served a large church in Columbus, Ohio, and Baptist Walter Rauschenbusch, who taught church history at Rochester Theological Seminary, they strove to construct the kingdom of God on earth by basing political, economic, and social institutions and practices on biblical teachings. Although they did not disparage attempts to save individuals, advocates of social Christianity focused on devising ministries and organizing campaigns to remedy social ills, improve education and working conditions, and uplift the destitute. They established institutional churches that aided the poor, illiterate, and downtrodden and provided employment bureaus, savings banks, kindergartens, English classes, vocational training, recreational opportunities, and medical assistance. Social Gospelers also created denominational agencies and parachurch organizations to combat social ills. Many theologically liberal social activists reconceptualized heaven as closely connected with "the coming of God's kingdom on earth."[10] To them, social justice and the good life were not chiefly ideals to be realized in the afterlife, but goals Christians could achieve on earth.

In the two decades before World War I, most proponents of the Social Gospel, many other theological liberals, and some evangelicals espoused postmillennial eschatology, the idea that the kingdom of God would progressively penetrate and refashion the world, culminating with the Second Coming of Christ and the creation of heaven on earth. Postmillennialists believed that "the preaching of the gospel and the saving work of the Holy Spirit" would eventually Christianize the world and usher in "a long period of righteousness and peace commonly called the millennium."[11] Their conviction that the world would gradually become more righteous and serve as a place for the redeemed to live for a thousand-year golden age and (for many postmillennialists) an eternal home (in a renovated and rejuvenated state) helped inspire zealous efforts to improve social, economic, and political structures, norms, and practices. Such actions, they believed, would both hasten the arrival of the millennium and make the earth a more pleasant place to live until Christ returned. It also led many Social Gospelers to support the humanitarian imperialism of William McKinley and Theodore Roosevelt, the missionary diplomacy of

Woodrow Wilson and William Jennings Bryan, and World War I as crusade to end all wars and advance democracy, as the United States increasingly flexed its muscles in the world.

Deeply troubled by many people's abuse of alcohol and acceptance of evolution, revivalists, most of whom were premillennialists, viewed things very differently. To them, this world was sort of "a hell on earth," while heaven embodied a "pristine, halcyon image" of America's much more wholesome past. Speaking for many religious conservatives, Baptist A. C. Dixon, who served large congregations in Baltimore, Brooklyn, Boston, Chicago, and London between 1883 and 1919, argued that Christians were "strangers and pilgrims" who sought "a better country." The Christian hope, proclaimed A. J. Gordon, the founder and first president of Boston Missionary Training Institute (later Gordon College), is not to adapt to or transform current conditions, but rather to follow "the Lord in the upward path of glory."[12]

Most Social Gospelers downplayed depictions of heaven as a celestial realm where the saints worshipped God and received heavenly rewards and instead urged Christians to build God's kingdom on earth. For many Social Gospelers, Jonathan Butler argues, heaven was a "remote symbol with little immediate relevance." Liberal Baptist William Newton Clarke contended in his influential *Outline of Christian Theology* (1898) that Christians should expect "the long and steady advance of his spiritual kingdom" rather than the "visible return of Christ to the earth." "Our mission is not to get men into heaven," declared Baptist Harry Emerson Fosdick, who taught practical theology at Union Seminary in New York City and pastored First Presbyterian Church, but "to bring heaven to earth." He challenged Christians not to focus on the "rewards and possibilities" of the future life but to work to improve earthly conditions. "The true mark of a saved man," declared Charles Reynolds Brown, the dean of Yale Divinity School, "is not that he wants to go to heaven," but "that he is willing to go to China, or to Labrador, to the battlefield of France, or to the slums of a great city" to help build "the kingdom of God on earth."[13]

Although Walter Rauschenbusch valued individual salvation, he placed much greater emphasis on social salvation, on conforming social institutions and life to the norms of the kingdom of God. In *Christianity and the Social Crisis* (1907), the book that catapulted him from a relatively obscure Baptist seminary professor into the leading spokesperson for the Social Gospel, Rauschenbusch denigrated the otherworldly, individualistic concept of heaven that had characterized Christianity for centuries. It ignored the central teachings of Jesus and the epistles and diminished efforts to reform society. Moreover, seeking to avoid hell or obtain "a life without pain or trouble in heaven" was not Christian. A genuinely converted person strove to serve others and remedy social ills.[14]

Similarly, Johns Hopkins economist Richard Ely denounced the pervasive other-worldliness of traditional Christianity as an "unfortunate error" that had alienated the working class. He urged Christians to abandon the "narrow, negative, individualistic attitude" that concentrated only on "saving souls" and replace this "one-sided half-gospel" with one that emphasized redeeming both society and individuals. He labeled Christianity that did not include philanthropy "a monstrosity." The mission of Christianity, he asserted, is to establish "here a kingdom of righteousness" and to "redeem all our social relations."[15]

Other religious progressives shared this vision. Washington Gladden, for example, insisted that God's advancing kingdom would eventually establish the millennium, a perfect society on earth. When the millennium ended, God would create a new heaven on earth. Rejecting the premillennial view that Christ's Second Coming would be sudden, he declared that God's "kingdom of law and of love" would gradually arrive "with no breaks...interregnums...[or] cataclysms."[16] For Gladden, this eternal kingdom would be an earthly, not a celestial one. He claimed that evolutionary processes in the social, economic, and political spheres were steadily making the world a better place. Many of Gladden's sermons detailed the progress that had occurred in society, religion, morals, justice, and aesthetics. Gladden rejected the idea that "heaven is the antithesis of earth" and stressed the similarities between the two. Heaven is the completion of earth; it is the "homeland," not "a foreign land."[17]

"For many generations," complained Unitarian John Haynes Holmes, pastor of the Church of the Messiah in New York City, belief in immortality had inhibited Christians from waging war on social evils. However, he declared, "eternal life is just as much present with us here as it will [be]...over there." The calling of Christians was "not to anticipate a kingdom of heaven...beyond the grave, but to bring" the "kingdom of heaven" on earth. To achieve this, they must "abolish poverty, wipe out slums, alleviate inhuman conditions of toil, emancipate child laborers, heal the sick, compensate the injured, protect the aged," and help people realize their spiritual potential.[18]

William Adams Brown agreed that American Christians' preoccupation with paradise had often discouraged social reform. For many, "the other world" had "loomed so large that the concerns of this world" had "seemed petty." This did not need to be the case, however, because throughout history, belief in personal immortality had often inspired people to engage in social service. He rejoiced, moreover, that many Christians were "beginning to take Christ's prayer literally, and instead of abandoning earth" to "win heaven, we are trying to make earth like heaven."[19]

Some conservatives, by contrast, urged believers to focus more on heaven and highlighted the benefits of doing so. If a wise man planned to live in a foreign country, Theodore Cuyler, a Presbyterian pastor in New York City, analogized, he would learn "the language and customs of its people." David Gregg exhorted believers to "keep in touch with those who are in heaven" and "follow as closely as we can, day by day, the heaven-life." Thinking "more about heaven," R. A. Torrey argued, would help people better bear their earthly burdens, act more righteously, and conquer the power of greed and lust. Affirming (unintentionally) Karl Marx's argument that religion was an opiate, H. S. Hoffman, the pastor of a Reformed Episcopal Church in Philadelphia, contended that when people believed in a future state, they were disposed to patiently bear "their labors, privations and hardships." Their confidence that social inequalities would someday be abolished, if not on earth, then in the life to come, led many Christians to accept them. Social Gospelers abhorred this view.[20]

While conservatives emphasized that hope in heaven provided "great solace for life's misfortunes," "consolation in bereavement," and "compensation for failure," liberals like William Adams Brown were more likely to stress that focusing on heaven helped supply Christians with strength, courage, enthusiasm, and consecration to be "happier, stronger, and more successful" in their daily lives. Liberals also asserted that laboring to build God's kingdom on earth prepared people for heavenly life. The more individuals "absorbed the laws of the Kingdom" into their character, Rauschenbusch argued, the better equipped they were for the "life of heaven."[21]

HEAVEN: "A BUSY HIVE, A CENTER OF INDUSTRY"

Between 1890 and 1920, the United States became a more dynamic, energetic society. Driven by social Darwinist and racial theories, Protestant desires to establish foreign missions, the quest for raw materials and markets, and their growing power, Americans strove to obtain an overseas empire, expand their trade, and export their principles. Educational and economic opportunities increased, and individual fulfillment and happiness became much more important. Leisure became a commercial enterprise as millions frequented large dance halls, nickelodeons, movie theaters, amusement parks, and professional baseball games. As technological innovations, especially automobiles and electricity, made transportation and communication faster and life easier for millions, optimism abounded. The Boy Scouts, YMCAs, Protestant church brotherhoods, Student Volunteer Movement, and Men and Religion Forward Movement promoted vigorous activity, athletic competition, masculine values, and social service. Social commentators extolled hard work, sacrifice, and self-control and denounced lethargy and debt. The pace of life became quicker, and stimulants like coffee, sugar, chocolate, and Coca-Cola became popular among all classes. Horatio Alger's novels, books with titles such as *Pushing to the*

Front, How to Succeed or, Stepping-Stones to Fame and Fortune, and *The Secret of Achievement,* and sermons and lectures like Russell Conwell's famous "Acres of Diamonds" emphasized striving for success.[22] Meanwhile, other groups, organizations, and individuals strove to promote the social good, expand economic opportunities, improve social conditions, and stimulate Americans to engage in community service.[23] Mirroring these trends, both theological liberals and conservatives pictured an active heaven that featured personal growth, perpetual progress, and many different forms of service.

Some pastors, theologians, and evangelists continued to exalt the beatific vision and the wonder of basking in the presence and power of God and Jesus. Others followed Victorian Christians in stressing the homelike features of heaven. Lecturer and author S. D. Gordon, who wrote more than twenty-five devotional books, exulted that the redeemed would be "absorbed with our glorious King," and William Uylat trumpeted that heavenly residents would see Jesus' "grace and beauty and feel his magnetic force." "When I reach Heaven," gushed Billy Sunday, the most successful evangelist of the early twentieth century, "I won't stop to look for Abraham, Isaac, Jacob, Moses, Joseph, David, Daniel, Peter or Paul. I will rush past them all saying, 'Where is Jesus?'" Presbyterian pastor and evangelist J. Wilbur Chapman compared heaven with home, but he did not do so primarily to make heaven alluring but rather to encourage Christians to make their earthly residences reflect heaven. The domiciles of those who lived according to biblical teachings, he declared, could be "everything that Heaven is."[24] However, during these three decades, rhetoric about worship of the Trinity or heaven's homey features paled compared to other more culturally relevant themes of activism, reform, and progress.

Rejecting the idea that heaven was a place of eternal rest, many Christians during this era viewed it as "a busy hive, a center of industry."[25] People were "not made for rest but activity," proclaimed James Gray, the president of Moody Bible Institute. "Our employments," claimed Henry D. Kimball, a New York City evangelist and reformer, "will be as varied as our aptitudes." If the redeemed worshipped God only through praise and prayer, Gregg contended, "many faculties of the mind" would remain unemployed. As colaborers with Christ in His kingdom, Uylat averred, the saints would rule "over His household and His goods." They would deliver messages, teach, produce art, sing, play instruments, study many subjects, and go "on errands to…distant worlds." In heaven, George Hepworth stated, astronomers, chemists, and philosophers would all "have ample opportunity to investigate" their areas of interest. Using "the expanded powers" of their minds, the saints, avowed Levi Gilbert, would study and discover "the secrets of God's world." Unitarian Ida Craddock expected heaven to have stone cutters, masons, miners, architects, harness makers, blacksmiths, gardeners, spinners, weavers, and clerks.[26]

Traditional views of heaven, Rauschenbusch complained, stressed idleness. They appeared "to have been conceived by oppressed and exploited people who regarded labor as a curse and wanted rest more than anything else." Social Gospelers, by contrast, expected the saints to work productively and study, and they argued that acts of love and service would be the centerpiece of heaven. The saints would rejoice, Rauschenbusch exclaimed, when they saw men who had toiled in mines and shops and women who had labored in restaurants and laundries finally getting a college education.[27]

The future life, Rauschenbusch maintained, would also provide wonderful opportunities for reparation, kindness, and justice. In heaven, stockowners who had reaped large dividends from mill towns could become belated converts to the Social Gospel and work to improve the lives of those whose souls they had starved on earth. Men who had fathered children out of wedlock and abandoned them to poverty and vice could care for their children and help them fulfill their potential. In short, people could atone for their sins and shortcomings, he reasoned, by serving those they had mistreated on earth.[28]

Most controversially, Rauschenbusch suggested that if the concept of reincarnation became widely accepted, Social Gospelers could put it to good use. Those who had labored diligently to improve social conditions in an earlier life could return to earth to continue their work, enriched by their previous experiences and strong character. Moreover, reincarnation, if true, would provide "remarkable chances of retribution and purgation." A man who had forced women into prostitution could be reincarnated as a prostitute to "see how he likes it." A woman who had lived luxuriously on the proceeds of child labor could be reborn as a poor girl and work in a cotton mill. On the other hand, belief in reincarnation could deter the work of social reform because people might conclude that the poor were indigent because of their actions in their previous lives and refuse to help them. Current child laborers might be former exploiters and therefore "trying to uplift them" would be seen as interfering with divine justice. That conviction, he predicted, would "cut the nerve of the social movement much more" than preoccupation with heaven had.[29]

Both theological liberals and conservatives expected the saints, while engaged in worship and active service, to experience substantial personal growth. Heaven's inhabitants would have marvelous opportunities to learn, develop their characters, and advance spiritually. Religious liberals especially stressed growth in heaven. They contended that the saints would resume "the process of growth toward moral perfection" precisely where they stopped at death.[30] Abbott and Gladden argued that heaven is not primarily a place to escape earth's evils, dangers, limitations, and crushing burdens. Instead, they asserted, in the New Jerusalem people's spirits, hearts, and minds are completely liberated so that they can see and serve God and experience "tireless growth." William Newton Clarke repudiated the traditional conception of heaven as a place where people have no challenges because sin is impossible. Because heaven's residents continue to be "real moral agents," he countered, motive, volition, character, and responsibility are still important there.[31]

Heaven, liberals argued, would completely liberate the human spirit, strengthen the hearts of its residents, and increase the vigor of their minds so they could discover truth and realize their "divine possibilities." In heaven, asserted Newman Smyth, people's intellect grew continuously as they built upon their earthly skills and experiences. William Adams Brown expected the saints to progress morally as they trusted God more deeply, served others, fellowshipped with Christ, conformed to His character, and enjoyed a transformed nature. The saints' "illuminated minds and unwearied powers," Gladden alleged, would enable them to investigate the universe and comprehend God's wisdom more fully.[32]

Several authors emphasized that growth would be especially important for those who came to heaven as children. Since a third of humans died as children, Clarke argued, other saints would be assigned to help them develop, making heavenly life "intensely active and interesting." Burdett Hart insisted that children matured in heaven just as Jesus grew "in wisdom and stature and in divine grace" while He was on earth. Heaven's streets will be full of playing children who will gain divine knowledge and perfect character. Those who attained greater "spiritual experience and knowledge" on earth, Kimball maintained, would instruct the many who died as infants and millions of adults who died with "very meager spiritual enlightenment."[33]

"A PLACE OF PERFECT HAPPINESS" OR A "HOPELESSLY MATERIALISTIC" CONCEPT?

Because they were so interested in bringing heaven to earth, theological liberals provided far fewer descriptions of heaven than did religious conservatives. Moreover, the two groups tended to conceive of heaven quite differently. Revivalists sometimes stressed the fantastic beauty and amazing riches of heaven, exalting its incredible loveliness, magnificent colors, and sweet aromas.[34] France's Tuileries, England's Windsor Castle, and Austria's Schonbrunn, argued Billy Sunday, "are all dungeons compared with Heaven." For the revivalists, the afterlife was also a scholar's paradise, a place of "perfect knowledge." Evangelist R. A. Torrey was convinced that all the riddles about God, humanity, time, and eternity that perplexed people on earth would be solved in heaven.[35]

The New Jerusalem conservatives envisioned had none of the perennial problems that plagued humanity or any of the peculiar ills that afflicted their increasingly industrialized society. Paradise, Torrey proclaimed, had no poverty, demeaning labor, sickness, death, saloons, or filth. Sunday's heaven was "free from everything that curses and damns this old world," including pain, sin, poverty, "booze joints," "gambling hells," and tenements.[36] Based on her vision of heaven, Rebecca Springer concluded that it had no "sorrow...partings, disappointments, broken hopes, mislaid plans, night, or storms." The saints grew immeasurably, Hoffman asserted, while remaining "forever young in spirit" and possessing "bodies that cannot age, never become weary, and need no rest." Kimball insisted that heaven would have no cutthroat competition, dangerous, backbreaking toil, monotony, "unwholesome occupations," or underpaid work.[37]

John Haynes Holmes denounced conventional conceptions of heaven as "hopelessly materialistic," debasing, and sordid. Christians expressed "frank disgust" with the gardens, fruits, and harems of the Muslim paradise. But how, he asked, is the Islamic "dream any more degrading in essence than the golden streets, jewel-studded gates, and rivers of water of the 'holy city' of Revelation"? Christians' depiction of heaven, like those of Muslims, Native Americans' Happy Hunting Grounds, Greeks' Elysian Fields, and Norsemen's great hall, was principally a projection of what their own culture most valued. Jesus and Paul provided "no precise descriptions of the life to come." They offered only "a few vague" hints about "what they thought or hoped the future would be like." As a result, "the traditional Christian idea of heaven" was based primarily on Dante's *Divine Comedy* and John Milton's *Paradise Lost* and was similar to the "pietistic speculation" of these other religions. Christians, like these other groups, conceived of heaven "as a place where all human wishes" will be gratified, all needs satisfied, all disappointment and disaster avoided, and "unalloyed happiness" attained. Each of these specific depictions of heaven inevitably assumed the form and features of life which a particular society or religious group considered ideal. Because most people had lived "amid ugly and squalid conditions," Christian theologians and poets had pictured heaven as "a place of indescribable beauty and splendor." Heaven, Holmes concluded, "will most assuredly not be like anything that has thus far been described." He encouraged Christians to "frankly confess that we can never...know what immortality is like" because "heaven lies beyond our experience" and our "first-hand knowledge."[38]

THE RESURRECTION BODY AND THE INTERMEDIATE STATE

As did their counterparts in earlier eras, most Christians in the 1890–1920 period insisted that believers went directly to heaven after death. Some theologians contended that the deceased "slumbered in unconsciousness between death and resurrection," but the most widely held position was "that the souls of the redeemed had already entered into joy but awaited reunion with their bodies which moldered in the grave until the last trumpet." "That the reward of the righteous will be complete only when body and spirit are indissolubly joined in heaven," Kimball declared, "is the faith of all who hold both to the believer's conscious existence after death and to the final resurrection and glorification of the body." However, Christians disagreed about whether the righteous were allowed to enter heaven before their glory was consummated. Probably speaking for many, William Newton Clarke averred that "a doctrine of the resurrection that dispenses with the intermediate period of disembodiment" helped remove "the gloom of death."[39]

By the late 1800s, some Protestant liberals protested that the traditional idea of a future resurrection violated scientific teaching and argued that the concept of an intermediate state was indefensible. In *The Mode of Man's Immortality*, Methodist pastor and editor T. A. Goodwin maintained that the resurrection of a person's physical body was absurd. The resurrection did not involve a future reanimation of the body lying in the grave but "the rising of a spirit form from the earthly house at the moment of death."[40]

Lyman Abbott also rejected the idea of bodily resurrection. The phrase "resurrection of the body," he declared, "does not exist in the New Testament"; it "is borrowed from paganism." Moreover, in I Corinthians 15, Paul explicitly repudiated this doctrine, which improperly identified "the person with the tenement in which he dwells." Bodily resurrection made the idea of immortality "seem irrational" by connecting it with "the miraculous preservation of the decaying body." People would have celestial, not terrestrial, bodies in heaven. Even those alive at "the last great day," Abbott averred, "must pass through a transition" in which their mortal, corruptible bodies became immortal and incorruptible.[41]

Gladden claimed that the bodies individuals inhabited in the world to come were similar to those they had on earth. Although their heavenly bodies were free from the deformities and corruptions of their mortal bodies, their form and substance were almost identical. By the phrase *spiritual body*, Paul meant "a body that is perfectly under the control of the spirit." The saints no longer had "fleshly appetites" that clashed with the spiritual body's aspirations or infirmities that thwarted its endeavors. God constructed the resurrected body out of "enduring and incorruptible material" that aided, instead of impeded, spiritual growth. As with all other doctrines, Newman Smyth argued, Christians must adapt the "essential truth" of the resurrection to modern "conditions of thought." "Belief in the literal resurrection of the flesh" was one of the doctrine's "earlier and crude forms," he asserted, that "is as impossible for us now to accept…as it would be" to espouse "the old Ptolemaic astronomy." "The Christian hope," Smyth added, is that a person will exist as "body, soul, and spirit" and enjoy "the integrity of his whole nature."[42]

Clarke asserted that New Testament teaching about the resurrection implied that the saints would possess a body which the spirit could use. This vehicle would not be a restoration of people's earthly bodies, as the Jews of Jesus' day anticipated, but "a spiritual body," which unlike the fleshly body, was not "inextricably entangled with sin." People's present bodies, which belonged to the material order, had "no further use…after death." Rather, the bodies of the saints would be like Christ's glorified body.[43] Clarke, A. H. Strong, the president of Rochester Theological Seminary, and others claimed that the essential elements of human personality were incorporated into spiritual bodies that were unshackled at death and that therefore the bodies people had at death would not ever be resurrected.[44]

Others offered more traditional views. "We are not to be disembodied spirits in the world to come," Torrey declared, "but redeemed spirits, in redeemed bodies, in a redeemed society in a redeemed universe." "Our very bodies," he added, will be "dazzling…like the sun." Catholic Charles Callan argued that "the risen bodies of the just will be…spiritualized" and made more beautiful by far than they are on earth. "In the resurrection," each person "will retain his own distinct features and individual traits" unmarred by blemishes. Charles C. Hall insisted that Christ's incarnation sanctified and honored the whole nature of human beings and that His rising from the dead "in the fullness of Personality, clothed…with the glorious Body of His Resurrection" indicated the kind of bodies the saints possessed in heaven.[45]

"GLAD REUNIONS," "ENNOBLING COMPANIONSHIPS," AND "PALACES" OR "ASH-HEAPS"?

Theological conservatives, in an effort to persuade sinners to repent, put more emphasis on heavenly recognition, relationships, and rewards than did liberals. While noting that some Christians rejected the idea of heavenly recognition and admitting that no one could be certain that the saints would know each other in heaven, conservatives put forth numerous reasons they found this concept compelling. They insisted that this belief was almost universally held by Christians, taught in both testaments, and stressed by the apostle Paul, who repeatedly discussed the reunion of family members in the afterlife. Moreover, the concept was consistent with the fact that angels recognized each other, the desire for fellowship God implanted in people, and the necessity of individuals' memories continuing in heaven.[46] Theological conservatives also refuted objections to the concept, most notably that the saints' radically transformed bodies would make it impossible for people to recognize one another and that the realization certain loved ones were absent would mar the happiness of heaven. Even if people's appearance did change significantly, Hart argued, the saints could still identify each other just as blind people knew others or friends could "recognize each other in the dark." Kimball admitted that the question of how a mother could be happy in heaven while knowing that one of her children "is forever lost" was a very difficult one. While confessing that this question could not be answered satisfactorily, he noted that God "loves his creatures, is grieved by their rebellion," and had no "pleasure in the death" of sinners, and yet "is the fountain of all happiness." A few liberals also defended the conception of heavenly recognition. "What satisfaction would there be in talking to Isaiah or Paul," Rauschenbusch asked, if the redeemed did not "remember what books they wrote"?[47]

Although Christians in this period did not accentuate family reunion and fellowship in heaven as much as their antebellum and Gilded Age predecessors, their portraits of heaven typically included joyous, intimate relationships among the saints. Hart promised that families "will be restored in the new Paradise" and that husbands and wives would continue to love each other. "Paradise would lose its blessedness," Charles Strong alleged, "if our loved ones did not share in its bliss." Because all "obstacles to fellowship will be removed" and the saints will know each other fully, he avowed, their relationships will be "purer, holier and more lasting" than they were on earth. Torrey expected the saints to enjoy "high and ennobling companionships," while A. H. Strong asserted that they would cherish their friends even more than on earth. The saints will love God far more than one another, Catholic Charles Callan contended, but it "will not detract from or lessen their mutual love." Expressing the conviction of many, a popular hymn of the era declared:

Whom shall I meet in the unseen country,
Whom shall I meet in that land so fair?
Friends who have entered the upper glory,
Leaving behind all their grief and care.[48]

As did Christians in earlier eras, theological conservatives in this period stressed the rewards the redeemed received in heaven, primarily to motivate Christians to evangelize, lead holy lives, and seek intimacy with God. Much more than did their liberal counterparts who emphasized making earth like heaven, conservatives accentuated what individuals needed to do to prepare properly for paradise and enjoy its rewards. They also argued that saints would receive different types of compensation based on their levels of service and spirituality on earth.

Revivalists especially underscored heaven's treasures and rewards. While the saints were awarded five different crowns, J. Wilbur Chapman stated, the best crown, the crown of rejoicing, was given to those who led others to Christ. Helping to convert others, he insisted, was a privilege the angels longed to have, but it belonged only to believers on earth. The idea that all Christians "will have an equally glorious eternity," Torrey claimed, contradicted both the Bible and "sanctified common sense." "We are saved by faith," Torrey trumpeted, "but rewarded according to our own works."[49] The saints' recompense, he added, would "be richer or poorer" based on how faithfully they served Christ on earth, how much suffering they endured, and how much they had sacrificed for Him. Christians would also be judged by how well they had used their earthly resources.[50]

Other conservatives echoed these points. Concern only with our own salvation and not with service, argued A. C. Dixon, "is pathetic"; Christians' earthly lives would determine what roles they were assigned in heaven. People took their character and works with them to heaven. Both scripture and philosophy, Hart declared, taught that the saints received different rewards. Those who became most like Jesus and served Him the longest, most faithfully, and most fruitfully on earth, he insisted, would be closest to Him in heaven. This should inspire Christians to diligently follow Christ's teachings and earthly example. Some heavenly mansions, he averred, are "more superb than others." The parables of the talents and of the pounds both taught that what individuals harvested in heaven depended on what they sowed on earth. The scriptures pointed out, Gregg claimed, that some saints were superior to others in heaven; some ruled over ten cities and others over five. When nominal Christians "contrast their ash-heaps with the standing palaces" of devout Christians, he declared, "they will feel regret." The purer people's thoughts, the nobler their ambitions, the loftier their aspirations, declared Rebecca Springer, the higher their heavenly rank will be.[51]

"CLOTHED IN THE ROBE OF CHRIST'S RIGHTEOUSNESS"

Not surprisingly, theological conservatives placed more emphasis on how individuals get to heaven than did religious liberals. Stressing God's love and mercy, liberals expected almost everyone to go to heaven eventually because of their acceptance of the gospel either in this life or in a subsequent probationary period. Liberals rarely used the death of individuals to try to convert people; instead they primarily strove to console those who had lost loved ones. Speaking for many liberals, Gladden argued that the ransom (Christ's death was a payment to Satan to annul his just claims on humans), governmental (God publicly demonstrated His displeasure with sin by punishing Jesus, thereby preserving His position as the moral ruler of the universe), and substitutionary (Christ died to atone for human sins and reconcile people to God) theories, although widely held throughout church history, did not properly describe Christ's atonement. These judicial analogies did not properly explain the ethical and spiritual consequences of what Christ had done for humanity at Calvary. Andover Seminary professor George Harris denounced these theories for failing to base salvation on character, converting the "sympathy and love of Christ into legal fictions," and exalting the demands of God's justice above the consequences of His love. Christ's atonement was not "a ransom paid to the devil." It did not satisfy God's justice or vindicate divine government. Instead, His sacrificial example had great power to transform individuals.[52] Christ brought salvation, Gladden avowed, by identifying with the human condition, participating in human experiences, and suffering on the cross to show both God's love for humanity and hatred of sin. Jesus "bore our sins in fellowship with us, not in substitution for us." As their "redeeming partner," Christ endured "the retributive evils of their sins" to teach and stimulate people to despise and conquer sin. Christ's death displayed how much God loathed iniquity, declared William Newton Clarke; He served as the "sin bearer" in order to "win men." Rather than satisfying God's punitive justice, Christ's death exhibited God's righteousness, abhorrence of sin, and love of sinners.[53]

Clarke, like other liberals, emphasized the role that virtue and works played in determining people's eternal destiny. The Old Testament prophets and Jesus, they maintained, taught that God judged individuals on the basis of their "life and character" and sent them to the place "for which they are fit." Their understanding of God's nature led many Progressive Era liberals, like their Gilded Age predecessors, to espouse the idea of future probation. Clarke insisted that a loving God would give people who left this world in a state of moral incompleteness (the vast majority of humanity) a postmortem chance to change their condition. "A good God" would not allow many of those He created to "be forever lost to him." Moreover, the Bible implied that all people would eventually be "brought to holiness as God desires." "To be saved," Clarke announced, "is to be transformed from sinfulness into the likeness of God in Christ." Inspired by Christ's life and sacrificial death, many experienced this change on earth, but it could also occur after death.[54]

For Charles Reynolds Brown, the idea that Christ took the full penalty of human guilt upon Himself on the cross to appease God's wrath against humanity was "a frightful doctrine, unwarranted by the teaching of the Four Gospels." He argued that the Bible put forth three complementary views of salvation: by faith (preached by Paul), by works (stressed by James), and by love (proclaimed by John). Genuine faith, Brown argued, expressed itself in deeds. Fruitful work for God could spring only from faith, only works done in love were truly good, and genuine love depended upon faith and was demonstrated by service to others. To be saved, he declared, individuals must have "a filial relation to God" and live righteously. "The scriptural view of salvation," as exemplified in the parable of the Prodigal Son, is that it is not because of their works, opinions, or ceremonies, but because of their faith "that God is ready to forgive" His erring children, "to restore them to the family," and to aid them to act virtuously.[55]

A different view was held by Torrey, Sunday, Sam Jones, and other turn-of-the-twentieth-century revivalists, as well as evangelicals generally and Pentecostals who stressed the gifts of the Holy Spirit. They insisted that Christ's death on the cross atoned for human sin and that individuals must accept Jesus as their savior and Lord to go to heaven. Revivalists argued that good character and altruistic deeds played absolutely no role in procuring salvation and urged their hearers and readers to confess Jesus as their redeemer and King. To attain a "glorious eternity," Torrey contended, individuals must submit to Christ and serve Him. "Christ is the door to heaven," he proclaimed. Only those who experienced a new birth, were radically transformed by the Holy Spirit, and received new wills, affections, and thoughts would be admitted to God's eternal home. No matter how virtuous, educated, philanthropic, or cultured people were, Sunday declared, if they rejected Jesus, they were doomed. He denounced pictures of God as the great bookkeeper of heaven who recorded all the good and bad deeds every individual did, let into heaven those whose good acts surpassed their bad ones, and sent everyone else to hell. No one's works, no matter how numerous or noble, Sunday argued, could satisfy the debt he or she owed to God as a result of his or her sins. However, by dying on the cross, Christ paid people's debt for them, providing a way to reconcile them to God. Only those who accepted Christ's atonement on their behalf, who were "washed in the blood of the Lamb and clothed in the robe of Christ's righteousness," would be permitted to enter heaven. God would "slam the gate of heaven" shut on all who refused to repent and accept Jesus as their savior.[56]

HELL: ETERNAL PUNISHMENT OR TEMPORARY REHABILITATION?

Their conflicting interpretations of the Bible and differing views of God, sin, and salvation led theological liberals and conservatives to also espouse conflicting conceptions of hell. During this period, the traditional conception of hell was challenged even more than the conventional view of heaven.[57] Prior to the 1880s, only a few groups, most notably Unitarians, Universalists, and Seventh-Day Adventists, had directly attacked the concept of eternal damnation. However, led by the faculty at Andover Seminary in Boston, most liberals by the 1890s rejected the idea of hell as a place of eternal punishment, viewing it either as a temporary abode where the unredeemed were rehabilitated to fit them for heaven or as the suffering people endured on earth.[58]

George T. Knight, a professor at Tufts Seminary in Boston, noted in 1904 that "The New Hell" of both Protestants and Catholics was neither as densely populated nor as endless as the old one. Everyone agreed that all those dying as infants or children were saved, and Catholics seemed to imply that "great multitudes of non-Catholics" would go to heaven. "The notion of literal fire in hell" had long disappeared, and Catholics stressed that "the essence of eternal punishment is the loss of the 'Beatific Vision' of God." In fact, some commentators made hell so pleasant, Knight maintained, that "bad men" were likely to choose it "as a place of residence." Gertrude Slaughter agreed that hell "had lost its terrors."[59]

Some protested that the demise of hell removed an important incentive for moral behavior. The increasing unwillingness of Christians to view evil as "a palpable, omnipresent reality," Jackson Lears avows, seemed to be connected with "emergent theories that sin was socially determined rather than individually chosen." Both liberal theology and the positivistic social sciences seemed to absolve people of moral responsibility. The editors of *Scribner's* bemoaned the loss of the traditional Christian doctrine of the devil because it promoted "the idea that each man must bear his own burden and fight his own fight." By developing "the martial virtues," belief in Satan trained people to be virile, indomitable, and forceful and to improve "our national character."[60]

Influenced by portraits stressing God's love and minimizing His wrath, by the principles of the behavioral sciences, and by progressive reformers who called for the rehabilitation rather than the punishment of criminal offenders, many Americans in the early twentieth century rejected the traditional view of hell as a place of chastisement and torment. During the Progressive years, many states established juvenile courts, built adult reformatories, and adopted probation, indeterminate sentencing, and parole in an attempt to rehabilitate offenders and help them readjust to society. At the same time, Progressive ideology typically shifted the blame for criminal actions from individual moral failings to biological, psychological, or sociological factors.[61] Influenced by these trends, most theological liberals argued either that God gave those who had never heard the gospel on earth a chance to do so after death, that the wicked were annihilated when they died, or that the unrepentant went to heaven after enduring postmortem punishment for an indefinite period. Many denounced the conventional concept of hell as unjust because it penalized "finite sin with infinite punishment." Future punishment, contended Arthur Chambers, is "not everlasting but remedial and limited." The only value of punishment, declared historian G. Lowes Dickinson, was as a deterrent.

The orthodox concept of hell, he protested, was deeply flawed because it failed to reform its residents.[62]

Guided by his conception of justice rather than by biblical texts, Rauschenbusch repudiated the claim that people's destiny was "immediately and irrevocably settled" at death. Some people, he argued, deserved to spend time in hell, but no one deserved to be there forever. On the other hand, some converted individuals had treated others so badly that they should experience "a taste" of hell before being admitted to heaven. Permitting them to "go to heaven totally exempt" would be unjust. Rauschenbusch insisted that no one was beyond the reach of God's love and that God would eventually save everyone. He admitted that the doctrine that all would be saved judged sin too lightly, offended people's sense of justice, and deterred righteous conduct. However, he contended, belief that those who were saved solely as a result of Christ's atonement escaped all eternal penalties did even more to discourage self-discipline and upright behavior.[63]

If even a minority of people were in hell, Rauschenbusch averred, it would raise significant concerns about God's character. He renounced Jonathan Edwards's contention that Christians "should rejoice in the damnation" of those whom a sovereign God "abandoned to everlasting torment." Hell could be a permanent state only if God was an autocrat who ruled his subjects rather than a Father who loved His children. Many Protestants, Rauschenbusch alleged, had concluded that the pain of hell was the result, not of fire, but of separation from God. If, however, "God had not locked the door of hell from the outside" and people remained there because they preferred darkness, then the "most Christian souls in heaven" would invade hell to try to convince its residents to come to heaven. And they would be led by the One who detested the thought "of ninety-nine saved and one caught among the thorns."[64]

Although they held different opinions about it, Washington Gladden and Billy Sunday agreed that few ministers preached about hell in the late nineteenth and early twentieth centuries. Gladden claimed that hell's "most strenuous" defenders occasionally delivered a discourse on the topic and then rejoiced "that nothing more on that subject" was required for awhile. Sunday lamented that most of his listeners could not remember the last sermon they had heard on hell and promised them, "you'll hear about hell while I am here" because "God Almighty put hell in the Bible." Any preacher who ignored hell because people disliked it, he thundered, should "get out of the pulpit."[65]

While Moody rarely mentioned eternal punishment, Sunday and Sam Jones, like the Second Great Awakening revivalists, often discussed the dreadfulness of damnation. Torrey preached several sermons on the features of hell, and some other theological conservatives defended the traditional conception of hell, focusing mainly on its mental anguish.[66] "Do you think you can annihilate hell because you don't believe in it?" Sunday asked his audience. Whether its fire was literal or figurative, he reasoned, hell "must be an awful place if God loved us...enough" to sacrifice His Son "to keep us out of there." Invoking Blaise Pascal's famous wager, Sunday argued, "suppose there is no hell" and "death is eternal sleep." Those who followed scriptural teachings would live longer and be happier on earth and thus "lost nothing by believing and obeying the Bible...even if there is no hell." But if there is a hell, he warned, Christians will be saved from it while non-Christians would spend eternity there. Therefore, Christians won whether hell existed or not. In his influential *Systematic Theology*, A. H. Strong stressed that the Bible used the figures of eternal fire, the pit of the abyss, and outer darkness to describe the final state of the wicked. Those in hell lost all physical and spiritual good, suffered "the misery of an evil conscience," were "banished from God" and the saints, and dwelled under God's curse forever. Speaking for numerous conservatives, William C. Procter, writing in *The Fundamentals*, asked, "Could any material torments be worse than the moral torture of an acutely sharpened conscience," which compelled hell's residents to contemplate their "misspent time and misused talents," "omitted duties and committed sins," and neglected opportunities to repent and do good?[67]

While many liberals repudiated the traditional notion of hell and some conservatives defended it, most Christians simply ignored hell. American society's growing emphasis on compassion, social reform, and the environmental causes of crime, as well as their own discomfort with the doctrine of eternal torment, prompted many pastors and revivalists to employ enticing images of heaven rather than to vividly portray the horrors of hell. A Baptist minister claimed in 1889 that the doctrine of hell seldom intruded into the message of pastors, Sunday school teachers, or Christian workers. In 1916 the General Conference of the Methodist Church omitted almost all references to future punishment in its manual for conducting funeral services. Even many conservatives greatly reduced the population of hell by claiming that all those who died in infancy went to heaven. Moreover, when ministers and theologians did discuss hell, they typically argued that biblical descriptions of its torments were metaphors, minimized the severity of its punishment, and maintained that damnation was a consequence of sinners' actions rather than God's election, of "natural moral laws" rather than God's vindictiveness.[68]

Liberals and conservatives also continued to debate the concept of future probation that proponents of the New Theology had devised in the 1880s. This doctrine asserted that no one's future destiny was decided until he had a chance to respond to the gospel. Therefore, all those who never heard it on earth would have an opportunity after death.[69] Numerous conservatives denounced this idea. "Schemes of future probation," Torrey protested, "are pure speculations with absolutely no foundation in fact and contrary to the plain teaching of the Book that never lies." People must settle their eternal destiny "before the undertaker pumps embalming fluid" into them, declared Sunday. Thousands of biblical passages urged people to accept Christ as their savior now, argued S. D. Gordon; only one implied "a possible opportunity in a future life."[70]

THE NEW DEATH: "PASSING FROM ONE ROOM TO ANOTHER"

While deemphasizing hell, liberals put forth a new, milder view of death as an easy transition to another realm that completed the process of evolution. As the nineteenth century closed, James Moorhead explains, death was increasingly seen as "an event symbolizing continuity more than an abrupt divide." For several decades, the rural cemetery movement had labored to transform "burial places into pleasant parks" where people could go "for edification and diversion." Funerary art shifted from emphasizing emblems of mortality to depicting "the deceased in lifelike scenes." Meanwhile, "consolatory literature stressed the beauty of death and the ease of transition to a state of fulfillment not unlike, though assuredly more glorious than, the best moments of earthly existence."[71] Many embraced a sentimental view of death that diminished hell and stressed self-fulfillment and a celestial home, helping them cope with the shift from the stable communities of the early nineteenth century to "the more atomized mobile society" of the century's later decades. Surveying the American scene, an Englishman argued in 1899 that "the thought of death" had little effect on everyday life. The joy of life had replaced the fear of death, and the flames of hell were sinking low. The death of dying was evident in the greater popularity of cremation, "the disappearance of hell," the search for pleasure rather than wealth, and the increasing frequency of suicide. Moreover, funeral practices were changing. "We no longer shroud the house in black," explained Lyman Abbott, "we make it sweet with flowers"; Christians also substituted "hymns of victory" for "hymns of grief."[72]

For George A. Gordon and other liberals, "eternal life was a present possession." Death, Gordon argued, is just "a bend in the river around the spur of a mountain." "Liberals portrayed death as part of a natural evolution to immortality, and encouraged people to accept and celebrate their passage to a new life." Death, asserted Washington Gladden, involved "no serious break in the continuity of our experience." The saints' experience would be like someone who returned from a journey and found "his home improved and beautiful—many discomforts gone, the cramped rooms enlarged…[and] everything arranged the way" he liked. Similarly, Abbott encouraged Christians to "think of life as one and indivisible, of immorality as our possession here and now, [and] of death as normal change in an eternal process of growth." Death, he argued, is simply "pushing aside the portiere and passing from one room to another."[73]

Newman Smyth insisted that Darwinism demanded a reappraisal of death, immorality, and resurrection "in light of modern science." In *The Place of Death in Evolution* (1897), he contended that death did not frustrate life's good purposes. Instead, it promoted life by "burying the useless waste, removing the outworn garment, and providing ever-needed nutriment," enabling life to march "on to its height and joy." "In the Christian hope of endless life," Smyth claimed, death was not "a curse" but rather "a natural and often happy transition to…better life." Succinctly stated, death contributed to evolutionary progress.[74]

CONCLUSION

Many significant shifts occurred in American views of heaven between 1890 and 1920. During these three decades, technological innovation helped dramatically increase industrial and agricultural output and cures were discovered for many endemic diseases. The nation's population grew significantly, and per capita GNP increased almost fourfold. While many social problems remained, progress abounded as evident in railroad regulation, workmen's compensation, women's suffrage, a graduated income tax, the abolition of child labor, the initiative, referendum, and recall, pure food and drug laws, the conservation of natural resources, and many other "reforms." Paralleling these developments, greater numbers of Christians conceived of heaven as an active realm where the saints performed varied forms of service and grew substantially in knowledge, character, and spirituality.

For the first time in American history, a major theological rift divided the nation's Protestants, as many college and seminary professors and numerous pastors adopted some form of theological liberalism. Liberals sought to revise traditional Christian doctrines to make them more intellectually compelling and morally palatable to an increasingly educated, secular American citizenry. In the process, they rejected some aspects of the long-standing Christian conception of heaven and hell. Many liberals embraced the Social Gospel, urged believers to make implementing heaven's life and principles on earth their chief priority, accentuated the role character and virtue played in gaining entry to heaven, and insisted that most or all non-Christians would have a postmortem opportunity to respond to the gospel. More than liberals,

religious conservatives stressed the material and aesthetic aspects of heaven, speculated about the details of heavenly life, discussed celestial fellowship and rewards,
and emphasized the necessity of a new birth experience. After 1920, the theological
differences between these two camps intensified, erupting into the Fundamentalist-
Modernist controversy and contributing to even more divergent understandings of
heaven.

8

SHIFTING CONCEPTIONS OF HEAVEN FROM THE ROARING TWENTIES TO THE FABULOUS FIFTIES

The future life as a bottomless pit or as a perpetual religious serenade is...intolerable.
—HARRY EMERSON FOSDICK, *Spiritual Values and Eternal Life*

We do not purchase the right to enter heaven by any good works that we have done. We enter it through the merits of Jesus Christ alone and our trust in God's redeeming grace freely proffered in him.
—JOHN SUTHERLAND BONNELL, *Heaven and Hell*

Heaven is not related to a good life as a medal is related to a school examination; it is rather related to a good life as knowledge to study.
—BISHOP FULTON J. SHEEN, *Go to Heaven*

AMERICAN LIFE CHANGED dramatically from 1920 to 1960. This forty-year period witnessed the roaring twenties, the 1929 stock market crash, the Great Depression, World War II, the beginning of the cold war and a nuclear arms race, and the affluent, complacent fifties. The nation's population grew from 106 million in 1920 to 179 million in 1960, fueled in part by a baby boom following the war. These four decades opened with the first radio broadcast by KDKA in Pittsburgh in November 1920 and closed with television as an integral part of family life. They began with women gaining the right to vote in 1920 and ended with most women viewing their principal role as wives, mothers, and homemakers. The growth of corporations, new techniques of mass marketing, a surfeit of manufactured goods, consumer credit, new styles of dress, patterns of travel, and forms of entertainment, and a substantial assault on traditional moral values significantly altered America. Jazz, radio, movies, television, and a new generation of writers led by Sinclair Lewis, Ernest Hemingway, and William Faulkner helped changed the way many Americans thought and spent their leisure time. Nativism reared its ugly head, the Ku Klux Klan flourished in the 1920s, and blacks continued to suffer substantial discrimination. Prohibition, which took effect in 1920 and was repealed in 1933, was widely denounced as a flawed experiment that proved morality could not be legislated. The New Deal brought a flurry of government programs designed to put Americans back to work and end the depression. It also greatly enlarged the size and scope of the federal government and the power of the presidency, a trend that World War II and the cold war furthered. The war and its aftermath brought full employment, redistributed income, and significantly increased the nation's middle class. Emerging from the war as a superpower, the United States soon became embroiled in an ideological struggle and arms competition with its former ally the Soviet Union. Efforts to contain communism contributed to a massive buildup of the American military establishment and a crusade by Republican Senator Joseph McCarthy to ferret out Communists in the movie industry, politics, and other sectors of American society. During the 1950s, American scientists helped discover the structure of DNA, ended the scourge of polio, and sent satellites into space. Although racism continued, the Supreme Court overruled the "separate but equal" doctrine in *Brown v. the Board of Education* (1954) and demanded that public schools be integrated. The nation achieved unparalleled levels of prosperity, while poverty remained widespread but largely invisible.

On the religious scene, a battle erupted in the 1920s between fundamentalists and modernists over the infallibility and interpretation of the Bible, the nature of religious authority, the person and work of Jesus, and evolution. Especially heated among northern Baptists and Presbyterians, the conflict was waged both on the home front and the foreign mission field where, theological conservatives stressed, the salvation of millions of souls was at stake. Led by J. Gresham Machen of Princeton Seminary, they denounced liberalism as a new religion that denied Christ's deity and substitutionary atonement for human sin. Liberals countered that they were preserving the core truths of Christianity and making them plausible to modern people. They berated fundamentalists for misconstruing the Bible and called for tolerance of differing theological perspectives. Already disillusioned by the results of World War I and embroiled in their internecine skirmish, most conservative Christians and many liberal ones were deeply disturbed by the revolution in morals that flaunted Victorian values. Sensationalized and sexually suggestive stories filled tabloids, popular literature discussed Freudianism and other provocative topics, women smoked in public and wore skirts that bared their lower legs, youth challenged conventional norms, and dancing became widely accepted. During the 1920s, materialism triumphed over idealism, cynicism replaced optimism, and many questioned or rejected traditional religious values.

A religious depression paralleled the economic one in the 1930s, with lower levels of church attendance, reduced funds, diminished spiritual vitality, and fewer ministries. Unable to feed their families or upset by theological battles, the secular drift of the culture, or their declining status, thousands left the ministry.[1] In many ways, the Catholic Church flourished during the depression years as parochial school attendance remained high, its members gained greater political power, and it substantially assisted the urban poor. Nevertheless, Christianity exerted less influence on the national scene than in earlier periods of American history. As millions of Americans listened to radios daily and went to the movies weekly, the secular media competed with the church in shaping values, strongly influencing views of morality, marriage, recreation, and the good life.

When World War II erupted, most American religious leaders and laypeople endorsed a neutral, isolationist position. However, the rapid Nazi victories and the Japanese attack on Pearl Harbor on December 7, 1941, changed that. During the first half of the 1940s, the war preoccupied American attention and diverted many resources from religious enterprises. Unlike World War I, most Christians saw the new conflict not as a crusade to construct a better world, but a grim necessity to stop ruthless aggressors. The war prompted many combatants and civilians to "think more deeply about God," and their faith helped them "cope with the constant presence of possible death."[2] The traumatic events from 1930 to 1945, coupled with a premillennialist eschatology that expected the world to become worse and worse, led many fundamentalists to disengage from public life and see themselves as a persecuted minority. Meanwhile, the depression and the war undermined most liberals' belief in human goodness, societal progress, and the coming of God's kingdom on earth. Prodded by the critique of Neo-orthodox theologians, many liberals lamented that they had too fully embraced American culture and relinquished their prophetic role.

During the 1950s, church membership and attendance soared and thousands of churches were built, but many saw the decade's religious practices as superficial and hypocritical. Jewish sociologist Will Herberg protested that most Americans joined churches and synagogues to gain social benefits and did not understand the doctrines of their particular denominations or live by biblical principles.[3] During the decade, the words "under God" were added to the Pledge of Allegiance, "In God We Trust" was adopted as the national motto, Presidential Prayer Breakfasts began in Washington, and President Dwight Eisenhower's church attendance and religious rhetoric were widely applauded. Southern Baptist Billy Graham's evangelistic crusades drew large audiences and produced many converts. Graham, Catholic Bishop Fulton J. Sheen, and Reformed Church of America minister Norman Vincent Peale all reached millions through their best-selling books, syndicated newspaper columns, and radio and television programs. Movies (including such epics as *Ben Hur*, *The Ten Commandments*, and *The Robe*), books, and songs with religious themes were popular, and the sale of Bibles reached an all-time high.

While mainline Protestant denominations and Catholicism flourished and a record 69 percent of Americans belonged to a church or synagogue in 1959, the nation's Protestants were more divided than ever before. Millions continued to embrace fundamentalism, and its proponents built a network of congregations, Bible colleges, mission agencies, and parachurch organizations and effectively used radio and television programs to spread the gospel and their views. Led by Harry Emerson Fosdick, who helped launch the public phase of the fundamentalist-modernist controversy with his 1922 sermon "Shall the Fundamentalists Win?" and theologians Shailer Mathews, Paul Tillich, and Albert C. Knudson, Protestant liberals held many prestigious positions in seminaries, colleges, and publishing houses and pastored some of the nation's largest congregations. Meanwhile, two groups sought to develop a middle position between fundamentalists and liberals. Calling themselves "evangelicals," some ministers and laypersons created the National Association of Evangelicals in 1942, started *Christianity Today* magazine in 1956, and founded new seminaries, most notably Fuller in Pasadena, California, in 1947. Led by Reinhold and H. Richard Niebuhr, proponents of Neo-orthodoxy criticized both fundamentalism and liberalism and reasserted God's transcendence, human sinfulness, and Christ's divinity.[4]

Not surprisingly, the most popular views of heaven from 1920 to 1960 reflected the nation's increased religious diversity. Many of the same motifs of earlier eras remained important, especially heavenly recognition, implementing heavenly principles in this world, adopting a heavenly perspective toward earthly life, and preparing appropriately for heaven. Some of the same disagreements continued as well. However, new themes and perspectives also emerged. Many Christians repudiated traditional views of heaven, refused to speculate about heavenly life, or argued that preoccupation with heaven inhibited, rather than inspired, endeavors to improve conditions on earth or to live ethically. Moreover, while Catholics continued to exalt the beatific vision, few Protestants stressed a staple element of the pre–Civil War portrait of heaven: worshipping the Trinity. Neither group depicted heaven as an attractive, desirable home or emphasized family reunions or rewards as had many nineteenth-century Christians. Nor did Christians focus as much on building the kingdom of Heaven on earth as had their predecessors during the Progressive Era. However, numerous Christians continued to insist that heaven's residents grew intellectually, morally, and spiritually as they zealously served God and utilized all their gifts. During this era, the disagreement over the relative merit of faith and works as grounds for admission to heaven grew more intense. Conservative Protestants underscored God's saving action in Christ; Catholics stressed the role of the church, the sacraments, good works, and purification in purgatory; and liberal Protestants and Jews accentuated human character and agency. Finally, while some evangelicals and more fundamentalists endorsed the traditional doctrine of hell and some Catholics defended both hell and purgatory, most liberal Protestants repudiated the conventional concept and hell became even more unpopular among Americans.

Preoccupied with other issues, neither fundamentalists nor liberals placed much emphasis on the afterlife. Fundamentalists concentrated on converting sinners, equipping church members for ministry, defending biblical infallibility against liberal onslaughts, combating moral decline, and analyzing the final series of earthly events preceding Christ's Second Coming. They provided little description of what heaven would be like. Influenced by C. I. Scofield, many fundamentalists espoused dispensationalism, a doctrine that divided history into ages. They focused on the present dispensation—the "church age"—and the final dispensation—the millennium, Christ's thousand-year reign on earth—rather than on the afterlife. When evangelist William Biederwolf published a book about the hereafter in 1930, he admitted that it was "somewhat unusual" for fundamentalists like himself to discuss this topic and confessed that it was not "essential to the great plan of salvation."[5] Liberals meanwhile continued to focus much more on this world than the next one. For them, adapting the Christian message to modern culture, providing religious education, strengthening character, and improving social conditions were more important than either speculating about the afterlife or preparing people for it. Evangelicals generally devoted their energies to saving souls, nurturing believers, building flourishing congregations, defending orthodoxy, and attacking immorality. During these four decades, Americans clashed over the basis for admission to heaven, with fundamentalists and evangelicals arguing that individuals must be born again and most liberal Protestants, Catholics, and Jews stressing the importance of character, religious nurture, and good deeds. Rejecting belief in life after death, other liberal Protestants, Jews, and secular humanists accentuated achieving self-fulfillment on earth and attaining immortality through one's accomplishments or children.

THE NATURE OF HEAVEN: TRADITIONAL PORTRAITS AND NEW PERSPECTIVES

Although the portrait of heaven that some religious conservatives painted shared many similarities with those of earlier generations, many liberals claimed that it was no longer popular or plausible. Even those "who take…religion seriously," Charles Reynolds Brown, the dean of Yale Divinity School, observed in 1926, put little emphasis on "eternal blessedness." Christians talked extensively about useful earthly service but had "very little to say about going to heaven." Even on their deathbeds, he opined, the devout thought more about how their financial investments and life insurance policies would provide for their spouses and children than they did about their own prospects for eternal bliss. Presbyterian pastor John Sutherland Bonnell complained in 1956 that a secular, materialistic society had little interest in "the nature of the afterlife." Many Americans, he declared, found the symbolism of heaven as a city with gold streets, emerald walls, and gates of pearl repulsive. Baptists Shailer Mathews and Harry Emerson Fosdick and Quaker Rufus M. Jones contended that few Americans were still interested in eternal rewards and punishments. "The old dogmatisms" of "the future life as a bottomless pit or as a perpetual religious serenade," Fosdick proclaimed in 1927, had become intolerable. Popular preachers of earlier eras had been able to motivate multitudes to live moral lives by promising "a glorious future paradise as the consummation of man's endeavor." However, the present generation, Fosdick claimed, was more interested in fulfilling their earthly destiny and promise. The "appeal to postmortem rewards and punishments," Matthews claimed in 1933, "is distinctly out of fashion." A considerable number of Americans, he alleged, would prefer to cease to exist than live forever in the heaven most theologians and hymn writers portrayed. Many had redefined the term *immortality* to mean "postmortem influence, social persistence," or being absorbed by the "cosmic will." Speaking for many liberals, Baptist educator W. H. R. Faunce insisted that most Christians found the Book of Revelation's images of harps, crowns, and endless singing unbearable and disgusting.[6]

Meanwhile, some theological conservatives attempted to describe heaven, but admitted that biblical information about the subject was limited or lamented that Christians had little interest in the afterlife. Congregationalist pastor James Campbell contended that God did not discuss many of the issues about which people were curious, but He did supply enough information to stimulate faith, inspire hope, assuage sorrow, and banish fears. Edward Bounds, a Methodist minister and editor, pointed out that the Bible sought to "portray in human language things for which there are no earthly equivalents" to "stir and allure…and…instruct" people about the nature of heaven. William Biederwolf complained in 1930 that heaven was rarely discussed in church services or religious circles and that "many professing Christians" ignored the subject. In his early evangelistic crusades, Billy Graham, by contrast, provided vivid images of the afterlife. Heaven, he trumpeted, is "as real as Los Angeles, London, or Algiers," with "streets of gold, gates of pearl," and "fruit-bearing trees." The marriage feast of the Lamb after the Judgment Day would make banquets at Buckingham Palace or posh restaurants in Miami seem "like pauper meals."[7]

In these decades, neither conservative nor liberal Protestants placed much emphasis on worshipping the Trinity in heaven. Several authors lamented that articles, books, and sermons rarely discussed "the beatific vision, the essential characteristic of heaven."[8] A few Protestants did stress this theme. John MacNeill announced that "heaven's central glory is God; its chief attraction is Christ." The saints' "crowning experience" in heaven, Jesse T. Whitley averred, will be to share the

Savior's joy.[9] However, the dearth of similar statements by Protestants in this period is striking.

Catholics, by contrast, continued to accentuate this aspect of heaven. The disciples' three years of camaraderie with Christ, asserted J. P. Arendzen, was "nothing compared with the companionship" the blessed had with Him in heaven. "Although Christ is the great King, He will also be the intimate personal friend" of each heavenly resident. In heaven, Arendzen announced, the redeemed will view all things through the lens of the beatific vision. Fellow priest J. P. McCarthy argued that heaven's inhabitants will share God's life and "His complete beatitude;" they will possess and enjoy Him. "The joy of heaven," McCarthy concluded, is "to love God and be loved."[10]

No Catholic emphasized the beatific vision more than Martin Scott, a priest at the Church of St. Francis Xavier in New York City. The saints, he declared, will see the "infinite beauty of God" and share His bliss. Compared to God's splendor, "all the beauty of nature" and "the fascination of human attractiveness," Scott proclaimed, "is less than that…of a candle compared to the sun." Seeing God as "as He is…so ravishes" the saints that if they did not partake "of the divine nature" they would be unable to bear the joy. Heavenly residents will identify with God so completely that they will "freely and joyously desire only what He wills." They will also see Christ "face to face and know that He loves" them "inexpressibly more than anyone ever loved them on earth." Heaven, Scott avowed, is "the abode of inexpressible happiness." Heavenly joy gave individuals "a delirium of delight" that lasted forever. Most wonderful of all, "in heaven love is supreme, perpetual, inexhaustible, [and] all-satisfying."[11]

Bishop Fulton J. Sheen enjoyed immense popularity in the 1950s as a result of his half-hour weekly television show, *Life Is Worth Living*, which won him a *Time* magazine cover, an Emmy, and a place on the list of "most admired" Americans. Sheen argued that eternity will "be nothing like" anything people had ever "seen, heard or imagined." There will be "peace and a quiet without idleness," "profound knowledge of things without research," and "constant enjoyment without satiety." Heaven will combine all the best pleasures of earth while eliminating all its evils, diseases, and worries.[12]

Although they largely neglected the traditional theocentric depiction of heaven, both conservative and liberal Protestants during this period, like Sheen, portrayed paradise as a place where people realized their full potential, no longer battled evils, gained a sense of completion, and experienced ecstasy. Rejecting conceptions of heaven as a realm of white-robed, harp-playing, crown-wearing, bored saints who endlessly sang hymns, many pastors, professors, and authors depicted the afterlife as filled with challenges, variety, and service.[13] The Bible taught that heaven is "bustling with . . . activity," John Anderson declared. Since God, Jesus, the Holy Spirit, and the angels all work, so would the redeemed. The saints, asserted Presbyterian educator and author Loraine Boettner, will continue to grow, learn, and serve in the afterlife, but these endeavors will be neither trying nor tiring. Everyone, Campbell promised, would be assigned jobs based upon their "special aptitudes and powers." Episcopal rector Walter Russell Bowie argued that the saints fulfill all their potential because they are freed from all the restrictions and friction of earthly existence. In heaven, people had jobs that utilized their earthly "knowledge, experience and development" and experienced "unchecked growth and development . . . excitement and adventure."[14] The saints, Anderson averred, would study the treasures of "the great art gallery and museum of the universe." The least resident of heaven, Scott maintained, knows more about "art, science, history, [and] astronomy than the wisest of mankind."[15]

Theological conservatives and Catholics also stressed that heaven lacks earth's ills. In paradise, James Campbell declared, absolute love reigns and no discord exists. Others added that every earthly pain will be removed, "all fiery trials quenched, and all tears dried." Residents will experience no toil, anxieties, or temptations.[16] Heaven would have no slums, crowded apartment buildings, "ignorance, despair, debt," grinding toil, or "sweat shops." Nor would it have any gamblers, murderers, or meddlers. Regret, sorrow, frustration, and disappointment do not exist in heaven, Catholic J. P. Arendzen argued.[17]

Although some liberal Protestants accentuated these same themes, they tended to offer a less specific portrait of heaven. Charles Reynolds Brown declared that he had no idea what "the conditions or employments" of the future life would be. For liberals like Albert Knudson, the afterlife would be "continuous with the present," a life of service, progress, fellowship, "transcendent joy and peace," and moral growth. Fosdick reasoned that the afterlife provided increased opportunities for growth because living forever with one's current limitations would be "dreadful." He agreed with Reinhold Niebuhr that Christians did not have "any knowledge of either the furniture of heaven or the temperature of hell." "Immortality," Fosdick declared, "is a great adventure into the unseen and the unknown." Because pastors and theologians failed to emphasize this, many Americans either doubted heaven's existence or did not desire to go there. "The conventional heaven," he protested, "would be intolerable." It was like telling a grammar school pupil "with an earnest and aspiring mind" that he could never advance beyond his current state. "Annihilation would be far better."[18]

For some Protestant liberals, including theologian Paul Tillich, eternal life did not appear to involve existence beyond physical death. Rather, it seemed "to be a quality of life [on earth] gained through personal encounter with the Christian revelation."[19] Both Tillich and Niebuhr discussed the afterlife in figurative terms. "The biblical symbols" describing the hereafter, Niebuhr declared, "cannot be taken literally" because finite minds cannot "comprehend that which transcends and fulfills history." Some type of life after death may exist, but people could not count on it because it was totally beyond their experience. Niebuhr confided to a friend in 1938, "I do not believe in individual immortality." He also told a Scot that he did not have "the slightest interest in the empty tomb or physical resurrection." Moreover, like the Social Gospelers, he complained that their preoccupation with heaven caused some Christians to neglect their worldly responsibilities. Tillich labeled detailed accounts of the afterlife "absurd" because the Bible used symbolic, not literal, language to describe it. Tillich offered instead "a series of paradoxes, contradictions, and descriptions of what eternal life is not." Like Niebuhr, Tillich did not publicly deny life after death, but his 1952 book *The Courage to Be* "seemed to reject any claims of human immortality." He challenged the images of heaven that had developed during the two millennia of Christian history and urged other theologians to adopt "an abstract, philosophical understanding" of eternal life.[20]

Like some liberal Protestants, many Jews rejected belief in personal postmortem existence and argued that people lived on only through their children and contributions. As rabbi Milton Steinberg put it, an individual "may be immortal biologically, through his children; in thought, through the survival of his memory; in influence," through his personality continuing as a force in later generations; "and ideally, through his identification with the timeless things of the spirit." Jewish traditionalists, however, affirmed belief that the "human personality outlives its corporeal housing." A just God would make sure that individuals receive their just deserts in another world since they often do not receive them on earth. Traditionalists looked forward to a "purified world" where they could "enjoy the glory of God." Heaven is "the goal of holiness" and, therefore, "enforces the demand for moral endeavor upon earth."[21]

Despite his earlier statements, Niebuhr expressed hope in *The Nature and Destiny of Man* (1943) that Christians would spend eternity in heaven. He noted that modern minds took "the greatest offense" at the idea of the resurrection of the body and that most modern versions of Christianity had replaced it with the "idea of the immortality of the soul." Like all other conceptions that involved a consummation beyond history, both of these ideas were "beyond logical conception." "The hope of the resurrection," he stated, implied that "eternity will fulfill...the richness and variety" of the temporal process. "From a human perspective," the problem of the human "condition of finiteness and freedom" "can only be solved by faith...in the God who is revealed in Christ and from whose love neither life nor death can separate us." All defenses of the immortality of the soul strove to prove that some element in human nature "is worthy and capable of survival beyond death," but nothing could substantiate this point. Nevertheless, Christians must assert what seemed "logically inconceivable"—that finite humans could live forever in loving fellowship with God. In expressing the Christian hope, Niebuhr contended, Christians must simultaneously admit that "it doth not yet appear what we shall be" and confess that "we shall be like him" (I John 3:2).[22]

The Social Gospel movement declined in vitality after 1920. Its key leaders died, many Protestants became preoccupied with their fraternal theological disputes, and Americans' attention shifted from social reform to amusement, economic woes, and war. Correspondingly, few emphasized efforts to establish paradise on earth. One exception was R. R. Moton, Booker T. Washington's successor as president of Tuskegee Institute, who declared that his quest to construct heaven on earth gave him little time to think about the nature of the afterlife. Similarly, New York City rabbi Samuel Schulman insisted that Judaism taught people to work "to create the Kingdom of God here" rather than to focus on personal immorality. People should promote and practice rectitude, justice, and kindness "and leave the mysteries of the future world to God." On the other hand, some looked to heaven to rectify earth's social injustices. Wellesley College professor Vida Scudder argued that her privileged position "would be intolerable" if she did not believe that the earth's "starved and cheated masses" had "redress and enlarged opportunity in another world." Heaven was necessary, the editor of *The American Hebrew* contended, to satisfy "the demand for justice, righteousness, and love," which was rarely fulfilled on earth.[23] Many African Americans and lower-class whites expected the splendors of heaven to compensate for their earthly exploitation and privation.[24]

Others, especially theological conservatives, encouraged Christians to focus on heaven or argued that belief in heaven should influence people's earthly life. "Overworldliness, not other-worldliness," James Campbell complained in 1924, "is the besetting sin of the times." Jesus discussed heaven as "a present experience rather than [as] a future hope." Belief in the afterlife, Campbell maintained, provided "the deepest motives for right living in the present" and for striving to create "a fairer social order." Heaven, Bounds proclaimed, should "so fill" people's hearts, manner, conversation, and character that everyone would see that they are "strangers to this world." Having their names written and their treasures stored in paradise, he declared, should give Christians hope, assuage their grief, and make them "immune to the ills of this life." In a 1957 sermon Martin Luther King, Jr., argued that Christians "are a colony of heaven" whose "ultimate allegiance is to the empire of eternity." This should inspire them to work fearlessly to solve the nation's racial problems.[25]

Both conservatives and liberals urged Christians to implement heaven's principles and practices on earth. Earthly life, Campbell avowed, should be "governed by heavenly laws." The Bible taught that money could be invested on earth to achieve "good returns in the hereafter." Heaven and earth are so closely connected, he argued, that people could send their resources to "Heaven's treasure-house" and reclaim them after their arrival. "We think" of heaven, declared William Biederwolf, "as some place we are to go…when in reality it is the something we are to be." Learning about heaven could provide Christians with "inspiration, strength, and comfort" for daily living. Belief in life after death, Shailer Mathews asserted, helped make a "life of love and sacrifice" worthwhile on earth and provided a "compelling impulse" for emulating His actions.[26]

Several conservative pastors exhorted Christians to prepare properly for paradise. Because heavenly bliss depended largely on "what we are," John Sutherland Bonnell contended, believers should cultivate godly virtues. "The fullest measure of happiness" in heaven, Anderson argued, is based partly "upon our conduct here." Jesse T. Whitley urged Christians to develop the attitudes, "characters and tastes…that prevail" in their future abode, most notably humble "trust in divine mercy," purity, "grateful love," "self-denying service," and generosity "to the needy."[27]

From 1920 to 1960, Hollywood offered several portraits of heaven that featured popular religious teachings and cultural stereotypes of heaven. These movies also provided comfort, consolation, and cheer and advanced various social agendas. The most controversial movie was *Green Pastures* (1936), an adaptation of Marc Connelly's Pulitzer Prize–winning play, which Southern theater owners boycotted because of its all-black cast and depiction of God as an African American. To encourage whites to empathize with the exploitation and injustice blacks had suffered for centuries, the film presented several biblical episodes from the vantage point of contemporary African Americans residing in heaven and stressed that blacks and these biblical heroes had been similarly abused. *The Fighting Sullivans* (1944), based on the true story of five brothers who all died in World War II, conveyed a different, but equally important, cultural message. Ending with a reunion of the brothers marching into heaven, it taught that God would reward earthly valor in the afterlife. It helped comfort tens of thousands of Americans whose loved ones had been killed in the war or were still fighting overseas. Meanwhile, other movies such as *A Guy Named Joe* (1943) depicted paradise as a place of merriment where saints enjoyed reunions with loved ones or developed new friendships and angels tried to help people achieve earthly happiness. In the 1945 comedy *The Horn Blows at Midnight*, heaven "resembles a typical government office" and the saints "earn rewards for successfully completing celestial missions." *For Heaven's Sake* (1950) similarly portrayed paradise "as a benevolent bureaucracy where Angels oversee earthly affairs" as two celestial social workers tried to help a feuding couple reconcile in order to prepare the way for a yet-to-be conceived baby waiting in heaven for them. *It's a Wonderful Life* (1946) also featured an angelic intervention in earthly affairs as a hapless celestial agent helped a despairing, melancholy savings and loan manager by showing him what his town would be like without him. Although nominated for five Academy Awards, including best picture, the film was a box office failure, and only its repeated showings since the 1970s made it an American icon.[28]

FELLOWSHIP AND REWARDS IN HEAVEN

Christians in this period, especially conservative Protestants, devoted considerable attention to the topic of heavenly recognition. "No question connected with the future life," Presbyterian Robert Hough declared in 1947, "is more frequently and earnestly asked than, 'Shall we know one another in Heaven?'" As in earlier generations, many argued that the doctrine had strong scriptural support, was required by the Bible's emphasis on personal identity and memory in heaven, had been widely affirmed in all times and places, and accorded with reason. Moreover, they insisted, this concept was one of the most attractive features of the afterlife. The Word of God, William Biederwolf asserted, supplied a powerful basis "for believing this beautiful and consoling truth." "Not a book, chapter … verse … or even a word … from Genesis to Revelation," alleged John Anderson, contradicted the "thrilling doctrine" of heavenly recognition. Both the disciples' recognition of Jesus after His resurrection and Paul's teaching that the resurrection body retained its original appearance, identity, and individuality, Methodist Robert Dane Cook averred, indicated that the redeemed would know each other in heaven.[29] Biederwolf and many others claimed that heavenly recognition had always been "a universal belief of the human heart."[30] That everyone has a distinct individuality, various authors noted, made it highly probable that personal identity continued in the future abode.[31] Some asserted that the nature of love and fellowship required both that the saints must have personal identity and recognize each other.[32] "Heaven would lose a good part of its charm," Biederwolf reasoned, if its residents "did not know to whom" they were talking and did not "recognize the dear ones" they had "loved below." The prospect of seeing family and friends in the afterlife, Hough asserted, had sustained many during the "bereavements of life."[33]

Numerous authors discussed the difficulties with the doctrine of heavenly recognition. Only God could explain the apparent problem of how the saints could be happy if they recognized that some of their friends and family were not in heaven, Jesse T. Whitley declared, and He had not done so. Citing Jonathan Edwards, Robert Dane Cook asserted that the redeemed "would say 'Amen' to the damnation of those," including their parents, children, or siblings, whom God did not permit to enter "the heavenly abode, because they refused" His offer of "mercy in Christ." The saints would not grieve if some of their loved ones did not join them, Anderson added, because heaven was "a land of eternal rejoicing," not "a place of weeping and wailing." God loved these individuals even more than they did, and He did not mourn their absence.[34]

Some conservative and liberal Protestants and Catholics accentuated heavenly fellowship, but they generally paid less attention to it than previous generations had. "My first great pleasure" in paradise, declared Congregationalist pastor and temperance advocate Charles M. Sheldon, famous for his book *In His Steps*, "will be to meet again the dear ones I love. Then it will take me an eternity to…interview all the great minds of the ages." "One great thing we do know about the future world," Harry Emerson Fosdick proclaimed, is that we will converse with loved ones and friends. "Friendship, affection, [and] love," Father Martin Scott declared, would abound in the "heavenly home."[35] Others, including Billy Graham, expected fellowship with the larger "family of the redeemed" to be as important in heaven to individuals as communing with their loved ones. Going further, Anderson argued that "the ties of the New Birth will be stronger than those of the Natural Birth" because spiritual connections were superior to and took "precedence over all other relationships."[36]

As in the Progressive Era, Christians in these years focused little on heavenly rewards. Fosdick denounced the traditional focus on postmortem compensation as detrimental and undesirable. Those who did discuss this issue contended that heavenly rewards differed depending on people's character, holiness, and service on earth. John Sutherland Bonnell, for example, insisted that the saints received "different degrees of blessedness" and attained varying levels of "spiritual knowledge and development" in proportion to their earthly righteousness. A priest maintained that the saints' heavenly mansions are constructed of the materials their earthly lives supplied, making some much grander than others.[37] Numerous popular hymns, such as one written by Ira Stamphill in 1949, celebrated heavenly rewards:

> I'm not discouraged, I'm heaven bound…
> I want a mansion, a harp and a crown.…
> In that bright land where we'll never grow old.

CALVARY VERSUS CHARACTER

Conservatives and liberals disagreed not only about some of the features of heaven and the value of focusing on the afterlife, but also over the basis of salvation.

Although fundamentalists and evangelicals saw numerous issues differently, they concurred with the historic American Protestant position that, with the probable exception of infants and the mentally incapacitated and the possible exception of those who never heard the gospel message, only those who accepted Jesus as their personal savior and Lord would be permitted to enter heaven. Speaking for both groups, John Anderson declared that everyone "who believed that the Lord Jesus Christ is the Son of God, and the only Savior of the world...and who has personally trusted Him for life and salvation will certainly go to heaven." All those who died before reaching the age of accountability and "the feeble-minded," he added, would "surely go to heaven." Religious conservatives often protested that many professing Christians (primarily Catholics, liberal Protestants, and nominal church members) assumed that their fitness for heaven depended partly on what Christ did for them and partly on their own efforts. The only thing that qualified individuals for admission to heaven, they countered, "is the atoning work of the Lord Jesus Christ." As David I. Berger, who taught homiletics at (Presbyterian) Dubuque Theological Seminary in Iowa, succinctly put it, "We are not saved by [our] character but by Calvary." "We do not purchase the right to enter heaven by any good works that we have done," Bonnell proclaimed. "We enter it through the merits of Jesus Christ alone and our trust in God's redeeming grace freely proffered in him." To ensure they obtained a mansion in heaven, declared a female African Methodist Episcopal evangelist, people must be born again; only those with a "true ticket...stamped by...the Captain of the Good Ship Zion" would be admitted.[38] Perhaps because liberals insisted that upright character and good deeds played a major role in salvation, neither fundamentalists nor evangelicals, unlike Christians in earlier periods, placed much emphasis on the efforts of believers to work out their salvation by living righteous lives.

In his popular crusades and best-selling books of the 1950s, Billy Graham proclaimed that individuals must be born again to gain admission to heaven. While arguing that everyone must have "a decisive turning point" in his life, he maintained that conversion need not involve a traumatic, deeply emotional experience. On the other hand, Graham repudiated nineteenth-century theologian Horace Bushnell's theory of Christian nurture, which, in Graham's words, taught that "every child should grow up to be a Christian without ever knowing that he has not always been one." This supposition led liberal congregations to substitute "a false and improper use of religious training" "for the experience of a new birth." Graham maintained that "biblical conversion" involved an individual's repenting of sins and believing in Christ as her savior and God's regeneration of her heart. The first two steps were active, and the third was passive.[39] Although he accentuated God's holiness, justice, and wrath more than Dwight L. Moody or Billy Sunday, Graham, like them, placed greater emphasis on God's love, mercy, and grace. In his sermons, Graham attempted to make people anxious by showing that everyone had sinned and deserved "the worst kind of punishment." Then the evangelist explained that God had provided a way of redemption through Christ's death on the cross for sinful humanity. He concluded by explaining "how reasonably, simply, and quickly salvation" could be attained.[40] Speaking for evangelicals and fundamentalists, Graham repeatedly insisted that because people were sinners by nature, inheritance, and practice, they could not change their own hearts. Only Christ could transform individuals' sinful nature and reconcile them to God. No one could earn, inherit, or produce a second birth. Instead, God regenerated individuals by infusing divine life into their souls and implanting His nature in them. Salvation transformed people's hearts, changed their wills, and made them righteous in God's eyes.[41]

Liberals, by contrast, argued that religious experience and ethics, not doctrines and creeds, were the essence of Christianity. Dogmas like Christ's virgin birth, miracles, substitutionary atonement, and bodily resurrection are tentative and historically situated statements that express deeper religious sentiments and must periodically be revised in light of humanity's increasing knowledge. Liberals usually accentuated Christ's character and moral teachings while downplaying the metaphysical and supernatural. They also stressed God's love, the great worth of human beings, and the continual advancement of God's kingdom on earth. By His life and death, liberals averred, Jesus showed people how to live and love. Rather than atoning for sin and appeasing God's wrath, His death on Calvary supplied a marvelous model of sacrificial love and forgiveness. Because attaining eternal life, argued Charles Reynolds Brown, depended upon developing a worthy character by making "wise and right choices," everyone was responsible for their own destiny. Immortal life, he declared, is "an achievement...to be sought and won by spiritual effort." Those who walked in the light and strove to attain the highest end would "enter into life eternal."[42] Therefore, people should strive to act righteously, perform virtuous deeds, and improve society rather than focus on otherworldly salvation. Emulating Christ's example, they should serve and love others, not concentrate on their own future destiny. Numerous liberals concurred with Unitarians and Universalists that all people would ultimately be saved.[43]

Disagreeing with both conservative and liberal Christians, secular humanists, who became an important force in the 1930s, especially in intellectual circles, defined "salvation" as self-actualization or reaching one's own highest potential. In "Humanist Manifesto I," signed in 1933 by thirty-four prominent Americans including renowned philosopher John Dewey, they declared that belief in the supernatural "is either meaningless or irrelevant" to human fulfillment. "No deity will save us," the document bluntly proclaimed; "we must save ourselves" by "the complete realization of human personality" "in the here and now" and by working to create a "society in which people voluntarily and intelligently co-operate for the common good."[44]

Catholics, meanwhile, continued to teach that both Christ's sacrificial death and individuals' good works as mediated through the church's sacramental ministry and the purifying effects of purgatory were essential to salvation. Most Catholics saw obeying the Ten Commandments, attending church, taking communion, performing penance, praying, and doing good deeds as requirements for getting to heaven. Heaven, Martin Scott contended, is God's reward for achieving "victory in the warfare of life," the recompense God used to inspire loyalty to Him during the earthly pilgrimage, the destiny of those who lived righteously. All who obeyed God, he promised, will "reign with Him forever." Bishop Fulton Sheen argued similarly that heaven "is related to a…virtuous life…the same way that knowledge is related to study. One necessarily follows the other."[45]

Sheen explained further that individuals' eternal destiny depended on their "merits and demerits," their virtues and vices. When people died "in the state of grace" and God saw "a likeness of His own nature," He bid them to "come into the Kingdom prepared for you from all eternity." When individuals stand before the "majestic presence of almighty God," they do not plead, argue, or protest His judgment, because they see themselves as they truly are. If they see themselves as "clean and alive with the life of God," they run "to the embrace of love, which is heaven." If people see themselves as "slightly stained and the robes" of their "Baptism remediably soiled," they throw themselves "into the purifying flames of purgatory." If they see themselves as "irremediably vitiated, having no likeness whatever to the purity and holiness of God," they cast themselves into hell, recognizing that because of their unworthiness, impurity, and ungodliness, heaven would be hell for them.[46]

THE CONTINUED DEMISE OF HELL

The subject of hell is noticeably absent from most Protestant analyses of heaven and salvation from this period. In their classic sociological study *Middletown*, Robert and Helen Lynd noted that the idea of eternal punishment was receding. Many of those who did mention hell, especially theological liberals, condemned the concept. Fosdick denounced Jonathan Edwards's "awful sermon," "Sinners in the Hands of an Angry God," which caused women to faint and strong men to cling to "the pillars of the church in agony." This faulty picture of "the Eternal Arbiter on his judgment seat" filled souls "with terror and dismay." "Let us not torture ourselves with old pictures of hell as a place of unending punishment," declared Ralph Sockman, a renowned radio preacher and pastor of Christ (Methodist) Church in New York

City. "God is love, and love chastens only to redeem." Unitarians and Universalists denounced the doctrine of hell as "the foulest" conceivable assault on the character of God. Only those with hearts of stone "could be happy...knowing that half the human family, including many of their own loved ones, were in torments."[47]

A few evangelicals and some fundamentalists continued to maintain the long-standing Christian doctrine of hell as a literal place of physical and spiritual suffering. If Christians truly believed in the biblical depiction of hell, evangelist Hyman Appelman declared in 1947, they would weep, agonize, and plead "with lost souls to be reconciled to God through the Lord Jesus Christ." Although a handful of theological conservatives preached sermons warning people of the terrors of hell, Billy Graham noted in 1953 that the subject of hell was "very unpopular, controversial, and misunderstood." In his early crusades, Graham warned his audiences that hell is a lake of burning brimstone. He renounced as unbiblical the ideas that those who rejected God's plan of redemption were annihilated or had a second chance after death. By the late 1950s, however, the evangelist downplayed hellfire and stressed that hell is essentially "banishment from the presence of God." Although he did not repudiate hell, Graham focused more on its mental and emotional, rather than its physical, suffering. Hell's fire may signify "the burning desire of those who have been eternally banished from his presence." "Hell's torments," he added, will include suffering remorse and regret for earthly actions. Others stressed that the unredeemed had "no capacity for appreciating heaven" and thus would be miserable there. If given the freedom, they would search for a place more suitable to their "habitual state of mind" and natural inclinations and would eventually "land in hell."[48]

Meanwhile, some Catholics, led by Sheen, continued to strongly defend the traditional concepts of both hell and purgatory. After death, he asserted, individuals either went to heaven—"a state of perfect Love without suffering"—hell—"a state of suffering without Love"—or purgatory—"a state of Love with suffering." Sheen acknowledged that the idea of hell offended many mid-twentieth-century Americans and that most Westerners did not believe it existed. The doctrine of hell, he contended, was an integral part of "the organic whole of Christian truths," especially the principle that both justice and love demanded hell. Those who recognized that a just moral order undergirded the universe, Sheen argued, understood that "retribution beyond the grave" was necessary. "The martyr and the persecutor" could not be treated the same way after death. Those who rejected the love of an infinite God, Sheen declared, would be eternally separated from the source of "Life and Truth and Love." Christ was willing to pour "out His life's blood to redeem us from sin" because sin had a consequence as terrible as hell. "Hell exists," the bishop maintained, "for those who refuse to love" God, which was the only thing He could not forgive.[49]

Although Christianity had affirmed the doctrine of purgatory for sixteen centuries and the Catholic Church continued to teach this dogma, Sheen stated, Protestants and non-Christians repudiated it "as a mere product of the imagination, rather than as a fruit of sound reason and [divine] inspiration." "Belief in purgatory," he argued, had declined among Catholics because people had forgotten both "the purity of God and the heinousness of sin."[50] However, God's holiness and humanity's sin made purgatory inescapable. A just and perfect God, Sheen argued, allowed only the pure of heart to spend eternity with Him. If purgatory did not exist, God's justice "would be too terrible for words" because who dared to assert that he was "pure enough…to stand before the Immaculate Lamb of God." Martyrs, faithful missionaries, and devout monastics could do this, but they were "glorious exceptions." If there were no purgatory, divine justice would require that all the "beautiful souls" who died with even "slight imperfections" be consigned to hell. However, Sheen rejoiced, in purgatory, God's love balances His justice as he retouches "these souls with His Cross," as he refashions "them with the chisel of suffering," so that they "fit into the great spiritual edifice of the heavenly Jerusalem." Purgatory also enabled "the love of man" to assuage "the injustice of man," by allowing Christians on earth "to break the barriers of time and death," and through their prayers, sacrifices, and alms, help their loved ones move to heaven. Therefore, Sheen concluded, purgatory was a product of God's mercy.[51]

CONCLUSION

The divisions and disagreements among Protestants that began in the final decades of the nineteenth century intensified between 1920 and 1960. These differences helped produce competing perspectives of what heaven would be like and on what basis individuals would be admitted. Although most Protestants still agreed about aspects of the afterlife, their disagreements over its nature and the basis of salvation were significant. Meanwhile, their intramural conflict, as well as the shifting cultural attitudes generated by increasing secularization, skepticism, and assaults on orthodoxy, prompted all Protestants, including theologically conservative ones, to focus less on some topics that long had been staple aspects of traditional conceptions of heaven, most notably the relationship of the saints with God and Jesus, heavenly fellowship and rewards, and the existence of hell. Moreover, the growing size, influence, and assertiveness of American Catholics made their perspectives on heaven more important. Although Protestants, especially fundamentalists and evangelicals, and Catholics agreed on some of the features of heaven, they clashed on other issues, especially over how individuals gain entry, what the saints do there, and whether people must be purified in purgatory before being admitted.

The relatively complacent, conformist 1950s gave way to the turbulent 1960s, a decade characterized by the efforts of African Americans, Native Americans, women, Hispanics, and homosexuals to gain greater civil rights, as well as debates over the Vietnam War, a war on poverty, and great ideological ferment. In the midst of this maelstrom, new theologies emerged, promoting the liberation of the poor, blacks, and women, declaring God to be dead, and emphasizing teleological processes. These new theologies, coupled with the resurgence of evangelicalism, the rejuvenation of Catholicism after Vatican II, and the rise of multiculturalism, political correctness, and postmodernism, had great effects on American views of heaven in the final decades of the twentieth century.

9

NEW CURRENTS AND OLD

STREAMS, 1960–2000

The saints "see the Father, Son, and Holy Spirit face-to-face" and endlessly share "in their love and joy" and thereby find "eternal rest and fulfillment."
—EDMUND FORTMAN, *Everlasting Life after Death*

In heaven, God "will be at the center of everything. And His glory will be dominant."
—BILLY GRAHAM, *Facing Death*

After death people's "existence as individuated ego/organism" ceases and dissolves into "the cosmic matrix of matter/energy, from which new centers of individuation arise. It is this matrix, rather than our individuated centers of being, that is 'everlasting.'"
—ROSEMARY RADFORD RUETHER, *Sexism and God-Talk*

A teacher, a garbage collector, and a lawyer arrived together at the Pearly Gates. St. Peter informed them that in order to get into heaven, they each had to answer one question.

St. Peter asked the teacher, "What was the name of the ship that crashed into the iceberg? They just made a movie about it."

The teacher answered, "The Titanic," and St. Peter admitted him.

Concluding that heaven did not need all the odors that the garbage collector would bring with him, St. Peter decided to make the question a little harder: "How many people died on the ship?"

Fortunately the trash collector had just seen the movie. "1,228," he answered.

"That's right," Peter declared. "You may enter."

St. Peter then turned to the lawyer. "Name them."

THE LAST FORTY years of the twentieth century were a time of substantial ferment and change in American society. Tumult prevailed in the 1960s fueled by civil rights marches, boycotts, and sit-ins; race riots in major cities; a war in Vietnam that evoked great protest and caused societal discord; and renewed efforts to increase opportunities for women. Turmoil continued in the 1970s as a result of the United States' defeat in Vietnam, the Watergate scandal, President Richard Nixon's resignation, and a major economic recession. During the "Me Decade," self-absorption reigned as many focused on personal well-being and self-fulfillment. The 1980s are best known for affluence, the AIDS epidemic, a war against drugs, soaring federal deficits, nuclear arms agreements with the Soviets, and the fall of Communism in Eastern Europe. During the 1990s, the United States experienced a stock market boom, an information revolution ignited by the Internet, and greater consumerism and pursuit of leisure. The collapse of the Soviet Union in 1991 dramatically changed the world order, while at home, culture wars continued over abortion, homosexuality, and the nation's alleged moral decay.

The American religious scene shifted as well. In the 1970s, mainline Protestant denominations—especially the United Church of Christ, the Disciples of Christ, the United Methodist Church, the Presbyterian Church, USA, the Episcopal Church, and various Baptist denominations centered outside the South—while remaining a significant social and political force, began to experience a decline in membership and interest in evangelism and spiritual formation. Meanwhile, evangelical Protestant groups flourished. Contemporary evangelicalism is a large and diverse movement of Christians who emphasize the authority of the Bible, the centrality of the divine-human Jesus Christ, the importance of a new birth experience, and the responsibility of believers to evangelize. It includes Christians who belong to eight distinctive traditions: Lutheran, Reformed, Wesleyan, Pentecostal and charismatic, black evangelical, Anabaptist, former fundamentalist, and several white Protestant denominations, most notably the Southern Baptist Convention.[1] Many evangelical congregations, especially megachurches in major cities that drew from 5,000 to 30,000 worshippers on Sundays, grew in size and influence. Evangelicals created dozens of parachurch organizations to minister to diverse groups and advance various causes. Prompted by their concerns about government intrusion into private education, possible loss of their congregations' tax-exempt status, abortion, secularization, and declining moral standards, many evangelicals reentered the political arena in the late 1970s with the founding of several organizations that coalesced into the Religious Right. During these four decades, the Catholic Church experienced major changes as a result of Vatican II (1962–1965), especially more theological innovation, greater openness to interfaith dialogue, increased ecumenism, and revised liturgies. In the United States, liberation theology, the New Age, and Mormonism put forth portraits of heaven that clashed with traditional Christian ideas. Finally, the much greater reporting and scholarly investigation of near-death experiences helped increase interest in life beyond the grave.

Commentators reached very different conclusions about the importance of heaven in American life during these years. Almost all Western Christians, Colleen McDannell and Bernhard Lang observed in 1988, had been "influenced by a skeptical perspective on life after death." For many Christians, life after death "means existing only in the memory of their families and of God. Scientific, philosophical, and theological skepticism has nullified" the traditional Christian view of heaven "and replaced it with teachings that are minimalist, meager, and dry." Moreover, they concluded, Christians were much less eager than their predecessors to "discuss the details of heavenly existence." Rejecting the depictions of "earlier generations of ministers, scholars, and visionaries," many contemporary theologians portrayed heaven "as a symbolic, imaginative representation of the unknowable." "Rich and detailed accounts of the afterlife," which were widely "accepted in the nineteenth century," were often denounced "as absurd, crude, materialistic, or sheer nonsense."[2]

Other observers agreed. Although few church leaders "explicitly repudiate belief in a future life," noted an article in *The Westminster Dictionary of Christian Theology*, "the virtual absence of references to it in modern hymns, prayers, and popular apologetic indicates how little part it plays in the contemporary Christian consciousness." While superficially accepting "Christian teaching on the subject" of life after death, process theologian Norman Pittinger declared in 1980, most "regular church-going people" held views that were "not deeply rooted or profoundly felt." *Christianity Today* editor Philip Yancey concluded in 1989 that "older, biblical images of heaven" had lost their appeal for many Americans because they enjoyed in this life what earlier "generations could only anticipate" in paradise.[3]

Numerous authors argued that traditional conceptions of heaven seemed boring to sophisticated, jaded, self-indulgent moderns. "Our conventional images of heaven," Peter Kreeft, a Catholic professor at Boston College, declared, are insipid, "platitudinous and syrupy." "Playing harps and polishing halos," changeless perfection, and "abstract contemplation of changeless truth" "do not fulfill our need for creative work." Many Christians, Anne Sandberg asserted, had little enthusiasm for nebulous depictions of paradise as "blessed souls lounging upon a grassy sward, blissfully strumming harps or attending a great big, never-ending church service." Billy Graham contended that many people paid little attention to the wonderful biblical promises about heaven because the conventional images seemed implausible to them.[4]

On the other hand, several other factors indicate that Americans had considerable interest in heaven after 1975. During the last quarter of the twentieth century, dozens of books about heaven (mostly by evangelical Protestants) and near-death experiences were published. Polls repeatedly reported that a high percentage of Americans believed heaven existed and expected to go there.[5] Materials about the afterlife became popular, including "angelware" (items decorated with images of angels, including T-shirts, collector plates, salt and pepper shakers, and night-lights) and "heavenly" greeting cards (including sympathy cards that promised mourners reunion with their loved ones in heaven), as did songs about heaven and discussions of the afterlife on talk shows and in novels. In numerous television commercials, those who lived righteously on earth or made healthy lifestyle choices were rewarded in heaven with "superior consumer products" or enthralling parties. Among the period's most popular movies dealing with heaven are *Heaven Can Wait* (1978), *Oh, Heavenly Dog!* (1980), *Brainstorm* (1983), *The Heavenly Kid* (1985), *Made in Heaven* (1987), *Always* (1989), *Jacob's Ladder* (1990) *Hi Honey, I'm Dead* (1991), *White Light* (1991), *Defending Your Life* (1991), and *City of Angels* (1998). Mostly comedies, these films offered whimsical views of heaven replete with stereotypes and (from an orthodox Christian perspective) misconceptions. Caretaker angels, second chances, renewed relationships with family and friends, divine mercy, and discovering the meaning of life are prominent themes in movies about the hereafter. Especially popular was *Bill & Ted's Bogus Journey* (1991), in which two teenage "excellent dudes" traverse heaven and hell and find it very difficult to meet heaven's entrance requirement of serenity and enlightenment. Actress Diane Keaton examined conceptions of the afterlife in her documentary-style film *Heaven: The Ultimate Coming Attraction* (1987), which included discussion of traditional religious perspectives on the hereafter, clips of the afterlife from vintage films, and interviews of ordinary Americans.[6]

In the final years of the twentieth century, heaven also made inroads into television. The two most watched shows were Michael Landon's *Highway to Heaven*, which aired weekly from 1984 to 1989, and *Touched by an Angel*, which ran from 1994 to 2003. In each episode of *Highway to Heaven*, "probationary angels" helped people by promoting "peace, love, and understanding." The show depicted paradise as a warm place filled with deep joy and abundant laughter. In *Touched by an Angel*, angels aided humans at crossroads in their lives.[7]

The era's best-selling books on heaven included Betty J. Eadie's *Embraced by the Light* (1992) and Daniel Pinkwater's *The Afterlife Diet* (1995). Based on her alleged near-death experience, Eadie describes her conversations with angels, deceased friends, and Jesus. Pinkwater criticized American attitudes toward the overweight by portraying heaven as a place where body size, not morality, determines people's rewards. "Strictly segregated according to their body fat quotient," "svelte souls ascend to stellar ecstasy" while chubby ones "are relegated to a lesser realm." "Paradise is decidedly unpleasant for the plump" who are denounced as a "blot on the landscape" that mars heaven's beauty.[8]

Numerous songs about heaven became hits in the 1990s. Marty Robbins's "Hillbilly Heaven" (1993) describes a dream in which many deceased country stars relish the glories of heaven, while numerous rap songs, most notably Tupac Shakur's

"I Ain't Mad at Cha" (1995) and Puff Daddy's "I'll Be Missing You" (1997), focus on the afterlife. Shakur meets his heroes in heaven and asks that violent criminals be forgiven, while "I'll Be Missing You" laments the death of rapper Notorious B.I.G. and rejoices that relationships with loved ones will be restored in heaven. Especially popular was Eric Clapton's "Tears in Heaven" (1992). Written in response to the death of his four-year-old son, who fell from their fifty-third-story apartment, Clapton celebrates the bliss of celestial reunion. The song topped both the sales and request charts in 1992 and won the artist four Grammy Awards.[9]

During these years, many cartoons also depicted heaven. The characters in Bil Keane's *Family Circus* often speculated about the world to come. For decades, Gary Larson's *Far Side* cartoons lampooned heaven. In a typical one, an anxious Colonel Sanders arrives at the pearly gates and finds angry chickens guarding them. Heaven has long been a staple of political cartoons. After Richard Nixon's death in 1994, numerous cartoonists portrayed the former president basking in heaven while many others depicted him suffering in a smoky hell. When comedian George Burns died two years later at age 100, a cartoon in *Esquire* showed him arriving in paradise and proclaiming, "Gracie, I got the part!"[10]

ALTERNATIVE VIEWS OF HEAVEN AND SALVATION

In the years following 1960, a number of new forces challenged and competed with those of mainstream Christianity. One of the most prominent was liberation theology. In the 1960s, some Latin American theologians and priests, as well as Protestant pastors and professors, responded to their region's widespread poverty and oppression by calling on their respective churches to denounce exploitation and side with the indigent. In North America and other parts of the world, liberation theology principally appealed to those who prioritize ending economic, sexual, and racial discrimination. African-American theologians denounced the racism of white-dominated society, while feminist theologians attacked patriarchy. Asserting that God sides with the poor and the oppressed and that Jesus identified with the indigent and deplored economic and sexual exploitation, liberation theologians challenged the church to condemn, and work to end, injustice.

Liberationists rejected the traditional Christian understanding of salvation and heaven. They saw the terms *liberation* and *salvation* as closely related, if not identical. Liberation, asserted Jesuit professor Roger Haight, entails "social, economic, and political release" from oppression. God's saving grace affects not only people's "spiritual intentions but the whole of human existence." While liberationists did not ignore "the ultimate meaning of salvation…beyond history," he argued, they focused on how salvation changes life in this world. The church should proclaim the values of God's kingdom and "directly challenge the political economic, social, and cultural struc-tures" that cause human misery. Salvation is not primarily concerned with "the promise of immortality." In fact, the traditional concept of the afterlife, Haight warned, fre-quently led people to misunderstand salvation, which involved working to bring about God's reign on earth. Only those who actively promoted "corporate salvation here and now" could "legitimately hope" to attain "resurrection and ultimate salvation." Salvation's essential component is conversion, which requires emulating Jesus' life.[11]

Jesus clearly taught, Haight claimed, that God will evaluate people at the last judgment on the basis of whether they assisted or ignored the poor (Mt. 25:31–46). Only those who helped the destitute and needy were promised that they would commune "with Christ in the afterlife." God's kingdom will eventually liberate all creation and eliminate all earthly exploitation. Conversion demands that people not only change their convictions (theory) but more importantly that they alter their attitudes (practice) toward all their "personal, social, and religious relationships." Through His "torture, judicial condemnation, and crucifixion," Jesus set people free. Even though Jesus Christ is the "model of salvation" and God worked through Him "in a qualitatively unique and unsurpassable way," Haight argued, salvation is not "an exclusive Christian possession"—it had "been universally available in history."[12]

Black liberation theologians also stressed building God's kingdom on earth, attack-ing social injustice, and viewing salvation as a basis for action in this world rather than as a passport to heaven. In *A Black Theology of Liberation* (1970), James H. Cone, a professor at Union Theological Seminary in New York City, argued that "the kingdom of God is a black happening" that compelled blacks to challenge whites' unjust prac-tices. Repentance, he contended, had "nothing to do with" white versions of "morality or religious piety." Instead, it meant "casting one's lot with" the kingdom God was building in this world. Cone protested that salvation had usually been interpreted in ways that did "not threaten the security of the existing government." White Christianity encouraged the poor to long "for the next life," rather than to improve their earthly conditions. Whenever the indigent concentrated on the afterlife, Cone maintained, their oppressors could exploit them without any fear of reprisal. Although black slaves had reinterpreted salvation to enable them to endure their subjugation, after the Civil War, the black church had embraced the white definition of salvation as "an objective act of Christ in which God 'washes' away our sins in order to prepare us for a new life in heaven." Salvation did have a future component, Cone asserted, but it focused heavily upon the present. God's salvation required assisting "the Black Christ as he liberates his people from bondage." God's people must defy their oppres-sors and demand that justice be achieved on earth, not just in heaven.[13]

Cone denounced all eschatological perspectives that did "not challenge the present order" and led the oppressed to tolerate their unjust treatment. The white portrait of heaven was "fruitless for black people." Focusing on pearly gates and singing about "a great camp meeting in the Promised Land" did nothing to improve blacks' present situation. Blacks must resist whites' long-standing quest to entice them to "look forward to heavenly justice" and ignore present injustices, and must not "accept hell on earth" just because they had "a home over yonder." However, Cone urged blacks not to "reject the future reality of life after death—grounded in Christ's resurrection—simply because" whites had "distorted it for their own selfish purposes." Their faith that death is not the end, Cone avowed, should inspire blacks to "fight against overwhelming odds" against "the guns, atomic power, police departments, and every [other] conceivable weapon of destruction" their enemies possessed. If blacks truly believed that "death is not the last word, then they could" risk "death to obtain their freedom, knowing that man's ultimate destiny" is in God's hands.[14]

Feminist theologian Rosemary Radford Ruether similarly exhorted Christians to reject narcissistic concern about personal immortality or "the eternal meaning" of their individual lives and instead seek "to create a just and good community." Holy Wisdom would forge everlasting life out of people's finite struggle to obtain truth and meaning. Ruether concluded that after death people's "existence as individuated ego/organism" ceases and dissolves into "the cosmic matrix of matter/energy, from which new centers of individuation arise. It is this matrix, rather than our individuated centers of being, that is 'everlasting.'" She criticized Christians for teaching that "personal or individual ego," rather than "the total community of being," existed forever. Ruether labeled personal immortality "the apogee of male individualism and egoism" and contended that women historically had focused much less on life after death than had men.[15]

The New Age movement also offered an alternative view of the afterlife. After 1980, Americans displayed considerable interest in this eclectic, syncretistic worldview that involved a wide variety of individuals, organizations, ideas, and practices. It infiltrated many areas of contemporary American society, including psychology, education, medicine (acupuncture, Rolfing, kinesiology, and psychic healing), sociology, business, politics, science fiction, and movies (such as *Close Encounters of the Third Kind* and the *Star War* series). With diverse roots in Eastern religions (especially Hinduism and Buddhism), Gnosticism, and the occult (particularly magic, spiritualism, and divination), New Age philosophy rejects both monotheism and atheistic materialism and stresses mystical experiences that transcend space, time, and traditional moral concepts. The movement also draws from distinctly American sources—Transcendentalism (which imported Eastern mysticism to the United States in the mid nineteenth century), the Spiritualist movement, Helena Blavatsky's Theosophical Society, and the New Thought or Mind Cure movement of the last decades of the nineteenth century, which produced Christian Science. Its more immediate roots lie in the counterculture of the 1960s, in Eastern spiritual gurus and swamis, and in such Western critics as Alan Watts, Theodore Roszak, and Timothy Leary, who espoused various types of non-Christian mysticism.[16]

New Age advocates argued that the self is the prime reality and that liberated selves could produce a glorious new age of peace, light, and love. As people understand this, they can experience a radical change in their nature and become prototypes of the new humanity. For New Agers, physical death does not end the self; it is simply "a transition to another stage of life." Replacing the traditionally fatalistic, pessimistic Eastern concept of reincarnation with a much more upbeat American version, they viewed reincarnation as a means for achieving endless advancement. Some New Agers maintained that they had learned about their previous lives through either consulting channelers or seeing themselves in former incarnations. In a best-selling book, actress Shirley MacLaine, for example, claimed to have had thousands of lives, including ones as a harem dancer, a monk, a Russian ballet dancer, and a Peruvian Inca. In one former life, she allegedly saved an entire village from being destroyed.[17]

The Mormons, or the Church of Latter-day Saints, grew rapidly in the final decades of the twentieth century, bringing attention to their unique view of the afterlife. The Mormon conception of heaven shared some similarities with widely held nineteenth-century views. Both emphasized the importance of "love, family, progress, and work" in heaven and the nearness and resemblance of the other world to earthly life.[18] Like the proponents of future probation in the late nineteenth century, Mormons taught that people had postmortem opportunities for salvation. However, in other ways, Mormons departed from the Victorian view. They argued that because God is a person who has a tangible body, individuals can become gods by obeying the laws and ordinances of the LDS Church. Mormons also maintained that heaven consists of three different levels—the Celestial, Terrestrial, and Telestial kingdoms—and taught that couples could be married for eternity and procreate in paradise. Their spirit children take on bodies and populate other worlds. Unlike most other groups, Mormons contended that all the activities of heaven are distinctively religious in nature. Finally, while almost all other Christian conceptions of heaven are ecumenical, with no special privileges accorded to members of any particular denomination or to those holding any specific set of doctrines, in the LDS depiction of afterlife, their church is dominant and Mormons play distinctive roles.

While "the motifs of the modern heaven—eternal progress, love, and fluidity between earth and the other world," are "not fundamental to contemporary Christianity," Robert Millet, a professor at Brigham Young University, asserted, "what happens to people after they die is crucial to LDS teachings and rituals." For Mormons, earthly life is simply "one act in a long drama spanning several worlds and existences." Prior to their birth, individuals exist as "spirit children with their Heavenly Mother and Father." God places them on earth to choose the proper path.[19]

After death, souls travel to the spirit world, where they develop until the final resurrection. The unrighteous are tormented by their "guilt, fear, failure," and "the enslavement of their wills to Satan," while the godly reside in a paradise filled with forests, flowers, lakes, and extraordinary edifices. Residents of paradise can "think and act with…the vigor and enthusiasm" of their prime. The ungodly and ignorant have the opportunity in the spirit world to accept the LDS revelation, and Mormons continue to evangelize, teach, and shepherd others. In the spirit world, Mormons preach continually and prepare for the redemption of the earth's nations by presenting LDS doctrines and exhorting disobedient spirits to repent. They strive to convince Protestants, Catholics, Jews, Muslims, and the heathen to accept the baptism Mormons vicariously performed for them on earth. Meanwhile, "their selfless service" enables Mormon saints to progress. In addition, the LDS Church continues in the afterlife under the leadership of its president and priesthood.[20]

While Mormons can preach and teach in the spirit world, they cannot perform the earthly ordinances that are required for others to progress spiritually there. All those who do not accept Mormon doctrine on earth need to have various rituals, especially baptism and marriage, completed for them on earth to help them reach the Celestial Kingdom. Therefore, Mormons do genealogical research to identify specific deceased individuals (their headquarters in Salt Lake City has the world's largest collection of genealogical records) and perform rituals on their behalf. These rituals enable those who accept Mormon doctrine in the afterlife to gain admittance to the highest heaven. "It takes as much work," Theodore Burton explained, "to save a dead person as it does to save a living person."[21] Like numerous others who, since the late nineteenth century, have advocated a second probation, the Saints argued that people can be saved after death, but only through the work of Mormons.

After the millennium—Christ's 1,000-year rule on earth—the last judgment will occur, and all individuals will be "assigned either to one of three stages of glory or to an endless hell." Those who have earned the highest reward will reside in the Celestial Kingdom with God the Father and Jesus, which is subdivided into three levels. However, only those who merit the highest celestial glory by living righteously, espousing the proper beliefs, and performing the correct rituals, most notably being married for "time and eternity," experience "exaltation" and become gods. People who lived respectably but rejected the gospel of Jesus Christ on earth or accept the Christian message after death will inhabit the Terrestrial Kingdom. Those whose earthly lives were very immoral will dwell in the Telestial Kingdom after suffering for their sins in hell during the millennium.[22]

Those whose weddings are performed by justices of the peace or non-Mormon clergy are joined only until they die, but marriage ceremonies of Latter-day Saints in proper standing conducted in Mormon temples unite couples for eternity. Children born to couples after this special service are sealed to them for eternity, and those born to them before this temple marriage can be sealed through a later ceremony. Only families that are sealed stay together after death. For Mormons, the family is the primary celestial unit and couples married for eternity can procreate in the afterlife. Their "spirit children" are sent to "another earth to pass through the trials of mortality and obtain a physical body." Like God, those who populate the highest celestial realm rule over the innumerable worlds where spirit children who have taken on physical bodies reside. Moreover, in this "distinctively sectarian" afterlife, individuals need Mormon ordinances to advance spiritually.[23]

Mormons distinguish between immortality and eternal life. All those who qualify "for the second estate" receive immortality; "this free gift of God's grace" requires neither "righteousness nor rigorous attention to God's laws." Eternal life, the life God enjoys, by contrast, consists primarily of "possessing the fullness of the glory of the Father" and continuing "the family unit in eternity." Individuals qualify for eternal life by obeying the commandments the Mormon plan of salvation prescribes. "There is no salvation," wrote Millet and McConkie, for anyone either in this life or the world of spirits "who rejects the testimony of Joseph Smith [the founder of Mormonism] while professing loyalty to Peter, James, and John." However, as "a successful parent," God will "save far more of his children than he will lose," including billions of children who died before the age of accountability, multitudes who never heard the gospel message on earth but gladly received it in the spirit world, and massive numbers of those born during "the great millennial era." People obtain "a celestial body," Mormons asserted, "by developing celestial interests, appetites, propensities, desires, attitudes, and inclinations—that is, by living the gospel of Jesus Christ in full." Those who "think as God thinks, believes as he believes, act as he acts, and thus experience what he experiences" inherit salvation, the greatest of all God's gifts. These individuals "become equal with their Master in power, might, and dominion."[24]

As they had throughout American history, Jews also offered an alternative view of heaven during the final forty years of the twentieth century. The concepts of heaven and hell are integral to Christianity with its focus on salvation, but not to Judaism.[25] However, during these decades, American Jews discussed the afterlife more than in earlier eras. While Orthodox Jews argued that people lived forever, most Reform Jews and many Conservative Jews maintained that personal existence ended at death. Resurrection, asserted Orthodox rabbi Maurice Lamm, "is not beyond the capacity of an omnipotent God." Professor Eugene Borowitz declared that "having shared so intimately in God's reality in life," many Jews expected to "share it beyond the grave"; they trusted that their survival after death would be "personal and individual." Arlene Agus looked forward to being reunited with her family after death, studying the Torah with Moses, and seeing people receive compensation for their "crushing" hardships. By endowing people with souls, aspirations, and the potential for perfection—"characteristics that have no limit"—God clearly intended people "to be infinite." Belief in "a final accounting" after death, averred Blu Greenberg, motivated individuals to obey ethical laws on earth. Moreover, hope in the hereafter helped people deal with injustice and death, especially "the untimely death of an usually good person." For many Orthodox Jews, heaven is a place of never-ending study. The Jewish Renewal movement, which combined aspects of the human potential movement and therapeutic psychology with ancient Jewish texts to emphasize spiritual growth and the amelioration of society, also strongly reasserted the traditional Jewish view of the immortality of the soul.[26]

Disagreeing with this position, many Jews contended that people's existence ended at death and that individuals lived on primarily through their deeds. Harold Schulweis, a Conservative Jewish rabbi, insisted that Jews rarely asked about the afterlife even at funerals. While acknowledging that human beings continued to probe the mysteries of death because of curiosity, fear, sorrow over losing loved ones, "deep love for life," the "desire to remain creative," and the conviction that justice must ultimately prevail, rabbis Rifat Sonsino and Daniel B. Syme declared that "it is almost impossible...to fathom living a purposeful life 'forever'" and stressed that "there is no proof for life beyond the grave." Some Jews, most notably rabbi Richard L. Rubenstein, openly repudiated life after death. Like Rubenstein, who argued that humans arose "out of nothingness" and were "destined to return to nothingness," most Reform and Reconstructionist rabbis rejected belief in a bodily resurrection. Many Jews maintained that people lived on only through their offspring, religious community, and deeds. Modern Judaism, Schulweis contended, interpreted the hereafter symbolically and poetically, viewing heaven and hell not as places, but as states of mind and ways of living on earth. He and many others urged Jews to focus on improving this world, not getting to another one. Since the afterlife could not be proven, Syme reasoned, people should live as though this life "were the only one." People touched the future through their children, works, and "kindness and caring" for one another.[27]

MAINSTREAM CHRISTIAN CONCEPTIONS OF THE NATURE OF HEAVEN

While Protestants and Catholics continued to emphasize many of the same themes about heaven that were prominent in earlier eras, new trends emerged in the last four decades of the twentieth century. Many reasserted the more theocentric heaven espoused by countless Christians from the Puritans through the Second Great Awakening. More than Americans in any other previous era, Protestants, especially evangelicals, and some Catholics focused on heaven's relationship to earthly life.

Because numerous Catholics continued to accentuate the beatific vision and many conservative Protestants celebrated the saints' fellowship with God and Christ, the God-centered heaven became important again. "Theocentric minimalism," McDannell and Lang explain, was "probably the most widely accepted orthodox version of heaven" in the second half of the twentieth century. It "rejects all efforts to distract the saints from their primary focus on God." Many theological conservatives emphasized this perspective to help save the traditional view of heaven "from liberal disintegration." In heaven, Billy Graham asserted, God "will be at the center of everything." "The most important thing" about heaven, Hal Lindsey, author of best-selling *The Late Great Planet Earth* (1973), maintained, is that people will see God "face-to-face." The "joy of heaven," Catholic philosopher Peter Kreeft avowed, "is not primarily our joy but God's, not primarily the fulfillment of human desires, but of…God's desire—his single-minded love of us."[28] Numerous authors insisted that the principal activity in heaven will be fellowship with Jesus, heaven's "main attraction."[29]

Like the Puritans and the leaders of the First Great Awakening, many Christians in the late twentieth century described heaven as a majestic realm characterized by holiness, perfection, happiness, love, and phenomenal blessedness. McDannell and Lang's contention that after 1960 conservative Christians did "not return to the rich heavenly images of previous generations" is not true in America. "Heaven," asserted evangelical television talk show host John Ankerberg and apologist John Weldon, "will be an infinitely superb…paradise," "a place of indescribable love, beauty, peace, joy, happiness…adventure, and…fellowship with God" that is "beyond our wildest imagination." Much of the description of the New Jerusalem in Revelation, philosophers Gary Habermas and J. P. Moreland pointed out, emphasizes its beauty. "The radiant splendor" suggested by the figures of "jeweled foundations, the pearly gates, and…streets of gold," Calvin Theological Seminary professor Anthony Hoekema argued, "staggers the imagination." In heaven, exulted Randy Alcorn, "our every desire will be satisfied." The saints, proclaimed Daniel A. Brown, "will live on a perpetual and exhilarating high akin to the feeling we have now when we shout 'Yes' at…a clutch goal at the buzzer." Debate even raged over the size of heaven. While most took Revelation's descriptions to be figurative, others provided specific dimensions. Brown claimed that heaven covered "almost 65% of the continental US," and ascended "at a 63% angle for 750 miles" until peaking "at 1,500 miles (270x as high as Mt. Everest)," and Wilbur Smith concluded that heaven is ten times the size of Germany.[30]

Dominated by God's presence, heaven, many emphasized, is an ideal realm that is devoid of earthly ills and dominated by love. In the afterlife, Hoekema argued, the redeemed will know and serve God perfectly. The saints, Graham averred, will be like Jesus in knowledge, righteousness, and love. Heavenly residents, John MacArthur, Jr., popular author and president of The Masters' College, avowed, will never sin, experience guilt, or "need to apologize to anyone." Heaven, Anne Lotz argued, will have no suicide bombers, fiery infernos, school violence, car bombs, terrorists, air strikes, broken homes, wrecked lives, or shattered dreams. Heaven, Joni Tada, a quadriplegic inspirational author and speaker, rejoiced, contained no homeless shelters, orphanages, mental hospitals, abortion clinics, or nursing homes. Many insisted that love is paradise's "paramount quality" and "prevailing disposition." Altruism, asserted Fred Thompson, characterizes all its interpersonal relationships. Like God, the saints will be able to "love without sorrow or vulnerability," Kreeft claimed. Many of those who had near-death experiences, Sandberg pointed out, testified to heaven's "intense and wonderful love."[31]

Because sin is absent and love prevails, conservative Christians contended, God's home is a place of unity, harmony, tranquility, and justice. Heaven, argued Jesuit E. J. Fortman, has no conflict, hatred, wars, segregation or discrimination. The afterlife has no divisions, Alcorn asserted, based on race, class, sex, or doctrine. Several authors stressed that Revelation's declaration that heaven has no seas meant that no mysteries, separation, or turbulence existed there. Isaiah's vision of heaven, Calvin College professor Richard Mouw declared, indicated that "a political reckoning must occur." History's despicable rulers must stand trial publicly—"the unrighteous kings of Israel and Judah, the Egyptian pharaohs...the Roman caesars, Hitler, Stalin, [and] Idi Amin." "Believers who have been unjustly accused and punished by wicked rulers will be vindicated." Mouw expected accounts to "finally be settled between the Catholics and Protestants of Ireland, between Mennonite martyrs and their Calvinist persecutors, [and] between the Christian plantation owner and his Christian slaves."[32]

"USEFUL EMPLOYMENT" IN THE "FATHER'S INCREDIBLE HOUSE"

Many evangelicals and Catholics depicted heaven as a place of varied and vigorous activity. Heavenly residents will worship, serve, and rule, Alcorn asserted. All their activities, Don Baker insisted, will be perfectly tailored to their "tastes and abilities." The saints, Joni Tada speculated, might teach the nations how "how to beat their swords into plowshares" as well as patch the ozone layer. Moreover, people's intellectual curiosity, aesthetic instincts, social affinities, and strength would all be employed in heaven. Pastor W. A. Criswell, who served the huge First Baptist Church in Dallas, Wilbur Smith, and Tim LaHaye all claimed that during the millennial age, the saints would reign with Christ and rule over cities and regions on earth. This focus on heavenly tasks comports closely with how highly valued work was in late-twentieth-century America: Americans worked about 350 hours more per year than Europeans, reported deriving substantial fulfillment from their work, and strongly subscribed to the Protestant work ethic.[33]

Compared with earlier generations, Christians in this era placed much less emphasis on personal progress in heaven. Theologian Millard Erickson argued that heaven is a "state of completion" and therefore people "will not grow in heaven." The saints' perfection, J. Oswald Sanders countered, will be relative, like that of a child compared to a parent. Thus they can further grow and develop. John Gilmore disputed John Calvin and John Owen's contention that individuals had no possibility of improving because they became perfect when they entered paradise. If the saints always remained on the same level, he asserted, heavenly life would lack "challenge, variety, and interest." Others contended that the saints will continually grow in knowledge and truth, develop expanded powers of concentration, understanding, and memory, and comprehend God's work in history. Some Catholics insisted that "heaven will be a time for continual growth and moral progress" as the saints' minds and wills constantly became more "active and productive." Theologian E. J. Fortman anticipated galleries of art, literature, mathematics, psychology, physics, cosmology, theology, and intergalactic travel, which would enable heavenly residents to study and greatly expand their knowledge.[34]

UNUSUAL FEATURES OF HEAVEN

New attributes of heaven became important to Americans in this affluent, consumerist, pleasure-oriented age. Most of those who analyzed the issue of time in eternity concluded that heavenly time would involve a past and future but that the saints would either enjoy eternal youthfulness or that age would be irrelevant. "Eternity is not timelessness," declared Daniel Brown; "it is time without end." In heaven, Alcorn asserted, there will be "no more hurrying, no more delays, no more wasting of time or lack of it."[35]

In heaven, Kreeft alleged, people will be "the perfect age that includes all ages." A third of respondents in a 1988 *Newsweek* poll expected to be "the same age in heaven as when they die on earth." Several writers speculated that since Jesus was thirty-three when He received His resurrection body, the saints would appear to be "thirty-three eternalized." Although heavenly bodies will be ageless, Brown stated, the saints will probably "look like adults before they begin to age on earth." English professor Harry Blamires predicted that the redeemed would simultaneously enjoy "the vigor and freshness of youth and the wisdom and stability of age."[36]

Curiously, in an era marked deeply by the fight against Communism, some envisioned a heaven where all resources were shared. Rejecting the long-standing, popular concept of the saints having mansions in heaven, some contended that people had no private property. The saints do not receive "deeds to heavenly real estate," declared Gilmore. Its wealth "belongs equally to everyone."[37]

Pets were another topic of debate. Criswell insisted that no evidence indicates "that pets will be in heaven," and Gilmore stressed that "Scripture nowhere says animals have immortal souls," but others expected animals to be in heaven. Mouw noted that Isaiah pictured the Holy City as "populated by many animals." "Animals are some of God's best…ideas," argued Tada; "why would He throw out His greatest creative achievements?" Forty-three percent of respondents to a 2001 poll said that they expected pets to be in heaven.[38]

While most Christians concurred that marriage did not exist in heaven, they disagreed about whether sex and gender are part of paradise. The vast majority insisted that physical intercourse would not take place in heaven. Although the Bible provided no basis for believing that sex is necessary in heaven, Habermas and Moreland countered, this did not rule it out. While some argued that the saints will have no gender, others insisted that gender continues in heaven because it is an integral aspect of human beings that helps shape their "attitudes, thinking, perspective, and objectives." Being male or female, Gilmore maintained, is "built into the nucleus of every single cell in our body."[39]

Authors also disagreed about whether or not the saints are aware of what is happening on earth. Heaven's inhabitants, Kreeft and Criswell asserted, "see what happens on earth." The Bible taught, Criswell argued, that "when someone gives his heart to Jesus" on earth, those in heaven rejoice. Others reasoned that knowing what was happening on earth would mar the saints' happiness.[40]

ON EARTH AS IT IS IN HEAVEN

More than in any earlier period in American history, from 1960 to 2000 authors challenged Christians to focus on heaven. They urged believers to live as citizens of heaven and underscored the benefits of doing so. Some stressed that hope of heaven is the principal message of the Bible. Removing heaven from scripture, Presbyterian pastor Charles Ball contended, made the rest of its message meaningless. Numerous evangelicals quoted C. S. Lewis's admonition in *Mere Christianity*: "Aim at heaven and you'll get earth thrown in. Aim at earth and you'll get neither." Because heaven included the sphere "in this world where God rules," John MacArthur argued, Christians lived in the heavenly realm and their deepest spiritual experiences on earth were foretastes of paradise. "God calls us to be so heavenly minded," Baptist pastor Steve Lawson declared, "that we are of earthly good" and to "weigh every decision in the light of eternity."[41]

Both educator Joseph Stowell and writer Philip Yancey insisted numerous cultural values detracted attention from heaven, which had detrimental consequences. Stowell contended that several factors made heaven less important to many Christians: distorted perceptions of their future home; preoccupation with careers, families, and friendships; elevation of the material over the spiritual; belief that if they had enough faith, Christians could obtain "wealth, health, and happiness" on earth; and the impact of living in a skeptical society that rejected belief in an afterlife. Widespread denial of life after death, Yancey averred, led Americans to esteem youth, devalue the elderly, and spend billions to keep people alive just a little longer.[42]

Having a heavenly mindset, several claimed, provided important benefits. Making heaven their "primary point of reference," Stowell declared, radically changed individuals' posture toward God, possessions, people, pain, and pleasure. It also strengthened their commitment to moral purity and altered their sense of identity. Congregations that focused on heaven, he alleged, would also do more to help the poor. John MacArthur contended that focusing on heaven helped provide assurance of salvation, produce Christ-like character, protect people from yielding to temptations, and inspire sacrificial service. Reflecting on heaven, Lawson maintained, enabled Christians to know the "sovereign God and the glorified Christ more deeply," live more righteously, give more generously, and experience greater joy.[43]

Colossians 3:1, Stowell declared, commanded Christians to actively seek the things above. Because heaven is their true home, he argued, Christians are resident aliens and pilgrims on earth. They were part of a society that had radically different standards, values, and commitments than those of the world. Stowell challenged Christians to promote "the unique...principles, protocol, and practices" of heaven by working to further "righteousness, justice, compassion," forgiveness, "love, purity, patience, and wisdom." Kreeft exhorted Christians to recognize that Jesus had defeated death and hell and that victory over evil is assured.[44]

Richard Mouw lamented that Christians' belief in "pie in the sky" had sometimes served as an excuse for inaction on earth and led them to tolerate "wickedness in the present age." Those who viewed the Christian life as "a-lonely-journey-through-a-hostile-world" rarely worked to remedy "economic injustice or racial discrimination." Traveling to the New Jerusalem, he asserted, instead involved "identifying with those who are in need" and promoting peace and racial justice. Longing for heaven, he argued, should inspire diligent efforts to promote fairness, reconciliation, and righteousness on earth. Mouw praised "proponents of the 'social gospel,' advocates of 'liberation theology,' shapers of 'moral majorities,' and builders of Crystal Cathedrals" for trying to lay the groundwork for God's eternal city.[45]

Others insisted that those who focused on heaven often worked diligently to improve conditions on earth. "Otherworldliness is escapism," declared Kreeft, "only if there is no other world." If an afterlife exists, worldliness is escapism. Citing C. S. Lewis, apologist Dave Hunt argued that the Christians who focused the most on the next world were the ones who "did most for the present world." The apostles who converted the Roman Empire, the theologians and clergy who helped establish the Christian civilization of the Middle Ages, and "the English Evangelicals who abolished the slave trade" all significantly improved earthly life precisely because they were preoccupied with heaven.[46]

RECOGNITION, FELLOWSHIP, AND REWARDS

Evangelicals emphasized that the saints would know each other in heaven. Speaking for many, Habermas and Moreland declared that "Scripture plainly teaches that we will recognize others and fellowship with them in heaven." The Bible did not explicitly teach personal identity or mutual recognition following death, others insisted, but these concepts were implicit in its portrayal of judgment and the story of Lazarus and the rich man. Unlike their predecessors, Christians of this era rarely sought to refute objections to the doctrine of mutual recognition. Pastor W. A. Criswell argued that the saints would not remember their unsaved loved ones, while Habermas and Moreland reasoned that Christians did not presently understand why knowing that some of their loved ones were in hell would not diminish the saints' ecstasy in heaven.[47]

While a few accentuated heavenly fellowship with family and friends, late-twentieth-century Christians generally did not stress this theme as had their counterparts in most earlier eras. Christians, Jerry Walls stated, anticipated enjoying a richer and deeper fellowship in heaven than they had on earth, and Charles Ball expected heaven to "be a place of high and noble companionship." "Affection and intimacy," declared Daniel A. Brown, "will be common in heaven." Christians will love their spouses, children, and parents, asserted Alcorn, "even more than we did on earth." Unlike earlier periods, few emphasized the privilege and pleasure of communing with biblical heroes.[48]

Influenced by a society that honored personal achievements (evident in financial bonuses, academic degrees, halls of fame, athletic trophies, beauty pageants, and award shows), Christians during these years gave considerable attention to the subject of heavenly rewards. Some protested that the concept of rewards involved "selfishness and personal gain," which was difficult to reconcile with the nature of God or heaven. Kreeft counseled Christians to love God and do good because these actions were right, not to gain rewards. On the other hand, most writers insisted that heavenly rewards were powerful incentives to righteous earthly behavior and proper compensation for meritorious deeds and suffering. The saints, Anne Sandberg argued, will be assigned different mansions and positions and have different levels of happiness depending on their earthly dedication to Christ. Tim LaHaye asserted that "Jesus himself challenged" His followers to "lay up for yourselves treasures in heaven."[49] "The believer's profit-and-loss statement," he added, will determine "the degree of his reward." Many contended that heavenly recompense will be based on how much people accomplished in relation to their gifts and opportunities. Erwin Lutzer, pastor of the Moody Church in Chicago, maintained that those who are the most dependable on earth will have the greatest responsibility in heaven. Although Christians should serve others because they loved Christ rather than to attain a "better position in the Kingdom," Lutzer averred, Jesus often "motivated the disciples with the prospect of rewards" and their expectation of heavenly recompense inspired many biblical saints to promote God's kingdom. Lutzer and LaHaye argued that saints receive various crowns for different types of earthly work—those who love deeply are given the crown of righteousness; those who avoided the "pleasures of the world" and provided "profitable service" for Christ are granted the incorruptible crown; the crown of life is conferred on those who witnessed faithfully until their death; those who devoted their lives to saving souls receive the crown of rejoicing; and Bible teachers obtain the crown of glory.[50]

Most authors claimed that heavenly rewards consisted of positions and responsibilities much more than prizes and privileges. The treasures of heaven, Habermas and Moreland asserted, may be "capacities granted by God for greater service and personal growth." "Assignments...in glory," Criswell contended, will be based upon people's "ability...to rule." The more obedient individuals "are in this life," John MacArthur alleged, "the more responsibility" they will have "in the life to come."[51]

NEAR-DEATH EXPERIENCES

Accounts of out-of-body encounters with the spiritual world have a long history. Most notably, Swedish philosopher and mystic Emanuel Swedenborg (1688–1772) wrote twenty-five books about his trips to heaven and hell. However, public fascination with the subject exploded after the 1975 publication of physician Raymond Moody's *Life After Life: The Investigation of a Phenomenon—Survival of Bodily Death* and cardiologist Maurice Rawlings's *Beyond Death's Door*, both of which featured dozens of accounts of near-death experiences (NDEs). These NDEs commonly involved "feelings of peace and quiet; feeling oneself out of the body...meeting...one or more Beings of Light; a life review...seeing life differently"; and developing "new views of death." Moreover, many members of the medical profession and academic community documented these stories, making them more credible and respectable. Carol Zaleski contends that NDEs are "appealing for the same basic reason spiritualism and psychic research gained many adherents in the years after the Civil War: people aspire to immortality." Moreover, they can be used to support numerous worldviews, helping make them attractive in an era of "ideological diversity and fragmentation."[52]

Numerous investigators stressed the positive benefits of NDEs. Moody claimed that every subject he interviewed during twenty years of research "had a very deep and positive transformation." As a result of their experience, Moody argued, people lost the fear of dying and going to hell and love dominated their lives. They had a great respect for knowledge, a "profound appreciation of life," and deeper spirituality and took more personal responsibility. Rawlings reported similarly that many people described their encounters with the other world "as heavenly...exhilarating, or beyond expression."[53] Mally Cox-Chapman maintained that those who had NDEs had an enhanced self-image, improved relationships, greater purpose in work, and a richer spiritual life. Moreover, many visions of heaven included wonderful reunions with deceased loved ones, which should console those who longed to see family and friends again. "As a source of contemporary revelation," she added, "near-death experiencers receive the message we most need to hear" in late-twentieth-century America—"forgiveness and unconditional love." Many reported that they went through a quick life review that involved pardon and acceptance, not "crippling remorse." These people testified to what the mystics had asserted throughout history: "God's Presence is awesome...we are supposed to love one another and ourselves, and...when we die, we will go to be with God."[54]

Although admitting that "visits to the edge of Heaven cannot be proved," Cox-Chapman argued that "reasonable corroborative evidence" substantiated people's claims. That individuals described their encounters in the context of their own religious traditions did not discredit them. These near-death experiences, she maintained, helped many believe in heaven in the face of the doubt produced by "politics, science, psychology, and our personal histories." The journeys of eight million Americans "to the edge of the afterlife" did not prove that "God's dwelling place" existed, but their "richly compelling" stories provided persuasive evidence.[55]

A lively debated erupted in the 1980s over the nature of NDEs. Some scholars contended that NDEs had completely naturalistic explanations, while others defended their validity.[56] Physician Melvin Morse repudiated the argument that near-death experiences are "caused by a lack of oxygen to the brain, or drugs, or psychological stresses evoked by the fear of dying." Almost twenty years of scientific research, he maintained, had demonstrated "that these experiences are a natural and normal process." NDEs "are absolutely real," not hallucinations. Similarly, Cox-Chapman rejected the claims of skeptics that "drugs, oxygen deprivation...disassociation, temporal lobe stimulation, endorphin surge, anesthesia," or "even memories of birth" caused these experiences.[57]

Rawlings insisted that having a bona fide Christian NDE compelled people to tell others about it. While Betty Maltz's *My Glimpse of Eternity* (1977) and Richard Eby's *Caught Up into Paradise* (1978) set the pattern, the most dramatic and controversial account of a near-death experience in the last quarter of the twentieth century was probably Native-American Betty J. Eadie's *Embraced by the Light* (1992). During the time she was clinically dead, she met "Christ, the Creator and Savior of the earth" and felt "unconditional love." Eadie claimed that she traveled to many worlds "filled with loving, intelligent people" and discovered that "the vastness of space...was full of love and light—the tangible presence of the Spirit of God." A council of twelve men helped Eadie review her life, showed her the effects of her actions, and helped convince her to return to earth. Her experience gave Eadie a new energy to serve God and others.[58]

While Christians such as Norman Vincent Peale, Anne Sandberg, and Ralph Wilkerson saw NDEs as corroborating biblical accounts of heaven, others argued that they were highly suspect. Sandberg examined "hundreds of accounts of reliable witnesses who have experienced heaven in different ways," including many who "were declared clinically dead." Wilkerson chronicled similar stories in *Beyond and Back* (1977).[59] Others protested that many NDEs, especially ones that portrayed a "magnanimous, understanding, all-loving," "compassionate being," who found no fault with anyone, clashed with biblical teachings about the nature of God and heaven. Tim LaHaye noted several similarities between biblical teaching and the reports of NDEs, including that individuals maintained their personal identity, recognized loved ones and friends, and communicated with others. However, in NDEs God accepted everyone regardless of belief or character into His kingdom, Jesus was "not consistently presented as unique," sin appeared not to be judged, and travelers were "granted a second chance after death."[60]

Rejecting the idea that they were inspired by God, LaHaye argued that these experiences could be explained in four ways: they had "a physical basis in the nervous system"; a close brush with death released latent psychic powers "rendered dormant by the fall"; they were the result of "selective manipulation of some facts, exaggeration of others and perhaps…outright fabrication"; or they were demonic in origin. He concluded that the fourth explanation was the most plausible because these experiences did not glorify Jesus the way they would if they were truly from God. Habermas and Moreland observed that people's interpretation of their NDEs depended heavily on the concepts of the afterlife that were popular in different eras. This, coupled with the possibility that people's physical bodies might be causing these experiences, led them to argue that NDEs did not provide conclusive evidence for life after death or convincing descriptions of heaven. They concluded that while some aspects of these reported experiences might be occult in nature, not all NDEs were demonic.[61]

John Ankerberg and John Weldon claimed that one reason NDEs were so popular was that they seemed to deny the existence of hell. These alleged encounters with the other world also often repudiated the need for salvation through Christ by trivializing sin and accentuating works of righteousness. In addition, NDEs powerfully reinforced "a common, if mistaken, theme in modern culture—that God loves all persons unconditionally and will grant everyone entrance into heaven" because they are essentially good. Ankerberg and Weldon also expressed skepticism about NDEs because many of their primary investigators either had a "'New Age' interest, background, or philosophy" (including Raymond Moody, Elisabeth Kübler-Ross, Edgar Cayce, and Kenneth Ring) or were parapsychologists, psychic researchers, or occultists. However, they argued that the NDEs of Christians and non-Christians were very different and urged committed Christian who had these experiences not to conclude that they were "occult or deceptive unless such elements" were "clearly present." Ankerberg and Weldon lamented that many non-Christians who had had NDEs became "disoriented and confused" and "wrapped up in themselves." They also did not experience God as holy. Such NDEs provided a "false portrait of what death…involves biblically for the person outside of Christ." By contrast, others had "biblical near-death experiences" which led them to seek "a deep faith and more real experience of Christ."[62]

Numerous Christians questioned NDEs because many "experienced love, joy, and forgiveness from the light in the tunnel" even though they had not committed their lives to Christ. Some even claimed that Satan enabled non-Christians to have these delusions to deter them "from finding true salvation." More Christians probably agreed with philosopher Jerry Walls's conclusion that "NDEs have given many people fresh reason to hope for life after death." Although these experiences were not an essential ground for believing in the Christian doctrine of heaven, he argued, they did supply glimpses of "realities we know about from the revelation of Scripture and Christian tradition."[63]

Like conservative Christians in earlier eras, those living in the last four decades of the twentieth century maintained that salvation is a gift of God, not something individuals can earn. Habermas and Moreland protested that millions thought that "sincerity of belief is the only prerequisite to heaven." Many contended that the specific content of individuals' religious convictions did not matter as long as people genuinely believed them and strove to live by them. Influenced by a culture that stressed innate human goodness, downplayed the wrath of God, proclaimed that truth is relative to time, place, and circumstances, and shifted blame for wrong actions from individuals to psychological and sociological factors, many Americans assumed that their good deeds and sound character would get them to heaven. A 1988 Gallup survey found, for example, that three-quarters of Americans thought they had a "good or excellent" chance of going to heaven.[64] Numerous evangelicals countered that people's virtuous works, church attendance, faithfulness to religious rules, "good intentions, meditation, mystical enlightenment," and social service were all insufficient to get them to heaven. Citing a 1986 *USA Today* poll in which most respondents based their chances of being admitted to heaven on how upright their conduct was, John Gilmore complained that "we carry the American work ethic to the very gates of paradise."[65]

At the judgment, Billy Graham claimed, every person will have to answer the question "What Right Have You to Enter Heaven?" Individuals will answer in three different ways: they deserve heaven because they lived a good life; they do not know why they deserve to enter heaven or should care about going there; or they are entitled to go to heaven because they "believed in Jesus Christ and accepted Him" as their savior. Only those who gave the third response, Graham contended, will be allowed to enter heaven.[66]

Others agreed. "The Scriptures are clear," declared Gilmore; "we cannot negotiate, demand, or pay for salvation." "People cannot buy, earn, or inherit heaven, but they can miss it," warned Martha Boshart. The only way individuals can be admitted to heaven, evangelicals alleged, is to affirm that Jesus is the Son of God, ask God to forgive their sins, and invite Christ to take control of their life.[67] They stressed that no one is good enough to deserve heaven because God demands perfection, not simply consistently righteous behavior. Therefore, God permitted people to enter heaven only because "Christ paid the admission price" by dying on the cross for their sin. "Only Jesus' goodness is 'good enough' to get us to heaven," Ralph Muncaster asserted. Individuals are acceptable to God only if they are clothed in the One who led a perfect life. People can escape hell, LaHaye avowed, only by trusting in Christ's "finished work on Calvary's cross." There is "no other way" and "no second chance."[68]

Catholics, by contrast, argued that individuals are saved by faith and works. In *"Not by Faith Alone": The Biblical Evidence for the Catholic Doctrine of Justification* (1996), Robert Sungenis, the president of Catholic Apologetics International, maintained that to be saved, people must please God by both their faith and obedience. Because all people have sinned, they must be "redeemed through the atoning work of Christ." However, neither Jesus nor Paul said "anywhere in Scripture that one can be saved by faith alone." Paul taught that individuals are also justified by obeying God's law and loving God and their neighbors, that "faith must express itself through love in order to effectuate justification." James asserted that to be saved, individuals "must consciously add works to faith." Thus, for Catholics, Sungenis claimed, "justification is not a one-time event but an ongoing process." Those who have committed serious sins and refuse to repent "will be eternally condemned" at the last judgment. On the other hand, individuals who have "'pleased' God" by their "faith and works...will receive the eternal inheritance." Therefore, those who are "living a good Christian life" and loving God and their neighbors could be confident that "God will justify" them.[69]

After 1960, a variety of perspectives were put forth about how individuals can be saved and how many people would be. Most conservative Christians espoused one of three major stances—restrictivism, inclusivism, or postmortem evangelization. Advocated by Carl Henry, R. C. Sproul, Ronald Nash, and other, primarily Reformed, evangelicals, restrictivism declares that "God provides salvation only in Jesus Christ, and it is necessary to know about the work of Christ and exercise faith in Jesus before one dies...to be saved." Inclusivism, espoused by John Sanders and Clark Pinnock, maintains that God grants salvation to those who do not know about Christ "if they exercise faith in God" as they learn about Him "through creation and providence." Proponents of postmortem evangelization, sometimes also called divine perseverance, including Gabriel Fackre and Donald Bloesch, contend that those who die without hearing the gospel are given the opportunity to respond to it after death. Other theologians, including biblical scholar Norman Geisler, argued that all individuals have an opportunity to be saved before death because God somehow "sends more light" (possibly through dreams, or angels) to "those who respond to the light they have" through conscience and nature. Others suggested that "God may save those he knows would have believed in Christ had they heard the gospel." Some Roman Catholic theologians advocated "final option theory," a version of postmortem evangelization in which Christ confronts every person at the moment of death to give them an opportunity to repent and be saved. Some theologians, labeled unitive pluralists, most notably John Hick and Paul Knitter, rejected the view that Christ is the only savior and asserted that all the world's major religions lead to God.[70]

Many American Catholics also broadened their concept of salvation during the last decades of the twentieth century, arguing that New Testament texts offered wide possibilities of salvation or at least of "nondamnation." Some maintained that people who only had "implicit" faith could attain salvation. Those who obeyed God's law as they understood it through their consciences and performed good works would be saved.[71] Numerous Catholic theologians espoused a "final fundamental option," which gave both infants and adults who did not hear the gospel on earth a postmortem chance to accept or reject God. Jesuit E. J. Fortman expected almost all infants to choose God because they had no personal sin, evil habits, or sinful desire to inhibit them from doing so. He argued further that millions of aborted fetuses will awaken after death with "full liberty and complete knowledge" as adults and be given a chance to decide for or against God. All of them, Fortman predicted, would opt for God. Many American Catholics, he claimed, thought that either the majority of people or all people will be saved. Because God is loving and merciful and desires to save all individuals, Christians could reasonably "hope that all will be finally saved."[72]

Three main alternatives to "the biblical doctrine of salvation" had been offered to explain what happened to those who died without receiving Christ as their savior: annihilationism, universalism, and probationism. Arguing that those who did not go to heaven would cease to exist, biblical scholar and attorney Edward Fudge repudiated "the idea of conscious everlasting torment" as "a grievous mistake" and "a gross slander" against the loving heavenly Father. "The notion that the wicked will live forever in inescapable pain contradicts the clear, consistent teaching of Scripture." Apologist Robert Morey complained that annihilationists ignored explicit New Testament passages about everlasting punishment and used vague Old Testament ones to support their position.[73]

Morey identified three types of universalism: (1) "cheap universalism," the hope, without any theological foundation, that God will not judge people for their sins or send anyone to hell; (2) "philosophic universalism," the view of Eastern religions that people are part of the divine essence and ultimately become one with "God" or the universe; and (3) "pseudo-christian Universalism," which attempted to supply a biblical basis for why all people will be saved. Advocates of the third type of universalism, Morey explained, contended that because God is so loving and merciful He would save all people and punish no one eternally; that God's grace is triumphant and will ultimately save everyone; and the Bible's assertion that Christ died for everyone meant that all are saved. Responding to the first argument, he declared that the Bible emphasized God's wrath as well as His love and insisted that the universalist position produced a clash between God's love and justice. He added that the Bible never taught that God's love and mercy guaranteed no one would spend eternity in hell. Countering the second argument, Morey denounced universalists' "definition of grace" as "unscriptural" because they viewed it not as a gift but as a debt that God owed to all people. Moreover, their concept of "universal and triumphant grace" destroyed "the significance of both faith and unbelief," ignored the Bible's warning that those who did not repent would go to hell, removed the motivation for evangelism, and made biblical distinctions between the saved and unsaved nonsensical. Morey also repudiated the third universalist argument, declaring that "there is no biblical or logical warrant" for the inference "that the infinite sufficiency of the atonement must result in an infinite application." Catholic E. J. Fortman agreed that no biblical text explicitly stated or necessarily implied that "all will ultimately be saved." The passages universalists cited to defend their position did not imply that the wicked would receive "a further opportunity for salvation" after death. Moreover, the parables of Dives and Lazarus and the Last Judgment clearly taught that those who rejected Christ were not annihilated but rather experienced everlasting punishment.[74]

PURGATORY AND HELL

Debates over salvation often included discussions of purgatory and hell. While Catholics continued to defend the reality of purgatory, Protestants attacked the concept as nonbiblical. Catholic theologians admitted that neither the Old nor New Testament explicitly taught that a place or state of purification existed in the afterlife. However, this concept was implied in several biblical passages and by the early church's widespread practice of praying for the dead. Catholic scholars insisted that purgatory is necessary because many people are not spiritually prepared to enter heaven when they die. They generally rejected the idea that it includes literal fire or is a "temporary hell." Most of them portrayed purgatory as involving a gradual process of self-realization whereby individuals came to see themselves as God saw them. This painful experience helped them relinquish resentments and forsake selfishness, purged them of their sinfulness, and made them ready to commune with God. While many Catholic theologians viewed purgatory as state, condition, or process, Fortman insisted that it is also a physical place because people needed to interact with one another to perfect their love and prepare for heaven. He argued that individuals could avoid purgatorial punishments if "they died without any unforgiven venial sins" and paid off the "debt of temporal punishment in this life." Through fervent praying, deep love, and devout reception of the sacraments, individuals could "realize their defects and imperfections and gradually eliminate them." Like the martyrs, they could attain the maturity and perfect charity "required for immediate entry into glory." Protestants countered that purgatory is a human invention. Because Jesus Christ cleanses believers of all sin, Jack MacArthur, a pastor, author, and radio and television preacher, and Tim LaHaye asserted, it was not necessary for people to undergo "expiatory suffering in the fires of purgatory" to become "fit for heaven."[75]

Conservative Christians complained that many Americans considered the idea of hell "outdated" and therefore "usually ignored or…denied it." Most Americans were embarrassed by the concept of hell, and it was rarely mentioned in sermons. Some even denounced it as "infantile and obnoxious." Atheist George Smith pronounced "belief in eternal torment" Christianity's "most vicious and reprehensible doctrine." Speaking for many liberal Christians, Martin Luther King, Jr., declared that hell is not "a place of a literal burning fire." Rather, it "is a condition of being out of fellowship with God" and refusing to accept God's grace. Many Americans who believed that hell existed thought that only the most despicable individuals would go there.[76] Parodying the prevalent view, a 1988 *Far Side* cartoon displayed three doors leading into hell, designated "Terrorists," "Homicidal Maniacs," and "People who drive too slow in the fast lane."

Strikingly, few Catholics or evangelicals discussed hell between 1960 and 1990. None of the hundreds of documents Vatican II generated mentioned hell. Rejecting the traditional picture of hell as "terror in technicolor," Catholic theologians typically argued that hell is more "man's creation than God's." It was a destiny people chose by rejecting Christ. The essence of hell, they asserted, is the pain of loss and estrangement from God and others.[77] Evangelical Tim LaHaye complained that "the modern pulpit is strangely silent" on the subject of hell. Ministers who did not warn people about hell's horrors were shirking their responsibility because the New Testament contained fifty-three references to hell, most of which came directly from Jesus. Hell, LaHaye declared, "will be populated by…perverted, vicious, lustful, sinful, adulterous people." Nothing—"no police force, no moral standards, no code of decency"—will restrain its residents' depravity. God consigns people to hell, LaHaye maintained, "because they are not fit to enter heaven." Those who are not born again are "unprepared for the spiritual delights of heaven" and, therefore, "must spend eternity in the Lake of Fire." "God doesn't send unwilling people to hell," asserted John Gilmore. "They prefer it to heaven." God's judgment simply validates their decision.[78]

The 1990s brought renewed interest in hell. In 1991, both *Newsweek* and *U.S. News and World Report* featured articles on hell, with the latter article contending that "record numbers of Americans now believe in a netherworld and in a wide variety of after-death punishments." During the decade, evangelicals published several books defending the traditional view of hell.[79]

CONCLUSION

From 1960 to 2000, many Christians either continued to accentuate or reemphasized several long-standing themes about heaven, most notably the majesty and glory of God, the splendor of paradise, and heavenly worship and rewards. More than any previous era, stress was placed on the temporal and eternal benefits of focusing on heaven. Numerous developments made American perceptions of the afterlife more diverse and complicated: the efforts of the Catholic Church after Vatican II to adjust its theology and practice to modern times and Catholicism's increased acceptance in American society; the rise or growing importance of new theological positions and religious movements that held distinctive perspectives of heaven; the vastly larger number of reported near-death experiences and the substantial public interest in and scholarly discussion of them; the commercialization of heaven; and popularity of the hereafter as a subject for movies, television shows, and books. To counter these alternative perspectives, conservative Christians reasserted the traditional Christian conception of heaven through a plethora of books, sermons, and media productions. These developments helped pave the way for the onslaught of materials about heaven produced during the first decade of the twenty-first century and even greater fascination with the afterlife in the new millennium.

10

HEAVEN IN A POSTMODERN, ANXIETY-RIDDEN, ENTERTAINMENT-ORIENTED, THERAPEUTIC, HAPPINESS-BASED CULTURE

The thought of heaven puts all trouble and grief in perspective.
—MARK BUCHANAN, *Things Unseen*

Heaven is "the ultimate playground, created purely for our enjoyment."
—ANTHONY DESTEFANO, *A Travel Guide to Heaven*

You may not have known the reason at the time, and that is what heaven is for. For understanding your life on Earth.
—MITCH ALBOM, *The Five People You Meet in Heaven*

"God will supply us with everything we'll ever need to make us happy" in heaven.
—BILLY GRAHAM, "Billy Graham: Sports in Heaven? Far Greater Joy Lies in Store"

DURING THE NEW millennium, several major interrelated cultural trends, all with roots in earlier decades, helped shape American views of heaven and salvation. Especially significant were increased anxiety (caused by devastating terrorist attacks, severe economic recession, and global social problems), the impact of the therapeutic worldview (which exalted self-fulfillment and personal happiness), the emergence of an entertainment culture (which stressed pleasure and amusement), concerns about the breakdown of the family and the impoverishment of personal relationships, and the growing acceptance of a postmodern, relativistic perspective on life. Influenced by these trends, many Americans in the years after 2000 portrayed paradise as a place of comfort, self-actualization, bliss, enriching entertainment, and robust fellowship. Strikingly, while mainline Protestant and Catholic ministers and laypeople largely ignored heaven, the afterlife was a major theme in popular culture—movies, novels, television shows and specials, newspaper articles, songs, and jokes.

At the same time, a shift was evident in Americans' views of the admission requirements for heaven. Strongly influenced by a society that denied the possibility of absolute truth and prized tolerance, most Americans, including numerous evangelicals, rejected the traditional Christian position that only those who accept Jesus as their savior will go to heaven. Leading evangelicals, including Billy Graham and

Houston megachurch pastor Joel Osteen, retreated from this position, claiming that God alone knows who goes to heaven and why. Most Americans insisted that either people gained entry to paradise because of their moral virtue and good works or everyone went to heaven. While some evangelicals and Catholics defended the orthodox conception of hell, most Americans viewed hell as either nonexistent or as a temporary stop for punishment or purification on the way to heaven. A growing number of nonreligious Americans denied the existence of both heaven and hell.

Few mainline Protestant ministers discussed heaven at all. Americans heard about heaven far more often on late-night television than in church, asserted Methodist pastor Mark Ralls. "My own reticence to speak of heaven," he added, "places me at odds with the founder of my denomination." Like a lot of mainline ministers, Ralls felt caught between his belief in heaven and the potential embarrassment of preaching on the topic. Several factors produced this ambivalence: their dislike of using heaven to pressure people to convert or to raise money for ministries; their fear that heavenly mindedness would lead people to ignore their earthly obligations; and their seminary training which rarely, if ever, discussed heaven from a biblical, theological, or historical perspective. A Maryland minister contended that "most socially responsible pastors avoid preaching about the afterlife because it has been used to bludgeon non-believers and to endorse reckless military and environmental policies." Lutheran Martin Marty, a longtime professor of church history at the University of Chicago Divinity School, declared that many sermons during his childhood focused on "the geography of heaven and the temperature of hell," but today "the only time you hear of heaven is when somebody has died."[1]

Although Southern Baptists and most African-American denominations have retained a "robust heavenly vision," some claim that most evangelical communions have also retreated from heaven.[2] A seminary professor asserted that Rick Warren, author of the best-selling *The Purpose Driven Life*, preached an occasional sermon on heaven, but "his heart isn't in it." Meanwhile, Joel Osteen's "focus is firmly on the present tense, on *Your Best Life Now!*" Nathan Bierma of the Calvin Institute of Christian Worship complained that most Christians professed that heaven is "eternally important and then live as though it doesn't exist." Occasionally a church service or a funeral caused people to think about heaven, but few Christians had "a visceral, vital hope for heaven" that transformed their daily lives. Author Ted Dekker protested that most Christians were "preoccupied with finding" pleasure, happiness, and purpose "on earth rather than in the age to come."[3]

On the other hand, popular interest in heaven has increased substantially in recent years, as is evident in book sales, television and movie themes, and music. On television, in HBO's *Six Feet Under* and Showtime's *Dead Like Me*, deceased characters make cameo appearances and influence earthly events. In HBO's *Angels in America*, a miniseries adapted from Tony Kushner's Broadway play, which examines AIDS in the 1980s, angels play a central role by providing guidance and advice to troubled human beings. A pie maker on ABC's *Pushing Daisies* had the ability to bring the dead back to life. Songs about heaven, most notably Los Lonely Boys' "How Far Is Heaven?" and Mercy Me's "I Can Only Imagine," have played frequently on the radio.[4]

In various polls taken between 2002 and 2007, 76 to 89 percent of Americans said that they believe heaven exists. Somewhat smaller percentages (typically about 70) think that heaven is an actual place.[5] With churches downplaying heaven, many people seemed to derive their images from popular culture, which often conflicted with traditional Christian views. Basing their ideas on paintings, movies, songs, and novels, many Americans pictured a heaven where people received everything they wanted—more similar to the farm in *Field of Dreams* or the picturesque landscapes of *What Dreams May Come* than the biblical account. Most American Christians, Jeffrey Burton Russell, the author of *A History of Heaven*, contends, "have a better grasp of heaven's clichés than of its allures." They see it as "a boring place, or a silly myth, or something people invent in order to make themselves feel better, or all of the above."[6] Many envisioned St. Peter admitting people to heaven through pearly gates or the deceased becoming angels, both of which have no support in scripture.[7] Some censured the common American conception of heaven as vague, superstitious, and "almost meaningless."[8]

The attacks of September 11, 2001, shocked Americans and left them feeling vulnerable. The subsequent wars in Afghanistan and Iraq left thousands of American soldiers dead. Meanwhile, many Americans were also alarmed by the continuing struggle between Israelis and Palestinians and the attempts of Iran and North Korea to develop nuclear weapons. Although the United States suffered no more terrorist attacks during the remainder of the decade, terrorists continued their assaults overseas, killing thousands in the Middle East, Asia, and Europe. Other major problems afflicted the consciences of the sensitive and at least lurked in the recesses of the minds of others, especially the AIDS epidemic in Africa, the malnourishment of a fifth of the world's population, and numerous regional wars caused by ethnic, nationalistic, and religious factors.

Americans suffered other jolts to their well-being. The high price of oil called attention to global energy consumption, renewing fears that the world would not devise alternatives soon enough to sustain its current lifestyle when oil was depleted. Meanwhile, other environmental hazards, especially global warming, also provoked anxiety. In August 2005, Hurricane Katrina struck the Gulf Coast, killing over 1,400, making it the worst natural disaster in recent American history. The tragic results of the storm, coupled with a poorly managed and inadequate government response, contributed to further American frustration and disillusionment. In 2010, an underwater British Petroleum well leaked millions of gallons of oil into the Gulf of Mexico, destroying fish, polluting beaches, driving away tourists, and further hurting the region's economy.

A final assault on the American psyche was the recession of 2008–2010, the worst economic downturn since the Great Depression. Many banks collapsed, Wall Street experienced a meltdown as the New York Stock Exchange lost 40 percent of its value during 2008, thousands of businesses declared bankruptcy, the nation's unemployment rate surpassed 10 percent, and the stock portfolios and retirement accounts of millions drastically declined. Although the federal government passed a $787 billion stimulus package in 2009 and bailed out several major banks and corporations, millions of Americans lost their jobs or homes or both, and many others, fearful of losing them, reduced their spending and suffered a decline in their standard of living. Many worried about how to pay for food, gas, health care, and college for their children.

Many Americans felt awash in a sea of woes, and depictions of heaven expressed and addressed their concerns. The prospect of paradise provided a soothing antidote to the anxiety-arousing and disconcerting events that led most newscasts and newspaper headlines. Apprehensive people readily envisioned a heavenly realm where God will decisively rout all the forces that "threaten our security and comfort."[9] Heaven offered a pleasant respite from tragedy, despair, and perils. "By focusing on the glorious joy awaiting us in heaven," asserted author Barbara Johnson, people could "laugh…when life's storms" dumped them "on the rocky shore, beaten and bedraggled." Baptist pastor and lecturer Don Piper claimed that his ninety-minute sojourn in heaven enabled him to comfort individuals "who are facing death…or have suffered the loss of a loved one" by assuring them that "heaven is a place of unparalleled…joy." In heaven, assured David Shibley, the president of an evangelistic organization, God would lovingly explain the reason for "every pain, disappointment, and heartache" people experienced on earth. All of earth's problems, including drug trafficking, pornography, and murder, Raymond Hylton, the pastor of the First Presbyterian Church in Evanston, Illinois, promised, are absent from heaven.[10]

The influence of postmodernism and cultural and ethical relativism on American society in the new millennium has been profound, affecting views of salvation, heaven, and hell. Postmodernists reject the concept of metanarratives, or worldviews, that provide cohesion and meaning for cultural life. Because humans cannot know the truth about reality, postmodernists contend, the best they can do is tell stories that make sense to them. Christians, Jews, Muslims, Buddhists, Hindus, secular humanists, Marxists, and many other groups all have stories that satisfy them and make life meaningful, but no group's narrative is any truer than another. Postmodernists adopt a pragmatic test for truth: instead of asking "Is something true?" they inquire "Does it serve my needs?" No objective, universal, or revealed truth exists, they claim. Rather, truth "is socially constructed."[11] As cultural relativists, postmodernists maintain that societies, not transcendent norms, define social good. This perspective has deeply permeated contemporary American life, contributing to the widely held view that truth is whatever individuals find convincing and pleasing. Typically ignoring the fact that postmodernism is itself a metanarrative, many Americans have accepted its premises.[12] The widespread belief that all (or at least many) views are equally plausible and that tolerance of differences is the supreme virtue has powerfully impacted traditional views of biblical interpretation, heaven, hell, and salvation.

HEAVEN: "THE ULTIMATE PLAYGROUND"

The United States has become an entertainment culture. Contemporary Americans have much more leisure time than earlier generations, as the workweek has gradually decreased from 70 hours in 1850 to 40 today, while over the same span, life expectancy has increased from 39 to 78. Experiencing enjoyable leisure is a primary goal for most Americans. While acknowledging that leisure provides significant physical, psychological, and relational benefits, some warn that the nation's exaltation of amusement has numerous negative consequences.[13] In his influential book *Amusing Ourselves to Death*, Neil Postman protested that "politics, religion, news, athletics, education and commerce" had been "transformed into congenial adjuncts of show business." Las Vegas, "a city entirely devoted to the idea of entertainment," he asserted, is "a metaphor of our national character and aspiration." It embodies "the spirit of a culture in which all public discourse increasingly takes the form of entertainment." Television had made religion into a form of entertainment, eliminating "everything that makes religion an historic, profound and sacred human activity"—ritual, dogma, tradition, theology, and the "sense of spiritual transcendence."[14]

Today's Americans have untold entertainment options. Television offers hundreds of channels to surf, with programs to suit almost every type of taste. The average American adult watches between four and five hours of television per day, many youth (and adults) play video games for twenty or more hours each week. Pornography has become a huge industry in the United States and is readily available.[15] The United States directory of gaming properties lists more than 1,500 casinos, horse tracks, dog tracks, resorts, and cruise ships. Americans bet on almost everything imaginable, especially card games and sporting events, and gambling generates revenues of about $100 billion per year. Professional sports events—baseball, football, basketball, golf, tennis, and others—are well attended and very popular television fare. Testifying to our national priorities, movies stars and athletes earn considerably more than presidents and senators. Despite all these entertainment options, many Americans battle boredom. The expectations that movies, television, and advertising create make ordinary life seem tedious.[16]

Before the 1920s, when the Christian worldview was more widely accepted, most Americans expected life to be difficult and tiresome. Contentment was exalted as a virtue, and boredom was considered "a sign of weakness, a sin or a lack of moral fiber."[17] Influenced by the media, schools, and their parents, most Americans today, by contrast, think they are entitled to happiness and the fulfillment of their desires, which makes it more difficult for them to cope with frustration, disappointment, hard work, or lack of leisure time or physical or emotional stimulation.[18]

While fear that heaven may be boring has been a concern since the Gilded Age, it reached epidemic proportions in the new millennium. "Perhaps the greatest obstacle to a robust belief in heaven," noted Carol Zaleski, "is the curious notion that a life of eternal blessedness would be boring." Many worried that heaven would be a never-ending church service. "It reminds me," says Zaleski, "of the story about the little girl who asked whether, if she were very good up in heaven, they'd let her go down to play in hell on Saturday afternoons." Some people say, Randy Alcorn noted, "I'd rather be having a good time in hell than be bored in Heaven." "After an hour or so of church," wrote Mark Buchanan, "I can get distracted and cranky....My eyes glaze, my mind fogs, my belly growls. I find myself fighting back yawns....And I'm the pastor. Is heaven church forever?" In a Gary Larson's *Far Side* cartoon, a man with wings sits on a cloud in heaven, marooned, all alone, with nothing to do. The caption expresses his despair: "Wish I'd brought a magazine."[19]

In response, some authors and ministers portrayed heaven as the great entertainment center in the sky. Especially noteworthy is Anthony DeStefano's 2003 best seller, *A Travel Guide to Heaven*. For DeStefano, the CEO of Priests for Life, a Catholic antiabortion organization, heaven is "Disney World, Hawaii, Paris, Rome, and New York all rolled up into one." "Heaven is like a five-star hotel" where the saints can "experience all the new and exciting sensory pleasures...the entire resort has to offer." Filled with mountains, rivers, canyons, oceans, and beaches, paradise will be "a feast for the senses." Assisted by His "heavenly travel assistants," a playful God, "the king of all travel agents," has spent 4.6 billion years creating His incredible resort. "Heaven is a pleasure palace, a fairyland, a nature preserve...a great big family reunion, and a never-ending vacation, all rolled into one. It's the ultimate adventure for travelers of all ages."[20]

Heaven, DeStefano argued, pulsates with energy and provides "a vast wonderland of activities" and "fascinating possibilities." Its inhabitants can fish with Ernest Hemingway, "play catch with Joe DiMaggio," "discuss literature with Jane Austen," listen to Albert Einstein explain how the universe works, or take "piano lessons from Mozart." The saints can learn new languages, master new hobbies, and study new subjects. They will read and write books, create art, and attend and perform at concerts. All the work they do "in heaven will be more satisfying and more exciting than anything" they did on earth. If God is powerful and intelligent enough to create the universe, DeStefano reasoned, then He can "keep us amused for eternity!"[21]

Publishers Weekly declared that "many readers will find DeStefano's...exciting picture of heaven compelling," comforting, and fascinating. *AudioFile*, by contrast, protested that "this bizarre account of" the contours of heaven combines "the best of religion" with "the worst of puerile, fatuous fantasy." Although the Catholic layperson "tries to support his feel-good Disneyesque theories with biblical quotations and vague ideas entwined with bouncy faith and optimism," "only the most gullible and childish will believe this Richard-Simmons-style pep talk about the afterlife." Literary critic Adam Kirsch denounced as disingenuous DeStefano's depiction of heaven where residents are "thinner, younger, and prettier" than they were on earth and "race from one game, hobby, or exotic sight to the next, 'having fun' for eternity," where "no detail is too small" for a "cruise-director God" to arrange. Charles Colson, the founder of Prison Fellowship, complained similarly that DeStefano's heaven where God caters "to our every whim" misrepresented the ultimate purpose of heaven, which is not self-centered enjoyment, but worship and service of God and others.[22] Moreover, the problem of the "hedonistic paradox"—that those who make happiness their goal never find fulfillment—raised the question of whether this entertainment-oriented heaven could truly satisfy its residents.[23]

THE TRIUMPH OF THE THERAPEUTIC

In his 1966 book, *The Triumph of the Therapeutic,* Philip Rieff predicted that a psychological perspective would soon conquer all other modes of understanding society and personal identity. Historian Christopher Lasch argued in 1979 that "the contemporary climate is therapeutic, not religious." People "hunger not for personal salvation...but for...the momentary illusion of personal well-being, health and psychic security." "Plagued by anxiety, depression, vague discontents, [and] a sense of inner emptiness," Americans sought "neither individual self-aggrandizement nor spiritual transcendence but peace of mind." Many described, some applauded, and others bemoaned the nation's "therapeutic culture." In the United States, psychological categories provide the principal explanation of the meaning of life and help shape businesses, churches, the courts, popular entertainment, schools, and families.[24]

Eva S. Moskowitz contended in *In Therapy We Trust: America's Obsession with Self-Fulfillment* that "the worship of the psyche" dominates the current age. Although Americans are divided over many other matters, she asserted, they agree that "feelings are sacred and salvation lies in self-esteem, that happiness is the ultimate goal and psychological healing [is] the means" to achieve it. This therapeutic gospel, she declared, has three major tenets: all other activities and achievements are valuable only to the extent that they make us happy; all problems have underlying psychological causes; and these problems can be remedied. Americans' nearly universal acceptance of this gospel, Moskowitz maintained, was evident in the focus on psychological health, emotional problems, and self-esteem on numerous television talk shows, most notably *Geraldo*, *Oprah*, *Ricki Lake*, *Montel Williams*, and *Jenny Jones*, dozens of books such as *Your Sacred Self*, and school programs such as Massachusetts' "I Am a Good Person Curriculum." Forty percent of Americans belonged to support groups to help them deal with problems such as codependency, alcoholism, and drug addiction. The nation celebrated therapeutic holidays such as National Depression Screening Day and National Anxiety Disorder Day. Ads on public transportation beckoned riders to call 1–800-Feeling.[25] People are encouraged to share their feelings, no matter how intimate or "unwelcome they may be to others" because repression of feelings is considered psychologically harmful.[26] Philosopher Mike W. Martin argued that the therapeutic model has powerfully affected ethical understanding. Americans "blend and blur morality and mental health.... Character faults have become personality disorders." They seek moral advice from psychologists and therapists instead of philosophers, theologians, and pastors.[27]

Rieff maintained that as the therapeutic triumphed in American society, "psychological man" who was "born to be pleased" and viewed the psychotherapist as a "secular spiritual guide" was replacing "religious man" who was "born to be saved." Rieff asserted that "by its very nature" a therapeutic society negated "the sacred order." Obsessed with individual self-fulfillment and self-realization, it eliminated "the concept of transcendence." Numerous educators, pastors, and cultural critics denounced the therapeutic perspective's impact on contemporary Christianity. New York University professor Paul Vitz protested that psychology "had become a substitute for faith," a new religion that promoted self-worship.[28] Lasch denounced the therapeutic mentality as a false religion that strove "to liberate people from" submitting "to a higher authority," so they could "focus more obsessively on their own emotional needs." Albert Mohler, Jr., the president of Southern Baptist Theological Seminary in Louisville, complained that the "critical epistemological question" for Americans was no longer "What is true?" but rather "What makes me feel good?" or "What makes me feel authentic, healthy and happy?"[29] The therapeutic worldview asserted that all Americans "are either in therapy or in denial." The typical Christian bookstore, Mohler lamented, contains rows of books that taught this therapeutic perspective on life and simply added a few biblical verses to try to "make it Christian."[30] "The therapeutic culture's well-adjusted person," averred Boston College professor William Kilpatrick, might possess a "serene sense of self," but he was unprepared to die and blind "to the beatific vision" of heaven.[31] Keith G. Meador and Shaun C. Henson maintained that the church has played a major role in propagating the view that individuals are beings who need therapy rather than sinners who need salvation. Professor E. Brooks Holifield showed how pastoral care in America has shifted in recent decades from focusing on the salvation of souls to helping individuals achieve self-actualization. The therapeutic worldview, Meador and Henson asserted, promoted "fear of aging, suffering, and dying," encouraging people to ignore the gospel's message of dying to Christ in order to prepare for heaven.[32]

Despite these concerns, the therapeutic perspective has become a staple part of recent portraits of heaven. In two phenomenally popular books—Mitch Albom's *The Five People You Meet in Heaven* (2003) and Alice Sebold's *The Lovely Bones* (2002)—the afterlife is about introspection and self-actualization. It is "the place where you listen to your inner child, repair your self-esteem, and finally reach closure." Both stories begin with the death of their main characters; Eddie, an eighty-three-year-old amusement park maintenance worker dies heroically trying to save a little girl from a runaway ride, while Susie, a fourteen-year-old girl, is raped and murdered by a sadistic neighbor. In Albom's and Sebold's therapeutic afterlife, these characters must come to terms with their past. Eddie is forced to grapple with the seeming meaninglessness of his earthly life, while Susie struggles to accept the effect her tragic death has on her parents and brother. Rather than earth serving as a school to prepare people for heaven, in these novels, heaven exists to explain the meaning of individuals' earthly lives. In paradise, a former social worker functions as Susie's "intake counselor," and Susie joins a support group for the girls her neighbor murdered. For her and Eddie, "heaven is a journey of self-discovery, an eternal program of personal development."[33]

In Albom's story, which also aired as a movie on ABC, Eddie, who felt lonely, aimless, and insignificant on earth, encounters five carefully selected individuals. The first one explains, "Each of us was in your life for a reason. You may not have known the reason at the time," but heaven exists to help you understand your life on earth. "The greatest gift God" can give Eddie is to enable him to discover the purpose of his life, which will give him the peace he desires.[34] Albom teaches that lives intersect in unexpected ways. "Seemingly inconsequential acts of sacrifice and love impact others in ways we could never imagine."[35] The individuals he meets in heaven assure Eddie that people care about him, that he was a good person, and that his life had meaning. He reconciles with his father, who had treated him cruelly and who he blamed for his lack of career fulfillment and loss of hope. Eddie also receives forgiveness from some he inadvertently hurt on earth. Eddie is shown "a pier filled with thousands of people, men and women, fathers and mothers," and many children from the past, present, and ones yet to be born who are enjoying or would someday enjoy the amusement park "because of the simple, mundane things Eddie had done...the accidents he had prevented, [and] the rides he had kept safe."[36]

Susie's heaven is "tailor-made" to fulfill her "childish fantasies." It contains a high school where the boys all behave and the only textbooks are *Seventeen*, *Glamour*, and *Vogue*. She is surrounded by an ice cream parlor, bucolic landscapes, soccer fields, puppies, Victorian cupolas, and affable dogs. Nevertheless, she experiences little contentment because she is preoccupied with earthly events. As in a series of therapy sessions, her involvement with earth must go on until she resolves her "issues." Only after she approves of various earthly events that occurred after her death does she experience psychic wholeness. Similarly, in Albom's heaven, Eddie must, as in a counseling relationship, review the course of his life to make sense of it. He accomplishes this by conversing with the five people whose lives he has most significantly affected and who have most powerfully influenced him. Albom and Sebold, Adam Kirsch argued, are "the products of our affluent, post-religious society—not pious enough to be concerned with God and not hungry enough to fantasize about food. Instead, the afflictions they want heaven to cure are the very ones our wealth seems to aggravate: loneliness, alienation, [and] emotional deprivation." In Albom's and Sebold's visions of heaven, God is largely absent. Instead, the suffering, self-fulfillment, and psychological health of individuals are its central features.[37] Consumerism, individualism, and the therapeutic mindset have made personal choice the supreme cultural value as well as a primary component of the American vision of the afterlife.[38]

Albom and Sebold's heaven is so appealing, Mark Ralls contended, because Americans are "enamored with the therapeutic." The contemporary focus on self-fulfillment leads many to worry that they will no longer "possess the memories, desires and affections that made" their "earthly life unique." They desire a heaven that will ensure their personal identity and validate rather than repudiate their earthly existence. As a result, many Christians do not find the traditional theocentric portrait of heaven attractive, so pastors must portray heaven as more than a "never-ending Sunday school" where the saints are lost in the "wonder, love and praise" of God. They must describe the rich relationships that will exist there and help their parishioners establish "an emotional connection to heaven."[39]

Novels like Albom's and Sebold's offer readers the psychic comfort that someday they will make sense of their earthly existence and be reunited with loved ones. Eddie complains that he lived in the same apartment for years, fixed amusement park rides, and did "nothing to be proud of." Albom and Sebold reassured Americans who longed for meaning and fulfillment, that in the afterlife they will understand their important contributions. The popularity of these novels, Ralls claimed, testified that Americans desired to go to heaven not simply to survive death or receive compensation for their earthly struggles but also to make sense of their existence.[40]

While Ralls argued that these novels suggested ways ministers could make heaven more alluring, columnist David Brooks denounced Albom's fable for catering to "the easygoing narcissism" of our "psychobabble nation." The book and others like it, Brooks protested, portrayed heaven as simply "an excellent therapy session." One's friends and divine helpers told the deceased how wonderful they were and helped them reach closure. "In this heaven, God and his glory are not the center of attention." Rather, it was all about the saints. Hurts, not sins, were washed away. "The language of trauma and recovery" replaced the rhetoric of good and evil. God's justice, virtue, and a moral framework were absent. Rather than centering on loving and serving God, heaven focused on its residents feeling good about themselves, understanding how special they are, and mystically connecting with each other. Brooks protested that instead of offering people who feel lonely and insignificant "the rich moral framework of organized religion or rigorous philosophy" and "reminding them of the tough-minded exemplars of the Bible and history," books like Albom's threw "seekers remorselessly back upon themselves."[41]

James Bryan Smith's *Room of Marvels* (2004) trumpets similar therapeutic themes. Its primary character, Tim, receives a visionary guided tour of "the wonders that await him" in heaven, where his departed loved ones (he has recently lost a close friend, his mother, and his daughter) already reside. In Smith's heaven, residents strip off masks, are vulnerable, abandon their fears, and understand why things happened as they did on earth so that they can experience love. "To get into deeper heaven," Tim must give up the "restless anxieties and the self-deceiving defense mechanisms" that prevent him "from loving freely" and learn to be open and authentic and to trust. Everyone has a "room of marvels" in heaven that consists of all the ways they "touched other people's lives." These rooms are filled with souvenirs of the love that heavenly inhabitants exhibited on earth—the things they "did for other people." Movies of the saints' lives, which require several days to watch, reveal "the little acts of kindness that turned people's lives around." By conversing with his loved ones in heaven, Tim realizes that "the only things worth seeking [on earth] are treasures in heaven," which are best achieved by acts of love and patient enduring of suffering.[42]

HEAVEN AND THE PURSUIT OF HAPPINESS

Personal happiness is a major theme in our therapeutic culture, and more than the people of any other nation, Americans eagerly and anxiously pursue happiness.[43] Just look at the bookstore shelves: *14,000 Things to Be Happy About*; *33 Moments of Happiness*; *101 Ways to Happiness*; *7 Strategies for Wealth and Happiness*; *Absolute Happiness*; *Happiness That Lasts*; *Happiness Is Your Destiny*; *Happiness Is No Secret*; *Happiness Is a Choice*; *Happiness Without Death*; and *Find Happiness in Everything You Do*. In *Authentic Happiness: Using the New Positive Psychology to Realize Your Potential for Lasting Fulfillment* (2002), Martin Seligman claimed that research demonstrates that happiness "can be lastingly increased." Those who embrace positive psychology, he argued, could achieve "the upper reaches" of happiness by focusing on positive emotions, traits, and institutions "such as democracy, strong families, and free inquiry." These things help produce the virtues that in turn generate positive emotions.[44] Similarly, Ed Diener and Robert Biswas-Diener argued in *Happiness: Unlocking the Mysteries of Psychological Wealth* (2008) that people can attain "psychological wealth" and happiness by focusing on such factors as their "attitudes toward life, social support, spiritual development, material resources, health, and the activities" in which they engage. However, data indicate that material and scientific advances are not making people in the West happier with their lives, and many recent political, social, and economic developments are making happiness hard to achieve.[45]

Happiness has thus become a key ingredient in many recent portrayals of heaven. Obsession with happiness and consumption, sociologist Wade Clark Roof asserted, has led many, including some evangelicals, to picture heaven as a realm of affluence, comforts, and bliss. It is very "reassuring to know," wrote Barbara Johnson, "that our departed loved ones are…happy and healthy and enjoying all the amenities that come with living next door to God." "God will supply us with everything we'll ever need" to be happy in heaven, declared Billy Graham. "Imagine what we will accomplish," Michael Wittmer proclaimed, "after working a few million years without the limitations of sin!" People may have "the athleticism of Michael Jordan, the mind of Albert Einstein, and the creativity of Charles Dickens." The saints, Randy Alcorn declared, will make new discoveries, have banquets, drink coffee and wine, eat peanuts and chocolate, and experience abundant joy. God will replace sexual intercourse with something even better, and heaven's residents will continue to enjoy "the best part of sex"—"relational intimacy." "Music, dancing, storytelling, art, entertainment, drama, and books" will abound, and the saints will enjoy many of the same "activities, games, skills, and interests" they do on earth—as well as many new ones. Ted Dekker chastised Christians for seeking to find pleasure, happiness, and purpose "on earth rather than in the age to come." Doing so prevented them both from understanding "the bliss that awaits them" in heaven and from attaining earthly happiness. Unless Christians insatiably longed for "the hope of glory," they would "never enjoy this life."[46]

HEAVEN: "THE GREATEST FAMILY REUNION OF ALL"

Most Americans greatly value intimate relationships and close friendships, and many contemporary portraits of heaven emphasize being reunited with family and friends. Throughout American history, numerous theologians and pastors have portrayed the saints as being so consumed by their worship of God that they pay little attention to one another. Most American Christians, however, have followed Augustine in seeing the adoration of God and the joys of heaven as enhanced by corporate worship and interpersonal relationships. "Almost everyone who believes in heaven," alleged Yale professor Peter S. Hawkins, "imagines that those we love best in this life will be those we love in eternity." Ray Hylton described heaven as a place of "unhindered fellowship," and Don Piper called it "the greatest family reunion of all." Our love for others there, Baptist pastor and inspirational speaker Bruce Milne maintained, "will be immeasurably richer, deeper and mutually more satisfying" than on earth. Many echoed the words of Cardinal Theodore McCarrick, former archbishop of Washington, DC: "I'm looking forward to meeting my mom and dad and the rest of my family." Alcorn expected husbands and wives to be even closer in heaven than they were on earth.[47]

The depiction of heaven as a place of amazing delight, bliss, and enchantment is hardly new. Thomas Aquinas promised that the saints would enjoy "perfect pleasure" and the fulfillment of "every human desire," and numerous Puritans stressed the splendors of paradise. However, for medieval Catholic theologians and Puritan ministers, this everlasting bliss sprang primarily from being able to gaze upon and commune directly with God rather than from the entertainment and excitement heaven would supply. Although the themes of personal fulfillment, self-discovery, personal happiness, amusement, and fellowship have been pervasive in portrayals of heaven produced in the new millennium, some continued to emphasize the beatific vision and the saints' fellowship with God and Christ. "The pleasures of this life," argued Old Testament scholar Bill T. Arnold, "are not obliterated by union with, and enjoyment of, God in heaven." Rather, "all such pleasurable experiences" will likely be "enjoyed in heaven in a holy way that acknowledges God as their source." The saints, declared priest Joseph M. Champlin, will derive happiness and peace principally from seeing "God face to face." Fellow Catholic Peter C. Phan, a professor of social thought at Georgetown University, rejoiced that the redeemed will experience the "beatific vision of the divine essence." The focal point of paradise, Mark Buchanan exalted, is "Christ seated at the right hand of God" "reigning with God in power, justice, and mercy." In his vision of heaven, Don Piper heard hundreds of songs simultaneously worshipping God and praising Christ "for all he has done for us and how wonderful he is." Although he portrayed paradise primarily as a pleasurable playground, Anthony DeStefano argued that nothing else in heaven will "compare with the thrill of meeting God." If God did not protect the saints, the sheer ecstasy of being in His presence would annihilate them.[48] As the Christian rock group MercyMe put it in their 2001 song, "I Can Only Imagine," which received substantial airtime on both Christian and mainstream radio stations throughout the decade:

> Surrounded by Your glory, what will my heart feel
> Will I dance for you Jesus or in awe of you be still
> Will I stand in your presence or to my knees will I fall…

HEAVEN'S RELATIONSHIP TO EARTH

While many contemporary portraits of heaven emphasized comfort, entertainment, self-fulfillment, and happiness, others stressed that belief in heaven should inspire Christians to lead more godly lives on earth and to work to make the world a more righteous, just, and healthy place. Those who argued that after the final judgment the saints would dwell on a renovated earth were especially likely to accentuate these themes. "The purpose of heaven," Nathan Bierma averred, "is not to make us happy but to make things right," to restore shalom, "the right alignment of everything," and wholeness. Sadly, many Christians viewed heaven as a "retirement paradise" rather than a place they built on earth by their diligent labor. Christians should not seek to escape from the evils and problems of the world, but to renew it. How were those who would comprise Christ's "welcoming party" "preparing for his arrival"? Would Jesus come back to an earth that had been treasured, cared for, and managed responsibly for His glory? "This planet is more than just a stopover on" our "way to heaven," added Michael Wittmer. It is our "final destination."[49] Bierma challenged Christians to live in two worlds simultaneously—"the world as it is and the world as it was meant to be—and will be again." They should embrace "the strange tension between…the already and the not yet—the initial triumph of the first coming of Christ and the promise of his second one." Living in the hope of heaven, Bierma maintained, involves recognizing "the gap between what the world is and what it was created to be," realizing the role that Christ's death played in closing this gap, and longing for God to permanently close this gap by bringing heaven to earth. Christians could reduce this breech by promoting righteousness and justice, managing the resources of the world wisely, living responsibly, and producing minimal waste. Similarly, Phan declared that because the world is "our permanent home," Christians must be ecologically responsible.

"The new heaven and the new earth," he added, is "this universe...transformed by the divine power." Doing God's will on earth as it is done in heaven, Philip Yancey argued, involved providing homes, food, and water for all who lack them, pursuing economic and political justice, promoting peace between nations, living harmoniously with nature, and taking care of the sick.[50]

More than in earlier periods, Christians stressed that after the final judgment, God will either renovate or recreate the earth as a place for the saints to dwell for eternity. God "will renew the earth and restore it to His original intent," asserted editor Lee Wilson and Joe Beam, founder of LovePath International, a Christian organization devoted to improving marriages, to create "a perfect home" for the saints and Himself. Recognizing that God would refurbish the earth to serve as the residence of the saints, Bierma argued, was essential to understanding the cosmic scope of God's redemption. Believers, Wittmer contended, will eventually be reunited with their resurrected bodies and return to earth. Many Christians mistakenly thought that the goal was to escape earth, but people "were made to live here." Therefore, the departure of Christians from this world is the first part of a round-trip journey.[51]

Both Bierma and Mark Buchanan argued that people's conception of heaven significantly shaped their understanding of earthly life. Bierma urged Christians to reject four things almost everyone sought—power, success, wealth, and recognition—and to realize that their current life was not simply a temporary excursion before they began an eternal holiday in heaven. Rather, human culture and relationships provided "a sneak preview of heaven." The biblical picture of heaven, he concluded, was intended to make people seek to bring it on earth. Jesus, Buchanan alleged, "would be puzzled by our preoccupation with heaven as something that is exclusively hereafter." "Heaven starts now." He urged believers to emulate Peter, Paul, John, and thousands of Christian martyrs and missionaries who were "so enthralled with heaven" that they risked everything for its sake.[52]

Others maintained that the prospect of heaven had additional practical benefits. C. John Steer, pastor of Autumn Ridge Church, a large, nondenominational congregation in Rochester, Minnesota, insisted that it encouraged Christians to persevere, helped assuage their grief, stimulated them to lay up treasures above, and prompted them to pursue purity. It also challenged non-Christians to consider their eternal destiny. "If we view this life as a sort of boot camp for the afterlife," wrote David Shibley, our perceptions and actions will be different. William Wilberforce, Mother Teresa, and millions of lesser known heavenly minded people had built "thousands of hospitals, shelters, clinics, children's homes, schools and colleges...in heaven's honor." Engaging in "faithful, fruitful service for Christ on Earth" to gain eternal rewards, Shibley added, was a powerful incentive. The promise of heaven, Ted Dekker avowed, could stimulate people to live righteously and victoriously. He urged Christians to so run the race of life that they stored up treasures there.[53]

HOW DO PEOPLE GET TO HEAVEN?

While many evangelicals continued to argue that only those who accepted Jesus Christ as their personal savior go to heaven, most Americans disagreed. A 2008 Pew Forum on Religion & Public Life survey reported that Americans were evenly divided on how to attain eternal life: 30 percent insisted that people gain eternal bliss based on their beliefs, while 29 percent said that people's actions were the most important factor. Ten percent of respondents asserted that both belief and actions were crucial. While 64 percent of white evangelical Protestants claimed that individuals' beliefs determine whether they go to heaven, 61 percent of Catholics argued that actions or works are the key to gaining admittance to paradise.[54] Forty-five percent of evangelicals stated that individuals must believe in Jesus Christ to be saved, while another 19 percent gave more generic responses, "citing belief in God or, more simply, 'belief' or 'faith' as most important." White mainline Protestants and black Protestants were more evenly divided than white evangelicals and Catholics about how eternal life is attained. Thirty-three percent of mainline Protestants saw actions as most important, 25 percent claimed that belief is most important, and 10 percent stated that entry to heaven depends on a combination of both. Forty-three percent of black Protestants asserted that faith is paramount in achieving eternal life, while 27 percent pinpointed actions as the principal factor.[55]

The survey also found that 65 percent of all Christians believed that people can obtain eternal life by practicing many different religions. Eighty percent of white mainline Protestants, black Protestants, and white Catholics and 72 percent of evangelicals who said that "many religions can lead to eternal life cite at least one non-Christian religion that can do so."[56]

While most Americans who had a religious affiliation adopted a nonexclusivist approach to faith, 29 percent maintained that their faith is the only one that can lead to eternal life. This was especially true for white evangelical Protestants (49 percent) and black Protestants (45 percent).[57] As these statistics demonstrate, the views of some Americans are not logically consistent. As pollster George Barna explained, millions of Americans "contend that they will experience eternal salvation because they confessed their sins and accepted Christ as their savior, but also believe that a person can do enough good works to earn eternal salvation."[58]

Speaking for many evangelicals, Anne Graham Lotz declared that the only "way to go to heaven" is to "accept Jesus as your personal savior." Every individual will someday stand before God, wrote Rick Warren, who will audit our lives; we must pass "a final exam" before entering heaven. Because God wants us to pass, "he has given us the questions in advance...: 'What did you do with my Son Jesus Christ?' [and] 'What did you do with what I gave you?'" "We can never be saved because of what we do," Billy Graham proclaimed, "because God's standard is nothing less than perfection," which we will never achieve. A single sin would keep people out of heaven. Therefore, individuals "can only be saved because of what Jesus Christ," the perfect One, did for them by covering their sin. To be saved, Graham instructed, "simply believe that Christ has taken away your sins, and then receive Him into your heart and life."[59] Jokes also expressed the evangelical position. A man dies and approaches the Pearly Gates. Saint Peter tells him that heaven has become crowded so he has devised a point system to determine who would be admitted. Anyone who reaches 100 points may enter. The man tells Peter that he assisted the poor, for which Peter awards him three points. The man adds that he tithed, and Peter gives him another point. The man asserts that he had never sworn. Peter adds one more point. In despair, the man cries that at this rate he could get in to heaven only by the grace of God. "Come on in!" Peter replies.

Like the Catholics in the Pew survey, some priests asserted that both faith and works were necessary to salvation. Leo J. Trese's *Seventeen Steps to Heaven* include seeking to deepen one's understanding of the Christian faith, striving to win others to Christ, avoiding sin, going to confession and receiving communion regularly, and serving others. He urged people "to die, not only free from mortal sin, but free also from any venial sins or unpaid penance that might delay our entrance into Heaven." The principal purpose of last rites, he maintained, was "to cleanse us from whatever 'remains of sin' might impede our immediate flight to God." But some Catholics, like Anthony DeStefano, explained salvation in almost evangelical terms. Through the crucifixion, God "purchased our tickets to heaven." No one can provide his own ticket to heaven; individuals must invite God into their hearts, worship, pray, and obey Him. "A Protestant might describe union with God as accepting Jesus Christ as your personal savior and being born again," DeStefano maintained, while "a Catholic might urge you to make the Eucharist...the center of your life."[60]

Both Billy Graham and Joel Osteen appeared to deny that people must believe in Christ as their savior to be admitted to heaven, causing considerable consternation among evangelicals. On Robert Schuller's *Hour of Power* in 1997, Graham declared that everyone who "loves Christ or knows Christ, whether they're conscious of it or not," were "members of the body of Christ." God called Christians, Muslims, Buddhists, and nonbelievers to Himself. Some "may not even know the name of Jesus, but they know in their hearts that they need something they don't have, and they turn to the only light they have" and, as a result, they will go to heaven. In a 2006 interview in *Newsweek*, Graham was asked whether he believed "heaven will be closed to good Jews, Muslims, Buddhists, Hindus or secular people." He responded, "Those are decisions only the Lord will make.... I don't want to speculate about all that." God "gave his son for the whole world, and I think he loves everybody regardless of what label they have."[61] Osteen pastors the Lakewood Church in Houston, the nation's largest congregation, which draws over 30,000 people every weekend. Its televised services air in more than 100 countries. He has written two best-selling books—*Your Best Life Now: 7 Steps to Living at Your Full Potential* (2004) and *Become a Better You: 7 Keys to Improving Your Life Every Day* (2007). On the television show *Larry King Live*, King asked Osteen about who went to heaven. "What if you're Jewish or Muslim [and] you don't accept Christ at all?" The megachurch pastor responded, "I'm very careful about saying who would and wouldn't go to heaven. I don't know." King asked if Jews and Muslims were wrong for not believing in Christ for salvation. Osteen replied, "I don't know if I believe they're wrong.... [O]nly God will judge a person's heart. I spent a lot of time in India with my father. I don't know all about their religion. But I know they love God.... I've seen their sincerity." In response to Osteen's apparent agreement with a caller's claim that "Jesus is the way, the truth and the light and the only way to the father is through him," King stated that "So then a Jew is not going to heaven?" Osteen answered, "I can't judge somebody's heart.... It's not my business to say...this one is or this one isn't [going to heaven]. I just say, here's what the Bible teaches and I'm going to put my faith in Christ." When King asked, "What about atheists?" Osteen replied, "I'm going to let God be the judge of who goes to heaven and hell. I just...present the truth.... I believe it's a relationship with Jesus."[62]

Countless Christians complained that most Americans either do not think "they need to be 'saved' from or by anyone or anything" or believe that their own efforts will save them.[63] Alan F. Segal, author of *Life after Death: A History of the Afterlife in Western Religion* (2004), asserted that "most Americans believe they will be saved no matter what they [do or] are."[64] Many Americans affirmed the message of Maria Shriver's children's book, *What's Heaven?* and an episode of the *Simpsons* in which St. Peter tells Homer he must return to earth to do a good deed before he will be admitted: if you are good, you go to heaven.[65]

Theologically conservative Christians continued to refute universalism. Universalists argued, Kenneth Boa and Robert Bowman, Jr., stated, that because God is both all-loving and all-powerful, he "will find a way to save everyone." Universalists cited a variety of biblical texts to support their contention that Jesus' death on the cross atoned for the sins of every person and therefore all will be redeemed. These texts allegedly stressed that God sought to save "all" individuals or "the world." The context of these passages, Boa and Bowman countered, demonstrated that they did not teach universal salvation. The words "all" and "world" did not refer "to every single individual human being in history," but rather to the world-wide scope of Christ's redemption, or to all types of people, or in some cases to both Jews and Gentiles. Cardinal Avery Dulles, Professor of Religion and Society at Fordham University until his retirement in 2008, lamented that many Christians mistakenly assumed that "everyone, or practically everyone, must be saved." The New Testament taught "the absolute necessity of faith for salvation" and that everyone faced only two possibilities—"everlasting happiness in the presence of God" or "everlasting torment in the absence of God."[66]

THE DEMISE OF HELL?

Although many either applauded or lamented its alleged disappearance, significant percentages of Americans continued to affirm belief in hell. And while hell was seldom the subject of sermons, conservative Christians discussed it in books, blogs, and articles. Various polls conducted between 2003 and 2007 reported that between 69 and 74 percent of Americans believed in hell.[67] A 2004 Gallup poll found belief in hell to be more prevalent among Republicans, frequent churchgoers, Southerners, and those who never attended college. However, most Christians, including many evangelicals and conservative Catholics, were much more reluctant than those in earlier generations to say that many or even some would go to hell. Boston University religion professor Stephen R. Prothero asserted that in the 1970s and 1980s, many born-again Christians had little trouble declaring, "'You're going to hell if you don't believe this.' Now they say, 'Jesus is my Savior and Lord, but what is up with you is a mystery.'" Hell is rarely, if ever, mentioned from the pulpits of mainline churches, Peter Stanford claimed. Purgatory and limbo are almost totally ignored, and most people assume, but hardly ever directly state, that "we are all bound for some sort of heaven." The *Catechism of the Catholic Church* asserts that some individuals may "choose to reject God's offer of friendship and love," a decision that will be confirmed by their dying without repenting. Peter C. Phan insisted, however, that a loving God will not punish people eternally because doing so would be vindictive and would not improve them morally. Although Christians cannot be absolutely certain that no one will be damned, he added, they must hope that hell eventually will be empty.[68]

Many evangelicals were troubled by the complaint that their position "unfairly consigns most of humanity, including those who have never heard of Christ, to

Hell."[69] Some responded by arguing that "the punishment of Hell is reserved for people who have willingly and knowingly" rejected God rather than all those who have not accepted Jesus as their savior.[70] Meanwhile, some theological conservatives joined many liberal Christians in maintaining that those who rejected God's gracious offer of salvation would be annihilated rather than spend eternity in hell. Edward William Fudge, a biblical scholar and attorney, took this position in his *The Fire That Consumes: The Biblical Case for Conditional Immortality*. "Scripture nowhere suggests," Fudge declared, "that God is an eternal torturer.... The idea of conscious everlasting torment" is "a grievous mistake" and "a gross slander against the heavenly Father." "The Bible repeatedly warns that the wicked will 'die,' 'perish' or 'be destroyed.'" The view that the unredeemed "will live forever in inescapable pain contradicts the clear, consistent teaching of Scripture" by making the wages of sin everlasting torment rather than death. The Bible taught that the lost "will be destroyed, both body and soul, forever."[71]

On the other hand, others defended the traditional doctrine of hell, accentuated the awfulness of hell, and lamented the lack of sermons about hell. "Jesus mentioned hell more than he did heaven," Ann Graham Lotz pointed out. Christians must evangelize because "a lot of people" were heading to hell. Similarly C. John Steer stressed that twelve of the twenty New Testament references to hell come directly from Jesus. Christ taught that hell is as real and "as eternal as heaven." It "is a place of physical, emotional, relational and spiritual suffering" that is devoid of light, love, mercy, and kindness. "The agony of hell," Ray Hylton proclaimed, is its total separation from God. Hell's residents, declares Phan, are alienated from God and the redeemed and consequently cannot fulfill "the deepest longings of the human heart."[72] Although many proponents of the traditional view explained the fires of hell as metaphorical and contended that its pains are emotional and spiritual rather than physical, they insisted that the Bible taught that the lost will be punished eternally.[73]

MICHAEL JACKSON'S DEATH AND MEMORIAL SERVICE

The response to Michael Jackson's death and the memorial service held for him during the summer of 2009 help illuminate how death, heaven, hell, and salvation are viewed in contemporary America. The memorial service at Los Angeles's Staples Center was the second-biggest media event of the year, surpassed only by Barack Obama's inauguration.[74] The audience of 20,000 included 2,500 credentialed journalists and thousands of ordinary Americans chosen by lottery from the 1.6 million who applied. The story dominated cable television news and radio programming for more than a week. Patterned after black church services with inspiring songs followed by "fiery, emotional speeches," the memorial service was carried by nineteen different television networks and watched by thirty-one million people.[75]

Americans expressed great sorrow and loss, displayed curiosity about Jackson's will, debts, and the custody battles over his three children, and reminisced about and celebrated Jackson's life, music, and legacy. Family members, politicians, ministers, and a host of celebrities from the entertainment and sports world, including Magic Johnson, Brooke Shields, Queen Latifah, Mariah Carey, Usher, Al Sharpton, and John Mayer, participated in Jackson's memorial service. The ceremony blended Christian elements with Hollywood spectacle, adulation, and grief. Lucious Smith, the pastor of the Friendship Baptist Church in Pasadena who closed the service in prayer, called Jackson "an idol, a hero and even a king." The service featured the Andrae Crouch Choir, Lionel Richie, and Jennifer Hudson all performing "songs of salvation to huge applause."[76] Richie sang a moving rendition of The Commodores' "Jesus Is Love," which includes the words:

'Cause Jesus is love…
And I know He's mine forever…
And His words will be our salvation

As Jackson's casket was brought to the front of the stage, a choir sang Crouch's "Soon and Very Soon," which seemed to have a double meaning:

Soon and very soon we are going to see the King.
Hallelujah, Hallelujah, we're going to see the King.…
Yeah, no more cryin' there, we are going to see the King.

Martin Luther King, Jr.'s children, Bernice King and Martin Luther King III, called Jackson's life "inspired by God." Bernice declared that he was "full of the unconditional love of God. He was indeed a shining light, like our father Martin, and in remembrance of Michael may we all be inspired to go and let our lights shine." Expressing a view that is frequently asserted when public figures die, Stevie Wonder declared, "God is good and…as much as we may feel that we need Michael here with us, God must have needed him far more."

Jackson's eclectic religious background fit well with America's seeker-sensitive, pluralistic society. He was raised as a Jehovah's Witness and claimed that he did missionary work for this sect for many years after his musical career began. He was exposed to Islam through his brother Jermaine, and some incorrectly reported that he had become a Muslim. During his trial for child molestation in 2005, Jackson sought emotional support and spiritual assistance from the Kabbalah movement, a worldview derived from Jewish mysticism that Madonna helped popularize. At various times, Jackson received spiritual guidance from Orthodox Jewish rabbi Shmuley Boteach and New Age guru Deepak Chopra. Rumors also spread that he had become a Christian in his last days by praying with his friend Andrae Crouch and his twin sister Sandra, which they denied.[77]

Meanwhile, Bill Keller, an "Internet evangelist," consigned Jackson to hell. Keller repudiated the claim of some "high profile Christians" that Jackson "is now at peace in Heaven." Keller argued that the pop star was in torment in hell because he had not repented of his sins and accepted Jesus as his savior. Jackson's "great humanitarian deeds" and generous gifts to charities were commendable, but people could not buy their way into heaven.[78]

Jackson's family and friends sought to use his memorial service to rehabilitate his image, which had been under heavy attack for many years because of his eccentric behavior, indictment for child abuse, numerous plastic surgeries, many lawsuits, and seemingly bad career choices. The ceremony also celebrated Jackson's life, achievements, and music. He was praised as a trailblazer in African-American civil rights and a great humanitarian. The day after the service, the U.S. House of Representatives Foreign Affairs Committee passed a 1,500-word resolution recognizing Jackson "as a global humanitarian and a noted leader in the fight against worldwide hunger and medical crises" and honoring his contributions to "the worlds of arts and entertainment, scientific advances in the treatment of HIV/AIDS, and global food security."[79]

Many reactions to the media's treatment of Jackson's death and memorial service were negative. Kim Masters, a *Daily Beast* entertainment writer, declared that "celebrating Jackson's gifts is" appropriate, but "making him into a saint" is not. Turning "Jackson into a deity is a willing suspension of belief in what we know to be true." Fox TV commentator Bill O'Reilly denounced the extensive adulation of Jackson as "grandstanding and pathetic."[80] A comment on the *Variety* website lambasted the ceremony as "a grotesque and vulgar display" that demonstrated the United States' moral and cultural bankruptcy.[81] Richard Roeper complained that while millions were worshipping and weeping for Jackson, "a wildly controversial figure, an icon and a hero to some and a devil to others," "a lot of good people, from soldiers who fought in Iraq to teachers who devoted their lives to education to folks who lived quiet, decent, selfless lives," who were "also being put to rest this week," were largely ignored.[82]

As with another legendary American musician, Elvis Presley, rumors quickly began to circulate that Jackson either had not actually died or had been seen in the spirit world. A YouTube video showed Jackson's "ghost haunting the hallways" of his Neverland Ranch, and a website was created (michaeljacksonhoaxdeath.com) that asked "Is Jacko Really Dead?"[83]

Jackson's eclectic memorial service and the diverse response to his death illustrate the status of contemporary American views of the nature of the afterlife and of the grounds upon which individuals gain admittance to heaven. They display the deep desire of most Americans to conclude that everyone, no matter what they believe about God and Jesus and no matter how much their behavior violates Christian morality (or even common standards of decency), goes to heaven. Although some dissent from this position, many assume that in the final analysis the good deeds of most people (including Michael Jackson) outweigh their sins, shortcomings, and moral lapses and that a benevolent and merciful God will welcome all but the most heinous, debauched, brutal people into His eternal kingdom when they die.

CONCLUSION

The first decade of the twenty-first century was a difficult one for most Americans. Natural disasters, economic woes, terrorism, and seemingly intractable social problems at home and abroad produced a large amount of anxiety. Americans were deeply divided over a host of political and social issues. They also disagreed about the nature of the afterlife and the grounds for admission to heaven. A high percentage of Americans affirmed that there is an afterlife, but many of them pictured it as quite different from the traditional Christian conception. Cultural trends and norms led many to view engaging in entertainment, attaining self-understanding, and achieving personal happiness as much more important in paradise than worshipping and serving God. Influenced by postmodernism, relativism, and society's stress on tolerance, most Americans publicly stated or implied that almost everyone, except the extremely wicked, will go to heaven, a belief that is based largely on compassion, self-interest, and speculation. Privately, Americans were much more divided. Almost identical numbers of Americans maintained that belief is the key to being admitted to heaven as said that conduct is the principal determinant. Most churches provided little teaching about heaven through sermons, Sunday school classes, Bible studies, or other forums; few Americans read books or articles about heaven; and most Americans were biblically illiterate. Therefore, their portraits of heaven were largely derived from popular culture, projections of their own desires, and myths. As religious and ideological diversity increase in American society, our views of the afterlife and salvation are likely to become even more varied and possibly more contentious.

CONCLUSION

SOME IDEAS ABOUT heaven have remained remarkably stable throughout American history. Despite changing circumstances, Christians have generally agreed that the saints' communion with and worship of God the Father and Jesus will be central to heavenly life. They have concurred that heaven will be more spectacular and beautiful than anyone can imagine and that its life will be far more enjoyable than earth's. They have envisioned a heaven where the saints recognize family and friends and enjoy closer relationships with them than they did on earth. Social events, work, service of others, leisure activities, and spiritual growth will all continue in heaven. Americans have portrayed heaven as a destination and a reward, "relief from earthly trials," a perpetual "reunion with those we love," and humanity's "real home" and "true country." Heaven has been described as "the New Jerusalem and Paradise Regained, the community of Saints and the eternal Eucharist," "everlasting Easter and a million Christmases," and "the eternal ... ever growing experience of God."[1]

While these themes have been perennial, other aspects of American depictions of heavenly life have changed significantly over time, as has the relative importance of various features. Although almost all Christians have based their portraits of paradise on biblical passages, they have emphasized different ones, and their interpretations of the same texts has often differed substantially. Theological liberals have tended to interpret biblical references to heaven more figuratively and conservatives more literally.[2] However, both groups' conceptions of heaven have been strongly shaped by their cultural settings, and the topics they accentuated often reflected the major societal trends of their eras. Thus the particular conditions, problems, needs, and tendencies of various periods have powerfully affected American portraits of heaven. These factors especially helped determine which themes received the most emphasis in different decades. What Mark Schantz wrote about the antebellum years is true of Americans in all eras: "heaven was a tabula rasa upon which" they inscribed "their most profound hopes and aspirations. As poets, novelists, and theologians grappled with heaven, they loosed their imaginations, sometimes basing their ideas in dreams, sometimes in rational thought, sometimes in the authority of the Bible." Heaven, he added, appealed very strongly to antebellum (and many other) Americans "precisely because of the freedom it gave them to conjure perfect worlds that suited individual imaginations."[3] "Beliefs about Heaven," declared Mally Cox-Chapman, "like attitudes about food, child rearing, and clothes, go through fashions." "Beliefs about the afterlife," she insisted, "are a complex alchemy of religious legacy, visions, dreams, intuitions, and experiences of reasonable people," and I would add, biblical interpretation, theological perspective, and the social climate. As a result, the importance Christians have placed on fellowship with family and friends, relationships with the heroes of the Bible and church history, heavenly rewards and service, personal growth, self-understanding, happiness, and amusement has differed substantially over the course of time.

As we have seen, what Americans perceived to be the chief features of heavenly life varied from era to era. The Puritans emphasized the splendor of heaven, the grandeur of God the Father and Jesus, and the intimate communion the saints would enjoy with them. Jonathan Edwards, George Whitefield, and other leaders of the First Great Awakening echoed these themes, but Edwards also accentuated heaven's astounding love. The revivalists of the Second Great Awakening struck similar notes while fending off challenges from Unitarians, deists, and free thinkers. During the middle decades of the nineteenth century, the predominant image of heaven was as a celestial home where the saints rejoined their loved ones. Slaves expected heaven to provide freedom, dignity, justice, and compensation for their earthly exploitation and suffering. Heavenly rest was a major theme from the Puritans until the Civil War, but as leisure time and earthly comforts increased for many Americans, it became less important. On the other hand, concern that heaven might be boring began only after the Civil War. Until then, life for most people involved constant work and little entertainment, and few expressed fear that heavenly life might be monotonous, dull, or routine.

As American society placed more emphasis on education, individual success, and personal development in the postbellum years, views of heaven began to stress activism and progress. The Gilded Age heaven focused more on personal growth than ever before. During the late nineteenth century, evangelicals and theological liberals began to disagree over some of heaven's features, God's method of salvation, and hell's nature and duration. Progressive Era Christians highlighted the service the saints would render and the progress they would attain in knowledge, character, and spirituality. From 1890 to 1920, theological conservatives generally concentrated on helping people get to heaven and emphasized celestial rewards and fellowship, while proponents of the Social Gospel strove to replicate the conditions of heaven on earth. As American society focused more on individual fulfillment and creature comforts from 1920 to 1960, heaven was often depicted as a place where people achieved their full potential, transcended earth's limitations, gained a sense of completion, and experienced immense pleasure. During these years, theological conservatives and liberals disputed whether admission to heaven depended principally upon being spiritually regenerated or having a Christ-like character.

In the final forty years of the twentieth century, Christians underscored the eternal and temporal benefits of thinking about heaven more than earlier eras. Alternative perspectives on heaven arose, thousands of Americans reported having near-death experiences, and heaven became an important theme in television shows and movies. During the first decade of the twenty-first century, heaven was depicted as a site for achieving self-understanding, an entertainment center, and a place of personal happiness as much as a realm for worshipping and serving God.

From the Puritans to the present, Americans have disagreed sharply about the value of focusing on heaven. Building on the long Christian tradition that encourages people to experience glimpses of heaven on earth through meditating, worshipping, fellowshipping with other believers, and appreciating the beauty of the world, many have argued that contemplating heaven stimulates Christians to develop a closer relationship with God, live righteously, evangelize, and work to remedy social ills. Therefore, they have exhorted individuals to ponder their future intimate relationship with God and the wonders of heavenly life. Others who argue that Jesus came to bring the kingdom of God to earth have complained that concentrating on heaven leads people to neglect their earthly responsibilities, especially their duty to improve social conditions and help the poor and oppressed. They have also protested that those who viewed heaven as a future compensation for their earthly exploitation and suffering have done little to try to change their circumstances. Speculation about the afterlife detracts from people's principal calling to create a just and righteous society. Biblical representations of heaven should not be seen as ends in themselves but as pointing toward conditions that can be realized on earth either in the present or after the final consummation.[4]

At the same time, the complaint that people have been so preoccupied with earthly affairs that they have ignored the afterlife or have misunderstood its nature has been constant. At the end of the eighteenth century, Timothy Dwight contended that many wanted to gain admission to heaven, but few properly understood what that entailed. People love this world too much, Henry Harbaugh lamented in 1853, because they have "not sufficiently thought" about "a better" one. "This world is too much with us; Heaven, too little," bemoaned James Campbell in 1924. "During the last fifteen years," John MacArthur, Jr., observed in 1988, the only people who seemed interested "in the life to come are those involved in cults, Eastern religions, psychic circles, or those who have made studies of near-death experiences."[5]

Although individuals and groups have presented their views of the afterlife with great zeal and confidence, the American history of heaven involves few "formal definitions," "doctrinal debates," or "heresy trials" because the bases for constructing portraits of heaven are too broad, complex, and subjective to permit them.[6] The Bible has supplied the dominant images for most American depictions of heaven, but its vision of paradise is shrouded in substantial mystery and symbolism, making it very challenging to devise an "orthodox" concept of heaven.

Some argue further that heaven is too mysterious and incomprehensible to picture correctly, so trying to do so is foolhardy. Others counter that because people are imaginative creatures who are animated much more by pictures than abstract ideas, visualizing helps us conceptualize heaven. It is better to portray heaven "as a concrete place" with specific features even if we make mistakes, Carol Zaleski maintains, "than to be deprived of all pictures." Agreeing with her, countless Americans have supplied visual images of heaven to entice sinners to repent, stimulate people to live morally, and comfort believers.

Colleen McDannell and Bernhard Lang contend that although theocentric (focusing on the worship and glory of God) and anthropocentric (focusing on the relationships, activities, and development of the saints) images of heaven coexist, one of them is usually dominant in a particular place and time. Moreover, they insist, the history of heaven cannot properly be viewed as "a simple alternation" between these two models. "Some pictures of heaven are strongly theocentric, depicting the blessed as caught up in an endless rapture of adoration," Zaleski asserts, while others are primarily anthropocentric, focusing on the sociability of the saints. However, "a more adequate [and biblically accurate] picture of heaven," she concludes, "would be theocentric and anthropocentric at once."[7]

Several aspects of the most widely accepted American conceptions of heaven are paradoxical. Many Christians maintain that admittance to heaven is by God's grace, but people must fiercely battle temptations and evil until they die to get there. They must obey God's commandments, live holy lives, and express their faith through their actions. A second paradox (at least for evangelicals) is that good deeds do not earn people entry into heaven, but they will be rewarded there. Moreover, while these future rewards help motivate Christians to evangelize, nurture other believers, and live righteously, these actions are to be done principally to glorify God and aid others, not to achieve personal praise or fame or to gain eternal recompense. However, the redeemed will receive higher status, greater opportunities, and even better "crowns" and "mansions" because of their earthly deeds and service. Nevertheless, everyone will be delighted with their heavenly circumstances, and no one will be jealous of other saints' greater blessings and privileges.[8] A third tension is how the saints can be happy in heaven if some (or many) of their loved ones are not there. Although Christians have tried to explain this potential problem in various ways, none of their explanations is ultimately satisfying, at least on this side of eternity. And, finally, how can heaven truly be stimulating if its residents have no challenges to confront, no obstacles to overcome, no temptations to avoid, and no problems to solve? These things play a large role in making earthly life meaningful for many people, and their absence from heaven would seemingly make it difficult to experience fulfillment and exhilaration.

GETTING TO HEAVEN

Material conditions in America have improved significantly during the past 400 years. Americans today eat better, receive much better medical care, live longer, have more leisure time and options, enjoy more "creature comforts," labor-saving devices, and opportunities for travel, and have numerous other advantages over their predecessors. Because life has become physically comfortable and culturally enriching for many Americans, we might expect the afterlife to be less important than it was in earlier periods, but heaven continues to be very attractive and appealing to millions. Although contemporary Americans enjoy many physical and material blessings unknown to their ancestors, they still struggle with emotional, relational, and spiritual problems. Moreover, certain nonmaterial "needs" remain constant over time: desire for companionship, love, purpose, forgiveness, and, many believe, an intimate relationship with the Creator. Americans live longer, but the recognition that an average life span pales compared to everlasting life prompts many to think about their future destiny: is there a heaven, and if so, how can I get there? The four most common answers to the latter question have been: by trust in Jesus Christ as the divine-human Savior, by upright conduct and good deeds, by a combination of belief and works, or by God admitting everyone regardless of their belief and behavior.

While theologically conservative Christians from seventeenth-century Puritans to twenty-first-century evangelicals have concurred that individuals must repent of their sins, trust Jesus Christ as their savior, follow Him as their Lord, and be regenerated by the Holy Spirit, they have disagreed about how difficult it is to do this and the severity of the challenges they confront on the road to heaven as they "work out their salvation." Throughout American history, the necessity of having a conversion from sinfulness to godliness has been a defining element in the "broad evangelical stream of religious life," even among many "who also might be described in catechetical or theologically liberal terms."[9] More than any other group of American Christians, the Puritans taught that conversion involved a series of stages. In their sermons, devotional manuals, and personal narratives, Puritans explained the process of conversion, urged people to respond to God's redeeming grace, and exhorted one another to persevere in the faith. During the First Great Awakening, many pastors and revivalists continued to emphasize that salvation was God's sovereign act, but they also claimed that it involved a great deal of subsequent resolve and struggle on the part of Christians. Countless evangelists, from Charles Finney in the 1830s to Billy Graham today, by contrast, have argued that people can decide at any time that they want to be born again and that individuals can be saved "quickly and easily."[10] Throughout American history, revivalists have typically used both "fear and shock" and "love and reward," although the emphasis has gradually shifted from the former to the latter. Since the Second Great Awakening (1800–1840), evangelists have often warned sinners that if they did not respond to altar calls immediately, they might regret it forever: they might die suddenly, yield to doom, lose interest in spiritual matters, be inhibited by a hardened heart, or no longer be wooed by the Holy Spirit.[11] From the Gilded Age to the present, religious and cultural pluralism has steadily increased and the argument that all religions provide paths to heaven has constantly grown stronger. Since the 1960s, more and more Americans have denounced the position that only those who accept Christ as their savior go to heaven as unwarranted, unjust, and intolerant.[12]

The central debate among evangelical Protestants over how salvation occurs has been between Calvinists and Arminians. Prior to the Second Great Awakening, the Calvinist view was dominant. It stressed that salvation is God's doing: He chooses, calls, and brings people into fellowship with Himself through His irresistible grace. Jesus died at Calvary to fulfill God's justice, pay the price for the sins of the elect, and reconcile them to God. To gain entry to heaven, individuals must receive Jesus Christ as their savior and Lord and have His righteousness imputed to them (declared to be theirs). Because individuals are totally depraved, they cannot respond to God's gracious offer until the Holy Spirit makes them spiritually alive (regeneration). Because God enables those He has elected to persevere, their passport to paradise is guaranteed. The Holy Spirit indwells those He regenerates, transforming their character and relationships and empowering them to live righteous lives. Believers' union with Christ is eternally planned, effected at their conversion, and continues forever.[13]

Since the Second Great Awakening, the Arminian perspective has been more popular in America than the Calvinist position. For Arminians, sin is not a condition of the soul, but a choice of the will. Therefore, people are free, responsible moral agents who can repent and have faith. As revivalist Charles Finney argued, repentance entails individuals changing their fundamental approach to life from selfishness to benevolence, affirming the truths of scripture, and ceasing to commit outward sins.[14] Finney and other Arminians rejected the Calvinist belief that redemption is completely God's work and maintained instead that "both God and sinners are active in regeneration." When the Holy Spirit confronts individuals with God's message of salvation, they "change the disposition of their hearts and then turn themselves to God." Finney argued that regeneration involved a change in a person's preferences, will, moral character, and spiritual direction. At its heart was a shift "from selfishness to love."[15] For Arminians, the usual order of steps in salvation "is prevenient grace, repentance, faith, the new birth, and continued obedience."[16]

Finney insisted that Adam's sin was not imputed to humanity, that Christ did not atone for the sins of the elect, and that His righteousness was not accredited to Christians. Instead, God forgives and accepts those who restructure their lives around Him and obey His moral laws. God declares people to be righteous, Finney maintained, because they actually are righteous.[17] Other Arminians have also rejected the concept of substitutionary atonement, contending that Christ did not endure the punishment sinners deserved because sin and guilt could not be transferred to Him.[18]

During the past century, the debate over the nature of salvation between theological conservatives and liberals has become more heated and important than the one between Calvinists and Arminians. Most theological liberals have rejected the idea that people must be spiritually reborn to go to heaven. They have repudiated or reinterpreted the doctrines of original sin and human depravity and maintained that individuals are children of God in whom He dwells. Speaking for them, Congregationalist pastor and editor Lyman Abbott (1835–1922) averred that Christ came to develop "the latent divinity he has implanted in us."[19] Liberals have typically seen salvation as a process of ethical maturation that occurs as people follow the principles of Jesus. They have contended that although all people are children of God who are redeemed by His love, they have drifted away from Him and must be restored to fellowship with God, practice biblical morality, and labor to improve social conditions.[20] Following the ideals of Jesus and aligning their minds, wills, and values with His, Shailer Mathews argued, enriches people's personalities.[21] For liberals, the focus of the Christian faith is primarily on individuals' lifelong spiritual and moral growth, not their affirmation of any particular theological tenets.

Another liberal, Paul Tillich, considered the essential "human problem" not to be disobedience to God "but estrangement from the ground of being," others, and one-self. In salvation, individuals overcome their anxiety and alienation as they are grasped by the New Being, the Christ-power, "or the power of creative transforma-tion." People are saved or personally reintegrated, Tillich contended, by faith, which he defined as "ultimate concern" or "infinite passion" about spiritual, social, political, or intellectual matters.[22] For Tillich, salvation is "the process of becoming whole," of realizing one's full potential. People are saved by participating in and being accepted and transformed by the New Being. Rejecting belief in life after death, Tillich pos-ited a this-worldly salvation whereby people had faith in, surrendered to, and expe-rienced the love of the Ground of All Being.[23]

Abbott, Walter Rauschenbusch, and many other liberals defined both sin and sal-vation largely in social rather than individual terms and stressed working with the spirit of Christ as it permeated all facets of life—"political, industrial, social, scientific, and artistic."[24] Some, like John Bennett, who served as president of Union Theological Seminary in New York City during the 1960s, exhorted Christians to repent of their racial injustice, economic exploitation, and militarism, not simply their individual sins, and work to end these practices.[25]

In addition, liberals argued that God was not a monarch whose wrath must be placated so that He could be reconciled with His subjects. Rather than remitting penalties charged against them, Abbott alleged, the Divine Lover wooed His chil-dren so that He could forgive their sin and improve their character. Justification by faith meant that those who embraced Christ's companionship could "be made vir-tuous" even though they had been guilty of rejecting God. God, Mathews explained, wanted people to imitate Christ's life and principles in order to progress morally and spiritually, be reconciled to Him and to one another, experience fraternity, and cre-ate a more righteous society.[26]

Like theological liberals, Unitarians have rejected the concept of Christ's substitu-tionary atonement. They argued that "salvation is by character"; Jesus saved people "solely by helping them become better, not by vicariously atoning for their sins." The moment any of God's children sincerely sought forgiveness for his sins, "God freely and joyfully" forgave him without requiring that an innocent person suffer "in the place of the guilty."[27]

Liberation theologians have defined "sin in terms of unjust political, economic, and social structures" and ignored "personal repentance from sin and faith in Christ as Savior" as the means of gaining entry to heaven. Liberationists have generally viewed salvation "corporately rather than individually," "structurally rather than spiritually," and as this-worldly rather than otherworldly. Salvation centers on restructuring politics, economics, and social relationships to achieve justice. As

James Cone asserted, God's salvation is not "mystical communion" with Him, or "a pietistic state of inwardness bestowed on the believer," but His deliverance of people from social and political oppression.[28]

Many Catholics have also disagreed with the evangelical position that people get to heaven solely by trusting Christ as their savior and Lord and having His righteousness imputed to them. Those who participate in the sacraments, especially baptism and the Eucharist, "are united with or incorporated into Christ in a substantial sense."[29] Most Catholics have held that God saves individuals on the basis of Christ's merits and by means of baptism, which cancels their previous sins and infuses new habits of grace into their souls. Justification is not God's pronouncement that people are righteous but the lifelong process whereby individuals actually become righteous. Jesus' death secured forgiveness for everyone, but it is efficacious only for those who are joined to His body, the Catholic Church, through baptism. The surplus merit earned by Christ and extraordinary saints is deposited in the Treasury of Merits and can be transferred to less virtuous Christians.[30] The traditional Catholic position declares that individuals are "not justified by exercising saving faith in the finished work of Christ"; rather, they may "become justified through a life-time of obedience to Church teachings and nourishment from the Church's sacraments."[31] Those who have not achieved sufficient virtue in this life go to purgatory to be purified and made fit to enter heaven. Prayers and masses on their behalf can reduce the length of people's stay in purgatory.

Until Vatican II (1962–1965), Catholics taught that salvation was impossible outside the Catholic Church. Although Vatican II reasserted that faith and baptism are required for salvation, during the past four decades many American Catholic theologians have claimed that people can be saved through the "baptism of desire" or the "non-specific implicit faith" they possess. God recognizes the desire of those who want to participate in the church but have no opportunity to do so.[32] Some Catholics contended that "the great majority of men" will be saved this way.[33] While Catholics have increasingly argued that many outside the church will be saved on the basis of Christ's redemptive work, they have usually asserted that these individuals cannot "be fully saved without the aid of the Church" because doing so would undercut the core of Catholicism.[34]

Throughout American history, various groups and individuals have either denied that an afterlife exists or argued that humans cannot know if there is life after death. Atheists, agnostics, and secular humanists have contended that "salvation" involves either self-actualization or some type of earthly fulfillment. Others have argued that a new birth is unnecessary, at least for some people. For example, in *The Varieties of Religious Experience* (1901) Harvard psychology and philosophy professor William

James claimed that "some healthy-minded and well-adjusted" individuals, especially those "who harbor no ill-will toward God or others and who have no consciousness of sin," do not need to have a conversion experience. Others are temperamentally incapable of being regenerated. Many, James claimed, can have "a rich and satisfying life" without being born again.[35]

Today's American Christians espouse three main perspectives on salvation: particularism, pluralism, and universalism. Particularists maintain that salvation comes exclusively "through faith in God's special acts in history, culminating in Jesus Christ."[36] Some particularists argue, however, that we do not know how a merciful, righteous God will treat those who have never heard the Christian message.[37] Pluralists (also called inclusivists) assert that individuals can be saved by following any of the world's major religions. They insist that their position promotes tolerance, expresses the reality that "varying cultural and historical contexts preclude absolutist religious claims," and is supported by the fact that no religious group's followers are morally superior to those of others.[38] Inclusivists, primarily some Protestant liberals and post–Vatican II Catholic theologians, contend that God's saving grace is available in all places and times. Although Jesus Christ is the "final expression and norm" of God's revelation, to be saved, individuals must simply trust and obey God under whatever form they know Him.[39]

Since the 1880s, increasing numbers of American Christians have espoused the position that all people will eventually gain entry to heaven. Recently, many of its advocates have shifted the rationale for universal salvation from "the benevolence of God or the inconsequence of sin" to "the triumph of Christ's cross." They argue that Christ's victory over Satan through His death on the cross and His resurrection provides a basis for all to be saved. Several factors have led more Americans to conclude that everyone will be saved: society's emphasis on tolerance, pluralism, and relativism; their understanding of justice; and their belief that evangelizing the world is hopeless.[40]

Evangelicals counter that those who willingly reject belief in and commitment to Christ will not go to heaven. They insist that the biblical passages cited by proponents of universal salvation do not support their position and contend that scripture repeatedly presents God's offer of salvation as conditional: individuals must "believe it, receive it, and obey it." They also stress that Jesus used "clear, unambiguous language" to warn people about the "awful truth of eternal punishment." He frequently distinguished between two types of people (sheep and goats, those who build on the sand and those who build on the rock), two paths (broad and narrow), and two destinies (heaven and hell). His admonitions, Kenneth Kantzer avows, cannot be reconciled with universalism, annihilationism, or some type of future probation.[41]

CONCLUSION

Interest in heaven will undoubtedly continue to ebb and flow in response to the nation's religious climate and social, political, and economic conditions. While some themes will probably always be paramount, others are likely to wax and wane as the cultural and intellectual milieu changes. Although American Christians revere and read the same Bible, their depictions of heaven will always differ because of their conflicting approaches to interpreting scripture, life experiences, needs, priorities, and social settings. The Bible's few descriptions of heaven are rather vague and veiled. The information individuals provide about heaven based on their alleged near-death experiences must be treated as speculation. People can devise symbols or myths, consider heavenly visions, and rationally reflect about the nature of heaven, but they cannot provide concrete, indisputable information about the afterlife.[42] Because the sources of knowledge about heaven are so limited, Americans will continue to imagine it differently based in part on personal and social factors.

Some denounce "rich and detailed accounts of the afterlife," which were widely accepted in the nineteenth century and still offered by some today, as "absurd, crude, materialistic, or sheer nonsense." In an effort to develop a more rational, acceptable, and plausible heaven, many theologians' description of the hereafter is very minimal. Others supply a "meager picture of heaven" because they limit their portrait to what the Bible actually reveals about it.[43] Rejecting this "minimalist" description, some pastors and authors today offer highly imaginative, detailed portraits of paradise. While "scientific, philosophical, and theological skepticism" has challenged traditional views of heaven, fuller portraits still abound.[44]

What does the future hold for heaven? Polls since the 1970s have consistently shown that high percentages of Americans believe in heaven, typically around 80–90 percent.[45] Secularization has not had as great an effect in the United States as it has in Europe. While Sam Harris, Christopher Hitchens, Daniel Dennett, and others have vigorously attacked Christianity and promoted the "new atheism" and 15 percent of Americans identify themselves as agnostic, atheist, or having no religious preference, belief in the afterlife has remained high.[46] This testifies to the longing of many to live forever in pleasurable surroundings, be reunited with their loved ones, have meaningful experiences, and see cosmic justice prevail. As American society becomes increasingly pluralist and tolerant, portraits of heaven are likely to become even more eclectic and inclusive.

American conceptions of heaven, especially since the Gilded Age, have focused more and more on meaningful activity and work. Throughout its history, America has been viewed as a land of opportunity, a place where people can succeed if they labor diligently. Individuals have been expected to contribute to society through their talents, character, and arduous work. They have also been expected to discharge their civic responsibilities, promote the common good, and help their nation fulfill its potential. Those who have failed to live by the Puritan work ethic have been considered derelict and suspect.[47]

Significant numbers of Americans have seen their country as unique among the world's nations and believed that they were constructing a type of heaven on earth. Beginning with John Winthrop and the Puritans, many Americans have used biblical terms to define their mission. They have seen themselves as a "chosen people" who had "an errand in the wilderness" to create "the new Israel" or the "new Jerusalem." America was "the promised land," the site of "a new Heaven and a new earth," "the redeemer nation." Throughout American history, numerous conceptions of heaven have been intertwined with efforts to bring the millennium on earth by fulfilling our calling to be light and salt and to spread Christianity, republicanism, and free enterprise to the world.[48]

"The whole drama of history," wrote Reinhold Niebuhr, "is enacted in a frame of meaning too large for human comprehension."[49] Certainly this is also true about heaven. The concept is cloaked in mystery, and heaven's nature and purposes are far beyond full human understanding in this world. Nevertheless, depictions of heaven provide encouragement, inspiration, and hope. On the whole, these portraits have encouraged efforts to improve earthly life by supplying constructive models of a better life and helping to stimulate many individuals to promote justice and righteousness and treat each other better. Concentrating on heaven has sometimes diverted attention from efforts to rectify earth's maladies and improve its life. However, those who have focused on heaven, inspired by its ideals and their desire to spend eternity there, have frequently lived by its principles and worked to reproduce its finest features in this world.

Notes

FRONT MATTER

1. Harry Blamires, *Knowing the Truth about Heaven and Hell: Our Choices and Where They Lead Us* (Ann Arbor, MI: Servant, 1988), 127.

2. John MacArthur, Jr., *Heaven: Selected Scriptures* (Chicago: Moody Press, 1988), 13; W. A. Criswell and Paige Patterson, *Heaven* (Wheaton, IL: Tyndale House, 1991), 20.

3. The Barna Group, "Born Again Christians," http://www.barna.org/FlexPage.aspx?Page+Topicc&TopicID=8.

4. For Swedenborgian views of heaven, see Colleen McDannell and Bernhard Lang, *Heaven: A History* (New Haven, CT: Yale University Press, 1988), 181–95, 198–203, 209–11, 212–17. For contemporary American Jewish and Muslim perspectives of heaven, see Lisa Miller, *Heaven: Our Enduring Fascination with the Afterlife* (New York: HarperCollins, 2010). Spiritualist views are examined in R. L. Moore, *In Search of White Crows: Spiritualism, Parapsychology, and American Culture* (New York: Oxford University Press, 1977); B. E. Carroll, *Spiritualism in Antebellum America* (Bloomington: Indiana University Press, 1997); Ann Braude, *Radical Spirits: Spiritualism and Women's Rights in Nineteenth-Century America* (Bloomington: Indiana University Press, 1997).

5. Miller, *Heaven*, 215.

INTRODUCTION

1. *Gates Ajar* alone sold 180,000 copies in the United States and England before 1900. During these years, only Harriet Beecher Stowe's *Uncle Tom's Cabin* (1852) sold more copies (Colleen McDannell and Bernhard Lang, *Heaven: A History* [New Haven, CT: Yale University Press,

1988], 228, 265). As an example of jokes about heaven, see Donald Capps, *A Time to Laugh: The Religion of Humor* (New York: Continuum, 2005), 30–33, and passim. Especially important analyses of NDES are Raymond Moody's *Life After Life: The Investigation of a Phenomenon—Survival of Bodily Death* (Harrisburg, PA: Stackpole Books, 1976) and Maurice Rawlings's, *Beyond Death's Door* (Nashville, TN: Thomas Nelson, 1978).

2. See "Rising Belief in Hell, Angels, Devil, Heaven," *Christian Century* 121 (June 15, 2004), 14 (this poll also reported that 70 percent of Americans believe in hell); Richard N. Ostling, "Heaven and Hell," June 17, 2006, http://legacy.decaturdaily.com/decaturdaily/religion/060617/heaven.shtml.

3. See Mark Ralls, "Reclaiming Heaven: What Can We Say about the Afterlife?" *Christian Century* 121 (Dec. 14, 2004), 34–39. One exception to this trend has been mainline churches where heaven, like Timbuktu, "is treated as if it were a term for something foreign and far away" (34). Also see Peter Stanford's *Heaven: A Guide to the Undiscovered Country* (New York: Palgrave Macmillan, 2004).

4. Carol Zaleski, *Otherworld Journeys: Accounts of Near Death Experience in Medieval and Modern Times* (New York: Oxford University Press, 1987), 99. See also Allan Kellehear, *Experiences Near Death* (New York: Oxford University Press, 1996), 76; Jerry L. Walls, *Heaven: The Logic of Eternal Joy* (New York: Oxford University Press, 2002), 134–37.

5. Another very popular song is Eric Clapton's "Tears in Heaven."

6. Alan F. Segal, *Life after Death: A History of the Afterlife in the Religions of the West* (New York: Doubleday, 2004), 11, 710; quotations in that order; Paul A. Carter, *Spiritual Crisis of the Gilded Age* (DeKalb: Northern Illinois University Press, 1971), 88.

7. Henry Ward Beecher, *Yale Lectures on Preaching*, 3rd series (New York: J. B. Ford, 1887), 320; John Haynes Holmes, *Is Death the End?* (New York: G. P. Putnam's Sons, 1915), 285–86; John Shea, *What a Modern Catholic Believes about Heaven and Hell* (Chicago: Thomas More, 1972), 83.

8. Increase Mather, *Meditations upon the Glory of the Heavenly World* (Boston: T. Green, 1711), 15 (cf. Jonathan Edwards, "Nothing upon Earth Can Represent the Glories of Heaven," in *Works*, 22 vols. [New Haven, CT: Yale University Press, 1992], 14: 137–60); James McGready, "The Christian's Journey to the Heavenly Canaan," in James Smith, ed., *The Posthumous Works of the Reverend and Pious James McGready, Late Minister of the Gospel in Henderson, Kentucky*, 2 vols. (Nashville, TN: Lowry and Smith, 1833), 1: 326 (cf. Robert M. Patterson, *Paradise: The Place and State of Saved Souls between Death and the Resurrection* [Philadelphia: Presbyterian Board of Publication, 1874], 148; Henry Ward Beecher, *"The Heavenly State" and "Future Punishment": Two Sermons* [New York: J. B. Ford, 1871], 78–9, 81, 99; Dwight L. Moody, "The Eternal Life Indescribable," in Samuel Fallows, ed., *The Home Beyond or, Views of Heaven, and Its Relation to the Earth, Moody, Spurgeon, Talmage, and Over Four Hundred Other Prominent Thinkers and Writers* [Chicago: Coburn and Newman, 1884], 298); James M. Campbell, *Heaven Opened: A Book of Comfort and Hope* (New York: Fleming H. Revell, 1924), 76 (cf. John MacArthur, Jr., *Heaven: Selected Scriptures* [Chicago: Moody Press, 1988], 37); Bill T. Arnold, "Vegetarians in Paradise: Based on Isaiah 11:6–7 and 65:25, Will We Be Vegetarians in the New Heaven and Earth as Adam and Eve Were before the Fall?" *Christianity Today* 48 (Oct. 1, 2004), 104.

9. Jonathan Edwards, "Heaven Is a World of Love," in Stephen J. Nichols, *Heaven on Earth: Capturing Jonathan Edwards' Vision of Living in Between* (Wheaton, IL: Crossway Books, 2006), 129. Cf. Timothy Dwight, "The Remoter Consequences of Death: The Happiness of Heaven," in *Theology*

Explained and Defended, in a Series of Sermons, 5 vols. (Middletown, CT: Clark and Lyman, 1818–19), 5: 521; Burdett Hart, *Aspects of Heaven* (New York: American Tract Society, 1896), 119.

10. W. G. Heslop, *Heaven: Our Father's House, Our Heavenly Home, God's City of Gold* (Grand Rapids, MI: Peniel Press, 1937), 95 (quotation); A. H. Strong, *Systematic Theology* (Rochester, NY: E. R. Andrews, 1886), 585; Elizabeth Stuart Phelps, *Beyond the Gates* (Boston: Houghton Mifflin, 1889), 118ff.; Woodbury Davis, *The Beautiful City and the King of Glory* (Philadelphia: Lindsay and Blakiston, 1860); Dwight L. Moody, "The Heavenly City," in Fallows, *Home Beyond*, 319; Edward M. Bounds, *Heaven: A Place, A City, A Home* (Grand Rapids, MI: Baker, 1975 [1921]); Randy Alcorn, *Heaven* (Wheaton, IL: Tyndale House, 2004), 240–46.

11. Rufus Clark, *Heaven and Its Scriptural Emblems* (Philadelphia: John E. Potter, 1852), 105; Augustus C. Thompson, *The Better Land; or, The Believer's Journey and Future Home* (Boston: Gould and Lincoln, 1854); William Branks, *Heaven Our Home: We Have No Saviour But Jesus and No Home But Heaven* (Boston: Roberts Brothers, 1864); J. Wilbur Chapman, *When Home Is Heaven* (New York: Fleming H. Revell, 1917); Don Baker, *Heaven: A Glimpse of Your Future Home* (Portland, OR: Multnomah Press, 1983); Joni Ereckson Tada, *Heaven: Your Real Home* (Grand Rapid, MI: Zondervan, 1996); Anne Lotz, *Heaven: My Father's House* (Nashville, TN: W Publishing Group, 2001).

12. H. S. Hoffman, *Life Beyond the Grave* (Philadelphia: Union Press, 1899), 21, 24; Peter Kreeft, *Heaven: The Heart's Deepest Longing* (San Francisco: Ignatius Press, 1989), 162; Gary Habermas and J. P. Moreland, *Beyond Death: Exploring the Evidence for Immortality* (Wheaton, IL: Crossway Books, 1998), 339–40; Anthony DeStefano, *A Travel Guide to Heaven* (New York: Doubleday, 2003), 6; Adam Kirsch, "Paradise Lite: In Heaven, You'll Be Thinner, Happier, and Smarter—Or So Americans Think," Feb. 5, 2004, http://www.slate.com/id/2095002. See also Charles Colson, "An Everlasting Playground: Understanding the Nature of Heaven," *BreakPoint*, Mar. 23, 2004.

13. R. A. Torrey, *Real Salvation and Whole-Hearted Service* (New York: Fleming H. Revell, 1905), 72 (quotation); William T. Ellis, *Billy Sunday: The Man and His Message* (Philadelphia: John C. Winston, 1914), 417; Hal Lindsey with C. C. Carlson, *The Terminal Generation* (Old Tappan, NJ: Fleming H. Revell, 1976), 180. Cf. Timothy Dwight, "Heaven," in *Theology*, 1: 289; Henry Harbaugh, *The Heavenly Home; or, the Employments and Enjoyments of the Saints in Heaven* (Philadelphia: Lindsay & Blakiston, 1853), 30; Tada, *Heaven*, 29; Gilmore, *Probing Heaven*, 91–92, 103–5.

14. John G. Stackhouse, "Harleys in Heaven: What Christians Have Thought of the Afterlife, and What Difference It Makes Now," *Christianity Today*, June 2003, 40; Ebenezer Pemberton, *Heaven the Residence of the Saints* (Boston: D. Kneeland, 1770), 13; A. A. Hodge, *Evangelical Theology: A Course of Popular Lectures* (Carlisle, PA: Banner of Truth, 1976), 400. Cf. Mather, *Meditations*, 4, 247; MacArthur, *Heaven*, 91, 97.

15. Dwight, "Heaven," 1: 292; Anne Sandberg, *Seeing the Invisible* [Plainfield, NJ: Logos International, 1977], 185 (cf. Peter J. Kreeft, *Everything You Ever Wanted to Know About Heaven* [San Francisco: Harper & Row, 1982], 62; John Gilmore, *Probing Heaven: Key Questions on the Hereafter* [Grand Rapids, MI: Baker Book House, 1989], 169–70); Daniel A. Brown, *What the Bible Reveals about Heaven* (Ventura, CA: Regal, 1999), 189.

16. Mather, *Mediations*, 78; James M. MacDonald, *My Father's House, or, The Heaven of the Bible* (Philadelphia: Bradley, 1869), 94; "Heaven" in Alfred Nevin, ed., *Encyclopedia of the*

Presbyterian Church in the United States of America (Philadelphia: Presbyterian Publishing House, 1884), 314. Cf. Dwight, "Heaven," 1: 289; Asa Mahan, "Employments of Heaven" in Fallows, *Home Beyond*, 357; Hoffman, *Life*, 289; Clark, *Scriptural Emblem*, 85; Billy Graham, *Facing Death and the Life After* (Waco, TX: Word Books, 1987), 253.

17. Thompson, *Better Land*, 93; Walter Rauschenbusch, *A Theology for the Social Gospel* (New York: Macmillan, 1917), 235; Jay D. Robison, *Life after Death? Christian Interpretation of Personal Eschatology* (New York: Peter Lang, 1998), 211. Cf. John Sutherland Bonnell, *Heaven and Hell: A Present-Day Christian Interpretation* (New York: Abingdon Press, 1956), 25; Alcorn, *Heaven*, 274.

18. J. M. Killen, *Our Friends in Heaven* (Cincinnati: L. Swormstedt & A. Poe, 1857), 20–21; quotation from 21; J. Aspinwall Hodge, *Recognition after Death* (New York: Robert Carter & Brothers, 1889), 23, 28; quotations in that order; Gilmore, *Probing Heaven*, 328–29, 338; quotation from 328. Cf. Mather, *Mediations*, 227; Clark, *Scriptural Emblems*, 107; Thompson, *Better Land*, 73–86; Fallows, "Summary of Reasons for Recognition," in Fallows, *Home Beyond*, 381–83; T. DeWitt Talmage, "Shall We Know Each Other?" in ibid., 384; John J. Kerr, *Future Recognition: or, The Blessedness of Those "Who Die in the Lord"* (Philadelphia: Hooker, 1847); G. J. T. Whitley, *What Jesus Said about Heaven: A Study in the Four Gospels* (Nashville, TN: Cokesbury Press, 1925), 71.

19. Edwards, "Heaven," 124; Ellis, *Billy Sunday*, 417. Cf. Charles Hodge, *Systematic Theology*, 3 vols. (Grand Rapids, MI: Eerdmans, 1952 [1872]), 3: 861; Torrey, *Real Salvation*, 74; Thompson, *Better Land*, 86.

20. Edwards, "Heaven," 131; Phillips Brooks, "The Sea of Glass Mingled with Fire," in *Twenty Sermons* (New York: Macmillan, 1897), 125; Alcorn, *Heaven*, 261. Cf. Strong, *In Paradise*, 84; Whitley, *What Jesus Said*, 83.

21. Dwight, "Heaven," 1: 294. Cf. A. C. Dixon, *Heaven on Earth* (Greenville, SC: Gospel Hour, 1897), 65–66; Robert M. Patterson, *Vision of Heaven for the Life on Earth* (Philadelphia: Presbyterian Board of Publication, 1877), 318; David Gregg, *The Heaven-Life or Stimulus for Two Worlds* (Chicago: Fleming H. Revell, 1895), 23, 94, 113, 124; Lyman Abbott, "Life, Growth, and Heaven," *Outlook* 104 (Aug. 2, 1913), 741–42; Habermas and Moreland, *Beyond Death*, 323.

22. Kreeft, *Heaven*, 168–213. Cf. Gilmore, *Probing Heaven*, 126; Mark Buchanan, *Things Unseen: Living with Eternity in Your Heart* (Sisters, OR: Multnomah, 2002).

23. James Pierpont, *False Hopes of Heaven to Be Dreaded and Deprecated* (Boston: T. Green, 1712), 8, 18; quotations in that order; Whitefield's sermon, Sept. 29, 1770, as quoted in "George Whitefield," *Christian History and Biography*, http://www.christianitytoday.com/history/special/131christians/whitefield.html; Moody, "Heaven—Its Happiness," 38; Graham's statement is at http://www.kansascity.com/2010/11/10/2413878/billy-graham-salvation-isnt-about.html. Cf. Mather, *Mediations*, 258; Bonnell, *Heaven and Hell*, 29; Graham, *Facing Death*, 215–16; Alcorn, *Heaven*, 35.

24. George Whitefield, "Christ the Support of the Tempted," http://www.anglicanlibrary.org/whitefield/sermons/19.htm; Gilmore, *Probing Heaven*, 196; George Gallup with William Proctor, *Adventures in Immortality* (New York: McGraw-Hill, 1982), 59, 182; "Many Americans Say Other Faiths Can Lead to Eternal Life: Most Christians Say Non-Christian Faiths Can Lead to Salvation," Dec. 18, 2008, http://pewresearch.org/pubs/1062/many-americans-say-other-faiths-can-lead-to-eternal-life.

25. George N. Marshall, *The Challenge of a Liberal Faith* (Boston: Skinner House, 1991), 222. See also Jack Mendelsohn, *Being Liberal in an Illiberal Age: Why I Am a Unitarian Universalist*

(Boston: Beacon Press, 1985); John Sias, *100 Questions that Non-Members Ask about Unitarian Universalism* (Nashua, NH: Transition, 1994); John A. Buehrens and Forrest Church, eds., *A Chosen Faith: An Introduction to Unitarian Universalism* (Boston: Beacon Press, 1998).

26. Kenneth Cauthen, *The Impact of American Religious Liberalism* (New York: Harper and Row, 1962), 11. See, for example, William Adams Brown, *Christian Theology in Outline* (New York: Charles Scribner's Sons, 1906), 258–60, 412–23; Rauschenbusch, *Theology*, 223–39; Albert Knudson, *The Doctrine of Redemption* (Nashville, TN: Abingdon Press, 1933), passim.

27. See Francis A. Sullivan, *Salvation Outside the Church? Tracing the History of the Catholic Response* (New York: Paulist Press, 1992); Robert A. Sungenis, *Not by Faith Alone: The Biblical Evidence for the Catholic Doctrine of Justification* (Santa Barbara, CA: Queenship, 1997); Leo J. Trese, *Seventeen Steps to Heaven: A Catholic Guide to Salvation* (Manchester, NH: Sophia Institute Press, 2001).

28. *Justification by Faith: Lutherans and Catholics in Dialogue*, VII (Minneapolis: Augsburg, 1985), 14. For example, more than twice as many Catholics as Protestants (43 percent to 20 percent) agreed with the statement "Heaven is a divine reward for those who earn it by their good life." See George Gallup, Jr., and Jim Castelli, *The American Catholic People: Their Beliefs, Practices, and Values* (Garden City, NY: Doubleday, 1987), 18. Also see chapter 11.

29. Leo Baeck, *The Essence of Judaism* (New York: Schocken Books, 1948), 13–14, 36–37, 44, 70–71, 88, 118–19, 166, 195, 218–19; quotation from 88. See also Emil L. Fackenheim, *What Is Judaism? An Interpretation for the Present Age* (New York: Summit Books, 1987), 35, 130; Milton Steinberg, *Basic Judaism* (Northvale, NJ: Jason Aronson, 1987), 94–95; Michael L. Satlow, *Creating Judaism: History, Tradition, Practice* (New York: Columbia University Press, 2006), 162.

30. Dana Evan Kaplan, *American Reform Judaism: An Introduction* (New Brunswick, NJ: Rutgers University Press, 2003), 34; Marc Lee Raphael, *Judaism in America* (New York: Columbia University Press, 2003), 24–26; William Scott Green and Jed Silverstein, "The Doctrine of the Messiah," in Jacob Neusner and Alan J. Avery-Peck, eds., *The Blackwell Companion to Judaism* (Oxford, UK: Blackwell, 2000), 247–67; Benjamin Brown, "Orthodox Judaism," in ibid., 311–33; Daniel Gordis, "Conservative Judaism," in ibid., 334–53; Elliot N. Dorff, "Ethics of Judaism," in ibid., 373–92; M. A. Meyer, *Response to Modernity: A History of the Reform Movement in Judaism* (New York: Oxford University Press, 1988), 228–29.

31. McDannell and Lang, *Heaven*, 175.

32. McDannell and Lang, *Heaven*, 287 (quotation), 277, 327–31.

33. For example, F. J. Boudreaux, *The Happiness of Heaven* (Baltimore: Murphy, 1875 [1870]), 138–40.

34. See Robert Goldenberg, "Bound Up in the Bond of Life: Death and Afterlife in Jewish Tradition," in Hiroshi Obayashi, ed., *Death and Afterlife: Perspectives of World Religions* (New York: Greenwood Press, 1992), 97–108.

CHAPTER 1

1. J. I. Packer, "Why We Need the Puritans," foreword to Leland Ryken, *Worldly Saints: The Puritans as They Really Were* (Grand Rapids, MI: Academie Books, 1986), xvi; Charles Hambrick-Stowe, *The Practice of Piety: Puritan Devotional Disciplines in Seventeenth-Century New England* (Chapel Hill: University of North Carolina Press, 1982), 53 (quotation); Ryken, *Worldly Saints*,

12–16. See also Allen Carden, "The Word of God in Puritan New England: Seventeenth Century Perspectives on the Nature and Authority of the Bible," *Andrews University Seminary Studies* 18 (Spring 1980), 1–16.

2. Packer, "Puritans," ix.

3. Packer, "Puritans," x–xv; quotations from x.

4. See, for example, George Marsden, "America's 'Christian' Origins: Puritan New England as a Case Study," in Mark A. Noll, George M. Marsden, and Nathan O. Hatch, *The Search for Christian America* (Westchester, IL: Crossway Books, 1983), 28–47. See also Henry Warner Bowden, *American Indians and Christian Missions: Studies in Cultural Conflict* (Chicago: University of Chicago Press, 1981), 104–33; Alden T. Vaughan, *New England Frontier: Puritans and Indians, 1620–1675* (Boston: Little, Brown, 1965).

5. M. M. Knappen, *Tudor Puritanism: A Chapter in the History of Idealism* (Chicago: University of Chicago Press, 1939), 102; J. Sears McGee, *The Godly Man in Stuart England: Anglicans, Puritans, and the Two Tables, 1620–1670* (New Haven, CT: Yale University Press, 1976), 255; Ryken, *Worldly Saints*, 12 (quotation); Robert G. Pope, *The Half-Way Covenant: Church Membership in Puritan New England* (Princeton, NJ: Princeton University Press, 1969).

6. Colleen McDannell and Bernhard Lang, *Heaven: A History* (New Haven, CT: Yale University Press, 1988), 178.

7. Packer, "Puritans," xv. See Robert Middlekauff, *The Mathers: Three Generations of Puritan Intellectuals, 1596–1728* (London: Oxford University Press, 1971); Mason Lowance, Jr., *Increase Mather* (New York: Twayne, 1974); Michael Hall, *The Last American Puritan: The Life of Increase Mather, 1639–1723* (Middletown, CT: Wesleyan University Press, 1988); Kenneth Silverman, *The Life and Times of Cotton Mather* (New York: Harper and Row, 1984).

8. Increase Mather, *Meditations upon the Glory of the Heavenly World* (Boston: T. Green, 1711), 14, 20–21; first quotation from 14, second from 21; James Hillhouse, *A Sermon Concerning the Life* (Boston: Green, 1721), 93.; Edward Tompson, *Heaven the Best Country* (Boston: B. Green, 1712), 2–10, 16, 19–21. I have retained the Puritans' capitalization.

9. Cotton Mather, *Coelestinus: A Conversation in Heaven, Quickened and Assisted, with Discoveries of Things in the Heavenly World* (Boston: S. Kneeland, 1723), 51; Mather, *Meditations*, 98, 222–24, 247; first quotation from 224, second from 247; "bliss awaiting," quoted in Middlekauff, *The Mathers*, 185; Increase Mather, *A Plain Discourse* (Boston, 1713), 7. Cf. Mather, *Meditations*, 24.

10. Mather, *Meditations*, 11, 23, quotation from 23; Hillhouse, *Sermon*, 49; Michael Wigglesworth, *The Day of Doom* (Tucson, AZ: American Eagle, 1991), 93. The entire first edition of this book, 1,800 copies, were purchased in its first year of publication and the book went through twelve more editions during the next century and "gained a respect and authority in the lives of the Puritans perhaps second only to the Bible" (Introduction, 1).

11. Don Kistler, ed., William Gearing, *The Glory of Heaven: The Happiness of the Saints in Glory* (Orlando, FL: Soli Deo Gloria, 2005), 62–63, quotations in that order; Hillhouse, *Sermon*, 40.

12. Hillhouse, *Sermon*, 71, 69, 70; quotations in that order; Edward Pearse, *The Great Concern: Or, a Serious Warning to a Timely and Thorough Preparation for Death…* (Boston: B. Green, 1705), 70 (first quotation), 24, 161, 162 (second quotation). Cf. Gearing, *Glory of Heaven*, 231.

13. Mather, *Meditations*, 5, 239, 240, 237, 71, 238; Nathaniel Henchman, *A Holy and Useful Life* (Boston: Kneeland, 1721), 37; Wigglesworth, *Day of Doom*, 76.

14. Edward Taylor, "A Crown of Life," in Donald E. Stanford, ed., *The Poems of Edward Taylor*, 2 vols. (Chapel Hill: University of North Carolina Press), 1: 32; 2: 38, 41–42.

15. Mather, *Meditations*, 82–83, quotation from 82; Hillhouse, *Sermons*, 67; Gearing, *Glory*, 227, 225, quotation from 227.

16. Mather, *Plain Discourse*, 8 (first quotation); Gearing, *Glory*, 81; Increase Mather, "Meditations on Death, and on the Heavenly-Country, Which Believers Go into at the Hour of Death," in Mather, *Meditations on Death, Delivered in Several Sermons…* (Boston: T. Green, 1707), 166 (second quotation); Increase Mather, *Meditations on the Glory of the Lord Jesus Christ, Delivered in Several Sermons* (Boston: B. Green, 1705), 165. Cf. Increase Mather, *The Believers Gain by Death* (Boston: B. Green, 1713), 21.

17. Pearse, *Great Concern*, 150, 154, 155; quotations in that order; Mather, "Heavenly-Country," 114–15 (quotations) (cf. Mather, *Believers Gain*, 25); Mather, "Heavenly-Country," 122, 113, 149, 155; Mather, *Meditations*, 27.

18. Mather, *Believers Gain*, 27–29; first quotation from 27, second from 28. On the subject of calling, see John Cotton, "The Christian Calling," in Perry Miller and Thomas H. Johnson, eds., *The Puritans: A Sourcebook of Their Writings*, 2 vols. (New York: Harper and Row, 1963), 1: 319–27, and Cotton Mather, *A Christian at His Calling* (Boston: B. Green and J. Allen, 1701).

19. Gearing, *Glory of Heaven*, 244–48; quotation from 244; Mather, *Coelestinus*, 44; Increase Mather, "Meditations on Death: And on the Believer's Deliverance from the Fear of It," in Mather, *Meditations on Death*, 46; Mather, *Believers Gain*, 18 (quotation) (cf. Mather, *Meditations*, 73); Pearse, *Great Concern*, 24, 170; quotation from 170.

20. Jack P. Greene, *Pursuits of Happiness: The Social Development of Early Modern British Colonies and the Formation of American Culture* (Chapel Hill: University of North Carolina Press, 1988), 23–24; quotation from 23; James Axtell, *The School upon a Hill: Education and Society in Colonial New England* (New Haven, CT: Yale University Press, 1974).

21. Mather, "Meditations on Death: And on the Believer's Deliverance," 47–48; quotations in that order (cf. Mather, *Meditations*, 81, 130, 131–33); Hillhouse, *Sermons*, 66–67; first two quotations from 66, the remainder from 67.

22. Mather, *Meditations*, 227, 229, 231; quotation from 227 (cf. Mather, *Believers Gain*, 20); Hillhouse, *Sermons*, 73; Gearing, *Glory of Heaven*, 229 (cf. Samuel Lee, *The Great Day of Judgment* [Boston: B. Green, 1692], 22); Mather, "Meditations on Death: And on the Believer's Deliverance," 48. See also Hillhouse, *Sermons*, 82.

23. Hillhouse, *Sermons*, 83–85; first quotation from 83, second from 84; Pearse, *Great Concern*, 163, 24, 170; quotations in that order; Mather, *Lord Jesus Christ*, 164.

24. Mather, "Meditations on Death: And on the Believer's Deliverance," 14; Henchman, *Useful Life*, 26–27; quotation from 27.

25. Mather, *Meditations*, 118; Middlekauff, *The Mathers*, 203 (see Mather, *Meditations*, 108–50; Jonathan Mitchel, *A Discourse of the Glory to Which God Hath Called Believers* [Boston: B. Green, 1721], 45–49; Cotton Mather, "Triparadisus," unpublished manuscript, American Antiquarian Society); Mather, *Meditations*, 117–50 (cf. Henchman, *Useful Life*, 30); Mather, *Meditations*, 53, 85; quotations in that order; Hillhouse, *Sermons*, 66–68, first quotation from 67, second from 68; Mather, *Meditations*, 135–49.

26. Middlekauff, *The Mathers*, 321; Henchman, *Useful Life*, 26; Hillhouse, *Sermons*, 65.

27. Mather, "Heavenly-Country," 170 (first quotation) (cf. Henchman, *Useful Life*, 7–8); Mather, *Meditations*, 32 (second quotation) (cf. Mather, *Believers Gain*, 15–16); Mather,

Meditations, 33–34, 39, 185; third quotation from 33 (cf. Gearing, *Glory of Heaven*, 230); Mather, "Heavenly-Country," 119 (fourth quotation); Mather, *Meditations*, 246 (fifth quotation), 176; Hillhouse, *Sermons*, 97, 104–05.

28. Mather, *Plain Discourse*, 26–27 (second quotation from 27); Mather, *Meditations*, 41 (first quotation); Mather, *Lord Jesus Christ*, 164 (third quotation); Mather, *Coelestinus*, 54.

29. Packer, "Puritans," xiv. On New England's mortality rate, see Douglas McManis, *Colonial New England: A Historical Geography* (New York: Oxford University Press, 1975), 66–68; Philip J. Greven, Jr., *Four Generations: Population, Land, and Family in Colonial Andover, Massachusetts* (Ithaca, NY: Cornell University Press, 1970), 21–40; David E. Stannard, "Death and the Puritan Child," in Alden T. Vaughan and Francis J. Bremer, eds., *Puritan New England: Essays on Religion, Society, and Culture* (New York: St. Martin's Press, 1977), 238–39, 242–43.

30. Henchman, *Useful Life*, 36.

31. Mather, *Meditations*, 254–55; quotations in that order. "It is surely a great Favour of God," he added, "to have a Quick and an Easie Passage into his Heavenly Kingdom" (273).

32. Mather, *Believers Gain*, 31.

33. Henchman, *Useful Life*, 36; Increase Mather, "Meditations on Sudden Death. Occasioned by Several Late Sudden Deaths in Boston, as Well as in Several Other Towns in New England," in Mather, *Meditations on Death, Delivered in Several Sermons*, 109 (first quotation); Increase Mather, *A Sermon Wherein Is Declared that the Blessed God Is Willing to Be Reconciled to the Sinful Children of Men* (Boston: B. Green, 1713), 102 (second quotation) (cf. Thomas Hooker, *An Exposition of the Principles of Religion* [London, 1645], 13; Hooker, The *Soules Exaltation* [London: John Haviland, 1638], 132, 135–37, 175; Hooker, *The Application of Redemption, by the Effectual Work of the Word, and Spirit of Christ, for the Bringing Home of Lost Sinners to God* [London: Peter Cole, 1657]).

34. Mather, *Plain Discourse*, 15–16, quotations in that order; Increase Mather, *A Sermon Wherein Is Declared that the Blessed God Is Willing to Be Reconciled to the Sinful Children of Men* (Boston: B. Green, 1713), 129; Cotton Mather, *Heavenly Considerations: or the Joy of Heaven over Them that Answer the Call of Heaven* (Boston: T. Green, 1706), 15 (first quotation); Mather, *Coelestinus*, 10–15; second quotation from 15; Pearse, *Great Concern*, 143. Cf. Solomon Stoddard, *The Safety of Appearing at the Day of Judgment in the Righteousness of Christ: Opened and Applied* (Boston: D. Henchman, 1729) and Solomon Stoddard, *A Guide to Christ, or, The Way of Directing Souls that Are under the Work of Conversion...* (Boston: D. Henchman, 1735).

35. Mather, *Plain Discourse*, 17, 26, 65–68; first two quotations from 17, third from 26.

36. Hambrick-Stowe, *Practice of Piety*, 199, 198; quotations in that order. Cf. David D. Hall, *The Faithful Shepherd: A History of the New England Ministry in the Seventeenth Century* (Cambridge, MA: Harvard University Press, 2006), 162. See John Cotton, *Gods Mercie Mixed with His Justice, or, His Peoples Deliverance in Times of Danger* (London: G. Miller, 1641), 17; Hooker, *Application of Redemption, First Eight Books*, 132; Thomas Shepard, *The Parable of the Ten Virgins Opened & Applied*, 2 vols. (London, 1660), 1: 78–79, 128, 157; 2: 167.

37. Hillhouse, *Sermon*, 12, 11, 22, 15, 16, quotations in that order with the last two from 16. Thomas Hooker, *The Christians Two Chiefe Lessons* (London: P. Stephens and C. Meredith, 1640), 64. Cf. Richard Baxter: "Sitting will lose you heaven, as well as you run from it....If the way to heaven be not far harder than the world imagines, then Christ and his apostles knew not the way, or else have deceived us" (Baxter, *The Saint's Everlasting Rest* [New York: Robert Carter and Brothers, 1855], 16).

38. Hall, *Faithful Shepherd*, 154. See John Adams Albro, ed., *Works of Thomas Shepard*, 3 vols. (New York: G. Olms, 1971), 2: 259; Thomas Shepard, *The Sound Believer: A Treatise of Evangelical Conversion. Discovering the Work of Christs Spirit, in Reconciling of a Sinner to God* (London: J. Cotterel, 1671), 11, 50, 54, 8, 94, 96, 118, 111; Thomas Hooker, *The Application of Redemption…*, 2nd ed. (London: Peter Cole, 1659), 14, 11, 30, 320. On Hooker, see Frank Shuffleton, *Thomas Hooker, 1586–1647* (Princeton, NJ: Princeton University Press, 1977), and George H. Williams et al., eds., *Thomas Hooker: Writings in England and Holland, 1626–1633* (Cambridge, MA: Harvard University Press, 1975). Twenty-seven volumes of Hooker's sermons were published in the seventeenth century. Many of them focus on "Hooker's specialty, the morphology of religious conversion." He discusses the process of conversion and how God brings individuals to salvation without violating their wills. Hooker "saw…true conversion…as the result of a long and often painful process," and he emphasized "introspection, meditation, and self-examination" (Everett Emerson, *Puritanism in America: 1620–1750* [Boston, MA: Twayne, 1977], 96). Also see Norman Pettit, *The Heart Prepared: Grace and Conversion in Puritan Spiritual Life* (New Haven, CT: Yale University Press, 1966).

39. Hambrick-Stowe, *Practice of Piety*, 21, 70. He called my attention to many sources in this section. For descriptions of the Puritan process of conversion, see Charles Lloyd Cohen, *God's Caress: The Psychology of Puritan Religious Experience* (New York: Oxford University Press, 1986), 75–110; and Patricia Caldwell, *The Puritan Conversion Narrative: The Beginnings of American Expression* (New York: Cambridge University Press, 1983).

40. Patrick Ker, *The Map of Man's Misery…Being a Perpetual Almanack of Spiritual Meditations…* (Boston, 1692), title page; Hambrick-Stowe, *Practice of Piety*, 219, 98 (first, second, and fourth quotations); Thomas Shepard, *Theses Sabbaticae: or, The Doctrine of the Sabbath* (London: John Rothwell, 1649), 79 (third quotation).

41. Claudia Durst Johnson, *Daily Life in Colonial New England* (Westport, CT: Greenwood Press), 28; Hambrick-Stowe, *Practice of Piety*, 200 (quotation); Increase Mather, *Ichabod or, A Discourse, Shewing What Cause There Is to Fear that the Glory of the Lord Is Departing from New-England* (Boston: T. Green, 1702), 31. Cf. Solomon Stoddard, *The Sufficiency of One Good Sign to Prove a Man to Be in a State of Life* (Boston, 1703), 17.

42. Stannard, "Death and the Puritan Child," 236.

43. Shepard, *Sincere Convert*, 134 (first quotation); David D. Hall, *Worlds of Wonder, Days of Judgment: Popular Religious Beliefs in Early New England* (Cambridge, MA: Harvard University Press, 1989), 138 (second quotation). See also Samuel Willard, *The Child's Portion* (Boston: S. Green, 1684) and John Allin, *The Spouse of Christ Coming Out of Affliction* (Cambridge, MA: S. Green, 1672).

44. James Pierpont, *Sundry False Hopes of Heaven* (Boston: T. Green, 1712), xiv (first quotation), xviii (second quotation), 23; Hall, *Faithful Shepherd*, 165; first and second quotations; Albro, *Works of Shepard*, 2: 350; third and fourth quotations; Mather, *Coelestinus*, 16–25; quotation from 20.

45. Hall, *Worlds*, 205 (both quotations), 135; Kenneth P. Minkema, "The East Windsor Conversions Relations, 1700–1725," *Connecticut Historical Society Bulletin* 51 (Winter 1986), 27; Edward S. Morgan, ed., *The Dairy of Michael Wigglesworth, 1653–1657: The Conscience of a Puritan* (New York: Harper Torchbook, 1965), 118; Increase Mather, *A Discourse Concerning the Uncertainty of the Times of Men* (Boston: B. Green, 1697), in Miller and Johnson, *Puritans*, 1: 348. Hall called my attention to these sources.

46. See Cotton Mather, *The Temple Opening*... (Boston: B. Green, 1709), 30–31.

47. Hall, *Worlds*, 205 (quotation), 208; Leonard Hoar, *The Sting of Death Unstung* (Boston: John Foster, 1680), 3, 6–7, 9–11, 21–22.

48. On this issue of worry, see Samuel Willard, *The Mourners Cordial against Excessive Sorrow* (Boston: Benjamin Harris and John Allen, 1691), 21, 42, 71–72; Tompson, *Heaven*, 67. See also James Janeway, *A Token for Children* (Boston: T. Green, 1700).

49. Hambrick-Stowe, *Practice of Piety*, 197 (first quotations); John Cotton, *A Briefe Exposition with Practicall Observations upon the Whole Book of Ecclesiastes* (London, 1657), 47; Cotton Mather, *Preparatory Meditations upon the Day of Judgment* (Boston: B. Green, 1692), 27 (see also Worthington Chauncey Ford, ed., *Diary of Cotton Mather*, 2 vols. [New York: F. Ungar, 1957], 1: 372); Cotton Mather, *Parentator: Memoirs of Remarkables in the Life and Death of the Ever-Memorable Dr. Increase Mather* (Boston: B. Green, 1724), 36–37, 48; Thomas Shepard, "Journal," in Michael McGiffert, ed., *God's Plot: The Paradoxes of Puritan Piety: Being the Autobiography & Journal of Thomas Shepard* (Amherst: University of Massachusetts Press, 1994), 85–86; Anne Bradsteet, "As Weary Pilgrim," in Robert Hutchinson, ed., *Poems of Anne Bradstreet* (New York: Dover, 1969), 77–78; Mitchel, quoted in Cotton Mather, *Magnalia Christi Americana or, The Ecclesiastical History of New-England, from Its First Planting in the Year 1620 unto...1698. In Seven Books* (London: T. Parkhurst, 1702), 2: 111. See also David Stannard, *Puritan Way of Death: A Study in Religion, Culture, and Social Change* (New York: Oxford University Press, 1977), 79.

50. Hambrick-Stowe, *Practice of Piety*, 199 (see John Corbet, *Self-Imployment in Secret* [Boston: Brunning, 1684]); Mather, *Plain Discourse*, 62–63, quotations from 63.

51. Mather, *Meditations*, 262, 264, 265; quotation from 264. Cf. Mather, *Plain Discourse*, 63–64. In *Awakening Soul-Saving Truths*...(Boston: S. Kneeland, 1720), Mather described those destined for salvation as a "remnant" and a "little flock" (68–70, 75–76, 84–87). Cf. Thomas Shepard, *The Sincere Convert*...(London, 1640), 94, 121, 124–25, 264. The belief of some Puritans in infant salvation contradicted their view that the number of residents of heaven would be comparatively small. See also Peter J. Thuesen, *Predestination: The American Career of a Contentious Doctrine* (New York: Oxford University Press, 2009), 45, who called my attention to the last two sources. Mather contended that God admitted "all Children of Godly Parents dying in their Infancy" into heaven. God had "taken them into His Covenant," which was "a Covenant of Life." Since they had "not Violated the Covenant; it was reasonable to "hope that GOD has given them Eternal Life in *Heaven*" where they could attain the perfection they had no chance to obtain in this world (*Meditations*, 95). Since about half of all individuals died in infancy, and many of them had been included in the covenant, the number of heaven's residents would logically be much larger than most Puritans anticipated.

52. Mather, *Plain Discourse*, 34–57; first quotations from 36, second from 48, third from 57, fourth from 34.

53. Pierpont, *False Hopes*, 41, vi–vii, 37; first quotation from vi, second and third from 37; Stannard, "Death and the Puritan Child," 245; James Fitch, *Peace the End of the Perfect and Upright*...(Boston: S. Green, 1673), 6; Pearse, *Great Concern*, 27, 25; all quotations from 27 except for the last sentence, which is from 25; Mather, *Meditations*, 269, 273, 275; first quotation from 273, second from 275; Mather, *A Plain Discourse*, 71–72. Cf. Cotton Mather, *An Heavenly Life: A Christian Taught How to Live in an Infallible & Comfortable Perswasion of the Divine Love* (Boston: S. Kneeland, 1719), 2, 22, and passim.

54. Hambrick-Stowe, *Practice of Piety*, 190.

55. Increase Mather, *Heavens Alarm to the World* (Boston: John Foster, 1681), 8, 10, "To the Reader"; first quotation from 8, second from 10.

56. Mather, *Heavens Alarm*, 6, "To the Reader," 13, 15, quotations in that order. See also Johnson, *Daily Life*, 27.

57. Hall, *Faithful Shepherd*, 255. See Increase Mather, *Some Important Truths about Conversion: Delivered in Sundry Sermons* (Boston: S. Green, 1684), 207; Increase Mather, *The Greatest Sinners Exhorted and Encouraged to Come to Christ, and that Now without Delaying...* (Boston, 1686), sig. A3 verso. See also Samuel Willard, *A Brief Discourse of Justification...* (Boston: S. Green, 1686), 130–31; and Allin, *Spouse of Christ*, 9.

58. Solomon Stoddard, *The Fear of Hell Restrains Men from Sin*, Don Kistler, ed. (Morgan, PA: Soli Deo Gloria, 2003), 17–18; quotations in that order; Stephen R. Holmes, *God of Grace and God of Glory: An Account of the Theology of Jonathan Edwards* (Grand Rapids, MI: Eerdmans, 2001), 211; Samuel Danforth, *The Cry of Sodom Enquired Into* (Cambridge, MA: Marmaduke Johnson, 1674), 12; Hillhouse, *Sermons*, 131; Mather, *The Mystery of Christ Opened and Applyed in Several Sermons* (Boston: Richard Pierce, 1686); Thomas Shepard, *The Sincere Convert* (London: E. Flesher, 1646), 72. Cf. Increase Mather, *The Times of Men Are in the Hand of God* (Boston: John Foster, 1675), 4; Increase Mather, *The Greatest Sinners Exhorted and Encouraged to Come to Christ...* (Boston: Richard Pierce, 1686), 66–67; Increase Mather, *Solemn Advice to Young Men...* (Boston: B. Green, 1695), 33; Cotton Mather, *Warnings from the Dead...* (Boston: B. Green, 1693), 4; Joshua Moodey, *An Exhortation to a Condemned Malefactor* (Boston: Richard Pierce, 1686), 64; Pearse, *Great Concern*, 18, 170; Joseph Alleine, *An Alarm to Unconverted Sinners* (Boston: D. Kneeland, 1767 [1716]), 20–21, 113. On Puritan views of hell, see Carl R. Trueman, "Heaven and Hell: (12) In Puritan Theology," *Epworth Review* 22:3 (1995), 75–85. Puritans argued that those in hell could see heaven, thereby increasing their pain, while those in heaven could see hell, increasing their joy (79–80). Also see D. P. Walker, *The Decline of Hell: Seventeenth Century Discussions of Eternal Torment* (Chicago: University of Chicago Press, 1964).

59. Stoddard, *The Fear of Hell*, 3–7; first and two quotations from 3; third from 5, fourth from 7; fifth from 4.

60. Mather, *Believers Gain*, 22, 13, quotation from 13; Pearse, *Great Concern*, 32, 31; quotations in that order.

61. Pearse, *Great Concern*, 38, 1; Hambrick-Stowe, *Practice of Piety*, 241.

62. Harry S. Stout, *The New England Soul: Preaching and Religious Culture in Colonial New England* (New York: Oxford University Press, 1986), 157–58, 27, 129, 36; quotation from 157.

63. Thuesen, *Predestination*, 55–56, 66, 68; first quotation from 55, second from 66, third from 68; Cotton Mather, *The Everlasting Gospel: The Gospel of Justification by the Righteousness of God...* (Boston: B. Green, 1700), 65; John Cotton, *A Briefe Exposition with Practicall Observations upon the Whole Book of Ecclesiastes* (London, 1657), 244. See also Anne Bradstreet, "Autobiographical Passages," in Hutchinson, *Poems of Bradstreet*, 183–84. On the role of works in Puritan theology, see Cohen, *God's Caress*, 69–71, 87, 111–33, 221; Perry Miller, *The New England Mind: From Colony to Province* (Cambridge, MA: Harvard University Press, 1953), 410–14.

64. Stout, *New England Soul*, 6. "Seldom, if ever before, did so many people hear the same message of purpose and direction over so long a period as did the New England 'Puritans'" (3). For the relationship of apocalyptic and otherworldly themes in Puritan preaching to times of grave danger, revival, and political and social upheaval, see 8 and passim. Puritans typically fasted

because of various troubles such as sickness, death, drought, military defeats, political problems, and family friction (Hall, *Worlds*, 233).

65. Hall, *Worlds*, 6.

66. Hall, *Worlds*, 3 (first quotation), 7, 241 (second quotation); Stout, *New England Soul*, 4 (third quotation). See also Richard Godbeer, *The Devil's Dominion: Magic and Religion in Early New England* (Cambridge, UK: Cambridge University Press, 1992).

67. See Hall, *Worlds*, passim. Hall notes that those who migrated to New England in the seventeenth century were largely "of 'middling' status—yeomen, artisans, merchants, and housewives" who could explain basic biblical principles (5). He adds that "the clergy were successful in persuading many of the colonists to adopt their understanding of religion" (11). See, for example, George Selement and Bruce Woolley, eds., *Thomas Shepard's Confessions* (Boston: Colonial Society of Massachusetts, 1981), 41, 69, 71, 77–78, 86–87, 168–70, 211–12.

68. Greene, *Pursuits of Happiness*, 22–26. See also Timothy H. Breen and Stephen Foster, "The Puritans' Greatest Achievement: A Study of Social Cohesion on Seventeenth-Century Massachusetts," *Journal of American History* 60 (June 1973), 5–22.

CHAPTER 2

1. See Jonathan Edwards, "The Eternity of Hell Torments," http://www.biblebb.com/files/edwards/eternity.htm; Edwards, "Wrath upon the Wicked to the Uttermost," in Edward Hickman, ed., *The Works of Jonathan Edwards*, 2 vols. (Carlisle, PA: The Banner of Truth Trust, 1992), 2: 122–25; Edwards, "The Justice of God in the Damnation of Sinners," in ibid., 1: 668–79; and Edwards, "The Torments of Hell Are Exceedingly Great," in Kenneth P. Minkema, ed., *Sermons and Discourses, 1723–1729*, vol. 14 of Harry S. Stout, ed., *The Works of Jonathan Edwards* (New Haven, CT: Yale University Press, 1998), 301–31. See also Edwards, "Children Ought to Love the Lord," in Edwards, *Sermons and Discourses, 1739–1742*, vol. 22, in Harry S. Stout, Nathan O. Hatch, and Kyle P. Farley, eds., *The Works of Jonathan Edwards* (New Haven, CT: Yale University Press, 2003). On recent efforts to downplay Edwards's emphasis on hellfire, see Conrad Cherry, *The Theology of Jonathan Edwards: A Reappraisal* (Bloomington: Indiana University Press, 1990), 58; R. W. Jenson, *America's Theologian: A Recommendation of Jonathan Edwards* (Oxford, UK: Oxford University Press, 1988), 101; and Stephen R. Holmes, *God of Grace and God of Glory: An Account of the Theology of Jonathan Edwards* (Grand Rapids, MI: Eerdmans, 2001), 199–200. Holmes points out that although Edwards employed the threat of hell in several other sermons, in his major published works he wrote almost nothing about hell (216).

2. On Edwards's life, see Iain Murray, *Jonathan Edwards: A New Biography* (Carlisle, PA: Banner of Truth Trust, [1987]); George Marsden, *Jonathan Edwards: A Life* (New Haven, CT: Yale University Press, 2003); Perry Miller, *Jonathan Edwards* (Lincoln: University of Nebraska Press, 2005); and Philip Gura, *Jonathan Edwards: America's Evangelical* (New York: Hill and Wang, 2005).

3. "George Whitefield: Sensational Evangelist of Britain and America," http://www.christianitytoday.com/ch/131christians/evangelistsandapologists/whitefield.html?start=2. On Whitefield's life, ministry, and influence, see John Pollock, *George Whitefield and the Great Awakening* (Garden City, NY: Doubleday, 1972); Harry Stout, *The Divine Dramatist: George Whitefield and the Rise of Modern Evangelicalism* (Grand Rapids, MI: William B. Eerdmans, 1991);Frank Lambert, *Pedlar in Divinity: George Whitefield and the Transatlantic Revivals,*

1737–1770 (Princeton, NJ: Princeton University Press, 1994); and Jerome Dean Mahaffey, *Preaching Politics: The Religious Rhetoric of George Whitefield and the Founding of a New Nation* (Waco, TX: Baylor University Press, 2007). See also George Whitefield, *The Journals of George Whitefield* (Carlisle, PA: Banner of Truth Trust, 1960) and George Whitefield, *The Letters of George Whitefield, for the Period 1734–1742* (Carlisle, PA: Banner of Truth Trust, 1976).

4. Ebenezer Pemberton, *Heaven the Residence of the Saints Occasioned by the Sudden and Much Lamented Death of the Rev. George Whitefield* (Boston, 1771), 17. See Milton J. Coalter, *Gilbert Tennent, Son of Thunder: A Case Study of Continental Pietism's Impact on the First Great Awakening in the Middle Colonies* (New York: Greenwood Press, 1986); George W. Pitcher, *Samuel Davies: Apostle of Dissent in Colonial Virginia* (Knoxville: University of Tennessee Press, 1971); James Tanis, *Dutch Calvinistic Pietism in the Middle Colonies: A Study in the Life and Theology of Theodorus Jacobus Frelinghuysen* (The Hague, Holland: Martinus Nijhoff, 1967).

5. See Jon Butler, "Enthusiasm Described and Decried: The Great Awakening as Interpretive Fiction," *Journal of American History* 69: 2 (1982), 305–25; John Kent, *Wesley and the Wesleyans* (Cambridge, UK: Cambridge University Press, 2002); Frank Lambert, *Inventing the "Great Awakening"* (Princeton, NJ: Princeton University Press, 1999). On the First Great Awakening, see also Edwin Scott Gaustad, *The Great Awakening in New England* (Chicago: Quadrangle Books, 1968); J. M. Busted and John Van de Wetering, *What Must I Do to Be Saved? The Great Awakening in Colonial America* (Hinsdale, IL: Dryden, 1976); Harry S. Stout, *The New England Soul: Preaching and Religious Culture in Colonial New England* (New York: Oxford University Press, 1986); W. R. Ward, *The Protestant Evangelical Awakening* (Cambridge, UK: Cambridge University Press, 1992); Mark Noll, *The Rise of Evangelicalism: The Age of Edwards, Whitefield, and the Wesleys* (Downers Grove, IL: InterVarsity Press, 2003); and Thomas S. Kidd, *The Great Awakening: The Roots of Evangelical Christianity in Colonial America* (New Haven, CT: Yale University Press, 2007); Patricia Bonomi, *Under the Cope of Heaven Religion, Society, and Politics in Colonial America* (New York: Oxford University Press, 1986); Nathan Hatch, *The Sacred Cause of Liberty* (New Haven, CT: Yale University Press, 1977).

6. See Conrad Cherry, *The Theology of Jonathan Edwards: A Reappraisal* (Garden City, NY: Anchor Books, 1966); Robert W. Jenson, *America's Theologian: A Recommendation of Jonathan Edwards* (New York: Oxford University Press, 1988); Nathan O. Hatch and Harry S. Stout, eds., *Jonathan Edwards and the American Experience* (New York: Oxford University Press, 1988); Sang Hyun Lee and Allen Guelzo, eds., *Edwards in Our Time: Jonathan Edwards and the Shaping of American Religion* (Grand Rapids, MI: Eerdmans, 1999); David W. Kling and Douglas A. Sweeney, *Jonathan Edwards at Home and Abroad: Historical Memories, Cultural Movements, Global Horizons* (Columbia: University of South Carolina Press, 2003); D. G. Hart, Sean Michael Lucas, and Stephen J. Nichols, *The Legacy of Jonathan Edwards: American Religion and the Evangelical Tradition* (Grand Rapids, MI: Baker Academic, 2003); Gerald R. McDermott, *One Holy and Happy Society: The Public Theology of Jonathan Edwards* (University Park: Pennsylvania State University Press, 1992); William J. Danaher, Jr., *The Trinitarian Ethics of Jonathan Edwards* (Louisville, KY: Westminster John Knox Press, 2004).

7. John H. Gerstner, *Jonathan Edwards on Heaven and Hell* (Grand Rapids, MI: Baker, 1980), 9; Jonathan Edwards, sermon on Isaiah 3:10 (1722) in Gerstner, *Edwards*, 12.

8. Jonathan Edwards, "The Many Mansions" (1737), in M. X. Lesser, ed., *Jonathan Edwards: Sermons and Discourses, 1734–1738* (New Haven, CT: Yale University Press, 2001), 737–38 (first,

second, and fourth quotations from 737, third from 738); Jonathan Edwards, Miscellany no. 952, Hickman, *Works*, 2: 633 (fifth quotation); Jonathan Edwards, "The Everlasting Love of God" (1736), in Lesser, *Jonathan Edwards*, 480 (sixth, seventh, and eighth quotations). See also Jonathan Edwards, *A History of the Work of Redemption*, vol. 9, John F. Wilson, ed., in *The Works of Jonathan Edwards* (New Haven, CT: Yale University Press, 1989), 118–19.

9. Jonathan Edwards, Miscellany no. 721, Hickman, *Works*, 2: 628 (quotation); Edwards, "Nothing upon Earth Can Represent the Glories of Heaven" (ca. 1724), in Minkema, *Sermons*, 14: 137–60; Edwards, Miscellany no. 743, Hickman, *Works*, 2: 631.

10. Jonathan Edwards, "Heaven Is a World of Love," in Stephen J. Nichols, *Heaven on Earth: Capturing Jonathan Edwards' Vision of Living in Between* (Wheaton, IL: Crossway Books, 2006), 121–22; quotations in that order; Edwards, "The Christian Pilgrim; Or, The True Christian's Life a Journey Toward Heaven," in Hickman, *Works*, 2: 244 (third quotation); Edwards, "Heaven," 125 (fourth quotation); Edwards, "True Saints, When Absent from the Body, Are Present with the Lord," Hickman, *Works*, 2: 28 (fifth and sixth quotations).

11. Jonathan Edwards, Sermon on Romans 2: 10, why the vision of God is the ultimate joy of the blessed, in Carol and Phillip Zaleski, eds., *The Book of Heaven: An Anthology of Writings from Ancient to Modern Times* (Oxford, UK: Oxford University Press, 2000), 174–75; first quotation from 174, second from 175; Edwards, "Christian Pilgrim," 244; Jonathan Edwards, Miscellany no. 679, Hickman, *Works*, 2: 626.

12. Edwards, "True Saints," 2: 28–29; first three quotations from 28, fourth and fifth from 29; Edwards, Miscellany no. 957, Gerstner, *Edwards*, 16 (sixth quotation); Edwards, Miscellany no. 934, Hickman, *Works*, 2: 637 (seventh quotation).

13. Edwards, "Heaven," 130 (first quotation), 129 (second and third quotations), 125 (fourth quotation); Edwards, Miscellany no. 5, Hickman, *Works*, 2: 618 (fifth quotation).

14. Edwards, "Christian Pilgrim," 243 (first and second quotations); Edwards, Miscellany no. 1059, Hickman, *Works*, 2: 637 (third quotation); Edwards, Miscellany no. 585, ibid., 2: 625.

15. Edwards, Miscellany no. 952, 2: 634 (first, third, fifth and sixth quotations); Edwards, "True Saints," 2: 32 (second quotation); Edwards, Miscellany no. 1126 in Hickman, *Works*, 2: 636 (fourth quotation).

16. Jonathan Edwards, "The Excellency of Christ," in Wilson H. Kimnach, Kenneth P. Minkema, and Douglas Sweeney, eds., *The Sermons of Jonathan Edwards: A Reader* (New Haven, CT: Yale University Press, 1999), 181–82 (first quotation), 194 (sixth and seventh quotations); Edwards, Miscellany no. 571, Hickman, *Works*, 2: 623 (second quotation); Edwards, "True Saints," 2: 28 (third, fourth, fifth, eighth, ninth, and tenth quotations) (cf. Edwards, Miscellany no. 741, Hickman, *Works*, 2: 629; Edwards, *A Treatise Concerning Religious Affections*, in ibid., 1: 280); Marsden, *Edwards*, 326, summarizing Edwards's "True Saints" (eleventh quotation).

17. Kidd, *Awakening*, 130–35.

18. See Marsden, *Edwards*, 185; Jonathan Edwards, "Personal Narrative," in John E. Smith, Harry S. Stout, and Kenneth P. Minkema, *A Jonathan Edwards Reader* (New Haven, CT: Yale University Press, 1995), 293. For Sarah's euphoric spiritual experiences, see Marsden, *Edwards*, 240–49. See also Douglas Winiarski, "Souls Filled with Ravishing Transport: Heavenly Visions and the Radical Awakening in New England, 1742," *William and Mary Quarterly*, 3rd ser., 61 (Jan. 2004), 3–46.

19. Jonathan Edwards, Miscellanies nos. 105, 435, Hickman, *Works*, 2: 618, 2: 621; Edwards, Miscellany no. 777, Yale MSS, quoted in Sang Hyun Lee, *The Philosophical Theology of Jonathan*

Edwards (Princeton, NJ: Princeton University Press, 2000), 140 (first quotation); Jonathan Edwards, "The Wisdom of God, Displayed in the Way of Salvation" (1733) http://articles.christiansunite.com/article3398.shtml (second, third, and fourth quotations).

20. Kidd, *Great Awakening*, 15 (first quotation); Gura, *Edwards*, 31 (second quotation), 58; Marsden, *Edwards*, 135–36.

21. Jonathan Edwards, Miscellany no. 701, Hickman, *Works*, 2: 626 (first quotation); Edwards, Miscellany no. 371, ibid., 2: 620 (second quotation); Edwards, Miscellany, no. 1089, ibid., 2: 638; Edwards, Miscellany no. 372, ibid., 2: 620 (third quotation); Edwards, Miscellany no. 529, ibid., 2: 622 (fourth and fifth quotations) (cf. Edwards, "True Saints," 2: 30); Edwards, Miscellany no. 1089, 2: 639 (sixth quotation); Edwards, Miscellany no. 555, Hickman, *Works*, 2: 622 (seventh quotation); Edwards, Miscellany no. 1137, ibid., 2: 640; Gerstner, *Edwards*, 32 (eighth quotation).

22. Jonathan Edwards, Miscellany no. 430, Hickman, *Works*, 2: 621; Edwards, Miscellany no. 432, ibid., 2: 621 (first quotation); Edwards, Miscellany 105, 2: 618; Edwards, Miscellany, no. 571, 2: 624 (remainder of quotations). Cf. Edwards, "Sermon on Romans 2: 10," 174.

23. Edwards, "Heaven," 131; Edwards, "Many Mansions," 738; Edwards, Miscellany no. 188, Hickman, *Works*, 2: 619 (first quotation); Edwards, "Praise, One of the Chief Employments of Heaven," ibid., 2: 913–17 (second quotation from 913); Theodore Frelinghuysen, "The Believer's Well-founded Expectation of Future Glory," in Joel Beeke, ed., *Forerunner of the Great Awakening: Sermons by Theodorus Jacobus Frelinghuysen* (Grand Rapids, MI: Eerdmans, 2000), 182; Jonathan Edwards, Miscellany no. 152, Hickman, *Works*, 2: 618.

24. Edwards, "True Saints," 2: 30–31; first and third quotations from 30, second from 31; Edwards, Miscellany no. 430, 2: 621 (fourth quotation); Edwards, "Heaven," 131–32 (fifth quotation).

25. Jonathan Edwards, "Serving God in Heaven" in *The Works of Jonathan Edwards*, Vol. 17, *Sermons and Discourses, 1730–1733*, Mark Valeri, ed. (New Haven, CT: Yale University Press, 1999), 256–60; first and second quotations from 256, third from 257, fourth and fifth from 259, sixth from 260.

26. Edwards, "Many Mansions," 739–40; first quotation from 740, second and third from 739; Samuel Davies, "The Mediatorial Kingdom and Glories of Jesus Christ," in *Sermons on Important Subjects*, 3 vols. (New York: T. Allen, 1792), 1: 287–88; Whitefield is quoted in William Warren Sweet, *The Story of Religion in America* (New York: Harper and Brothers, 1939), 142. On the Awakening's inclusion of these groups, see Kidd, *Great Awakening*, 61, 213–33; Mark A. Noll, *The History of Christianity in the United States and Canada* (Grand Rapids, MI: Eerdmans, 1992), 105–9; Catherine A. Brekus, *Strangers and Pilgrims: Female Preaching in America, 1740–1845* (Chapel Hill: University of North Carolina Press, 1998).

27. Edwards, Miscellany no. 571, 2: 623–24; first quotation from 623 (cf. Edwards, "True Saints," 27); Edwards, "Excellency of Christ," 194 (second quotation); Edwards, *History of the Work of Redemption*, 497 (third quotation); Edwards, Miscellany no. 952, 2: 634; George Whitefield, "Christ's Transfiguration," http://www.biblebb.com/files/whitefield/GW030.htm.

28. Edwards, Miscellany no. 952, 2: 634 (first quotation); Edwards, "Heaven," 123 (second quotation); Jonathan Edwards, sermon manuscript on Hebrews 11:16 (Jan. 1754), Jonathan Edwards Collection, Beinecke Library, Yale University, quoted in Nichols, *Heaven*, 114 (third and fourth quotation); Jonathan Edwards, Miscellany no. 182, Hickman, *Works*, 2: 619 (fifth quotation); Edwards, "Christian Pilgrim," 243–46; Edwards, Miscellany no. 206, ibid., 2: 619 (sixth quotation).

29. Edwards, Miscellany no. 639, Hickman, *Works*, 2: 625 (first quotation); Edwards, "Heaven," 125 (third quotation), 126–27 (second quotation), 128; Edwards, Miscellany no. 555, 2: 622 (fourth quotation).

30. Marsden, *Edwards*, 253 (first quotation), 19–21, 349 (sixth quotation); Samuel Hopkins, *The Life and Character of the Late Reverend Mr. Jonathan Edwards* (Boston, 1765), quoted in David Levin, ed., *Jonathan Edwards: A Profile* (New York: Hill & Wang, 1969), 42–43 (second, third, and fourth quotations); Gura, *Edwards*, 59 (fifth quotation). On the Edwardses' marriage, also see Elizabeth Dodds, *Marriage to a Difficult Man: The Uncommon Union of Jonathan & Sarah Edwards* (Philadelphia: Westminster Press, 1971).

31. Whitefield, "Christ's Transfiguration."

32. Edwards, "True Saints," 2: 28; Edwards, Miscellany no. 565, Hickman, *Works*, 2: 623; Edwards, Miscellany, no. 743, 2: 632; Edwards, Miscellany no. 1126, 635; quotations in that order.

33. Edwards, Miscellany no. 743, 2: 630 (first two quotations); Edwards, Miscellany no. 743, 2: 631 (third quotation); Edwards, *Work of Redemption*, 503, 505, 506; last three quotations in that order. See also Edwards, Miscellanies no. 809 (516) and no. 710 (336–38) in *The Works of Jonathan Edwards*, Vol. 18, *The "Miscellanies,"* 501–832, Ava Chamberlain, ed. (New Haven, CT: Yale University Press, 2000).

34. Jonathan Edwards, Miscellany, no. 775, Hickman, *Works*, 2: 632 (first quotation); Edwards, "Degrees of Glory," in Lesser, *Jonathan Edwards*, 614 (second quotation), 620; Edwards, "Many Mansions," 740 (third quotation).

35. Edwards, "Degrees of Glory," 616–18, quotations in that order; George Whitefield, "The Eternity of Hell-Torments," in *Seventy-Five Sermons on Various Important Subjects* (London: W. Baynes, 1812), 393.

36. Edwards, "Degrees of Glory," 625 (first and second quotations), 624 (third), 621 (fourth), 622 (fifth).

37. Edwards, "Degrees of Glory," 618–19, 615, 620–21; quotation from 618; Marsden, *Edwards*, 191.

38. Edwards, "Heaven," 138 (first quotation); Edwards, Miscellany no. 565, 2: 623 (second quotation); Gerstner, *Edwards*, 13 (third quotation) (Edwards, sermon on Luke 22:20, Edwards' Collection, Beinecke Library, 4); Nichols, *Heaven*, 83 (fourth quotation).

39. Edwards, "True Saints," 2: 27 (first quotation); Edwards, "Heaven," 136 (remainder of quotations).

40. Jonathan Edwards, "Justification by Faith Alone," in Lesser, *Jonathan Edwards*, 193 (first quotation); Edwards, Miscellany no. 367; sermon on Titus 3:5, 3, as quoted by Gerstner, *Edwards*, 20 (second quotation); Edwards, "The Free and Voluntary Suffering and Death of Christ," in Lesser, *Jonathan Edwards*, 514; Edwards, Sermon on Col. 1:12 (2), Stockbridge Indians, Aug. 1756, 1, quoted in Gerstner, *Edwards*, 9 (third quotation); Edwards, "Heaven," 135 (fourth quotation); Edwards, "Sinners in the Hands of an Angry God," in *American Sermons: The Pilgrims to Martin Luther King, Jr.* (New York: Library of America, 1999), 361 (fifth quotation); Edwards, "Christian Pilgrim," 246 (sixth quotation). See also Edwards, "The Reality of Conversion" (1740) in Kimnach, Minkema, and Sweeney, *Sermons*, 80–104; Edwards, "He That Believed Shall Be Saved" (1751), in ibid., 111–20.

41. Winthrop S. Hudson and John Corrigan, *Religion in America* (New York: Macmillan, 1992), 81.

42. George Whitefield, "On Regeneration," http://www.apibs.org/classics/gw049.htm (first four quotations); George Whitefield, "Marks of a True Conversion," http://www.anglicanlibrary.org/whitefield/sermons/23.htm (last quotation).

43. Jonathan Edwards, "Fast Days in Dead Times," in Lesser, *Jonathan Edwards*, 65 (first three quotations); Edwards, "The Way of Holiness," in Kimnach, Minkema, and Sweeney, *Sermons*, 3 (fourth quotation); George Whitefield, "The Folly and Danger of Being Not Righteous Enough," http://www.biblebb.com/files/whitefield/gw009.htm; Frelinghuysen, "Scarcely Saved," 80; Samuel Finley, "The Madness of Mankind" (1754), in *American Sermons*, 452–53; quotations in that order.

44. Jonathan Edwards, "The Unreasonableness of Indetermination in Religion," in Lesser, *Jonathan Edwards*, 96–101; first three quotations from 96, fourth from 97, fifth from 99, sixth from 101; Edwards, "Christian Pilgrim," 245 (seventh quotation).

45. George Whitefield, "The Almost Christian," http://www.anglicanlibrary.org/whitefield/sermons/43.htm.

46. Whitefield, "Christ's Transfiguration." Some contended that punishing individuals for all eternity because they enjoyed "the pleasures of sin for a season" is inconsistent with God's justice. Whitefield chastised them for arraigning "the Almighty at the bar" of their "shallow reasoning." Simply "thinking or calling God unjust," Whitefield insisted, did not make Him unjust (Whitefield, "The Eternity of Hell-Torments," 391).

47. George Whitefield, "Christ the Support of the Tempted," http://www.anglicanlibrary.org/whitefield/sermons/19.htm.

48. Edwards, "Christian Pilgrim," 246 (first quotation); Edwards, "Unreasonableness," 103; Edwards's sermon on Isa. 35:8, 1722 or 1723, 4, quoted in Gerstner, *Edwards*, 10 (second quotation); Edwards, "Way of Holiness," 4 (third quotation); (cf. Samuel Davies, "The General Resurrection," in *Sermons*, 3: 377); Edwards, "Many Mansions," 745 (fourth quotation); Edwards, "Heaven," 137 (fifth quotation); Jerry Walls, *Heaven: The Logic of Eternal Joy* (New York: Oxford University Press, 2002), 39, analyzing Edwards, "The Way of Holiness" (sixth quotation); Edwards, "Christian Pilgrim," 246. For debates over the issue of assurance of salvation during the First Great Awakening, see Kidd, *Great Awakening*, 126–27.

49. Edwards, "Christian Pilgrim," 2: 243–46; quotations from 2: 242.

50. Whitefield, "On Regeneration."

51. George Whitefield, "Persecution Every Christian's Lot," http://www.biblebb.com/files/whitefield/gw055.htm.

52. Edwards, "Heaven," 136 (first quotation); Edwards, "Many Mansions," 743–45; quotations in that order.

53. Jonathan Edwards, Miscellany no. 889, Hickman, *Works*, 632; Edwards, "Christian Pilgrim," 245; quotations in that order.

54. Edwards, "Sinners," 353. See also Edwards, "Heaven," 135.

55. Holmes, *God of Grace*, 211–12; Jonathan Edwards, Sermon on Isa. 66:23, June 1742, 1, as quoted by Gerstner, *Edwards*, 34; Edwards, "The End of the Wicked Contemplated by the Righteous," Hickman, *Works*, 2: 208; quotations in that order. See also Edwards, "Wicked Men Useful in Their Destruction Only," ibid., 2: 125–29.

56. Holmes, *God of Grace*, 214; Jonathan Edwards, Miscellany no. 279, as quoted in Gerstner, *Edwards*, 34. For an analysis of this point, see Holmes, *God of Grace*, 233–39; Jerry Walls, *Hell: The Logic of Damnation* (Notre Dame, IN: University of Notre Dame Press, 1992); and Bruce W. Davidson, "Reasonable Damnation: How Jonathan Edwards Argued for the Rationality of Hell," *Journal of the Evangelical Theological Society* 38 (March 1995), 47–56.

57. George Whitefield, "The Eternity of Hell-Torments," http://www.reformed.org/documents/index.html?mainframe=/documents/Whitefield/WITF. See also Whitefield, "The

Method of Grace," ibid. While Whitefield was reluctant to describe hell, Jon Butler argues, Gilbert Tennent "seemed to delight in doing so." See Jonathan Butler, *Softly and Tenderly: Jesus Is Calling: Heaven and Hell in American Revivalism, 1870–1920* (Brooklyn, NY: Carlson, 1991), 25. For example, see Gilbert Tennent, *Solemn Warning to the Secure World* (Boston: S. Kneeland & T. Green, 1735).

CHAPTER 3

1. Helena M. Wall, *Fierce Communion: Family and Community in Early America* (Cambridge, MA: Harvard University Press, 1990), 128. See also George Taylor, *The Transportation Revolution, 1815–1860* (New York: Rinehart, 1951); Charles G. Sellers, *The Market Revolution: Jacksonian America, 1815–1846* (New York: Oxford University Press, 1991); Christopher Clark, "Household Economy, Market Exchange and Rise of Capitalism in the Connecticut Valley 1800–1860," *Journal of Social History* 13 Winter (1979), 169–89.

2. Gregg Frazer coined this term in "The Political Theology of the American Founding" (paper presented at a Symposium on Religion and Politics, Calvin College, May 1, 2004), 1–2.

3. See James H. Hutson, *Religion and the New Republic: Faith in the Founding of America* (Lanham, MD: Rowman & Littlefield, 2000); Daniel L. Dreisbach, Mark D. Hall, and Jeffry H. Morrison, *The Founders on God and Government* (Lanham, MD: Rowman & Littlefield, 2004); Daniel L. Dreisbach, Mark D. Hall, and Jeffry H. Morrison, *The Forgotten Founders on Religion and Public Life* (Notre Dame, IN: University of Notre Dame Press, 2009).

4. Amanda Porterfield, "Protestant Experience in America: Conclusion," in Protestant Experience in Greenwood Press' Daily Life in America, http://dailylife.greenwood.com (quotation); on Allen, see C. A. Jellison, *Ethan Allen: Frontier Rebel* (Syracuse, NY: Syracuse University Press, 1969) and Michael A. Bellesiles, *Revolutionary Outlaws: Ethan Allen and the Struggle for Independence on the Early American Frontier* (Charlottesville: University Press of Virginia, 1993). Palmer edited two short-lived journals: *Temple of Reason* (1801–1803) and *Prospect: View of the Moral World* (1803–1805). See E. Palmer, *Posthumous Pieces... To Which Are Prefixed a Memoir of Mr. Palmer...* (London: R. Carlile, 1824); John Murray, *Letters and Sketches of Sermons*, 3 vols. (Boston: Joshua Belcher, 1812–1813); Stephen A. Marini, *Radical Sects of Revolutionary New England* (Cambridge, MA: Harvard University Press, 1982); and R. E. Miller, *The Larger Hope: The First Century of the Universalist Church in America, 1779–1870* (Boston: Unitarian Universalist Association, 1979).

5. On the Second Great Awakening, see Whitney R. Cross, *The Burned-Over District: The Social and Intellectual History of Enthusiastic Religion in Western New York, 1800–1850* (Ithaca, NY: Cornell University Press, 1950); Charles I. Foster, *An Errand of Mercy: The Evangelical United Front, 1790–1837* (Chapel Hill: University of North Carolina Press, 1960); Dickson D. Bruce, *And They All Sang Hallelujah: Plain-Folk Camp-Meeting Religion, 1800–1845* (Knoxville: University of Tennessee Press, 1974); Paul E. Johnson, *A Shopkeeper's Millennium: Society and Revivals in Rochester, New York, 1815–1837* (New York: Hill and Wang, 1978); Nathan O. Hatch, *The Democratization of American Christianity* (New Haven, CT: Yale University Press, 1989); David W. Kling, *A Field of Divine Wonders: The New Divinity and Village Revivals in Northwestern Connecticut, 1792–1822* (University Park: Pennsylvania State University Press, 1993).

6. James B. Smith, ed., *The Posthumous Works of the Reverend and Pious James M'Gready, Late Minister of the Gospel, in Henderson, Kentucky*, 2 vols. (Nashville, TN: Lowry and Smith, 1833),

1: 285. See also John Boles, *The Great Revival: Beginnings of the Bible Belt* (Lexington: University Press of Kentucky, 1996).

7. James McGready, "Funeral Sermon," *Works*, 2: 299, 290, first quotation from 299, second and third from 290. Cf. 1: 326; Ebenezer Pemberton, *Heaven the Residence of the Saints Occasioned by the Sudden and Much Lamented Death of the Rev. George Whitefield* (Boston: D. Kneeland, 1770), 7; *Memoir, Select Thoughts and Sermons of the Late Rev. Edward Payson,* Asa Cummings, comp., 3 vols. (Harrisonburg, VA: Sprinkle, 1987), 1: 585; Charles Finney, *The Guilt of Sin: Evangelistic Messages* (Grand Rapids, MI: Kregel, 1965), 64; John Witherspoon, "The Happiness of the Saints in Heaven," in *The Works of the Rev. John Witherspoon*, H. Rondel Rumburg, comp., 2 vols. (Harrisonburg, VA: Sprinkle, 2002), 2: 260; John Eidsmoe, "Framer of the Framers," http://www.accessmylibrary.com/coms2/summary_0286-36585543_ITM.

8. McGready, "The Divine Authority of the Christian Religion," *Works*, 1: 2; McGready, "Funeral Sermon," 296; *Works*, 1: 330; first quotation from 2, second and third quotations from 330. Cf. John Rodgers, "The Faithful Servant Rewarded: A Sermon," in *Works of Witherspoon*, 1: 10; Payson, *Memoir*, 2: 69–70; Ezra Stiles, *A Funeral Sermon, Delivered at the Interment of the Reverend Mr. Chauncey Whittelsey* (New Haven, CT: Greens, 1787), 18, 19, 22; quotations in that order.

9. Timothy Dwight, "Heaven," in *Theology; Explained and Defended, in a Series of Sermons*, 5 vols. (Middletown, CT: Clark and Lyman, 1818), 1: 289 (first quotation), 295; Dwight, "The Remoter Consequences of Death: The Happiness of Heaven," *Theology*, 5: 518 (second quotation), 545 (third quotation), 541 (fourth quotation); Payson, *Memoirs*, 1: 537 (first quotation); Edward Payson, "The Feeling and Employment of Saints in Heaven," in Payson, *Memoir*, 2: 605 (second and third quotations); Payson, *Memoir*, 1: 538 (fourth and fifth quotations); Witherspoon, "Happiness of the Saints," 2: 262; James Dana, *The Heavenly Mansions: A Sermon Preached…at the Interment of the Reverend Ezra Stiles* (New Haven, CT: Thomas and Samuel Green, 1795), 12.

10. McGready, "Funeral Sermon," 2: 285; McGready, *Works*, 2: 96 (quotation); Levi Hart, *A Funeral Sermon* (New London: Printed by T. Green, 1787), 15; Payson, *Memoirs*, 1: 538.

11. Payson, *Memoir*, 1: 577–84; first four quotations from 584, fifth from 578. Payson also argued that the saints would no longer require food or sleep or be cognizant of time. Heaven had no colors, shapes, or tangible things, but every object would "appear incomparably more real, substantial and durable" than any earthly objects (*Memoir*, 3: 598).

12. Witherspoon, "Happiness of the Saints," 2: 257–59, 263; first quotation from 258, second from 257, third from 263, fourth from 259.

13. Payson, *Memoir*, 3: 599–601; quotations from 599; Witherspoon, "Happiness of the Saints," 2: 260, 265; quotations in that order; McGready, "Funeral Sermon," 2: 291; Hart, *Funeral Sermon*, 15–16; Ebenezer Pemberton, *Heaven the Residence of the Saints Occasioned by the Sudden and Much Lamented Death of the Rev. George Whitefield* (Boston and London, 1771), 9; Timothy Dwight, "The Remoter Consequences of Death: The Rewards of the Righteous," in *Theology*, 5: 512, 514, Dwight, "Remoter Consequences: Heaven," 5: 523, first quotation from 523; Dwight, *A Discourse, Preached at the Funeral of…Elizar Goodrich* (New Haven, CT: Greens, [1797]), 20 (second and third quotations).

14. Dwight, "Happiness of Heaven," 5: 522; Witherspoon, "Happiness of the Saints," 2: 261; Dwight, "Heaven," 1: 295; quotations in that order.

15. Lyman Beecher, *The Autobiography of Lyman Beecher* (Cambridge, MA: Belknap Press, 1961), 2: 418; Payson, *Memoir*, 1: 406–7; first quotation from 406, second and third from 407.

16. Charles G. Finney, *So Great Salvation* (Grand Rapids, MI: Kregel, 1965), 105; Charles G. Finney, *Sermons on the Way of Salvation* (Oberlin, OH: Edward J. Goodrich, 1891), 286–90; first quotation from 290, second from 286. See David Nelson, *Infidelity: Its Cause and Cure; Including a Notice of the Author's Unbelief, and the Means of His Rescue* (New York: American Tract Society, 1841). This type of testimony, Finney argued, provided no stronger evidence for heaven than the Bible did. Those who rejected the teaching of the Bible would not believe these accounts. Skeptics would counter either that these persons were not actually dead or that they brought back unreliable reports about the afterlife (*Way of Salvation*, 286).

17. Witherspoon, "Happiness of the Saints," 2: 266; Stiles, *Funeral Sermon,* 21; Asahel Nettleton, "The Death of the Righteous," in Bennet Tyler, comp., *Asahel Nettleton: Sermons from the Second Great Awakening* (Ames, IA: International Outreach, 1995), 28; Dwight, "Happiness of Heaven," 5: 547, 549; Dwight, "The Rich Man and Lazarus," in *Sermons by Timothy Dwight*, 2 vols. (New Haven, CT: Hezekiah Howe and Durrie & Peck, 1828), 2: 303. Cf. Dwight, *Discourse,* 20.

18. McGready, "Funeral Sermon," 2: 295; John Witherspoon, *Treatise on Regeneration,* in *Works,* 1: 209; Payson, *Memoir,* 1: 574.

19. Witherspoon, "Happiness of the Saints," 2: 255, 267–69; quotation from 269; Hart, *Funeral Sermon,* 18. See also Dana, *Heavenly Mansions,* 22, 37.

20. Witherspoon, "Happiness of the Saints," 2: 270; Dwight, "Heaven," 1: 294; McGready, "Funeral Sermon," 2: 310; Payson, "Saints in Heaven," 607–8; Charles G. Finney, *Lectures on Revivals of Religion* (New York: Leavitt, Lord, 1835), 15; Dana, *Heavenly Mansions,* 37; Payson, *Memoir,* 2: 70–72; first quotation from 70, second from 71.

21. Ann Lee Bressler, *The Universalist Movement in America, 1770–1880* (New York: Oxford University Press, 2001), 20; Stephen Watts, *The Republic Reborn: War and the Making of Liberal America, 1770–1820* (Baltimore: Johns Hopkins University Press, 1987), 113; quotations in that order. See also Wall, *Fierce Communion,* 130–33.

22. Lyman Beecher, *A Sermon Delivered at the Funeral of Henry Obookiah...* (Elizabethtown, NJ: Ebson Hart, 1819), 36; Dwight, "Happiness of Heaven," 5: 549, 539–42; Dwight "Heaven," 1: 289; first quotation from 549, second from 289, third from 539; Stiles, *Funeral Sermon,* 22; Dana, *Heavenly Mansions,* 12; McGready, "Funeral Sermon," 2: 307, 302, 305; quotation from 305; Finney, *Guilt of Sin,* 61–62. Although he rejected orthodox views of God, Christ, and salvation, Ethan Allen pictured a dynamic, active, energetic heaven where learning and intellectual development continued forever as everyone gained "greater understanding and deeper wisdom." See Ethan Allen, *Reason the Only Oracle of Man* (New York: Kraus, 1970), 128–29, 136; J. Kevin Graffagnino and H. Nicholas Muller, III, eds., *The Quotable Ethan Allen* (Barre: Vermont Historical Society, 2005), 242–43; quotation from 242.

23. Dwight, "Happiness of Heaven," 5: 546–47, 549; quotation from 546.

24. Stiles, *Funeral Sermon,* 14–15; Ezra Stiles, *A Sermon Delivered at the Ordination of the Reverend Henry Channing* (New London, CT: T. Green, 1787), 39–40; first and second quotations from 14, third and fourth from 15, fifth from 39.

25. Dana, *Heavenly Mansions,* 6–10; first quotation from 9, second from 10; Payson, *Memoir,* 2: 607. On the relationship of commercial life to moral experience and spirituality in the early 1800s, see Richard Rabinowitz, *The Spiritual Self in Everyday Life: The Transformation of Personal Religious Experience in Nineteenth-Century New England* (Boston: Northeastern University Press, 1989), 228–29.

26. Unitarians, distinguished by their rejection of the Trinity, gained strength within New England Congregationalism in the late 1700s. In 1805, Unitarian Henry Ware was appointed the Hollis Professor of Divinity at Harvard. These developments prompted Congregationalists to establish Andover Seminary in 1808 and to increasingly combat Unitarian views of biblical authority and interpretation and of salvation and spiritual maturity. This rift among Congregationalists led in 1825 to the formation of the American Unitarian Association. Boston became the stronghold of Unitarianism, as many of the city's intelligentsia, businessmen, and civil leaders adopted its tenets. See Conrad Wright, *The Beginnings of Unitarianism in America* (Hamden, CT: Archon Books, 1976).

27. See Norman Cousins, ed., *The Republic of Reason: The Personal Philosophies of the Founding Fathers* (San Francisco: Harper and Row, 1988), 141–44, 279–81; Herbert M. Morais, *Deism in Eighteenth Century America* (New York: Columbia University Press, 1934), chap. 4; James D. Hart, *The Popular Book: A History of America's Literary Taste* (Westport, CT: Greenwood Press, 1976), 35–37; Albert Post, *Popular Free Thought in America, 1825–1850* (New York: Columbia University Press, 1943), chap. 1.

28. See Rabinowitz, *Spiritual Self*, 230–31; Paul Mattingly, *The Classless Profession: American Schoolmen in the Nineteenth Century* (New York: New York University Press, 1975), 44.

29. William Ellery Channing, "A Letter to the Rev. Samuel C. Thacher…" (Boston, 1815), http://www.americanunitarian.org/lettertothacher.htm (these words were part of a statement of faith Unitarian ministers had recently adopted); Ballou, *Treatise*, 92, 111–18, 188–91; Bressler, *Universalist Movement*, 27; Allen, *Reason*, 346–47, 352–53; Bellesiles, *Revolutionary Outlaws*, 223; Palmer, *Principles*, 231.

30. William Ellery Channing, "Means of Promoting Christianity," in *Works of William E. Channing*, 5 vols. (Boston: American Unitarian Association, 1872), 5: 333–37; first quotation from 333, second from 334.

31. Bellesiles, *Revolutionary Outlaws*, 223 (quotation), 225–26, 228; Allen, *Reason*, 285–92, 359–63; Palmer, *Principles*, 179.

32. Palmer, *Principles*, 133, 142, 206; quotations in that order; Allen, *Reason*, 466.

33. Kerry S. Walters, *Elihu Palmer's 'Principles of Nature' Text and Commentary* (Wolfeboro, NH: Longwood Academic), 160–61; quotations in that order; Allen, *Reason*, 467–69; first quotation from 467, second from 468; Bellesiles, *Revolutionary Outlaws*, 226, 239, 228; Allen, *Reason*, 188, 222, 226–32.

34. First quotation from Nathan Perkins journal entry, May 26, 1789, 61; second quotation from Ethan Allen to Benjamin Stiles, Nov. 16, 1785, *Quotable Ethan Allen*, 46. See also Uzal Ogden, 1789, in *Quotable Ethan Allen*, 46.

35. See, for instance, Dwight, *Theology Explained and Defended* (1795) and *The Nature and Danger of Infidel Philosophy* (1798). See also Morais, *Deism*, chap. 6; Ralph H. Gabriel, *Religion and Learning at Yale* (New Haven, CT: Yale University Press, 1958), chap. 4.

36. Timothy Dwight, *Triumph of Infidelity* (n.p., 1788), iii; Dwight, *American Museum* 2 (1787): 171, 408–10; Dwight, *Travels in New-York and New-England*, Barbara M. Solomon, ed., 4 vols. (Cambridge, MA: Harvard University Press); Bellesiles, *Revolutionary Outlaws*, 239 (quotation).

37. Thomas Jefferson to Thomas B. Parker, May 15, 1819, The Thomas Jefferson Papers, Library of Congress; Jefferson to William Canby, Sept. 18, 1813, Andrew A. Lipscomb and Albert Ellery Bergh, eds., *The Writings of Thomas Jefferson*, 20 vols. (Washington, DC: Thomas Jefferson

Memorial Association, 1905), 13: 377; Jefferson to King, ibid., 14: 197–98; quotations in that order. Washington, "To the General Assembly of the PCUSA," May 1789, in Dorothy Twohig, ed., *Papers of George Washington, Presidential Series*, 11 vols. (Charlottesville: University Press of Virginia, 1987–2000), 2: 420 (cf. George Washington to Bryan Fairfax, Jan. 20, 1799, John C. Fitzpatrick, ed., *The Writings of George Washington*, 37 vols. [Washington, DC: GPO, 1931–42], 37:94–95); Benjamin Franklin to Ezra Stiles, Mar. 9, 1790, http://www.beliefnet.com/resourcelib/docs/44/Letter_from_Benjamin_Franklin_to_Ezra_Stiles_1.html; John Adams to Adrian van der Kemp, Jan. 30, 1814, Adams Papers (microfilm), reel 95, Library of Congress.

38. Elias Boudinot, *The Age of Revelation* (Philadelphia: Maxwell, 1801), 74; Benjamin Rush, *The Autobiography of Benjamin Rush*, George Corner, ed. (Princeton, NJ: Princeton University Press, 1948), 166; Andrew Jackson, May 29, 1845, statement, quoted in Robert Remini, *Andrew Jackson and the Course of American Freedom, 1822–1832* (New York: Harper & Row, 1981), 519. Cf. Lewis Henry Boutell, *The Life of Roger Sherman* (Chicago: A. C. McClurg, 1896), 272–73.

39. Dwight, *Discourse*, 28 (first quotation); Dwight, "The Disappointments Which Will Take Place at the Day of Judgment," in *Sermons*, 2: 369–77, 389; Nettleton, "The Destruction of Hardened Sinners," in *Sermons*, 63 (first quotation); Nettleton, "The Certain Destruction of All Who Do Not Seek Salvation Rightly," in ibid., 135–36; second quotation from 136, third from 135 (cf. Nettleton, "Regeneration," in ibid., 149; Nettleton, "The Necessity of Regeneration No Matter of Wonder," in ibid., 426; Dwight's series of 20 sermons on regeneration in his *Theology*, 3: 3–295); Dwight, "Long Life Not Desirable," in *Sermons*, 2: 285, 292.

40. McGready, "The New Birth," *Works*, 2: 71 (first quotation), 82 (second), 100, 70 (third), 71 (fourth), 92 (fifth and sixth), 102 (seventh), 106 (eighth); McGready, "Funeral Sermon," 2: 331 (ninth).

41. Payson, *Memoir*, 1: 586 (first quotation); 3: 591 (second); 2: 78 (third); Payson, "The Difficulty of Escaping the Damnation of Hell," in ibid., 2: 203 (fourth); *Memoir*, 1: 500 (fifth); Payson, "Saints in Heaven," 2: 604 (sixth).

42. Charles Finney, *God in You* (New Kensington, PA: Whitaker House, 1998), 24, 30 (first quotation), 31 (second quotation), 32; Charles Finney, *God's Love for a Sinning World* (Grand Rapids, MI: Kregel, 1966), 98; Finney, *God in You*, 32 (third and fourth quotations), 43, 39 (fifth quotation); Finney, *God's Love*, 115, 117 (sixth quotation), 102, 109, Finney, *God in You*, 43 (seventh quotation), 60.

43. Finney, *God's Love*, 102–3, 111–12, 116; quotation from 116.

44. Finney, *Guilt of Sin*, 42.

45. Mark Noll, *A History of Christianity in the United States and Canada* (Grand Rapids, MI: Eerdmans, 1992), 176–77, quotation from 176.

46. See James W. Fraser, *Pedagogue for God's Kingdom: Lyman Beecher and the Second Great Awakening* (Lanham, MD: University Press of America), 69; Lyman Beecher and Asahel Nettleton, *Letters of the Rev. Dr. Beecher and Rev. Mr. Nettleton on the "New Measures" in Conducting Revivals of Religion* (New York: G. & C. Carvill, 1828).

47. John W. Nevin, *The Anxious Bench* (Chambersburg, PA: German Reformed Church, 1844), passim; William McLoughlin, *Billy Graham, Revivalist in a Secular Age* (New York: Ronald Press, 1960), 77. Rabinowitz argues that religious experience and what it meant to be a Christian shifted significantly from 1790 to 1860. These changes include the criterion for being a Christian moving from "well-understood 'objective' standards...toward more interpersonal and personal judgments," less focus on "the cognitive faculties of the mind" and more on "the affective and volitional

faculties," and viewing being a Christian as "a continuous, developmental process by which moral activity and personal devotion" became "routine ways of life" (*Spiritual Self*, 217–18).

48. Bressler, *Universalist Movement*, 7.

49. Robert A. Morley, *Death and the Afterlife* (Minneapolis: Bethany, 1984), 224. On Chauncy, see Charles H. Lippy, *Seasonable Revolutionary: The Mind of Charles Chauncy* (Chicago: Nelson-Hall, 1981); Wright, *Unitarianism*, 185–99. William Gordon, *The Doctrine of Final Universal Salvation Examined and Shewn to Be Unscriptural* (Boston, 1783); Peter Thacher, *That the Punishment of the Finally Impenitent Shall Be Eternal* (Salem, 1783); and Samuel Hopkins, *Inquiry Concerning the Future State of Those Who Die in Their Sins* (Newport, 1783) are all responses to Chauncy's pamphlet *Salvation for All Men* published in 1782.

50. Bressler, *Universalist Movement*, 58.

51. See Ernest Cassara, ed., *Universalism in America: A Documentary History* (Boston: Beacon Press, 1971), 21–22; Thomas Whittemore, *Life of Rev. Hosea Ballou*, 4 vols. (Boston: J. M. Usher, 1854–1855); John C. Adams, *Hosea Ballou and the Gospel Renaissance of the Nineteenth Century* (Boston: Universalist Pub. House, 1903); Ernest Cassara, *Hosea Ballou: The Challenge to Orthodoxy* (Boston: Universalist Pub. House, 1961).

52. Cassara, *Universalism*, 21; Bressler, *Universalist Movement*, 9, 19, 58 (quotation). See also Elmo A. Robinson, *American Universalism: Its Origin, Organization, and Heritage* (New York: Exposition Press, 1970); David Robinson, *The Unitarians and the Universalists* (Westport, CT: Greenwood Press, 1985). Bressler argues that Universalism was especially attractive in New England's subsistence farming communities where "an egalitarian social structure marked by minimal class distinctions" prevailed (21–22).

53. Cassara, *Universalism*, 29–30; Bressler, *Universalist Movement*, 55; Timothy Dwight, *Duration of Future Punishment* (New York: American Tract Society, 183-?), Tract no. 181, 11–12, quotations in that order.

54. Bennet Tyler, *Nettleton and His Labours: The Memoir of Dr. Asahel Nettleton Remodelled in Some Parts by Andrew A. Bonar* (Edinburgh: Banner of Truth Trust, 1975), 399–400, 417.

55. Lemuel Haynes, "Universal Salvation: A Very Ancient Doctrine," in *American Sermons: The Pilgrims to Martin Luther King Jr.* (New York: Library of America, 1999), 533–36. On Haynes, see John Saillant, *Black Puritan, Black Republican: The Life and Thought of Lemuel Haynes, 1753–1833* (New York: Oxford University Press, 2003).

56. See Cassara, *Universalism in America*, 16–17, 26.

57. Bressler, *Universalist Movement*, 37–38. See also Donald H. Meyer, *The Instructed Conscience* (Philadelphia: University of Pennsylvania Press, 1972).

58. The poem was published in the *Theological Magazine*, as quoted in *American Sermons*, 537. I have not been able to determine its author or date of publication. See also Bressler, *Universalist Movement*, 31.

59. Morley, *Death and the Afterlife*, 225–27; Charles G. Finney, *Charles G. Finney: An Autobiography* (New York: Fleming H. Revell, 1876), 48–51; Finney, *God in You*, 56; Garth Rosell and Richard Dupuis, eds., *The Original Memoirs of Charles G. Finney* (Grand Rapids, MI: Zondervan, 2002), 39 (quotation).

60. Finney, *God's Love*, 97; Finney, *Way of Salvation*, 162; Finney, *God's Love*, 98; quotations in that order.

61. Bressler, *Universalist Movement*, 38. See Seth Crowell, *Strictures on the Doctrine of Universal Salvation Wherein the Doctrine Is Disproved on the Principle of the Moral Government of God*

(New York, 1821); Adam Empie, *Remarks on the Distinguishing Doctrine of Modern Universalism* (New York, 1824), 25; Joel Parker, *Lectures on Universalism* (New York, 1841), 164. Bressler called my attention to these sources.

62. McGready, "The New Birth," 2: 70; Stiles, *Henry Channing*, 13; Payson, *Memoir*, 3: 590; Finney, *Guilt of Sin*, 70. Cf. Timothy Dwight, *A Sermon the Death of Mr. Ebenezer Grant Marsh . . .* (Hartford, CT: Hudson and Goodwin, 1804), 17; Dwight, "Day of Judgment," 2: 391.

63. Finney, *God in You*, 61; Nettleton, "Necessity of Regeneration," 426, 431; quotation from 426.

64. For example, Dwight, *Future Punishment*, 10.

65. Palmer, *Principles*, 208–10; first and second quotations from 208, third and fourth from 209, fifth from 210.

66. Dwight, *Future Punishment*, 3–10; first and third quotations from 10, second from 7; Finney, *Way of Salvation*, 273.

67. Finney, *Way of Salvation*, 271–76, 151 (quotation); McGready, "The Doom of the Impenitent," in *Works*, 2: 167.

68. Charles G. Finney, *Principles of Revival*, Louis Gifford Parkhurst, Jr., ed. (Minneapolis: Bethany House, 1987), 155 (quotations); Finney, *Way of Salvation*, 154; McGready, *Works*, 2: 108 (see also Finney, "Why Sinners Hate God," in *Sermons on Important Subjects* [New York: John S. Taylor, 1836], 144–64); Nettleton, "Necessity of Regeneration," 426–29; quotation from 428; McGready, "Divine Authority," 1: 2.

69. Theodore S. Wright, *A Pastoral Letter, Addressed to the Colored Presbyterian Church in the City of New York* (New York: Sears and Martin, 1832), 7–8; Finney, *God's Love*, 113 (first quotation); Finney, *Way of Salvation*, 154–55, 205; second quotation from 155, third from 205, fourth from 207; Finney, *Way of Salvation*, 256 (fifth quotation), 284 (sixth quotation); Dwight, "The Final Interview," in *Sermons*, 2: 338. Cf. Dwight, "Day of Judgment," 2: 394; Dwight, "The Rich Man and Lazarus," in *Sermons*, 2: 298–99.

70. Dwight, *Marsh*, 6; Finney, *Way of Salvation*, 56; Nettleton, "Greater Sinners," 130–31. Cf. Bruce Kuklick, ed., *Joseph Bellamy: Works*, 2 vols. (New York: Garland, 1987), 1: 483–84.

71. McGready, "The New Birth," 2:112, 92; McGready, "The Doom of the Impenitent," 2: 178–80; McGready, "Nature and Tendency of Unbelief," in *Works*, 2: 164–65; first quotation from 112, second from 92, third and sixth from 179, fourth from 178, fifth from 180; Payson, *Memoir*, 3: 594–95 (first quotation); Payson, "The Punishment of the Wicked Dreadful and Interminable," in ibid., 2: 320, 322, 326 (second quotation). See also Payson, "Punishment of the Impenitent Inevitable and Justifiable," in ibid., 2: 434.

72. Samuel Hopkins, "A Dialogue Between a Calvinist and a Semi-Calvinist," in *Works of Samuel Hopkins*, 3 vols., Bruce Kuklick, ed. (New York: Garland, 1987), 143–57; quotation from 147.

73. Hopkins, *Works*, Kuklick, ed., 2: 459–63; first two quotations from 459, third and fourth from 460, fifth from 461, remainder from 463. See also Joseph Conforti, *Samuel Hopkins and the New Divinity Movement: Calvinism, the Congregational Ministry, and Reform in New England between the Great Awakenings* (Grand Rapids, MI: Christian University Press 1981); William K. Breitenbach, "Unregenerate Doings: Selflessness and Selfishness in New Divinity Theology," *American Quarterly* 34 (Winter 1980), 479–502.

74. Noll, *History of Christianity*, 328–29.

CHAPTER 4

1. Mark S. Schantz, *Awaiting the Heavenly Country: The Civil War and America's Culture of Death* (Ithaca, NY: Cornell University Press, 2008), 40.

2. Ann Douglass, "Heaven Our Home: Consolation Literature in the Northern United States, 1830–1880," *American Quarterly* 26 (Dec. 1974), 502.

3. Douglass, "Heaven Our Home," 512; William Branks, *Heaven Our Home: We Have No Saviour But Jesus and No Home But Heaven* (Boston: Roberts Brothers, 1864), 5; Henry Harbaugh, *Heaven: or An Earnest and Scriptural Inquiry into the Abode of the Sainted Dead* (Philadelphia: Lindsay & Blakiston, 1853), 3, 20; Adeline Bayard, *Views of Heaven* (Philadelphia: American Sunday School Union, 1877), 45 (third quotation). See James Moorhead, *World without End: Mainstream American Protestant Visions of the Last Things, 1880–1925* (Bloomington: Indiana University Press, 1999), 58ff. *Harper's Weekly*'s notice of the publication of Branks's book emphasized that to him, heaven "is a home, with a great, and happy and loving family in it" (Dec. 5, 1863, 784).

4. Elizabeth Stuart Phelps, *Chapters from a Life* (Boston: Houghton, Mifflin, 1897), 97; Charles O. Jackson, "Death in American Life," in Jackson, ed., *Passing: The Vision of Death in America* (Westport, CT: Greenwood Press, 1977), 232. See "Annexation of Heaven," *Atlantic Monthly* 53 (Jan. 1884), 139–40.

5. Moorhead, *World without End*, 59–60; quotations in that order.

6. Elizabeth Stuart Phelps, *The Gates Ajar*, Helen Sootin Smith, ed. (Cambridge, MA: Harvard University Press, 1964), 74 (first quotation), xxi (second), 16 (third), 49 (fourth and fifth), 17 (sixth and seventh), 51, 49 (eighth).

7. Phelps, *The Gates Ajar*, 52, 54, 56, 60–61, 65–66; first quotation from 52, second from 54, third from 61, fourth from 60.

8. Phelps, *The Gates Ajar*, 95, 131, 110, 157; first quotation from 95, second from 157.

9. Phelps, *The Gates Ajar*, first three quotations from 130, fourth and fifth from 95, remainder from 129.

10. Smith, "Introduction," vii, xxix, xxxi; quotations in that order.

11. Alister E. McGrath, *A Brief History of Heaven* (Malden, MA: Blackwell, 2003), 152; E. S. Phelps, *Austin Phelps: A Memoir* (New York: Scribner, 1891), 18.

12. Phelps, *Chapters from a Life*, 118–19; quotation from 118; Daniel R. Goodwin, *Christian Eschatology, or, Doctrine of the Last Things* (Philadelphia: McCalla and Stavely, 1885), 37; Mark Twain, "Eruption," in Bernard De Voto, ed., *Selected Short Stories of Mark Twain* (New York, 1940), 247; T. J. Jackson Lears, *No Place of Grace: Antimodernism and the Transformation of American Culture, 1880–1920* (New York: Pantheon Books, 1981), 24.

13. Harbaugh, *Heaven*, 13, 19; first quotation from 13, remainder from 19; Henry Harbaugh, *The Heavenly Recognition; or An Earnest and Scriptural Discussion of the Question, Will We Know Our Friends in Heaven?* (Philadelphia: Lindsay & Blakison, 1856 [1851]) 11th ed., 116–17, quotation from 117; James William Kimball, *Heaven, "My Father's House"* (Boston: John A. Whipple, 1882), 200; James William Kimball, *Heaven* (Boston: Gould and Lincoln, 1857), 266; quotations in that order.

14. James M. MacDonald, *My Father's House, or, The Heaven of the Bible: A Book of Consolation* (Philadelphia: Bradley, 1869), 237–38; William B. Sprague, *Sermons by the Late Rev. Edward D. Griffin, D.D., To Which Is Prefixed a Memoir of His Life,* 2 vols. (New York: John S. Taylor,

1839), 2: 296; Kimball, *Heaven*, 251–53, 167, 224, 262; first quotation from 251, second from 224. Cf. George Cheever, *The Power of the World to Come* (New York: Robert Carter and Brothers, 1853), 225; Kimball, *Heaven*, "*My Father's House*," 197, 188; Gardiner Spring, *Death and Heaven: A Sermon* (New York: John S. Taylor, 1838), 10; Henry Harbaugh, *The Heavenly Home; or, the Employments and Enjoyments of the Saints in Heaven* (Philadelphia: Lindsay & Blakiston, 1853), 279–81, 284, 294, 296.

15. John J. Kerr, *Future Recognition* (Philadelphia: Herman Hooker, 1847), 140–41; first two quotations from 140, third from 141; MacDonald, *My Father's House*, 57, 58, 60, 59, 63; quotations in that order.

16. Rufus W. Clark, *Heaven and Its Scriptural Emblems* (Philadelphia: John E. Potter, 1852), 218–19; first two quotations from 218, third from 219; Branks, *Life in Heaven*, 61; Kimball, *Heaven*, 237 (cf. MacDonald, *My Father's House*, 171, 238); George Wood, *Future Life or Scenes in Another World* (New York: Derby and Jackson, 1858), 32.

17. Schantz, *Awaiting*, 51 (first quotation), 50, (second); MacDonald, *My Father's House*, 115; Sprague, *Griffin*, 436; Clark, *Scriptural Emblems*, 70, 148; quotations in that order; Kerr, *Future Recognition*, 55; Wood, *Future Life*, x. Cf. Branks, *Heaven Our Home*, 81.

18. Sprague, *Griffin*, 1: 439–40, 442 (first quotation from 439), 2: 296 (second quotation), third quotation from 439–40, fourth from 2: 298.

19. Sprague, *Griffin*, 1:438 (quotation), 2: 298; Clark, *Scriptural Emblems*, 85; Sprague, *Griffin*, 2: 443–44; first quotation from 443, second from 444; Kerr, *Future Recognition*, 61, 95, 58; quotations in that order; William Ellery Channing, "A Discourse at the Ordination of the Rev. Frederick A. Farley," in *American Sermons: The Pilgrims to Martin Luther King, Jr.* (New York: Library of America, 1999), 555.

20. Harbaugh, *Heaven*, 278, 281, 283; first quotation from 281, second and third from 283; Harbaugh, *Heavenly Home*, 304–5 (fourth quotation). Branks argued that the saints might know about life on earth by seeing it; God telling them about it; making personal visits to earth; and guardian angels or deceased friends giving them information (*Life in Heaven*, 177–85).

21. Sprague, *Griffin*, 2: 300; Woodbury Davis, *The Beautiful City and the King of Glory* (Philadelphia: Lindsay & Blakiston, 1860), 249, 252; quotations in that order.

22. Wood, *Future Life*, 205, 207, 310–11, 67; first quotation from 207, second from 311, third from 67.

23. Augustus C. Thompson, *The Better Land; or, The Believer's Journey and Future Home* (Boston: Gould and Lincoln, 1854), 203, 206; quotations in that order; Sprague, *Griffin*, 1: 437; Archibald Alexander, *Thoughts on Religious Experience* (Philadelphia: Presbyterian Board of Publ., 1841), 513–14. Cf. Harbaugh, *Heavenly Home*, 305, 314–17, 319.

24. Sprague, *Griffin*, 1: 433–35; first quotation from 434, second from 435 (cf. Harbaugh, *Heaven*, 10); William Branks, *Life in Heaven: There, Faith Is Changed into Sight, and Hope Is Passed into Blissful Fruition* (Boston: Roberts Brothers, 1865), 41–47, 307; quotations from 41; Kerr, *Future Recognition*, 155. See also Timothy Shay Arthur, *Steps toward Heaven: Or, Religion in Common Life; a Series of Lay Sermons for Converts in the Great Awakening* (New York: Derby & Jackson, 1858).

25. Schantz, *Awaiting*, 62.

26. Nancy F. Cott, *The Bonds of Womanhood: "Woman's Sphere" in New England, 1780–1835* (New Haven, CT: Yale University Press, 1977), 63–100, 136; Lears, *No Place of Grace*, 15–16 (quotation from 16); Carroll Smith-Rosenberg, *Disorderly Conduct: Visions of Gender in Victorian*

America (New York: Oxford University Press, 1985), 13, 16, 21, 23, 89, 198–99. See also William E. Bridges, "Family Patterns and Social Values in America, 1825–1875," *American Quarterly* 17 (Spring 1965), 3–11; Kathryn Kish Sklar, *Catherine Beecher: A Study in Domesticity* (New Haven, CT: Yale University Press, 1973); Daniel Scott Smith, "Family Limitation, Sexual Control and Domestic Feminism in Victorian America," in Mary S. Hartman and Lois W. Banner, eds., *Clio's Consciousness Raised: New Perspectives on the History of Women* (New York: Octagon Books, 1976), 119–36; Martha Vicinus, ed., *A Widening Sphere: Changing Roles of Victorian Women* (Bloomington: Indiana University Press, 1977).

27. Colleen McDannell, *The Christian Home in Victorian America, 1840–1900* (Bloomington: Indiana University Press, 1986), 83. See also Timothy Shay Arthur, *Our Homes: Their Cares, and Duties, Joys and Sorrows* (Cincinnati: H. C. Peck and Theo. Bliss, 1856); Catherine Beecher and Harriet Beecher Stowe, *The American Woman's Home* (New York: J. B. Ford, 1869); Henry Boardman, *The Bible in the Family; or, Hints on Domestic Happiness* (Philadelphia: Lippincott, 1854); Samuel Phillips, *The Christian Home* (New York: Gurdon Bill, 1865); Catherine Sedgwick, *Home* (New York: J. Monroe, 1850); John Ware, *Home Life: What It Is, and What It Needs* (Boston: W. V. Spencer, 1866); Mary Teresa Carroll, *Glimpses of Pleasant Homes* (New York: Catholic Publ. Society, 1869).

28. Cheever, *World to Come*, 221; Branks, *Heaven Our Home*, 9, 77, 87, 89–90; first quotation from 9, second from 77, third from 87; J. M. Killen, *Our Companions in Glory: or, Society in Heaven Contemplated* (New York: Anson D. F. Randolph, 1862), 124, 184; quotations in that order; Harbaugh, *Heavenly Home*, 21–22. Cf. Sprague, *Griffin*, 2: 294–95; Branks, *Heaven Our Home*, 83, 81; McDannell, *Christian Home*, 83. See Joseph Thompson and Charles H. Spurgeon, *Home Worship...For Daily Use in Family and Private Devotions* (New York: A. C. Armstrong, 1883), 822.

29. J. Duncan, *The Mourner's Friend; or, Recognition of Friends in Heaven* (Lowell, MA: N. L. Dayton, 1850), 35; F. W. P. Greenwood, *Sermons of Consolation* (Boston: William D. Ticknor, 1842), 209. See *James Freeman Clark's Autobiography, Diary and Correspondence*, Edward Everett Hale, ed. (Boston: Houghton, Mifflin, 1891), 410; James Freeman Clark, *Manual of Unitarian Belief*, 13th ed. (Boston: Unitarian Sunday-School Society, 1889), 59–60 (James Farrell, *Inventing the American Way of Death, 1830–1920* [Philadelphia: Temple University Press, 1980], 29, called my attention to these sources).

30. Kimball, *Heaven*, 231, 234; Kimball, *"My Father's House,"* 204; MacDonald, *My Father's House*, 238, 252; quotation from 238; Sprague, *Griffin*, 2: 299.

31. See Stephanie McCurry, *Masters of Small Worlds: Yeoman Households, Gender Relations, and the Political Culture of the Antebellum South Carolina Low Country* (New York: Oxford University Press, 1995), 171–76; Jean E. Friedman, *The Enclosed Garden: Women and Community in the Evangelical South, 1830–1900* (Chapel Hill: University of North Carolina Press, 1985), 11, 49; Ann E. Loveland, *Southern Evangelicals and the Social Order, 1800–1860* (Baton Rouge, Louisiana State University Press, 1980), 7; Elizabeth Finisher to Nancy Cowen, Aug. 23, 1846, Nancy H. Cowan Papers, Perkins Library, Duke University, quoted in McCurry, *Masters*, 174.

32. Sarah Gould, comp., *The Guardian Angels, or, Friends in Heaven* (Boston: Higgins and Bradley, 1857), 214; Harriet Beecher Stowe, *Uncle Tom's Cabin*, Elizabeth Emmons, ed. (New York: Norton Critical Edition, 1994), 254ff.

33. Sprague, *Griffin*, 1: 436, 2: 299; first quotation from 436, second and third from 299; Thompson, *Better Land*, 86; Harbaugh, *Heavenly Recognition*, 129–30, 194; first quotation from

129, remainder from 130; J. M. Killen, *Our Friends in Heaven: or, The Mutual Recognition of the Redeemed in Glory Demonstrated* (Philadelphia: Presbyterian Board of Publ., 1855), 123; Gould, comp., *Guardian Angels*, 214.

34. Schantz, *Awaiting*, 61; Branks, *Heaven Our Home*, 149; Thompson, *Better Land*, 73, 77; quotations in that order. Cf. Killen, *Our Companions*, 22.

35. Clark, *Scriptural Emblems*, 107; Thompson, *Better Land*, 78, 80–81; first quotation from 80, second from 81 (cf. Branks, *Heaven Our Home*, 157); Harbaugh, *Heavenly Recognition*, 126, 134–35, 137, 149, 118, 124; quotations from 149; Sharp, *Recognition of Friends*, 10; Duncan, *Mourner's Friend*, 11.

36. Clark, *Scriptural Emblems*, 104–5; Branks, *Heaven Our Home*, 154; Thompson, *Better Land*, 85; Killen, *Our Companions*, 20–21, 23, quotation from 23. Cf. William Mountford, *Euthanasy; or Happy Talk towards the End of Life* (New York: D. Appleton, 1849), 462; Daniel Sharp, *Recognition of Friends in Heaven: A Discourse* (Boston: John Putnam, 1844), 7. Schantz, *Awaiting*, called my attention to the Mountford, Sharp, Duncan, and Greenwood sources in this section.

37. Killen, *Our Companions*, 24–26. The biblical descriptions of the last judgment and various passages that taught people are accountable to God, Killen alleged, all imply the "continued exercise of memory" (26); Kerr, *Future Recognition*, 83. Cf. Harbaugh, *Heavenly Recognition*, 182.

38. Killen, *Our Companions*, 28–30; first two quotations from 28, third from 29; Harbaugh, *Heavenly Recognition*, 119–22; quotation from 120.

39. Killen, *Our Companions*, 107, 115, 108, 115; quotation from 115, Harbaugh, *Heavenly Recognition*, 178.

40. Harbaugh, *Heavenly Recognition*, 239, 233, 235–36; first quotation from 239, second from 235.

41. Harbaugh, *Heavenly Recognition*, 244; Killen, *Our Companions*, 157; Harbaugh, *Heavenly Recognition*, 245 (first quotation), 241 (second and third quotations).

42. Harbaugh, *Heavenly Recognition*, 243, 246–47; quotations in that order.

43. Killen, *Our Companions*, 165–66, 168; first quotation from 165, second from 166, third from 168; Harbaugh, *Heavenly Recognition*, 253, 262, 264–66, 268; first quotation from 253, second and third from 265, fourth from 268. Cf. MacDonald, *My Father's House,* 253.

44. Harbaugh, *Heavenly Recognition*, 274, 276; quotations in that order; Thompson, *Better Land*, 84. Cf. Branks, *Heaven Our Home*, 177, 308; Killen, *Our Companions*, 184.

45. Harbaugh, *Heavenly Recognition*, 277, 282, 285–87, 280; first quotation from 285, second from 280.

46. Harbaugh, *Heavenly Home*, 345, 350; first two quotations from 345, third from 350; Cheever, *World to Come*, 253, 250, 251; quotations in that order. For example, see Theodore Cuyler, *The Empty Crib: A Memorial of Little Georgie. With Words of Consolation for Bereaved Parents* (New York: R. Carter and Brothers, 1869); Nehemiah Adams, *Agnes and the Key of Her Little Coffin* (Boston: S. K. Whipple, 1857). Later examples include Theodore Cuyler, *God's Light on Dark Clouds* (New York: Baker and Taylor, 1882) and Cuyler, *Beulah-Land: or Words of Cheer for Christian Pilgrims* (New York: American Tract Society, 1896).

47. Harbaugh, *Heavenly Home*, 351, 357, 352, 353; first quotation from 351, second from 357, third from 352; William Holcombe, *Our Children in Heaven* (Philadelphia: J. B. Lippincott, 1869), 98, 103–4; first quotation from 98, second from 104. Cf. William Simonds, *Our Little Ones in Heaven* (Boston: Gould & Lincoln, 1858); Augustus C. Thompson, *Gathered Lilies; or, Little*

Children in Heaven. (Boston: Gould & Lincoln, 1858). He argued that those dying as children remained children in heaven: "Children in heaven…what a goodly throng!…(33). God took them "for the sake of his garden above" (39) and for their own sakes (42). He sheltered and placed them in "richer soil" (42). Recognizing this could give bereaved parents balm for their stricken hearts (53). Cf. also William Edward Schenck, ed., *Children in Heaven or, the Infant Dead Redeemed by the Blood of Jesus* (Philadelphia: Presbyterian Board of Publ., 1865), a compilation of short essays by three dozen authors on various topics related to this subject.

48. Sean A. Scott, "Earth Has No Sorrow That Heaven Cannot Cure: Northern Civilian Perspectives on Death and Eternity during the Civil War," *Journal of Social History* 41 (Summer 2008), 854–55; first quotation from 854, second and third from 855. Indiana Quaker quotation: Anna Starr to William Starr, Oct. 5, 1861, William C. Starr Papers, Indiana Historical Society, Indianapolis; "others regarded" quotation: M. Buffington to Schuyler and Lucia Hendryx, Jan. 25, 1865, Schuyler V. R. Hendryx Papers, Minnesota Historical Society, St. Paul; a mother in Flint: N. Lounsbury to George and Elmina Lounsbury, Feb. 16, 1864, George W. Lounsbury Papers, IHS; all as cited by Scott, "Earth Has No Sorrow," 855. Cf. Sylvia D. Hoffert, " 'A Very Peculiar Sorrow': Attitudes toward Infant Death in the Urban Northeast, 1800–1860," *American Quarterly* 39 (Winter 1987), 605–7, 611–13, and Hoffert, *Private Matters: American Attitudes toward Childbearing and Infant Nurture in the Urban North, 1800–1860* (Urbana: University of Illinois Press, 1989), 177–80, 183–87. She explains why many parents in New England accepted the idea that all those dying in infancy gained admission to heaven.

49. Sprague, *Griffin*, 1: 445; Kimball, *Heaven*, 261 (first quotation); Kimball, *Heaven*, "My Father's House," 12, 15, 23, 212 (second quotation), 217.

50. Kimball, *Heaven*, 247.

51. Sprague, *Griffin*, 1: 459, 450, 451, 452, 456; first quotation from 459, second from 450, third from 452; Harbaugh, *Heaven*, 77–78; quotations from 77; MacDonald, *My Father's House*, 200. Both pre- and postmillennialists "confused the millennial period with the heavenly afterlife" (Douglas, "Heaven Our Home," 511). Both groups increasingly stressed that "this earth, purified and transfigured, would be the locus of the millennium." Premillennialist examples include John Lillie, *The Perpetuity of the Earth: A Discourse Preached Before the Premillennial Advent Association* (New York, n.p., 1842); Henry F. Hill, *The Saint's Inheritance; or the World to Come* (Boston: G. P. Carter, 1873 [1852]); and Anna Silliman, *The World Jubilee* (New York: M. W. Dodd, 1856). Consequently, "the millennial debate became part of a larger discussion over the nature of heaven: kingdom or home?" (Douglas, "Heaven Our Home," 512).

52. Kimball, *Heaven*, 15–16. Many Americans struggled with the traditional view that unless individuals displayed overt signs of accepting Christ as their savior, there was no basis for believing they had gone to heaven. Mary Livermore, for example, "could not reconcile her sister's [Rachel's] death at age fifteen] "with her parents' belief that an individual who had not shown obvious signs of receiving God's grace might not go to heaven." She protested that at Rachel's funeral "not one word was uttered of assurance that…she had entered into a larger, nobler, and happier life." See Mary Livermore, *The Story of My Life*, (Hartford, CT, A.D. Worthington, 1897), 134–46; Mary A. Livermore, "Two Years on a Virginia Plantation," *Ladies Repository* 41 (Feb. 1869), 129 (second quotation); Wendy Hamand Venet, "The Emergence of a Suffragist: Mary Livermore, Civil War Activism, and the Moral Power of Women," *Civil War History* 48.2 (2002), 147 (first quotation).

53. Clark, *Scriptural Emblems*, 116–17 (quotation); Cheever, *World to Come*, 241. Kimball, *Heaven*, 16, 246–47, first quotations from 246, second from 247.

54. Lyman Beecher, *Autobiography, Correspondence, Etc. of Lyman Beecher*, 2 vols., Charles Beecher, ed. (New York: Harper and Brothers, 1864), 1: 292–300; Schantz, *Awaiting*, 25–26; Louisa May Alcott, *Little Women* (Boston: University Press, 1880 [1868]), 498–501; William Sprague, *Letters on Practical Subjects to a Daughter* (New York: D. Appleton, 1834), 275–77. Farrell, *Inventing*, 37, 40, 232, called my attention to Beecher and Sprague. See also *The Faithful Mother's Reward: Narrative of the Conversion and Happy Death of J.P.B.* (Philadelphia: Presbyterian Board of Publ., 1853); Dickson D. Bruce, Jr., "Death as Testimony in the Old South," *Southern Humanities Review* 12 (Spring 1978), 123–32; Christopher Crocker, "The Southern Way of Death," in Kenneth Moreland, ed., *The Not So Solid South* (Athens: University of Georgia Press, 1971), 114–29.

55. Sprague, *Griffin*, 1: 465, 589, 592–93, 596; first quotation from 465, second from 589, third and fourth from 592, fifth from 466. Cf. Cheever, *World to Come*, 263; H. H. Dobney, George Storrs, and Vincent L. Dill, *Endless Life Only in Christ: The Scripture Doctrine of Future Punishment: An Argument in Two Parts* (New York: Bible Examiner, 1856).

CHAPTER 5

1. See Winthrop D. Jordan, *The White Man's Burden: Historical Origins of Racism in the United States* (New York: Oxford University Press, 1974), 87–98; Thomas S. Kidd, *The Great Awakening: The Roots of Evangelical Christianity in Colonial America* (New Haven, CT: Yale University Press, 2007), 213–32; David Brion Davis, *The Problem of Slavery in Western Culture* (Ithaca, NY: Cornell University Press, 1966), 165–66, 206–22. See Stephanie McCurry, *Masters of Small Worlds: Yeoman Households, Gender Relations, and the Political Culture of the Antebellum South Carolina Low Country* (New York: Oxford University Press, 1995), 174–75.

2. Timothy L. Smith, "Slavery and Theology: The Emergence of Black Christian Consciousness in Nineteenth-Century America," *Church History* 41 (Dec. 1972), 502. For the content of white preaching and teaching directed toward slaves, see Charles C. Jones, *The Religious Instruction of the Negroes in the United States* (Savannah, GA: John M. Cooper, 1842), 256–60; and Norman R. Yetman, *Life under "The Peculiar Institution"; Selections from the Slave Narrative Collection* (New York: Holt, Rinehart and Winston, 1970), 91–92, 117, 151, 227, as identified by Smith.

3. Norrece T. Jones, Jr., "Slave Religion in South Carolina: A Heaven in Hell?" *Southern Studies* 1 (Spring 1990), 7; Thomas Webber, *Deep Like the Rivers: Education in the Slave Quarter Community, 1831–1865* (New York: W. W. Norton, 1978), 48; Alexander Glennie, *Sermons Preached on Plantations to Congregations of Slaves* (Freeport, NY: Books for Libraries, 1971 [1844]), 4–5, 22–26 (see also Charles Joyner, *Down by the Riverside: A South Carolina Slave Community* [Urbana: University of Illinois Press, 1984], 156; Lewis V. Baldwin, "'A Home in Dat Rock': Afro-American Folk Sources and Slave Visions of Heaven and Hell," *Journal of Religious Thought* 41: 1 [1984], 39); Jones, *Religious Instruction*, 19; Janet Duitsman Cornelius, *Slave Missions and the Black Church in the Antebellum South* (Columbia: University of South Carolina Press, 1999), 129 (second quotation). See also Charles C. Jones, *A Catechism of Scripture, Doctrine and Practice...for the Oral Instruction of Colored Persons* (Savannah, GA: J. M. Cooper, 1837); and William Capers, *Catechism for Little Children and for Use on the Missions to the Slaves in South Carolina* (Charleston, SC: J. S. Burges, 1833); *Proceedings of the Meeting in Charleston, S.C., May*

13–15, 1845, on the Religious Instruction of the Negroes, Together with the Report of the Committee and the Address to the Public (Charleston, SC: B. Jenkins, 1845).

4. Jones, "Slave Religion," 7.

5. Baldwin, "Home," 40.

6. Daniel Baker, *A Series of Revival Sermons* (Georgia: n.p., 1847), 185–86; William Mumford Baker, *The Life and Labours of Reverend Daniel Baker…* (Louisville, KY: Lost Cause Press, 1961 [1858]), 457, 474.

7. Quoted in Marie Jenkins Schwartz, *Born in Bondage: Growing Up Enslaved in the Antebellum South* (Cambridge, MA: Harvard University Press, 2000), 121.

8. Quoted in John Cade, "Out of the Mouths of Ex-Slaves," *Journal of Negro History*, 20: 3 (1935), 329.

9. Baldwin, "Home," 40 (for an example, see Polly Cancor in George P. Rawick, ed., *The American Slave, A Composite Autobiography, Mississippi Narratives*, 31 vols., Supplement, no. 1, vol. 7, pt. 2 [Westport, CT: Greenwood Press, 1977], 344–45; Baldwin called my attention to the Cade and Cancor sources); Henry Box Brown, *Narrative of Henry Box Brown* (Boston: Brown and Stearns, 1849), 45. See also Bethany Veney, *The Narrative of Bethany Veney, a Slave Woman* (Worcester, MA: Press of George H. Ellis, 1889), 7–8 (my attention was called to these sources by Webber, *Deep*, 48); Ted Ownby, "Patriarchy in the World Where There Is No Parting? Power Relations in the Confederate Heaven," in Catherine Clinton, ed., *Southern Families at War: Loyalty and Conflict in the Civil War South* (New York: Oxford University Press, 2000), 237–38, 240; quotation from 240.

10. U. B. Phillips, *American Negro Slavery: A Survey of the Supply, Employment, and Control of Negro Labor as Determined by the Plantation Regime* (Baton Rouge: Louisiana State University Press, 1918), 314; Orlando Patterson, *Slavery and Social Death: A Comparative Study* (Cambridge, MA: Harvard University Press, 1982), 73–74 (my attention was called to these sources by Young, "Spirituality and Socialization," 184–85); Lawrence W. Levine, *Black Culture and Black Consciousness: Afro-American Folk Thought from Slavery to Freedom* (Oxford, UK: Oxford University Press, 1978), 44; James H. Cone, *The Spirituals and the Blues: An Interpretation* (New York: Seabury Press), 86–87, 101.

11. Baldwin, "Home," 42; Levine, *Black Culture*, 123.

12. Albert J. Raboteau, *A Fire in the Bones: Reflections on African-American Religious History* (Boston: Beacon Press), 187.

13. Smith, "Slavery and Theology," 510–11. Smith is especially critical of Benjamin May, *The Negro's God as Reflected in His Literature* (Boston, 1938). See W. E. B. DuBois, *The Souls of Black Folk* (New York: Fawcett, 1961), 183; Sterling Stuckey, "Through the Prism of Folklore: The Black Ethos in Slavery," *Massachusetts Review* 9 (Summer 1968); Levine, *Black Culture*, 21–55; Eugene Genovese, *Roll, Jordan, Roll* (New York: Pantheon Books, 1972), 161–82.

14. Baldwin, "Home," 38, 42; quotations in that order.

15. Baldwin, "Home," 56; David R. Roediger, "And Die in Dixie: Funerals, Death, & Heaven in the Slave Community 1700–1865," *Massachusetts Review* 22 (Spring 1981), 181. See also Sterling Brown, "Negro Folk Expression: Spirituals, Seculars, Ballads and Work Songs," in August Meier and Elliot Rudwick, eds., *The Making of Black America*, 2 vols. (New York: Atheneum, 1974), 2: 213. For songs that focus on heaven, see M. F. Armstrong, Helen W. Ludlow, and Thomas P. Fenner, *Hampton and Its Students, with Fifty Cabin and Plantation Songs…* (New York: G. P. Putnam, 1874), 173–255.

16. Genovese, *Roll, Jordan*, 252; Julius Lester, *To Be a Slave* (New York: Dial Press, 1968), 79.

17. Raboteau, *Fire*, 187.

18. Jones, "Slave Religion," 17; Anderson Edwards in Rawick, *American Slave*, part II, 9; Joyner, *Riverside* 167; Cone, *Spirituals*, 88–90; Frederick Douglass, *Life and Times of Frederick Douglass* (New York: Crowell Collier, 1962 [1892]), 159–60; Sarah Bradford, *Harriet Tubman: The Moses of Her People* (New York: Corinth Books, 1961 [1886]), 27–28; Howard Thurman, *The Negro Spiritual Speaks of Life and Death* (New York: Harper and Brothers, 1947), 17, 27–28, 38, 51; Genovese, *Roll, Jordan*, 248–49, 252; quotation from 248. Webber, *Deep*, 143.

19. Mechal Sobel, *The World They Made Together: Black and White Values in Eighteenth-Century Virginia* (Princeton, NJ: Princeton University Press, 1989), 174; Roediger, "Die in Dixie," 183; Baldwin, "Home," 39; L. Alex Swan, *Survival and Progress: The Afro-American Experience* (Westport, CT: Greenwood Press, 1981); Mechal Sobel, *Trabelin' On: The Slave Journey to an Afro-Baptist Faith* (Westport, CT: Greenwood Press, 1979); Genovese, *Roll, Jordan*, 247–48. West African influence was especially evident in black funeral and burial practices. Most slaves "believed that the spirit of the dead had to be comforted, protected, and sustained in its journey to the afterlife" (Baldwin, "Home," 50). See also Sobel, *World*, 174, 218; Olli Alho, *The Religion of the Slaves: A Study of the Religious Tradition and Behaviour of Plantation Slaves in the United States, 1830–1865* (Helsinki: Academia Scientiarum Fennica, 1976), 159–62; Albert Raboteau, *Slave Religion: The "Invisible Institution" in the Antebellum South* (New York: Oxford University Press, 1978), 230–31; Newbell N. Puckett, *Folk Beliefs of the Southern Negro* (London: H. Milford, 1926), 92–94.

20. Charles Ball, *Fifty Years in Chains* (New York: Dover, 1970 [1837]), 219; Roediger, "Die in Dixie," 178; Sobel, *World*, 200–1; Sobel, *Trabelin' On*, 145, 234, 247; Rawick, *American Slave*, 18: 149–50; Joana T. Isom in Rawick, ed., *Mississippi Narratives*, Supplement, no. 1, vol. 8, pt. 3, 1099; Sterling Stuckey, "Through the Prism of Folklore: The Black Ethos in Slavery," in Eric Foner, ed., *America's Black Past: A Reader in Afro-American History* (New York: Harper & Row, 1970), 102; William E. Hatcher, *John Jasper, The Unmatched Negro Philosopher and Preacher* (New York: Fleming H. Revell, 1908), 180; quotation from Baldwin, "Home," 44.

21. William F. Allen, *Slave Songs of the United States* (New York: A. Simpson, 1867), 46. See also Thomas P. Fenner, *Religious Folk Songs as Sung on the Plantation* (Hampton, VA: Institute Press, 1909), 8, 63–65; J. B. T. Marsh, *Jubilee Singers and Their Songs* (Mineola, NY: Dover, 2003), 240–41; Thomas Wentworth Higginson, *Army Life in a Black Regiment* (East Lansing: Michigan State University Press, 1960), 205; William F. Allen et al., *Slave Songs: The Complete 1867 Collection of Slave Songs* (Milwaukee: H. Leonard, 1965), 46, 53; Natalie Curtis Burlin, *Negro Folk-Songs*, 4 vols. (New York: G. Schirmer, 1918), 1: 37–42.

22. Cone, *Spirituals*, 99–101; Baldwin, "Home," 48; quotations from Negro spirituals. See also William H. Holcombe, "Sketches of Plantation Life," *Knickerbocker Magazine* 57 (June 1861), 631.

23. Baldwin, "Home," 47. See also Genovese, *Roll, Jordan*, 199; Jacob Stroyer, *Sketches of My Life in the South* (Salem, MA: Newcombe and Gauss, 1898), 41; Webber, *Deep*, 89.

24. DuBois, *Souls*, 183; Webber, *Deep*, 87.

25. Smith, "Slavery and Theology," 503; Cone, *Spirituals*, 102; Rawick, *American Slave*, 16: 49; Escott, *Slavery Remembered*, 112; Genovese, *Roll, Jordan*, 207.

26. Cone, *Spirituals*, 91–93; Hammon, *Address*, 120.

27. Genovese, *Roll, Jordan*, 250; Escott, *Slavery Remembered*, 115; Smith, "Slavery and Theology," 512.

28. Cone, *Spirituals*, 92–95; Baldwin, "Home," 56 (quotation); Roediger, "Die in Dixie," 182; Thurman, *Deep River,* 113.

29. Cornelius, *Slave Missions*, 20–21 (quotation from 21); Robert Calhoon, *Evangelicals and Conservatives in the Early South, 1740–1861* (Columbia: University of South Carolina Press, 1988), 135; Norrece T. Jones Jr., *Born a Child of Freedom, Yet a Slave: Mechanism of Control and Strategies of Resistance in Antebellum South Carolina* (Middletown, CT: Wesleyan University Press, 1990), 157; Webber, *Deep*, 86 (second quotation).

30. Baldwin, "Home," 39, 50; Webber, *Deep*, 89 (quotation). See also John S. Mbiti, *Death and the Hereafter in the Light of Christianity and African Religion* (Kampala, Uganda: Makerere University, 1973), 11–19.

31. Baldwin, "Home," 53, 55; quotation from 55.

32. Quoted in Raboteau, *Slave Religion*, 291.

33. Sobel, *World*, 214, 226 (e.g., Stith Mead, *Letterbook, 1792–1795*, June 12, 1793, 24, Virginia Historical Society; *[An] Authentic Account of the Conversion and Experience of a Negro* [n.p., 1812], 3); Jupiter Hammon, *An Address to the Negroes of the State of New York* (1787), in William Dudley, ed., *Slavery: Opposing Viewpoints* (San Diego: Greenhaven Press, 1992), 120 (first quotation); Ball, *Fifty Years*, 220–22. See also Mia Bay, *The White Image in the Black Mind: African-American Ideas about White People* (New York: Oxford University Press, 2000), 182; Levine, *Black Culture*, 34.

34. Douglass, *Life and Times*, 41 (first quotation); Webber, *Deep*, 85 (second quotation); Garnet quoted in Smith, "Slavery and Theology," 505–6. See Henry H. Garnet, *An Address to the Slaves of the United States of America ...* (New York: Arno Press, 1969), 92–94. Cf. Frederick Douglass, *My Bondage and My Freedom* (New York: Auburn, 1855), 241–46, 423; Richard M. Dorson, *American Negro Folktales* (Greenwich, CT: Fawcett, 1967), 160; Brown, *Narrative*, 18–19.

35. Webber, *Deep*, 85; for an example, see a letter to the *Southern Workman* 26 (1897), 210, summarizing the view of slaves before the Civil War, as cited by Levine, *Black Culture*, 35.

36. Ball, *Fifty Years*, 136 (first quotation), 220–21 (second and third quotations); Jones, "Slave Religion," 8; Roediger, "Die in Dixie," 180.

37. Levi J. Coppin, *Unwritten History* (Philadelphia: A.M.E. Book Concern, 1919), 54; Baldwin, "Home," 44. See Genovese, *Roll, Jordan*, 251ff.

38. Baldwin, "Home," 52.

39. Phillip Shaw Paludan, "Religion and the American Civil War," in Randall M. Miller, Harry S. Stout, and Charles Reagan Wilson, eds., *Religion and the American Civil War* (New York: Oxford University Press, 1998), 30, claims that ninety-four books were published about heaven in the ten years following the war.

40. Drew Gilpin Faust, "Christian Soldiers: The Meaning of Revivalism in the Confederate Army," *Journal of Southern History* 53 (Feb. 1987), 83.

41. Faust, "Christian Soldiers," 64; Sidney J. Romero, *Religion in the Rebel Ranks* (Lanham, MD: University Press of America, 1983), 129; James I. Robertson, Jr., *Soldiers Blue and Grey* (Columbia: University of South Carolina Press, 1989), 172.

42. Robertson, *Soldiers*, 172; Gardiner H. Shattuck *A Shield and Hiding Place: The Religious Life of the Civil War Armies* (Macon, GA: Mercer University Press, 1987), 14.

43. Shattuck, *Shield*, 14–17; quotation from 15. See Gilbert Haven, "The Church and the Negro," 1863, in *National Sermons: Sermons, Speeches and Letters on Slavery and Its War*…(Boston: Lee and Shepard, 1869), 367; Cyrus Bartol, *The Remission by Blood: A Tribute to Our Soldiers and the Sword*…(Boston: Walker, Wise, 1862) 4–5, 8–9; Horace Bushnell, *Reverses Needed: A Discourse Delivered on the Sunday after the Disaster of Bull Run* (Hartford, CT: L. E. Hunt, 1861). See also Harry S. Stout, *Upon the Altar of the Nation: A Moral History of the Civil War* (New York: Penguin Books, 2006), 42–43 and passim.

44. Shattuck, *Shield*, 15; Ernest Lee Tuveson, *Redeemer Nation: The Idea of America's Millennial Role* (Chicago: University of Chicago Press, 1968) 191, 202; James H. Moorhead, *American Apocalypse: Yankee Protestants and the Civil War, 1860–1869* (New Haven, CT: Yale University Press, 1978), 56–65.

45. Gerald F. Linderman, *Embattled Courage: The Experience of Combat in the American Civil War* (New York: Free Press, 1987), 10, 107–8.

46. Shattuck, *Shield*, 17. See also Samuel J. Watson, "Religion and Combat Motivation in the Confederate Armies," *Journal of Military History* 58 (Jan. 1994), 47–53.

47. It was the nation's most gruesome war in terms of the number of soldiers who died, the percentage of participants who were killed, the percentage of deaths in relationship to the total national population, and the number of injuries in proportion to combatants. Drew Gilpin Faust, "The Civil War Soldier and the Art of Dying," *Journal of Southern History* 67 (Feb. 2001), 1 (first quotation), 2 (second), 5–6 (third); Mark S. Schantz, *Awaiting the Heavenly Country: The Civil War and America's Culture of Death* (Ithaca, NY: Cornell University Press, 2008), 15. See also Nicholas Marshall, "'In the Midst of Life We Are in Death': Affliction and Religion in Antebellum New York," in Nancy Isenberg and Andrew Burstein, eds., *Mortal Remains: Death in Early America* (Philadelphia: University of Pennsylvania Press, 2003), 176–86.

48. Faust, "Art of Dying," 6–8, 10, 12–14, 16, 22, 32; first quotation from 14, second from 16; Schantz, *Awaiting*, 18. For examples of dying soldiers' professions of faith, see James B. Rogers, *War Pictures: Experiences and Observations of a Chaplain in the U.S. Army, in the War of the Southern Rebellion* (Chicago: Church & Goodman, 1863), 182; Frank Perry to J. Buchannon, Sept. 21, 1862, in Mills Lane, ed., *Dear Mother: Don't Grieve About Me. If I Get Killed, I'll Only Be Dead: Letters from Georgia Soldiers in the Civil War* (Savannah, GA: Library of Georgia, 1990), 189, all as cited by Faust, 22–26. She provides examples of obituaries from the *Daily South Carolinian* and the *Richmond Daily Whig*. For other examples, see Robert Lewis Dabney, *A Memorial of Lieut. Colonel John T. Thornton of the Third Virginia Cavalry, C.S.A.* (Richmond, VA: Presbyterian Committee of Publ., 1864), 6, 8; Sean A. Scott, "'Earth Has No Sorrow That Heaven Cannot Cure': Northern Civilian Perspectives on Death and Eternity During the Civil War," *Journal of Social History* 41 (Summer 2008), 850. In "Healing the Nation: Condolence and Correspondence in Civil War Hospitals," *Proteus* 17:2 (2000): 34–38, Jane E. Schultz discussed the role nurses played in writing condolence letters.

49. Faust, "Art of Dying," 33–34; quotation from 33. In many cases, however, grieving Americans gained no solace even from this substitute form of the Good Death. Based on her postwar investigation, Clara Barton concluded that 45 percent of the 315,555 Northern soldier graves were marked "unknown" and an additional 43,973 soldiers who died had no known graves. See Ishbel Ross, *Angel of the Battlefield: The Life of Clara Barton* (New York: Harper, 1956), 87.

50. Schantz, *Awaiting*, 2–3, 38; first and second quotations from 2, third and fourth from 38. For an example of heaven as a material place, see *Views of Heaven* (Philadelphia: American Sunday School Union, 1877). For sources that either confirm or challenge this view, see Marshall, "In the Midst of Life," 176–80; James M. McPherson, *For Cause and Comrades: Why Men Fought in the Civil War* (New York: Oxford University Press, 1997), 62–76; Steven E. Woodworth, *While God Is Marching On: The Religious World of Civil War Soldiers* (Lawrence: University Press of Kansas, 2001), 40–51; Scott, "Earth Has No Sorrow," 843–66; Lewis O. Saum, *The Popular Mood of Pre-Civil War America* (Westport, CT: Greenwood Press, 1980), 78–104; James J. Farrell, *Inventing the American Way of Death, 1830–1920* (Philadelphia: Temple University Press, 1980), 4–7, 44–98; Robert V. Wells, *Facing the "King of Terrors": Death and Society in an American Community, 1750–1990* (New York: Cambridge University Press, 2000), 126–33, 137–38, 148–68; James H. Moorhead, *World Without End: Mainstream American Protestant Visions of the Last Things, 1880–1925* (Bloomington: Indiana University Press, 1999), 17, 58–61; and Mary Louise Kete, *Sentimental Collaborations: Mourning and Middle-Class Identity in Nineteenth-Century America* (Durham, NC: Duke University Press, 2000), 6–7, 34–37, 66–77, 94–105.

51. Schantz, *Awaiting*, 68–69, 108–11; first quotation from 68, second from 69; Gary Laderman, *The Sacred Remains: American Attitudes toward Death, 1799–1883* (New Haven, CT: Yale University Press, 1996), 132; McPherson, *For Cause*, 76–178. See also Alice Fahs, *The Imagined Civil War: Popular Literature of the North and South 1861–1865* (Chapel Hill: University of North Carolina Press, 2001), 94; Schantz, *Awaiting*, 108–11.

52. Watson, "Combat Motivation," 31–32 (see also Faust, "Christian Soldiers," 75); Drew Gilpin Faust, *This Republic of Suffering: Death and the American Civil War* (New York: Alfred A. Knopf, 2008), 175. For example, W. H. Christian, *The Importance of a Soldier Becoming a Christian* (Richmond, VA: Soldiers' Track Association, 1863?), 3.

53. Linderman, *Embattled Courage*, 8–9. Linderman cites the following sources to support his points: Jesse W. Reid, *History of the Fourth Regiment of S. C. Volunteers* (Greenville, SC: Shannon, 1892), 24; William T. Poague, *Gunner with Stonewall* (Jackson, TN: McCowat-Mercer Press, 1957), 66; James B. Sheeran, *Confederate Chaplain: A War Journal*, Joseph T. Durkin, ed. (Milwaukee: Bruce, 1960), 6; Robert J. Burdette, *The Drums of the 47th* (Indianapolis: Bobbs-Merrill, 1914), 47; and George C. Eggleston, *A Rebel's Recollections* (Cambridge, MA: Riverside Press, 1875), 197. See also "For the Soldier's Paper," *Soldier's Paper*, Aug. 15, 1863, 3; "The Dying Soldier," *Soldier's Paper*, Sept. 1, 1863, 1.

54. Woodworth, *Marching*, 249; Peter S. Carmichael, "Christian Warriors," *Columbiad* 3 (Summer 1999): 92; McPherson, *For Cause*, 76.

55. Ro. Ryland, "A Letter to a Son in a Camp," July 17, 1861, in J. William Jones, *Christ in the Camp, or, Religion in Lee's Army* (Richmond: B. F. Johnson, 1887), 28. Jones's book includes his own accounts of events he witnessed and the reports of others that he collected.

56. Jones, *Camp*, 19.

57. For Southern examples, see Jones, *Camp*, 60–64, 102–3, 119, 402, 406–10, 418, and William W. Bennett, *A Narrative of the Great Revival Which Prevailed in the Southern Armies...* (Harrisonburg, VA: Sprinkle, 1989 [1876]), 146, 162–63, 170. For Northern examples, see Richard N. Ellis, ed., "The Civil War Letters of an Iowa Family," *Annals of Iowa* 39 (Spring

1969), 585; Larry M. Logue, ed., *The Civil War Soldiers: A Historical Reader* (New York: New York University Press, 2002), 477.

58. Jones, *Camp*, 402; Bennett, *Narrative*, 110; Burdette, *Drums of the 47th*, 192 (cf. Robert G. Carter, *Four Brothers in Blue* [Austin: University of Texas Press, 1978], 428, 456; Robert Stiles, *Four Years under Marse Robert* [Washington, DC: Neale, 1903], 149–51; Joseph Hopkins Twichell to his brother, April–July 1861, in Peter Messent and Steve Courtney, eds., *The Civil War Letters of Joseph Hopkins Twichell: A Chaplain's Story* (Athens: University of Georgia Press, 2006), 34. Cf. "Anecdotes for Our Soldiers," No. 94, 15; "Anecdotes for Our Soldiers," No. 95, 7.

59. Jones, *Camp*, 98, 100, 101; quotations in that order; Schantz, *Awaiting*, 64–65; James B. Ramsey, *True Eminence Founded on Holiness: A Discourse Occasioned by the Death of Lieut. Gen. T. J. Jackson*…(Lynchburg, VA: Virginian Water-Power Presses, 1863), 8–9. See also Daniel W. Stowell, "Stonewall Jackson and the Providence of God," in Miller, Stout, and Wilson, *Religion*, 187–207.

60. Archibald Alexander, "Christ's Gracious Invitation," Evangelical Tract Society, Petersburg, VA, No. 188, 11–12; first and second quotations from 11, third and fourth from 12.

61. Scott, "No Sorrow," 853; Warren B. Armstrong, *For Courageous Fighting and Confident Dying: Union Chapels in the Civil War* (Lawrence: University Press of Kansas), 24. See, for example, James C. Duram and Eleanor A. Duram, eds., *Soldier of the Cross: The Civil War Diary and Correspondence of Rev. Andrew Jackson Hartsock* (Manhattan, KS: Military Affairs/Aerospace Historian, 1979), 169.

62. George Remley to Jane Remley, June 16, 1863, in Julie Holcomb, ed., *Southern Sons, Northern Soldiers: The Civil War Letters of the Remley Brothers, 22nd Iowa Infantry* (DeKalb: Northern Illinois University, 2004), 74.

63. For Southern examples, see Jones, *Camp*, 204, 417, 419, 421, 424, 433, 584, 593. For Northern examples, see Scott, "No Sorrow," 854–55; Letter No. 4, "The Dying Soldier's Letter to His Wife," in A. S. Billingsley, *From the Flag to the Cross: Or, Scenes and Incidents of Christianity in the War*…(Philadelphia: New World, 1872), 114.

64. Faust, *Republic of Suffering*, 180; Reid Mitchell, *The Vacant Chair: The Northern Soldier Leaves Home* (New York: Oxford University Press, 1993), 141 (see also Phillip Shaw Paludan, *"A People's Contest": The Union and the Civil War, 1861–1865* [New York: Harper & Row, 1988], 364–70); Ownby, "Patriarchy," 234 (first and second quotations), 237 (third and fourth), 239 (fifth and sixth), 240. Strikingly, also absent were fellow soldiers, friends, slaves, and in most cases, extended family members. Their "heaven consisted of small mixed-gender units of family members" (238).

65. Faust, *Republic of Suffering*, 180. For a Jewish example of this theme, see Rebecca Gratz to Ann Boswell Gratz, Sept. 12, 1861, in David Philipson, ed., *Letters of Rebecca Gratz* (Philadelphia: Jewish Publication Society of America, 1929), 427.

66. Samuel Blackwell Gulledge to "Mother and Father," July 12, 1861, in *Letters to Lauretta, 1849–1863, from Darlington, S.C., and a Confederate Soldiers' Camp*, W. Joseph Bray Jr. and Jerome J. Hale, eds. (Bowie, MD: Heritage Books, 1993), 164; William L. Nugent to Eleanor Smith Nugent, Jan. 22, 1864, in *My Dear Nellie: The Civil War Letters of William L. Nugent to Eleanor Smith Nugent*, William M. Cash and Lucy Somerville Howorth, eds. (Jackson: University Press of Mississippi, 1977), 156. Cf. Isaac Jackson, *Some of the Boys: The Civil War Letters of Isaac Jackson, 1862–1865* (Carbondale: Southern Illinois University Press, 1960), 145. Woodworth identifies all these sources in *Marching*, 45.

67. William Dudley Gale to Kate Gale, Mar. 1, 1863, Gale and Polk Family Papers, Southern Historical Collection, Wilson Library, University of North Carolina at Chapel Hill, in *Southern Women and Their Families, in the Nineteenth Century: Papers and Diaries* (University Publishers of America), Series A, Reel 2; William W. Hassler, ed., *The General to His Lady: The Civil War Letters of William Dorsey Pender to Fanny Pender* (Chapel Hill: University of North Carolina Press, 1965), 57; both as cited by Ownby, "Patriarchy," 236; David Humphrey Blair to his parents, Aug. 8, 1864, David Humphrey Blair Papers, Civil War Miscellaneous Collection, USAMHI, as cited by Woodworth, *Marching*, 51; H. Wayne Morgan, ed., "A Civil War Diary of William McKinley," *Ohio Historical Quarterly* 69 (July 1960), Aug. 16, 1861. Cf. James C. Bates, *A Texas Cavalry Officer's Civil War: The Diary and Letters of James C. Bates*, Richard Lowe, ed. (Baton Rouge: Louisiana State University Press, 1999), 305; Bennett, *Narrative*, 108, 161; Twichell to his mother, Apr. 26, 1863, in Messent and Courtney, *Joseph Hopkins Twichell*, 229.

68. Schantz, *Awaiting*, 65; Augusta Jane Evans, *Macaria; or, Altars of Sacrifice*, Drew Gilpin Faust, ed. (Baton Rouge: Louisiana State University Press, 1992), 329, 402; quotations in that order.

69. Woodworth, *Marching*, 43; Schantz, *Awaiting*, 60.

70. J. Miles Pickens to Richard Franklin Simpson, Oct. 1, 1863, in Guy R. Everson and Edward H. Simpson, Jr., eds., *"Far, Far from Home": The Wartime Letters of Dick and Tally Simpson, Third South Carolina Volunteers* (New York: Oxford University Press, 1994), 293.

71. Aurelius Lyman Voorhis, Diary, Apr. 2, 1865, as cited in Woodworth, *Marching*, 43; Alfred Tyler Fielder, *The Civil War Diaries of Capt. Alfred Tyler Fielder, 12th Tennessee Regiment Infantry, Company B, 1861–1865*, Ann York Franklin, ed. (Louisville, KY: privately published, 1996), 55–56; Thomas B. Hampton to Jestin Hampton, Aug. 9, 1863, as cited by Faust, *Republic of Suffering*, 175 (cf. Frances Brokenbrough, *A Mother's Parting Words to Her Soldier Boy* [Petersburg, VA: Evangelical Tract Society], No. 127, 6); Jones, *Camp*, 433, 436. Cf. W. H. McIntosh, *James C. Sumner, the Young Soldier Ready for Death* (Chapel Hill: Academic Affairs Library, University of North Carolina at Chapel Hill, 2000); Bennett, *Narrative*, 169.

72. Woodworth, *Marching*, 43; Pickens to Simpson, Oct. 1, 1863, in Everson and Simpson, *"Far from Home,"* 293. Cf. Alexander, *Gracious Invitation*, 10.

73. Callaway, *Civil War Letters*, 153–54; *Sketches of the Life of Captain Hugh A. White, of the Stonewall Brigade by His Father* (Columbia: South Carolinian Steam Press, 1864), 26. Cf. Bennett, *Narrative*, 174–76; Mattie Spafford in Jeffrey D. Marshall, ed., *A War of the People: Vermont Civil War Letters* (Hanover, NH: University Press of New England, 1999), 311–12. Woodworth, *Marching*, 46, called my attention to Callaway and Spafford.

74. Scott, "No Sorrow," 859; Woodworth, *Marching*, 41. On the crisis over how to view God's providence during the Civil War, see Mark A. Noll, *The Civil War as a Theological Crisis* (Chapel Hill: University of North Carolina Press, 2006), 75–94.

75. Robertson, *Soldiers*, 217.

76. Jones, *Camp*, 390; W. B. Wellons, "The Confederate Army as a Field for Religious Labor," *Messenger*, Dec. 15, 1864, 1; Bennett, *Narrative*, 413; Bell Irvin Wiley, *The Life of Johnny Reb: The Common Soldier of the Confederacy* (Indianapolis: Bobbs-Merrill, 1943), 184–86.

77. Faust, "Christian Soldiers," 68–69; Woodworth, *Marching*, 246. Cf. Robertson, *Soldiers*, 188; Kurt O. Berends, "'Wholesome Reading Purifies and Elevates the Man': The Religious Military Press in the Confederacy," 134, in Miller, Stout, and Wilson, *Religion*, 135. See also Larry J. Daniel, *Soldiering in the Army of Tennessee* (Chapel Hill: University of North Carolina Press,

1991), 115–25; Robert J. Miller, *Both Prayed to the Same God: Religion and Faith in the American Civil War* (Lanham, MD: Lexington Books, 2007), 121–29.

78. Faust, "Christian Soldiers," 72–73, 75, 82, 88.

79. Steven E. Woodworth, "The Meaning of Life in the Valley of Death," *Civil War Times Illustrated* 42 (Dec. 2003), 55–58. See also Michael Barton, *Goodmen: The Character of Civil War Soldiers* (University Park: Pennsylvania State University Press, 1981).

80. Faust, "Christian Soldiers," 67.

81. Robertson, *Soldiers*, 182; Bell Irvin Wiley, *The Life of Billy Yank: The Common Soldier of the Union* (Indianapolis: Bobbs-Merrill, 1952), 269; John Cowper Granbery, "Introduction," in Jones, *Camp*, 14–15.

82. Woodworth, *Marching*, 56, 53; quotations in that order; Watson, "Combat Motivation," 39 (third quotation). See also Wiley, *Johnny Reb*, 190; Bennett, *Narrative*, 93, 206, 215, 358; Jones, *Camp*, 287; G. W. Nichols, *A Soldier's Story of His Regiment (61st Georgia)* (Kennesaw, GA: Continental, 1961 [1898]), 38.

83. Woodworth, *Marching*, 210. See also John Wesley Brinsfield et al., *Faith in the Fight: Civil War Chaplains* (Mechanicsburg, PA: Stackpole Books, 2003), 79–80; Jones, *Camp*, 525.

84. Woodworth, *Marching*, 211.

85. For example, *Tribute of Respect to the Memory of Rev. John Todd Edgar, D.D., Pastor of the First Presbyterian Church, Nashville, Tennessee* (Nashville, TN: John T. S. Fall, 1860), 24; L. H. Blanton, *Funeral Sermon on the Death of Rev. John W. Griffin, Chaplain of the 19th VA Regt.* (Lynchburg: Virginian Power-Press, 1865), 8.

86. Berends, "Wholesome Reading," 139. See also Faust, *Republic of Suffering*, 174. As an example of this approach, see A. M. Poindexter, *Why Will Ye Die?* (Raleigh, NC: n.p., 186-). On the conversion process, see Anne C. Loveland, *Southern Evangelicals and the Social Order, 1800–1860* (Baton Rouge: Louisiana State University Press, 1980), 70–71.

87. Wiley, *Johnny Reb*, 184.

88. *Confederate Baptist,* June 17, 1863; *Biblical Recorder,* Oct. 8, 1862; *Why Will You Die?* (Petersburg, VA, 1863?).

89. Berends, "Wholesome Reading," 141, 137; quotations in that order. He provides the following examples: "The Blood of Atonement," *Mississippi Messenger,* July 15, 1863, 2; "You Are in Danger," ibid., Feb. 16, 1865, 1; "Repent Ye," ibid., Feb. 16, 1865, 1; George Kramer, "Eternal Punishment," *Soldier's Paper,* June 18, 1863, 3; and "Simplicity of Faith," *The Soldier's Visitor,* Oct. 1863, 7.

90. Faust, "Civil War Soldier," 28. Catholic chaplains and nurses exhorted penitent, dying soldiers to be baptized.

91. Alice Chapin to [Lucius Chapin], letter fragment, n.d., Lucius Chapin Papers, Box 2, Indiana Historical Society; D. A. Lough to James Lough, Oct. 21, 1864 and D. A. Lough to William Lough, Nov. 30, 1864, Lough Family Papers, Box 2, Cincinnati Historical Society, as cited in Scott, "No Sorrow," 856 (Jones, *Camp*, 502, provides numerous examples of Southern soldiers trusting in Christ for their salvation); Bennett, *Narrative*, 163. Cf. Reuben Pierson to his father, in Thomas W. Cutrer and T. Michael Parrish, eds., *Brothers in Gray: The Civil War Letters of the Pierson Family* (Baton Rouge: Louisiana State University Press, 1997), 230; Marshall, *War of the People*, 311–12. See Woodworth, *Marching*, 41, for other examples.

92. Brinsfield et al., *Faith in the Fight*, 79.

93. Shattuck, *Shield*, 87; Stephen E. Ambrose, *Upton and the Army* (Baton Rouge: Louisiana State University Press, 1964), 34; Woodworth, *Marching*, 61.

94. George H. Allen, *Forty-Six Months with the Fourth R.I. Volunteers, in the War of 1861–1865* (Providence, RI: J. A. and R. A. Reid, 1887), 148; Charles B. Haydon, *For Country, Cause and Leader: The Civil War Journal of Charles B. Haydon*, Stephen W. Sears, ed. (New York: Ticknor and Fields, 1993), 180, 183. Woodworth, *Marching*, 106, called my attention to these sources.

95. For example, Ira S. Dodd, *The Song of the Rappahannock: Sketches of the Civil War* (New York: Dodd, Mead, 1898), 158–59. See also Linderman, *Embattled Courage*, 107.

96. Faust, "Art of Dying," 26. See Bennett, *Narrative*, 243–44. Some argued that faithful military service could substitute for faith in Christ as a ticket to heaven (Faust, "Art of Dying," 27). An Illinois soldier could not imagine "the soul of a soldier who had died in the defense of his country being consigned to an orthodox hell, whatever his opinion might be of the plan of salvation" (David Cornwell, quoted in Earl J. Hess, *The Union Soldier in Battle: Enduring the Ordeal of Combat* [Lawrence: University Press of Kansas, 1997], 143).

97. Scott, "No Sorrow," 856; Helen Sharp to John Sharp, April 23, 1862, in George Mills, ed., "The Sharp Family Civil War Letters," *Annals of Iowa* 34 Jan. (1959): 495; Rhoda Eggleston to Hubert Eggleston, August 28, [1863], Hubert N. Eggleston Papers, Minnesota Historical Society; both as cited by Scott, "No Sorrow," 856.

98. Scott, "No Sorrow," 856.

99. *Blood upon the Door Posts; or, Means of Safety in the Time of Danger* (Petersburg, VA: Evangelical Tract Society), No. 72, 2.

100. Brokenbrough, *Mother's Parting Words*, 4. For other examples of evangelistic tracts, see *Jesus, the Soldier's Friend. By a Young Lady of Virginia* (Raleigh, NC: Raleigh Register Steam Power Press, 1863); *The Soldier's Great Want* (Petersburg, VA: Evangelical Tract Society, 1863?), No. 250.

101. Wiley, *Johnny Reb*, 178; Joseph H. Martin, *Sufferings of the Lost* (Raleigh, NC: n.p., 186-).

102. Woodworth, *Marching*, 46–47; Hamlin Alexander Coe, *Mine Eyes Have Seen the Glory: Combat Diaries of Union Sergeant Hamlin Alexander Coe* (Rutherford, NJ: Fairleigh Dickinson University Press, 1975), 164.

103. Robertson, *Soldiers*, 182 (quotation); Hess, "Holding On," 477; Thompson, *13th New Hampshire*, 112. Also see Evan Rowland Jones, *Four Years in the Army of the Potomac: A Soldier's Recollections* (London: Tyne, 1881), 190.

104. Quoted in Linderman, *Embattled Courage*, 254.

105. Scott, "No Sorrow," 857.

CHAPTER 6

1. Robert Wiebe, *The Search for Order, 1877–1920* (New York: Hill and Wang, 1967), 5–6; quotation from 5. On the Gilded Age, also see Nell Irvin Painter, *Standing at Armageddon: The United States, 1877–1919* (New York: W. W. Norton, 1987); Sean Dennis Cashman, *America in the Gilded Age: From the Death of Lincoln to the Rise of Theodore Roosevelt* (New York: New York University Press, 1993); Rebecca Edwards, *New Spirits: Americans in the Gilded Age, 1865–1905* (New York: Oxford University Press, 2006).

2. See Mark Twain and Dudley Warner, *The Gilded Age: A Tale of Today* (New York: Oxford University Press, 1996 [1873]).

3. Alan Trachtenberg, *The Incorporation of America: Culture and Society in the Gilded Age* (New York: Hill and Wang, 1982), 52, 39; quotations from 39. See also John D. Buenker and Joseph Buenker, eds., *Encyclopedia of the Gilded Age and Progressive Era* (Armonk, NY: Sharpe

Reference, 2005); H. Wayne Morgan, ed., *The Gilded Age: A Reappraisal* (Syracuse, NY: Syracuse University Press 1970); Joel Shrock, *The Gilded Age* (Westport, CT: Greenwood Press, 2004); Sean Dennis Cashman, *America in the Gilded Age: From the Death of Lincoln to the Rise of Theodore Roosevelt* (New York: New York University Press, 1984); Rebecca Edwards, *New Spirits: Americans in the Gilded Age, 1865–1905* (New York: Oxford University Press, 2006); Robert W. Cherny, *American Politics in the Gilded Age, 1868–1900* (Wheeling, IL: Harlan Davidson, 1997); Charles W. Calhoun, ed., *The Gilded Age: Essays on the Origins of Modern America* (Wilmington, DE: Scholarly Resources, 1996); Mark Wahlgren Summers, *Party Games: Getting, Keeping, and Using Power in Gilded Age Politics* (Chapel Hill: University of North Carolina Press, 2004).

4. Trachtenberg, *Incorporation*, 3–5, 8: first quotation from 3–4, second from 5; Josiah Strong, *Our Country: Its Possible Future and Its Present Crises* (New York: Baker and Taylor, 1885), quotation from 147.

5. Wiebe, *Search for Order*, xiii, 14, 39–44; quotation from 39.

6. Trachtenberg, *Incorporation*, 47, 72.

7. Wiebe, *Search for Order*, 57; T. J. Jackson Lears, *No Place of Grace: Antimodernism and the Transformation of American Culture, 1880–1920* (New York: Pantheon Books, 1981), 4, 6; quotation from 4.

8. By the 1890s, this cadre of celebrated preachers also included Russell Conwell, George A. Gordon, Washington Gladden, Lyman Abbott, Newell Dwight Hillis, Frank W. Gunsaulus, Charles M. Sheldon, Charles A. Parkhurst, Josiah Strong, Graham Taylor, and others whose fame was more regional than national. See Winthrop Hudson, *The Great Tradition of the American Churches* (Gloucester, MA: Peter Smith, 1970), 159.

9. On Beecher see, Debby Applegate, *The Most Famous Man in America* (New York: Doubleday, 2006). By the early 1880s, Beecher had publicly stated his acceptance of evolution, rejection of Calvinism, and repudiation of eternal punishment. On Talmage, see Charles Eugene Banks, *Life and Works of T. DeWitt Talmage* (Chicago: Monroe, 1902); John Rusk, *The Authentic Life of T. DeWitt Talmage: The Greatly Beloved Divine* (Vancouver: J. M. MacGregor, 1902); David Gregg and Louis Banks in "Publisher's Preface," in T. DeWitt Talmage, *The Earth Girdled: The World as Seen To-Day* (New Haven, CT: Butler and Alger, 1896), 38–39. Hudson, *Great Tradition*, 163 (quotation); James Bryce, *The American Commonwealth*, 2 vols. (New York: Macmillan, 1888), 2: 775.

10. Sydney Ahlstrom, "Introduction," in Ahlstrom, ed., *Theology in America: The Major Protestant Voices from Puritanism to New Orthodoxy* (Indianapolis: Hackett, 2003), 58–68; first quotation from 66, third from 67; Jackson, *No Place*, 20–22; second quotation from 21.

11. Elizabeth Stuart Phelps, *The Gates Ajar*, Helen Sootin Smith, ed. (Cambridge, MA: Harvard University Press, 1964), vi.

12. Jonathan Butler, *Softly and Tenderly Jesus Is Calling: Heaven and Hell in American Revivalism, 1870–1920* (Brooklyn, NY: Carlson, 1991), 162; T. DeWitt Talmage, "The Joy to Come!" in Mary Lowe Dickinson, ed., *Heaven, Home and Happiness* (New York: Christian Herald, 1901), 376.

13. Butler, *Softly and Tenderly*, 162, 144–45, first two quotations from 162, third from 144, fourth from 145; T. DeWitt Talmage in Samuel Fallows, ed., *The Home Beyond, or, Views of Heaven and Its Relation to Earth by Moody, Spurgeon, Talmage, and Over Four Hundred other Prominent Thinkers and Writers* (Chicago: Coburn and Newman, 1884), 311; Austin Phelps, "What Do We Know of the Heavenly Life?" in Phelps, *My Portfolio: A Collection of Essays* (New York: Charles

Scribner's Sons, 1882), 280; F. J. Boudreaux, in James Daly, *Heaven: An Anthology* (New York: Longmans, Green, 1935), 97. Cf. W. G. T. Shedd, *Sermons to the Spiritual Man* (New York: Charles Scribner's Sons, 1884), 170.

14. Butler, *Softly and Tenderly*, 148, 153, 5; Ira Sankey, comp., *Sacred Songs and Solos, and Songs of Love and Mercy* (London: Morgan and Scott, 1877). See Douglas Davies, "Christianity," in Jean Holm, *Sacred Place* (New York: Pinter, 1994), 37.

15. Applegate, *Most Famous Man*, 14 (first quotation); Beecher as quoted in Hudson, *Great Tradition*, 188.

16. Robert M. Patterson, *Paradise: The Place and State of Saved Souls between Death and the Resurrection* (Philadelphia: Presbyterian Board of Publ., 1874), 148; William R. Alger, *The Destiny of the Soul: A Critical History of the Doctrine of a Future Life* (New York: Greenwood Press, 1968 [1860]), 573; T. DeWitt Talmage, "Paul's Valedictory," in Talmage, *Sermons: First Series* (New York: Funk and Wagnalls, 1885), 331 (cf. W. G. T. Shedd, *Sermons to the Natural Man* [New York: Charles Scribner, 1871], 2–3; Shedd, *Spiritual Man*, 171; Howard Crosby, "Heaven, A Place Prepared by Christ," in Fallows, *Home Beyond*, 296; G. W. Quinby, *Heaven Our Home: The Christian Doctrine of Resurrection* [Augusta, ME: Gospel Banner, 1882], 205); Henry Ward Beecher, *"The Heavenly State" and "Future Punishment": Two Sermons* (New York: J. B. Ford, 1871), 78–79, 99, first quotation from 78, second from 99; Henry Ward Beecher, "The Necessities of Correct Belief," in *Sermons*, 2 vols. (New York: Harper & Brothers, 1868), 2: 294 (third quotation); Phillips Brooks, *Twenty Sermons* (New York: E. P. Dutton, 1903), 72.

17. Dwight L. Moody, *Heaven: How to Get There* (Springdale, PA: Whitaker House, 1982 [1880]), 5 (first quotation) 13 (third and fourth quotations); Moody, "Not Wrong to Speculate about Heaven," in Fallows, *Home Beyond*, 312 (second quotation). Moody added that everything the Bible taught about the future state agreed with people's "idea of right," "reasonable fears," and personal experiences (Moody, *Conversion, Service, and Glory* [London: Morgan and Scott, 1885], 267).

18. Lears, *No Place*, 6; Richard Rabinowitz, *The Spiritual Self in Everyday Life: The Transformation of Personal Religious Experience in Nineteenth-Century New England* (Boston: Northeastern University Press, 1989), 236–38; first quotation from 237, second from 238; Shedd, *Spiritual Man*, 79 (first quotation); Shedd, *Natural Man*, 13–16. Whether people resided in heaven or hell, they would have "an open and unavoidable vision of God." Those who delighted in this view would be blessed, Shedd explained, while those who loathed it would be miserable (16). See also W. G. T. Shedd, *Dogmatic Theology*, 3 vols. (New York: Charles Scribner's Sons, 1888), 2: 664; Charles Hodge, *Systematic Theology*, 3 vols. (New York: Charles Scribner's, 1883), 3: 860; A. A. Hodge, *Outlines of Theology for Students and Laymen* (Grand Rapids, MI: Zondervan, 1972 [1879]), 578.

19. Daniel Goodwin, *Christian Eschatology or Doctrine of the Last Things* (Philadelphia: McCalla & Stavely, 1885), 36; Dwight L. Moody, "Heaven: Its Happiness," in Moody, *Heaven*, 40; Phelps, "Heavenly Life," 277; F. J. Boudreaux, *The Happiness of Heaven* (Manchester, NH: Sophia Institute Press, 1999 [1871]), 7–9; quotation from 9; Boudreaux, *Happiness of Heaven*, 33 (second quotation), 111 (third quotation); Boudreaux in Daly, *Anthology*, 19 (fourth quotation).

20. Dwight L. Moody, "Christ Is in Heaven," in Fallows, *Home Beyond*, 295 (quotation); Moody, "Christ in Heaven," in Dickinson, *Heaven*, 368; T. DeWitt Talmage, "Employment in Heaven," in Talmage, *Life's Looking Glass: Companion, Counsellor, and Guide* (Toronto: C. R. Parish, 1899), 406; Talmage, "Paul's Valedictory," 334; J. L. Dagg, "The Christian Hope for

Heaven," in Fisher Humphreys, ed., *Nineteenth Century Evangelical Theology* (Nashville, TN: Broadman, 1983), 363; originally in Dagg, *Manual of Theology* (Philadelphia: American Baptist Publication Society, 1871); Kenneth Osbeck, *Beyond the Sunset: 25 Hymns Stories Celebrating the Hope of Heaven* (Grand Rapids, MI: Kregel, 2001), 25. Cf. Robert Patterson, *Paradise the Place and State of Saved Souls between Death and Resurrection* (Philadelphia: Presbyterian Board of Publ., 1874), 187; Fanny J. Crosby's 1894 hymn "My Savior First of All."

21. Phillips Brooks, *The New Song in Heaven* (New York: E. P. Dutton, 1907), 18, 10–11, 22–26; quotation from 22. On the other hand, Brooks's view of eternal life was closely connected with his emphasis on the value of human personality. "Heaven," he stated, "is the soul finding its own perfect personality in God" (Alexander V. G. Allen, *Life and Letters of Phillips Brooks*, 3 vols. [New York: E. P. Dutton, 1901], 2: 481). See Gillis Harp, *Brahmin Prophet: Phillips Brooks and the Path of Liberal Protestantism* (Lanham, MD: Rowman & Littlefield, 2003), 187.

22. Moody, *Conversion*, 350; Samuel Spear, *Meditations on the Bible Heaven* (New York: Funk & Wagnalls, 1886), 228; Patterson, *Paradise*, 199 (cf. Dagg, "Christian Hope," 364; Phelps, "Heavenly Life," 278); "Heaven," in Alfred Nevin, ed., *Encyclopedia of the Presbyterian Church in the United States of America* (Philadelphia: Presbyterian Publishing House, 1884), 315.

23. Dagg, "Christian Hope," 361, 364; quotations in that order; Lucy Larcom, *As It Is in Heaven* (Boston: Houghton, Mifflin, 1891), 26; Boudreaux, *Happiness*, first quotation from 143, second from 38.

24. Shedd, *Spiritual Man*, 323, 325 (first quotation); Shedd, *Natural Man*, 11, 24 (second quotation); "Heaven," in Nevin, *Encyclopedia,* 315 ("perfect purity"); Boudreaux, *Happiness*, 38. Cf. Goodwin, *Christian Eschatology*, 35; Patterson, *Paradise*, 168.

25. Lears, *No Place*, 11–12; quotation from 11; Spears, *Meditation*, 217; Phelps, "Heavenly Life," 273; T. DeWitt Talmage, "Royal Womanhood," in Talmage, *Life's Looking Glass* (Toronto: C. R. Parish, 1890), 401–2. Cf. L. L. Hamline, "No Regrets in Heaven," in Fallows, *Home Beyond*, 345–46; Talmage, "A Haven of Rest," in Dickinson, *Heaven*, 349; Henry C. Potter, "No Care in Heaven," in ibid., 314; Patterson, *Paradise*, 160, 180–84; Hodge, *Systematic Theology*, 3: 860.

26. Trachtenberg, *Incorporation*, 80, 48 (first quotation), 43, 54 (second quotation); Henry George, *Social Problems* (Chicago: Belford, Clarke, 1883), 147; Edwards, *New Spirits*, 56 (third quotation); Moody, "Heaven: Its Certainty," in Moody, *Heaven*, 58; J. Edmosson, "Heaven [Is a?] Happy Place," in Fallows, *Home Beyond*, 369.

27. Phillips Brooks to Elizabeth K. Mitchell, May 30, 1872, in Allen, *Life and Letters*, 2: 176; Boudreaux, *Happiness*, 84.

28. Shedd, *Spiritual Man*, 315–16; quotation from 316; Shedd, *Natural Man*, 23–25; second quotation from 23, third from 24; Dagg, "Christian Hope," 361–62; quotation from 362; Patterson, *Paradise*, 150; Talmage, "Paul's Valedictory," 333; Ellen White, *Heaven* (Nampa, ID: Pacific Press, 2003), 149–50, 152, 155–56, 159; quotation from 156. Cf. Hodge, *Systematic Theology*, 3: 860; Phelps, "Heavenly Life," 273.

29. T. DeWitt Talmage, "The Resurrection," in Talmage, *Sermons Delivered in the Brooklyn Tabernacle* (New York: Funk and Wagnalls, 1885), 227, 229; quotations in that order. See Clifford Putney, *Muscular Christianity: Manhood and Sports in Protestant America, 1880–1920* (Cambridge, MA: Harvard University Press, 2001); Gail Bederman, *Manliness and Civilization: A Cultural History of Gender and Race in the United States, 1880–1917* (Chicago: University of Chicago Press, 1995); E. Anthony Rotundo, *American Manhood: Transformations in Masculinity from the Revolution to the Modern Era* (New York: BasicBooks, 1993). Putney identifies Social

Gospeler Josiah Strong, psychologist G. Stanley Hall, and Theodore Roosevelt as leading proponents of muscular Christianity. "To energize the churches and counteract the supposedly enervating effects of urban living," they promoted competitive sports, exercise, and physical fitness. During the late nineteenth century, YMCAs adopted athletic programs to help build character. Decrying the "feminization of American culture," many politicians, professors, and journalists emphasized masculine values, vigorous activity, and sports. Concerned that the nature's middle- and upper-class managers were becoming physically weak and effete, many reformers encouraged them to exercise at gyms or home, play sports, and camp to strengthen themselves (1–4; first quotation from 1, second from, 4).

30. Alger, *Destiny*, 715, 717–18; first three quotations from 715, next four from 717, remainder from 718.

31. Elting E. Morison, *From Know-How to Nowhere: The Development of American Technology* (New York: Basic Books, 1974); Putney, *Muscular Christianity*, 6; Brooks, *Twenty Sermons*, 125 (quotation); Brooks, *New Song*, 17; T. DeWitt Talmage, "A Half Hour in Heaven," in J. Ward Gamble and Charles Morris, eds., *Trumpet Blasts or Mountain Top Views of Life* (Nashville, TN: Southwestern, 1892), 500, 502, 508, quotations in that order; Talmage, "The Resurrection," 229–30; quotation from 229.

32. Edwards, *New Spirits*, 71–79; Walter Licht, *Industrializing America: The Nineteenth Century* (Baltimore: Johns Hopkins University Press, 1995); Patterson, *Paradise*, 146, 123, 145, 159, 178; quotation from 146 (see also Robert M. Patterson, *Vision of Heaven for the Life on Earth* [Philadelphia: Presbyterian Board of Publ., 1877], 54, 57); "Heaven," 315; White, *Heaven*, 65, 146, 152; quotation from 146; Dagg, "Christian Hope," 363–64; quotation from 363; Talmage, "Employment in Heaven," 406–17 (Talmage argued that God would use earthly soldiers to defeat evil angels and conquer rebellious worlds); Asa Mahan, "Employments of Heaven," in Fallows, *Home Beyond*, 357; Phelps, "Heavenly Life," 275; A. A. Hodge, *Evangelical Theology: A Course of Popular Lectures* (Carlisle, PA: Banner of Truth, 1976 [1890]), 400. Cf. Hodge, *Outlines*, 578; James P. Boyce, "The Final States of the Righteous and Wicked," in *Abstract of Systematic Theology* (Philadelphia: American Baptist Publication Society, 1887) at http://founders.org/library/boyce1/toc.html.

33. Trachtenberg, *Incorporation*, 38, 41, 45–46, 26, 77; John Kasson, *Civilizing the Machine: Technology and Republican Values in America, 1776–1900* (New York: Grossman, 1976); Lears, *No Place*, 7–8; Henry Ward Beecher, "From Glory to Glory," in Fallows, *Home Beyond*, 306 (first two quotations); Mahan, "Employments," 90 (third quotation); E. D. Morris, *Is There Salvation after Death?* (New York: A. C. Armstrong & Son, 1887), 17; Hodge, *Systematic Theology*, 3: 860; Quinby, *Heaven*, 211, 232–33, quotation from 211. Cf. Hodge, *Outlines*, 580; D. M. Reid, "Progression in Heaven," in Fallows, *Home Beyond*, 323; Patterson, *Paradise*, 156, 201.

34. Larcom, *Heaven*, 148 (first quotation), 140–41, 138, 71 (second quotation).

35. Goodwin, *Christian Eschatology*, 36. The biblical descriptions "of the scenes and employments of the heavenly state," he added, "are for the most part figurative."

36. For example, Samuel Fallows, "Summary of Reasons for Recognition," in Fallows, *Home Beyond*, 381–83; T. DeWitt Talmage, *Heavenly Recognition* (New York: Thomas Y. Crowell, 1897); Randolph S. Foster, *Beyond the Grave* (New York: Philips & Hunt, 1879), 206; Alger, *Destiny*, 569, 572–73; first quotation from 569, second from 575. "In the life beyond the grave," Alger maintained, people might be able to recognize their earthly companions "directly, either by spiritual

sight or by intuitive feeling," or indirectly by comparing common recollections, or "the mediation of angels," or by some other arrangement God "especially prepared for that purpose" (272–73).

37. George Zabriskie Gray, *The Scriptural Doctrine of Recognition in the World to Come* (New York: T. Whittaker, 1875), 10, 73, 45, 74; quotation from 10; Patterson, *Paradise*, 118, 122; Foster, *Beyond the Grave*, 200, 224, 194, 195–98, 217; first quotation from 200, second from 224, third from 194, fourth from 195, fifth and sixth from 197, seventh from 198, eighth from 217; Talmage, "Shall We Know Each Other?" in Fallows, *Home Beyond*, 384. Cf. William M. Punshon, "Recognition in Heaven Is a Fact," in ibid., 416; M. Rhodes, *Recognition in Heaven* (Philadelphia: Lutheran Publication Society, 1880).

38. J. Aspinwall Hodge, *Recognition after Death* (New York: Robert Carter & Brothers, 1889), 16–31, 172–73; first quotation from 30, second from 31; Boudreaux, *Happiness*, 111–12; quotation from 111. Cf. Quinby, *Heaven*, 257–60.

39. Hodge, *Recognition*, 23, 25, 28–29; first quotation from 25, second from 28; Foster, *Beyond the Grave*, 221, 222, 191; quotations in that order; Patterson, *Vision of Heaven*, 160; Newman Smyth, *The Orthodox Theology of To-day* (New York: Charles Scribner, 1881), 145, 152; quotation from 145; Hodge, *Systematic Theology*, 3: 860–61; Boudreaux in Daly, *Anthology*, 50; Talmage, "Employments of Heaven," 414; Talmage, "Lazarus and Dives," 331; T. DeWitt Talmage, "Jesus in Heaven," in Fallows, *Home Beyond*, 320 (quotation); Moody, *Great Joy. Comprising Sermons and Prayer-Meeting Talks* (New York: E. B. Treat, 1877), 76; Larcom, *Heaven*, 147; Boudreaux, *Happiness*, 102–4. Cf. Dagg, "Christian Hope," 363; Patterson, *Paradise*, 160–61; Alger, *Destiny*, 575.

40. Trachtenberg, *Incorporation*, 45; Spear, *Meditations*, 118, 130, quotation from 118 (cf. Moody, "Heaven: Its Riches," in Moody, *Heaven*, 88); Smyth, *Orthodox Theology*, 132–34; quotation from 132; Patterson, *Vision of Heaven*, 305–6; Patterson, *Paradise*, 204–6; Boudreaux, *Happiness*, 125, 136; quotation from 136; Hodge, *Outlines*, 579; Henry Ward Beecher, *Norwood, or, Village Life in New England* (New York: Charles Scribner, 1868), 372.

41. Moody, "Heaven: Its Riches," 76–77; Moody, "Heaven: Its Happiness," 53–54 (quotation from 53); Henry Ward Beecher, "On the Decadence of Christianity," in *Sermons*, 1: 399; Beecher, "The Heavenly State," 94 (quotations in that order); Brooks, *Twenty Sermons* 74; Brooks, *New Song*, 29 (quotations in that order); Matthew Simpson, "The Cloud of Witnesses," in Fallows, *Home Beyond*, 477; Simpson, "The Sainted Dead Interested in the Living," in ibid., 472 (quotation); T. DeWitt Talmage, "The Ministry of Tears," in *American Sermons: The Pilgrims to Martin Luther King, Jr.* (New York: Library of America, 1999), 693–94; Smyth, *Orthodoxy Theology*, 101–3; quotation from 101.

42. Henry Ward Beecher, *Royal Truths* (Boston: Ticknor and Fields, 1866), 25; Brooks, *Twenty Sermons*, 125; Moody, *Conversion*, 280; Moody, "Heaven: Its Certainty," 69 (all quotations); Larcom, *Heaven*, 28; White, *Heaven*, 90; Patterson, *Vision of Heaven*, 318 (second quotation); Boudreaux, *Happiness*, 124 (first quotation), 177, 135 (second quotation).

43. Dwight L. Moody, "The Way to God," in James Bell, ed., *The D. L. Moody Collection: The Highlights of His Writings, Sermons, Anecdotes, and Life Story* (Chicago: Moody Press, 1997), 121, 124; Moody, "What Salvation Is," in Moody, *You Will Live Forever* (New Kensington, PA: Whitaker House, 1997), 42 (first two quotations); Moody, "Heaven: Its Rewards," in Moody, *Heaven*, 99 (third quotation); Moody, "Heaven," in Warren W. Wiersbe, comp., *Classic Sermons on Heaven and Hell* (Grand Rapids, MI: Kregel, 1994), 16 (cf. Moody, "Heaven: Its Inhabitants," in Moody, *Heaven: How to Get There*, 32; *Fifty Evenings with Dwight L. Moody* (Philadelphia:

C. H. Yost, 1876), 176ff.); T. Dewitt Talmage, "Money Cannot Buy Heaven," in Fallows, *Home Beyond*, 334 (quotation); Talmage, "The Heavenly Harvests," in Gamble and Morris, *Trumpet Blasts*, 514; Talmage, "The Gate Keepers," in Dickinson, *Heaven*, 397 (see also Talmage, "Fit for Heaven," in ibid., 354; Talmage, "Last Things," in Talmage, *Sermons, First Series*, 194–95); Shedd, *Natural Man*, 20, 38; quotations in that order. Cf. James P. Boyce, "Regeneration and Conversion," in *Systematic Theology*, 379; A. J. Gordon, *The Ministry of the Spirit* (Philadelphia: American Baptist Publication Society, 1894), 102; White, *Heaven*, 12.

44. Henry Ward Beecher, "Christianity a Vital Force," in *Sermons*, 2: 317–18; Beecher, "What Will You Do with Christ?" in *Sermons*, 1: 352; quotations in that order. Cf. Beecher, "The Necessity of Correct Belief," 2: 294–319; Phillips Brooks, "All Saints' Day," in *Sermons* (New York: E. P. Dutton, 1878), 134–35; quotations from 134.

45. Harp, *Brahmin Prophet*, 175–78, quotation from 177. See also John Fox, "Phillips Brooks as a Theologian," *Presbyterian and Reformed Review* 6 (July 1895), 393–413; C. G. Brown, "Christocentric Liberalism in the Episcopal Church," *Historical Magazine of the Protestant Episcopal Church* 37 (1968), 5–38; and Jerome F. Politzer, "Theological Ideas in the Preaching of Phillips Brooks," *Historical Magazine of the Protestant Episcopal Church* 33 (1964), 157–69.

46. Henry Ward Beecher, "Preparing for Death," in Charles Wallis, ed., *The Funeral Encyclopedia* (New York: Harper and Brothers, 1953), 127; Gary Dorrien, *The Making of American Liberal Theology: Imagining Progressive Religion, 1805–1900* (Louisville, KY: Westminster John Knox Press, 2001), 402. William McLoughlin argues that although Beecher's view of salvation differed sharply from that of "the emotional experiences of the revival meeting," he still believed that a new birth was necessary. "The seed of the old Adam still had to die and be reborn even though God was immanent in Nature" (*The Meaning of Henry Ward Beecher: An Essay on the Shifting Values of Mid-Victorian America, 1840–1870* [New York: Alfred A. Knopf, 1970], 74–80, quotation from 78); Hudson, *Great Tradition*, 168, quoting statements by George A. Gordon, "The Theological Problem for To-Day," in *The New Puritanism: Papers* (Freeport, NY: Books for Libraries Press, 1972 [1897]), 169.

47. Alger, *Destiny*, 719 (first and second quotations), 720 (third, fifth, and sixth quotations), 722 (fourth quotation).

48. Moody, "Heaven: Its Rewards," 99; Shedd, *Natural Man*, 353, 339 (quotation); Beecher, *Royal Truths*, 243; Henry Ward Beecher, *Life Thoughts, Gathered from the Extemporaneous Discourses of HWB by One of His Congregation* (Boston: Phillips, Sampson, 1858), 266; Beecher, *Norwood*, 372; quotations in that order. Cf. Augusta Moore, *Notes from the Plymouth Pulpit* (New York: Derby & Jackson, 1859), 259.

49. Spear, *Meditations*, 228–29; Shedd, *Natural Man*, 32–34; quotation from 33; Larcom, *Heaven*, 147.

50. George Marsden, *Fundamentalism and American Culture* (New York: Oxford University Press, 2006), 25. See also Frank Hugh Foster, *The Modern Movement in American Theology* (New York: Fleming H. Revell, 1939), 16–27.

51. Hudson, *Great Tradition*, 161, 194; first and second quotations from 164, third and from 194.

52. See Gabriel Fackre, "Divine Perseverance," in John Sanders, ed., *What About Those Who Have Never Heard? Three Views on the Destiny of the Unevangelized* (Downers Grove, IL: InterVarsity Press, 1995), 71; Thomas P. Field, "The 'Andover Theory' of Future Probation," *Andover Review* 7 (May 1887), 461–75; Andover Seminary, *The Andover Case* (Boston: Stanley and Usher, 1887).

53. Daniel Day Williams, *The Andover Liberals: A Study in American Theology* (New York: Octagon Books, 1970), 66.

54. Smyth, *Orthodox Theology*, 101, 111–12; first from quotation 101, second from 111, third from 111–12; 125, 183, 185; fourth quotation from 125.

55. Smyth, *Orthodox Theology*, 185, 125–26; 138; first and second quotation from 185, third from 126.

56. Smyth, *Orthodox Theology*, 127, 131–32; first and second quotations from 127, third from 131.

57. William, *Andover Liberals*, 66, 70–73, 86; quotation from 86. See also Orpheus T. Lanphear, *It Is Contrary to Congregationalism to Appoint as Missionaries Those Who Hold the Hypothesis of Future Probation* (Beverly, MA: n.p., 1893?). Edward Morris noted in *Is There Salvation After Death?* (New York: A. C. Armstrong & Son, 1887) that Christians held four different theories about how individuals change from a state of sinfulness to one of full perfection in the intermediate life: (17) 1. the evolutionary theory—people change chiefly through their own actions; 2. the educational theory—the "processes of training and chastisement" are "providentially brought to bear on the soul" (19); 3. the purgatorial theory—imperfect believers are divinely punished only to prepare them for heaven; and 4. the probationary theory—many will be saved during the intermediate state by responding to the gospel message (20).

58. James Strong, *The Doctrine of a Future Life from a Scriptural, Philosophical, and Scientific Point of View* (New York: Eaton & Mains, 1891), 101–8; first quotation from 101, second and third from 102, fourth from 103, fifth from 105, sixth from 108; Hodge, *Outlines of Theology*, 555–56; all quotations from 556. See also William De Loss Love, *Future Probation Examined* (New York: Funk and Wagnalls, 1888) and his *Christ Preaching to the Spirits in Prison* (Boston: Congregational Publication Society, 1883).

59. Spear, *Meditations*, 131; Goodwin, *Christian Eschatology*, 27–31, 60–63; quotations from 29. See Love, *Future Probation*; Thomas Field, *The "Andover Theory" of Future Probation* (Amherst, MA: n.p., 18–); Justin Edwards Burbank, *Future Probation: What the Scriptures Teach Concerning It* (Concord, NH: John P. Kelley, 1890); William Glen Moncrieff, *Future Probation: Is that Awaiting Any of the Unrighteous?* (Cleveland: Taylor Austin, 1891); Margaret Lamberts Bendroth, *A School of the Church: Andover Newton across Two Centuries* (Grand Rapids, MI: Eerdmans, 2008).

60. Hodge, *Systematic Theology*, 3: 749–57, 764; first quotation from 752, second from 757, third and fourth from 764; Hodge, *Outlines*, 557; Goodwin, *Christian Eschatology*, 7–8.

61. Henry Ward Beecher, *"The Heavenly State" and "Future Punishment": Two Sermons* (New York: J. B. Ford and Co., 1871), 83, 105, 109; quotations in that order.

62. Quoted in Hudson, *Great Tradition*, 171. See also Beecher, "Progress of Thought in the Church," *North American Review* 135 (Aug. 1882), 111; Beecher, sermon, *Christian Union*, July 14, 1880; Lyman Abbott, *Henry Ward Beecher: A Sketch of His Career* (Hartford, CT: American, 1887), 114–16. Abbott underwent a similar transition in his views in the 1880s. See Ira V. Brown, *Lyman Abbott, Christian Evolutionist: A Study in Religious Liberalism* (Cambridge, MA: Harvard University Press, 1963), 130–45.

63. E. L. Youmans, "Concerning Belief in Hell," *Popular Science Monthly* 12 (Mar. 1878), 627–30; Octavius Brooks Frothingham, "The Dogma of Hell," in *American Sermons*, 681, 684–86; first quotation from 681, second from 686, third from 684. On the decline of belief in Satan and hell across the Atlantic, see Edward Langton, *Satan, a Portrait* (London: Skeffington, 1947) and Geoffrey Rowell, *Hell and the Victorians* (Oxford, UK: Clarendon Press, 1974). William James

also questioned the traditional conception of hell. See William James, *The Principles of Psychology*, 2 vols. (New York: Dover, 1950 [1890]), 1: 127.

64. Butler, *Softly and Tenderly*, 41, 5; quotation from 41; James H. Moorhead, "Between Progress and Apocalypse: A Reassessment of Millennialism in American Religious Thought, 1800–1880," *Journal of American History* 71 (Dec. 1984), 540 (quotation); Moorhead, "The Erosion of Postmillennialism in American Religious Thought, 1865–1925," *Church History* 53 (Mar. 1984), 70; Butler, *Softly and Tenderly*, 2, 43; quotation from 2. Moody occasionally preached about hell. See "Hell," undated sermon, http://www.biblebelievers.com/moody_sermons/m7. html.

65. Hodge, *Outlines*, 582–85; first quotation 582, second 583; Shedd, *Natural Man*, 28–30; Goodwin, *Christian Eschatology*, 60–61; quotation from 61. See also Shedd, *The Doctrine of Endless Punishment* (Minneapolis: Klock and Klock, 1980). In his *Dogmatic Theology* (New York: Scribner, 1888–94), 3 vols., Shedd devoted two pages to heaven and eighty-seven pages to eternal punishment.

66. Talmage, "Lazarus and Dives," in Talmage, *Sermons: First Series*, 330–31, 334; Talmage, "The Resurrection," 230–31; first quotation from 329, second from 330.

67. Dwight L. Moody, "On Being Born Again," in *American Sermons*, 678; Ellen White, "Heaven Would Be Torture to the Rebellious," in White, *Heaven*, 114–15. Cf. Spear, *Meditations*, 229.

CHAPTER 7

1. On the Social Gospel, see Charles Howard Hopkins, *The Rise of the Social Gospel in American Protestantism* (New Haven, CT: Yale University Press, 1940); Henry May, *Protestant Churches and Industrial America* (New York: Harper, 1949); Ronald C. White, *Liberty and Justice for All: Racial Reform and the Social Gospel (1877–1925)* (San Francisco: Harper & Row, 1990); Susan Curtis, *A Consuming Faith: The Social Gospel and Modern American Culture* (Baltimore: Johns Hopkins University Press, 1991); Gary Scott Smith, *The Search for Social Salvation: Social Christianity and America, 1880–1925* (Lanham, MD: Lexington Books, 2000).

2. William R. Hutchison, *The Modernist Impulse in American Protestantism* (Cambridge, MA: Harvard University Press, 1976), 95–99, 113–22, 2; quotation from 2; Bradley J. Longfield, *The Presbyterian Controversy: Fundamentalists, Modernists, and Moderates* (New York: Oxford University Press, 1991), 19; William E. Hordern, *A Layman's Guide to Protestant Theology* (New York: Macmillan, 1968), 73–110.

3. James Moorhead, *World without End: Mainstream American Protestant Visions of the Last Things, 1880–1925* (Bloomington: Indiana University Press, 1999), 57 (quotation); Rebecca Edwards, *New Spirits: American in the Gilded Age, 1865–1905* (New York: Oxford University Press, 2006), 90–92, 94.

4. Moorhead, *World without End*, 57 (first quotation); David Gregg, *The Heaven-Life or Stimulus for Two Worlds* (Chicago: Fleming H. Revell, 1895), 109; James H. Moorhead, "The Erosion of Postmillennialism in American Religious Thought, 1865–1925," *Church History* 53 (Mar. 1984), 71–72; quotation from 72. For example, William N. Clarke, *An Outline of Christian Theology* (New York: Charles Scribner's Sons, 1909), 450.

5. Moorhead, *World without End*, 61. For example, Gregg, *Heaven-Life*, 44, 56, 57, 62–63; Lucy Larcom, *As It Is in Heaven* (Boston: Houghton, Mifflin, 1891), 27–28.

6. Levi Gilbert, *The Hereafter and Heaven* (Cincinnati: Jennings and Graham, 1907), 174–81; first quotation from 175, second from 177, third from 174, fourth from 181.

7. William Adams Brown, *The Christian Hope: A Study in the Doctrine of Immortality* (New York: Charles Scribner's Sons, 1912), 18 (first, third, and fourth quotations), 195 (second quotation), 128 (fifth quotation), 196 (sixth quotation). Cf. Charles H. Strong, *In Paradise or the State of the Faithful Dead: A Study from Scripture on Death and After-Death* (New York: Thomas Whittaker, 1893), 111.

8. Mark Twain, "Extract from Captain Stormfield's Visit to Heaven," in Twain, *Tales, Sketches, Speeches, and Essays, 1891–1900*, 2 vols. (New York: Library of America, 1992), 2: 838, 843, 846, 851–52; all quotations from 838. Jeremiah, Homer, Buddha, Muhammad, and Shakespeare all reside in Twain's ecumenical heaven, and everyone who does not receive their proper reward on earth gets it in heaven.

9. Mark Twain, *Letters from Earth*, Letter IV, in Twain, *Tales*, 2: 885–90; first three quotations from 885, fourth from 887, fifth and sixth from 886. See also Twain's critique of denominationalism in "Captain Simon Wheeler's Dream Visit to Heaven," in Howard G. Baetzhold and Joseph B. McCullough, eds., *The Bible According to Mark Twain* (Athens: University of Georgia Press, 1995), 190–94, his lampooning of evangelist Sam Jones in "A Singular Episode: The Reception of Rev. Sam Jones in Heaven," in ibid., 198–202, and his "Etiquette for the Afterlife: Advice to Paine," in ibid., 208–10.

10. James J. Farrell, *Inventing the American Way of Death, 1830–1920* (Philadelphia: Temple University Press, 1980), 84.

11. Lorraine Boettner, "Postmillennialism," in Robert G. Clouse, *The Meaning of the Millennium* (Downers Grove, IL: InterVarsity Press, 1977), 118. See Moorhead, "Erosion of Postmillennialism," 61–77; Jean B. Quandt, "Religion and Social Thought: The Secularization of Postmillennialism," *American Quarterly* 25 (Oct. 1973), 390–409.

12. Jonathan Butler, *Softly and Tenderly Jesus Is Calling: Heaven and Hell in American Revivalism, 1870–1920* (Brooklyn: Carlson, 1991), 140; A. C. Dixon, *Heaven on Earth* (Greenville, SC: Gospel Hour, 1897), 9; A. J. Gordon, "The Open Way to Heaven," in Charles Wallis, ed., *The Funeral Encyclopedia* (New York: Harper and Brothers, 1953), 54.

13. Butler, *Softly and Tenderly*, 95; Clarke, *Outline*, 444; Harry Emerson Fosdick, *The Assurance of Immortality* (New York: Association Press, 1918), 4; Charles Reynolds Brown, *A Working Faith* (Chapel Hill: University of North Carolina Press, 1926), 81–82.

14. Walter Rauschenbusch, *Christianity and the Social Crisis* (New York: Macmillan, 1910), 160–90, 202–10; Rauschenbusch, *A Theology for the Social Gospel* (New York: Macmillan, 1917), 108 (quotation). See also Colleen McDannell and Bernhard Lang, *Heaven: A History* (New Haven, CT: Yale University Press, 1988), 334.

15. Richard Ely, *Social Aspects of Christianity* (New York: T. Y. Crowell, 1889), 53, 63ff., 26–27, 148–50, 86, 53; first and fourth quotation from 53, second from 148, third from 86. Cf. Clarke, *Outline*, 447–48.

16. Jacob H. Dorn, *Washington Gladden: Prophet of the Social Gospel* (Columbus: Ohio State University Press, 1966), 193–95; Washington Gladden, Christmas Sermon, 1893, Gladden Papers, quoted in Dorn, *Washington Gladden*, 194.

17. Dorn, *Washington Gladden*, 190, 194–95; Washington Gladden, *How Much Is Left of the Old Doctrines?* (Boston: Houghton Mifflin, 1899), 303–16; first quotation from 303, second from 307.

18. John Haynes Holmes, *Is Death the End?* (New York: G. P. Putnam's Sons, 1915), 347, 353–57; first quotation from 353, second and third from 354, fourth from 355, fifth from 357.

19. Brown, *Christian Hope*, 196, 199, 197; first quotation from 196, second from 197.

20. Theodore L. Cuyler, *Beulah-Land: or Words of Cheer for Christian Pilgrims* (New York: American Tract Society, 1896), 183; Gregg, *Heaven-Life*, 100, 84, 124, 113; quotations from 84; R. A. Torrey, "Heaven: What Sort of Place," in Torrey, *Real Salvation and Whole-Hearted Service* (New York: Fleming H. Revell, 1905), 72; H. S. Hoffman, *Life Beyond the Grave* (Philadelphia: Union Press, 1899), 21.

21. Brown, *Christian Hope*, 193 (cf. Hoffman, *Life Beyond the Grave*, 234); Rauschenbusch, *Theology*, 239.

22. See Warren Zimmermann, *The First Great Triumph: How Five Americans Made Their Country a World Power* (New York: Farrar, Straus and Giroux, 2002); John Milton Cooper, Jr., *Pivotal Decades: The United States, 1900–1920* (New York: W. W. Norton, 1990), 3–16; Maureen A. Flanagan, *America Reformed: Progressives and Progressivisms, 1890s–1920s* (New York: Oxford University Press, 2007), 181–97; John Kasson, *Amusing the Millions: Coney Island at the Turn of the Century* (New York: Hill and Wang, 1978); Kathy Peiss, *Cheap Amusements: Working Women and Leisure in Turn-of-the-Century New York* (Philadelphia: Temple University Press, 1986); Steven A. Reiss, *Touching Base: Professional Baseball and American Culture in the Progressive Era* (Urbana: University of Illinois Press, 1999); Clifford Putney, *Muscular Christianity: Manhood and Sports in Protestant America, 1880–1920* (Cambridge, MA: Harvard University Press, 2001), 7; Edwards, *New Spirits*, 88–91, 96. Orison Swett Marsden, who founded *Success Magazine* in 1897, wrote these three books. In 1900, the United States had the world's largest school enrollment in term of "numbers and percentage of the population" (Cooper, *Pivotal Decades*, 3).

23. See Flanagan, *America Reformed*, 122–31; James Kloppenberg, *Uncertain Victory: Social Democracy and Progressivism in European and American Thought, 1870–1920* (New York: Oxford University Press, 1986); Daniel Rodgers, *Atlantic Crossings: Social Politics in a Progressive Age* (Cambridge, MA: Harvard University Press, 1998); Morton Keller, *Regulating a New Society: Public Policy and Social Change in America, 1900–1930* (Cambridge, MA: Harvard University Press, 1994).

24. S. D. Gordon, *Quiet Talks about Life After Death* (New York: Fleming H. Revell, 1920), 45; William Uylat, *The First Years of the Life of the Redeemed After Death* (New York: Abbey Press, 1901), 164; Billy Sunday, "Heaven," in John R. Rice, ed., *The Best of Billy Sunday* (Murfreesboro, TN: Sword of the Lord, 1965), 342; J. Wilbur Chapman, *When Home Is Heaven* (New York: Fleming H. Revell, 1917), 18–21; quotation from 20. Cf. Burdett Hart, *Aspects of Heaven* (New York: American Tract Society, 1896), 67.

25. Uylat, *First Years*, 191.

26. James M. Gray, *Progress in the Life to Come* (New York: Fleming H. Revell, 1910), 35; Henry D. Kimball, *Beyond the Horizon, or, Bright Side Chapters on the Future Life* (New York: Eaton & Mains, 1896), 217–18 (cf. Gordon, *Life After Death*, 42); Gregg, *Heaven-Life*, 44; Uylat, *First Years*, 191, 205; quotations in that order (cf. Strong, *Paradise*, 115, 117; Henry S. Belden, *Heaven* [Akron, OH: New Werner, 1912], 122, 132, 134); George Hepworth, *They Met in Heaven* (New York: E. P. Dutton, 1894), 142; Gilbert, *The Hereafter*, 181; Ida C. Craddock, *The Heaven of the Bible* (Philadelphia: J. B. Lippincott, 1897), 49–54. Cf. Mary Sparkes Wheeler, *As It Is in Heaven* (Philadelphia: Ziegler, 1906), 344; Rebecca Springer, *Within the Gates* (Dallas: Christ for the

Nations, 1979 [1899]), 36; A. H. Strong, *Systematic Theology* (New York: Fleming H. Revell, 1907), 585; Charles Reynolds Brown, *The Social Message of the Modern Pulpit* (New York: Charles Scribner's Sons, 1912), 259; Lyman Abbott, *The Other Room* (New York: Outlook, 1903), 92.

27. Rauschenbusch, *Theology*, 235–37; quotation from 236.

28. Rauschenbusch, *Theology*, 237.

29. Rauschenbusch, *Theology*, 230–32; first and second quotations from 230, third and fourth from 232. Rauschenbusch admitted that some of these ideas were simply "personal fancy about a fascinating subject." The only things Christians could know with assurance were that God would forever love His children; "that the law of love and solidarity" would function more effectively in heaven than on earth; and that "salvation, growth and solidarity" were best advanced by service (238).

30. Kenneth Cauthen, *The Impact of American Religious Liberalism* (New York: Harper and Row, 1962), 55. For example, William Adams Brown, *Christian Theology in Outline* (New York: Charles Scribner's Sons, 1906), 258–60, 412–23; Rauschenbusch, *Theology*, 223–39.

31. Lyman Abbott, "Life, Growth, and Heaven," *Outlook* 104 (Aug. 2, 1913), 741–42; quotation from 742; Gladden, *How Much*, 303; Clarke, *Outline*, 467–72; quotation from 467.

32. Farrell, *Inventing*, 86; Smyth, *Immortality*, 64, 52; Brown, *Christian Hope*, 178; Gladden, *How Much*, 318. Cf. Holmes, *Death*, 289–99, 349; Abbott, "Life, Growth, and Heaven," 741–42; Charles Cuthbert Hall, *The Redeemed Life After Death* (New York: Fleming H. Revell, 1905), 49.

33. Clarke, *Outline*, 468–69; quotation from 469; Hart, *Heaven*, 121, 127, 130; quotation from 121; Kimball, *Horizon*, 226, 229; quotations in that order.

34. For example, Torrey, "What Sort of Place," 73.

35. William T. Ellis, *"Billy" Sunday: The Man and His Message* (Philadelphia: John C. Winston, 1914), 341; Torrey, "What Sort of Place," 74 (quotation), 79. See also Charles Callan, *Out of Shadows into Light* (Baltimore: John Murphy, 1913), 44–45.

36. R. A. Torrey, "Catching a Glimpse of Heaven," in *Heaven or Hell* (New Kensington, PA: Whitaker House, 1985), 73–75, quotation from 75; R. A. Torrey, *What the Bible Teaches* (New York: Fleming H. Revell, 1898), 491–92; Ellis, *"Billy" Sunday*, 417–20 (quotation from 418); Sunday, "Heaven," 339–42.

37. Rebecca Ruter Springer, *My Dream of Heaven*, in Calvin Miller, ed., *Images of Heaven: Reflections on Glory* (Wheaton, IL: Harold Shaw, 1996), 113; Hoffman, *Life Beyond the Grave*, 288–91, 299; quotation from 290; Kimball, *Horizon*, 216.

38. Holmes, *Death*, 276–77, 280–81, 284–86; first, second, and sixth quotations from 284, third and fourth from 276, fifth from 277; seventh from 285, eighth from 286, ninth from 287, tenth from 288.

39. Moorhead, *World without End*, 64 (see Geoffrey Rowell, *Hell and the Victorians: A Study of the Nineteenth-Century Theological Controversies concerning Eternal Punishment and the Future Life* [Oxford, UK: Clarendon Press, 1974], 18–23); Kimball, *Horizon*, 73; Clarke, *Outline*, 459, 466; quotation from 459.

40. T. A. Goodwin, *The Mode of Man's Immortality: or the When, Where, and How of the Future Life* (New York: Fords, Howard, and Hulbert, 1879), 168.

41. Abbott, *Other Room*, 72, 75, 73, 76–77; first three quotations from 72, fourth from 73.

42. Gladden, *How Much*, 307–10; first two quotation from 308, third from 309; Smyth, *Modern Belief*, 55–56; first two quotations from 55, third from 56.

43. Clarke, *Outline*, 454–57; first quotation from 455, second from 457.

44. Strong, *Systematic Theology*, 231. See also "The Resurrection and Modern Thought," *Homiletic Review* 89 (Apr. 1925), 318–20; James H. Moorhead, "'As Though Nothing at All Had Happened': Death and Afterlife in Protestant Thought, 1840–1925," *Soundings* 67 (Winter 1984), 462.

45. Torrey, "What Sort of Place," 73; Torrey, *The Return of the Lord Jesus* (Los Angeles: Bible Institute, 1913), 59; quotations in that order; Callan, *Shadows*, 68–69; quotations in that order; Hall, *Redeemed Life*, 56. See also Butler, *Softly and Tenderly*, 161.

46. Hoffman, *Life Beyond the Grave*, 187–206; Kimball, *Horizon,* 235–38, 244–46; Sunday, "Heaven," 345; Gordon, *Life After Death*, 36.

47. Hart, *Heaven*, 186; Kimball, *Horizon,* 239–41; first and third quotations from 239, second from 241; Rauschenbusch, *Theology*, 235.

48. Hart, *Heaven*, 119, 177; quotations in that order; Strong, *Paradise*, 77, 84, 75–76; first quotation from 77, second from 75 (cf. *Billy Sunday Speaks* [New York: Chelsea House, 1970], 193; Sam Jones, "Sowing and Reaping," in *Sam Jones' Sermons* [Chicago: Rhodes & McClure, 1886], 415); Torrey, "What Sort of Place," 74–75; quotation from 74; Strong, *Systematic Theology*, 585; Callan, *Shadows*, 49 (cf. Belden, *Heaven*, 128; Uylat, *First Years*, 195); Ada Blenkhorn, "The Unseen Country," in William Phillips Hall, J. Wilbur Chapman, and W. S. Weeden, *Christian Hymns*, No. 1 (Philadelphia: Hall-Mack, 1899), no. 63.

49. Butler, *Softly and Tenderly*, 118; J. Wilbur Chapman, *The Ivory Palaces of the King* (Chicago: Fleming H. Revell, 1893), 66; Chapman, *Home*, 127; R. A. Torrey, "Time and Eternity Contrasted," in Torrey, *The Gospel for Today: New Evangelistic Sermons for a New Day* (New York: Fleming H. Revell, 1922), 148; Torrey, *Bible Teaches*, 493; quotations in that order.

50. Torrey, "Time and Eternity," 148, 149, 150, 144; quotation from 149.

51. Dixon, *Heaven on Earth*, 43, 68; quotation from 43; Hart, *Heaven*, 140–51; first quotation from 144, second from 150–51; (cf. Callan, *Shadows*, 44, 46); Gregg, *Heaven-Life*, 161, 142, 129, 131, 148, 145; quotation from 129; Springer, *Gates*, 15, 25; quotations from 15; Strong, *Systematic Theology*, 585.

52. Farrell, *Inventing*, 92–93; Gladden, *How Much* 175–87; George Harris, *Moral Evolution* (Boston: Houghton Mifflin, 1896), 407–8.

53. Gladden, *How Much*, 189–92; quotations from 192; Clarke, *Outline*, 332–49; quotation from 339. Cf. Newman Smyth, *Christian Facts and Forces* (New York: Charles Scribner's Sons, 1887), 210–24.

54. Clarke, *Outline*, 469–77, 480; first quotation from 472, second from 473, third and fourth from 480.

55. Charles Reynolds Brown, *The Larger Faith* (Boston: Pilgrim Press, 1923), 167–68 (first quotation); Brown, *The Main Points: A Study in Christian Beliefs* (Boston: Pilgrim Press, 1911), 140–45; second quotation from 141–42, third from 145. Cf. Brown, *Working Faith*, 47–87.

56. Torrey, "Time and Eternity," 146–47; first quotation from 146; Torrey, "Catching a Glimpse," 77 (second quotation); Torrey, "The New Birth," in Torrey, *Heaven or Heaven*, 82; Ellis, *"Billy" Sunday*, 411, 415, 389; Billy Sunday, "Christ's Atonement for Our Sins: Central Doctrine of Christian Faith," in Rice, *Best of Billy Sunday*, 264; Sunday, "Heaven," 346 (first quotation); *Billy Sunday Speaks*, 192 (second quotation). Cf. Sam Jones, "What Must I Do to Be Saved?" in *Sam Jones' Sermons*, 418–33; Belden, *Heaven*, 82–83; Hart, *Heaven* 180; L. W. Munhall, "The Doctrines That Must Be Emphasized in Successful Evangelism," in R. A. Torrey et al., *The Fundamentals: A Testament to the Truth*, 5 vols. (Grand Rapids, MI: Baker Book House, 1970

[1910–15]), 4:156–67; George W. Lasher, "Regeneration—Conversion—Reformation," in ibid., 4:133–38. John A. Broadus, the president of Southern Baptist Theological Seminary in Louisville, accused those who did not believe that Christ's substitutionary atonement was necessary for salvation as having inadequate views of sin and God. By stressing only God's mercy and love, they ignored God's holiness and justice. Christ's crucifixion satisfied God's wrath against sin, enabling Him to forgive those who accepted Christ's sacrifice on their behalf ("Necessity of the Atonement," in Vernon Latrelle Stanfield, ed., *Favorite Sermons of John A. Broadus* [New York: Harper and Brothers, 1959], 96, 94).

57. Butler, *Softly and Tenderly*, 68.

58. See Moorhead, "As Though Nothing," 456, and Farrell, *Inventing*, 84, who called my attention to the periodical articles in this section. See also Lyman Abbott, "The Present Hell," *Outlook* 104 (July 12, 1913), 556–57; *Progressive Orthodoxy: A Contribution to the Interpretation of Christian Doctrines* (Boston: Houghton Mifflin, 1892), 67–111; S. D. McConnell, *The Evolution of Immortality* (New York: Macmillan, 1901), 139.

59. George T. Knight, "The New Hell," *North American Review* 179 (July 1904), 128–35; first quotation from 129, second from 134, third from 135; Gertrude E. T. Slaughter, "Death-Doors and Asphodel," *North American Review* 204 (Dec. 1916), 917. Knight cited Francis Patton, the president of Princeton University, as contending that the number of the lost would be about the same proportion of the population confined to prisons on earth; Charles Briggs of Union Theological Seminary as arguing that the number of those in hell would be "inconsiderable"; and George Gordon and Amory Bradford, the president of the General Conference of Congregationalists, as maintaining that all people would eventually be saved (129–30). Knight complained that many pictured hell as similar to some of America's "reform prisons" that were "made so comfortable and honorable" that they failed to achieve their purpose (135). Cf. Frederick A. Fernald, "Ancient and Modern Ideas of Hell," *Popular Science Monthly* 37 (Aug. 1890), 489–501; George Wolfe Shinn, "What Has Become of Hell?" *North American Review* 170 (June 1900), 837–49; "Abolishing Hell-Fire by Vote," *Literary Digest* 45 (Aug. 3, 1920), 194; Lyman Abbott, "Why I Believe We Do Not Die," *Ladies Home Journal* 27 (Mar. 1910), 22.

60. T. J. Jackson Lears, *No Place of Grace: Antimodernism and the Transformation of American Culture, 1880–1920* (New York: Pantheon Books, 1981), 45; "The Passing of the Devil," *Scribner's* 25 (Apr. 1899), 508. See also Edward H. Jewett, *Diabolology: The Person and Kingdom of Satan* (New York: T. Whittaker, 1890).

61. See Eugene Smith, "The Old Penology and the New," *North American Review* 184 (Jan. 4, 1907), 80–86; Thomas G. Blomberg and Karol Lucken, *American Penology: A History of Control* (New York: Aldine de Gruyter, 2000), 70–75, 83–89, 99–100; Blake McKelvey, *American Prisons: A History of Good Intentions* (Montclair, NJ: Patterson Smith, 1977), 24–29, 38–39, 234–67.

62. Moorhead, "As Though Nothing," 456; Thomas Percival Beyer, "The Art of Everlasting Life," *Forum* 51 (Apr. 1914), 484–88 (quotation from 484); Arthur Chambers, *Our Life After Death: Or the Teaching of the Bible Concerning the Unseen World* (Philadelphia: George W. Jacobs, 1902), 208; G. Lowes Dickinson, *Is Immortality Desirable?* (Boston: Houghton Mifflin, 1909), 25–26.

63. Rauschenbusch, *Theology*, 232–35; quotations from 233.

64. Rauschenbusch, *Theology*, 233–34; all quotations from 234.

65. Washington Gladden, "Under the Laws of His Own Moral Nature, and by His Own Volition, Man Fixes His Own Destiny," in *That Unknown Country or, What Living Men Believe concerning Punishment after Death* (Springfield, MA: C. A. Nichols, 1891), p. 387 (Moorhead argues that this collection of essays "provides an excellent gauge of opinions on hell in the late 1800s" ["Erosion of Postmillennialism," 71]); Billy Sunday, "What Shall the End Be?" in Ellis, *"Billy" Sunday*, 187. See also Sunday, "Tormented in Hell," in Curtis Hutson, comp., *Great Preaching on Hell* (Murfreesboro, TN: Sword of the Lord, 1989), 123–33.

66. Moody seemed very uncomfortable with the doctrine of hell and preferred stressing God's love (Butler, *Softly and Tenderly*, 79). See R. A. Torrey, *Soul-Winning Sermons* (Westwood, NJ: Fleming H. Revell, 1956 [1925]), 231–48; Torrey, "God's Blockades on the Road to Hell," in Hutson, *Great Preaching*, 195–209; Samuel Jones, "Not Polite to Believe in Hell," 233–34; "The Localities of Hell," 234; and "Greedy for Hell," 236–37, all in *Sam Jones' Gospel Sermons* (Chicago: Rhodes and McClure, 1898).

67. Ellis, *"Billy" Sunday*, 397, 399; first two quotations from 397, third from 399; Strong, *Systematic Theology*, 587; William C. Procter, "What Christ Teaches Concerning Future Retribution," in Torrey et al., *Fundamentals*, 3: 58.

68. H. O. Rowlands, "The Present Drift in Eschatology," *Baptist Quarterly Review* 11 (Oct. 1889), 411; Edwin Locke, ed., *Journal of the Twenty-Seventh General Conference of the Methodist Episcopal Church* (New York: Methodist Book Concern, 1916), 1354–60; Moorhead, "Erosion of Postmillennialism," 71 (quotation); Moorhead, "As Though Nothing," 455, 457. He cites as examples of this last point Charles Hodge, *Systematic Theology*, 3 vols. (New York: Scribner, Armstrong, 1874–75), 3: 537; William G. T. Shedd, *The Doctrine of Endless Punishment* (New York: Charles Scribner's Sons, 1887), 15, 147, 159; and G. Frederick Wright, *An Inquiry Concerning the Relations of Death to Probation* (Boston: Congregationalist Publishing Society, 1882), 44–47.

69. See Daniel Day Williams, *The Andover Liberals: A Study in American Theology* (New York: Octagon Books, 1970), 65ff.

70. R. A. Torrey, *The Voice of God in the Present Hour* (New York: Fleming H. Revell, 1917), 107; Billy Sunday, *New York Times*, Apr. 9, 1917, 4; Gordon, *Life After Death*, 183. Cf. Sam Jones, *Quit Your Meanness* (Cincinnati: Cranston & Stowe, 1886), 79–90, 156–66; Procter, "What Christ Teaches," 60.

71. Moorhead, "Erosion of Postmillennialism," 69. See David E. Stannard, ed., *Death in America* (Philadelphia: University of Pennsylvania Press, 1975); Charles O. Jackson, *Passing: The Vision of Death in America* (Westport, CT: Greenwood Press, 1977); and Farrell, *Inventing*.

72. Moorhead, "As Though Nothing," 466; Jacob Joseph, "The Dying of Death," *Review of Reviews* 20 (Sept. 1899), 364–65; Lyman Abbott, "There Are No Dead," *Outlook* 104 (Aug. 30, 1913), 979.

73. Moorhead, *World without End*, 58 (first quotation); George A. Gordon, *The Witness to Immortality in Literature, Philosophy and Life* (Boston: Houghton Mifflin, 1893), 238; Farrell, *Inventing*, 13 (second quotation); Gladden, *How Much*, 313; Abbott, "No Dead," 980 (first quotation); Abbott, *Other Room*, 14 (second quotation), 21, 91–92. Cf. Clarke, *Outline*, 449–50.

74. Moorhead, *World without End*, 65 (first quotation); Smyth, *Place of Death*, 154; Farrell, *Inventing*, 89–90.

CHAPTER 8

1. See Robert T. Handy, *The American Religious Depression, 1925–1935* (Philadelphia: Fortress Press, 1968).

2. Tom Brokaw, *The Greatest Generation* (New York: Random House, 1998), 55.

3. Will Herberg, *Protestant-Catholic-Jew: An Essay in the American Religious Sociology* (Garden City, NY: Doubleday, 1956), especially 49–57, 85–113, 276–77.

4. On fundamentalism, see George M. Marsden, *Fundamentalism and American Culture* (New York: Oxford University Press, 2006); Joel A. Carpenter, *Revive Us Again: The Reawakening of American Fundamentalism* (New York: Oxford University Press, 1997). On liberalism, see Lloyd J. Averill, *American Theology in the Liberal Tradition* (Philadelphia: Westminster Press 1967); Kenneth Cauthen, *The Impact of American Religious Liberalism* (New York: Harper & Row, 1962); W. R. Hutchinson, ed., *American Protestant Thought in the Liberal Era* (Lanham, MD: University Press of America, 1984). Bradley J. Longfield estimates that by 1920, liberals controlled about half of the nation's Protestant seminaries and publishing firms and about a third of all Protestant congregations. See "Liberalism/Modernism, Protestant," in Daniel Reid et al., eds., *Dictionary of Christianity in America* (Downers Grove, IL: InterVarsity Press, 1990), 647. On evangelicalism, see George Marsden, *Reforming Fundamentalism: Fuller Seminary and the New Evangelicalism* (Grand Rapids, MI: Eerdmans, 1987); D. G. Hart, *That Old-Time Religion in Modern America: Evangelical Protestantism in the Twentieth Century* (Chicago: Ivan R. Dee, 2002); Garth M. Rosell, *The Surprising Work of God: Harold John Ockenga, Billy Graham, and the Rebirth of Evangelicalism* (Grand Rapids, MI: Baker Academic, 2008). On Neo-orthodoxy, see Richard Wightman Fox, *Reinhold Niebuhr: A Biography* (New York: Pantheon Books, 1985); Robin W. Lovin, *Reinhold Niebuhr and Christian Realism* (New York: Cambridge University Press, 1995); Douglas John Hall, *Remembered Voices: Reclaiming the Legacy of "Neo-Orthodoxy"* (Louisville, KY: Westminster John Knox Press, 1998); Heather Warren, *Theologians of a New World Order: Reinhold Niebuhr and the Christian Realists, 1920–1948* (New York: Oxford University Press, 1997).

5. On dispensationalism, see Colleen McDannell and Bernhard Lang, *Heaven: A History* (New Haven, CT: Yale University Press, 1988), 338–40; Timothy P. Weber, *Living in the Shadow of the Second Coming: American Premillennialism, 1875–1925* (New York: Oxford University Press, 1979); *The Scofield Reference Bible* (New York: Oxford University Press, 1967 [1917]), 5, 1250; C. I. Scofield, *Addresses on Prophecy* (New York: Gaebelein, 1910), 130 (McDannell and Lang called my attention to the last two sources);William Biederwolf, *The Adventures of the Hereafter* (New York: R. R. Smith, 1930), viii.

6. Charles Reynolds Brown, *A Working Faith* (Chapel Hill: University of North Carolina Press, 1926), 66–67; quotations in that order (cf. John Herman Randall and J. H. Randall, Jr., *Religion and the Modern World* [New York: Stokes, 1929], 66–67, 206; Harry Elmer Barnes, *The Twilight of Christianity* [New York: Vanguard Press, 1929], 281–82);John Sutherland Bonnell, *Heaven and Hell: A Present-Day Christian Interpretation* (New York: Abingdon Press, 1956), 23, 21; quotations in that order; Rufus M. Jones, in Sydney Strong, ed., *We Believe in Immortality: Affirmations by One Hundred Men and Women* (New York: Coward-McCann, 1929), 124; Harry Emerson Fosdick, *Spiritual Values and Eternal Life* (Cambridge, MA: Harvard University Press, 1927), 36, 14, quotations in that order; Shailer Mathews, *Immortality and the Cosmic Process* (Cambridge, MA: Harvard University Press, 1933), 4–5; quotations in that order; W. H. R. Faunce, in Jacob Helder, ed., *Greatest Thoughts on Immortality* (New York: Richard R. Smith,

1930), 103. Cf. Charles W. Eliot in ibid., 107. For liberals like Mathews, God was not "an entity objective to the universe." Rather God stood for "our conception of those personality-producing activities of the cosmos with which we are organically connected." This perspective, he avowed, conserved the most important features of the conventional view of immortality while avoiding its "recourse to rewards and punishments" (Mathews, *Immortality*, 39, 48; first and second quotation from 39, third from 48).

7. James Campbell, *Heaven Opened: A Book of Comfort and Hope* (New York: Fleming H. Revell, 1924), 21, 53; Edward Bounds, *Heaven: A Place, A City, A Home* (Grand Rapids, MI: Baker Book House, 1975 [1921]), 38; Biederwolf, *Adventures*, 103–4; quotation from 104; *Picture Post* (London), Mar. 20, 1954, 40 (first quotation); Graham's 1955 radio message, "Heaven," published by the BGEA; Columbia State, Mar. 10, 1950, 7-B (second quotation). See also "Religion: The New Evangelist," *Time*, Oct. 25, 1954, 58.

8. Desmond J. Leahy, *St. Augustine on Eternal Life* (London, 1939), xi–xii. Cf. J. P. McCarthy, *Heaven* (New York: P. J. Kenedy & Sons, 1958), 8.

9. John MacNeill, *Many Mansions: Sermons on the Future Life* (New York: Richard R. Smith, 1930), 194; Jesse T. Whitley, *What Jesus Said About Heaven: A Study in the Four Gospels* (Nashville, TN: Cokesbury, 1925), 82. Cf. Bounds, *Heaven*, 50; Robert Ervin Hough, *The Christian after Death* (Chicago: Moody Press, 1947), 103; Campbell, *Heaven Opened*, 147, 149.

10. J. P. Arendzen, *Heaven Sense: What the Scripture and the Catholic Church Really Teach about Heaven* (Manchester, NH: Sophia Institute, 2004), originally *The Church Triumphant* (New York: Macmillan, 1928), 37, 38, 47, 60; first quotation from 37, second from 38; McCarthy, *Heaven*, 83, 92; quotations in that order.

11. Martin J. Scott, *What Is Heaven* (New York: P. J. Kenedy & Sons, 1936), 65, 64, 72, 131, 154, 78, 150, 102; quotations in that order.

12. Fulton J. Sheen, *Go to Heaven* (New York: McGraw-Hill, 1960), 232–33; first quotation from 233, the remainder from 232. On Sheen, see Thomas C. Reeves, *America's Bishop: The Life and Times of Fulton J. Sheen* (San Francisco: Encounter Books, 2001).

13. Walter Russell Bowie, "Our Reach to Heaven," in Charles Wallis, ed., *The Funeral Encyclopedia* (New York: Harper and Brothers, 1953), 52; MacNeill, *Mansions*, 196.

14. John Anderson, *The Heaven of the Bible: A Devotional and Inspirational Book* (Morristown, TN: Triangle Press, 1934), 291, 248; quotations in that order (cf. Shaw, *Life after Death*, 53; Adolph C. Ferber, *Where is Heaven?* (New York: Pageant Press, 1955), 194; Bonnell, *Heaven and Hell*, 26); Lorraine Boettner, *Immortality* (Grand Rapids, MI: Eerdmans, 1956), 91–97; Campbell, *Heaven Opened*, 120, 123 (quotation) (cf. MacNeill, *Mansions*, 204; Vance H. Webster, "Life's Dimensions," in Wallis, *Funeral Encyclopedia*, 114; Shaw, *Life after Death*, 55; Hough, *Christian after Death*, 106; Whitley, *What Jesus Said*, 83–91; Bounds, *Heaven*, 50); Bowie, "Our Reach to Heaven," 52; George W. Coleman in Strong, *Immortality*, 89–90 (quotation). Cf. Benjamin Goodfield, "Gracious Interpretations," in Wallis, *Funeral Encyclopedia*, 69; William E. Brooks, "In My Father's," in ibid., 63; Biederwolf, *Adventures*, 144–48; Robert Dane Cook, *The Heavenly City: A Devotional Exposition of the Christian Hope* (Dallas: Mathis and Van Nort), 113.

15. Anderson, *Heaven*, 217, 221 (quotation); Scott, *Heaven*, 125. Cf. John Macintosh Shaw, *Life after Death: The Christian View of the Future Life* (Toronto: Ryerson Press, 1945), 52; Hough, *Christian after Death*, 113–14, 93–94; McCarthy, *Heaven*, 123.

16. Campbell, *Heaven Opened*, 141; Bounds, *Heaven*, 62 (quotation); Whitley, *What Jesus Said*, 100.

17. Anderson, *Heaven*, 294; W. G. Heslop, *Heaven: Our Father's House, Our Heavenly Home, God's City of Gold* (Grand Rapids, MI: Peniel Press, 1937), 103; Biederwolf, *Adventures*, 146–47 (quotation); Arendzen, *Heaven Sense*, 61, 65, 68. Cf. Hough, *Christian after Death*, 107.

18. Charles R. Brown in Strong, *Immortality*, 106; Albert Knudson, *The Doctrine of Redemption* (Nashville, TN: Abingdon Press, 1933), 504–5; Fosdick, *Eternal Life*, 36–37: first quotation from 36; Fosdick, "The Eternal Victories over the Temporal," in Fosdick, *On Being Fit to Live With: Sermons on Post-war Christianity* (New York: Harper & Brothers, 1946), 215–16; second and third quotations from 215, remainder from 216. Cf. Ralph W. Sockman, "Life Can Be Eternal," in G. Paul Butler, ed., *Best Sermons*, Vol. VII: *1959–1960* (New York: Thomas Y. Crowell, 1959), 7. See Reinhold Niebuhr, *The Nature and Destiny of Man: A Christian Interpretation*, 2 vols. (New York: Charles Scribner's Sons, 1941–43), 2: 294.

19. Cauthen, *Religious Liberalism*, 242.

20. Fox, *Reinhold Niebuhr*, 215; Niebuhr to Waldo Frank, Apr. 26, 1938, Frank Papers; Niebuhr to Norman Kemp-Smith, Feb. 9, 1940, Kemp-Smith Papers, both as cited by Fox, 215; Paul Tillich, *Systematic Theology*, 3 vols. (Chicago: University of Chicago Press, 1963), 3: 408 (first quotation); McDannell and Lang, *Heaven*, 328–30; second and third quotations from 328, fourth from 329, fifth from 330.

21. Milton Steinberg, *Basic Judaism* (New York: Harcourt, Brace and World, 1947), 196–97 (first quotation), 199 (second quotation); Leo Baeck, *The Essence of Judaism* (New York: Schocken Books, 1948), 184 (third quotation), 185 (fourth quotation). Steinberg insisted that no other tenet of Judaism had been "more divergently construed" as had "the form of the hereafter" (197), and Baeck argued that the Old Testament, while not denying belief in life after death, said little about it (184).

22. Niebuhr, *Nature and Destiny*, 2: 294–98; first quotation from 294, second, third, fourth, and fifth from 295, sixth from 297, seventh from 298.

23. R. R. Moton in Strong, *Immortality*, 63; Samuel Schulman in ibid., 136–37, quotations in that order; Vida Scudder in ibid., 109; Isaac Landman in ibid., 161.

24. Benjamin Mays and Joseph Nicholson, *The Negro's Church* (New York: Arno Press, 1969 [1933]), 17, 59, 70–75, 92–93; Robert S. Lynd and Helen Merrell Lynd, *Middletown: A Study in American Culture* (New York: Harcourt, Brace, 1931), 405–6.

25. Campbell, *Heaven Opened*, 132–33, 75–76; first and third quotations from 132, second from 75; Bounds, *Heaven*, 125, 120–21; first quotation from 125, second from 120; Martin Luther King, Jr., "The Role of the Church in Facing the Nation's Chief Moral Dilemma," in Davis W. Houck and David E. Dixon, eds., *Rhetoric, Religion, and the Civil Rights Movement* (Waco, TX: Baylor University Press, 2006), 220. Ralph Abernathy, on the other hand, trying to help blacks cope with their earthly trials and defeats, reminded them that "this world ultimately is not our home" and that "we are citizens of another world" ("Trying to Get Home Without Jesus" [1961 sermon] in ibid., 436). Cf. Anderson, *Heaven*, 68; Lowell Russell Ditzen, "Why Do One's Best When the World Is Going to Hell?" in G. Paul Butler, ed., *Best Sermons*, 1951–1952 edition (New York: Macmillan, 1952), 202–3.

26. Campbell, *Heaven Opened*, 125, 128, 86, 87, 131; first quotation from 125, second from 86, third from 87; Biederwolf, *Adventures*, 195, 104; quotations in that order; Shailer Matthews in Strong, *Immortality*, 92.

27. Bonnell, *Heaven and Hell*, 25; Anderson, *Heaven*, 283; Whitley, *What Jesus Said*, 93–103; first quotation from 93, second from 98, third from 96. Cf. Cook, *Heavenly City*, 90.

28. See Miriam Van Scott, *Encyclopedia of Heaven* (New York: St. Martin's Press, 1999), 127–28, 109–10, 130–31, 141–42, 11–12; first quotation from 141, second from 142, third from 111.

29. Hough, *Christian after Death*, 89; Biederwolf, *Adventures*, 76; Anderson, *Heaven*, 249, 251; quotations from 249; Cook, *Heavenly City*, 135, 138, quotation from 135.

30. Biederwolf, *Adventures*, 70; Cf. Hough, *Christian after Death*, 90.

31. MacNeill, *Mansions*, 72–73; Daniel A. Poling in Strong, *Immortality*, 75; Bonnell, *Heaven and Hell*, 25; Biederwolf, *Adventures*, 73.

32. Whitley, *What Jesus Said*, 71; Hough, *Christian after Death*, 91.

33. Biederwolf, *Adventures*, 70; Hough, *Christian after Death*, 89.

34. Whitley, *What Jesus Said*, 71–72; Cook, *Heavenly City*, 130; Anderson, *Heaven*, 278.

35. Charles M. Sheldon in Strong, *Immortality*, 98; Fosdick, "Eternal Victories," 217–18; Scott, *Heaven*, 122. Cf. Biederwolf, *Adventures*, 68; Arendzen, *Heaven Sense*, 44, 62.

36. Billy Graham, *My Answer* (Garden City, NY: Doubleday, 1960), 200; Anderson, *Heaven*, 277.

37. Fosdick, "A Great Year for Easter," in Harry Emerson Fosdick, *Living Under Tension: Sermons on Christianity Today* (New York: Harper Brothers, 1941), 250; Bonnell, *Heaven and Hell*, 28; McCarthy, *Heaven*, 58–60, 68. Cf. Biederwolf, *Adventures*, 122; Arendzen, *Heaven Sense*, 63; Cook, *Heavenly City*, 81.

38. Anderson, *Heaven*, 294–95; Hough, *Christian after Death*, 123–26; David I. Berger, "Confident Dying," in Wallis, *Funeral Encyclopedia*, 125 (cf. Biederwolf, *Adventures*, 151); Bonnell, *Heaven and Hell*, 29; Mrs. Raiff, "Get the Right Ticket" (1927), in Bettye Collier-Thomas, *Daughters of Thunder: Black Women Preachers and Their Sermons, 1850–1979* (San Francisco: Jossey–Bass, 1998), 172. Cf. Ella Eugene Whitfield, "Salvation Is a Discovery Found in Jesus Christ" (1926), in ibid., 157–59; John Roach Straton, "God's Way of Life for Man," in Straton, *The Old Gospel at the Heart of the Metropolis* (New York: George H. Doran, 1925), 108–20; Carl F. H. Henry, "Christ on the Margins of Life," in Butler, *Best Sermons, 1959–1960*, 75; James M. Gray, *How to Get Right with God* (New York: Fleming H. Revell, 1925), 9–14; Bob Jones, *Bob Jones' Revival Sermons* (Wheaton, IL: Sword of the Lord, 1948), 94–106.

39. Billy Graham, *Peace with God* (Garden City, NY: Doubleday, 1953), 106–7, 143–44; first quotation from 143, second from 144, third from 107.

40. William McLoughlin, *Billy Graham: Revivalist in a Secular Age* (New York: Ronald Press, 1960), 132–33; quotations from 133.

41. See Graham, *My Answer*, 209; Graham, *Peace with God*, 135–39.

42. Charles Reynolds Brown, *Have We Outgrown Religion?* (New York: Harper & Brothers, 1932), 189–90, 193, 197; first two quotations from 189, third and fourth from 190. For most residents of Middletown, "what you believe is not so important as the kind of person you are." See Robert S. Lynd and Helen Merrill Lynd, *Middletown in Transition: A Study in Cultural Conflicts* (New York: Harcourt, Brace, 1937), 416.

43. On the liberal position, see Harry Emerson Fosdick, "Christ Himself Is Christianity," in Fosdick, *On Being Fit*, 193–98; Fosdick, "Christian Faith—Fantasy or Truth?" in ibid., 38; Fosdick, "The Essential Elements in a Vital Christian Experience," in ibid., 187; Georgia E. Harkness, *Understanding the Christian Faith* (Nashville, TN: Abingdon-Cokesbury Press, 1947), 106–20. On universal salvation, see Unitarian-Universalist Association, "What Do Unitarians Believe?" in J. Gordon Melton, ed., *American Religious Creeds*, vol. 3 (New York: Triumph Books, 1991), 16; Fosdick, *Dear Mr. Brown: Letters to a Person Perplexed about Religion* (New York: Harper, 1961),

110–13; Nels Ferre, *The Christian Understanding of God* (New York: Harper, 1951), 229–30; Tillich, *Systematic Theology*, 3: 406–9; Tillich, *The New Being* (New York: Scribner's, 1955), 175–79; Tillich, *The Shaking of the Foundations* (New York: Scribner's, 1949), 76–86.

44. http://www.jjnet.com/archives/documents/humanist.htm. See also Corliss Lamont, *Humanism as a Philosophy* (New York: Philosophical Library, 1949).

45. Scott, *Heaven*, 69, 52, 33, 59; first quotation from 59, second from 69; "Heaven Grows in Us," in Fulton Sheen, *Through the Year with Fulton Sheen: Inspirational Readings for Each Day of the Year* (Ann Arbor, MI: Servant Books, 1985), 222.

46. Sheen, *Heaven*, 213–15; first quotation from 213, second from 214, remainder from 215.

47. Lynd and Lynd, *Middletown*, 416; Fosdick, "Christian Faith," 67; Sockman, "Life Can Be Eternal," 8; "What Do Unitarians Believe?" 16. Cf. Gerald Kennedy, "Gamblers at the Cross," in Butler, *Best Sermons*, 1951–1952, 123; *What Is Hell?* (New York: Harper and Brothers, 1930), a collection of essays by leading British theologians, philosophers, and church leaders.

48. Hyman J. Appelman, *Hell: What Is It?* (Grand Rapids, MI: Zondervan, 1947), 20; Graham, *Peace with God*, 73–76; first quotation from 73; *Time*, Oct. 25, 1954, 58 (see the sermons of Appelman, John R. Rice, H. A. Ironside, John Linton, and Fred Barlow in Curtis Hutson, comp., *Great Preaching on Hell* [Murfreesboro, TN: Sword of the Lord, 1989] and Carlyle B. Haynes, *Life, Death, and Immortality* [Nashville, TN: Southern Publishing Association, 1952], 219–64; 333–57; Harry Buis, *The Doctrine of Eternal Punishment* (Philadelphia: Presbyterian and Reformed, 1957); H. M. S. Richards, *What Jesus Said* [Nashville, TN: Southern Publishing Association, 1957], 370–84); Stanley High, *Billy Graham: The Personal Story of the Man, His Message, and His Mission* (New York: McGraw-Hill, 1956), 63–64 (second quotation); Graham's 1957 radio message, "Immortality," quoted in *Billy Graham Christian Worker's Handbook*, 146, http://www.hbclz.org/Content/10048/28321.pdf (third quotation); Graham, *My Answer*, 201 (fourth quotation); Cook, *Heavenly City*, 90.

49. Fulton J. Sheen, *A Fulton Sheen Reader* (St. Paul: Carillon Books, 1979), 159–62; first and second quotation from 160; third from 161, fourth from 162, fifth from 159.

50. Sheen, *Reader*, 153 (first and second quotations) Sheen, *Heaven*, 216 (third quotation).

51. Sheen, *Reader*, 153–57; first and second quotations from 154, third and fourth from 155, fifth from 156. Theologically conservative Protestants agreed with Sheen's contention that God's holiness prohibited sinful human beings from entering heaven. They argued, however, that because of Christ's death on the cross, God imputed Christ's righteousness to those who accepted Him as their savior. Thus God viewed the redeemed as righteous and accepted them into His presence. In this way, God satisfied His own demands of justice and holiness while also demonstrating His amazing love.

CHAPTER 9

1. See Bruce Shelley, "Evangelicalism," in Daniel G. Reid et al., eds., *Dictionary of Christianity in America* (Downers Grove, IL: InterVarsity Press, 1990), 416; Mark Noll, *American Evangelical Christianity: An Introduction* (Malden, MA: Blackwell, 2001); Barry Hankins, *American Evangelicals: A Contemporary History of a Mainstream Religious Movement* (Lanham, MD: Rowman & Littlefield, 2008).

2. Colleen McDannell and Bernhard Lang, *Heaven: A History* (New Haven, CT: Yale University Press, 1988), first three quotations from 352, fourth from 307, fifth from 308, sixth from 322.

3. Paul Badham, "Death," in Alan Richardson and John Bowden, eds., *The Westminster Dictionary of Christian Theology* (Philadelphia: Westminster, 1984), 146; Norman Pittinger, *After Death: Life in God* (New York: Seabury Press, 1980), 11; Philip Yancey, *I Was Just Wondering* (Grand Rapids, MI: Eerdmans, 1989), 212–14; first quotation from 214, second from 213. Cf. Joseph M. Stowell, *Eternity: Reclaiming a Passion for What Endures* (Chicago: Moody Press, 1995), 57; A. J. Conyers, *The Eclipse of Heaven: The Loss of Transcendence and Its Effect on Modern Life* (South Bend, IN: St. Augustine's Press, 1999), 22; Jerry L. Walls, *Heaven: The Logic of Eternal Joy* (New York: Oxford University Press, 2002), 10; John Gilmore, *Probing Heaven: Key Questions on the Hereafter* (Grand Rapids, MI: Baker, 1989), 126.

4. Peter Kreeft, *Everything You Ever Wanted to Know About Heaven but Never Dreamed of Asking* (San Francisco: Ignatius Press, 1990), 5, 12, 85; second phrase from 5, remainder from 12; Anne Sandberg, *Seeing the Invisible* (Plainfield, NJ: Logos International, 1977), 3; Billy Graham, *Facing Death: And the Life After* (Waco, TX: Word Books, 1987), 221–22. Cf. Joni Eareckson Tada, *Heaven: Your Real Home* (Grand Rapid, MI: Zondervan, 1995), 18; J. Oswald Sanders, *Heaven: Better by Far* (Grand Rapids, MI: Discovery House, 1994), 18; Leighton Ford, "A Religious View of Life after Death," in Kimberly Benton, ed., *Life After Death: Fact or Fiction?* (San Diego: Greenhaven Press, 2004), 49; Gilmore, *Probing Heaven*, 174.

5. For example, a 1990 Gallup poll found that 78 percent of Americans believed in heaven and 80 of that group expected to spend eternity there. See Mally Cox-Chapman, *The Case for Heaven: Near-Death Experiences as Evidence of the Afterlife* (New York: G. P. Putnam's Sons, 1995), 187.

6. Miriam Van Scott, *Encyclopedia of Heaven* (New York: St. Martin's Press, 1999), 18, 129, 239, 246, 3–4; 135, and passim; quotation from 3.

7. Van Scott, *Encyclopedia of Heaven*, 138, 154–55; quotation from 138.

8. Van Scott, *Encyclopedia of Heaven*, 197, 7–8, 62; first quotation from 7, second from 8.

9. Van Scott, *Encyclopedia of Heaven*, 222, 247, and passim.

10. Van Scott, *Encyclopedia of Heaven*, 57.

11. Roger Haight, *An Alternative Vision: An Interpretation of Liberation Theology* (New York: Paulist Press, 1985), 22, 183–84, 134–36, 129–31; first and second quotations from 22, third and fourth from 183, fifth from 134, sixth from 136.

12. Haight, *Alternative Vision*, 45, 52–54; first quotation from 45, second from 54, third from 53, fourth from 131; fifth from 136. Cf. Jon Sobrino, *Christology at the Crossroad* (Maryknoll, NY: Orbis, 1976); Philip Berryman, *Liberation Theology: The Essential Facts about the Revolutionary Movement in Latin America and Beyond* (New York: Pantheon, 1987); Robert McAfee Brown, *Liberation Theology* (Louisville, KY: Westminster John Knox Press, 1993).

13. James H. Cone, *A Black Theology of Liberation* (Philadelphia: Lippincott, 1970), 220–27; first quotation from 220, second from 220–21, third from 221, fourth and fifth from 224, sixth from 225, seventh from 227.

14. Cone, *A Black Theology*, 241–48; first three quotations from 241, fifth from 242, fourth, sixth, and seventh from 247, eighth and ninth from 248. See also James H. Cone, *Black Theology and Black Power* (New York: Seabury Press 1969); Gayraud S. Wilmore, *Black Religion and Black Radicalism* (Garden City, NY: Doubleday, 1972); Cone, *The God of the Oppressed* (Minneapolis: Seabury Press, 1975); Cornel West, *Prophesy Deliverance! An Afro-American Revolutionary Christianity* (Philadelphia: Westminster Press, 1982); Cone, *For My People: Black Theology and the Black Church* (Maryknoll, NY: Orbis, 1984); Rufus Burrow, *James H. Cone and Black Liberation Theology* (Jefferson, NC: McFarland, 1994).

15. Ruether, *Sexism and God-Talk*, 256–58, 235–36; first quotation from 258, second and third from 257, fourth from 235. On feminist liberation theology, see also Mary Daly, *Beyond God the Father: Toward a Philosophy of Women's Liberation* (Boston: Beacon Press, 1973); Beverly W. Harrison, *Making the Connections: Essays in Feminist Social Ethics* (Boston: Beacon Press, 1986); Susan Brooks Thistlewaite and Mary Potter Engel, eds., *Lift Every Voice* (San Francisco: Harper and Row, 1990). For a female Native American view, see Vine Deloria, *God Is Red* (New York: Grosset and Dunlap, 1973), 169–87. Numerous evangelical Protestants criticized liberation theology, especially its Christology and view of salvation. For most liberationists, Humberto Belli and Ronald H. Nash protested, Jesus is not "the incarnate Son of God," but "a human revolutionary" who strove to deliver people from their earthly oppression. Some liberationists, they complained, "suggest that the poor are saved simply because they are poor." Belli and Nash insisted that people needed to be freed from sin more than oppression (Humberto Belli and Ronald H. Nash, *Beyond Liberation Theology* [Grand Rapids, MI: Baker, 1992], 63–64; quotations from 63). See also Paul C. McGlasson, *Another Gospel: A Confrontation with Liberation Theology* (Grand Rapids, MI: Baker, 1994), 37, 73–74, 87, 89. Many process theologians espoused a position similar to Ruether's: all that has existed is somehow "fulfilled or perfected" in the "end," thereby making people's transient existence individually or historically meaningful (John B. Cobb, Jr., and Jeanyne B. Slettom, eds., *The Process Perspective: Frequently Asked Questions about Process Theology* [St. Louis: Chalice Press, 2003], 106). See also John B. Cobb, Jr., *God and the World* (Philadelphia: Westminster Press, 1969); Delwin Brown, Ralph E. James, Jr., and Gene Reeves, eds., *Process Philosophy and Christian Thought* (Indianapolis: Bobbs-Merrill, 1971); Bernard M. Loomer, "Process Theology: Origins, Strengths, Weaknesses," *Process Studies* 16 (Winter 1987), 245–54; George R. Lucas, Jr., *The Genesis of Modern Process Thought: A Historical Outline with Bibliography* (Metuchen, NJ: Scarecrow Press, 1983); Cobb, *Matters of Life and Death* (Louisville, KY: Westminster John Knox Press, 1991).

16. I am indebted to Douglas Groothuis, "The New Age Movement," in Reid et al., *Dictionary*, 809–10. See also Groothuis, *Unmasking the New Age* (Downers Grove, IL: InterVarsity Press, 1986). The most important expositions of the New Age philosophy are Marilyn Ferguson's *The Aquarian Conspiracy: Personal and Social Transformation in the 1980s* (Los Angeles: J. P. Tarcher, 1980), Fritjof Capra's *The Turning Point: Science, Society, and the Rising Culture* (New York: Simon and Schuster, 1982), and Ken Wilber's *A Brief History of Everything* (Boston: Shambhala, 1996). Numerous magazines, most notably *Body and Soul*, *What Is Enlightenment?* and *Yoga Magazine*, advanced New Age ideas.

17. James Sire, *The Universe New Door: A Basic Worldview Catalog* (Downers Grove, IL: InterVarsity Press, 2004), 194 (quotation); Shirley MacLaine, *Dancing in the Light* (New York: Bantam, 1985), 353–59, 366.

18. McDannell and Lang, *Heaven*, 313. My analysis of Mormon views of the afterlife depends heavily upon their book. On the close relationship Mormons see between this world and the afterlife, see Parley P. Pratt, *Key to the Science of Theology* (Salt Lake City: Deseret Book, 1965), 126–27.

19. Robert L. Millet, *Life After Death: Insights from Latter-Day Revelation* (Salt Lake City, Deseret, 1999), 2; McDannell and Lang, *Heaven*, 314 (last two quotations).

20. McDannell and Lang, *Heaven*, 314 (first quotation), 315 (third quotation); Robert L. Millet and Joseph F. McConkie, eds., *The Life Beyond* (Salt Lake City: Bookcraft, 1986), 18 (second quotation), 64. See also Bruce R. McConkie, *The Millennial Messiah: The Second Coming of the*

Son of Man (Salt Lake City: Deseret, 1982), 284–85; *Doctrines and Covenants*, 138: 57, http://scriptures.lds.org/dc/contents. For an overview of early Mormons' views on salvation and heaven, see Mary Ann Meyers, "Gates Ajar: Death in Mormon Thought and Practice," in David E. Stannard, *Death in America* (Philadelphia: University of Pennsylvania Press, 1975), 112–33.

21. McDannell and Lang, *Heaven*, 316 (first quotation); Theodore Burton, *God's Greatest Gift* (Salt Lake City: Deseret, 1977), 237; E. W. Fugal, "Salvation of the Dead," in D. H. Ludlow, ed., *Encyclopedia of Mormonism* (New York: Macmillan, 1992), 1257–59.

22. See *Doctrines and Covenants*, 76: 74–75, 84, 100–6.

23. McDannell and Lang, *Heaven*, 317–18, 320–21; first quotation from 317, second from 320, third from 321; Millet and McConkie, *Life Beyond*, 26 (fourth quotation); Duane S. Crowther, *Life Everlasting* (Salt Lake City: Bookcraft, 1971), 340 (fifth quotation).

24. Millet and McConkie, *Life Beyond*, 132–33, 55, 137, 126, 131; first two quotations from 132, third from 55, fourth from 137, fifth from 126, sixth and seventh from 131. See *Doctrine and Covenants* 132:19. The LDS *Articles of Faith* state that "through the Atonement of Christ, all mankind may be saved, by obedience to the laws and ordinances of the Gospel" (1:3).

25. Robert Goldenberg, "Bound Up in the Bond of Life: Death and Afterlife in the Jewish Tradition," in Hiroshi Obayashi, ed., *Death and Afterlife: Perspective of World Religions* (New York: Greenwood Press, 1992), 99.

26. Maurice Lamm, *The Jewish Way in Death and Mourning* (New York: Jonathan David, 1969), 230; Eugene Borowitz, "Covenant Theology," in Rifat Sonsino and Daniel B. Syme, eds., *What Happens After I Die?: Jewish Views of Life After Death* (New York: UAHC Press, 1990), 114–15; quotation from 114 (see also "What We Believe," in *Reform Judaism Today*, Book 2 [New York: Behrman, 1977], 480; Arlene Agus, "Outrage and Faith," in Sonsino and Syme, *What Happens*; quotations from 121; Blu Greenberg, "Is There Life after Death?" in ibid., 89, 90; quotations in that order; Lisa Miller, *Heaven: Our Enduring Fascination with the Afterlife* (New York: HarperCollins, 2010), 232; H. Freeman and G. Scholem, "Academy on High," in Michael Berenbaum and Fred Skolnik, eds., *Encyclopedia Judaica* (Detroit: Macmillan Reference USA, 2007), 1: 353–54; Jeffrey K. Salkin, "New Age Judaism," in Jacob Neusner and Alan J. Avery-Peck, eds., *The Blackwell Companion to Judaism* (Oxford, UK: Blackwell, 2000), 365–66. See also Ronald B. Gittlesohn, *Wings of the Morning* (New York: UAHC Press, 1969), 347–48; Arthur A. Cohen, "Resurrection of the Dead," in Cohen and Paul Mendes-Flohr, eds., *Contemporary Jewish Religious Thought* (New York: Scribner's, 1987), 807–13; Kevin Madigan and Jon Levenson, *Resurrection: The Power of God for Christians and Jews* (New Haven, CT: Yale University Press, 2008).

27. Harold Schulweis, "Immortality through Goodness and Activism," in Sonsino and Syme, *What Happens*, 98–100; Rifat Sonsino and Daniel B. Syme "Introduction," in ibid., 6, 4, 7; quotations in that order; Richard L. Rubenstein, "The Making of a Rabbi," in Ira Eisenstein, ed., *Varieties of Jewish Belief* (New York: Reconstructionist Press, 1966), 179 (see also 194–95); Gittelsohn, *Wings*, 354–62; Bernard S. Raskas, "A Jewish View of Immorality," *The American Rabbi* 19 (Aug. 1986), 57–59; Alexander M. Schindler, "Here and Hereafter," in Sonsino and Syme, *What Happens*, 75–76; Rifat Sonsino and Daniel B. Syme, "Two Personal Statements" in ibid., 142–43; quotations in that order.

28. McDannell and Lang, *Heaven*, 345 (they argued that this perspective, which they attributed primarily to fundamentalists, Neo-orthodox Protestants, and Catholics, was the most widely accepted one during the twentieth century, but I am not convinced this is true for the years before

1960); Graham, *Facing Death*, 223, 230; quotation from 223; Hal Lindsey, *There's a New World Coming* (Santa Ana, CA: Vision House, 1973), 273;Peter Kreeft, *Heaven: The Heart's Deepest Longing* (San Francisco: Ignatius Press, 1989), 157. Cf. Norman Vincent Peale, *Life beyond Death* (Grand Rapids, MI: Zondervan, 1996), 14; Paul Marshall, *Heaven Is Not My Home: Learning to Live in God's Creation* (Nashville, TN: Word, 1998), 238; Anne Lotz, *Heaven: My Father's House* (Nashville, TN: W Pub. Group, 2001), 92; John MacArthur, Jr., *Heaven: Selected Scriptures* (Chicago: Moody Press, 1988), 35; Oliver B. Greene, *Heaven and Other Sermons* (Greenville, SC: Gospel Hour, 1969), 202; Randy Alcorn, *Money, Possessions, and Eternity* (Wheaton, IL: Tyndale House, 1989), 332, 342, 340; R. C. Sproul, *Surprised by Suffering* (Wheaton, IL: Tyndale House, 1989), 156, 161; Sandberg, *Seeing*, 179; Tada, *Heaven*, 61, 64; Smith, *Heaven*,190; Daniel A. Brown, *What the Bible Reveals about Heaven* (Ventura, CA: Regal, 1999), 40–41; Edmund Fortman, *Everlasting Life After Death* (New York: Alba House, 1976), 231, 326–27.

29. W. A. Criswell and Paige Patterson, *Heaven* (Wheaton, IL: Tyndale House, 1991), 72 (quotation). Cf. Steven Lawson, *Heaven Help Us! Truths about Eternity That Will Help You Live Today* (Colorado Springs: NavPress, 1995), 81, 86, 90; Gary Habermas and J. P. Moreland, *Beyond Death: Exploring the Evidence for Immortality* (Wheaton, IL: Crossway, 1998), 275; Thomas Ice and Timothy J. Demy, *What the Bible Says About Heaven & Eternity* (Grand Rapids, MI: Kregel, 2000), 37; Jill Briscoe, *Heaven and Hell* (Wheaton, IL: Victor, 1990), 26; John Guest, *Making Sense of Life: When Our Real Home Is Heaven* (Grand Rapids, MI: Baker, 1994), 112–14; Ralph Wilkerson, *Beyond and Back: Those Who Died and Lived to Tell It* (Anaheim, CA: Melodyland Productions, 1977), 261–62; Richard Mouw, *When the Kings Come Marching In: Isaiah and the New Jerusalem* (Grand Rapids, MI: Eerdmans, 1983), 68; Gilmore, *Probing Heaven*, 276.

30. McDannell and Lang, *Heaven*, 352; John Ankerberg and John Weldon, *The Facts on Near-Death Experiences* (Eugene, OR: Harvest House, 1996), 39–40; Habermas and Moreland, *Immortality*, 148; Gary R. Habermas and J. P. Moreland, *Immortality: The Other Side of Death* (Nashville, TN: Thomas Nelson, 1992), 275; Anthony A. Hoekema, *The Bible and the Future* (Grand Rapids, MI: Eerdmans, 1979), 285 (cf. Greene, *Heaven*, 131; Sandberg, *Seeing*, 179; Fred Thompson, *What the Bible Says about Heaven and Hell* [Joplin, MO: College Press, 1983], 254–55; Briscoe, *Heaven and Hell*, 16;Charles Ferguson Ball, *Heaven* [Wheaton, IL: Victor, 1978], 45; Ford, "Life after Death," 49; Lawson, *Heaven*, 104–5, 134; Stowell, *Eternity*, 69, 72–73); Alcorn, *Money*, 355–56; quotation from 356; Brown, *Heaven*, 192, 199; quotations in that order; Smith, *Heaven*, 246. Cf. MacArthur, *Heaven*, 62; Thompson, *Heaven and Hell*, 249; Greene, *Heaven*, 127; Graham, *Facing Death*, 247; Hal Lindsay and C. C. Carlson, *The Terminal Generation* (Old Tappan, NJ: Fleming H. Revell, 1976), 209; Harry Blamires, *Knowing the Truth about Heaven and Hell: Our Choices and Where They Lead Us* (Ann Arbor, MI: Servant, 1988), 113; Kreeft, *Everything*, 47; Gilmore, *Probing Heaven*, 114; Briscoe, *Heaven and Hell*, 25; Sproul, *Surprised by Suffering*, 164; Jack MacArthur, *Exploring in the Next World* (Minneapolis: Bethany Fellowship, 1967), 137; Wilkerson, *Beyond and Back*, 266–67.

31. For example, see Thompson, *Heaven and Hell*, 240; Alcorn, *Money*, 350; Hoekema, *Future*, 285; Graham, *Facing Death*, 253–54; MacArthur, *Heaven*, 59–60, 97; quotation from 60; Lotz, *Heaven*, 94, 97, 40–41; quotation from 94; Tada, *Heaven*, 69 (cf. Ball, *Heaven*, 26; Alcorn, *Heaven*, 353; Brown, *Heaven*, 189–92); Thompson, 247–50; Kreeft, *Everything*, 39 (quotation); Kreeft, *Heaven*, 154; Sandberg, *Seeing*, 85–86.

32. Fortman, *Everlasting Life*, 332; Alcorn, *Money*, 352 (cf. Graham, *Facing Death*, 230; Gilmore, *Probing Heaven*, 277; Mouw, *Kings*, 45; Kreeft, *Everything*, 190); Ball, *Heaven*, 65; Sproul,

Surprised by Suffering, 153; MacArthur, *Heaven*, 44; Mouw, *Kings*, 31–33; first quotation from 31, second and third from 32, fourth from 32–33. Cf. Gilmore, *Probing Heaven*, 275.

33. For example, see Ice and Demy, *Heaven & Eternity*, 23; Ball, *Heaven*, 65–69; Alcorn, *Money*, 362–68; Don Baker, *Heaven: A Glimpse of Your Future Home* (Portland, OR: Multnomah, 1983), 16–17; Tada, *Heaven*, 69 (quotation), 49 (cf. Thompson, *Heaven and Hell*, 239; Kreeft, *Everything*, 13–14; MacArthur, *Heaven*, 107; Marshall, *Heaven*, 241; Douglas Connelly, *After Life: What the Bible Really Says* [Downers Grove, IL: InterVarsity Press, 1995], 101–3; Habermas and Moreland, *Beyond Death*, 271; Criswell and Patterson, *Heaven*, 44–45, 49); Criswell and Patterson, *Heaven*, 44; Smith, *Heaven*, 193; Tim LaHaye, *Life in the Afterlife* (Wheaton, IL: Tyndale House, 1980), 69; Samuel P. Huntington, *Who Are We?: The Challenges to America's National Identity* (New York: Simon and Schuster, 2004), 72–74; Cindy S. Aron, *Working at Play: A History of Vacations in the United States* (New York: Oxford University Press, 1999), 236.

34. Millard Erickson, *Christian Theology* (Grand Rapids, MI: Baker, 1998), 1240; Sanders, *Heaven*, 71–74; Gilmore, *Probing Heaven*, 279–82; quotation from 281 (cf. Thompson, *Heaven and Hell*, 241); Habermas and Moreland, *Beyond Death*, 271, 277; Baker, *Heaven*, 18; Brown, *Heaven*, 111; Tada, *Heaven*, 43, 45; John Shea, *What a Modern Catholic Believes about Heaven and Hell* (Chicago: Thomas More Press, 1972), 86–87; Fortman, *Everlasting Life*, 234–38, 333–35; first quotation from Shea, 86, second from Fortman, 238. Cf. John J. Heaney, *The Sacred and the Psychic* (New York: Paulist Press, 1984), 23ff.

35. Brown, *Heaven*, 203; Alcorn, *Money*, 357. See also Gilmore, *Probing Heaven*, 153–61; Blamires, *Knowing*, 124.

36. Kreeft, *Everything*, 56; Brown, *Heaven*, 235; Blamires, *Knowing*, 124. Cf. Habermas and Moreland, *Beyond Death*, 280; Gilmore, *Probing Heaven*, 284; Baker, *Heaven*, 13.

37. Gilmore, *Probing Heaven*, 301. See also Kreeft, *Everything*, 43.

38. Criswell and Patterson, *Heaven*, 71; Gilmore, *Probing Heaven*, 132; Mouw, *Kings*, 7; Tada, *Heaven*, 55. Cf. Kreeft, *Everything*, 45; Brown, *Heaven*, 91; "Do Pets Go to Heaven?" http://www.beliefnet.com/Inspiration/Angels/2001/04/Do-Pets-Go-To-Heaven.aspx. See also Cynthia Rylant, *Dog Heaven* (New York: Blue Sky Press, 1995) and *Cat Heaven* (New York: Blue Sky Press 1997).

39. For example, see Criswell and Patterson, *Heaven*, 62–63; Brown, *Heaven*, 237; Habermas and Moreland, *Beyond Death*, 280; Baker, *Heaven*, 12 (first quotation); Gilmore, *Probing Heaven*, 224–25 (second quotation).

40. Kreeft, *Everything*, 34; Criswell, *Heaven*, 57–58; for example, see Baker, *Heaven*, 15.

41. Ball, *Heaven*, 47, 109 (cf. Walls, *Heaven*, 13; Brown, *Heaven*, 33); for example, Stowell, *Eternity*, 94; MacArthur, *Heaven*, 18–19, quotation from 19; Steven Lawson, *Heaven*, 10–13; first quotation from 10, second from 12. Cf. Dave Hunt, *Whatever Happened to Heaven* (Eugene, OR: Harvest House, 1988), 1; Alcorn, *Money*, 18–19, 339; Habermas and Moreland, *Immortality*, 196.

42. Stowell, *Eternity*, 70–77; Yancey, *Wondering*, 217–19.

43. Stowell, *Eternity*, 96–114, 59; quotation from 97; MacArthur, *Heaven*, 119; Lawson, *Heaven*, 22–25; quotation from 22. Cf. Alcorn, *Money*, 375.

44. Stowell, *Eternity*, 119, 88–89, 138–54; first quotation from 128, second from 119; Kreeft, *Heaven*, 183. Cf. Ice and Demy, *Heaven & Eternity*, 57; Peale, *Beyond Death*, 36, 110, 125–26; Lawson, *Heaven*, 183, 133; Greene, *Heaven*, 18; Tada, *Heaven*, 23, 15, 87, 47, 193; Smith, *Heaven*, 139, 141; Brown, *Heaven*, 229; Habermas and Moreland, *Immortality*, 144.

45. Mouw, *Kings*, 22, 70, 74, 72; quotations in that order.

46. Kreeft, *Heaven*, 168–70, 176; quotation from 168; Hunt, *Heaven*, 298, quoting Lewis, *Mere Christianity* (New York: Macmillan, 1952), 119. Cf. Hoekema, *Future*, 287; Marshall, *Heaven*, 248, 250; Conyers, *Eclipse*, 182, 48.

47. Habermas and Moreland, *Beyond Death*, 278; see for example, Peale, *Beyond Death*, 43; see Gilmore, *Probing Heaven*, 328, who argued that almost everyone believed this doctrine; Criswell and Patterson, *Heaven*, 59–60; Habermas and Moreland, *Beyond Death*, 282.

48. Walls, *Heaven*, 40; Ball, *Heaven*, 31, 14; quotation from 142; Brown, *Heaven*, 234; Alcorn, *Money*, 360. Cf. Gilmore, *Probing Heaven*, 329; Habermas and Moreland, *Immortality*, 145; Jack Hayford, *I'll Hold You in Heaven: Healing and Hope for the Parent Who Has Lost a Child through Miscarriage, Stillbirth, Abortion, or Early Infant Death* (Ventura, CA: Regal, 1990).

49. See Daniel C. Boyle, *Secrets of a Successful Employee Recognition System* (Portland, OR: Productivity Press, 1995); Steven Kerr, ed., *Ultimate Rewards: What Really Motivates People to Achieve* (Boston: Harvard Business School Press, 1997); John de Graaf, David Wann, and Thomas H. Naylor, *Affluenza: The All-Consuming Epidemic* (San Francisco: Berrett-Koehler, 2001); Peter C. Whybrow, *American Mania: When More Is Not Enough* (New York: W. W. Norton, 2005); for example, see Smith, *Heaven*, 187; Kreeft, *Everything*, 20; Sandberg, *Seeing*, 180–81; LaHaye, *Afterlife*, 64, 61; quotations from 64. He added that Christian service done for any other purpose than to glorify Christ would be exposed as wood, hay, and straw and consumed by fire. Cf. Graham, *Facing Death*, 225.

50. LaHaye, *Afterlife*, 58–59; Sandberg, *Seeing*, 70; Habermas and Moreland, *Immortality*, 154; Ball, *Heaven*, 73; Tada, *Heaven*, 58; Erwin W. Lutzer, *Your Eternal Reward: Triumph and Tears at the Judgment Seat of Christ* (Chicago: Moody Press, 1998), 14, 19, 16, 17; first quotation from 16, second from 17; LaHaye, *Afterlife*, 60–70; quotations from 60. Cf. Lutzer, *Eternal Reward*, 152–55; Wilkerson, *Beyond and Back*, 247–50.

51. Habermas and Moreland, *Immortality*, 155, 196; quotations in that order; Criswell and Patterson, *Heaven*, 42; MacArthur, *Heaven*, 114, 105; quotation from 105. Cf. Tada, *Heaven*, 89.

52. See Raymond Moody, *Life After Life* (Covington, GA: Mockingbird, 1975), 14–15; Cox-Chapman, *Case for Heaven*, 6 (first quotation) (cf. Melvin Morse, "Foreword," in Betty J. Eadie, *Embraced by the Light* [Placerville, CA: Gold Leaf Press, 1992], ix; Ankerberg and Weldon, *Facts on Near-Death Experiences*, 16); Carol Zaleski, *Otherworld Journeys: Accounts of Near Death Experience in Medieval and Modern Times* (New York: Oxford University Press, 1987), 99 (second quotation); Walls, *Heaven*, 136 (third quotation).

53. Raymond A. Moody, *The Light Beyond* (Toronto: Bantam, 1988), 27–40; first quotation from 27, second from 38; Maurice Rawlings, *Beyond Death's Door* (Nashville, TN: Thomas Nelson, 1978), 79, 90; quotation from 90. Rawlings found that interviewees had as many bad experiences as had good ones, but they usually accentuated the good ones and tried to forget the bad ones (Maurice S. Rawlings, *To Hell and Back* [Nashville, TN: Thomas Nelson, 1993], xi, 48). See also Rawlings, *Beyond Death's Door*, and Rawlings, "Hell Is for Real," *Christian Life*, Jan. 1979, 32–33, 55–56, 78.

54. Cox-Chapman, *Case for Heaven*, 17–20, 48–49, 58 (first quotation), 64 (second quotation), 193 (third quotation).

55. Cox-Chapman, *Case for Heaven*, 10 (first quotation), 48–49, 186 (second quotation), 194 (third quotation). On heavenly reunions, see also Maggie Callanan and Patricia Kelley, *Final Gifts: Understanding the Special Awareness, Needs, and Communications of the Dying* (New York: Poseidon Press, 1992); Rawlings, *Beyond Death's Door*, 100.

56. For example, see Susan Blackmore, *Dying to Live* (Buffalo: Prometheus, 1991). She examines four explanations—the consistency, reality, paranormal, and transformation arguments, which are summarized in Walls, *Heaven*, 137–40.

57. Morse, "Foreword," viii; Cox-Chapman, *Case for Heaven*, 5. See also Bruce Greyson, "The Near Death Experience Scale: Construction, Reliability, and Validity," *Journal of Nervous and Mental Disease* 171 (June 1983), 369–75; Greyson, "Near-Death Encounters with and without Near-Death Experiences: Comparative NDE Scale Profiles," *Journal of Near-Death Studies* 8 (Mar. 1990), 151–61.

58. Rawlings, *To Hell and Back*, 57–58; Eadie, *Embraced*, 31, 53, 41, 86–88, 109–13, 118–20, 42; first quotation from 53, second from 41, third from 88, fourth from 86–87.

59. Sandberg, *Seeing*, 5. Cf. Peale, *Beyond Death*, 142–44. After studying NDEs cross-culturally, Karlis Osis and Erlendur Haraldsson concluded that reports never describe "what 'life' after death is really like—its activities, purposes, joys and sorrow, customs, social structure" (*At the Hour of Death* [New York: Avon, 1977], 197). See also Marvin Ford, *On the Other Side* (Plainfield, NJ: Logos International, 1978).

60. For example, see Rawlins, *To Hell and Back*, 57; LaHaye, *Afterlife*, 119–22; first quotation from 121, second from 122.

61. LaHaye, *Afterlife*, 123–25; first quotation from 123, second and third from 124 (these alternatives are based on Mark Albrecht and Brooks Alexander, *The Journal of the Spiritual Counterfeits Project* [April 1977]); Habermas and Moreland, *Immortality*, 93, 101. Their assessment is based in part on Zaleski's *Otherworld Journeys*.

62. John Ankerberg and John Weldon, *Facts on Life After Death* (Eugene, OR: Harvest House Publishers, 1992), 10, 16–18 (first quotation from 18); Ankerberg and Weldon, *Facts on Near-Death Experiences*, second quotation from 32, third and fifth from 37, fourth from 26, sixth from 34, seventh from Nina Helene, February 2, 1996, letter to Ankerberg and Weldon, 35. These observations largely depend on the research of Helene, P. M. H. Atwater, and Cherie Sutherland. See P. M. H. Atwater, *Coming Back to Life: The Aftereffects of the Near-Death Experience* (New York: Dodd, Mead, 1988); Atwater, *Beyond the Light: What Isn't Being Said About Near Death Experience* (New York: Birth Lane, 1994); Cherie Sutherland, *Reborn in the Life: Life After Near-Death Experiences* (New York: Bantam, 1995). See also Douglas Groothuis, *Deceived by the Light* (Eugene, OR: Harvest House, 1995).

63. Rawlings, *To Hell and Back*, 47 (first two quotations); Walls, *Heaven*, 159–60; quotations in that order.

64. Habermas and Moreland, *Immortality*, 157; "Eternal Destinations: Americans Believe in Heaven, Hell," May 25, 2004, http://www.gallup.com/poll/11770/eternal-destinations-americans-believe-heaven-hell.aspx. See, for example, Thomas Harris, *I'm OK, You're OK* (New York: Harper & Row, 1969); Robert H. Knight, *The Age of Consent: The Rise of Relativism and the Corruption of Popular Culture* (Dallas: Spence, 1998); Sharon Lamb, *The Trouble with Blame: Victims, Perpetrators, and Responsibility* (Cambridge, MA: Harvard University Press, 1996); Nicholas A. H. Stacey, *Living in an Alibi Society: A Catalogue of Pretensions* (London: Rubicon, 1988); Francis J. Beckwith and Gregory Koukl, *Relativism: Feet Firmly Planted in Mid-Air* (Grand Rapids, MI: Baker, 1998).

65. Baker, *Heaven*, 23 (quotation); Criswell, *Heaven*, 32; Ralph, Muncaster, *Can We Know for Certain We Are Going to Heaven?* (Eugene, OR: Harvest House, 2001), 27–28; Jean Becker,

"What Are Your Chances of Going to Heaven?" *USA Weekend*, Dec. 19–21, 1986; Gilmore, *Probing Heaven*, 193–95; quotation from 194; Sanders, *Heaven: Better by Far*, 144.

66. Graham, *Facing Death*, 215–16; first three quotations from 215, fourth from 216.

67. Gilmore, *Probing Heaven*, 195; Martha Boshart, *Heaven: Who's Got the Tickets and How Much Do They Cost?* (Uhrichsville, OH: Barbour, 2001), 20; for example, see Baker, *Heaven*, 23; MacArthur, *Exploring*, 135; Ice and Demy, *Heaven & Eternity*, 34. (see notes 29, 33, and 44 and the cover of the book)

68. Gilmore, *Probing Heaven*, 135; Muncaster, *Can We Know*, 27; LaHaye, *Afterlife*, 36–37; quotations in that order. Cf. Lutzer, *Eternal Reward*, 17.

69. Robert Sungenis, *"Not by Faith Alone": The Biblical Evidence for the Catholic Doctrine of Justification* (Santa Barbara, CA: Queenship, 1996), 115, 217, 116, 294, 515–16; first five quotations in that order; last two quotations from 515.

70. John Sanders, "Introduction" in Sanders, ed., *What About Those Who Have Never Heard? Three Views on the Destiny of the Unevangelized* (Downers Grove, IL: InterVarsity Press, 1995), 12–15; first quotation from 12, the remainder from 13. See also Ronald Nash, *Is Jesus the Only Savior?* (Grand Rapids, MI: Zondervan, 1994); James Borland, "A Theologian Looks at the Gospel and World Religions," *Journal of the Evangelical Theological Society* 33 (Mar. 1990), 3–11; Norman Geisler, *Options in Contemporary Ethics* (Grand Rapids, MI: Baker, 1981), 32; William Craig, "No Other Name: A Middle Knowledge Perspective on the Exclusivity of Salvation through Faith in Christ," *Faith and Philosophy* 6 (Apr. 1989), 176; John Hick, *An Interpretation of Religion: Human Responses to the Transcendent* (New Haven, CT: Yale University Press, 1989); Paul Knitter, *No Other Name? A Critical Survey of Christian Attitudes Toward the World Religions* (Maryknoll, NY: Orbis, 1985).

71. Yves Congar, *The Theology of Salvation* (Boston: St. Paul Edition, 1960), 68ff; Fortman, *Everlasting Life*, 202.

72. Fortman, *Everlasting Life*, 181–82 (first quotation), 204–7; William J. Dalton, *Salvation and Damnation* (Butler, WS: Clergy Book Service, 1977), 80 (second quotation). See also Vincent Wilkins, *From Limbo to Heaven* (New York: Sheed and Ward, 1961); Robert Novell, *What a Modern Catholic Believes about Death* (Chicago: Thomas More Press, 1972); Shea, *Heaven and Hell*, 74–75.

73. Ball, *Heaven*, 88; Edward William Fudge and Robert A. Peterson, *Two Views of Hell: A Biblical & Theological Dialogue* (Downers Grove, IL: InterVarsity Press, 2000), 20, 80; quotations in that order; Robert Morey, *Death and the Afterlife* (Minneapolis: Bethany House, 1984), 215–17, 219. See also Robert A. Peterson, *Hell on Trial: The Case for Eternal Punishment* (Phillipsburg, NJ: Presbyterian and Reformed, 1995), 11–14, 161–79, 195–98; David George Moore, *The Battle for Hell: A Survey and Evaluation of Evangelicals' Growing Attraction to the Doctrine of Annihilationism* (Lanham, MD: University Press of America, 1995); MacArthur, *Exploring*, 101. For defenses of annihilationism, see LeRoy Edwin Froom, *The Conditionalist Faith of Our Fathers*, 2 vols. (Washington, DC: Review and Herald, 1965–66) 1: 105–11, 286–302, 404–14, 486–97; Edward Fudge, *The Fire That Consumes: A Biblical and Historical Study of Final Punishment* (Houston: Providential Press, 1982), 173–78, 243–50, 295–307.

74. Morey, *Death*, 231–33, 237–39; first quotation from 231, second from 232, third from 237, fourth from 238, fifth from 239; Fortman, *Everlasting Life*, 192–94; quotations from 192. Cf. Sanders, *Heaven*, 114.

75. Fortman, *Everlasting Life*, 149–51, 156–66, 167–68; first quotation from 167, the remainder from 168 (see also George Maloney, *The Everlasting Now* [Notre Dame, IN: Ave Maria Press,

1979], 74; Robert Ombres, *Theology of Purgatory* [Butler, WS: Clergy Book Service, 1978]; R. J. Bastian, "Purgatory," in *New Catholic Encyclopedia*, 15 vols. [New York: McGraw Hill, 1966], 2: 1037; Kreeft, *Everything*, 21–22); MacArthur, *Exploring*, 103 (quotation); LaHaye, *Afterlife*, 35. Cf. Hunt, *Heaven*, 97.

76. Habermas and Moreland, *Immortality*, 157; Gallup poll as cited by Cox-Chapman, *Case for Heaven*, 53; George H. Smith, *Atheism: The Case Against God* (Buffalo, NY: Prometheus, 1979), 299; Martin Luther King, Jr., "What Happened to Hell?" *Ebony* (Jan. 1961), 52. The percentage of Americans who believed in hell ranged from 54 in 1965 to 85 in 1994. Very small percentages of people (typically 4 to 6 in various surveys) expected to reside there after death. See "Religious Beliefs of Americans," http://www.religioustolerance.org/chr_poll3.htm#salv.

77. Cox-Chapman, *Case for Heaven*, 53; Fortman, *Everlasting Life*, 196–98. For example, Robert W. Gleason, *The World to Come* (New York: Sheed and Ward, 1958), 115ff; Patrick Fannon, *The Changing Face of Theology* (Milwaukee: Bruce, 1968), 89; Heaney, *Sacred*, 231; Maloney, *Everlasting Now*, 109.

78. LaHaye, *Afterlife*, 105–6, 108, 116–17; first quotation from 105, second and third from 116, fourth from 117; Gilmore, *Probing Heaven*, 269. See also Criswell and Patterson, *Heaven*, 91; MacArthur, *Exploring*, 106.

79. "The Rekindling of Hell," *U.S. News and World Report*, Mar. 25, 1991, 56ff; "Heaven," *Newsweek*, Mar. 27, 1991, which included a survey on hell. See also "Heaven and Hell: Who Will Go Where and Why," *Christianity Today* 35 (May 27, 1991), 29–39. For books by evangelicals on hell, see Peterson, *Hell on Trial*; Larry Dixon, *The Other Side of the Good News: Confronting the Contemporary Challenges to Jesus' Teaching on Hell* (Wheaton, IL: Victor, 1992); D. A. Carson, *The Gagging of God: Christianity Confronts Pluralism* (Grand Rapids, MI: Zondervan, 1996), 515–36; Daniel P. Fuller, *The Unity of the Bible: Unfolding God's Plan for Humanity* (Grand Rapids, MI: Zondervan, 1992), 187–203.

CHAPTER 10

1. Peter Stanford, *Heaven: A Guide to the Undiscovered Country* (New York: Palgrave Macmillan, 2002), 11; Mark Ralls, "Reclaiming Heaven: What Can We Say about the Afterlife?" *Christian Century* 121 (Dec. 14, 2004), 39, 34 (quotation); "Who Do We Meet in Heaven?" Jan. 23, 2005, http://www.ccpc.bowiemd.org/sermons/jan232005.doc (Maryland pastor); Marty is quoted in David Van Biema, "Does Heaven Exist?" *Time*, Mar. 24, 1997, http://www.time.com/time/magazine/article/0,9171,986097,00.html.

2. Van Biema, "Does Heaven Exist?"

3. Thomas Long, "Imagine There's No Heaven: The Loss of Eschatology in American Preaching," *Journal for Preachers*, Advent 2006, 26; Nathan Bierma, *Bringing Heaven Down to Earth: Connecting This Life to the Next* (Phillipsburg, NJ: Presbyterian and Reformed, 2005), 2, 6; quotations in that order; Ted Dekker, *The Slumber of Christianity: Awakening a Passion for Heaven on Earth* (Nashville, TN: Thomas Nelson, 2005), 10.

4. In *Afterlife* (Boise, ID: G3 Media, 2009) Guy Smith provides other recent examples of heaven and hell in popular culture.

5. See Lisa Miller, "Why We Need Heaven: In Troubled Times, The Afterlife Beckons with Visions of Dark-Eyed Virgins, Gardens and Palaces, the Bliss of God's Eternal Presence and the Joy of Uniting with Loved Ones," *Newsweek*, Aug. 12, 2002, http://www.newsweek.

com/2002/08/11/why-we-need-heaven.html; John Leland, "The Nation: Afterlife for Everyone," *New York Times*, Dec. 21, 2003, http://www.nytimes.com/2003/12/21/weekinreview/the-nation-afterlife-for-everyone-heaven-comes-down-to-earth.html?scp=15&sq=Afterlife&st=nyt; Dana Blanton, "10/28/05 Fox Poll: More Believe in Heaven Than Hell," http://www.foxnews.com/story/0,2933,173838,00.html; Dalia Sussman, "Poll: Elbow Room No Problem in Heaven," Dec. 20, 2005, http://abcnews.go.com/US/Beliefs/story?id=1422658; Alec Gallup and Frank Newport, *The Gallup Poll: Public Opinion 2007* (Lanham, MD: Rowman & Littlefield, 2008), 258.

6. Van Biema, "Does Heaven Exist?"

7. See Bierma, *Bringing Heaven*, 10–11; Miller, "Why We Need Heaven."

8. Richard N. Ostling, "Heaven and Hell," http://legacy.decaturdaily.com/decaturdaily/religion/060617/heaven.shtml. Ostling cites Jeffrey Burton Russell, author of *Paradise Mislaid: How We Lost Heaven and How We Can Regain It* (New York: Oxford University Press, 2006), to support this claim.

9. "Who Do We Meet in Heaven?" Jan. 23, 2005, http://www.ccpc.bowiemd.org/sermons/jan232005.doc.

10. Mark Buchanan, *Things Unseen* (Sisters, OR: Multnomah, 2002), 94; Barbara Johnson, *Laughter from Heaven* (Nashville, TN: W Pub. Group, 2004), 4; Don Piper, *90 Minutes in Heaven: A True Story of Death and Life* (Grand Rapids, MI: Revell, 2004), 194; David Shibley, *Living as If Heaven Matters: Preparing Now for Eternity* (Lake Mary, FL: Charisma House, 2007), 179; Ray Hylton, "New Heaven and New Earth," Mar. 1, 2009, sermon at First Presbyterian Church, New Castle, PA.

11. Albert Mohler, Jr., "Ministry Is Stranger than It Used to Be: The Challenge of Postmodernism," http://www.albertmohler.com/article_read.php?cid=2.

12. James Sire, *The Universe Next Door: A Basic Worldview Catalog* (Downers Grove, IL: Intervarsity Press, 2004), 211–41.

13. See Leland Ryken, *Redeeming the Time: A Christian Approach to Work and Leisure* (Grand Rapids, MI: Baker, 1995), 61–63, 67, 187–88, 239, 266. See also Quentin J. Schultze et al., *Dancing in the Dark: Youth, Popular Culture, and the Electronic Media* (Grand Rapids, MI: Eerdmans, 1991), esp. 250–77.

14. Neil Postman, *Amusing Ourselves to Death: Public Discourse in the Age of Show Business* (New York: Viking, 1985), 3–4 (first quotation), 3 (second and third), 116 (fourth), 117 (fifth).

15. See Frank Rich, "Naked Capitalists," *New York Times Magazine*, May 20, 2001, 51, http://www.nytimes.com/2001/05/20/magazine/naked-capitalists.html.

16. See http://us.casinocity.com/; http://www.americangaming.org/Industry/factsheets/statistics_detail.cfv?id=7; Richard Winter, *Still Bored in a Culture of Entertainment* (Downers Grove, IL: InterVarsity Press, 2002), 38.

17. Winter, *Still Bored*, 80. Winter argues that this was true before 1800, but I put the date much later.

18. Patricia Meyer Spacks, *Boredom: The Literary History of a State of Mind* (Chicago: University of Chicago Press, 1995), 259–60.

19. Carol Zaleski, "When I Get to Heaven: Picturing Paradise," *Christian Century* 120 (Apr. 5, 2003), 25–26 (quotations in that order); Randy C. Alcorn, *Heaven* (Wheaton, IL: Tyndale House, 2004), 393; Buchanan, *Things Unseen*, 66; Max Lucado, "You're Expected," *Today's Christian Woman* (Jan./Feb. 2008), 32 (cartoon). Cf. Michael E. Wittmer, *Heaven Is a Place on Earth: Why*

Everything You Do Matters to God (Grand Rapids, MI: Zondervan, 2004), 16; Anthony DeStefano, *A Travel Guide to Heaven* (New York: Doubleday, 2003), 103; Leo J. Trese, *Seventeen Steps to Heaven: A Catholic Guide to Salvation* (Manchester, NH: Sophia Institute Press, 2001), 66; Billy Graham, http://www.greaternycrusade.org/MyAnswer_Article.asp?ArticleID=1590; Joe Beam and Lee Wilson, *The Real Heaven: It's Not What You Think* (Webb City, MO: Covenant, 2006), 95.

20. DeStefano, *Travel Guide*, 6 (first quotation), 15 (second), 42 (third), 90 (fourth), 175 (fifth).

21. DeStefano, *Travel Guide*, 106 (first quotation), 107 (second), 110 (third), 113, 124 (fourth), 177–78.

22. The *Publishers Weekly* and *AudioFile* reviews are at http://www.amazon.com/Travel-Guide-Heaven-Anthony-DeStefano/dp/product-description/0385509898; Adam Kirsch, "Paradise Lite: In Heaven, You'tl Be Thinner, Happier, and Smarter—or So Americans Think," Feb. 5, 2004, http://www.slate.com/id/2095002/; BreakPoint with Charles Colson Commentary #040323, Mar. 23, 2004. Cf. Joseph M. Stowell, *Eternity: Reclaiming a Passion for What Endures* (Chicago: Moody Press, 2005), 78.

23. Darrin M. McMahon, *Happiness: A History* (New York: Atlantic Monthly Press, 2006), 460–61.

24. Philip Rieff, *The Triumph of the Therapeutic: The Use of Faith after Freud* (New York: Harper & Row, 1966); Christopher Lasch, *The Culture of Narcissism: American Life in an Age of Diminishing Expectations* (New York: Norton, 1979), 42. See also William Kilpatrick, "Faith & Therapy," *First Things*, Feb. 1999, 21–26.

25. Eva S. Moskowitz, *In Therapy We Trust: America's Obsession with Self-Fulfillment* (Baltimore: Johns Hopkins University Press, 2001), 1–8, quotations from 1. See also Frank Furedi, *Therapy Culture: Cultivating Vulnerability in an Uncertain Age* (New York: Routledge, 2004); Jonathan B. Imber, ed., *Therapeutic Culture: Triumph and Defeat* (New Brunswick, NJ: Transaction, 2004); Thomas W. Strahan, "The Influence of Therapeutic Culture on Abortion Decisions of the U.S. Supreme Court," *Association for Interdisciplinary Research in Values and Social Change* 16: 4 (2002), http://www.lifeissues.net/writers/air/air_vol16no4_2002.html; Thomas Szasz, "The Theology of Therapy: The Breach of the First Amendment through the Medicalization of Morals," *New York University Review of Law and Social Change* 5 (Spring 1975), 127–35.

26. Paul Beston, "Sharing Way Too Much," *Wall Street Journal*, Apr. 21, 2005. See also Christina Hoff Sommers and Sally Satel, *One Nation under Therapy: How the Helping Culture Is Eroding Self-Reliance* (New York: St. Martin's Press, 2005).

27. Mike W. Martin, *From Morality to Mental Health: Virtue and Vice in a Therapeutic Culture* (New York: Oxford University Press, 2006), 3. Cf. James Davison Hunter, *The Death of Character: Moral Education in an Age without Good or Evil* (New York: Basic Books, 2000), 147.

28. Rieff, *Triumph*, 24–25; Kilpatrick, "Faith & Therapy," 24 (second quotation), 21 (third quotation). See Paul Vitz, *Psychology as Religion: The Cult of Self-Worship* (Grand Rapids, MI: Eerdmans, 1977).

29. David Brooks, "Hooked on Heaven Lite," *New York Times*, Mar. 9, 2004, http://www.nytimes.com/2004/03/09/opinion/09BROO.html (first quotation); Albert Mohler, Jr., "Truth and Contemporary Culture," in Andreas J. Kostenberger et al., *Whatever Happened to Truth?* (Wheaton, IL: Crossway, 2005), 61–62, quotation from 61. Cf. William Kilpatrick, *Psychological*

Seduction (Nashville, TN: T. Nelson, 1983); Stanley Grenz, *The Social God and the Relational Self* (Louisville, KY: Westminster John Knox Press, 2001), 96.

30. Albert Mohler, Jr., "Preaching with Culture in View," in Mark Dever et al., *Preaching the Cross* (Wheaton, IL: Crossway, 2007), 81.

31. Kilpatrick, "Faith & Therapy," 26.

32. Keith G. Meador and Shaun C. Henson, "Growing Old in a Therapeutic Culture," *Theology Today*, July 2000, http://findarticles.com/p/articles/mi_qa3664/is_200007/ai_n8904371/?tag=content;col1; E. Brooks Holifield, *A History of Pastoral Care in America: From Salvation to Self Realization* (Nashville, TN: Abingdon, 1983). See also Arthur Frank, *The Wounded Storyteller: Body, Illness, and Ethics* (Chicago: University of Chicago Press, 1995), 83.

33. Kirsch, "Paradise Lite" (first quotation); Ralls, "Reclaiming Heaven," 37 (second and third quotations).

34. Mitch Albom, *The Five People You Meet in Heaven* (New York: Hyperion, 2003), 35.

35. Ralls, "Reclaiming Heaven," 36.

36. Albom, *Five People*, passim, quotation from 193.

37. All quotations from Kirsch, "Paradise Lite."

38. Ralls, "Reclaiming Heaven," 36.

39. Ralls, "Reclaiming Heaven," 36 (first and third quotations), 37 (second quotation).

40. Albom, *Five People*, 65; Ralls, "Reclaiming Heaven," 37.

41. Brooks, "Hooked on Heaven Lite."

42. James Bryan Smith, *Room of Marvels* (Nashville, TN: Broadman & Holman, 2004), back cover (first quotation), 67 (second), 70, 75, 107 (third and fourth), 123 (fifth), 132–33 (sixth). Some authors stressed therapeutic themes in their biblical and theological analyses of heaven. See, for example, Bruce Milne, *Message of Heaven and Hell* (Downers Grove, IL: InterVarsity Press, 2003), who argues that all the potential of every saint will find "complete and satisfying expression" (200). Two other novels that focus on heaven are Myla Goldberg's *Bee Season* (2000) and Marilynne Robinson's Pulitzer Prize–winning *Gilead* (2005).

43. McMahon, *Happiness*, 473, who called my attention to these books on happiness.

44. Martin E. P. Seligman, *Authentic Happiness: Using the New Positive Psychology to Realize Your Potential for Lasting Fulfillment* (New York: Free Press, 2002), xii–xiii.

45. Ed Diener and Robert Biswas-Diener, *Happiness: Unlocking the Mysteries of Psychological Wealth* (Malden, MA: Blackwell, 2008), 3–4; quotation from 3. Surveys of Americans, conducted since the 1950s, for example, reveal that the percentage of those reporting that they are "happy" has remained constant (60), while those describing themselves as "very happy" has decreased from 7.5 to 6 percent. See Richard Layard, "Happiness: Has Social Science a Clue?" http://www.lse.ac.uk/collections/LSEPublicLecturesAndEvents/events/2003/20030106t439z001.htm; Layard, *Happiness: Lessons from a New Science* (New York: Penguin, 1995); David G. Myers, *The Pursuit of Happiness: Who Is Happy—and Why?* (New York: William Morrow, 1992).

46. Roof is quoted in Leland, "Afterlife for Everyone"; Johnson, *Laughter*, 5; "Billy Graham: Sports in Heaven? Far Greater Joy Lies in Store," May 25, 2007, http://seattlepi.nwsource.com/graham/314278_billy26.html (quotations); Wittmer, *Heaven*, 207, 204; quotations in that order; Alcorn, *Heaven*, 297–98, 338 (first quotation), 403 (second), 410 (third); (cf. Piper, *90 Minutes*, 24); Dekker, *Slumber of Christianity*, 10–11, 171–74, 178; first quotation from 10, second from 10–11, third from 11.

47. Peter S. Hawkins, "Surprise Ending: Imagining Heaven," *Christian Century* 123 (Nov. 14, 2006), 34; Hylton, "New Heaven"; Piper, *90 Minutes*, 25; Milne, *Heaven and Hell*, 138; McCarrick's statement is from *Heaven—Where Is It? How Do We Get There? Barbara Walters Explores the Meaning of Heaven and the Afterlife*, http://abcnews.go.com/2020/Beliefs/story?id=2734704&page=1; Alcorn, *Heaven*, 336. Cf. Bierma, *Bringing Heaven*, 131; DeStefano, *Travel Guide*, 66, 69, 72, 76.

48. Thomas Aquinas, *Summa Contra Gentiles*, Book III: *Providence,* part I, V. J. Bourke, trans. (Notre Dame, IN: University of Notre Dame Press, 1975), 208; Bill T. Arnold, "Vegetarians in Paradise: Based on Isaiah 11:6–7 and 65:25, Will We Be Vegetarians in the New Heaven and Earth as Adam and Eve Were before the Fall?" *Christianity Today* 48 (Oct. 1, 2004), 104; Joseph M. Champlin, *Preparing for Eternity: A Catholic Handbook for End-of-Life Concerns* (Notre Dame, IN: Ave Maria Press, 2007), 69–70; quotation from 69; Peter C. Phan, *Responses to 101 Questions on Death and Eternal Life* (New York: Paulist Press, 1997), 77–78; Buchanan, *Things Unseen*, 97; Piper, *90 Minutes*, 30–31; quotation from 31; DeStefano, *Travel Guide*, 127–36; quotation from 133. Cf. Kenneth Boa and Robert Bowman, Jr., *Sense & Nonsense about Heaven and Hell* (Grand Rapids, MI: Zondervan, 2007), 168–69.

49. Bierma, *Bringing Heaven*, 156, (first quotation), 64 (second, third, and fourth); Wittmer, *Heaven*, back cover. Cf. John Stackhouse, Jr., "Preface," 10, and Amy Sherman, "Salvation as Life in the (New) City," 147–52, both in Stackhouse, ed., *What Does It Mean to Be Saved? Broadening Evangelical Horizons of Salvation* (Grand Rapids, MI: Baker Academic, 2002).

50. Bierma, *Bringing Heaven*, 145 (first and second quotations), 149 (third), 150, 62; Phan, *Responses*, 127; Philip Yancey, *Rumors of Another World: What on Earth Are We Missing?* (Grand Rapids, MI: Zondervan, 2003), 189.

51. Beam and Wilson, *Real Heaven*, 69; Bierma, *Bringing Heaven*, 137, 139; Wittmer, *Heaven*, 17, 74, 206 (quotation). Cf. Boa and Bowman, *Sense & Nonsense*, 163; C. John Steer, "A New Heaven and a New Earth," Feb. 12, 2006, sermon at Autumn Ridge Church, Rochester, MN; David Bryant, *Christ Is All! A Joyful Manifesto on the Supremacy of God's Son* (New Providence, NJ: New Providence, 2005), 91; David Van Biema, "Christians Wrong About Heaven, Says Bishop," *Time*, Feb. 7, 2008. [see http://www.time.com/time/world/article/0,8599,1710844,00.html] For earlier statements, see Albert M. Wolters, *Creation Regained* (Grand Rapids, MI: Eerdmans, 1985); Wayne Gruden, *Systematic Theology: An Introduction to Biblical Doctrines* (Grand Rapids, MI: Zondervan, 1994), 1158.

52. Bierma, *Bringing Heaven*, 171, 182 (quotation); Buchanan, *Things Unseen*, 100, 102, 67; quotations in that order. Cf. Michael D. Williams, "Heaven Is a Place on Earth: Why Everything You Do Matters to God," *Presbyterion* 31 (Spring 2005), 56–58; Quentin J. Schultze, *Here I Am: Now What on Earth Should I Be Doing?* (Grand Rapids, MI: Baker, 2005), 26.

53. C. John Steer, "Are You Ready for Heaven?" Aug. 11, 2002, sermon at Autumn Ridge Church, Rochester, MN, 5–6; Milne, *Heaven and Hell*, 290–92; Shibley, *Heaven Matters*, 46, 36, 110; quotations in that order; Dekker, *Slumber of Christianity*, 115–16. Cf. Keri Wyatt Kent, "Your Kingdom Come," *Today's Christian Woman* (Jan./Feb. 2008), 34–36; John Bevere, *Driven by Eternity* (New York: Warner Faith, 2006).

54. The remaining 30 percent of Americans says that some other factor "is the key to eternal life," "they don't know what leads to eternal life," or "they don't believe in eternal life."

55. Ten percent of evangelicals contended that beliefs and actions are both essential to salvation, so 74 percent of them consider specific beliefs to be necessary to salvation. "Many Americans

Say Other Faiths Can Lead to Eternal Life: Most Christians Say Non-Christian Faiths Can Lead to Salvation," Dec. 18, 2008, http://pewresearch.org/pubs/1062/many-americans-say-other-faiths-can-lead-to-eternal-life. See also "30% —Tickets to Paradise," July 14, 2009, http://pewre-search.org/databank/dailynumber/?NumberID=701.

56. "Many Americans Say."

57. "Many Americans Say." A survey conducted by *AARP* magazine in 2007 obtained similar results: 29 percent of those who believe heaven exists declared that "the prerequisite" for entry "is to 'believe in Jesus Christ.'" Twenty-five percent of respondents said all who "are good" get in. Ten percent said that all who "believe in one God" are admitted, while another 10 percent stated that everyone gets into heaven regardless of their beliefs or actions. See Bill Newcott, "Is There Life After Death?" *AARP*, Sept./Oct. 2007, 68. Lisa Miller cites a *Newsweek* poll that found that 75 percent of Americans "believe that their actions on earth determine whether they'll go to heaven" ("Why We Need Heaven").

58. "Christianity Is No Longer Americans' Default Faith," The Barna Update, http://www.barna.org/barna-update/article/12-faithspirituality/15-christianity-is-no-longer-american-default-faith

59. Lotz made this statement on *"Making It through the Pearly Gates,"* *Today Show* special, Nov. 14, 2008; http://video.msn.com/video.aspx?mkt=en-us&vid=b6c86420-e323-49ce-9858-70d14b6a926e (cf. Buchanan, *Things Unseen*, 99); Rick Warren, *The Purpose-Driven Life* (Grand Rapids, MI: Zondervan, 2002), 34; "Billy Graham's My Answer," http://www.billygraham.org/articlepage.asp?articleid=3895.

60. Trese, *Seventeen Steps*, quotation from 86; DeStefano, *Travel Guide*, 166–69; first quotation from 166, second from 168–69.

61. Jon Meacham, "Pilgrim's Progress," http://www.msnbc.msn.com/id/14204483/. For examples of negative reactions, see Robert E. Kofahl, "Billy Graham Believes Catholic Doctrine of Salvation without Bible, Gospel, or Name of Christ," http://www.biblebb.com/files/tonyqa/tc00-105.htm; Ken Silva, "Wider Mercy: You Just May Be Saved Whether You Know It or Not," http://apprising.org/2009/01/wider-mercy-you-may-be-saved-whether-you-know-it-or-not/; http://www.mercifultruth.com/graham.htm; Texe Marrs, "Billy Graham Exposed!," http://www.jesus-is-savior.com/Wolves/billy_graham_exposed.htm

62. See "CNN Larry King Live: Interview with Joel Osteen," June 20, 2005, http://transcripts.cnn.com/TRANSCRIPTS/0506/20/lkl.01.html. For negative reactions, see Terry Watkins, "Joel Osteen: True or False?" http://www.av1611.org/osteen.html; "Joel Osteen Can't Tell You the Gospel/Doesn't Know Who's Going to Hell," http://www.rapidnet.com/~jbeard/bdm/exposes/osteen/king.htm; Albert Mohler, Jr., "Taking the Measure of Joel Osteen," Jan. 17, 2008, http://www.albertmohler.com/radio_show.php?cdate=2008-01-17. Shortly after the interview on *Larry King Live*, Osteen issued an apology for his lack of clarity, stating, "I believe with all my heart that it is only through Christ that we have hope in eternal life. Jesus declared in John 14 'I am the way, the truth and the life. No one comes to the Father but by me.'" Only later did he realize that he "had not clearly stated that having a personal relationship with Jesus is the only way to heaven." http://carolinachristianconservative.blogspot.com/2005/06/joel-osteen-apologizes-for-larry-king.html. However, because of subsequent statements Osteen has made in sermons, books, and interviews, many evangelicals continue to criticize his view of salvation.

63. Winter, *Still Bored*, 89.

64. Quoted in Newcott, "Life After Death," 68.

65. Bierma, *Bringing Heaven*, 179.

66. Boa and Bowman, *Sense & Nonsense*, 82–85; first quotation from 82, second from 85; Avery Cardinal Dulles, "The Population of Hell," *First Things*, May 2003, http://www.firstthings.com/article/2008/08/the-population-of-hell-23.

67. See Humphrey Taylor, "The Religious and Other Beliefs of Americans 2003," http://www.harrisinteractive.com/harris_poll/index.asp?PID=359; "Rising Belief in Hell, Angels, Heaven, Devil," *Christian Century*, June 15, 2004, http://findarticles.com/p/articles/mi_m1058/is_12_121/ai_n6145195/ reporting on a Gallup poll; Blanton, "More Believe in Heaven than Hell"; Gallup and Newport, *The Gallup Poll*, 258.

68. See Albert L. Winseman, "Eternal Destinations: Americans Believe in Heaven, Hell," May 25, 2004, http://www.gallup.com/poll/11770/eternal-destinations-americans-believe-heaven-hell.aspx; Prothero is quoted in Leland, "Afterlife for Everyone"; Stanford, *Heaven*, 20–21; quotation from 21; Phan, *Responses*, 85–87; quotation from 85.

69. Boa and Bowman, *Sense & Nonsense*, 120.

70. Beam and Wilson, *Real Heaven*, 34.

71. Edward William Fudge and Robert A. Peterson, *Two Views of Hell: A Biblical & Theological Dialogue* (Downers Grove, IL: InterVarsity Press, 2000), 20 (first quotation), 21 (second), 80 (third and fourth).

72. Lotz's statement is in *Heaven—Where Is It?*; C. John Steer, "Is There Life After Death?" Nov. 29, 1998, sermon at Autumn Ridge Church, Rochester, MN, 2; Hylton, "New Heaven"; Phan, *Responses*, 81.

73. Fudge and Peterson, *Two Views of Hell*, 85–126. Cf., for example, Millard Erickson, *Christian Theology* (Grand Rapids, MI: Baker, 1985), 1235.

74. "Poignant Service Says Goodbye to M.J., the Man," Associated Press, http://www.huffingtonpost.com/2009/07/07/los-angeles-braces-for-mi_n_226803.html

75. "Michael Jackson: A Requiem for a King," http://www.latimes.com/news/local/la-me-jackson-memorial8-2009jul08,0,199118.story?page=1.

76. "A Historic Farewell to Michael Jackson," *Toronto Star*, July 8, 2009, http://www.thestar.com/news/world/article/662541.

77. See "Religion Thriller: Michael Jackson & Faith," http://www.boston.com/news/local/articles_of_faith/2009/07/michael_jackson.html; Mark Moring, "Was Michael Jackson a Christian?" June 29, 2009, http://blog.christianitytoday.com/ctliveblog/archives/2009/06/was_michael_jac.html; Michael Jackson, "My Childhood, My Sabbath, My Freedom," Dec. 2000, http://www.beliefnet.com/Faiths/2000/12/My-Childhood-My-Sabbath-My-Freedom.aspx?p=1; Steve Waldman, "Michael Jackson's Sad Childhood & Joyful Sabbaths," July 7, 2009, http://blog.beliefnet.com/stevenwaldman/2009/07/michael-jacksons-god-michael-j.html.

78. "World's Leading Internet Evangelist Claims Michael Jackson Is in Hell," http://www.earnedmedia.org/lp0629.htm.

79. "House Resolution Honoring Michael Jackson Awaits Vote…," http://www.startribune.com/politics/50211002.html.

80. Both are quoted in "Michael Jackson Memorial Reviewed: 'Weird, Fun and Sad,'" http://www.guardian.co.uk/news/blog/2009/jul/08/michael-jackson-memorial-reviews.

81. "King of Pop Michael Jackson Gets Royal Send Off," http://economictimes.indiatimes.com/News/News-By-Industry/ET-Cetera/King-of-Pop-Michael-Jackson-gets-royal-send-off-/articleshow/4751637.cms?curpg=2.

82. Richard Roeper, "Circus around Jackson's Death Mirrors His Life: Some Say He Is Not Dead, Others Claim to Have Seen His Ghost," http://www.suntimes.com/news/roeper/1654449,CST-NWS-roep07.article.

83. Roeper, "Circus."

CONCLUSION

1. Peter Kreeft, as quoted in David Van Biema, "Does Heaven Exist?" *Time*, Mar. 24, 1997, 71.

2. Those who interpret heaven largely in symbolic terms, like Reinhold Niebuhr and Paul Tillich, have been more influenced by prevailing philosophical, theological, and scientific trends than by cultural and social ones.

3. Mark S. Schantz, *Awaiting the Heavenly Country: The Civil War and America's Culture of Death* (Ithaca, NY: Cornell University Press, 2008), 47, 52; quotations in that order Mally Cox-Chapman, *The Case for Heaven: Near-Death Experiences as Evidence of the Afterlife* (New York: G. P. Putnam's Sons, 1995), 35, 190; quotations in that order.

4. Colleen McDannell and Bernard Lang, *Heaven: A History* (New Haven, CT: Yale University Press, 1988), 335.

5. Timothy Dwight, "The Remoter Consequences of Death: The Happiness of Heaven," in *Theology; Explained and Defended, in a Series of Sermons*, 5 vols. (Middletown, CT: Clark and Lyman, 1818), 5: 530; Henry Harbaugh, *Heaven; or An Earnest and Scriptural Inquiry into the Abode of the Sainted Dead* (Philadelphia: Lindsay & Blakiston, 1853), 11, 23 (quotation); James Campbell, *Heaven Opened: A Book of Comfort and Hope* (New York: Fleming H. Revell, 1924), 131; John MacArthur, Jr., *Heaven: Selected Scriptures* (Chicago: Moody Press, 1988), 72. Cf. Theodore L. Cuyler, *Beulah-Land: or Words of Cheer for Christian Pilgrims* (New York: American Tract Society, 1896), 197; Billy Graham, *Facing Death and the Life After* (Waco, TX: Word, 1987), 221.

6. McDannell and Lang, *Heaven*, 357. The debate about the nature of hell, especially the type and duration of its punishment, has in many ways been more intense.

7. Carol Zaleski, "When I Get to Heaven: Picturing Paradise," *Christian Century* 120 (Apr. 5, 2003), 29; McDannell and Lang, *Heaven*, 357–58; quotation from 358.

8 Many Christian have contended that the saints will lay the crowns God gives them at Christ's feet in gratitude for His redeeming sacrifice rather than retain them as a source of personal benefit.

9. Charles Hambrick-Stowe, *Charles G. Finney and the Spirit of American Evangelicalism* (Grand Rapids, MI: Eerdmans, 1996), 15.

10. See Billy Graham, *Peace with God* (Garden City, NY: Doubleday, 1953), 134; William McLoughlin, *Billy Graham: Revivalist in a Secular Age* (New York: Ronald Press 1960), 77 (quotation).

11. McLoughlin, *Graham*, 132–33; quotation from 132.

12. As discussed in the previous chapter, about 35 percent of lay American Christians believe that individuals can obtain entry to heaven through their commitment to other religions. See "Many Americans Say Other Faiths Can Lead to Eternal Life: Most Christians Say Non-Christian Faiths Can Lead to Salvation," Dec. 18, 2008, http://pewresearch.org/pubs/1062/many-americans-say-other-faiths-can-lead-to-eternal-life. However, another poll found that 65 percent of mainline ministers and 96 percent of evangelical strongly agreed that "Jesus Christ is the only

path to salvation." See Erin Curry, "Study: Most Protestants Believe Jesus Is Only Way to Salvation," *Baptist Press*, Oct. 14, 2004, http://www.bpnews.net/bpnews.asp?id=19349. The survey compared ministers whose denominations are affiliated with the NAE and the NCC.

13. Louis Berkhof, *Systematic Theology* (Grand Rapids, MI: Eerdmans, 1941), 449; John Murray, *Redemption Accomplished and Applied* (Grand Rapids, MI: Eerdmans, 1955), 165; Anthony Hoekema, *Saved by Grace* (Grand Rapids, MI: Eerdmans, 1989), 57, 64.

14. Charles Finney, *Lectures on Systematic Theology*, J. H. Fairchild, ed. (Whittier, CA: Colporter Kemp, 1944), 365–66, 374.

15. Finney, *Systematic Theology*, 224.

16. Demarest, *Cross and Salvation*, 287.

17. Finney, *Systematic Theology*, 333, 320. See Warfield's critique of Finney's understanding of justification in *Studies in Perfectionism*, Samuel G. Craig, ed. (Philadelphia: Presbyterian and Reformed, 1958), 152–65.

18. For example, John Miley, *Systematic Theology*, 2 vols. (New York: Hunt and Eaton, 1892–94), 2: 168–69, 172, 176, 178, 181; J. Kenneth Grider, "Governmental Theory of the Atonement," in Richard S. Taylor, ed., *Beacon Dictionary of Theology* (Kansas City, MO: Beacon Hill, 1984), 240. Cf. R. Larry Shelton, "Initial Salvation," in Charles W. Carter, ed., *A Contemporary Wesleyan Theology*, 2 vols. (Grand Rapids, MI: Zondervan, 1983), 1: 502–5. See Demarest, *Cross and Salvation*, 354–55, 155.

19. Lyman Abbott, *The Evolution of Christianity* (Boston: Houghton Mifflin, 1893), 250. See Kenneth Cauthen, *The Impact of American Religious Liberalism* (New York: Harper & Row, 1962), 98–99, 221, 263; William Hutchison, *The Modernist Impulse in American Protestantism* (New York: Oxford University Press, 1976), 186–87, 252–53. Liberals generally argued that sin had environmental or psychological explanations.

20. Bruce Demarest, *The Cross and Salvation: The Doctrine of Salvation* (Wheaton, IL: Crossway, 1997), 279, 322. For example, Abbott, *Evolution*, 254–56. This section depends heavily on Demarest's book.

21. Shailer Mathews, *The Gospel and the Modern Man* (New York: Macmillan, 1912), 75; Mathews, *The Faith of Modernism* (New York: Macmillan, 1924), 100–3.

22. Paul Tillich, *Dynamics of Faith* (London: Harper, 1957), 1, 2, 4, 8, passim. Cf. Tillich, *Systematic Theology*, 3 vols. (Chicago: University of Chicago Press, 1951–63), 3: 130, 134, 223. See also Demarest, *Salvation*, 243.

23. David F. Wells, *The Search for Salvation* (Downers Grove, IL: InterVarsity Press, 1978), 85–86; quotation from 85; Tillich, *Systematic Theology*, 2: 166, 177.

24. Walter Rauschenbusch, *Walter Rauschenbusch: Selected Writings*, Winthrop Hudson, ed. (New York: Paulist Press), 75.

25. John C. Bennett, *Christian Realism* (New York: Charles Scribner's Sons, 1947), 82. See also Bennett, *Social Salvation: A Religious Approach to the Problem of Social Change* (New York: Charles Scribner's Sons, 1935).

26. Demarest, *Salvation*, 349; Lyman Abbott, *What Christianity Means to Me* (New York: Macmillan, 1921), 140; Mathews, *Modernism*, 182. See also Gary Dorrien, *The Making of American Liberal Theology: Imagining Progressive Religion, 1805–1900* (Louisville, KY: Westminster John Knox Press, 2001), 399–400; Dorrien, *The Making of American Liberal Theology: Idealism, Realism, and Modernity, 1900–1950* (Louisville, KY: Westminster John Knox Press, 2003), 38–39, 54–55, 103, 117, 193, 238, 250, 277, 281, 294, 344, 411.

27. Unitarian-Universalist Association, "What Do Unitarians Believe?" in J. Gordon Melton, ed., *American Religious Creeds*, vol. 3 (New York: Triumph, 1991), 16.

28. Demarest, *Salvation*, 238, 280, 35–56; James Cone, *God of the Oppressed* (New York: Seabury, 1975), 229. See also Hugo Assmann, *Theology for a Nomad Church* (Maryknoll, NY: Orbis, 1976), 38.

29. Demarest, *Salvation*, 317; for example, Karl Adams, *The Spirit of Catholicism* (New York: Macmillan, 1955), 19–22.

30. Demarest, *Salvation*, 350; for example, John A. Hardon, *The Catholic Catechism* (New York: Doubleday, 1975), 169.

31. Wells, *Salvation*, 141–42; quotation from 142.

32. Demarest, *Salvation*, 283. See John J. King, *The Necessity of the Church for Salvation in Selected Writings of the Past Century* (Washington, DC: Catholic University of America Press, 1960).

33. Gregory Baum, "Baptism," in Karl Rahner, ed., *Encyclopedia of Theology: The Concise Sacramentum Mundi* (New York: Crossroad, 1982), 77. Cf. Richard O'Brien, *Catholicism* (Minneapolis: Winston, 1981), 738.

34. Wells, *Salvation*, 146.

35. William James, *The Varieties of Religious Experience: A Study in Human Nature* (New York: Longmans, Green, 1928), 79–90, 114; quotations from Demarest, *Salvation*, 290.

36. Okholm and Phillips, "Introduction," in Okholm and Phillips, eds., *Four Views on Salvation in a Pluralistic World* (Grand Rapids, MI: Zondervan, 1996), 17. For a defense of particularism, see Ronald Nash, *Is Jesus the Only Savior?* (Grand Rapids, MI: Zondervan, 1994); R. Douglas Geivett and W. Gary Phillips, "A Particularist View: An Evidentialist Approach," in Okholm and Phillips, *Four Views*, 213–50.

37. For example, Arthur T. Pierson, *The Crisis of Missions; or The Voice Out of the Cloud* (New York: Baker & Taylor, 1886), 297; Samuel H. Kellogg, *Handbook of Comparative Religion* (New York: Student Volunteer Movement, 1908), 174; W. G. T. Shedd, *Dogmatic Theology* (New York: Charles Scribner's Sons, 1889), 2: 706ff. Other proponents of this position have held out even greater hope for the unevangelized. See James S. Dennis, *Foreign Missions After a Century* (London: Oliphant, Anderson, and Ferrier, 1894), 202–3; Robert H. Glover, *The Progress of World-Wide Missions* (New York: George H. Doran, 1924), 25. James Davison Hunter's survey of evangelicals in the mid-1980s found that one-third of them believed that "the only hope for Heaven is through personal faith in Jesus Christ except for those who have not had the opportunity to hear of Jesus Christ." See *Evangelicalism: The Coming Generation* (Chicago: University of Chicago Press, 1987), 35. Hunter noted that while the majority of evangelicals held a traditional position on salvation, there was a "pervasive uneasiness" about "who is relegated" to hell that "may portend a greater cultural accommodation" (47–48).

38. John Hicks and Paul F. Knitter, *The Myth of Christian Uniqueness: Toward a Pluralistic Theology of Religions* (Maryknoll, NY: Orbis, 1987), vii–xii; Okholm and Phillips, "Introduction," 17. In 1993, almost two-thirds of Americans agreed that all religions teach similar things and that none of them is superior to the others. See George Barna, *Absolute Confusion* (Ventura, CA: Regal, 1993), 15.

39. Okholm and Phillips, "Introduction," 25. For defenses of inclusivism, see Clark Pinnock, *A Wideness in God's Mercy: The Finality of Jesus Christ in a World of Religions* (Grand Rapids, MI: Zondervan, 1992); John Sanders, *No Other Name: An Investigation into the Destiny of the*

Unevangelized (Grand Rapids, MI: Eerdmans, 1992); and Clark Pinnock and Robert C. Brow, *Unbounded Love: A Good News Theology for the 21st Century* (Downers Grove, IL: InterVarsity Press, 1994).

40. See Bernard Ramm, "Will All Men Be Finally Saved?" *Eternity*, Aug. 1964, 22; Harold O. J. Brown, "Will Everyone Be Saved?" *Pastoral Renewal* 11 (June 1987), 13; Leighton Ford, "Do You Mean to Tell Me that in This Modern, Humanistic, Pluralistic, Tolerant Society You Still Believe in Hell?" *Worldwide Challenge*, Sept./Oct. 1983, 20; Richard J. Bauckham, "Universalism: A Historical Survey," *Themelios* 4:2 (1979), 48–54.

41. Wells, *Salvation*, 68–69; first two quotations in that order; Kenneth S. Kantzer, "Troublesome Questions," *Christianity Today* 31 (Mar. 20, 1987), 45. See also James I. Packer, "The Way of Salvation, Part III: The Problem of Universalism," *Bibliotheca Sacra* 130 (Jan. 1973), 3–11; Kantzer, "The Claims of Christ and Religious Pluralism," in *Evangelism on the Cutting Edge*, Robert E. Coleman, ed. (Old Tappan, NJ: Fleming H. Revell, 1986), 15–29; Roger Nicole, "Universalism: Will Everyone Be Saved?" *Christianity Today* 31 (Mar. 20, 1987), 38; Timothy K. Beougher, "Are All Doomed to Be Saved? The Rise of Modern Universalism," in Paul R. House and Gregory A. Thornbury, eds., *Who Will Be Saved? Defending the Biblical Understanding of God, Salvation, and Evangelism* (Wheaton, IL; Crossway, 2000), 100–4; Robin A. Parry and Christopher H. Partridge, eds., *Universal Salvation? The Current Debate* (Grand Rapids, MI: Eerdmans, 2003); Gregory MacDonald, *The Evangelical Universalist* (Eugene, OR: Cascade, 2006).

42. McDannell and Lang, *Heaven*, 350. Karlis Osis and Erlendur Haraldsson argue that those who have NDEs never explain "what life after death is really like—its activities, purposes, joys, sorrows, customs, [and] social structure" (*At the Hour of Death* [New York: Avon, 1977], 197).

43. McDannell and Lang, *Heaven*, 322–23, 335–45; first quotation from 322, second from 336. They cite the following works to support their argument: Joe Bayly, "What Heaven Will Be Like," *Moody Monthly* 76:8 (1975–1976), 25–27; Charles F. Baker, *A Dispensational Theology* (Grand Rapids, MI: Grace Bible College, 1971), 5, 583; Hal Lindsey, *The Late Great Planet Earth* (Grand Rapids, MI: Zondervan, 1970); Karl Barth, *Church Dogmatics*, 5 vols., G. W. Bromiley, trans. (Edinburgh: Clark, 1960), 3: 624; Karl Rahner, *Theological Investigations*, David Bourke, trans. (London: Darton, Longman, and Todd, 1875), 13: 174.

44. McDannell and Lang, *Heaven*, 352.

45. "More Believe in God than Heaven" (2004), http://www.foxnews.com/story/0,2933,99945,00.html; "Poll: Elbow Room No Problem in Heaven" (2005), http://abcnews.go.com/US/Beliefs/story?id=1422658; "Comparing U.S. Religious Beliefs with Those in Other Mainly Christian Countries," http://www.religioustolerance.org/rel_comp.htm; George Gallup and D. M. Lindsay, *Surveying the Religious Landscape* (Harrisburg, PA: Morehouse, 1999); "World: Religiosity (III)—Belief in Heaven and Hell," http://micpohling.wordpress.com/2007/05/27/world-religiosity-iii-belief-in-heaven-and-hell; Andrew Kohut and Bruce Stokes, *America Against the World: How We Are Different and Why We Are Disliked* (New York: Times Books, 2006), 105.

46. Sam Harris, *Letter to a Christian Nation* (New York: Knopf, 2006); Christopher Hitchens, *God Is Not Great: How Religion Poisons Everything* (New York: Twelve, 2007); Daniel Dennett, *Breaking the Spell: Religion as a Natural Phenomenon* (New York: Penguin, 2007). See "American Religious Identification Survey (ARIS) 2008," 2, http://www.americanreligionsurvey-aris.org/reports/ARIS_Report_2008.pdf.

47. Samuel P. Huntington, *Who Are We? The Challenges to America's National Identity* (New York: Simon and Schuster, 2004), 75; Peter N. Stearns, *From Alienation to Addiction: Modern American Work in Global Historical Perspective* (Boulder, CO: Paradigm, 2008).

48. See Huntington, *Who Are We?* 65.

49. Reinhold Niebuhr, *The Irony of American History* (New York: Scribner, 1952), 88.

Index

Abbott, Lyman
  on death 156
  on funeral practices 155
  as a proponent of New Theology 113, 135
  on the resurrection body 146
  on salvation 233, 234
  on self-development in heaven 143–44
  on sin 234
Abednego 91
Abernathy, Ralph 294n25
Abraham 5, 37, 38, 76, 79
Adam 13, 64, 123, 233
Adams, John 48, 59
Adams, Samuel 48
Afghanistan War, the 206
Afterlife Diet, The (1995)
agnostics 235
Agus, Arlene 186–87
AIDS 206, 225
Albom, Mitch 1, 2, 4, 212–14
Alcorn, Randy
  on activities in heaven 5, 189
  on boredom in heaven 209
  on the fellowship of the saints 193, 216
  on the fulfillment of the saints' desires 188, 215

  on heaven's lack of divisions 189
  on time in heaven 190
Alcott, Louisa May 85, 86
Alger, Horatio 141–42
Alger, William R.
  on heaven not being a place 119
  on heavenly recognition 122, 281–82n36
  on humans' limited knowledge of heaven 115
  on salvation 126, 127
Allen, Ethan
  attack of on Christian orthodoxy 48, 57–58
  attack upon by Christian clergy 58
  consignment of to hell 68
  denial of original sin of 58
  exaltation of reason of 57, 58
  on heaven 258n22
  on Jesus 57
  on salvation 57
  on universalism 58
Alexander, Archibald 77
Alighieri, Dante 76, 123, 145
Allen, George 106
American Bible Society 103
American Federation of Labor 110
American Nervousness (1884) 117
American Revolution 30–31, 47

American Unitarian Association 259n26

Amin, Idi 189

Amusing Ourselves to Death (1985) 208

Anabaptists 47, 178

Anderson, John
  on the fellowship of the saints 170
  on heaven as an active place 164–65
  on heavenly recognition 169
  on preparing for heaven 168
  on the saints' vastly increased knowledge 165
  on salvation 171

Andover Theological Seminary 71, 74, 113, 128, 129

Andrae Crouch Choir 224

angels
  comparison of saints with 32
  as conveying people to heaven 53
  deceased infants as 83
  different degrees of glory of 39
  exaltation of saints above 56
  fallen 43, 67
  fellowship of the saints with 14, 38, 53, 79, 123
  guardian 16, 76, 168, 180, 206
  as having only one trial 129
  as part of NDEs 180
  as recognizing each other 147
  as rejoicing when souls are converted 34
  residing of in heaven ix, 33, 39, 52, 84
  role of in conversion 149, 199
  saints as becoming 206
  service of God of 77, 165
  as teaching the saints 83, 86
  as worshipping God in heaven 14, 57, 92

Ankerberg, John 188, 197

annihilation 68, 129, 165, 200, 223

Anxious Bench, The (1844) 62

apostles, the
  evangelism of 193
  fellowship of the saints with 16, 53, 79, 92, 123, 133
  on the glory of heaven 54
  power over purgatory of 131
  on salvation 130, 246n37
  support of for justice for slaves 91
  worship of God in heaven of 51

Appleman, Hyman 174

Aquinas, Thomas 37, 79, 216

Arendzen, J. P. 164, 165

Arminians 41, 62, 233

Arnold, Bill T. 3, 216

atheists 47, 63, 221, 235, 237

atonement of Christ
  importance of to salvation 83, 84, 91, 105, 125
  nature of 21, 57, 61, 63, 64, 67, 126, 201, 234
  theories of 65, 127, 135, 149–50, 159, 172, 233

Augustine 79, 216

Austen, Jane 209

Australian Aboriginals 1

Authentic Happiness: Using the New Positive Psychology to Realize Your Potential for Lasting Fulfillment (2002) 215

Babylonians 1

Baeck, Leo 294n21

Baker, Daniel 89

Baker, Don 189

Baldwin, Lewis 91

Ball, Charles 92, 95, 96

Ball, Charles (pastor) 191, 193

Ballou, Horace 48, 57, 63

Baptists 30, 59, 159, 178, 205

Barna, George 219

Bartol, Cyrus 97

Barton, Clara 272n49

Baxter, Richard 246n37

Beam, Joe 218

Beard, George M. 117

Become a Better You: 7 Keys to Improving Your Life Every Day (2007) 221

Beecher, Henry Ward
  on character and virtue 111
  on cultural values influencing portraits of heaven 3
  on the evanescence of earthly life 115
  on focusing on heaven 124
  on heavenly rewards 124
  on hell 131
  on holiness and good works 127
  on limited knowledge of heaven 115
  optimism of about cultural improvement 114
  on the permanence of heaven 115
  on preparing for heaven 125
  prominence of 112
  as a proponent of New Theology 113
  on the saints' growth 121
  on salvation 126, 283n46

Beecher, Lyman 49, 52, 55, 62

Beethoven, Ludwig 76

Bell, Alexander Graham 120
Bellamy, Edward 110
Belli, Humberto 298n15
Bennett, John 234
Berends, Kurt 105
Berger, David 171
Between the Gates (1887) 71, 113
Beyond and Back (1977) 196
Beyond Death's Door (1978) 195
Beyond the Gates (1883) 71, 113
Biederwolf, William 162, 163, 167–68, 169
Bierma, Nathan 205, 217, 218
Biswas-Diener, Robert 215
Black Theology of Liberation, A (1970) 182
Blackmore, Susan 303n56
Blair, David 102
Blamires, Harry 191
Blavatsky, Helena 183
Bloesch, Donald 199
Boa, Kenneth 221–22
Boettner, Loraine 165
Bolingbroke, Henry St. John 58
Bonnell, John Sutherland 162–63, 168, 170, 171
Borowitz, Eugene 186
Boshart, Martha 198
Boteach, Shmuley 225
Boudinot, Elias 48, 59
Boudreaux, F. J.
  on the beatific vision 115
  on the fellowship of the saints 123
  on heaven as home 114
  on heavenly recognition 122
  on heavenly rewards 124
  on heaven's absence of earthly woes 118
  on love in heaven 117
  on preparing for heaven 125
  on purity in heaven 117
Bounds, Edward 163, 167
Bowie, Walter Russell 165
Bowman, Jr., Robert 221–22
Boy Scouts 141
Boyce, James P. 112
Bradford, Amory 290n59
Bradstreet, Anne 22
Branks, William
  on the fellowship of the saints 86
  on focusing on heaven 77
  on heaven as home 71, 78, 263n3
  on heavenly recognition 80, 86

on the saints' fellowship with Christ 75
Briggs, Charles 290n59
British Petroleum oil leak 207
Broadus, John A. 290n56
Brooks, David 214
Brooks, Phillips
  on the evanescence of earthly life 115
  on focusing on heaven 124
  on heaven as an active place 5, 119
  on heaven's absence of earthly woes 118
  as a leading Gilded Age minister 112
  optimism of about cultural improvement 114
  on the permanence of heaven 115
  on preparing for heaven 125
  as a proponent of New Theology 113
  on the saints' fellowship with God and Christ 115, 280n21
  on salvation 126
Brown, Charles Reynolds
  on Americans' reduced interest in heaven 162
  on the atonement 50
  on bringing heaven to earth 139
  on limited knowledge of heaven 165
  on salvation 150–51, 172
Brown, Daniel
  on age in heaven 190–91
  on the fellowship of the saints 193
  on heaven as enjoyable 4, 188
  on the size of heaven 188
  on time in heaven 190
Brown, Henry Box 89
Brown, William Adams
  on focusing on heaven 141
  on personal development in heaven 137, 144
  on preoccupation with heaven discouraging social reform 140
  as a proponent of New Theology 113, 135
Brown University 30
Brown v. the Board of Education (1954) 159
Bryan, William Jennings 135, 138
Buchanan, Mark 204, 209, 216, 218
Buddha 286n8
Buddhism viii, 183, 207, 220, 221
Bunyan, John 20, 79
Burns, George 181
Burton, Theodore 185
Bushnell, Horace 97, 112, 125, 171
Butler, Jonathan 113, 132, 139

Callan, Charles 147, 148
Callaway, Joshua 103
Calvin, John
  on the fellowship of the saints 37
  influence of on Puritans 5, 10
  people's desire to fellowship with in heaven 5, 79
  on the perfection of the saints 190
Calvinists
  belief in election of 63
  as persecutors of Mennonites 189
  Puritans as 19, 26
  view of salvation of 41, 56, 62, 65, 105, 232–33
Campbell, James
  on the biblical description of heaven 3, 163
  on focusing on heaven 167
  on heaven's absence of earthly woes 165
  on implementing heaven's principles on earth 167–68
  on lack of focus on heaven 230
Carey, Mariah 224
Carnegie, Andrew 109
Carroll, Charles 48
Carter, Paul 3
Cartwright, Peter 63
Catechism of the Catholic Church 222
Catholic Church
  as Christ's body on earth 235
  doctrine of purgatory of 129, 175
  flourishing of during the 1930s 159
  major changes to as a result of Vatican II 176, 178, 203
  view of salvation of 235
Catholics
  and the "baptism of desire" 235
  on the beatific vision 116, 152, 161, 164, 188, 216
  on the fellowship of the saints 170
  growing importance of 175, 203
  on the growth of the saints 190
  on the happiness and holiness of heaven 117
  on heaven as an active place 189
  on heavenly rewards 170
  on heaven's absence of earthly woes 165
  on heaven's relationship to earthly life 188
  on hell 152, 162, 174, 202, 205, 222
  as immigrants during the Gilded Age 109
  as a peril 111

prevalence of in the United States viii
as proponents of the Social Gospel 135
and purgatory 130–31, 162, 173, 174, 175, 201, 222, 235
on salvation 6–7, 100, 152, 161, 162, 171, 173, 199, 200, 219, 220, 222, 235, 243n28
theocentric view of heaven of 8, 115, 299n28
and the Treasury of Merits 235
Caught Up into Paradise (1978)
Cayce, Edgar 197
Chambers, Arthur 152
Champlin, Joseph M. 216
Channing, William Ellery 57, 71, 112
Chapin, Alice 105
Chapman, J. Wilbur 142, 149
Chauncy, Charles 33, 62, 76
Cheever, George 78, 83
Chopra, Deepak 225
Christ in the Camp: Religion in the Confederate Army (1887) 100
Christian Nurture (1847) 125
Christian Science 183
Christianity and the Social Crisis (1907) 139
Christianity Today 161
church fathers, the 53, 79, 84, 129
Civil War, the
  as America's most tragic and psychically devastating war 98
  belief in heaven as contributing to the carnage of 99, 100
  and belief in heaven as inspiring soldiers 96–97, 99, 100–101
  and belief in heaven as motivating conversion 102–103
  as a challenge to fundamental assumptions about life's value 98
  as contributing to interest in heaven 2, 8, 97
  efforts to convert soldiers during 96
  extensive focus on heaven during 96–97, 107
  extremely high rates of casualties in 98, 272n47
  factors that motivated and sustained combatants in 99–100
  and the fellowship of the saints 79
  and grief 71, 99, 101
  and heaven as a place of family reunion 97, 99, 100, 101, 102, 108
  and heaven as a source of comfort and consolation 97, 100, 102

and heaven's absence of earthly woes 103
and the importance of Christian beliefs to
    soldiers 96, 100
as the most religious war in history 96, 107
and participants' conception of heaven 99
and the relationship between sin and
    victory 97–98
religious explanations for 97
revivals during 104
soldiers as agents of redemption 97
and speculation about heaven 103
as validating the model of the "Good Death" 98
and views of hell 103, 107
and views of salvation 103–7
Clapton, Eric 181
Clark, James Freeman 79, 80
Clark, Rufus 75, 76
Clarke, William Newton
    on the advancement of God's kingdom 139
    on the atonement 150
    on future probation 150
    as a proponent of New Theology 113, 135
    on the resurrection body 146, 147
    on salvation 150
    on self-development in heaven 144
Coe, Alexander 107
cold war, the 159
College of New Jersey (Princeton) 30, 42
Colson, Charles 210
Commodores, The 224
Cone, James 94, 182–83, 235
Confederacy, the
    on its cause as God's cause 97
    Christian faith as maintaining the morale
        of 97
    and its Christian heritage and convictions 97
    and its fight to defend the Southern way of
        life 97
    and its use of Bible to justify slavery 97
Confederate soldiers 89, 102, 274n64
Congregationalists 26, 30, 128, 259n26
Connelly, Marc 168
Conservative Jews 7, 186, 187
consolatory literature 70, 71, 155
Conwell, Russell 142
Cook, Robert Dane 169, 170
Corbet, John 23
Cotton, John 13, 22
Council of Trent, the 7

Courage to Be, The (1952) 166
Cox-Chapman, Molly 195, 196, 228
Craddock, Ida 142
Criswell, W. A. 190, 191, 193, 194
Cromwell, Oliver 76
Crosby, Fanny 118
Crouch, Andrae 225
Crouch, Sandra 225
Cult of True Womanhood, the 78, 86
Currier and Ives 78
Cuyler, Theodore 140–41

Dagg, J. L. 115, 117, 119, 120
Dana, James 51, 54, 55, 56
Danforth, Samuel 18–19, 24
Daniel 79, 91
Dartmouth 30
David 76, 79, 142
Davies, Samuel 30, 36, 41
Davis, Jefferson 97
Davis, Woodbury 76
Day of Doom, The (1662) 13, 244n10
death, view of 155–56. See also
    "Good Death," the
Death of God theology 8, 176
deists
    challenge to orthodox conceptions of
        salvation of 46, 69, 228
    characteristics of 57–58
    denial of biblical orthodoxy of 48
    rejection of Christ's divinity of 48, 57
    on the role of character and virtue in
        salvation 48, 57
    view of Jesus of 57
Dekker, Ted 205, 215, 219
Dennett, Dennis 237
DeStefano, Anthony 2, 3, 209–10, 217, 220
Devil, the. See Satan
Dewey, John 172
Dickens, Charles 215
Dickinson, G. Lowes 152–53
Diener, Ed 215
DiMaggio, Joe 209
Disciples of Christ 178
dispensationalism 162
Divine Comedy, The 145
Dixon, A. C. 139, 149
Dorrien, Gary 126
Douglas, Ann 70

Douglass, Frederick 91, 94, 95
Dulles, Avery 222
Duncan, J. 79
Dwight, Timothy
    attack of on the views of Ethan Allen 58–59
    on the fellowship of the saints 53
    on focusing on heaven 54
    on the happiness of heaven 52
    on a heavenly perspective toward earthly life 5
    on hell 66, 68
    on the joys of heaven 4
    on the progress of the saints 55
    on roles in heaven 55
    on the saints' relationship with God 50
    on salvation 60, 230
    on the splendor of heaven 50
    on universalism 63, 64

Eadie, Betty J. 180, 196
Eby, Richard 196
Edison, Thomas 120
Edmosson, J. 118
Edwards, Jonathan
    on activities in heaven 5
    on assurance of salvation 44
    on the beatific vision 32
    as a Calvinist 41, 56
    on Christ's role in heaven 33
    criticism of the view of hell of 131
    defense of First Great Awakening of 33–34
    description of heaven of 3
    on desiring heaven 43
    on the diversity of heaven's residents 36
    on the fall 35
    family life of 38
    on the fellowship of the saints 5, 8, 37–38
    on God's love in heaven 3, 3–33, 36, 37–38, 43, 45, 228
    on good works 39, 41–42
    on the happiness of heaven 32, 33, 34, 36, 40
    on heavenly recognition 37
    on heavenly rewards 39–40
    on hell 29–30, 38, 42, 44–45, 169, 250n1
    on holiness as a prerequisite for heaven 43
    impact of the view of heaven of 45
    on the large number of heaven's residents 36
    life of 30
    people's desire to fellowship with in heaven 79
    on preparation for heaven 44
    on previews of heaven 40
    recreation of 34
    on the resurrection body 37
    role of in the First Great Awakening 30, 31
    on the saints' activities in heaven 35–36
    on the saints' communion with God 32, 51
    on the saints' fellowship with biblical heroes and angels 38
    on the saints' relationship with Christ 33
    on the saints residing eternally in heaven 38–39
    on the saints' vastly increased knowledge 34–35
    on salvation 40–44, 45
    on the Second Coming 39
    and the sermon "Heaven is a World of Love" 29
    and the sermon "Sinners in the Hands of an Angry God" 24, 29, 173
    sermons of about heaven 1, 31
    on soul sleep 38
    on the splendor of heaven 31–32
    story of an intemperate neighbor of 61–62
    theocentric view of heaven of 8, 31–32
    on worship in heaven 35
Egyptians (ancient) 1
Einstein, Albert 210, 215
Eisenhower, Dwight 160
Elijah 38, 53, 80
Ely, Richard 140
Embraced by the Light (1992) 180, 196
Emerson, Ralph Waldo 112
end times 2, 24, 26, 33, 162
Enoch 49, 53
Episcopalians 178
Erickson, Millard 190
Escott, Paul 93
evangelical liberalism. See New Theology
evangelicals
    activities of 113, 162
    books about heaven by 2
    criticism of 112
    in England 193
    on the fellowship of the saints 193
    flourishing of 178
    on growth and progress in heaven 121
    on heavenly recognition 169, 193
    on heavenly rewards 148–49, 193–94

importance of in America viii
and parachurch organizations 178
political involvement of 178
and the rejection of future probation 128, 129,
    154–55
resurgence of in the mid-twentieth
    century 161
view of heaven of 135, 157
view of hell of 132, 135, 153–55, 174, 202, 203
view of salvation of 86, 94, 149, 151, 162, 171,
    198, 199, 219, 220, 222, 230, 231–32, 314n37
Evans, Augusta Jane 102
Eve 64
*Examination of the Doctrine of Future
    Retribution, An* (1834) 63

Fackre, Gabriel 199
farmers' alliances 110
Faulkner, William 158
Faust, Drew Gilpin 98, 101
feminist theology 8, 183
Fielder, Alfred 103
Finley, Samuel 42
Finney, Charles
    as an Arminian 56, 233
    on the atonement 65, 233
    contributions of 49
    critique of Universalism of 65
    debate of with Universalists 63
    as an evangelist 62
    on good works 65
    on hell 66, 67–68
    on the imputation of Adam's sin 233
    invention of "new measures" by 62
    as a leader of the Second Great
        Awakening 49, 233
    narration of a story of Jonathan Edwards
        by 61–62
    on near-death experiences 53
    people wanting to fellowship with in
        heaven 123
    on revivals as a foretaste of heaven 54
    on the saints' vastly increased knowledge 55
    on salvation 61–62, 65, 232, 233
    on signs of salvation 65–66
    on the splendor of heaven 49
Fire that Consumes, The (1994) 223
First Great Awakening, the
    focus of on heaven 2, 45

George Whitefield's role in 30
impact of 30–31
and the importance of being born again 45
Jonathan Edwards' role in 30
and mystical experience 33
on the obstacles to getting to heaven 46
Fiske, John 112
Fitch, James 23
Five People You Meet in Heaven, The (2003) 2,
    212–14
Fortman, E. J. 189, 190, 200–1
Fosdick, Harry Emerson
    on Americans' reduced interest in heaven 163
    on bringing heaven to earth 139
    critique of the conventional portrait of heaven
        of 165
    on the fellowship of the saints 170
    on heaven as a great adventure 165
    on heavenly rewards 170
    on hell 173
    on improving earthly conditions 139
    as a leader of the modernists 161
    on limited biblical information about
        heaven 165
Foster, Randolph 122, 123
founding fathers, the 48, 59
Francis of Assisi 123
Franklin, Benjamin 48, 59
Free Religious Association 131
free thinkers 46, 69, 228
Frelinghuysen, Theodore 30, 35, 41, 42
Freudianism 159
Frothingham, Octavius Brooks 131–32
Fudge, Edward William 200, 223
Fuller Theological Seminary 161
fundamentalists 161
    and the afterlife 8, 162
    battle of with modernists 159
    and dispensationalism 162
    goals of 162
    view of heaven 175, 299n28
    view of hell of 161, 174
    view of salvation of 162, 171, 172
    withdrawal of from public life 160
Fundamentalist-Modernist controversy 157,
    159
Fundamentals, The (1910–1915) 154
Future Life or Scenes in Another World (1858)
future probation 6, 128–29, 154–55, 184, 186

Gale, William 102
gambling 208
Garnet, Henry 95
Gast, John 121
Gates Ajar, The (1869) 2, 71–73, 113, 239n1
Gearing, William 13, 14, 15, 16
Geisler, Norman 199
General Conference of the Methodist Church 154
Genovese, Eugene 92, 96
George, Henry 117
Gilbert, Levi 136–37, 142
Gilded Age, the
  conception of occupations during 120
  conspicuous consumption of 110
  and corporations 110
  depressions during 110
  development of the social sciences during 109
  discrimination against African Americans during 109
  emphasis on bureaucracy and technical rationality in 115
  emphasis on physical fitness and sports in 118
  as an era of great anxiety 111, 117–18
  faith in progress of 119
  immigration during 109, 111
  importance of private religious experience during 115
  improved material conditions during 117, 121
  and increasing bureaucracy 111
  industrialization during 109, 110
  industriousness during 119
  labor problems of 110
  quantitative ethic of 111
  political corruption during 109–10
  social problems of 111, 117
  strikes and labor riots during 110
  and technological innovation 120
Gilmore, John
  on growth in heaven 190
  on heavenly recognition 5
  on hell 202
  on ownership in heaven 191
  on pets in heaven 191
  on salvation 198
  on sex in heaven 191
Gladden, Washington
  on death 155–56
  on God's creation of a new heaven on earth 140
  on hell 153
  as a leader of the Social Gospel 134, 138
  on preparation for heaven 141
  as a proponent of New Theology 113
  on the resurrection body 146
  on salvation 150
  on self-development in heaven 143–44
  on theories of the atonement 149–50
Glennie, Alexander 88
Gnosticism 183
Godey's Lady's Book 83
Goliath 76
"Good Death," the 85, 98, 100, 272n47
Goodwin, Daniel 115–16, 121, 130, 131, 132
Goodwin, T. A. 146
Gordon, A. J. 115, 139
Gordon, Augustus 100
Gordon, George A. 113, 155, 290n59
Gordon College 139
Gordon, S. D. 142, 155
Gould, Jay 109
Gould, Sarah 79
Graham, Billy
  on belief in Christ for salvation 6, 171–72, 198, 204–5, 220–21, 232
  crusades of 160
  on the fellowship of the saints 170
  on the happiness of heaven 215
  on hell 174
  on the implausibility of conventional images of heaven 179
  on the saints being like Jesus 189
  view of heaven of 1, 163, 188
Grange movement 110
Grant, Ulysses S. 109, 118
Gray, George Zabriskie 122
Gray, James 142
Greeks (ancient) 1, 99, 145
Greenberg, Blu 187
Greenwood, F. W. P. 79
Gregg, David 136, 141, 142, 149
Griffin, Edward
  on the fellowship of the saints 79
  on focusing on heaven 77
  on heavenly rewards 54
  on hell 85
  on the nature of heaven 75, 77
  on the saints' fellowship with biblical heroes 79

on the saints' fellowship with God 74
on the saints' vastly increased
knowledge 75–76
on where the saints will reside eternally 84
Guardian Angels, or, Friends in Heaven, The (1857)

Habermas, Gary
on heavenly recognition 193
on heavenly rewards 194
on near-death experiences 196
on salvation 198
on sexual intercourse in heaven 191
on the splendor of heaven 188
Haight, Roger 181–82
Half-Way Covenant of 1662, the 11–12, 26
Hall, Charles C. 147
Hall, David 27
Hall, G. Stanley 281n29
Hammon, Jupiter 95
Hampton, Thomas 103
Handel, George Frideric 76
*Happiness: Unlocking the Mysteries of
Psychological Wealth* (2008)
Harbaugh, Henry
on the beauty of heaven 75
books of about heaven 71
on the fellowship of the saints 79, 81–82, 86
on heaven as home 71, 78
on heavenly recognition 80, 81, 82–83, 86
on lack of focus on heaven 230
on limited knowledge of heaven 73–74
on the saints' awareness of earthly life 76
on the salvation of infants 83
on where the saints will reside eternally 84
Harris, Sam 237
Hart, Burdett 144, 148, 149
Hart, Levi 51, 52, 54, 148, 149
Harvard College 15, 26
Haven, Gilbert 97
Hawkins, Peter S. 216
Haydn, Franz Joseph 76
Haydon, Charles B. 106
Hayes, Lemuel 64
Haymarket Square bombing 110
Hazard of New Fortune, A (1890) 111
heaven. *See also* various groups and individuals
absence of earthly woes in 103, 117–18,
144–45, 164, 189
absence of mystery in 189

as an active place 119–21, 137, 142, 143, 156,
164–65, 189–90, 228, 258n22
activities in 3, 5, 34, 55, 77, 120, 121, 133, 142,
165, 184, 189, 209–10, 215, 227, 303n59
as an actual place 4, 8, 206, 273n50
and African Americans 167, 168, 205. *See also*
slavery
age in 190–91
anthropocentric conception of 8, 70,
71–73, 230
art in 5, 72, 73, 120, 121, 142, 165, 190, 210, 215
assault on the traditional conception of 48,
69, 72, 113, 137, 144, 145, 165, 179
baffling nature of ix, 230, 237, 238
basis of admission to vii, 2, 5–7, 9, 204–5,
226. *See also* salvation
beauty of vii, 4, 13, 50, 55, 70, 75, 86, 89, 144,
145, 188, 227
biblical teaching about vii–viii, 3, 5, 17, 31, 35,
39, 53, 55, 58, 73–73, 76, 77, 79, 80–81, 107,
115, 121–22, 124, 125, 129, 149, 152–53, 169,
191–94, 196, 197, 206, 230, 237
cartoons about 181, 209
commercialization of 2, 179, 203
as compensation for earthly suffering 7, 13,
90, 167, 187, 194, 214, 228, 229
concern about Christians focusing on too
much 229, 238
concern about Christians ignoring 230
critique of whites' portrait of 182–83
as a delusion 3
description of in near-death experiences 195
Elizabeth Stuart Phelps' depiction of 71–73
as an entertainment center 4, 168, 209–10,
228
as an eternal home 3, 8, 70–71, 72, 77–80,
101, 113, 142, 155, 161, 227, 228
fear of boredom in 209, 228
fellowship of the saints in 5, 8, 16, 39, 53, 70,
79, 113, 123, 148, 168, 170, 193, 216, 227
foretastes of 38, 40, 54, 78, 192, 197, 218, 229
great interest in 179–80, 231
harmony of 31, 52, 189
highly imaginative portraits of 2, 179, 230, 237
hymns about 78, 114, 116, 148, 155, 163, 164,
170, 179, 269n15
importance and benefits of focusing on 18,
54, 77, 86, 124–25, 140–41, 167, 191–93,
203, 207, 229, 238

heaven (*continued*)

as an incentive for conversion 70, 89, 113, 230, 231

and the intermediate state ix, 6, 16, 33, 34, 38, 132, 145–47, 185, 287n57

Islamic view of 67, 145

Jewish view of 9, 101, 186–87

jokes about vii, 2, 177, 204, 240n1

liberation theology's view of 181–83

limited knowledge of ix, 73–74, 114–15, 163, 237

marriage in 185–86, 191

minimalist descriptions of 179, 237

Mormon view of 184–86

movies about viii–ix, 2, 168–69, 180, 203, 204, 206, 229

music in 5, 12–13, 16, 35, 51, 53, 72, 76, 116, 120, 124, 133, 136, 137, 215, 216

mutual recognition in 5, 70, 80–83, 113, 121–23, 147–48, 169–70, 193

as a narcotic 3, 192–93

and the nature of the resurrection body 17, 37, 40, 77, 145–47, 169, 190–91

novels about ix, 1, 2, 71, 83, 85, 86, 108, 179, 180, 204, 206, 212–14, 308n42

ownership in 191

paradoxes of American conceptions of 230–31

personal identity in 4–5, 80–81, 122, 169, 193, 196, 213

pets in 191

as a place of great knowledge 4, 15–16, 34–35, 55,75–76, 118, 165

as a place of justice and reparation 9, 45, 75, 90, 91, 93, 94, 96, 143, 167, 174, 183, 228

as a place of love 3, 14, 29, 31–33, 36, 37–38, 40, 43, 45, 50, 53, 69, 113, 117, 133, 143, 164, 165, 170, 184, 188, 189

as a place of rest 8, 16, 20, 21, 36, 40, 64,76, 77, 87, 96, 102, 103, 137, 142, 143, 177, 228

as a place of safety and security 3, 4, 27–28, 118, 207

as a place of work, service, and progress 3, 8, 34, 49, 55, 69, 75, 113, 119–21, 133, 136, 142–44, 156, 161, 164, 165, 184, 190, 228, 229, 234, 237

polls about 2, 6, 179, 190, 191, 198, 206, 237, 243n28, 297n5

popular culture's effect on beliefs about viii–ix, 2, 168, 206, 226, 305n4

portraits of influenced by cultural values viii, 2–3, 7–9, 26–28, 33–34, 36, 38, 55, 56, 69, 70, 73, 75–76, 78, 86, 87, 89, 90–94, 96, 97, 99–103, 107–8, 114, 115, 117–21, 136–38, 139 141–45, 156, 161, 179, 182–83, 207, 208–17, 226, 228, 237

as portrayed in art 1, 2, 3, 206

as portrayed in music viii, 1, 2, 3, 91–92, 93, 99, 179, 180–81, 204, 206, 217

and the post-resurrection state ix, 16, 38

preparation for life in 14, 22–23, 44, 54–55, 65, 113, 125, 141, 168

Puritan view of 10–18

reduced interest in 179, 192, 205, 226

relationship of to building God's kingdom on earth 138, 139, 141, 161, 167, 194, 217–18, 229, 238

relationship of to earthly life 161, 167–68, 184, 188, 217–19, 238

replication of the life of on earth 228, 229, 238

rewards in 9, 12, 13, 14, 17–18, 25, 39–40, 45, 49, 50, 55–56, 69, 77, 81, 84, 88, 90, 99, 113, 122, 123–24, 135, 139, 147, 148–49, 161, 163, 168, 175, 170, 180, 194, 203, 218, 228, 231, 312n8

saints' fellowship with and worship of the Trinity in 8, 13, 14, 31, 50, 51, 69, 74, 86, 103, 115, 116–17, 136, 142, 161, 163–64, 188, 189, 216, 227, 228

saints' knowledge about earthly events in 2, 34–35, 76, 213, 191

sex in 189, 191

sexual intercourse in 137, 191, 215

size of 188

as a source of encouragement, inspiration, and hope vii, 3, 7, 8, 40, 99, 141, 168, 187, 205, 215, 217, 238

Southerners view of 101–2

splendor of vii, 12–16, 31, 50, 55, 61, 70, 74, 75, 86, 89, 115, 119, 124, 145, 167, 188, 203, 216, 227, 228

television commercials about 179–80

television shows about viii–ix, 180, 203, 204, 205–6, 229

theocentric conception of 7, 8, 14, 31–32, 49, 70, 73, 113, 116, 117, 164, 187–88, 213, 230

as a therapeutic center 4, 210–14, 228

time in 190

varied views of vii–viii, 3, 7–8, 113, 133, 175, 178, 226, 228, 230, 237

Heaven Our Home (1864) 71

hell. *See also* various groups and individuals

  basis for punishment in 223

  biblical teaching on 66, 85, 153, 154, 174, 201, 223

  Catholic view of 202, 205

  cartoons about 202

  changing conception of during the Gilded Age 131–33

  conflicting views of during the Progressive era 151–55

  decreasing belief in 154, 173–74, 202, 284–85n63

  Elizabeth Stuart Phelps' view of 73

  evangelical defense of 202, 203, 205, 222, 223

  Jesus' emphasis on 223, 236

  liberal Protestant view of 151–53

  little emphasis on 202, 222, 85–86

  Michael Jackson consigned to 225

  nature of punishment in 44, 66–67, 131, 132, 174, 200, 223

  as nonexistent 205

  as a place of temporary punishment or purification 205

  polls about 222, 305n76

  portraits of influenced by cultural values 86, 107, 152–53

  Puritan's view of 23, 24–25, 27, 69, 249n58

  renewed interest in during the 1990s 202–3

  and the Second Great Awakening 66

  seeming denial of in near-death experiences 197

  urban revivalists' view of 153–54

  view of Octavius Brooks Frothingham on 131–32

  view of Samuel Hopkins on 68–69

Hemingway, Ernest 158, 209

Henchman, Nathaniel 14, 16, 17, 19

Henry, Carl 199

Henry, Patrick 48

Henson, Shaun C. 212

Hepworth, George 142

Herberg, Will 160

Hick, John 200

Hillhouse, James

  on the beatific vision 13–14

  on heaven as compensation for earthly suffering 13

on heaven as a place of great knowledge 16

on heavenly fellowship 16

on heavenly rewards 17–18

on heavenly worship 16

on hell 24

on the resurrection body 17

on the saints' conformity to God's will 14

on salvation 20

on the splendor of heaven 12–13

Hinduism viii, 183

Hispanics 176

History of Heaven, A (1997) 206

Hitchens, Christopher 237

Hitler, Adolf 189

Hoar, Leonard 22

Hodge, A. A.

  on heavenly rewards 124

  on the intellectual aspects of heaven 4, 120

  as a leading Reformed theologian 112

  opposition of to future probation 130

  view of hell of 132

  view of purgatory of 131

Hodge, Charles

  on the beatific vision 115

  on the fellowship of the saints 123

  as a leading Reformed theologian 112

  on the saints' intellectual growth 121

  on salvation 131

  view of purgatory of 130–31

Hodge, J. Aspinwall 5, 122–23

Hoekema, Anthony 188, 189

Hoffman, H. S. 141, 145

Holcombe, William 83

Holifield, E. Brooks 212

Holmes, John Haynes 3, 140, 145

Holmes, Stephen 44

Homer 286n8

Homestead Works strike 110

homosexuals 176, 178

Hooker, Thomas 20, 247n38

Hopkins, Samuel 38, 68–69

Hough, Robert 169

Howe, John 76

Howe, Julia Ward 97

Howells, William Dean 111

Hudson, Jennifer 224

Hudson, Winthrop 127

Humanist Manifesto I 172

Hume, David 58

Hunt, Dave 193
Hunter, James Davidson 314n37
Hurricane Katrina 206
Hylton, Raymond 207, 216, 223

"I Am a Good Person Curriculum" 210
Ignatius of Loyola 123
immigration 109, 111, 134
In His Steps (1897) 170
In Therapy We Trust: America's Obsession with Self-Fulfillment (2001) 211
Internet, the 178
Iraq War, the 206, 225
Isaac 38, 76, 79, 142
Isaiah 5, 53, 148, 189, 191
Islam 67, 68, 145, 224

Jackson, Andrew 59
Jackson, Charles 71
Jackson, Jermaine 224
Jackson, Michael 223–26
Jackson, Stonewall 100, 101
Jacob 38, 79, 142
James, the apostle 150, 186, 199
James, William 235–36, 284–85n63
Jay, John 48, 59
Jefferson, Thomas 48, 59
Jehovah's Witnesses 224
Jewish Renewal movement 187
Jews. *See also* Conservative Jews, Orthodox Jews, Reconstructionist Jews, Reform Jews
    as immigrants 109
    less interest of in the afterlife than Christians 9, 162
    on the necessity of heaven 9
    rejection of belief in personal existence after death of 166
    view of heaven of viii, 1, 101, 186–87
    view of salvation of 6–7, 161, 162, 221
Jim Crow laws 134
John, the apostle 5, 49, 79, 150, 186, 218
Johnson, Barbara 207, 215
Jones, Charles Colsock 88
Jones, J. William 100, 273n55
Johnson, Magic 224
Jones, Jr. Norrece 88
Jones, Rufus 163
Jones, Samuel 135, 151, 153, 286n9

Jordan, Michael 215
Joshua 123

Kabbalah movement 225
Kantzer, Kenneth 236
Keane, Bil 181
Keaton, Diane 180
Keller, Bill 225
Ker, Patrick 20
Kerr, John 74, 75, 76, 77, 81
Killen, J. M. 5, 78, 79, 80–81, 82
Kilpatrick, William 212
Kimball, Henry 142, 144, 145, 146, 148
Kimball, James W. 74, 75, 79, 84, 85
King, Bernice 224
King, Larry 221
King, Jr., Martin Luther 167, 202
King, III, Martin Luther 224
King Philip's War 26
King William's War 26
Kirsch, Adam 210, 213
Knight, George T. 152, 290n59
Knights of Labor 110
Knitter, Paul 200
Knudsen, Albert C. 161, 165
Kreeft, Peter
    on age in heaven 190
    on the benefits of focusing on heaven 193
    on Christ's victory over death and hell 192
    on conventional images of heaven 179
    on heavenly rewards 194
    on love in heaven 189
    on the saints' awareness of earthly events 191
    theocentric view of heaven of 188
Ku Klux Klan, the 158
Kubler-Ross, Elisabeth 197
Kushner, Tony 206

Lafollette, Robert 135
LaHaye, Tim
    defense of hell of 202
    on heavenly rewards 194, 302n49
    on near-death experiences 196–97
    on purgatory 201
    on the saints reigning with Christ 190
    on salvation 198–99
Lamm, Maurice 186
Landon, Michael 180
Lang, Bernhard 178–79, 188, 230

Larcom, Lucy 117, 121, 123, 125, 127
Larson, Gary 181, 209
Lasch, Christopher 210, 211
Late Great Planet Earth, The (1973)
Lawson, Steve 192
Lears, T. J. Jackson 73, 111, 115, 117, 152
Leary, Timothy 184
Lee, Robert E. 100
Levine, Lawrence 90
Lewis, C. S. 191–92, 193
Lewis, Sinclair 158
liberal Protestantism
  belief in universalism of 172
  beliefs of 135
  on combating social ills and injustices 234
  criticism of 115
  efforts of to make Christianity more
    intellectually compelling 156
  as embracing American culture 160
  emphasis of on religious experience, ethics,
    and social progress 113
  factors contributing to the development
    of 112
  goals of 135, 162
  on growth and progress in heaven 121
  growth of in the 1930s 8
  on heaven viii, 135, 143–44, 156
  on heaven as a state of mind 8
  on hell 152–53, 161
  on holiness and good works 127
  influence of 112, 135
  interpretation of scripture of 227–28
  leaders of 161
  precursors of 112
  and the Social Gospel 135, 156
  view of the atonement of 127, 135, 150, 153, 159,
    172, 234
  view of doctrine of 172
  view of evolution of 112
  view of future probation (*see* New Theology)
  view of humanity of 112, 233
  view of salvation of 6, 126, 149–51, 161, 162,
    171, 172, 233, 234
  view of sin of 233, 313n19
  work of to bring God's kingdom 112–13
liberation theology
  black version of 182–83
  critique of 298n15
  emphasis of on building God's kingdom on

  earth 8, 182, 193
  feminist version of 183
  view of heaven of 178, 181–83
  view of salvation of 181–82, 234–35
  view of sin of 234
*Life after Death: A History of the Afterlife in
    Western Religion* (2004)
*Life After Life: The Investigation of a
    Phenomenon—Survival of Bodily Death*
    (1975)
Lincoln, Abraham 97, 112
Lindsey, Hal 4, 188
Little Women (1868) 85
Livermore, Mary 267n52
Livingstone, David 123
Lonely Boys, Los 2, 206
Longfield, Bradley 292n4
Lovely Bones, The (2002) 2, 212–14
Lotz, Anne Graham 189, 220, 223
Lough, David 105
Luther, Martin 5, 40, 79
Lutherans 7, 178
Lutzer, Erwin 194
Lynd, Helen 173
Lynd, Robert 173

MacDonald, James 4, 74, 75, 84
Macaria; or Altars of Sacrifice (1864) 102–03
MacArthur, Jack 201
MacArthur, Jr. John 189, 192, 194, 230
Machen, J. Gresham 159
MacLaine, Shirley 184
MacNeill, John 163
Madonna 225
Mahan, Asa 120
mainline Protestants
  decline of viii, 178
  description of heaven of 1
  flourishing of 160
  ignoring of heaven of 104, 205, 240n3
  view of hell of 222
  view of salvation of 219
Maltz, Betty 196
The Map of Man's Misery (1685) 20
Marsden, Orison Swett 287n22
Martin, Mark 211
Marty, Martin 205
Marx, Karl 3, 141
Masters, Kim 225

Mather, Cotton
  on assurance of salvation 20
  death of the children of 18
  on focusing on heaven 18
  on heaven as trouble-free 15
  on heavenly rewards 17
  influence of 12
  on preparation for heaven 22
  on salvation 19
  writings of about heaven 12
Mather, Increase
  on the atonement 19
  on the beatific vision 14
  on Christ in heaven 14–15
  on Christ's Second Coming 24
  on the end times 24
  on focusing on heaven 18
  on grief 19
  on heaven as compensation for earthly
    suffering 13
  on heaven as an inspiration for evangelism 25
  on heaven as a place of great happiness 12, 215
  on heaven as a place of great knowledge 4, 16
  on heaven as trouble-free 15
  on heavenly recognition 16
  on heavenly rewards 18
  heavenly visions of 22
  on heavenly worship 16
  on hell 24
  influence of 12
  on the journey to heaven 15, 23
  on preparation for death 22, 24
  on preparation for salvation 21
  rejection of soul sleep of 16
  on the resurrection body 17
  roles of 12
  on the saints' conformity to God's will 14
  on the saints' spending eternity in heaven 38
  on salvation 19, 23, 248n51
  on the splendor of heaven 13
Mathews, Shailer
  on Americans' reduced interest in heaven 162
  on implementing heaven's principles on
    earth 167–68
  as a leader of the modernists 161
  on salvation 233, 234
Mayer, John 224
McCarrick, Theodore 216
McCarthy, J. P. 164

McCarthy, Joseph 159
McConkie, Joseph F. 186
McDannell, Colleen 178–79, 188, 230
McGready, James
  on the absence of sin and Satan in heaven 52,
    118
  on the diversity of heaven 54
  on good works 65
  on hell 66, 67, 68
  as a leader of the Second Great Awakening 49
  on the progress of the saints 55
  as a revivalist 49
  on the saints' fellowship with Christ 51
  on salvation 60
  on the splendor of heaven 49, 50
McKinley, William 102, 138
McLoughlin, William 62, 284n57
Meador, Keith G. 212
"Me Decade" 177
Men and Religion Forward Movement, the 141
Mennonites 189
MercyMe 206, 217
Mere Christianity (1952) 191
Meschach 91
Mexicans 1
Middlekauff, Robert 17
*Middletown: A Study in Contemporary American
  Culture* (1929)
Miller, Lisa viii–ix
Miller, Perry 11
Millet, Robert 184, 186
Milne, Bruce 216, 308n42
Milton, John 123, 145
Mitchel, Jonathan 17, 22
Mitchell, Reid 101
Mode of Man's Immortality, The (1879) 146
Mohler, Albert 211–12
Moody, Dwight
  on biblical teaching about heaven 1, 115
  on the fellowship of the saints 123
  on God's wrath and justice 171
  on good works 127
  on heaven as a place of worship 116
  on heaven's absence of earthly woes 118
  on hell 132, 153, 285n64, 291n66
  on the importance of learning about
    heaven 115
  people wanting to fellowship with in
    heaven 5

premillennialism of 114
on preparing for heaven 125
on the saints' fellowship with Christ 115
on the saints' fellowship with God 115
on salvation 6, 125
on the unsaved being unhappy in heaven 132
as an urban revivalist 111
and the use of heaven to win converts 132
view of heaven of 114, 279n17
Moody, Raymond 195, 197
Moorhead, James 132, 156
Moreland, J. P.
  on heavenly recognition 193
  on heavenly rewards 194
  on near-death experiences 196
  on salvation 198
  on sexual intercourse in heaven 191
  on the splendor of heaven 188
Morey, Robert 200–1
Morgan, Edmund 11
Mormons
  baptism for the dead of 185
  on the beatific vision 50
  genealogical research of 185
  and immortality versus eternal life 186
  and marriage for eternity 185–86
  rapid growth of 184
  on the relationship between this world and
    the afterlife 298n18
  on salvation 299n20, 299n24
  on three stages of glory in heaven 185
  view of heaven of 1, 8, 178, 184–86, 299n20
Morris, Edward 284n57
Morse, Melvin 196
Moses
  identification of slaves with 91
  people wanting to fellowship with in
    heaven 5, 79, 123, 142, 187
  at Christ's transfiguration 38
  as recognizable in heaven 80
Moskowitz, Eva S. 211
Moton, R. R. 167
Mouw, Richard 189, 192–93
Mozart, Wolfgang 76, 210
Muhammad 107, 286n8
Muncaster, Ralph 198
Munger, Theodore 113
Murray, John 48, 62
"muscular" Christianity 118, 119, 136, 281n29

Muslims
  salvation of 220, 221
  view of heaven of viii, 1, 145
  worldview of 207
My Glimpse of Eternity (1977) 196
Mystery Hid from Ages, or the Salvation of All
  Men, The (1784)

Nash, Ronald 199, 298n15
National Association of Evangelicals 161
Nationalist clubs 110
Native Americans
  confining of to reservations 134
  discrimination against 110
  efforts of to gain greater civil rights 176
  and the First Great Awakening 15, 36
  as fleeing before "civilizing" agents 121
  and heaven viii, 1, 145
  missionary efforts of Edwards to 30
  relationship of with the Puritans 11
  removal of from the East 49
  and the Social Gospel 135
Nature and Destiny of Man, The (1943) 166
Near-death experiences
  accounts of 195, 196
  critique of 196–97
  debate over the validity of 196
  descriptions of 195, 303n59
  as focusing attention on heaven 2, 195
  as helping to validate belief in heaven 195,
    197
  history of 194–95
  increased reporting and scholarly
    investigation of 178
  increased scientific scrutiny of 195
  increasing attractiveness of 195
  positive benefits of 195
  and the Second Great Awakening 52
  seeming denial of hell of 197
  speculative nature of 237
  and William Tennent 53
Nelson, David 53
Neo-orthodoxy 8, 160, 161, 299n28
Nettleton, Asahel
  denunciation of Universalism by 63–64
  on the fellowship of the saints 53
  on hell 67, 68
  as a leader of the Second Great
    Awakening 49

Nettleton, Asahel (*continued*)
  repudiation of Finney's "new measures" by 62
  on salvation 60
  on the signs of salvation 65–66
Nevin, John W. 62
New Age movement, the
  description of 183
  influence of 183
  influence of on NDE investigators 197
  proponents of 298n16
  roots of 183
  view of the afterlife of 1, 8, 178
  view of death of 184
New Deal, the 158–59
New Theology
  on the atonement 149–50
  on future probation 128–29, 150, 154
  leaders of 113
  origins of 113
  view of Christ of 127
  view of death of 155–56
  view of salvation of 126, 127–28, 150–51
New Thought movement, the 183
Niebuhr, H. Richard 161
Niebuhr, Reinhold
  denial of personal immortality by 166
  on figurative descriptions of the afterlife 166
  hope of in eternal life 166–67
  influences on 312n2
  as leader of Neo-orthodoxy 161
  on limited biblical information about
    heaven 165
  on the meaning of history 238
90 Minutes in Heaven (2004) 2
Nixon, Richard 177, 181
Noah 5
Norwood, or, Village Life in New England
  (1868) 124, 127
"Not by Faith Alone": *The Biblical Evidence for
  the Catholic Doctrine of Justification*
  (1996) 199
Nugent, William 102

Obama, Barack 223
O'Reilly, Bill 225
Orthodox Jews 7, 166, 186–87
Osteen, Joel 205, 220–21, 310n62
*Our Country Its Possible Future and Its Present
  Crises* (1885) 110–11

Owen, John 190
Ownby, Ted 89, 101

Palmer, Elihu
  attack of on Christian orthodoxy 48, 57–58
  denial of life after death of 58
  exaltation of reason of 57, 58
  on good works 66
  rejection of eternal punishment of 66
  repudiation of Christ's atonement of 58
  view of Christ of 57
  view of salvation of 57
Paradise Lost (1667) 145
Park, Edward A. 71
Pascal, Blaise 154
Patterson, Orlando 89
Patterson, Robert
  on growth and service in heaven 120
  on heavenly recognition 122
  on heavenly rewards 124
  on limited knowledge of heaven 114
  on preparing for heaven 125
  on the saints' vastly increased knowledge 118
  on worship in heaven 116
Patton, Francis 290 n. 59
Paul, the apostle
  as enthralled with heaven 218
  evangelistic work of in heaven 77
  fellowship with in heaven 5, 79, 123, 142, 148
  on heavenly recognition 80, 122, 147
  on the inability of language to describe
    heaven 49
  on Jesus' descent into Hades 128
  as providing a vague description of
    heaven 145
  on the resurrection body 17, 146, 169
  and salvation by faith 23, 126, 150, 199
  on the saints' awareness of life on earth 76
  on slaves' requirement to obey their
    masters 88
  survival of a shipwreck by 85
  vision of heaven of 53
  willingness of to postpone the joys of
    heaven 15
Payson, Edward
  on activities in heaven 51–52
  on the diversity of heaven 54
  on good works 65
  on heavenly rewards 54, 56

on hell 68
on the nature of heavenly life 257n11
on preparing for heaven 54–55, 56, 65
on the saints' relationship with Christ 51
on the saints' relationship with God 50–51
on salvation 60–61
vision of heaven of 52–53
Peale, Norman Vincent 160, 196
Pearse, Edward
on the difficulty of getting to heaven 23
on heaven as an inspiration for evangelism 25
on heavenly worship 16
on the journey to heaven 15
on preparing for salvation 25
on salvation 19
on sinlessness in heaven 15
theocentric view of heaven of 14
Pemberton, Ebenezer 4, 52
Pender, William Dorsey 102
Pentecostals 151, 178
Pequot War, the 26
Peter, the apostle
as admitting people to heaven 177, 206, 220, 221
and Christ's transfiguration 38
as enthralled with heaven 218
people's desire to fellowship with in heaven 5, 79, 123, 142
teachings of 186
Phan, Peter C. 216, 217, 222, 223
Phelps, Austin
on heaven as home 71, 114
on heaven as a place of service 120
on the saints' fellowship with God 115
on the saints' perfect health 117
view of heaven of 73
Phelps, Elizabeth Stuart 2, 71–73, 86
Phillips, U.B. 89
Pickens, J. Miles 103
Pierpont, James 6, 21, 23
Pilgrim's Progress, The (1678) 20
Pinkwater, Daniel 180
Pinnock, Clark 199
Piper, Don 2, 207, 216
Pittinger, Norman 179
Place of Death in Evolution, The (1897) 156
political corruption 109–10
Polynesians 1
Populists 11

pornography 208
Postman, Neil 208
postmillennialism 114, 138, 267n51
postmodernism 176, 207–8, 226
postmortem evangelization 199
premillennialism 114, 139, 140, 160, 267n51
Preparatory Meditations upon the Day of Judgment
Presbyterians 30, 59, 62, 159, 178
Presidential Prayer Breakfasts 160
Presley, Elvis 225
Principles of Nature (1802) 58, 66
process theology 298n15
Procter, William C. 154
Progressive era, the
abundant consumer goods available during 136
emphasis on hard work during 141
expansion of American trade during 141
higher standard of living during 136
increased leisure time during 136
increased pace of life during 141
major theological rift during 156
mission efforts during 141
new forms of entertainment during 136, 141
progress during 156
technological innovations of 141
Progressive movement, the 135
Progressive orthodoxy. See New Theology
Prohibition 158
Prosser, Gabriel 94
Protestant men's brotherhoods 141
Prothero, Stephen R. 222
Puff Daddy 180
Pullman Company Strike 110
purgatory 7, 129, 130–31, 201–2, 222
Puritans
assessment of 11
on assurance of election 21, 22, 26
on the beatific vision 13–14
as Calvinists 19, 26, 56
concern for education of 11, 15
descriptions of 10
and election 19, 26, 27
emphasis on the Bible of 10, 11, 16, 250n67
emphasis on calling of 10
emphasis on God's providence of 10, 11, 25
emphasis on introspection of 11, 27
emphasis on worship of 16

Puritans (*continued*)
  and the end times 24, 26
  on focusing on heaven 18
  and folk religion 27
  goals of 10
  great interest in heaven of 2, 12, 18, 25, 27
  on the happiness of heaven 12
  on heaven as compensating for earthly
    suffering 13
  on heaven as an inspiration for evangelism 25
  on heaven as a trouble-free place 15
  on a heavenly perspective of earthly life 12
  on heavenly rewards 17–18, 26
  on heavenly worship 16
  on hell 23, 24–25, 27, 69, 249n58
  and infant mortality 18–19
  on the journey to heaven 15, 23
  impact of 10
  as the New Israel 11
  origins of 10
  and preparing for death 19–22
  on preparing for heaven 14, 22–23
  on preparing for salvation 20–21, 25
  quest of to construct a Christian society 11,
    27–28
  rejection of soul sleep of 16
  on the resurrection body 17
  on the saints' conformity to God's will 14
  on the saint's fellowship 16
  on the saints' vastly increased
    knowledge 15–16
  self-righteousness of 11
  sermons of 26, 27, 249–50n64
  shortcomings of 11
  on the splendor of heaven 12–13
  on the stages of salvation 20, 21, 232
  stereotyping of 10–11
  stringent legal system of 11
  theocentric view of heaven of 8, 12–14
  theological understanding of 11
  view of good works of 12, 25–26, 249n63
  view of salvation of 12, 19–20
  worldview of 26–27, 250n67
Purpose Driven Life, The (2002) 205
Putney, Clifford 281n29

Quakers 47
Queen Latifah 224
Quinby, G. W. 121

Rabinowitz, Richard 115, 260–61n47
Ralls, Mark 205, 213–14
Rauschenbusch, Walter
  criticism of otherworldly conceptions of
    heaven of 139
  emphasis of on social salvation 139, 234
  on future probation 153
  on growth in heaven 143
  on heaven providing opportunities for
    reparation and justice 143
  on heavenly recognition 5, 148
  on hell 153
  on knowledge about heaven 288n29
  as a leader of the Social Gospel 134, 138
  and preparation for heaven 141
  on reincarnation 143
  on sin 234
Rawlings, Maurice 195, 196, 302n53
Reason the Only Oracle of Man (1784) 58, 59
recession of 2008–2010 207
Reconstructionist Jews 187
Reform Jews
  on heaven as a spiritual state 9
  origins of 7
  rejection of the bodily resurrection of 9
  view of the human task of 7
  view of immortality of 9, 186, 187
Reformers, the 53, 79, 84, 129
rehabilitation of prisoners 152
reincarnation 143, 184
religious depression of the 1930s 159
religious revival of the 1950s 160
Rieff, Philip 210, 211
Ring, Kenneth 197
Ritchie, Lionel 224
Robison, Jay D. 5
Rockefeller, John D. 109
Roediger, David 91, 92
Roeper, Richard 225
Romans (ancient) 1
Romantics 66, 99
Roof, Clark Wade 215
Room of Marvels (2004) 214
Roosevelt, Theodore 135, 137, 138, 281n29
Roszak, Theodore 184
Rousseau, Jean Jacques 58
Rubenstein, Richard L. 187
Ruether, Rosemary 183
Rush, Benjamin 48, 59

Russell, Jeffrey Burton 206
Rutgers 30

Sacred Songs and Solos (1877) 114
Saint Patrick 123
salvation
    African-American view of 182, 219
    Arminian view of 233
    assurance of 19, 21, 26, 83, 100, 192, 255n48,
        267n52
    as based on belief in Christ viii, 6, 12, 43, 49,
        69, 84, 91, 103, 151, 171, 198–99, 204, 219,
        231–32, 296n51, 310n57
    as based on good works 6, 7, 48, 59, 63, 106,
        131, 162, 173, 198, 200, 205, 219, 226, 295n42
    Catholics view of 6–7, 100, 152, 161, 162, 171,
        173, 199, 200, 219, 220, 222, 235, 243n28
    debates over the nature of in the early national
        era 48
    as depending on humans' response to God's
        offer 232, 233
    earning of by dying in battle 105, 277n96
    evangelicals' view of 86, 94, 149, 151, 162, 171,
        198, 199, 219, 220, 222, 230, 231–32, 314n37
    and efforts to convert slaves 88
    factors promoting during the Civil
        War 107–8
    the final fundamental option view of 200
    as God's sovereign act 19, 26, 41, 232
    and the "Good Death" 98–99
    hymns about 106
    the inclusive view of 199
    of infants 63, 70, 83, 86, 152, 171, 200, 248n51
    jokes about 220
    Jonathan Edwards's view of 40–44
    liberal Protestant view of 6, 126, 149–51, 161,
        162, 171, 172, 233, 234
    mainline Protestant views of 219
    mid-nineteenth century Protestants' view
        of 84–85, 86
    and the new birth experience viii, 27, 30, 41,
        45, 56, 58, 60, 65, 125, 151, 157, 162, 170, 171,
        178, 202, 220, 232, 233, 235–36
    Reformed view of 62, 65, 105, 232–33
    the particularist view of 236
    the pluralistic view of 236
    polls about 6, 206, 219, 309nn54–55, 310n57,
        312–13n12, 314n37
    postmortem opportunities of 199

    predestination and 41
    Puritan view of 231–32
    and regeneration 10, 19, 20, 21, 23, 35, 41, 56,
        60, 62, 63, 65, 67, 125, 126, 171, 172, 229, 232,
        233, 236
    the restrictive view of 199
    Second Great Awakening and 56–57, 60–66
    the unitive pluralist view of 200
    varied paths to 199, 200, 232, 236
    views of in the 1960–2000 period 198–201
Sandberg, Anne 4, 179, 189, 194, 196
Sanders, J. Oswald 190
Sanders, John 199
Satan
    Christ's death as a ransom to 149, 150
    Christ's victory over 236
    claim of to own the world 11
    decline of belief in 284n63
    exclusion from heaven of 118
    as the father of evil 64
    and hell 24, 43, 67, 85
    necessity of combating 26, 54, 152
    as nonexistent 64
    opposition of to God 20, 34
    as providing delusional NDEs 197
    temptations of 15, 22, 52, 64, 75
    as ultimately defeated 13, 105
Schantz, Mark 80, 99, 228
Schuller, Robert 220
Schulweis, Harold 187
Scofield, C. I. 162
Scott, Martin 164, 165, 173
Scott, Sean A. 83, 106
Scudder, Vida 167
Sebold, Alice 1, 2, 4, 212–14
Second Great Awakening, the
    as a Benevolent Empire 49
    and challenges to orthodox view of
        salvation 57, 62, 69
    critique of Universalism of 64–65
    and diversity in heaven 54
    and focusing on heaven 54
    emphasis of on heaven 49, 69
    emphasis of on hell 49, 66, 69, 85, 95
    and the fellowship of the saints 49, 53–54
    on good works 65
    and the growth of the saints 49
    and heavenly recognition 49
    and heavenly rewards 49, 53, 55–56

Second Great Awakening, the (*continued*)
  impact of 49
  and the importance of heaven to earthly life 49
  leaders of 49
  on the progress of the saints 55
  response of to Finney's "new measures" 62
  on salvation 56–57, 60–66
secular humanists 162, 172–73, 235
Segal, Alan 2–3, 221
self-help groups 210
Self-Imployment in Secret (1684) 23
Seligman, Martin 215
sentimentalism 114
Seventeen Steps to Heaven (2001) 220
Seventh-Day Adventists 151
Sewall, Samuel 18
Shadrach 91
Shakespeare, William 123, 286n8
Shakur, Tupac 180
Sharp, Helen 106
Sharp, John 106
Sharpton, Al 224
Shaw, Timothy 78
Shea, John 3
Shedd, W. G. T.
  on heaven as a place of great knowledge 118
  on holiness in heaven 117
  as a leading Reformed theologian 112
  on moral character 127
  on people's vision of God in the afterlife 279n18
  on the saints' fellowship with God 115
  on salvation 125–26
  on suffering 127
  view of hell of 132
Sheen, Fulton
  on the absence of earthly woes in heaven 164
  defense of purgatory of 175
  on hell 173, 174
  influence of 160, 164
  on salvation 173
  on the splendor of heaven 164
Sheldon, Charles M. 170
Shepard, Thomas 20, 21, 22
Sherman, Roger 48
Shibley, David 207, 218
Shields, Brooke 224
Shriver, Maria 221
Simpson, Matthew 124
slave owners 88, 89–90, 189

assignment of slaves to a subordinate place in
  heaven by 87
conception of heaven 89
culpability of before God 95
few of permitted to enter heaven 87
hell as a punishment for 95
reconciliation of with former slaves in
  heaven 189
and use of heaven and hell to promote
  obedience 88, 89–90
and use of religion to control slaves 88, 89
view of slaves as commodities 93
slaves
  alleged acceptance of whites' view of
    Christianity of 89
  alleged visits to heaven of 92
  belief in heaven as inspiration of 94
  and heaven as compensation for earthly
    deprivation and dehumanization 87, 90,
    91, 92–94, 182
  identification of with Moses and Jesus 91
  impact of Western African heritage on 92, 95,
    270n19
  on opposition to conversion of 88
  reconciliation of with former owners in
    heaven 189
  on the relationship of blacks and whites in
    heaven 95–96
  on salvation 87, 91, 94
  spirituals of 91–92, 94
  and the Underground Railroad 94
  version of the gospel of 88, 90
  view of heaven of 8, 87–96
  view of hell of 87, 91, 95, 96
  on whites' acceptance into heaven 95–96
Smith, George 201
Smith, Guy 305n4
Smith, Helen Sootin 73
Smith, James Bryan 214
Smith, Joseph 186
Smith, Lucious
Smith, Timothy 90, 94
Smith, Wilbur 188, 190
Smyth, Newman
  on death 156
  on the fellowship of the saints 123
  on focusing on heaven 124
  on future probation 128–29
  on heavenly rewards 124

as a proponent of New Theology 113
on the resurrection body 146
on self-development in heaven 144
social Darwinism 141
Social Gospel
accomplishments of 135
activities of 134–35, 138
advocates of 134, 156
attempt of to promote justice on earth 8
decline of in the 1920s 166
effort of to bring heaven to earth 139, 140
effort of to reconstruct society 135, 138
goals of 134–35
key leaders of 134
as postmillennialists 138
on service and growth in heaven 8, 138
and theological liberalism 135
weaknesses of 135
Social Problems (1883)
Sockman, Ralph 173–74
Sonsino, Rifat 187
soul sleep 16, 38, 122
Southern Baptists 178, 205
Spear, Samuel 116, 117, 124, 127, 130
Spencer, Herbert 112
Spiritualists viii, 1, 183, 239n4
Sprague, William 85
Springer, Rebecca 145, 149
Sproul, R. C. 199
Spurgeon, Charles 5
Stalin, Joseph 189
Stamphill, Ira 170
Stanford, Peter 222
Steer, C. John 218, 223
Steinberg, Milton 166, 294n21
Stiles, Ezra 50, 53, 55–56, 65, 68
Stoddard, Solomon 24–25, 30, 41
Stout, Harry 26, 27, 249n64
Stowe, Harriet Beecher 78, 79, 83, 86, 102
Stowell, Joseph 192
Strong, A. H. 147, 148, 154
Strong, Charles 148
Strong, James 129
Strong, Josiah 110, 281n29
Stuart, J. E. B. 100
Stuart, Moses 71
Student Volunteer Movement 141
Sufferings of the Lost (186–) 107
Sunday, Billy

on the beauty of heaven 144
on fellowship with Jesus in heaven 142
on the fellowship of the saints in heaven 5
on future probation 155
on God's wrath and justice 171
on heaven as an actual place 4, 206
on heaven's absence of earthly woes 145
on hell 153, 154
on the nature of God 171
on salvation 151
Sungenis, Robert 199
Swedenborg, Emanuel 194
Swedenborgians viii
Syme, Daniel B. 187

Tada, Joni Eareckson 189, 191
Talmage, T. DeWitt
on the fellowship of the saints 123
on focusing on heaven 124
on heaven as an active place 119–20
on heaven as a home 114
on heaven as a place of great knowledge 118
on heaven as a place of joy 113–14
on heaven's absence of earthly woes 117
on heavenly recognition 122
on hell 132–33
as a leading Gilded Age minister 112
on limited knowledge of heaven 115
on the resurrection body 118–19
on the saints' fellowship with Christ 115
on the saints' varied employments 120
on salvation 125
Tammany Hall 109
Taylor, Edward 14
television 208
Tennent, Gilbert 30, 56
Tennent, William 53, 56
Teresa of Avila 123
Teresa, Mother 218
terrorist attacks 206
theistic rationalists 48, 56–57
Theosophical Society 183
Thompson, Augustus
on activities in heaven 77
on children in heaven 267n47
on heavenly recognition 82
on personal identity in heaven 4, 80
on the saints' fellowship with historical
figures 79

Thompson, Fred 189
Thuesen, Peter 26
Tillich, Paul
  denial of personal existence after death of 165,
    234
  discussion of the afterlife in figurative terms of 166
  on human estrangement from God 234
  influences on 312n2
  as a modernist leader 161
  repudiation of conventional view of heaven of 166
  on salvation 234
  on "ultimate concern" 234
Torrey, R. A.
  on the atonement 151
  on the fellowship of the saints 148
  on focusing on heaven 141
  on future probation 155
  on heaven as an actual place 4
  on heaven as a scholar's paradise 144
  on heavenly rewards 149
  on heaven's absence of earthly woes 145
  on the resurrection body 147
  on salvation 151
  view of death of 155–56
Trachtenberg, Alan 110
Transcendentalism 183
Travel Guide to Heaven, A (2003) 2, 3, 209–10
Treatise on the Atonement, A (1805) 63
Trese, Leo J. 220
Triumph of the Therapeutic, The (1966) 210
Tubman, Harriet 91, 94
Turner, Nat 94
Twain, Mark 73, 110, 137–38, 286nn8–9
Twitchell, Joseph Hopkins 102

Uncle Tom's Cabin (1852) 79, 102, 239n1
Union, the 97
Unitarians
  on the atonement 234
  challenge of to orthodox conceptions of
    salvation 46, 69, 228
  denial of Christ's divinity of 57
  emphasis of on human goodness 66
  growth of 259n26
  on punishment after death 64, 151
  rejection of hell of 174
  on the role of good deeds in salvation 6, 234
  on the role of character in salvation 56–57
  view of Jesus of 57, 127

United Church of Christ 178
United Methodist Church 178
United States Christian Commission 103
United States House of Representatives Foreign
    Affairs Committee 225
universalism 129, 236
  critiques of 63–64, 65, 200–1, 221–22, 236
  increasing belief in 236
  types of 200–1
Universalists
  on the atonement 65
  attacks on 130
  attractiveness of the beliefs of 261n52
  belief of that all will be saved 62–63, 66
  challenge of to orthodox conceptions of
    salvation 46, 69
  debate of with Finney 63
  denial of Christ's divinity of 57
  as a denomination 62–63
  and eternal punishment 132
  on punishment after death 64, 151
  rejection of hell by 174
  on the role of character in salvation 56–57
  on the role of good deeds in salvation 6
  view of Jesus of 57
Universalist Magazine 63
Upton, Emory 106
urban revivalists
  conception of heaven of 111, 113–14, 144
  emphasis of on heavenly rewards 149
  as premillennialists 114, 138
  reduced focus on of hell 131–32
  and the use of heaven to win converts 132
Usher 224
Uylat, William 142

Vanderbilt, George W. 110
Varieties of Religious Experience, The (1901)
    235–36
Vatican II 178, 202, 235
Vesey, Denmark 94
Victorian values 159
video games 208
Vietnam War, the 176, 177
Vitz, Paul 211
Voltaire 58

Walls, Jerry 193, 197
Wanamaker, John 136

Ware, Henry 259n26
Warner, Dudley 110
Warner, Susan 78, 86
Warren, Rick 205, 220
Washington, Booker T. 167
Washington, George 47, 48, 59
Watts, Alan 184
Webber, Thomas 88
Weldon, John 188, 197
Wesley, John 123
What's Heaven? (1999)
White, Hugh A. 103
White, Ellen 118, 120, 125, 133
Whitefield, George 228
   as a Calvinist 41, 56
   on the diversity of heaven 36–37
   on the fellowship of the saints 38
   on good works 43
   on hell 43, 45
   on heavenly rewards 39
   life of 30
   people wanting to fellowship with in
      heaven 123
   on personal recognition in heaven 38
   on the resurrection body 37
   role of in First Great Awakening 30, 36
   on salvation 6, 41–43, 45
Whitley, Jesse T. 163–64, 168, 169
Wiebe, Robert 109
Wigglesworth, Michael 13, 14
Wilberforce, William 218
Wilkerson, Ralph 196

Williams, Daniel 128
Wilson, James 48
Wilson, Lee 218
Wilson, Woodrow 135, 138
Winchester, Elhanan 62
Winthrop, John 63, 238
Witherspoon, John
   as a Christian founding father 48
   contributions of 50–51
   on the diversity in heaven 54
   on the fellowship of the saints 53
   on focusing on heaven 54
   on the saints' relationship with
      God 51
   on the saints' worship 52
   on salvation 60
   on the splendor of heaven 50
Wittmer, Michael 215, 217, 218
Wonder, Stevie 224
Wood, George 75, 76–77
Woodsworth, Steven 105
World War I 98, 138, 139, 159, 160
World War II 98, 158, 159, 160, 168
Wright, Theodore 67

Yale College 26, 30, 58
Yancey, Philip 179, 192, 218
Yellow Fever Outbreak of 1853 98
YMCA 103, 141, 281n29
Your Best Life Now! (2004) 205

Zaleski, Carol 195, 209, 230